Encyclopedia of
AFRICAN-AMERICAN HERITAGE
Second Edition

Encyclopedia of
AFRICAN-AMERICAN HERITAGE
Second Edition

Susan Altman

Special writing and research by
Joel Kemelhor

Consultants
Dr. Arnold H. Taylor B.A., M.A., Ph.D.
Dr. Debra Newman Ham B.A., M.A., Ph.D.
Dr. Arthur Burt B.A., M.A., Ph.D.

Facts On File, Inc.

Encyclopedia of African-American Heritage, Second Edition

Second Edition copyright © 2000 by Susan Altman

First Edition copyright © 1997 by Susan Altman

Maps copyright © 2000, 1997 by Facts On File, Inc.

Facts On File, Inc.
11 Penn Plaza
New York NY 10001

Library of Congress Cataloging-in-Publication Data

Altman, Susan.
Encyclopedia of African-American heritage / Susan Altman ; special writing and research by Joel Kemelhor.—2nd ed.
p.   cm.
Includes bibliographical references and index.
ISBN 0-8160-4125-3 (hardcover)
1. Afro-Americans—Encyclopedias. 2. Afro-Americans—History—Encyclopedias.
3. Africa—Civilization—Encyclopedias. I. Kemelhor, Joel. II. Title.
E185 .A455 2000
973′.0496073′003—dc21   00-049449

Facts On File books are available at special discounts when purchased in bulk quantities for businesses, associations, institutions, or sales promotions. Please call our Special Sales Department in New York at 212/967-8800 or 800/322-8755.

You can find Facts On File on the World Wide Web at http://www.factsonfile.com

Text design by Joan M. Toro
Cover design by Cathy Rincon

Printed in the United States of America

VB Hermitage 10 9 8 7 6 5 4 3 2 1

This book is printed on acid-free paper.

*To my mother and father, who have always
been an inexhaustible source of strength
and encouragement.*

CONTENTS

Foreword   ix

Introduction   xi

Entries A to Z   1

Bibliography   333

Index   339

FOREWORD

In addition to the rich and varied history of Africans on their ancestral continent, this encyclopedia chronicles Africans who were captured and sold as slaves to the far corners of the earth. A small number of these involuntary emigrants from the continent (or their descendants) were able to return to Africa after years of absence. Within the last century, particularly since the decolonization of Africa, Africans have been studying and living in many nations throughout the world. People now refer to this movement of African people to and from the continent for over a millennium as the "African diaspora."

This volume provides thorough yet succinct information about Africans who remained on the continent as well as those in the diaspora. The author concentrates most of her attention on indigenous Africans and blacks in the United States but also includes information about descendants of the African motherland who were involuntary and voluntary immigrants to the Caribbean, Latin America, Europe, and Asia. Although most of the individuals described herein were intellectual, political, military, scientific, or educational leaders, the author also gives careful attention to musicians, artists, literary figures, and athletes.

Almost all of the subjects covered in the brief entries of this text offer a gateway to extensive further study. Along with the carefully distilled information about each subject, some entries include bibliographic information about biographies, historical works, artistic and musical expressions, and literary accomplishments. Full-length autobiographies and biographies are available for most of the individuals described in this volume. The bibliography at the end of the text suggests additional sources for the study of the history and culture of the people of the African diaspora. Most local public libraries could supply interested students with rich additional material on the subjects covered in this encyclopedia. Research libraries at major universities may yield more in-depth sources for the study of the African diaspora as will the invaluable resources at the Library of Congress in Washington, D.C.

Although many who pick up this volume will use it only as a reference work and peruse just a few entries at a time, I recommend that any who are sincerely interested in learning about the African diaspora curl up and read this work from cover to cover as I did. Not, I should add, because this is not an excellent reference work, it is, but because it affords such a thorough introduction to the subject. I have been a student of the African diaspora for almost three decades, yet I met men and women on the pages of this volume whose acquaintance I had not made in the annals of the National Archives or the Library of Congress. Susan Altman is a compelling author who breathes life into this history for her readers.

–Debra Newman Ham
Professor of History,
Morgan State University

INTRODUCTION

The vast tapestry of African and African-American history forms an intricate design, weaving together good and evil, freedom and slavery, justice and repression. It is a history that has touched that of almost every major civilization since the beginning of recorded time. The remains of the earliest humans were found in Africa, and the continent was home to advanced cultures that influenced much of the ancient world.

Because the range of African and African-American history and culture is so vast and this encyclopedia is subject to space limitations, profiles of many well-known figures, particularly in the fields of sports and entertainment, have been omitted, in part because information about them is readily available elsewhere.

In compiling this encyclopedia, I had the help and support of many individuals. In particular, I would like to thank Joel Kemelhor, Susan Lechner, Chip and Nancy Lupu, Chuck Jeffreys, Nancy and Alan Shestack, Nicole Evans, Jeorge Watson, Rev. James Gordon Emerson, Professor Paul Butler, Professor Charles Craver, Dean Edwin Dorn, Jerry Anderson, Bernard Ingold, and my parents, Norman and Sophie Altman. All were supportive, providing me with advice and information. Several were also critical in helping me maintain an "edge," a sense that one is sometimes speaking for those anonymous men, women, and children whose voices were silenced but whose stories remain to be told.

I am also indebted to Dr. Arnold Taylor of Howard University, Dr. Debra Newman Ham of Morgan State University, and Dr. Arthur Burt of Howard University for their painstaking review of the manuscript and their advice, guidance, and recommendations. I would also like to thank my editors: Nicole Bowen, Emily Ross, and Hilary Poole.

Encyclopedia of
AFRICAN-AMERICAN HERITAGE
Second Edition

A

Aaron, Henry ("Hank") (1934–) *baseball player*
Hank Aaron is best known as the baseball player with the Atlanta Braves who broke Babe Ruth's record of 714 home runs. Born in Mobile, Alabama, the third of eight children, Aaron began his professional career in 1952 with the Indianapolis Clowns of the Negro American League. The Clowns paid him $200 a month, and Aaron led the league with a .467 average his first season. The Braves, then based in Milwaukee, purchased his contract for $10,000 in 1954. Three years later, he was named National League MVP. When it became clear that he would probably break Babe Ruth's record, Aaron received thousands of hate-filled letters, some of which threatened his life. However, he went on to hit his 715th home run on April 8, 1974, in a game against the Los Angeles Dodgers. He retired in 1976 with a home run total of 755. Aaron became a vice president with the Atlanta Braves and was elected to the Baseball Hall of Fame in 1982. "I had to break that record," he said. "I had to do it for Jackie [ROBINSON] and my people and myself and for everybody who ever called me a nigger."[1] His autobiography is entitled *I Had a Hammer: The Hank Aaron Story.*

Portrait of Hank Aaron in uniform during his rookie year with the Milwaukee Braves (*Archive Photos*)

Abbott, Robert Sengstacke (1870–1940)
newspaper publisher
Robert Abbott was a newspaper publisher and founder of the Chicago *Defender,* one of the most important African-American newspapers in the country. The first edition of the *Defender,* which came out in 1905, ran four pages. Abbott sold it door-to-door himself for four cents a copy. As the *Defender* grew in size and influence, it developed a

[1] Columbus Salley, *The Black 100.* New York: Citadel Press, 1994, p. 316.

1

nationwide black readership previously ignored by the white press. The paper's militant demands for political, economic, and social justice caused it to be banned in many southern towns during World War I. Abbott later served on the Chicago Commission of Race Relations and was active in the fight to ensure that African Americans participated in Franklin Roosevelt's New Deal programs.

Abele, Julian Francis (1881–1950) *architect*

Julian Abele was the architect who designed the Philadelphia Museum of Art, much of Duke University, the Philadelphia Free Library, Widener Library at Harvard, and the building that is now the Institute of Fine Arts at New York University. In 1902, Abele became the first African-American student to graduate from the University of Pennsylvania School of Architecture. He then spent four years in Paris where he studied at the Ecole des Beaux-Arts and came to the attention of Philadelphia architect Horace Trumbauer. When he returned to the United States, he joined Trumbauer's architecture firm and became chief designer in 1909. Abele vacationed regularly in Europe, where he spent numerous hours sketching Gothic cathedrals and other buildings, and this European influence is evident in many of his designs. Because of his race, he received little public recognition during his years at the Trumbauer firm, and many of the company's clients were unaware of his work on their designs. However, architectural historians credit Julian Abele as being the primary designer on many major projects in addition to the ones listed above.

Abernathy, Ralph David (1926–1990) *civil rights leader*

After serving in the armed forces during World War II, Ralph Abernathy attended Alabama State College, where he was president of the student body, and Atlanta University. He bacame a baptist minister in 1948. In 1951 he joined the teaching faculty of Alabama State College. Later, he joined the First Baptist Church in Montgomery, Alabama, as pastor. There he became a close friend of MARTIN

Doctor Ralph Abernathy *(SCLC)*

LUTHER KING JR. and helped found the Montgomery Improvement Association, the organization that directed the 1955 MONTGOMERY BUS BOYCOTT. In 1957, he, King, and several others founded what later became the SOUTHERN CHRISTIAN LEADERSHIP CONFERENCE (SCLC). In 1968, Abernathy became SCLC president, resigning in 1977 when he ran unsuccessfully for Congress. Earlier, he had helped plan the historic 1963 MARCH ON WASHINGTON. Abernathy helped plan and worked on many civil rights marches and protests until his death in April 1990. His autobiography is titled *And the Walls Came Tumbling Down.*

abolitionist movement

The abolitionist movement was a political and social movement to end slavery. The idea that slavery was morally wrong first gained widespread acceptance in the United States during the American Revolution. Abigail Adams, the wife of John Adams, spoke for many when she wrote that it was hypocritical for colonists to demand liberty for themselves while denying it to slaves. Other well-known whites who advocated an end to slavery included Benjamin Franklin, Thomas Paine, the marquis de Lafayette, Noah Webster, and John Jay, the first chief justice of the U.S. Supreme Court.

Massachusetts courts abolished slavery in that state in 1783, noting that the new state constitution declared that "all men are born free and equal." Pennsylvania had moved even earlier, in 1780, to provide for gradual emancipation. By 1804, all states north of Delaware had passed laws aimed at freeing their slaves, and abolitionists had succeeded in outlawing slavery in all territory covered by the Northwest Ordinance of 1787. Congress outlawed the transatlantic slave trade as of January 1, 1808. However, the federal government was not sympathetic to the antislavery movement. In 1835, President Andrew Jackson asked Congress to outlaw mail distribution of abolitionist literature in the South. A year later, the House of Representatives instituted a gag rule whereby antislavery petitions were set aside instead of being considered. Abolitionists argued that the gag rule violated the First Amendment right to petition for redress of grievances, but it was not overturned until 1845. Other major abolitionist political battles in the United States involved the Missouri Compromise, the Kansas-Nebraska Act, the FUGITIVE SLAVE LAW, the DRED SCOTT case, the AMISTAD mutiny, and the CREOLE MUTINY.

The Abolitionist Societies

The New England Anti-Slavery Society was formed in 1831, under the leadership of William Lloyd Garrison, who was to become the leading white spokesperson for militant abolition. Two years later, a more moderate group, encouraged by developments in Great Britain, founded the American Anti-Slavery Society in Philadelphia. Within three years, it was able to field 70 lecturers and distribute four periodicals. Another major abolitionist organization, The American and Foreign Anti-Slavery Society, which emphasized political action, was set up in 1840. Though blacks were very active in these groups, they had begun organizing on their own even earlier. By 1830, African Americans in the

northern United States had formed at least 50 committees to help fugitive slaves escape and to raise money to purchase others still held in captivity.

Abolitionist Writings

The best-known abolitionist newspaper was William Lloyd Garrison's *Liberator.* Approximately 90 percent of its 450 first-year subscribers were African American, even though it was issued at a time when slaves were generally forbidden to learn to read, let alone subscribe to a newspaper, and free blacks were often too poor to buy one. Another important paper was the *North Star,* published by FREDERICK DOUGLASS. Such papers were a favorite target of proslavery mobs. In 1837, shortly after his printing presses were wrecked for the third time, abolitionist editor Elijah Lovejoy was murdered by a proslavery mob in Alton, Ohio.

People caught with abolitionist newspapers or literature in their possession were often subjected to physical abuse and criminal charges. A Georgia man who had subscribed to the *Liberator* was tarred and feathered, set on fire, and then whipped by a mob. A Maryland court sentenced a free African American named Samuel Green to 10 years in prison merely for having a copy of Harriet Beecher Stowe's UNCLE TOM'S CABIN in his possession. However, the most explosive piece of abolitionist writing was *David Walker's Appeal.* Published in 1829, it was so incendiary that the *Richmond Enquirer* refused even to mention it by name for fear slaves might learn of it. Abolitionists' arguments attacked slavery on several fronts. They maintained that it was contrary to the ideals of freedom and democracy, that it was economically wasteful and harmful to free laborers, that it created problems of arson and revolt that threatened even nonslaveholding whites, and that it was a cruel, vicious practice that was un-Christian and morally wrong. In spite of the violent reaction they frequently incurred, abolitionists continued to make an impact, even among slaveholders. In commenting on his four years of work helping others escape, one ex-slave said,

> I don't know to this day how he [Mr. Tabb, his owner] never knew what I was doing. I used to

CHRONOLOGY OF THE ANTISLAVERY MOVEMENT IN THE UNITED STATES

1619   Twenty Africans are imported to Jamestown. They are regarded as indentured servants rather than slaves.

1661   Virginia House of Burgesses recognizes chattel slavery as legal.

1733   Spanish Florida offers freedom to slaves escaping from British colonies.

1735   Georgia forbids importation or use of slaves. Statute is later repealed.

1774   Importation of slaves is banned by the Massachusetts legislature, but the legislation is blocked by royal governor Thomas Gage.

Connecticut forbids the importation or sale of slaves but allows ownership.

Continental Congress bans the importation of slaves after December 1, 1774. The southern colonies ignore this bill, which has no enforcement provision.

Rhode Island frees slaves brought in after December 1, 1774, but does not liberate slaves already in bondage.

1775   Virginia's royal governor, Lord Dunmore, offers freedom to male slaves who enlist in the British army during the American Revolution (about 800 eventually do).

1776   Delaware's new constitution forbids the importation of slaves.

A resolution by the Second Continental Congress asks that no more slaves be imported into the colonies.

1777   Vermont's state constitution is the first to ban ownership of slaves.

1780   Pennsylvania provides for the gradual emancipation of all slaves. It also becomes the first state to permit interracial marriage.

Massachusetts abolishes slavery through legislation, a law upheld by the state supreme court in 1783. This also applied to Maine, which was then a territory of Massachusetts.

1783   New Hampshire forbids chattel slavery.

Virginia, Maryland, and Delaware agree to ban the African slave trade.

1787   Slavery is forbidden in the Northwest Territory by the Ordinance of 1787. The area is later divided into the states of Ohio, Indiana, Illinois, Michigan, Wisconsin, and parts of Minnesota.

1804   New Jersey forbids future bondage, but slavery continues due to a grandfather clause. By 1830, about two-thirds of the people still enslaved in the North are in New Jersey.

1807   Congress bans the African slave trade as of January 1, 1808, as provided for in Article I, Section 9 of the Constitution.

1817   New York schedules complete abolition by July 4, 1827.

1820   The Missouri Compromise admits Maine to the Union as a free state and Missouri as a slave state and closes U.S. territory north of 36°30′ to slaveholders.

1831   *Liberator* begins publication, becoming the leading abolitionist newspaper.

1832   New England Anti-Slavery Society is founded.

1842   The U.S. Supreme Court, while supporting the Fugitive Slave Act of 1793, holds that state and local authorities are not bound to aid in recovery of escaped slaves.

1844   The Liberty Party, opposed to any expansion of slave territory, nominates James G. Birney for president. He gets less than 3 percent of the vote.

1848   Slavery is banned in the Oregon Territory, which later becomes the states of Oregon, Idaho, Washington, and parts of Montana.

1850   The Compromise of 1850 admits California as a free state, bans the slave trade in the District of Columbia, but supports the idea of popular sovereignty to determine whether territories enter the Union as free or slave states.

(Continued)

CHRONOLOGY OF THE ANTISLAVERY MOVEMENT IN THE UNITED STATES (Continued)

1854   Opponents of the 1854 Kansas-Nebraska Act organize what later becomes the Republican Party. The act established the territories of Kansas and Nebraska and left the question of slavery there to be decided by the settlers. The effect was to override the Missouri Compromise of 1820, which would have outlawed slavery in both territories.

Growing abolitionist sentiment results in strong opposition to the Ostend Manifesto, a proposal to acquire Cuba as a slaveholding territory.

1855   Massachusetts enacts a personal liberty law to protect black residents, rejecting the Fugitive Slave Law in the Compromise of 1850.

1856   Five proslavery settlers in Kansas are killed by John Brown and his men in the Pottawatomie Creek Massacre.

The Republican Party platform calls for admitting Kansas as a free state.

1860   The merchant ship *Erie* is seized by federal forces with a cargo of 890 slaves. Her captain, Nathaniel Gordon, is hanged in 1862.

1861   The Civil War begins. The First Confiscation Act emancipates slaves within Union army lines in the area of "the rebellion."

Slavery is banned in the Nebraska Territory.

1862   Congress forbids slavery in all nonstate territories and in the District of Columbia. Owners are promised compensation.

Second Confiscation Act emancipates all slaves whose owners are in rebellion against the United States.

1863   Emancipation Proclamation is issued January 1, freeing all slaves in the Confederacy. It does not apply to the border states—Delaware, Maryland, Kentucky, and much of Missouri—or areas under Union control.

1864   Maryland's state constitution is amended to abolish slavery.

1865   The Thirteenth Amendment is passed, abolishing slavery throughout the United States and its territories.

take some awful chances, and he knew I must have been up to something. Sometimes I think he did know and wanted me to get the slaves away that way so he wouldn't have to cause hard feelings [in the white community] by freeing 'em. I think Mr. Tabb used to talk a lot to Mr. John Fee. Mr. Fee . . . used to always tell us—we never let our owners see us listening to him though—that God didn't intend for some men to be free and some men be in slavery. He used to talk to the owners, too, when they would listen to him, but mostly they hated the sight of John Fee.[1]

Abolitionist Political Parties

The first abolitionist political party was the Liberty Party, which was founded in 1840. It nominated

[1] B. A. Botkin, ed., *Lay My Burden Down*. Chicago, Ill.: University of Chicago, 1973, p. 188.

James Birney (an abolitionist editor who was nearly killed in 1836) for president in 1840 and 1844, but it was unable to win more than 60,000 votes. The Free Soil Party, which opposed the extension of slavery into new western territories, was organized in 1847 and ran Martin van Buren for president the following year. Its members were among the early supporters of the new antislavery Republican Party, which was founded in 1854.

End of Slavery

Slavery in the United States came to an end with the Civil War (1861–65), during which President Abraham Lincoln issued the EMANCIPATION PROCLAMATION freeing all slaves in Confederate-held territory, and afterward, with the 1865 ratification of the THIRTEENTH AMENDMENT to the Constitution freeing all slaves in U.S. territory. Elsewhere, abolitionists in Britain were able to get that country to outlaw the African slave trade in 1807. Twenty-six years later, shocked by the brutality of the great 1831 BAPTIST WAR in Jamaica, Britain freed 780,000 colonial slaves after paying £20 million to their owners and instituting a forced labor APPRENTICESHIP program to ease the transition for the former owners. Slavery was finally abolished in Britain's New World colonies in 1838, but its continued existence was later ignored in Britain's African colonies. In Central and South America, the abolitionist fight gained momentum in conjunction with the struggle for independence from Spain and Portugal.

Although the United Nations outlawed slavery in its 1948 Universal Declaration of Human Rights, the practice was not prohibited by the Sultanate of Muscat and Oman until 1970. Though illegal, slavery continues to be practiced in several West African and Middle Eastern countries. As of 1996, between 90,000 and 300,000 persons were still enslaved in Mauritania, and thousands of others were in bondage in Sudan. Moreover, customs involving debt bondage, the selling of women and girls into marriage, and coercive child labor practices are still a major problem in many parts of the world.

See also DAVID WALKER.

Aborigines

A black ethnic group that has lived in Australia for approximately 40,000 years. Aborigines are sometimes called the People of the Dream, since they believe the universe began in "Dreamtime," a mystery time/place where the ancestors live and the physical and psychic worlds are linked. When Europeans arrived in Australia in 1788, there were around 300,000 Aborigines divided into perhaps 500 tribes; they spoke approximately 200 separate languages and 700 dialects. Though they often fought among themselves, they were linked by their religious beliefs. They lacked a formal political structure but were noted for their complicated marriage and kinship relationships. According to Aborigine culture, land belonged to the tribe rather than to individuals and could not be sold or transferred. They bitterly resisted white attempts to fence off land thereby limiting the Aborigines' ability to hunt.

Australia was first used as a British penal colony, and the whites initially sent there were either con-

victs or military guards. Because of their superb hunting skills, Aborigines were often hired to track down escaped prisoners—a practice that did not endear them to the convicts. The Australian colonial government failed to persuade the Aborigines to take up farming, and when the Aborigines persisted in maintaining their traditional lifestyle, a South Wales court in 1836 simply ruled that they were too scattered and disorganized to be able to claim title to any land. Aborigines were declared British subjects, and although the colonial government asked settlers to respect their rights, the settlers—many of them ex-convicts who had completed their sentences—were allowed to settle any disputes with them without trial on the theory that Aborigines were unable to understand judicial proceedings. In practice, this meant Aborigines were often beaten or murdered whenever conflicts with whites arose. Aborigines resisted through guerrilla warfare and by

An Aborigine throwing a spear. Hall's Creek, Kimberly, Australia, 1885 (*Library of Congress*)

killing specific Europeans whom they regarded as guilty of crimes against them. They also killed sheep, horses, and cattle belonging to settlers and burned settlers' homes. However, Aborigine weapons were no match for European firearms, and an estimated 20,000 Aborigines and 2,000–2,500 settlers were killed in this fighting. The combination of massacres, the destruction of the environment that supported the animals the Aborigines hunted, and the introduction of European diseases like cholera and influenza reduced the Aborigine population to approximately 60,000 by 1920. In 1976, the Australian government granted the Aborigine population a certain measure of autonomy.

Aborigines are famous for their boomerangs, though they also use spears that they throw 50 to 60 yards with the help of a *woomera,* a slinglike attachment that acts as an extension of the hunter's arm. They possess an extraordinary ability to mimic the sounds of numerous animals and insects and are known for their medicinal knowledge. Aborigines are also said to have unusual powers of mental telepathy.

Recommended Reading: Hughes, Robert. *The Fatal Shore.* New York: Random House, Vintage Books, 1988.

Abraham (Sohanac, Souanakke Tustenukle)
(ca.1790–ca.1871) *military adviser and interpreter*
Abraham was the primary adviser and interpreter to Micanopy, a chief of the Seminole Indians. Born a slave, Abraham escaped, possibly with the help of the British, during the War of 1812. After the British defeat, he settled among the Florida Seminole and rapidly gained an influential role.

At that time, the Seminole were the target of frequent complaints by Georgia planters for their willingness to shelter runaway slaves. Whites were also unhappy that runaways had been able to establish free black settlements along a 50-mile stretch of the Apalachicola River. To mollify the slaveowners, General Andrew Jackson, in 1816, ordered the invasion of what was then Spanish Florida in order to attack FORT NEGRO, a fortress that had been taken over by blacks after the British defeat. This was the beginning of the First Seminole War.

In 1825, Abraham accompanied Chief Micanopy to Washington, D.C., and he later served as an interpreter during the negotiations concerning the 1832 Treaty of Payne's Landing and the 1833 Treaty of Fort Gibson. Both of these treaties, which called for the removal of the Seminole from Florida, were bitterly resented. In 1835, war between the Seminole and the United States again broke out when the black wife of Chief Osceola was kidnapped and sold into slavery.

Abraham played a leading role in Seminole military operations and was active in encouraging resistance among slaves on the nearby plantations. However, the Seminole and their black allies were forced to agree to the Treaty of Fort Dade following a major defeat in 1837. This treaty was largely negotiated by Abraham, and it was his diplomatic skill that convinced the Indians to agree to it. The United States almost immediately violated the treaty, causing another outbreak of fighting, but peace was finally restored, thanks to Abraham's diplomatic maneuvers. He was shipped west with his family, though he continued to be involved in Indian affairs. Abraham was described by army officers who dealt with him as a "great" man who "ruled all the councils and actions of the Indians in this region."[1]

Abyssinia former name for ETHIOPIA.

Achebe, Chinua (1930–) *Nigerian novelist, poet, essayist, short story writer*
Achebe's first and most famous novel, *Things Fall Apart,* was published in 1958. Set in an Ibo village, it is the story of a wrestler and farmer named Okonkwo who watches colonialism destroy Ibo village society. The book's title is taken from W. B. Yeats' poem, "The Second Coming." During the Nigeria-Biafra civil war (1967–70), Achebe, an Ibo, served as a spokesperson for Biafra, the break-away region of Nigeria dominated by Ibo tribespeople. From 1972–75, he was a visiting professor of literature at the University of Massachusetts, and the following year he taught at the University of

[1] William Loren Katz, *Eyewitness: The Negro in American History.* New York: Pitman, 1971, p. 73.

Chinua Achebe (*Schomburg Center for Research in Black Culture*)

Connecticut. Achebe returned to his country in 1976 to become a professor of literature at the University of Nigeria. He is one of Africa's most popular writers and is the first African novelist to be widely read in Europe and the United States. He has used the novel to describe African life and traditions and the impact of European culture. In 1990 he was seriously injured in an auto accident and spent six months in a hospital and has since been confined to a wheelchair. In 1991, he joined the faculty at Bard College in New York. Achebe has said that his interest in literature stems from his sister, who introduced him to the art of storytelling when he was very young. Among his other works are *No Longer at Ease, Arrow of God, Beware Soul Brother, Girls at War and Other Stories,* and *Anthills of the Savannah.* In 1999, Achebe returned to Nigeria after a nine-year absence.

acquired immunodeficiency syndrome (AIDS)

An infectious disease caused by either of two related retroviruses known as *human immunodeficiency virus* (HIV). These attack the body's immune system by infiltrating the body's T cells, leaving the sufferer vulnerable to other illnesses, which eventually prove fatal. AIDS is spread primarily through contaminated blood and sexual contact. Infected mothers can also transmit the disease to their unborn children or to nursing infants. The disease can have an extremely long incubation period—as much as 10 years—before symptoms appear, although the victim can become infectious within a relatively short time. Various drugs can slow the progression of the disease, but as yet there is no cure.

AIDS has reached epidemic proportions in much of sub-Saharan Africa. According to two United Nations health organizations, UNAIDS and the World Health Organization, seven out of 10 HIV-positive adults (that is, adults who carry the HIV virus) lived in sub-Saharan Africa in 1998. Among infected children, nine out of 10 are in sub-Saharan Africa. In Botswana, Namibia, Swaziland, and Zimbabwe, one in five people between the ages of 15 and 49 is either an HIV carrier or has AIDS. In South Africa, in 2000, one in every five adults—4.2 million people—was believed to be HIV-positive, and the rate of new infections continues to increase rapidly. Zimbabwe President Robert Mugabe stated in 1999 that more than 1,200 Zimbabweans were dying each week from the disease. A shortage of burial space has led the Zimbabwe government to promote cremation to save space, in spite of the fact that this violates many cultural beliefs. Since the beginning of the epidemic, more than 11 million people in sub-Saharan Africa have died from AIDS—a number representing 83 percent of AIDS deaths worldwide. The rate of new infections in Africa is approximately 5,000 a day.

Since the majority of people with AIDS today are teenagers and adults under 50, the ages when many people become parents, AIDS is likely to cut population growth by as much as 5 percent in Africa as a whole, and by much higher percentages in countries with high infection rates. And because its victims are generally in their most productive years, AIDS will have a severe impact on Africa's economic, social, and political future. Officials in Swaziland have stated that 70 percent of the teachers in that small kingdom are HIV-positive and that education there is threatened as a result. It is estimated that the disease has made orphans of approximately 12.1 million children in Africa; at least 1 million children there are infected with the HIV virus. In Zambia, more than half the juvenile population has already lost one or both parents to the disease. Although the AIDS epidemic is worldwide, 95 percent of all AIDS orphans are in Africa. Traditionally, orphans in Africa have been cared for by the EXTENDED FAMILY. The large numbers of orphans now being created, however, are placing a great strain on this system. Medical treatment is expensive and often beyond the reach of those in need. In 1999, the Bristol-Myers Squibb Company donated $100 million for research and the training of doctors in Africa. Some researchers believe that unless a vaccine can be developed, AIDS may kill up to 40 percent of the population of sub-Saharan Africa within the next 30 years. Because of the potential of the disease to destroy the social, cultural, political, and economic infrastructure of many African countries and trigger wars and rebellions, the Clinton administration, in April 2000, formally designated AIDS as a threat to U.S. national security.

Aesop (Aethiop) (ca. 620–560 B.C.) *fabulist*

Aesop was the creator and collector of what is now referred to as *Aesop's Fables*. Although he lived in ancient Greece, Aesop is believed to have been a black slave from Phrygia, a region now in central Turkey. References to him by Aristotle and other ancient Greek scholars, and the fact that the Athenians erected a statue to him, indicate that at some point he was freed. His fables, which generally involve animals, have lasted more than 2,000 years and are still quoted for their wisdom and moral outlook. Among the everyday phrases that his fables have made popular are "don't count your chickens before they hatch," "sour grapes," and "look before you leap."

affirmative action

Social and legal means used to attack discrimination in education and employment; to encourage the hiring of African Americans, women, and certain other minorities; and to create greater diversity in schools and the workplace. Although discrimination in education and employment was prohibited by the Civil Rights Act of 1964, that statute did not address the need for affirmative-action programs. In a 1965 Executive Order, President Lyndon Johnson directed that contractors providing goods or services to the federal government engage in affirmative-action efforts to ensure that the percentage of blacks, women, and other minorities they hired be consistent with the percentage of blacks, women, and other minority groups in the local community. When contractors were found to be "underutilizing" any of these groups—that is, when the percentages of blacks, women, or other minorities being hired were significantly lower than the percentages of such groups in the local labor force—contractors were obliged to establish "goals" and "timetables" through which they would endeavor to hire greater numbers from the underrepresented groups until the percentage of minority workers being hired approached their percentage in the local labor force. Contractors that failed to make good-faith efforts to increase the numbers of minorities in their workforce were threatened with the loss of federal business. The Equal Employment Opportunities Act was passed in 1972 for the purpose of enforcing such plans.

When employers or labor unions have deliberately and pervasively engaged in discriminatory practices, some courts have ordered that a specific percentage of minority or female applicants be hired, until the percentage of those hired approximated the percentage of those in the local labor force. Such court-ordered, "remedial" affirmative-action plans have been reserved for extreme cases.

A number of private corporations have created voluntary affirmative-action programs designed to increase minority and female employment opportunities. Some consist simply of outreach programs designed to attract minority job applicants, while others provide limited preferential treatment to minority job-seekers. In *United Steelworkers v. Weber* (1979), the Supreme Court held that voluntary affirmative-action programs by private employers and labor unions that give preferential treatment to minority workers do not violate the nondiscrimination mandate of the Civil Rights Act, so long as the preferential treatment is used to eliminate conspicuous imbalances in traditionally segregated job classifications, does not cause the displacement of any current employees, does not act as an absolute bar to the advancement of any worker, and is used as a temporary measure until the percentage of the preferred minority group approaches its percentage in the labor force.

A number of public and private colleges and universities have established affirmative-action programs to eradicate the effects of past discrimination and to provide all students with a more diverse education experience. In *Regents of the University of California v. Bakke* (1978), the U.S. Supreme Court ruled that race could be a factor in admitting a student to a university, so long as no quotas were used. By the late 1980s the Supreme Court had begun to narrow the use of certain affirmative-action programs. It struck down a "set-aside" program by the City of Richmond that reserved a certain percentage of city contracts to firms owned by minority contractors, except in cases where past discrimination could be established. In *Adarand Constructors v. Peña* (1995), the Supreme Court found unconstitutional a federal statutory plan to encourage government entities to award certain contracts to minority-owned firms. The Court majority ruled that race-conscious programs could only be sustained where the government could demonstrate a "compelling state interest" necessitating the use of racial criteria. Preferential employment programs could be instituted only to eradicate the effects of prior discrimination in the specific employment area—not as part of an effort to overcome past discrimination in general.

In recent years, educational and employment affirmative-action programs have come under increasing attack. In *Hopwood v. State of Texas* (1996), the U.S. Court of Appeals for the Fifth Circuit threw out a University of Texas Law School program that separately considered the applications of minority applicants—even though that same law school had refused to admit African Americans until ordered to do so by the Supreme Court in the landmark case *Sweatt v. Painter* in 1950. In the late 1990s, California voters adopted Proposition 209, which outlawed consideration of ethnicity or gender by government agencies with respect to employment decisions or college admissions.

Affirmative action has resulted in a certain amount of white (and some black) resentment. Critics charge it is demeaning to women and minorities because it assumes they cannot achieve parity without special help and that it, in fact, constitutes "reverse discrimination" against persons who receive no preferences. Its proponents argue that discrimination against blacks has been so severe as to require special help in order to overcome its catastrophic impact. They claim that diversity in universities and the workplace benefits everyone in a heterogeneous society, and they further note that both employers and educational institutions have historically considered various factors—such as athletic or musical ability, family histories, etc.—when making hiring and college admission decisions, thus negating the belief that such determinations have always been based on academic achievement.

—Professor Charles Craver, George Washington
University Law School

Africa

The second-largest continent (ca. 11,677,240 sq. miles), Africa is an area of great geographical, political, and social diversity. The continent straddles the equator and is the site of four principal mountain ranges (Atlas, Ruwenzori, Drakensberg, and the Ethiopian highlands), tropical rain forests, vast grasslands, the world's largest desert (the SAHARA), the world's longest river (the NILE RIVER), the world's second-largest freshwater lake (Victoria), and the world's largest swamp (the SUDD). Africa also contains the main part of the Great Rift Valley that runs about 3,000 miles from Syria to Mozambique and is as much as 60 miles wide in places. Most of the world's diamonds are found in Africa, as are gold, oil, and other valuable deposits, and an abundance of plants and animals seen nowhere else in the world.

Africa's 700,000,000 people, who represent over 12 percent of the world's population, speak more than 800 languages. The remains of the earliest members of the human race were found there, and the continent has been home to many ancient civilizations, including EGYPT, KUSH, AXUM, CARTHAGE,

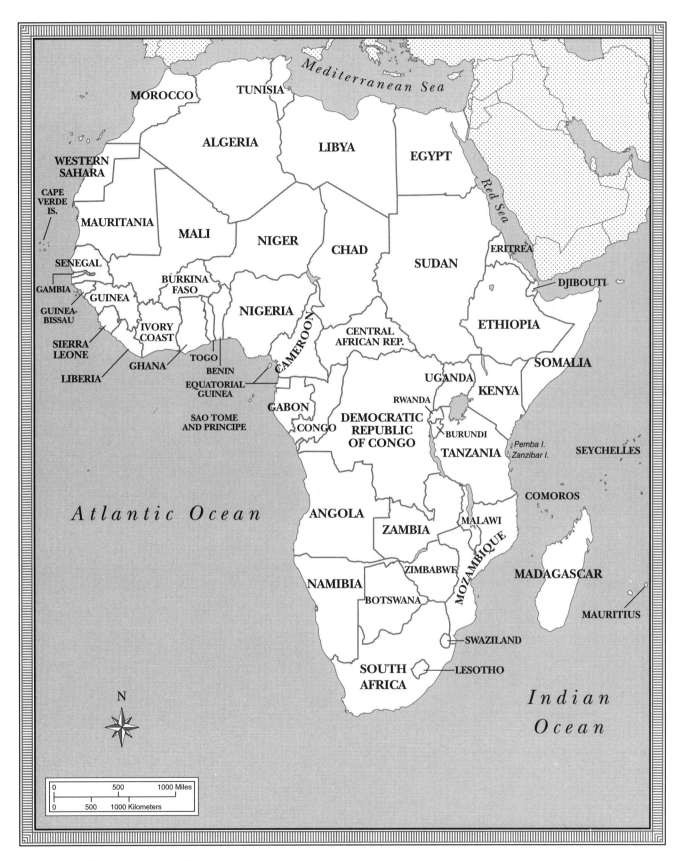

Nations of Africa (*Facts On File*)

Mask, Yaure people (*National Museum of African Art, Washington, D.C.*)

SONGHAI, EMPIRE OF MALI, KINGDOM OF GHANA, KANEM-BORNU, DAHOMEY, and ZIMBABWE.

Africans have engaged in profitable trade with Europeans and Asians throughout recorded history. However, this began to change in the early 1500s with the colonization of the Americas. European-run plantations in the New World required the services of enormous numbers of slaves, which led to the development of an immense transatlantic slave trade that lasted over 350 years. The transatlantic slave trade crowded out other commerce and plunged large sections of the continent into constant violence and warfare. This, in turn, led to the collapse of many African states and to Europe's eventual colonization of most of the continent. Africa is still suffering the results of this exploitation. Many sections of the continent are extremely poor and remain underdeveloped, and disease, drought, war, and civil disorder are continuing problems. However, Africa retains its rich diversity of peoples and resources. Before 1950, only four African countries were independent. In 2000, Africa counted 53 independent nations.

African contact with Americas before Columbus

A strong possibility exists that Africans reached the Americas prior to the arrival of Columbus in 1492, and they may have engaged in trade with Native Americans. Evidence of contact between Africans and Native Americans falls into several categories: artistic, archaeological, linguistic, agricultural, historical references, and navigational. In 1862, an immense carved head with African-like features was found in Central America. Similar carvings dating back to around 800 B.C. have been found since. Step pyramids, such as were built in Egypt, and Peruvian looms resembling those found in Africa have also been found. Certain plants, including strains of cotton and bananas, appear to have been introduced into the Americas from Africa prior to 1492. Numerous Native American words are similar to African ones, and African historical accounts tell of the Mali Empire's King Abubakari II, who set out across the Atlantic in 1311 but never returned. Aztec and Peruvian legends from the same period tell of dark-skinned men, and worship of black gods linked to travel and trade developed among Native Americans around this time. Early European explorers such as Balboa wrote of seeing African war captives in Indian villages and of hearing of isolated tribes of blacks. Finally, the flow of transatlantic ocean currents suggests the likelihood of African–Native American interaction. Such contact, if it did occur, probably took place at different times over the centuries.

Recommended Reading: Sertima, Ivan Van. *They Came Before Columbus.* New York: Random House, 1976.

African National Congress (ANC)

A political organization founded in South Africa in 1912 to counter government mistreatment of blacks and other minorities, the ANC was established in accordance with the nonviolent principles advocated by Mohandas K. Gandhi and initially focused on mass meetings and petitions. Most of its members are of XHOSA, ZULU, NDEBELE, or Sotho origin. As white oppression increased, the ANC began calling for strikes, boycotts, and civil disobedience and launched the Defiance Campaign in the 1950s. The government responded by arresting over 8,500 people.

In 1955, the ANC adopted its Freedom Charter, which called for a multiracial struggle against APARTHEID and equal rights for all South Africans. A split occurred in 1959 when a group called the Pan Africanist Congress (PAC) broke away to follow a more militant course. In 1960, a massacre occurred in Sharpeville, near Johannesburg, when police opened fire on a crowd of unarmed blacks who were demonstrating against South Africa's notorious pass laws. (These laws required all black Africans to carry passes and have official permission to be in cities and other areas.) In the Sharpeville Massacre, 69 people were killed and more than 400 were wounded, including many women and children. The government then banned both the ANC and the PAC.

The ANC went underground, forming a military wing called Umkhonto we Sizwe (Spear of the Nation) that targeted police and government agencies for attack. The government responded by arresting hundreds of ANC supporters, including NELSON MANDELA in 1962.

The ANC then became less visible but gained many new followers after the 1976 Soweto riots in which possibly as many as 1,000 people were killed. The organization also increased its diplomatic efforts abroad, winning aid from numerous countries in Europe, Africa, and the Soviet bloc. Steady pressure from the ANC and other groups finally led to South Africa's transition to democratic rule. ANC leader NELSON MANDELA was released from prison in 1990 and was elected president of South Africa in 1994. Both Mandela and African National Congress leader Chief Albert Luthuli are winners of the Nobel Peace Prize.

age groups/age sets

This is a widespread African tribal custom of forming associations according to age. Members of each age group are taught that they have a special rela-tionship to each other, and in some ethnic groups, individuals are considered responsible for the actions of others in their group. Thus, if an elder is insulted by someone of a younger age group, all members of the younger group can be fined. At the same time, all members of the older person's age group may share in the compensation. Each age group has certain rights, responsibilities, and social obligations in relation to the rest of the tribal unit, and while collective responsibility for misbehavior is no longer common, those in the same age group often cooperate in work and other matters throughout their lives. Members of the same age group are expected to think of each other as "brothers," and the age group custom, which emphasizes group solidarity, has been an important stabilizing force in traditional African society.

AIDS see ACQUIRED IMMUNODEFICIENCY

Ailey, Alvin (1931–1989) *dancer, choreographer*

The founder of the Alvin Ailey American Dance Theatre, Ailey studied dance after graduating from high school and became choreographer of the Lester Horton Theatre in 1953. A year later, he was chosen as the lead dancer in *House of Flowers*. In 1958, Ailey formed his dance company, which has showcased more than 200 African-American dancers, including Judith Jamison. More than 15 million people around the world have seen the company perform. In addition to performing himself, Ailey has choreographed Leonard Bernstein's *Mass* and Bizet's *Carmen*.

Akan

Akan is a language spoken in much of Ghana and parts of the Ivory Coast. The term Akan also refers to a person who speaks that language and to a number of medieval and precolonial West African states. The earliest Akan-speaking peoples traveled from the north to what is now Ghana in a series of migrations between the 11th and 13th centuries. They mixed with the people already in the area, established villages, and supported themselves through farming. By the 17th century, Akan peoples dominated the area and had formed a number of small states that traded with each other and with merchants as far away as Benin. Commerce in the Akan states revolved around salt, kola nuts, slaves, and gold, a metal in which the Akan-controlled area was extremely rich. In fact, Europeans later referred to the region as the Gold Coast. As trade increased, one Akan group, the ASHANTI, was eventually able to establish itself as the foremost military and commercial power in the region. Other major Akan groups included the Denkyira, the Akwame, and the FANTE. Akan is one of Ghana's national languages.

Aldridge, Ira Frederick (ca. 1807–1867) *actor*

Aldridge was described by critics as among the greatest Shakespearean actors of his time. It is thought that he was born in New York City, where he attended the African Free School. He became interested in the theater while still in his teens and moved to England in 1824 to further his career. In 1833, he appeared at the Theatre Royal, Covent Garden, in the role of *Othello*. He toured Europe in 1852 and was honored by the government of Haiti and by theatrical groups in Germany, Hungary, Switzerland, Russia, and other countries. He died while on tour in Poland.

Algeria

Africa's second-largest country. Capital: Algiers. Located on the Mediterranean coast, Algeria was a French colony that gained its independence in 1962 after a bitter revolt. The Sahara occupies much of the southern part of the country, with most of the population concentrated along the Mediterranean shore. In ancient times, what is now Algeria was occupied by Numidia, a country that was part of the Carthaginian Empire until it was temporarily granted independence by Rome after the Punic Wars. Ancient Roman ruins can still be seen, and it was in Algeria that St. AUGUSTINE spent much of his life and wrote *The City of God* in A.D. 412. Algeria was conquered by the Vandals in A.D. 430, and came under the control of the Byzantine Empire after the fall of Rome in A.D. 476. The Arab invasion in the

seventh and eighth centuries permanently established Islam in the area. Later the region was a base for Barbary pirates and a center of the slave trade.

The French invaded and colonized Algeria in 1830, after subduing the Arab and Berber population. In 1943, Ferhat Abbas gave voice to a growing nationalist movement with his "Manifesto of the Algerian People," which demanded a constitution and other reforms. Violent opposition to French rule began in 1945 with riots at the town of Setif that killed 100 Europeans and triggered a government crackdown that caused the deaths of 8,000 Muslims. It gained momentum in the 1950s under the leadership of the Front de Libération Nationale (FLN). The French were eventually forced out in 1962 in spite of the terrorist tactics of the Organisation de l'Armée Secrète (OAS), a renegade French army group backed by French settlers who wanted Algeria integrated into France. Tens of thousands of Algerians died in the revolt. A new socialist government under Ahmed Ben Bella was overthrown in 1963 and was succeeded by one under Col. Houari Boumédienne. Major progress regarding civil rights and the rights of women was threatened by violent opposition from Islamic fundamentalists who killed more than 100,000 Algerians after the Algerian military overturned the 1992 elections. In 1999, President Abdelaziz Bouteflika agreed to a peace with the Islamic Salvation Army, the main military wing of the rebel Islamic Salvation Front. A year later, in January 2000, he tried to end the continuing civil unrest by offering amnesty to rebel fighters. More than 1,000 rebels surrendered, and the Islamic Salvation Army officially announced its dissolution. However, other antigovernment organizations, including the Armed Islamic Group, rejected the offer and continued to murder civilians in an effort to bring down the government. Southern Algeria is the site of the ancient TASSILI-N-AJJER rock paintings, which date back to 8500 B.C.

Ali, Muhammad (Cassius Clay) (1942–)
heavyweight boxing champion

Ali, who was originally named Cassius Clay, became a professional boxer after winning a gold medal in

Muhammad Ali photographed during a press conference at the London (U.K.) Hilton, 1974 (*Express Newspapers/Archive Photos*)

the 1960 Olympics. He reached his boxing peak in his twenties at a time when the Civil Rights movement was already in full swing and the black power movement was beginning to gain momentum.

In 1964, after defeating Sonny Liston to become heavyweight champion, Clay announced that he had become a member of the NATION OF ISLAM and would thereafter be known by the Islamic name Muhammad Ali. The announcement was met with widespread criticism. Additional criticism followed his request for a draft deferment on grounds that he was a Muslim minister. Ali had previously been classified 1-Y after failing a preinduction mental test, but in 1966, he was suddenly reclassified A-1. He refused to be inducted into the army, saying "No Vietcong ever called me Nigger." As a result, he was sentenced to five years in prison and stripped of his boxing title by the World Boxing Association and his license to fight was revoked by the New York

State Athletic Commission. Ali remained free on bail while the case was appealed, and in 1970, Judge Walter Mansfield ruled that the athletic commission had acted illegally in denying him a license to box. In 1971, the U.S. Supreme Court overturned his conviction.

On March 8, 1971, Ali lost to Joe Frazier in what was called the "Fight of the Century." A second fight with Frazier in 1974 ended in an Ali victory. Ten months later, he fought heavyweight champion George Foreman and regained his title. In 1975, Ali met Joe Frazier for the third time for the "Thrilla in Manila" and won when Frazier's manager stopped the fight. He lost his title to Leon Spinks in 1978 but regained it seven months later.

When he retired in 1979, his boxing record was 56 wins, 3 losses. Ali often referred to himself as "the Greatest" and frequently used rhymes to taunt his opponents. He was the first man to win the heavyweight crown three times and is regarded as one of the most skillful boxers of all time. An Oscar-winning documentary called *When We Were Kings*, about Ali's 1974 fight with George Foreman, was released in 1996. He was honored at the 1996 Olympics in Atlanta.

Allen, Richard (1760–1831) *abolitionist and founder of the African Methodist Episcopal Church*
Born a slave, Richard Allen taught himself to read and write and earned enough money to purchase his freedom when he was 23. He became a Methodist minister in Philadelphia, but found himself unwelcome in white churches. In 1787, Allen and ABSALOM JONES founded the Free African Society, an abolitionist benevolent religious group. Allen also established the African Methodist Episcopal Church (A.M.E.), which would eventually become a national organization. When hundreds of people died during a yellow fever epidemic in Philadelphia in 1793, Allen and Jones arranged for members of the African-American community to act as nurses and undertakers. Along with JAMES FORTEN, the two men later organized a group of 2,500 African Americans to defend Philadelphia when the British threatened the city during the War of 1812.

Almoravids (Al-MORE-ah-vids)

The Almoravids were a fanatical BERBER/Moorish group of Muslim warriors. The sect began in the 11th century in what is now MAURITANIA, when a Berber holy man named Abdallah Ibn Yasin left MOROCCO and founded a monastery on an island in the Senegal River. His early followers were Sanhaja Berbers who were already in conflict with other Berber groups to the north and south. The Almoravid movement united the various Sanhaja clans and molded them into a victorious army able to dominate the trans-Sahara gold trade by 1055 with the capture of Sijilmasa (in Morocco) and Awdaghust (in Mauritania). Ibn Yasin was killed in 1059 and was succeeded by Abu Bakr ibn Umar. Under Abu Bakr, the Almoravids conquered the kingdom of GHANA in 1076 and founded the city of Marrakesh in Morocco in 1070. In 1087, Almoravid rule in West Africa came to an end when Abu Bakr was killed by rebelling tribes in what is now MALI. He was succeeded by Yusuf ibn Tashufin (Yusuf I), who overran all of Morocco and then responded to the request of the Muslim rulers of Spain to help prevent a Christian conquest there. Entering Spain with an army of 13,000 men and 6,000 Senegalese cavalrymen, the Almoravids massacred the 70,000 Christian troops of King Alphonso VI at the 1086 battle of Zalakah. They then took control of Spain from the local Moorish rulers. The Almoravids maintained control of Morocco and Spain until 1147, when they were overthrown by another Berber religious sect, the Almohads, under the leadership of Abd al-Mu'min.

Recommended Reading: Brett, Michael, and Elizabeth Fentress. *The Berbers.* Cambridge, Mass.: Blackwell Publishers, 1996.

American Colonization Society

An organization formed in 1816 to establish a black colony in Africa. The idea of resettling ex-slaves and free blacks in Africa or elsewhere was widely regarded by many people as a practical solution not only to slavery but to all racial problems in the United States. By 1832, more than a dozen state governments had agreed to back the idea, and approximately 15,000 black people eventually migrated to LIBERIA. But strong opposition to colonization soon developed among free African Americans who saw it as a means of eliminating black opponents to slavery. White slaveholders saw it the same way, and many of the leaders of the American Colonization Society were men sympathetic to the slave system. Two African-American leaders who strongly supported the idea of colonization were MARTIN DELANY and PAUL CUFFE. Cuffe went so far as to arrange to transport 38 blacks to Africa at his own expense. However, most black leaders rejected the idea of colonization, and the movement faded as abolitionist resistance to it grew. Back-to-Africa movements have been a recurrent phenomenon, supported by Henry McNeal Turner and MARCUS GARVEY, among others, and later found expression as part of the PAN-AFRICAN MOVEMENT.

Amistad

A U.S.-built slave ship on which a successful mutiny took place in 1839 under the leadership of an African named Joseph Cinqué. Cinqué had been shipped to Havana, Cuba, on the *Tecora* under conditions so terrible that more than one-third of the 500 captives aboard died. The Anglo-Spanish treaty of 1817 made it illegal to import slaves into Cuba, and the captives were secretly transferred to hidden barracoons (pens for holding slaves) on the island. After two weeks, Cinqué and 52 other captives were placed aboard the *Amistad,* where Cinqué managed to pry a nail out of the ship's hull and use it to undo the chains binding him and the others. They then killed the captain and most of the crew. The two slave owners, José Ruiz and Pedro Montes, who were also aboard, were allowed to live in exchange for agreeing to sail the ship back to Africa. However, Montes secretly changed direction each night in an effort to land the ship in the southern United States, where slavery was legal.

Instead, the *Amistad* landed in the north near Montauk Point on Long Island, where the ship was boarded by the U.S. Coast Guard. Cinqué and the other slaves were arrested and charged with mutiny and murder. The trial was held on January 7, 1840, in New Haven, Connecticut. By this time, abolitionist groups had rallied around the accused Africans, arguing that Cinqué and the others had every right to resist their enslavement. So much controversy was generated by the event that classes at Yale Law School were dismissed so students could attend the trial. The court ruled for the Africans, but the decision was appealed. When the Circuit Court of Appeals upheld the lower court's decision, the case was appealed to the U.S. Supreme Court. At this point, former president John Quincy Adams agreed to represent the Africans. A strong abolitionist, Adams was then in his seventies and almost blind. Nevertheless, he delivered an eight-hour argument before the Supreme Court, which ruled in favor of the Africans on March 9, 1841. Cinqué and the others were ordered freed, and they were shipped to Freetown, the settlement for freed slaves in Sierra Leone.

Recommended Reading: Jones, Howard. *Mutiny on the Amistad.* New York: Oxford University Press, 1987.

Anderson, Marian (1897–1993) *opera singer*

Marian Anderson was said by the great conductor Arturo Toscanini to have the kind of voice that is "heard only once in a hundred years." A contralto, she began singing as a child at Philadelphia's Union Baptist Church. In 1925, she won the Lewisohn Stadium Concert Award after competing against 300 other young singers. This was followed by a concert tour and an appearance as a soloist with the New York Philharmonic Orchestra. Anderson then traveled throughout the world, singing to packed audiences in country after country. But in 1939, she was barred from singing in Constitution Hall in Washington, D.C., because she was black. The incident made headlines across the country. In protest, First Lady Eleanor Roosevelt resigned from the Daughters of the American Revolution (D.A.R.), which owned Constitution Hall. She also arranged for Anderson to sing instead at the Lincoln Memorial, where she later performed before a crowd of 75,000.

In 1955, Marian Anderson became the first African American to sing at the Metropolitan Opera House in New York. Two years later, she toured Asia

Marian Anderson preparing to sing at the dedication of a mural commemorating her historic free concert on the steps of the Lincoln Memorial. January 6, 1943 (*Library of Congress*)

at the request of the State Department. In 1958, she was appointed a member of the U.S. delegation to the United Nations. Her autobiography is entitled *My Lord, What a Morning.*

Anderson, Osborne Perry (1830–1871)
abolitionist, African-American revolutionary
An Oberlin College student, Anderson was one of John Brown's raiders who staged the attack on HARPERS FERRY, West Virginia, in 1859. He managed to escape and later wrote a book, *A Voice from Harper's Ferry,* about his experiences. He served in the Union army during the Civil War.

Angelou, Maya (Marguerite Johnson)
(1928–) *poet, playwright, actress, dancer*
Born Marguerite Johnson in St. Louis, Missouri, Maya Angelou was the first African-American street-car conductor in San Francisco, taught drama and music in Ghana, edited a newspaper in Egypt, and studied cinematography in Sweden. She is especially noted for her series of autobiographies: *I Know Why the Caged Bird Sings* (1970), *Gather Together in My Name* (1974), *Singin' and Swingin' and Gettin' Merry Like Christmas* (1976), *The Heart of a Woman* (1981), and *All God's Children Need Traveling Shoes* (1986). She wrote the screenplay and score for the movie *Georgia, Georgia* and in the 1960s was asked by Dr. Martin Luther King Jr. to become the Northern coordinator for the Southern Christian Leadership Conference. In 1972, Angelou won a Pulitzer Prize for her book of poems, *Just Give Me a Cool Drink of Water 'fore I Diiie.* Maya Angelou was the first Reynolds Professor of American Studies at Wake Forest University. In 1993, she read her poem *On the Pulse of Morning* at President Bill Clinton's inauguration. She made her directing debut in 1998 with *Down in the Delta.*

Angola, People's Republic of
A country in southwestern Africa, bordering the Atlantic Ocean. Capital: Luanda. Angola has an area of almost 500,000 square miles and an estimated population of 8,960,000. The official language is Portuguese, though most Angolans also speak one of several BANTU languages. Oil is a major export.

The Portuguese arrived in Angola in the 16th century and attempted to develop a slave trade there as they had further north. The coastal area was then part of the Ndongo kingdom. (The Ndongo king's title, *ngola,* was the basis for the name *Angola.*) The Ndongo kingdom was part of the KONGO federation, but managed to gain its independence in 1556, thanks to the availability of Portuguese firearms. Initially, the Ngolas intended to establish a trading partnership with Portugal, but the Portuguese attempted to take control of their kingdom, and a series of wars resulted. Because of the constant violence and the gangs of slave traders roaming the countryside, Ndongo's leaders set up a new state farther inland. There, Queen NZINGA continued the fight against the Portuguese, defeating their forces in 1643, 1647, and 1648, but was eventually forced to come to terms with them in 1656. The Portuguese finally succeeded in gaining a loose control of the Angola coast around 1700.

Total Portuguese colonization of inland sections of the country occurred in 1925. In 1961, a revolt triggered a long-term guerrilla war led by the Movimento Popular de Libertação de Angola (MPLA), and Angola finally achieved its independence in 1975. A power struggle between the MPLA-run government and the União Nacional para a Independência Total de Angola (UNITA) resulted in a brutal civil war, which was aggravated by the fact that Angola was caught in the middle of the cold war struggle between the United States and the Soviet Union. A cease-fire led to elections in 1992, but fighting broke out again when UNITA leader Jonas Savimbi was defeated by MPLA leader Jose Eduardo Dos Santos. Full-scale civil war resumed in 1998. Lack of food is a major problem and much of the population is seriously malnourished. Because of the mines laid during the war, Angola now suffers one of the highest rates of amputees per capita of any country in the world.

animism
Animism is the religious belief, prevalent throughout much of Africa, that individual spirits live in

every person, animal, plant, and object. In general, animists believe that there is a single Supreme Creator of the universe but that it is not necessary to pray to Him since He is already friendly to people. Instead, people ask the spirits for help, a practice that often involves consulting herb doctors or diviners and the practice of magic.

To protect themselves from evil, animists often carry fetishes, which are charms or amulets such as dolls, wood carvings, stones, feathers, animal teeth, or pieces of bone. These fetishes are believed to be either inhabited or blessed by a spirit. The practice of wearing them is somewhat similar to the Western custom of wearing religious medals or placing religious symbols on walls or doorposts.

Unlike Western traditions, which emphasize the need to control or dominate nature, animist beliefs reflect a feeling that the individual is only a small part of the natural world and has a responsibility to remain in harmony with it. This harmony is produced in part through rituals marking childbirth, puberty, initiation into special groups, weddings, funerals, and other significant occasions.

Ancester veneration is an important aspect of animist religious life and is closely related to African traditions of EXTENDED FAMILY and clan obligations. In contrast to Western religious belief, which often attributes evil to outside forces such as the Devil, many Africans believe that bad luck or misfortune happens for personal reasons, such as failure to carry out a given ritual, placate a spirit, or show proper respect for a deceased ancestor. Spirits are believed to interact with each other and with people, causing both good and evil. For example, the spirit of a tree is said to draw strength from the spirits of the earth and the rain. If someone cuts the tree down, he or she is expected to plant a new tree so that the spirit of the old one will have someplace to live. Failure to do this can bring bad luck.

Some Africans believe that a person's shadow provides protection from evil or disturbed spirits, since the shadow is thought to represent the individual's soul. At night, when shadows cannot be seen, it is thought that one's soul wanders through the spirit world collecting dreams. Animist beliefs differ from tribe to tribe, but in general they reflect the idea that everything in the universe is related in some way to everything else and that all things—animals, plants, insects, rocks, trees, rivers—have a place and a purpose and should be regarded with respect.

apartheid

Apartheid is a rigid segregationist system set up in SOUTH AFRICA by the ruling white population shortly after the victory of the Nationalist Party in 1948. Black Africans had already been denied the vote even before the Union of South Africa was formed in 1910. The Group Areas Act of 1959 classified all South Africans by race (Black, White, or Coloured—meaning Indian, Asian, or mixed race), and all people were required to live within set racial boundaries. The cities were reserved for white occupation, and approximately 3.5 million black people lost their homes when they were forced to move. Many blacks were resettled in rural BANTUSTANS or "homelands" far from their original homes. Intermarriage was made illegal, and prison terms of up to seven years were imposed on persons convicted of engaging in interracial sex. All blacks were required to carry passes limiting their right to travel. The best jobs were reserved for whites, and black Africans were forbidden to go on strike. Apartheid laws were strictly enforced, and thousands of black Africans were beaten and/or imprisoned for even minor violations. The apartheid system was ended shortly before NELSON MANDELA became president in 1994.

Apollo Theater

famed New York theater that has showcased hundreds of leading African-American entertainers. Located at 253 West 125th Street in Harlem, the Apollo began as a burlesque house in 1914. Its audiences are considered the toughest to please, particularly on Amateur Night, and the theater is considered the ultimate test for African-American performers. Among those who have appeared on its stage are ELLA FITZGERALD, JAMES BROWN, Diana Ross and the Supremes, BESSIE SMITH, LOUIS ARMSTRONG, the Temptations, SARAH VAUGHN, BILLIE HOLIDAY, MICHAEL JACKSON, and ARETHA FRANKLIN.

apprenticeship system

The apprenticehip system was a labor system instituted by the British for ex-slaves following the Emancipation Act of 1833. The Emancipation Act freed all slaves in British territories as of August 1, 1834. Slave children under the age of six were to be freed immediately. All other slaves were required to participate in an apprenticeship program that forced them to work without pay for their former masters for 40 $\frac{1}{2}$ hours per week for the next four to six years. The masters were to continue to provide the former slaves with clothing, shelter, medical care, and either food or a plot of ground where they could grow their own provisions. The sum of twenty million pounds was to be divided among the former masters as compensation for the loss of their slaves. The stated purpose of the apprenticeship program was to prepare the ex-slaves for the rights and responsibilities of freedom. The real reason, however, was to keep them from deserting their former masters, thus creating a crisis in the workforce.

On some of the smaller British islands, such as Bermuda and Antigua, little or no undeveloped land was available, and ex-slaves had no choice but to continue working for their former owners or starve. On those islands, all slaves were freed unconditionally. In places such as Jamaica, Trinidad, St. Lucia, and Dominica, there were thousands of acres of unclaimed land available, and the forced apprenticeship system allowed the planters to keep their labor force.

In 1838, the apprenticeship program ended, and the former slaves became "full free." Thousands of them left to establish their own farms, and without their labor, many of the sugar and coffee plantations collapsed in bankruptcy.

The planters soon began to import indentured laborers from Germany, Scotland, Ireland, India, and China. Though a number of workers, including several thousand Africans, immigrated to the West Indies as part of this program, the majority either died, returned home, or left to take jobs away from the plantations.

The United States did not establish a British-style apprenticeship program after the Civil War, but during the early years of Reconstruction, thousands of African-American children who were orphaned, or whose parents were supposedly unable to care for them, were assigned by white judges to work as apprentices for white "guardians." Many of these children had relatives able to care for them, and the purpose of the program was really to provide a continuation of forced child labor. In many cases, the minors "in need of care" were over 16, and at least one had a wife and child of his own. The FREEDMEN'S BUREAU managed to overturn many of these court-ordered apprenticeships, which were bitterly resented in the black community.

In addition to creating these child apprenticeships, many southern states severely limited the rights of African Americans when negotiating labor contracts and instituted stringent vagrancy laws that forced many black people to accept employment they would otherwise have rejected. Thousands of blacks were also trapped by a peonage system that held people against their will and forced them (and often their children) to work for years to pay off minor and often fraudulent debts. Peonage labor, later ruled illegal, remained a serious problem in the South through the 1950s. The southern states also instituted prison chain-gang systems that forced thousands of prisoners, most of them black and many of them innocent or jailed for minor offenses, to work for long periods without pay on state construction projects. A variation of this involved convict-lease programs that leased convicts out to work for free for white employers willing to pay their fines. All of these programs were devised to create a pool of free, or nearly free, black labor.

Arabs

Semitic people from the Arabian Peninsula who invaded North Africa in the seventh century A.D. and were partly responsible for the spread of Islam across much of the continent. Arab influence in Egypt and East Africa is of long-standing duration because of extensive trade contacts going back to ancient times. Arab linguistic and cultural influence is seen in Swahili, which includes many Arabic words.

In the seventh century, Arab armies invaded Egypt, establishing the Umayyad dynasty, which ruled from 640 to 750. The capture of Carthage in

698 secured Arab dominance along the North African coast. The Arabs loosely divided the region into eastern and western sections, with the east extending from the Sinai across Egypt and Libya and the west (The Maghreb—from the Arabic word for "the west") including northern Algeria, Tunisia, and Morocco. The Arabic language, Arabic numerals, and Arabic currency were introduced.

Captured Berber/Moorish warriors were inducted into Arab armies and then subjected to extensive religious indoctrination. Efforts to encourage ordinary BERBERS to accept Islam were limited, but those who did not convert were subjected to heavy taxes. Since translation of the Koran was forbidden, converts had to learn Arabic, which then became the language of daily life and commerce. In the eighth century, Arab armies, composed primarily of thousands of Moorish/Berber converts, moved across the Mediterranean into Spain (called al Andalus).

Arab traders were closely linked to East Africa's INDIAN OCEAN TRADE and the development of city-states such as KILWA and MOMBASA. In 1698, the

The great Friday prayer: The muezzin has called Muslims to prayer before the mosque (*United Nations*)

Omani Arabs gained control of ZANZIBAR and extended their influence over several East African cities. They were deeply involved in the slave trade.

Armistead, James (1760–1832) *American Revolution spy*

Born a slave, Armistead got his master's permission to join the forces of General Lafayette, the young Frenchman who was one of George Washington's chief allies. Armistead volunteered to serve as a spy and secured a position as an aide to British general Cornwallis. This enabled him to obtain information that led to an American victory at the 1781 siege of Yorktown, which brought an end to the Revolutionary War. The U.S. government rewarded Armistead with his freedom in 1786 and a yearly pension of $40. He later added "Lafayette" to his name in honor of his former commander. General Lafayette, in turn, became very active in the effort to abolish slavery.

Armstrong, Daniel Louis (1900–1971) *trumpeter and singer*

Born in poverty, Armstrong was raised by his grandmother in New Orleans, a city known for its bands and jazz musicians. He learned to play the cornet after being sent to the Colored Waif's Home at age 12 for firing a gun into the air on New Year's Day. He was released after a year and a half.

At age 17, he gained a mentor in Joe "King" Oliver, who was also a cornetist and who was then playing in Kid Ory's Jazz Band. When Oliver left for Chicago, Armstrong took his place in the band. Nicknamed "Satchelmouth," or just "Satchmo," Armstrong traveled to Chicago in 1922, where he joined King Oliver's Creole Jazz Band and made several classic records with them, including *Dippermouth Blues*.

Two years later, Armstrong moved to New York, where he began working with some of the finest musicians in the country. Returning to Chicago, he organized his own band, Louis Armstrong and the Hot Five. (It later became the Hot Seven.) Among their famous recordings was *West End Blues*.

After 1931, Louis Armstrong became the best-known jazz musician in the world. He toured

Portrait of jazz musician Louis Armstrong kissing his trumpet, late 1920s (*Archive Photos*)

Europe several times and appeared in a number of movies. Noted for the emotional force of his playing, unsurpassed technical skill, gruff voice, and "scat" singing (singing that uses syllables instead of words), Louis Armstrong is considered one of the select group who substantially altered the history of jazz. Songs associated with him include "Ain't Misbehavin'," "Hello Dolly," "What a Wonderful World," and "Sleepy Time Down South."

Recommended Reading: Armstrong, Louis. *Satchmo: My Life in New Orleans.* New York: Da Capo Press, Incorporated, 1986; Collier, James. *Louis Armstrong: An American Success Story.* New York: Macmillan Publishing Company, 1994.

Ashanti (Asante)

A major West African ethnic group that established the Ashanti confederation in the 17th century in what is now Ghana. According to legend, a spiritual leader named Anotchi visited the Ashanti chief Osai Tutu in 1697 and told him to assemble the other Ashanti leaders. Traditionally, each Ashanti man sits on his own personal stool when he attends a village meeting or conference. These stools are often elaborately decorated and represent part of a man's spirit. When the Ashanti chiefs gathered as Anotchi had asked, a stool of pure gold is said to have descended from heaven, landing directly in front of Osai Tutu—a sign that he should unite all the tribes and rule the Ashanti nation. Whatever the truth of the story, the Ashanti confederation grew rapidly by conquering nearby kingdoms whose rulers then became advisers to the Ashanti king and provided troops for the Ashanti army. In return, these kings were allowed to retain their authority in local affairs. Major expansion took place in the early 1700s under the Oyoko clan, and by 1750, the Ashanti kingdom had become the strongest military power in the region.

Located in an area where several trade routes came together, the kingdom was an important economic center with a strong trade in gold, kola nuts, and slaves. Its capital was located at Kumasi on the Pra River. During the 18th century, the kingdom evolved into a centralized bureaucratic state that spread over 150,000 square miles and had a population of 3 to 5 million people. The ever-expanding slave trade brought the Ashanti, who were themselves slave traders, into conflict with various other African and European groups. They were able to force the withdrawal of the Danes but were defeated by the British in the Ashanti War of 1873–1874, which was fought for control of ELMINA CASTLE.

In 1895, the British occupied Kumasi, deposed the Ashanti king, and established the Gold Coast colony. A few years later, in 1900, the British governor infuriated the Ashanti by demanding to sit on the Golden Stool, which does in fact exist and which is regarded as the soul of the Ashanti people. A major revolt took place that was put down with great difficulty. At one point, the Golden Stool was buried in order to protect it. Its hiding place was accidently discovered by some workmen in 1921, and some golden ornaments buried with it were stolen. In an effort to avert a riot, the British quickly jailed the thieves and arranged for the Golden Stool to be placed in the palace at Kumasi in Ghana, where it remains today. The Gold Coast colony became the Republic of Ghana in 1957. The Ashanti people are still noted for their goldwork and colorful KENTE CLOTH.

Ashe, Arthur Robert, Jr. (1943–1993) *tennis champion*

Ashe was born and grew up in Richmond, Virginia, where segregation kept him from playing on most public courts and from competing in many tournaments. After entering UCLA on a tennis scholarship, he became the first African-American man on a Davis Cup team (1963) and over the next 15 years set a record of 27 Davis Cup wins that stood until 1984. Ashe was also the first African American to win the men's singles title at Wimbledon, beating Jimmy Connors in four sets (1975). Forced to undergo quradruple bypass surgery following a heart attack in 1979, Ashe retired from active competition but was named captain of the U.S. Davis Cup team a year later. He became active in the movement to end apartheid in South Africa and authored several books, *A Hard Road to Glory: A History of the African-American Athlete* and two memoirs: *Off the Court* and *Days of Grace.* He also supported efforts to raise academic standards for college athletes. Ashe died of AIDS after becoming infected with the HIV virus during surgery.

Arthur Ashe (*Schomburg Center for Research in Black Culture*)

asiento

An *asiento* was a royal permit granting an individual or company an exclusive right to sell slaves in Spanish colonies. In return for the *asiento,* the Spanish king received a percentage of the profits of the sales. The first major *asiento* was granted in 1592 to a man named Gomes Reynal, who agreed to pay the Spanish king nearly one million ducats for the right to sell 38,250 slaves over a period of nine years. A minimum of 3,500 slaves per year had to be landed alive, and Reynal agreed to pay 10 ducats for each slave short of the 3,500 minimum. As other European countries gained a foothold in the slave trade, they too became involved in the competition for *asiento* rights. In 1713, the British acquired an *asiento* allowing them to deliver 4,800 slaves a year, or 144,000 over a 30-year period. In return for their monopoly, the British paid the Spanish king 200,000 crowns plus a tax of 33 $\frac{1}{3}$ crowns for every slave landed alive. By this time, the British (and the French) were also providing large numbers of slaves to their own colonies in addition to maintaining the foreign markets. During the Seven Years War (1756–63), English ships landed approximately 40,000 slaves in Guadeloupe and 10,000 in Cuba. By 1788, approximately two-thirds of all slaves carried in English ships were destined for the colonies of other nations.

Recommended Reading: Davidson, Basil. *The African Slave Trade.* Boston: Little, Brown, 1980.

Askia Muhammad Touré   See MUHAMMAD TOURÉ.

Attucks, Crispus (1723–1770) *runaway slave, leader of the colonist group in the Boston Massacre*
Attucks is sometimes said to be the first to have died in the fight for American Independence. After his escape from slavery, Attucks became a sailor and taught himself to read and write. On March 5, 1770, he was in Boston, Massachusetts, where a good deal of tension already existed between American colonists and British troops. A British soldier named Hugh Montgomery struck a young boy, and an angry crowd gathered, pelting Montgomery and the other soldiers with snow and ice. When more soldiers arrived, Crispus Attucks led the Americans in an attack on them. The soldiers fired on the crowd, killing Attucks and four other men in what is now known as the Boston Massacre. The deaths enraged the colonists. Attucks' body lay in state for three days, and thousands of people attended his funeral. The Boston Massacre became a major turning point in the events leading to the American Revolution.

Augustine, St. (354–430) *Catholic saint, bishop of Hippo*
Augustine was born in what is now Algeria. His mother, St. Monica, was a BERBER who raised him as a Christian. Augustine gave up Christianity when he went to school in Carthage, where he converted to Manichaeism, a faith that fused Zoroastrianism, Christianity, Buddhism, Taoism, and other Asian faiths. In 376 he traveled to Rome and then to Milan, supporting himself by teaching rhetoric. Inspired by St. Ambrose, the bishop of Milan, he returned to Christianity and was baptized on Easter Sunday, 387. In 391, Augustine traveled to the city

Crispus Attucks (*Library of Congress*)

of Hippo Regius in Algeria, where he became a Christian priest, and later a bishop, while combating what he saw as heresies among Christian sects. Around 400, he wrote *Confessions,* in which he repented a wild youth spent in Carthage. He also examined the nature of human memory and offered a theory of time. In 412 he wrote *City of God,* in which he defends Christianity against its critics. This work was prompted by the capture of Rome in 410 by Alaric's Visigoth forces. He sought to contrast two cities—the temporal metropolis that could be detroyed and the spiritual city that is eternal. In other writings he attacks various other faiths, including Manichaeism, and developed the idea that Christian faith is guaranteed by the authority of the Roman Catholic Church. St. Augustine died during the siege of Hippo by the Vandals in 430. His influence on Christian doctrine is considered by many to be second only to that of St. Paul. In his *Letters,* 17.2, St. Augustine described himself as "An African, writing for Africans . . . living in Africa."

Axum (Aksum)
An ancient kingdom centered in what is now Ethiopia and Eritrea. Urban development began in the area around the first century A.D. By the third century, Axum had grown powerful enough to conquer parts of the Arabian Peninsula, and in A.D. 300, under King EZANA, the state conquered the older

kingdom of KUSH and destroyed the city of MEROE. From its location on the Red Sea, Axum served as a natural bridge between Africa, India, Ceylon, and the various Arabian commercial centers. Exports included ivory, tortoiseshell, gold, emeralds, animal skins, and rhinoceros horn.

In 531, the Byzantine emperor Justinian sent an envoy to Axum who reported that the Axumite king wore a linen robe encrusted with gold and pearls and that his throne was a golden chariot drawn by four elephants. The kingdom had its own written language, Ge'ez, which is the ancestor of the modern Ethiopian languages Amharic, Tigre, and Tigrinya. Axum was also the first state in sub-Saharan Africa to mint its own coins.

In addition to its trade, Axum is noted for its tall, carved stone columns known as stelae. The most famous stood over 108 feet high and weighed approximately 750 tons. It is thought by some to be "the largest single block of stone ever quarried, carved, and set up in the ancient world."[1] The Axumites constructed large stone palaces, including one 40-room structure several stories high, and were noted for their ability to build in dry stone—that is, without the use of mortar. Agricultural focus was on wheat and other cereals and the maintenance of large herds of cattle, sheep, and goats. Success in this area was due in part to Axum's system of terraced hillside farming and irrigation systems. Christianity became the Axumite state religion under King Ezana in the fourth century, though it tended to isolate Axum culturally from its neighbors. The kingdom went into a decline after A.D. 700 and was destroyed by an Agaw chieftainess named Gudit (or Judith) in the 10th century in an unsuccessful attempt to drive out Christianity and restore Judaism.

[1] Graham Connah, *African Civilizations*. New York: Cambridge University Press, 1992.

Baker, Ella Josephine (1903–1986) *civil rights activist*

After graduating from Shaw University, Ella Baker moved to New York, where she became a member of a consumer advocacy group called the Young Negroes Cooperative League. In 1943, she became a field secretary for the NATIONAL ASSOCIATION FOR THE ADVANCEMENT OF COLORED PEOPLE (NAACP), a position that allowed her to meet many civil rights workers throughout the South. She was the first woman to become president of the NAACP's New York branch, where she led efforts to involve parents in fighting discrimination in the public schools. She worked closely with Bayard Rustin and A. Philip Randolph in efforts to raise money for the 1955 MONTGOMERY BUS BOYCOTT and for sharecroppers who had been evicted for civil rights activities.

In 1958, Baker traveled to Atlanta to coordinate a voting rights campaign for the SOUTHERN CHRISTIAN LEADERSHIP CONFERENCE (SCLC). Leaving the SCLC in 1960, she became closely involved with the student sit-in movement and helped found the STUDENT NON-VIOLENT COORDINATING COMMITTEE (SNCC). In 1964, Baker helped found the MISSISSIPPI FREEDOM DEMOCRATIC PARTY, which was to challenge the Mississippi Democratic party delegation to the 1964 Democratic presidential convention in Atlantic City.

Baker, Josephine (1906–1975) *dancer, singer*

Born in St. Louis, Baker left school at age eight to go to work. While still a teenager, she became a surprise sensation as a chorus girl in the Noble Sissle/Eubie Blake musical *Shuffle Along*. This was followed by a part in *Chocolate Dandies* and then a major role in *La Revue Nègre*, which opened in

Wearing a glamorous bias-cut satin gown, entertainer Josephine Baker strikes an alluring pose. (*Archive Photos*)

Paris in 1925. She left the show to join the world-famous Folies-Bergère and created a sensational act in which she appeared topless, wearing only a string of bananas. She appeared in several films, and her dancing inspired ballet choreographer George Balanchine to create a dance especially for her as part of a Ziegfeld Follies revue. During World War II, she acted as an undercover agent and was awarded the Legion of Honor by the French government.

Baldwin, James Arthur (1924–1987) *novelist, essayist, playwright*

James Baldwin grew up in Harlem and became a preacher at the age of 14. His early childhood was unhappy, and he spent hours alone reading and writing poetry, plays, and short stories. Though many laughed at his desire to write, he was encouraged by African-American poet Countee Cullen, who was one of Baldwin's junior high school teachers. Conflict with his stepfather caused Baldwin to leave home at age 17, but he drew on memories of that conflict in writing his first, and possibly best, novel, *Go Tell It on the Mountain.*

In 1944, Baldwin met author Richard Wright, who helped him win a Saxon award and encouraged him when Baldwin arrived in Paris in 1948. A year later, Baldwin's essay "Everybody's Protest Novel" was published. This essay, which was later included in his book *Notes of a Native Son* (1955), was bitterly resented by Wright, who believed Baldwin had attacked him in it. Baldwin denied it, but their friendship was severely damaged. *Go Tell It on the Mountain* was published in 1953, and Baldwin began work on a second novel, *Another Country,* and a play called *The Amen Corner.* Dissatisfied with his progress on them, he began what would be his favorite novel, *Giovanni's Room,* which was published in 1956.

Returning to the United States, Baldwin took part in sit-ins and helped raise money for the Civil Rights movement. In 1961, he published a book of essays, *Nobody Knows My Name,* which was a critical and financial success. He followed it a year later with *Another Country,* and, a year after that, with one of his most famous works, *The Fire Next Time.*

Leaning on a piece of wood, author James Baldwin stands in the middle of rubble, 1960s. (*Walter Daran/Archive Photos*)

He continued to write novels, short stories, essays, plays, and screenplays, including *Blues for Mr. Charlie, Going to Meet the Man, The Devil Finds Work, Tell Me How Long the Train's Been Gone,* and *The Evidence of Things Not Seen.*

Bambara (BAM-bah-rah)

African ethnic group related to the MANDINKA, and concentrated largely in Mali, the Ivory Coast, and southern Mauritania. They are noted for their exceptional artistic ability, particularly their antelope masks, which are among the best known in African art. The rise of two Bambara kingdoms in the 17th century, though relatively small and short-lived, helped check the spread of Islam in West Africa.

Bambara art: Chi wara kun headdress (*National Museum of African Art, Washington, D.C.*)

Banneker, Benjamin (1731–1806)

mathematician, astronomer

Banneker was born free in Baltimore County, Maryland, and spent his life on his parents' farm. His grandmother, an English indentured servant named Molly Welsh, taught him to read and write. At age 12, Banneker began attending school, where he displayed a strong talent for mathematics, often making up math puzzles for the fun of solving them. While in his late teens, he saw a pocket watch for the first time and decided to build a clock himself. After spending two years carving all the gears from wood, he constructed the first clock ever made in America with nonimported parts. It kept perfect time for over 40 years.

Around 1771, Banneker became friendly with the Ellicotts, five Quaker brothers who had purchased land adjoining his property. From them, Banneker borrowed various science books, from which he taught himself astronomy. When an Ellicott cousin, Major Andrew Ellicott, was appointed to Pierre L' Enfant's team to conduct a survey of what would later become Washington, D.C., Banneker was hired to assist him. He maintained the field astronomical clock and compiled astronomical and other necessary mathematical data.

In 1791, and again in 1792, Banneker compiled an ephemeris, an astronomical report providing mathematically computed positions for the various stars and planets for every day throughout the year. He sent a copy of the 1792 ephemeris to Thomas Jefferson, along with a letter promoting the abolition of slavery. Jefferson was so impressed with Banneker's work that he forwarded it to the Académie des Sciences in Paris. The ephemeris, along with a good deal of antislavery material, became a part of *Benjamin Banneker's Pennsylvania, Delaware, Maryland and Virginia Almanack and Ephemeris, for the Year of Our Lord, 1792.* The almanac sold well, and Banneker continued publishing almanacs and/or ephemerics until 1804. His work was often cited by abolitionists as proof that blacks were the equal of whites in intelligence and sensitivity.

Bantu

A term referring to millions of African people who share similar languages and, often, similar cultures, and to the languages themselves. Bantu dialects, of which there are almost 100, are unusual in that they not only incorporate many onomatopoetic words (words that imitate a sound, such as the English words "buzz" or "hiss") but also words that imitate a motion or sensation. For example, a butterfly fluttering in the air is described "ro pha-pha-pha-pha." A frog that takes three hops and then jumps into a pond is "khele ro: noni-noni-noni-djamaaa." Bantu speakers are known for their picturesque speech, which often involves the use of proverbs, riddles, and unusual comparisons. For example, a person who eats too much may be described as "a pot breaking on all sides."

Many Bantu peoples practice polygamy (the practice of a man having more than one wife) and maintain extended family relationships. This leads to concepts of group responsibility, so that a man will hold himself responsible for the debts of deceased relatives. However, individual responsibility is also taken very seriously in Bantu cultures. If, for example, a person were to lend a man a knife, and the man then killed someone with it, the first person is considered equally to blame for lending a weapon to someone who could not be trusted with it. Bantu peoples frequently engage in ancestor veneration and hold various animist beliefs in addition to being Muslims or Christians.

As Bantu-speaking peoples spread across the lower half of Africa 2,000 to 3,000 years ago, they pushed the Pygmies deep into the rain forests and the various Bushmen peoples into the Kalahari Desert region. The most widespread Bantu language is Swahili. Others that are widely spoken are Shona, Zulu, Lingala, Kongo, Bemba, Ganda, and Kikuyu.

bantustans (homelands)

Areas set aside, beginning in 1913, by the former white government of South Africa as independent African reserves or nations. They were called bantustans because the white government regarded all Africans as BANTU. More than 2 million black people (more than 70 percent of the black population) were forced to leave their homes and relocate in bantustans, which were assigned only 13 percent of South Africa's territory. Destitution and malnutrition were common, and in some homelands, infant mortality ran as high as 50 percent. By setting up these so-called "independent" bantustans, the former South African government tried to disavow all responsibility for thousands of black women, children, and old people who were no longer economically productive.

Baptist War

Violent uprising that took place in Jamaica in 1831 and did much to hasten the end of slavery throughout the British Empire. The rebellion began as a protest strike initiated by a slave named Samuel Sharpe. Sharpe, who was literate, was aware that the British Parliament was close to legislating an end to slavery. He urged slaves in St. James Parish to go on strike on December 27, after the Christmas holidays, and demand wages. The strike turned into a rebellion when a man, forced to watch the brutal whipping of his wife, struck the man beating her and other slaves came to the husband's defense.

The uprising rapidly spread to four other parishes, and within days, 50,000 slaves were in revolt. Only the presence of British troops kept other areas under control. Many slaves believed that the English king had already freed them and that their masters were holding them illegally. In addition to burning homes and sugarcane fields, the rebellious slaves destroyed bridges and set up roadblocks to prevent soldiers from coming to the aid of besieged whites. However, the insurgents were largely unarmed, and the uprising was put down after nine days. Four hundred slaves were killed before the revolt ended, and more than 100 men, including Sharpe, were later executed. At least another hundred were whipped. Fifteen whites also died.

The uprising was called the Baptist War because Sharpe was a British deacon and because several white Baptist ministers were later charged with inciting the rebellion. The brutality with which the uprising had been repressed, and the reports of atrocities against abolitionist white ministers, quickly circulated in England. There was widespread public protest and demands that slavery be ended immediately. The result was the Emancipation Act, which provided that as of August 1, 1834, all slave children under age six be set free immediately. Other slaves were to be apprenticed to their former masters for periods varying from four to six years, after which they were to be completely free.

Baraka, Imamu Amiri (LeRoi Jones) (1934–   )

poet, playwright, essayist, political activist, founder of the Black Arts Repertory Theater in New York

Baraka has taught at several universities, including Columbia, George Washington, and the University of New York at Stony Brook. Born LeRoi Jones, he took the name Imamu Amiri Baraka after becoming a Muslim. His Black Nationalist, and later Marxist, views strongly influenced his writing, which is noted for its emotional force and powerful command of language. His best-known plays are *Dutchman,* for which he won an Obie Award in 1964, *The Slave,* and *The Toilet.* In addition to producing a large volume of work, Baraka has had a major impact on a number of other African-American writers, including NIKKI GIOVANNI.

barracoons

pens or walled enclosures in which Africans were held prior to being loaded aboard slave ships. Here, captives might partially regain their strength after the brutal journey to the coast. However, the barracoons were filthy and overcrowded, and the slaves, who were generally stripped naked, were sometimes forced to live with goats and other animals. They were fed twice a day, usually boiled yams, beans, and rotten fish. The poor diet, extremely unsanitary conditions, and contaminated water created ideal disease conditions, and a death rate of only 11 percent of the confined slaves was considered quite good. Once slaves were sold, they were branded with their owners' names to prevent weaker, less valuable slaves from being substituted for them.

Barthe, Richmond (1901–1989) *sculptor*

Segregation prevented Barthe from studying art in his home state of Mississippi, and instead he attended the Art Institute of Chicago. His ability to express a sense of flow and movement derived partly from his own study of dance. Though noted for his many busts of African Americans, Barthe's favorite work reflected the racial problems of his times, such as *The Awakening of Africa* and *Mother and Son,* which portrays a mother holding the body of her son who has been lynched. His portrait of TOUSSAINT Louverture appears on Haitian coins, and his statues of Louverture and Jean-Jacques Dessalines are on display in that country. Though Barthe was the best-known black artist in the United States for many years, he was impoverished at the end of his life. His rent and medical bills were paid by actor James Garner, and in gratitude Barthe made Garner the subject of his last sculpture.

Basie, William ("Count") (1904–1984) *pianist, bandleader*

Basie began his career as an accompanist for silent movies. He later learned to play the organ by watching Fats Waller play at the Lincoln Theatre in Harlem. In 1928, he became the pianist for Walter Page's band, then joined Benny Moten's group a year later. In 1935, he and saxophonist Buster Smith

formed the *Buster Smith and Basie Barons of Rhythm* at the famous Reno Club in Kansas City. A bad contract with Decca Records prevented Basie from receiving any royalties for hits like *One O'Clock Jump, Jumping at the Woodside,* and many other classic recordings, even though he was one of the leading figures of the Big Band "Swing" era. Swing is a style of music in which two notes of equal value are played within a beat. The first note is held slightly longer than the second, creating a swinging, dance-like feeling. The Big Band sound, made accessible by radio, added enormously to the popularity of jazz, and Count Basie's bands were noted for their wealth of musical talent.

Recommended Listening: *The Best of Count Basie* (MCA Records).

Bates, Daisy Lee Gatson (1920–1999) *civil rights activist, newspaper publisher*

When Daisy Bates was an infant, her mother was murdered by three white men during a rape attempt. Her father left town after arranging for her to be raised by friends. She and her husband, Lucius Christopher (L.C.) Bates, settled in Little Rock, Arkansas, and, in 1941, began a weekly newspaper called the *State Press.* Though the paper did well initially, it lost many advertisers after running an angry story on the murder of an African-American soldier by a local policeman. Later, an anti-union judge had Mrs. Bates arrested after she ran a story denouncing him for sentencing three African-American men to a year in prison because they had been walking a picket line when another striker was murdered.

In response to the 1954 Supreme Court decision ending school segregation, the Little Rock school board developed a plan to desegregate Central High School in the fall of 1957. Daisy Bates, as president of the NATIONAL ASSOCIATION FOR THE ADVANCEMENT OF COLORED PEOPLE (NAACP) in Arkansas, organized the nine black students who would attend. On August 22, two weeks before school was scheduled to begin, a rock crashed through Bates' living room window. Attached to it was a note that read, "Stone this time. Dynamite next."

Daisy Lee Gatson Bates, American journalist, civil rights leader, and advocate of racial integration, in Little Rock, Arkansas, 1958 (*New York Times Co./Archive Photos*)

National Guard troops, sent in by Arkansas' segregationist governor Orval Faubus, prevented the black teenagers, known as the LITTLE ROCK NINE, from entering the school on September 4. Three weeks later, armed with a court order, the nine were admitted but were forced to leave when a mob surrounded the school. In the end, the nine teenagers were able to attend the school only under the protection of the 101st Airborne Division.

Throughout the year, Bates provided emotional support for the nine students and their families, who faced considerable harassment. In an attempt to intimidate Bates and the other civil rights leaders, city officials demanded information about NAACP members and finances. When the organization refused to turn over the information, Daisy Bates and other NAACP leaders were arrested. Their convictions were later overturned by the U.S. Supreme Court. During the year, two crosses were burned on the Bates' lawn, and two firebombs were tossed at the house. It became necessary to have guns readily available throughout the house, and Mr. Bates and several other men maintained an armed guard on the property for over a year. The *State Press*, which Daisy and L.C. Bates had begun 18 years earlier, was forced to close.

Recommended Reading: Bates, Daisy. *The Long Shadow of Little Rock*. Fayetteville, Ark.: 1987.

Bearden, Romare (1914–1988) *artist*
Born in North Carolina, Bearden graduated from New York University in 1935. He decided to become a painter while working as a political cartoonist for Baltimore's *Afro-American* newspaper. After serving in the army during World War II, Bearden studied art in Paris, where he met Matisse and Joan Miro. Returning to the United States, he again took up cartooning and also became a professional songwriter. He continued to paint, focusing on scenes from African-American life. In later years, he became noted for his unique collage work. Bearden was a founder of the Spiral meetings, which involved African-American artists who met in the early 1960s to discuss their responsibilities regarding art, the Civil Rights movement, and American society. Romare Bearden's work has been exhibited at the Hirshhorn Gallery in Washington, D.C., New York's Metropolitan Museum of Art, and the Museum of Modern Art (New York). He is a coauthor of *A History of African-American Artists*.

Bechet, Sidney (1897–1959) *jazz musician, composer*
Born in New Orleans in 1897, Sidney Bechet began playing professionally while still in his teens, performing with King Oliver, LOUIS ARMSTRONG, and Freddie Keppard. He was a master of both the clarinet and the soprano sax. Though highly regarded by other jazz musicians, Bechet never enjoyed the public acclaim in the United States that he achieved in France, where he moved permanently after 1951. He composed the very successful *Petite Fleur* and *Dans les Rues d'Antibes*, as well as the music for the

ballet *La Nuit est Une Sorcière*. Among others, he worked with JOSEPHINE BAKER, BESSIE SMITH, and DUKE ELLINGTON, and tutored Johnny Hodges.

Suggested Listening: *The Victor Sessions/Master Takes: The Complete Blue Note Recordings.*

Beckwourth, James Pierson   (1798–1866)
explorer, scout

Born in Virginia to a slave mother and white father, Beckwourth's family moved to Missouri while he was still a child. At age 19, he was taken to St. Louis and apprenticed to a blacksmith. However, after fighting with his master, he left for New Orleans, where he became a scout for the Rocky Mountain Fur Company. He soon became a legendary mountain man, famed for his hunting and fighting skills.

James P. Beckwourth (*Nevada Historical Society*)

In 1824, he was adopted by the Crow Indians and given the name "Bloody Arm" because of his courage in battle.

In 1837, Beckwourth left the tribe and joined the U.S. Army as a scout during the Second Seminole War. From there, he moved west and fought in California's revolt against Mexico (1846) and in the Mexican War (1846–1848). In 1850, while prospecting for gold in the Sierra Nevada he discovered what was later called Beckwourth Pass, which was of great importance to wagon trains heading for California.

In 1866, the U.S. government asked Beckwourth to use his influence with the Crow Indians to avoid warfare. The Crow welcomed Beckwourth and asked him to return to the tribe as a chief. One account says that when he refused, the Crow prepared a huge feast in his honor and then poisoned him in the belief they could at least keep his spirit with them. Other reports indicate the food poisoning was accidental and occurred elsewhere.

Belgian Congo

Belgian colony in what later became Zaire and is now DEMOCRATIC REPUBLIC OF CONGO. The colony was originally known as the CONGO FREE STATE and was the personal property of King Leopold II, who had succeeded in having his claims to more than 1 million square miles of the Congo basin recognized by European leaders at the Berlin Conference of 1884. Widespread atrocities in conjunction with rubber production forced Leopold to turn the Congo Free State over to the Belgian government in 1908, and the area was renamed the Belgian Congo. Though the worst excesses of the Free State era were curbed, a number of coercive labor practices continued. Changes were made in regard to land ownership, but age-old customs were ignored as the area was divided into political districts governed by Belgian-appointed chiefs with little or no traditional authority.

In the 1920s and 1930s, private development companies, facing serious labor shortages, built modern communities with health, education, and recreational facilities, but strict segregation remained the rule everywhere. Until 1955, Congolese were forbidden to attend college, and employment opportunities generally did not extend to professional and management jobs. There were no elections, and since political parties were banned, Congolese formed social and religious clubs that became the birthplace of the independence movement that erupted in the 1950s. A number of concessions were quickly elicited from the Belgian government, and the country gained independence in 1960.

Recommended Reading: Hochschild, Adam. *King Leopold's Ghost*. New York: Houghton Mifflin Co., 1998; Nelson, Samuel H. *Colonialism in the Congo Basin 1880–1940*. Athens, Ohio: Ohio University Center for International Studies, 1994.

Benin, Kingdom of

A West African kingdom located in what is now NIGERIA. According to tradition, the Edo-speaking people of Benin, who shared many cultural traditions with the YORUBA, asked the Yoruba king of IFE to send them a prince to act as their ruler. The king responded by sending Oranmiyan, who married the daughter of a Bini chief and fathered Eweka, the 14th-century ruler who founded the Benin Empire. Benin continued to grow, gradually becoming a powerful state under the rule of EWUARE THE GREAT (ca. 1440–1473). The capital was at Benin City, a prosperous metropolis with stately houses separated by an extensive network of broad streets and avenues. A lavish royal palace completed the picture. Benin is famous for its beautiful bronzes and carved ivories, which were designed as a historical record of the state and its kings.

Located on the coast, the kingdom was one of the first West African states to come in contact with the Portuguese (1485). A trade in pepper and slaves was rapidly established, but Portuguese influence in state affairs was limited. The king, or *oba,* was both the religious and political leader and had no interest in seeing his authority undermined by the introduction of Christianity. Also, the slave trade in Benin, while important, never achieved the scope it reached further along the coast. Benin, however, did practice human sacrifice, but agreed to abolish the

Head of an *oba* (king), Edo people of Benin (*National Museum of African Art, Washington, D.C.*)

practice along with slavery after signing a treaty with England in 1892. Failure to comply, coupled with the 1897 massacre of a British consul general and his party who had intruded upon a Bini religious festival marked by human sacrifice, resulted in a military action in which the *oba* was exiled, and the kingdom became a part of Britain's Niger Coast Protectorate.

Benin, Republic of

West African country. Capital: Porto Novo. A small, densely populated country, Benin is situated on the Atlantic between Nigeria and Togo. Its 62-mile shoreline was once known as the SLAVE COAST because of the huge number of slaves sold there. The powerful kingdom of DAHOMEY controlled the area until forced to become a French colony in 1894. In 1904, the region became a part of the

French West African Federation. After World War II, the people were granted greater civil rights, and the country, still known as Dahomey, became independent in 1960. Its name was changed to Benin in 1975. The country has been the site of numerous coups. In 1972, Lieutenant Colonel Mathieu Kerekou seized power and instituted a marxist regime that severely damaged the economy. Kerekou was deposed in 1990; a new constitution was introduced, and political prisoners were released. Multiparty elections were held in 1991. Kerekou returned to power in 1996 after being elected president. The Fon, who are famous for their art, constitute one of the country's major tribal groups. Benin is considered a birthplace of the VOODOO religion.

Berbers

Nomadic peoples who dominated areas of LIBYA, North Africa, and the SAHARA Desert after 2000 B.C. The term *Berber* applies to the languages spoken by these peoples and not to any specific physical characteristic, although Berbers, whose descendants include the TUAREG, are sometimes referred to as Africa's "white tribe" because of their light skin color. A mixture of Egyptian, West African, and southern European strains, Berbers range from dark-skinned desert residents to some blue-eyed inhabitants of the Atlas Mountains. Historically, dark-skinned Berbers were referred to as MOORS. Today, however, in countries like MAURITANIA, the term *Moor* or *white Moor* frequently is used to refer to light-skinned persons of Berber-Arab ancestry, as distinct from dark-skinned people belonging to West African tribal groups such as the FULANI, Halpular, Soninke, and WOLOF.

Famed as expert horsemen and fierce fighters, it was the Berbers who, according to the ancient historian Herodotus, first taught the Greeks to harness four horses to a chariot. Berber groups invaded EGYPT several times, engaged in trade with PHOENICIANS, Greeks, and other Mediterranean peoples, and established several North African kingdoms. In the fourth century, a Berber tribe called the Zenagas founded what would become the medieval empire of GHANA, although the state soon came under the rule of Soninke kings.

When the ARABS swept across North Africa in the seventh century, thousands of captured Berber warriors were inducted into Arab armies and were a major force in the invasion of Spain in 711. However, the Arabs in North Africa faced continuing resistance from various Berber tribes that finally exploded in widespread revolt in 1740. Numerous small Berber caliphates (Islamic kingdoms) were established, although the Arabs managed to regain control of North Africa after 30 years of fighting. In Spain, however, Abd ar-Rahman I, a Muslim of Arab-Berber descent and a supporter of the Umayyad Caliphate in Damascus, Syria, seized political control in 756. His Moorish successors were later pushed aside by ALMORAVID Berbers in the 11th century.

The invading Arab armies in North Africa resulted in the scattering of Berber groups and the intermingling of the two peoples. Additional racial diversity probably occurred as a result of marriages between Berber/Moorish warriors and Spanish women after the Arab-Berber invasion of the Iberian Peninsula in 711. Thousands of their descendants were driven out of Spain during the long Christian reconquest (1212–1492) and the Spanish Inquisition, and many returned to North Africa.

It is estimated that about 10 million North Africans still speak a Berber tongue as a first language. The word *Berber* is believed to come from the Roman word *barbari* meaning a barbarian whose language is unknown. North Africa's Barbary Coast is named for them. Famous people of Berber ancestry include St. AUGUSTINE.

Recommended Reading: Brett, Michael and Elizabeth Fentress. *The Berbers.* Cambridge, Mass.: Blackwell Publishers, 1996.

Beta Israel or Black Jews

Descendants of Jews, possibly from Egypt and the Arabian peninsula, who settled in what is now Ethiopia during the first century B.C. Many believe they arrived as much as 700 years earlier and are the descendants of the biblical King Solomon and the Queen of Sheba. When Ethiopia became Christian in the fourth century, these Black Jews moved to the

Lake Tana region, where they converted many of the local Agaw tribe. They have been isolated from the rest of the Jewish community for over 2,000 years, but in 1974, the chief rabbinate of Israel ruled that these Ethiopians were in fact Jewish and therefore eligible to emigrate to Israel if they so chose. In 1985, during a severe famine, the Israeli government flew more than 7,000 Ethiopian Jews to Israel during a three-month period. Another emergency airlift brought an additional 14,000 black Jews to Israel when Ethiopia was engulfed in civil war in 1991. At that time, Israel paid the Ethiopian government $35 million to allow the Beta Israel Jews to leave. Approximately 44,000 Ethiopian Jews—most of them under 15—have settled in Israel since 1977. They were formerly referred to as "Falashas," meaning "exiles" or "wanderers."

In 1999, DNA testing confirmed that members of the Lemba tribe, a Bantu-speaking people of southern Africa, were descended from Jews who had migrated from Senna, an ancient Jewish settlement in what is now Yemen. The Lemba practice circumcision and avoid eating pork. They claim that they were led out of Senna by a man named Buba more than 1,000 years ago.

Bethune, Mary Jane McLeod (1875–1995)
educator, civil rights leader

Born in Mayesville, South Carolina, the 15th of 17 children, Mary McLeod spent much of her childhood picking cotton and taking in washing and ironing. Determined to get an education, she walked five miles to and from school each day for six years. Later she attended Scotia Seminary in North Carolina and Moody Bible Institute in Chicago. After graduating from Moody in 1895, she became a teacher and two years later married Albertus Bethune. She and her husband had one son, Albert.

In 1904, the Bethunes moved to Florida, and Mrs. Bethune set up her own school, The Daytona Normal and Industrial School for Negro Girls. Tuition was 50 cents a week, and the student body consisted of just five girls. Within two years, there were 250 students, and the school, which would later become Bethune-Cookman College, was firmly established.

Mary McLeod Bethune *(Library of Congress)*

In 1911, when a student almost died after being refused help at a local whites-only hospital, Mrs. Bethune established a hospital for African Americans. Her success brought her national attention, and in 1920, she became a vice president of the National Urban League. Between 1924 and 1928 she also served as president of the National Association of Colored Women. She founded the National Council of Negro Women in 1935, and was Director of the Division of Minority Affairs in the National Youth Administration, a New Deal agency created under Franklin Roosevelt.

Mrs. Bethune was a personal friend of Eleanor Roosevelt, and an adviser to five presidents: Calvin Coolidge, Herbert Hoover, Franklin Roosevelt, Harry Truman, and Dwight D. Eisenhower. She insisted upon being addressed respectfully as Mrs. Bethune, and, while at Johns Hopkins Medical Center, ordered that two African-American physicians be allowed to monitor her treatment. Throughout her life, Mrs. Bethune emphasized education, self-respect, and pride in being African-American.

Biko, Stephen (BEE-kaw) (1946–1977) *founder of the Black Consciousness Movement in South Africa*
Stephen Biko was tortured and killed by security police for opposing the former white-ruled South African government. He formed the Black Consciousness movement to help black Africans develop self-reliance and move away from a psychological dependency on white liberals in the fight against apartheid. In 1968, Biko directed a walkout of black students from the multiracial but white-led National Union of South African Students and formed the all-black South African Students Organization. He rejected the idea of integration under a white-controlled government as "a one-way course, with the whites doing all the talking and the blacks listening."

In 1972, he helped found the Black People's Convention as a way of expanding Black Consciousness ideas and programs beyond students and into the black community at large. He was also a founder of Black Community Programs, an organization that ran various black self-help projects such as literacy and health programs. He was imprisoned several times and "banned" (restricted to a given area and not allowed to meet with more than one person at a time or be quoted). On August 18, 1977, Stephen Biko, along with a friend named Peter Jones, was arrested and jailed by Security Police. A month later, while still in detention, he was beaten to death by police. He is the subject of the Peter Gabriel song "Biko."

Recommended Reading: Woods, Donald. *Biko.* New York: Holt, 1987.

Black Codes

A series of laws passed by the Southern states immediately after the Civil War, during the period when blacks in the South were still unable to vote. Some of the new laws were beneficial, for example, those legalizing the marriages of former slaves. Others, such as those that allowed African Americans to own, buy, and sell property, tended to exist more in theory than in practice, since most blacks were too poor to buy land and many whites refused to sell it to them. Blacks were allowed to sue and be sued, but they were not permitted to testify against whites, and they could not serve on juries. Laws were also passed forbidding blacks and whites to marry and providing for segregated schools, trains, hotels, and restaurants.

However, the main purpose of the Black Codes was to reestablish slavery in everything but name, and many of the new laws involved labor rights. New vagrancy laws providing for the imprisonment of those who could not provide written proof of employment were used to force thousands of African Americans into signing labor contracts with white plantation owners that they otherwise would have rejected. Other laws made it difficult for blacks to work as craftsmen, peddlers, mechanics, or other self-employed professions. Statutes were passed requiring laborers who left their jobs before the expiration of their contracts to forfeit wages already earned. Opelousas, Louisiana, set up a pass system and forbade African Americans to live in towns except as servants. South Carolina forbade blacks to leave the plantations where they worked without the permission of the owner. Florida made "disrespect" a crime and allowed blacks who broke labor contracts to be whipped.

The Black Codes, backed by Ku Klux Klan violence, had an extremely negative effect on Northern public opinion. The furious reaction caused a number of the worst laws to be overturned. An angry Congress also passed an 1866 civil rights bill to protect African-American rights and the Reconstruction Act of 1867, which required that the Southern states give African-American men the right to vote.

See also CRIMINAL JUSTICE RIGHTS; LABOR AND PROPERTY RIGHTS.

Black Muslims

Term frequently used to refer to the NATION OF ISLAM in the 1960s. It was first introduced by historian C. Eric Lincoln in 1965.

See also ELIJAH MUHAMMAD.

Black Panther Party for Self-Defense

Militant political and social activist group founded by HUEY NEWTON and Bobby Seale in Oakland, Cali-

Black Panthers with their fists raised in a sign of black power, on the opening day of the Panther 21 Trial on 100 Centre Street in New York City, 1970 (*Roz Payne/Archive Photos*)

fornia in 1966. Its minister of information was Eldridge Cleaver, who had written a series of essays that were collected in his book *Soul On Ice* after his release from prison. The initial purpose of the Black Panther Party was to set up armed patrols that would follow police officers and intervene in cases of police misconduct. Party members were forbidden to use drugs or alcohol while on duty, and a 10-point political program included demands for full employment, exemption from military service for blacks, an end to police brutality, the release of all black men from prison, and a United Nations–supervised plebiscite to allow African Americans to determine their future.

The party established 40 chapters in northern and western cities, ran free breakfast programs for inner-city children, and set up a free health care clinic in Berkeley, California. However, its antipolice rhetoric elicited strong hostility from law enforcement authorities. Panther Bobby Hutton was killed by police in 1968. That same year, Huey Newton was convicted of voluntary manslaughter in the 1967 shooting of police officer John Frey. Gun battles between police and Panthers became a continuing phenomenon across the country, culminating in a 1969 police raid on a Chicago apartment in which Panthers Fred Hampton and Mark Clark were

killed. A year later, party chairman Bobby Seale and 13 other Panthers were charged in the torture-slaying of Panther Alex Rackley, who was mistakenly believed to be a police informer. Though many Panthers were sincere in wanting to help the black community, others saw an opportunity to extort money and divert program funds for personal gain. Internal power struggles, deaths, and disillusionment led to the fragmentation of the party in the 1970s.

black power movement

Social, cultural, and political phenomenon that grew out of the CIVIL RIGHTS MOVEMENT of the 1950s and 1960s. It gained its name from a cry, "Black Power!" raised by STOKELY CARMICHAEL in 1965 during a speech in Greenwood, Mississippi. It found expression in various African-American organizations, including the BLACK PANTHER PARTY FOR SELF-DEFENSE and the STUDENT NON-VIOLENT COORDINATING COMMITTEE. While differing substantially in many ways, these groups were united in rejecting white leadership (and often white membership) and in their desire for social, economic, and political control of black communities, particularly in regard to schools and police.

The Civil Rights movement had made enormous gains, but only with great difficulty and at tremendous human cost. The unwillingness of many whites to acknowledge the basic rights of African Americans gave rise to great bitterness, and the black power movement was characterized by a determination that black accomplishments and culture be properly recognized. African Americans took pleasure in wearing African-inspired hairstyles and fashions, particularly with the colors green, black, and red, symbolizing Africa, black people, and blood or revolution. The expression "Black Is Beautiful" became popular everywhere, and the "black power salute" was raised by athletes Tommy Smith and John Carlos during the presentation of their medals at the 1968 Mexico City Olympic Games.

The Civil Rights movement had projected an image of black people as decent, hardworking, nonviolent, law-abiding citizens who were being unfairly and illegally victimized. Similarities to their counterparts in white society were emphasized. The black power movement took a different approach, arguing that there existed a distinct black culture and insisting that it be recognized as valid. People took pride in their identity as black men and women, and linked self-awareness to a knowledge and appreciation of black history. Pressure was placed upon schools to incorporate black history programs into their curriculums. White society was condemned for ignoring black people in commercials, television programs, movies, and the arts. These protests got results. Many colleges and universities agreed to set up black studies departments. Manufacturers began advertising in black magazines and newspapers and using African-American actors in commercials. Local television stations began featuring black-oriented public service shows and hiring African-American reporters. Movies depicting black heroes (and heroines) who beat up evil whites were popular, though a number of people referred to these contemptuously as "blaxploitation" films. Nonetheless, the idea of regularly using African Americans in a range of roles once reserved for whites took root.

Blacks viewed the black power movement as pro-black, whereas whites often condemned it as antiwhite and pointed to civil rights gains, arguing that black power rhetoric endangered future advances. Such condemnation increased after riots broke out in many cities during the late 1960s. But to many African Americans, these complaints sounded suspiciously like past requests that blacks "go slow" and accept "gradual" advancement.

Of course, neither the Civil Rights movement nor the black power movement was a rigidly defined phenomenon, and the two overlapped considerably in their goals and methods. The Civil Rights movement—as its name indicates—emphasized obtaining civil and political rights, in fact as well as in theory. Its focus was voting rights, integrated schools, fair housing laws, an end to job discrimination, and legal access to hotels, restaurants, transportation, and all public places. It laid the groundwork for the black power movement's demands for acceptance and recognition of African-American history and culture and its efforts to free blacks from economic and political dependence on whites.

black Seminoles

African Americans, often runaway slaves, who lived among the Seminole Indians and were regarded as members of the tribe. They played a major role in the Seminole War, which was described by U.S. General Thomas Jessup as being "a Negro, not an Indian war." Further proof of this heavy black involvement is indicated by the fact that, when General Jessup's troops stormed an Indian camp in 1837, taking 55 members of Chief Osceola's personal bodyguards prisoner, 52 were black. In fact, historian Kenneth Porter described the final Seminole War as "a Negro insurrection with Indian support."[1]

Conflict between the Seminole Indians, who lived in Spanish-owned Florida, and the United States stemmed largely from the fact that the Seminoles provided shelter and protection to runaway slaves, who often returned to raid plantations in Georgia. Hundreds of these runaways settled in a 50-mile strip of land along the Apalachicola River. Their very presence served as an enticement to those still in bondage, and in 1816, slave-owner complaints led General Andrew Jackson to order military intervention. United States troops attacked and destroyed FORT NEGRO, an abandoned British post in Florida that had been taken over by about 300 blacks and 30 Seminole Indians after the British defeat in the War of 1812. This was the beginning of the Seminole Wars, which were to stretch over 40 years and cost the United States millions of dollars.

Among the leading black Seminoles involved in the conflict were ABRAHAM, JOHN HORSE, and John Caesar. Along with their Indian allies, the black Seminoles were eventually forced to move west to Oklahoma and Texas. Some also settled in Mexico. In an ironic twist of fate, the U.S. Army hired many black Seminoles as scouts following the Civil War, and several of them won the Congressional Medal of Honor.

[1] William Loren Katz, *The Black West.* Seattle, Wash.: Open Hand, 1987, p. 20.

black soldiers

In Africa

African military history goes back to the armies of ancient Egypt. Hausa cavalry in West Africa rode horses draped in quilted armor; the Ashanti and Tuareg were noted for their swordsmanship; and the kingdom of Dahomey was famous for its ruthless women warriors. African weaponry includes not only spears, clubs, and bows and arrows, but a wide variety of multibladed throwing knives, such as those of the Zande that are found nowhere else in the world. Spiked bracelets, wrist and finger knives, and hooked finger rings complete the arsenal. Africa also boasts two of the world's most famous military leaders: HANNIBAL, whom Napoleon called the great-est general of all time, and SHAKA, whose battle formations are still studied in military academies.

In the United States

REVOLUTIONARY WAR (1775–83)

Five thousand black men fought for the colonies during the American Revolution. Twenty thousand others fought for the British. Although whites were reluctant to arm blacks, African-American soldiers had already seen service during the French and Indian Wars (1689–1763) and in various colonial militias. Free black men enlisted in the army in the hope that freedom for the colonies would also mean an end to slavery; slaves enlisted as a means of winning their freedom. Black soldiers fought at the

Military band of the 107th U.S. Colored Infantry (*Library of Congress*)

battles of Lexington and Concord, and it was PETER SALEM who fired the fatal shot killing the British commander at Bunker Hill. However, the Continental army, responding to fears from slave owners, forbade the use of all black troops, slave and free, on October 8, 1775. The individual states followed the army's lead, although in many states, whites were allowed to hire blacks to serve as substitutes. As the war dragged on, many began to rethink this no-blacks policy, especially as the British, in November 1775, had offered to free all slaves willing to join their forces. The Continental army reversed itself and agreed to allow the recruitment of black soldiers, and in 1779, the Continental Congress even recommended the recruitment of slaves. When the war ended, American diplomats insisted that runaway slaves who had served in the British army be returned. The British refused and evacuated some 14,000 black soldiers, 1,100 of whom helped establish the British colony of Sierra Leone in Africa. In addition to the men mentioned above, other notable black soldiers included JAMES FORTEN, Lemuel Haynes, who was among the troops led by Ethan Allen in the attack on Fort Ticonderoga, and Salem Poor, who distinguished himself at Bunker Hill.

WAR OF 1812 (1812–15)

Both free blacks and slaves participated in the War of 1812. Ten to 25 percent of Oliver Hazard Perry's squadron at the 1813 Battle of Lake Erie were African-American sailors, and others served in British crews. New York's state militia contained two black regiments, and in Pennsylvania, ABSALOM JONES and RICHARD ALLEN organized a force of 2,500 blacks to defend Philadelphia in case of British attack. Andrew Jackson utilized the services of at least one black battalion at the Battle of New Orleans, as well as the mixed-race crew of pirate Jean Lafitte.

SEMINOLE WARS

See ABRAHAM; BLACK SEMINOLES; FORT NEGRO; JOHN HORSE.

CIVIL WAR (1861–65)

More than 200,000 black men served as Union soldiers and sailors during the Civil War; an estimated 38,000 died. Thousands of others were wounded or listed as missing in action. Twenty-four men received the Congressional Medal of Honor. Initially, blacks were not allowed to enlist in the Union army, although some were serving in federalized state militias and the navy. The all-black First Carolina volunteers, an unofficial unit made up of former slaves organized by Union general David Hunter, was formed in 1862. That same year, a slave named ROBERT SMALLS hijacked the Confederate ship *Planter* and surrendered it to the Union army.

The EMANCIPATION PROCLAMATION (January 1, 1863) made it possible for blacks to serve in the army, and thousands of African-American men rushed to enlist, despite the fact that it was Confederate policy to shoot or enslave captured black soldiers. Although black soldiers were paid less than whites and received inferior equipment and medical care, they distinguished themselves in numerous battles, including the assault on Port Hudson, Louisiana. Other critical campaigns were the battles of Fort Wagner and FORT PILLOW. One of the most famous black units was the FIFTY-FOURTH MASSACHUSETTS REGIMENT. By the end of the war, black military units made up almost 13 percent of the army.

FRONTIER WARS

The Reorganization Act of 1866 authorized the formation of four black regiments: the Twenty-fourth and Twenty-fifth Infantry and the Ninth and Tenth Cavalry. Known as the BUFFALO SOLDIERS, these men were stationed west of the Mississippi and assigned the task of protecting settlers from Indian attack. Many, including GEORGE JORDAN, were Civil War veterans. Black progress in the military was difficult. In 1877, Henry O. Flipper became the first black graduate of West Point, but he and others who followed him faced considerable discrimination and harassment.

SPANISH-AMERICAN WAR (1898)

When the battleship *Maine* sank in Havana harbor in 1898, at least 30 black sailors were among the 260 officers and men killed. The Twenty-fifth Infantry took the chief role in capturing the garrison at Santiago, Cuba, and soldiers from the Tenth

Cavalry participated in the famous charge up San Juan Hill. Black soldiers also saw action in the Philippines.

WORLD WAR I (1917–18)

More than 350,000 African-American men served in the armed forces during the war, 100,000 of them overseas. In 1918, HENRY JOHNSON of the famous 369th Infantry became the first U.S. soldier awarded the Croix de Guerre, France's highest military decoration. (The award was also won by Eugene Jacques Bullard [1894–1961], the first African-American combat pilot. Bullard joined the French Foreign Legion and then fought with France's Lafayette Escadrille Flying Corps. The U.S. Army Air Force wouldn't accept him because of his race.) Combat units and medical and recreational facilities were segregated, despite promises of nondiscrimination in the Selective Service Act.

WORLD WAR II (1941–45)

The military remained segregated, although there was an increase in the number of black officers. Famous black heroes included DORIE MILLER, who earned the Navy Cross for his actions at Pearl Harbor, and pilot Leonard Roy Harmon, for whom a navy ship is named. Prejudice continued to be a serious problem. Race riots broke out on military bases across the country, and a black soldier was lynched at Fort Benning. Additional violence broke out in numerous communities, especially in the South, as black soldiers stationed in the area refused

Black soldiers in World War II (*Library of Congress*)

to comply with segregationist customs. Discriminatory treatment within the military was also a problem. In one notorious case in which the navy later admitted racial prejudice was a factor, 258 black sailors at Port Chicago, California, were court-martialed and 50 sent to prison for refusing to load live ammunition without safeguards after an explosion killed 320, including 202 African Americans. Approximately 1,000,000 black men served in World War II, about 8.7 percent of the total U.S. forces.

POST–WORLD WAR II

In 1948, President Harry S. Truman issued Executive Order 9981, ending segregation in the armed forces. The Air Force integrated its personnel immediately. The other branches moved more slowly, and the last all-black army units were not disbanded until 1954. During the Korean War (1950–53), Private William Thompson became the first black soldier since the Spanish-American War to win the Medal of Honor. (African-American veterans of World Wars I and II awarded medals did not receive them until the 1990s.) In addition to integrating its units, the military instituted policies to desegregate schools on military bases, challenge discrimination in off-base housing, and oppose segregated facilities used by military personnel. In spite of integration, serious discrimination continued.

During the Vietnam War (1961–75) black Americans made up 9.8 percent of U.S. military forces. With the ending of the draft in 1973, the proportion of African Americans in the military doubled. Black men and women continued to enlist, and reenlist, in substantial numbers, while the number of white volunteers dropped. This led to a dramatic increase in the number of black officers. Even more startling has been the increase in the number of black women soldiers. Today, more than 40 percent of all enlisted women in the army are black. In the 1991 Persian Gulf War, 20 percent of troops in the combat zone were black. At that time, the chairman of the Joint Chiefs of Staff was COLIN POWELL, an African American.

See also ABRAHAM; BLACK SEMINOLES; BROWNSVILLE, TEXAS, AFFAIR; BENJAMIN O. DAVIS;

AFRICAN-AMERICAN MEDAL OF HONOR RECIPIENTS

Civil War (1861–65)

Anderson, Aaron (a.k.a. Sanderson)
Anderson, Bruce
Barnes, William H.
Beaty, Powhatan
Blake, Robert (escaped slave)
Bronson, James H.
Brown, William H.
Brown, Wilson

Carney, William Harvey
Dorsey, Decatur (escaped slave)
Fleetwood, Christian A.
Gardiner, James
Harris, James H.
Hawkins, Thomas R.
Hilton, Alfred B.
Holland, Milton Murray

James, Miles
Kelly, Alexander
Lawson, John
Mifflin, James
Pease, Joachim
Pinn, Robert
Ratcliff, Edward
Veal, Charles

Indian Campaigns (1861–1898)

Boyne, Thomas
Brown, Benjamin
Denny, John
Factor, Pompey
   (Black/Seminole; a.k.a. Facton)
Greaves, Clinton
Johnson, Henry

Jordan, George
Mays, Isaiah
McBryar, William
Paine, Adam
   (Black/Seminole)
Payne, Isaac
Shaw, Thomas

Stance, Emanel
Walley, Augustus
Ward, John
   (Black/Seminole)
Williams, Moses
Wilson, William O.
Woods, Brent

Interim (1871–1898)

Atkins, Daniel
Davis, John
Girandy, Alphonse

Johnson, John
Johnson, William
Noil, Joseph B.

Smith, John
Sweeney, Robert Augustus
   (double recipient)

Spanish-American War (1898)

Baker, Edward L., Jr.
Bell, Dennis

Lee, Fitz
Penn, Robert

Thompkins, William H.
Wanton, George H.

World War I (1914–18)

Stowers, Freddie (Awarded posthumously, April 24, 1991)

World War II (1941–45) (Awarded posthumously except Vernon Baker)

Baker, Vernon J.
Carter, Edward A.
Fox, John R.

James, Willy F., Jr.
Rivers, Reuben

Thomas, Charles L.
Watson, George

Korean War (1950–53)

Charlton, Cornelius H.
Thompson, William

Vietnam (1964–1973)

Anderson, James, Jr.
Anderson, Webster
Ashley, Eugene, Jr.
Austin, Oscar R.
Bryant, William Maud
Davis, Rodney Maxwell
Jenkins, Robert H., Jr.

Joel, Lawrence
Johnson, Dwight
Johnson, Ralph
Langhorn, Garfield M.
Leonard, Matthew
Long, Donald Russell
Olive, Milton Lee, III

Pitts, Riley L.
Rogers, Charles Calvin
Sargent, Ruppert L.
Sasser, Clarence Eugene
Sims, Clifford Chester
Warren, John E., Jr.

JOHN HORSE; HOUSTON MUTINY; THURGOOD MARSHALL; TUSKEGEE AIRMEN; CHARLES YOUNG.

Blake, James Hubert ("Eubie") (1883–1983)
musician, composer

Blake began studying the piano when he was six and started playing professionally at age 17. In 1915, he and Noble Sissle teamed up to write the song "It's All Your Fault." Six years later, the two, along with Flournoy Miller and Aubrey Lyles, created *Shuffle Along,* which became the most popular musical revue of the HARLEM RENAISSANCE. JOSEPHINE BAKER appeared in it as a chorus girl. Blake and Sissle followed *Shuffle* in 1924 with another hit, *Chocolate Dandies.* Among Blake's other songs were "Charleston Rag," "How Ya' Gonna Keep 'Em Down on the Farm," "I'm Just Wild About Harry," and "Love Will Find a Way." His life was the subject of the 1978 Broadway show *Eubie.*

Blakey, Art (Abdullah ibn Bulaina) (1919–1990) *jazz drummer, bandleader*

Abandoned as a young child, Blakey was taken in by a Pittsburgh woman against her husband's wishes. He learned to play the piano in a brothel where he was sent to live at age 11 and later claimed he switched to drums on orders from a gangster who put a gun to his head. By the time he was in the seventh grade, he was playing professionally. His ability led to engagements with musicians like Mary Lou Williams, Fletcher Henderson, Billy Eckstine, CHARLIE PARKER, and THELONIOUS MONK.

In 1947, Blakey and Miles Davis organized a group called the Seventeen Messengers. In 1955, he joined with Horace Silver to create the highly popular Jazz Messengers ensemble. Though Silver left the Messengers in 1956, Blakey attracted musicians such as CLIFFORD BROWN, Lee Morgan, Chuck Mangione, Donald Byrd, Wynton Marsalis, Wayne Shorter, and Keith Jarrett. Blakey was the first drummer to go to Africa to study percussion, and he adopted certain African techniques in his playing. Famous for his power and speed and his use of multiple drummers, Blakey was a leader in the development of the hardbop style that became popular in the 1950s.

Recommended Listening: *A Night at Birdland* (Blue Note); *Drum Suite* (Columbia); *The Freedom Rider* (Blue Note).

Bloody Sunday
The name given March 7, 1965, the day on which police in Selma, Alabama, attacked peaceful demonstrators who were marching to protest police brutality and demand voting rights.

See VOTING RIGHTS STRUGGLE.

blues
Music form created by African Americans, blues gets its name from the use of "blue notes," usually the third and seventh notes of a major scale, that are flatted or played below the intended pitch. Classic blues music follows a 12-bar structure with an opening line that is repeated and a third rhyming line. *"I got the blues so bad, it hurts my feet to walk/I got the blues so bad, it hurts my feet to walk/It have settled on my brain and it hurts my tongue to talk"* ("Lonesome House Blues").

The first blues songs originated in the Mississippi Delta during the 1890s, but the roots of blues music can be heard in the Negro SPIRITUALS and "call-and-response" songs sung during slavery. Blues-like fragments were heard after the Civil War and frequently dealt with the ex-slaves' newly gained freedom to go wherever they pleased: *"If anybody asks you who made up this song/Tell 'em it was——done been here and gone."* Though the blues grew out of the black experience, it was frequently condemned by black churches as "the Devil's music." The lyrics stressed everything from poverty, loneliness, and love, to racism, drinking, work, and sex. A number of blues musicians, including HUDDIE "Leadbelly" LEDBETTER, had spent time in jail, and their experiences were reflected in lyrics like *"It was early this mornin' that I had my trial/Ninety days on the county road, and the judge didn't even smile"* ("Chain Gang Blues"). Sardonic humor was a common ingredient: *"I wonder why they electrocute a man after the*

Blues musicians play guitars and sing in a crowded tavern on the South Side of Chicago, Illinois, April 1941. (*Anthony Potter Collection/Archive Photos*)

one o'clock hour of the night/Because the current is much stronger, when the folkses turn out all the lights" ("'Lectric Chair Blues"). Just as in the civil rights songs of the 1960s, early blues music often referred to specific sheriffs, judges, and/or prison bosses.

After the turn of the century, racism and poverty caused thousands of African Americans to move north to New York, Philadelphia, Cleveland, Chicago, and Detroit, bringing blues (and JAZZ) with them. Singers like Alberta Hunter and Victoria Spivey found work in urban clubs and dance halls, although others like BESSIE SMITH and GERTRUDE "MA" RAINEY continued to perform in the traveling minstrel and carnival shows that crisscrossed the South and Midwest. The first recorded blues song was Mamie Smith's "Crazy Blues," which was released by Okeh Records in 1920.

It sold 75,000 copies its first month and proved the commercial appeal of so-called RACE RECORDS. The Great Depression created serious problems in the music business, and blues singers were affected as well as others—in their lyrics as well as financially. *"Starvation in my kitchen, rent sign's on my do'"* ("Starvation Blues"). Blues have influenced the writing of African-American authors ranging from Langston Hughes to Alice Walker and can be heard in everything from boogie woogie and jazz to SOUL and rock and roll. Current blues singers include Robert Cray and B.B. KING.

Recommended Reading: Awmiller, Craig. *This House on Fire: The Story of the Blues.* Danbury, Conn.: Grolier, 1996. Oakley, Giles. *The Devil's*

Music: A History of the Blues. New York: Da Capo Press, 1997.

Bluford, Guion Stewart, Jr. (1942–) *astronaut*

Born in Philadelphia, Guion Bluford enlisted in the Air Force after graduating from Pennsylvania State University. He served as a fighter pilot in Vietnam, where he flew 144 missions and reached the rank of lieutenant colonel. After returning to the United States, he earned a Ph.D in aerospace engineering and was one of 35 out of 8,878 applicants accepted by the astronaut program at NASA. On August 30, 1983, Bluford became the first African American in space as a member of the crew of the STS-8 Orbiter *Challenger.* His primary responsibility, which he successfully accomplished, was the launching of a $45,000,000 Insat-1B communications and weather satellite. Bluford flew on two other space shuttle flights, in 1985 and 1991.

Bogle, Paul (unknown–1865) *leader of the Morant Bay Rebellion in Jamaica in 1865*

Though slavery officially ended in Jamaica in 1834, blacks continued to live under an economically repressive government controlled by white planters. The uprising began when black farmers from a village named Stony Gut refused to pay additional rent to white landowners in Morant Bay. Bogle, a black preacher from the village, led the uprising with the cry, "Cleave to the black! Color for color!" The rebels were able to take control of St. Thomas parish, but they were eventually overcome. One thousand blacks, including Paul Bogle, were hanged, 400 were flogged, and thousands of homes were burned to the ground in reprisal. Although it was really a local conflict, the uprising was termed a rebellion by Governor Eyre so as to obtain British permission to invoke martial law throughout the island.

Bontemps, Arna (1902–1973) *poet, novelist, editor, teacher*

Bontemps was the author of 25 books, including poetry, history, biography, fiction, and anthologies. He worked closely with Langston Hughes, Countee Cullen, and Claude McKay, and was one of the major figures of the HARLEM RENAISSANCE. The winner of the poetry prize from *Crisis* magazine and the ALEXANDER PUSHKIN poetry prize, Bontemps also wrote a number of books for children, including *Sad-Faced Boy, We Have Tomorrow, Story of the Negro,* and *Slappy Hooper.* His novels include *Black Thunder, Drums at Dusk,* and *God Sends Sunday.*

Botswana, Republic of

Small country of (231,800 sq. miles) located in south-central Africa. Capital: Gaborone. Eighty percent of the country is covered by the Kalahari Desert, with most of Botswana's people living in the narrow, fertile sector bordered by the Limpopo River.

A majority of the people are Tswana, a BANTU people who began moving into the area in the 14th century, gradually displacing the !KUNG SAN. Traditionally, the Tswana maintained a highly structured society with people living in villages and towns built around family clans. After 1852, bloody attacks by South African whites forced Tswana rulers to seek British protection, and the country became a British protectorate called Bechuanaland in 1885. The Tswana rulers managed to prevent a takeover of their country by British businessman Cecil Rhodes and later to avoid being incorporated into the Union of South Africa. The colony became self-governing in 1965 and independent in 1966 under president Seretse Khama. Botswana is the fourth-largest diamond producer in the world. AIDS has seriously threatened Botswana's future. Two-thirds of Botswana's 15-year-olds are expected to die of AIDS by age 50.

Boukman Revolt

A slave uprising that took place in the French colony of Saint-Domingue (Haiti) in 1791. It was led by Boukman, a Jamaican-born slave who had traveled from plantation to plantation the year before in an effort to persuade slaves to strike for wages. He was successful, in part because of his stature as a VOODOO priest, and the strike began on August 22, 1791. It quickly turned violent. Intense fighting broke out around Le Cap François, where close to 1,100 plantations were destroyed and more than 2,000 whites—men, women, and children—were killed. The colonial government struck back, slaughtering more than 10,000 slaves and mulattoes (people of mixed race). Many mulattoes in Saint-Domingue were legally free, although their rights were severely limited. However, they could own property and slaves, and many did. Though they had often sided with whites in previous uprisings, on this occasion, they allied themselves with the slaves. They switched sides, however, when the whites agreed to let free-born mulattoes become members of the colonial government.

The French Revolution had begun in 1789, and the Jacobin party in the French National Assembly in Paris initially refused to send French troops to Saint-Domingue in support of the slaveholding whites. Sensing a black victory, the mulattoes again switched sides and joined the slaves in an attempt to end white domination. Faced with an all-out war against the white population of Saint-Domingue and determined to save a valuable colony, the French National Assembly, in 1792, sent in 6,000 soldiers under Commissioner Léger Félicité Sonthonax and granted greater political rights to free mulattoes. The white planters resented the idea of mulatto political rights, and the mulattoes would not agree to Sonthonax's demand that amnesty be granted to rebelling slaves. The *petit blancs* (French term meaning "little whites" that was used to refer to small landowners, shopkeepers, and poor whites) rejected all three groups—slaves, mulattoes, and rich planters—and formed their own revolutionary group in the capital, Port-au-Prince, after burning much of the city to the ground. Sonthonax responded in August 1793 by issuing a decree freeing the slaves. This united the slaves behind him, but heavy fighting continued and many whites fled the colony. Though Boukman was killed in the fighting in 1791, his uprising was the beginning of the Haitian Revolution.

See also TOUSSAINT LOUVERTURE, HAITI, JEAN-JACQUES DESSALINES.

Brooks, Gwendolyn (1917–   ) *poet*

Gwendolyn Brooks was the first African American to win the Pulitzer Prize for poetry (1950). She was encouraged to write by her parents, as well as by writers like James Weldon Johnson and Langston Hughes.

Poet Gwendolyn Brooks wins the Pulitzer Prize for *Annie Allen*, 1950. (*Popperfoto/Archive Photos*)

Her first book of poetry, *A Street in Bronzeville* (1945), was followed by the Pulitzer Prize-winning *Annie Allen* in 1949. In 1953, Brooks published her only novel, *Maud Martha*. Other major works include *The Bean Eaters* (1960) and *In the Mecca* (1968).

Brooks made a point of writing about ordinary African Americans, saying that beauty could be found in the commonplace. Her popular poem *We Real Cool* focused on the problems of black youth, and other works explored racism and violence. Growing concern about African-American writers led her to market her work through black publishers. She also wrote an unusual autobiography called *Report from Part One*.

In addition to writing, Brooks taught at several colleges and universities. She has received numerous honorary degrees and was selected as a Library of Congress consultant in poetry and Poet Laureate of Illinois.

Brown, Claude (1937–   ) *writer*

Brown is known for his candid autobiography *Manchild in the Promised Land*, which described his life in a Harlem gang. As a child, Brown was sent to the Wiltwyck School for emotionally disturbed boys and then to Warwick Reform School. He later graduated from Howard University and became a lawyer. In 1976, he published a second book, *The Children of Ham.*

Brown, Clifford (1930–1956) *musician*

Brown toured Europe playing trumpet with Lionel Hampton, then joined ART BLAKEY'S quintet in 1953, after Charlie Parker recommended him to Blakey. A year later, Brown and Max Roach formed an electrifying new hard-bop group that included Sonny Rollins. Though Brown was killed in an automobile accident two years later, he is regarded as a brilliant performer and one of the greatest JAZZ trumpeters. Among his compositions are "Joy Spring" and "Dahoud."

Recommended Listening: *Jazz Immortal* (Pacific Jazz); *Brownie* (EmArcy).

Brown, James (1928–) *singer, songwriter*

In and out of trouble as a youth, Brown began singing with gospel groups in the late 1940s and learned to play the drums and organ. He soon branched out into rhythm and blues, gaining a considerable following among African Americans. In the 1950s, he and his group, The Famous Flames, signed with King Records, releasing his first big hit, "Please, Please, Please," in 1956. He rapidly became the top-ranked rhythm and blues singer in the country with hits like "Papa's Got a Brand New Bag," "Ain't That a Groove," and "It's A Man's, Man's World." His 1960s work also reflected the Civil Rights/black power movements with songs like "Say It Loud, I'm Black and I'm Proud." Noted for his high-energy performances, Brown is often referred to as the "Godfather of Soul."

Brown, William Wells (ca. 1814–1884)
abolitionist, author, historian, physician

Born a slave, Brown escaped in 1834 and became a conductor (guide) on the UNDERGROUND RAILROAD and lecturer for the ABOLITIONIST MOVEMENT. In 1847, he wrote his autobiography, *Narrative of William W. Brown, A Fugitive Slave, Written by Himself.* In 1849, he traveled to Europe, where he delivered over a thousand speeches against slavery. He also published a book about his travels. In 1853, he became the first African American to publish a novel, *Clotel; Or, The President's Daughter: A Narrative of Slave Life in the United States.*

Returning to the United States in 1854, Brown continued his abolitionist activities. He became a physician after the Civil War, though he continued his literary career. Between 1856 and 1880, he wrote two antislavery plays, four books on black history and biography, and an account of his travels through several former slave states in 1879–1880. His work provided biographical data on more than 100 African Americans, as well as information on black military history.

Brownsville, Texas, Affair

Incident that occurred August 1906, involving nine to 15 African-American soldiers from the Twenty-fifth Regiment. Brownsville had been placed off-limits to soldiers of the Twenty-fifth Infantry after a number of insults and harassment had culminated in a fight between a soldier and a white merchant. In protest, the soldiers shot up the town, killing one white person and wounding two others. When a military investigation failed to identify the soldiers involved and a local grand jury failed to return any indictments, President Theodore Roosevelt dishonorably discharged the entire battalion of 167 black men, thereby preventing its members from working in either the military or civil service capacity. The civil disability aspect of the order was revoked in January 1907, one week before the U.S. Senate launched an investigation into the matter. In 1909, Senator Joseph Foraker of Ohio, who earlier had condemned Roosevelt's action, was able to force the establishment of a court of inquiry to investigate each individual case, and allow those found innocent to reenlist and receive back pay. In 1972 the dishonorable discharge order was revoked.

The Brownsville affair had an extremely negative affect on African-American views. Up to that time, the black community had been very supportive of President Roosevelt because he had entertained BOOKER T. WASHINGTON at the White House in spite of strong white opposition. In fact, many black homes boasted so-called social equality pictures of Roosevelt and Washington together. Roosevelt's willingness to destroy the military careers of 167 men, six of whom had won the Medal of Honor, infuriated blacks across the nation, particularly as the news of the discharges was withheld until after the 1906 congressional elections so that the pro-Republican black vote would not be affected. Booker T. Washington did not publicly condemn Roosevelt, but he did appeal to Secretary of War William Howard Taft (later the 27th president) to stay the discharge order temporarily, hoping that Roosevelt would withdraw it when the anger of the black community became apparent. Roosevelt refused to rescind his decision.

Brown v. Board of Education of Topeka, Kansas
Lawsuit resulting in the 1954 Supreme Court decision that ended segregation in the public schools.
See EDUCATION.

Bruce, Blanche Kelso (1841–1898) *U.S. senator*
Born a slave, Bruce managed to acquire an education before running away to the free state of Kansas, where he opened a school. In 1865, he entered Oberlin College for a few months, then got a job on a riverboat. He settled in Mississippi in 1869, where he was elected to various offices including sheriff, superintendent of education, and tax collector of Bolivar County. He also became a wealthy plantation owner.

In 1874, Bruce became the second African American elected to the U.S. Senate from Mississippi. (HIRAM REVELS was the first.) During his term, he unsuccessfully opposed the Chinese Exclusion Act of 1878 as racially discriminatory. He also sought to integrate the armed forces and called for an investigation into the treatment of West Point cadet Johnson Whittaker, an African American, who was beaten by other cadets, then accused of lying and self-mutilation when he complained. After the

failure of the FREEDMAN'S SAVINGS AND TRUST COMPANY, Bruce succeeded in helping depositors regain some of their money.

Buffalo Soldiers
A term describing African-American soldiers who served in the U.S. Army regiments authorized by the Reorganization Act of 1866—specifically the Ninth and Tenth Cavalry and the Twenty-fourth and Twenty-fifth Infantry. The name is said to have originated with the Plains Indians, who likened the soldiers' bravery to that of the buffalo, and because the soldiers' curly black hair was reminiscent of a buffalo mane. A picture of a bison subsequently appeared on the Tenth Cavalry's regimental flag.

Illustration of Buffalo Soldiers marching along a mountain with their horses carrying their packs (*Archive Photos*)

During the first years of RECONSTRUCTION, President Andrew Johnson made a point of removing black troops from the South. As a result, the Buffalo Soldiers, many of whom were former slaves, were stationed west of the Mississippi, where they took part in the Indian Wars against Victorio, Sitting Bull, and Geronimo, escorted trains and stagecoaches, and provided protection for America's expanding web of railways and telegraph lines. Between 1870 and 1890, more than a dozen Buffalo Soldiers earned the Congressional Medal of Honor, with the first going to Sgt. Emanuel Stance, who rescued two white children who had been kidnapped.

During the 1898 Spanish-American War, both the Tenth Cavalry and the Twenty-fourth Infantry won commendations, seeing service in the battles of Santiago and San Juan Hill. Black troops were later sent to fight rebels in the Philippines. The four units remained together and fought in both world wars and Korea, before being integrated into the rest of the army in 1952. In 1992, the Buffalo Soldier monument was dedicated at Fort Leavenworth, Kansas. The dedication speaker was Gen. COLIN POWELL. The Buffalo Soldiers were the subject of a famous Bob Marley song.

Bunche, Ralph Johnson (1904–1971) *diplomat*

Ralph Bunche was the first African American to win the Nobel Peace Prize. While working on his masters degree at Harvard University, Bunche met Dr. PERCY JULIAN, who arranged for him to join the political science department at Howard University. In 1936, Bunche published *A World View of Race,* in which he stated that racial prejudice exists in order to justify economic exploitation. During World War II, he was part of the Office of Strategic Services, where his expertise on Africa was used in preparing the Allied invasion of the continent. He joined the State Department in 1944, where he became acting chief of the Division of Dependent Area Affairs. After the war, he was assigned to the United Nations, where he served as director of the Division of Trusteeship & Non-Self-Governing Territories, an office that dealt with the rights of people living under colonial rule. In 1950 Bunche was awarded the Nobel Peace Prize for his work in trying to resolve the conflict between Israel and the Arab states. His later diplomatic activities involved efforts to end fighting on Cyprus, supervising peacekeeping troops at the Suez Canal, and working to resolve a dispute between India and Pakistan.

Burke, Selma Hortense (1900–1995) *sculptor*

Burke began her professional career in sculpture when she moved to New York in 1935. In 1943, she won a competition sponsored by the Fine Arts Commission to create a profile drawing of Franklin Roosevelt. Finding no usable photographs of him (they were all 3/4 or full face), she arranged to meet with the president for 45 minutes, during which time she made several sketches of him. From these she created a bronze plaque that was used to design the portrait of Roosevelt that appears on the dime. Burke also created sculptures of MARY MCLEOD BETHUNE, BOOKER T. WASHINGTON, and JOHN BROWN.

Burkina Faso

West African country located north of Ghana. The capital is Ouagadougou (wah-gah-DEW-gu), but it is often called Ouaga (wah-gah). Before the French gained control of the area in the 1890s, Burkina Faso was ruled by a series of highly organized MOSSI kingdoms. The country became an official French colony in 1932, but the French failed to develop the area economically and instituted policies of forced labor and heavy taxation. The result was widespread resentment and revolt, and Burkina Faso became independent in 1960.

Burkina Faso, which is largely rural, is one of the five poorest nations on Earth, with the average person earning approximately $140 per year. The French called the area Upper Volta because of its three rivers: the Black Volta, the White Volta, and the Red Volta. The name was changed to Burkina Faso in 1984 after a 1983 coup led by Captain Thomas Sankara. Sankara emphasized preventive medicine, arranging for about 60 percent of the country's children to be vaccinated against measles, yellow fever, and meningitis. Efforts were made to build a small medical center in each village and to train medical technicians. In spite of this, infant mortality remains high, and the average lifespan is less than 50 years. Sankara also stressed education, and about 350 schools were built between 1983 and 1986. A guitarist who liked to compose "revolutionary music," Sankara had widespread popular support. However, he alienated Burkina Faso's powerful national unions and the landlords and was killed in a coup in 1987. A multiparty constitution was adopted in 1991.

Burkina Faso is located in Africa's SAHEL region, and its northern area is largely desert. The country's 9 million people, who are called Burkinabe, come from a number of tribal groups. French is the official language, though over 60 other languages are also spoken.

Burundi, Republic of

A small country (10,747 sq. miles) in East Africa. Capital: Bujumbura. Burundi was originally inhabited by Twa Pygmies, but these were gradually displaced by Hutu farmers who settled in the area after A.D. 1000. In the 16th century, another tribe, the Tutsi (or Watutsi), began entering the region and gradually established a feudalistic society in which the Hutu were subservient. In the late 1800s, Germany asserted sovereignty over what are now Burundi and Rwanda but was forced to surrender its colonial claims to Belgium after World War I. The Belgians maintained Burundi's social structure, keeping the Tutsi in control. Independence was granted in 1962.

In 1972, a massacre took place in which an estimated 100,000 Hutus were killed and 200,000 were forced to flee the country. Smaller massacres occured in 1988 (20,000 dead) and 1991 (1,000 killed). After 1988, Burundi's Tutsi political leaders sought reconciliation with the Hutus, and elections in July 1993 brought a Hutu leader, Melchior Ndadaye, to power. However, three months later, Ndadaye was the victim of a coup staged by the Tutsi-dominated army.

On April 6, 1994, Burundi's new Tutsi president, Cyprien Ntaryamira, was killed along with Rwanda's Hutu president, Juvenal Habyarimana, when their plane was shot down. In retaliation, Rwanda Hutus massacred more than 500,000 of that

Lidded basket, Tutsi people of Rwanda (*National Museum of African Art, Washington, D.C.*)

country's Tutsis. The Rwanda Tutsis then managed to gain control, and thousands of Rwanda Hutus fled to Burundi, where tensions were already high because of the genocide in Rwanda. Since the murders in Rwanda, thousands of Burundi Hutus have been killed in raids by Burundian Tutsi soldiers, and thousands more have fled into Tanzania.

On July 25, 1996, the Tutsi-dominated Burundi army ousted Hutu president Sylvestre Ntibantunganya and established a military government. (Ret.) Major Pierre Buyoya assumed the presidency, but Hutu militias retaliated, killing hundreds of Tutsi civilians. In an effort to separate Hutu civilians from Hutu rebels, the Tutsi-controlled military has forced thousands of Hutu people into "regroupment" camps or into exile. However, many in the crowded camps are suffering from hunger or disease, and in February 2000, the government agreed to dismantle 11 of them. Appoximately 100,000 people have died in the civil conflict since 1994.

Bushmen

A distinct group of people living in Africa's Kalahari Desert. They are graceful people, averaging around four foot eight inches in height, and are a light brown color. They are divided into several subgroups, the best known being the !KUNG SAN and the KHOI. Bushmen are noted for their unusual "click" languages, which not only involve frequent clicking sounds but which also include many specialized terms for things like the inside of the elbow and the back of the knee.

Since the desert is too dry for growing crops, Bushmen live by hunting and by gathering berries, roots, and various wild vegetables. They are extremely skilled at squeezing water from roots and melons and know where they can suck water up through the sand, using a straw. Although the scarcity of water prevents Bushmen from keeping livestock or pets, they are expert in imitating various animal cries and are knowledgeable about all animals, plants, and insects living in the desert.

Bushmen like tobacco, and almost all Bushmen, including children, smoke. They live in small, semipermanent camps called *werfs* and own little in the way of personal possessions. For centuries, Bushmen lived throughout Southern Africa, but they were pushed into the desert centuries ago by migrating BANTU peoples and later by Europeans. Today, Bushmen sometimes work as laborers and servants for Bantu and white farmers; this contact has exposed them to various illnesses, such as smallpox.

Bush Negroes

The name used to refer to slaves who escaped and established African-style settlements in the jungle interior of the colony of Dutch Guyana (now Suriname). The Bush Negroes planted fruit trees, plantains, and yams to feed themselves and to hide their newly built villages from soldiers. They also dug moats with sharpened stakes hidden under the water to repel military expeditions sent against them in retaliation for their raids on European plantations. The Dutch colonial government signed treaties with the two main Bush Negro groups in 1761 and 1767, guaranteeing their freedom in return for their promise not to accept any additional runaways or to come within a two-day overland journey or 10-hour boat trip of any white settlement.

busing

Busing was one method used to achieve school integration in the United States. The slow pace of school integration caused the U.S. Supreme Court to rule in a series of cases that widespread busing would be necessary to achieve desegregation. Actually, the busing of children was nothing new. For years, children all over the country had ridden buses to school. Throughout the South, black children had ridden buses to attend schools miles from their homes because they were not allowed to attend closer schools, which happened to be white. But while busing itself was not a new concept, the use of it to achieve integration often drew a furious response. This was especially true in Boston, where buses carrying black students were attacked by white demonstrators. White families there who participated in busing were also subjected to harassment. The extent to which busing could be used to promote integration was limited by the Supreme Court in 1974 when it ruled, in a split decision, that suburbs could not be compelled to participate in busing programs with city schools (*Miliken v. Bradley*).

C

calypso

A musical form that developed in 19th-century Trinidad, becoming the dominant sound in the Caribbean until REGGAE and salsa gained widespread popularity in the 1970s. Calypso lyrics emphasize political protest, sexual prowess, and "picong"—a kind of impromptu rhyming poking fun at a public figure or member of the audience. The musical patterns and rhythms that form calypso's base come originally from the West African "gayup," a call-and-response form of work song. In fact, the word *calypso* is believed to come from the African word *kaiso,* which is an exclamation of encouragement. With the end of slavery in Trinidad in 1834, calypso came into its own during carnival season (between New Year's and the beginning of Lent), when drum bands and stick fighters paraded while calypso singers traded "picong" insults. Drumming and stick fighting were banned by the British in 1880, but the music continued with drummers banging bamboo sticks together. These too were banned but reappeared in what eventually became steel drum bands. Early calypso stars included Lord Executor, Lord Invader, Attila the Hun, Roaring Lion, Mighty Destroyer, and Mighty Sparrow. Developing musical technology and American soul music led to "soul calypso," known as *soca.*

Cameroon, Republic of

West African country. Capital: Yaounde. The country is marked by a diverse terrain that includes tropical rain forests, deserts, mountains, swamps, and savannas. It is home to over 200 distinct ethnic groups, a situation that led to serious conflict in the 1950s and 1960s. Cameroon was the site of a large-scale slave trade, beginning in the late 15th century. Germany gained control of the region in the late 19th century but was forced to give up its claims to France and England following World War I.

The zone known as French Cameroons achieved complete independence in 1960 following several years of guerrilla warfare, and most of the British Cameroons zone voted to become part of the new state. The country's first president was Ahmadou Ahidjo. Under his rule, strikes were banned, and a significant number of political prisoners were held in jail, but the country was relatively stable. He resigned in 1982 but attempted an unsuccessful return a year later. An attempted coup in 1984 resulted in as many as 1,000 deaths before calm was restored. Opposition parties were legalized in 1990; however, Cameroon remains primarily a one-party state under President Paul Biya.

In 1986, the buildup of carbon dioxide gas under Lake Nyos resulted in an explosion that killed 1,746 people and 8,000 animals. To avoid a repetition of the disaster, scientists began work on siphoning toxic gas out of Lake Nyos and Lake Nonoun in 1999.

Cape Verde, Republic of

A country consisting of 10 islands and five islets off the west coast of Africa and considered a part of Africa. Its area is about 1,550 square miles, its population approximately 330,000 people. Capital: Praia. The islands were uninhabited when they were discovered in 1456 by a Portuguese named Luigi da Cadamosto. Six years later, Portuguese settlers arrived and began importing slaves from West Africa to work their vineyards. Because of its location about 350 miles off the African coast, Cape Verde became an important stop for ships carrying slaves to Europe and the Americas.

Although the islands originally appeared to be fertile (*verde* means "green"), they are extremely dry. One island has gone without rain for over 10 years, and the others enjoy precipitation only once or twice a year. As the population increased, soil erosion became a serious problem. That, in turn, led to recurring droughts and famine, causing over 40 percent of the population to die of starvation in 1773–75, 1830–33, and 1863–66.

The islands are located in whale-filled waters and attracted many U.S. whaling ships in the early 1800s. These ships frequently recruited crew members from the islands, and as a result, many Cape Verdeans have relatives in the United States. Portugal encouraged island residents to sign labor contracts obligating them to work on the cacao plantations of São Tomé, another Portuguese colony. Because of poverty, over 80,000 Cape Verdeans did so, even though they were treated little better than slaves.

Cape Verdeans began their struggle for independence under the leadership of Amilcar Cabral. They were joined in their effort by the people of Portuguese Guinea (now Guinea-Bissau) and achieved independence in 1975. Cape Verde is stable and has an excellent human rights record. About 38 percent of the people are of pure African ancestry, with 60 percent of mixed European and African heritage. The culture is a blend of African and Portuguese, and although Portuguese is the official language, many people speak Crioulo, a kind of African-Creole-Portuguese.

capoeira (CAP-oh-AIR-uh)
A martial arts style developed by slaves in Brazil, *capoeira* is thought to be derived from the West African courtship ritual called the "Zebra Dance," in which men fought to acquire brides. (Zebras are noted for their powerful kicks). During slavery, the dance and acrobatic elements of *capoeira* were emphasized to hide its fighting applications from the slave masters. Music was provided by drums, bells, and the *berimvau,* a one-string instrument similar to a bow and arrow. The songs, which provided the fighting rhythm, also were used to transmit coded information. Escaped slaves at the Palmares settlement in Brazil trained in *capoeira* for defense. Fighters utilize sweeps, kicks from a handstand position, flying kicks, head butts, and various punches. The original Angola *capoeira* emphasizes low-to-the-ground techniques. It evolved into what is known as *regional capoeira,* which incorporates flying kicks adopted from kung fu and other martial arts styles. In 1972, *capoeira* became the national martial arts style of Brazil.

Carmichael, Stokely (Kwame Turé, Kwame Touré) (1941–1998) *head of the Student Nonviolent Coordinating Committee (SNCC)*

Born in Trinidad, Stokely Carmichael and his family moved to the United States when he was 11. After graduating from Howard University in 1964, he began voter registration work with the STUDENT NON-VIOLENT COORDINATING COMMITTEE (SNCC). He was elected chairman of the organization in 1966 but was both criticized and praised for his radical views. A year earlier, he had popularized the cry "Black Power" during a famous speech in Greenwood, Mississippi. He resigned as chairman of SNCC in 1967 amid debate regarding continuing dependence on nonviolence and on the presence of whites in the organization. He traveled to Africa, where he became interested in Pan-Africanism, and also became involved with the BLACK PANTHER PARTY. In 1969 Carmichael moved to GUINEA, where he changed his name to Kwame Turé in honor of the African leaders Sékou Touré and KWAME NKRUMAH. Carmichael died on November 15, 1998.

Carrido, Juan (1500s) *explorer*

Juan Carrido was one of approximately 200 Africans who were part of Hernán Cortés' 1519 expedition to conquer Mexico. Carrido brought grains of wheat with him, which he planted as an experiment in 1521. This was the first wheat crop grown in the Americas.

Carson, Benjamin S. (1951–) *pediatric neurosurgeon*

Ben Carson was born in 1951 in Detroit, Michigan, the younger of two brothers. His parents divorced when he was young and he ran into serious difficulties at school. His classmates ridiculed him because of his learning problems and he developed a violent temper. His mother responded by limiting his television viewing and requiring him to read two books a week. Within a year, he had become first in his class. But when he was 14, he tried to stab another student. The knife broke when it struck the other child's belt buckle, and Carson ran home, locked himself in the bathroom, and prayed for help. He has said he never lost his temper again, and he remains extremely devout. He continued to read widely and decided to become a physician. He graduated with honors from high school and entered Yale University, where he earned a degree in psychology. Carson then entered medical school at the University of Michigan, where he developed an interest in neurosurgery. He worked as a resident at Johns Hopkins Hospital in Baltimore, Maryland, where he later became director of pediatric neurosurgery. In 1987, Carson made medical history when he successfully separated a pair of twins who were joined to each other at the back of the head. Previous attempts to separate twins joined in this way had always resulted in the death of one or both children. He has also successfully removed half the brains of several children suffering from multiple seizures. Carson typically performs 500 operations a year. He and his wife, Candy, have established The Carson Scholars Fund to provide college scholarships for poor children. Carson has written three books: *Gifted Hands; Think Big,* and *The Big Picture.*

Carthage

An ancient North African city founded by the PHOENICIANS in 814 B.C. in what is now Tunisia. By the sixth century B.C., it had become a major com-mercial center with a population of around 400,000. The Phoenicians settled Carthage as a base for their maritime activities, and this seagoing orientation continued throughout the city's history. The Carthaginian admiral HANNO led an expedition to establish a series of settlements between what are now Morocco and Senegal, and traveled as far south as Mt. Cameroon.

In the fifth century B.C., Carthage came into conflict with Greece and Sicily but managed to gain control over most of the western Mediterranean. Tension with Rome in the third century B.C. resulted in the Punic Wars, which finally ended with a Carthaginian defeat in 146 B.C. and the destruction of the city. Lost in the wreckage was the great Library of Carthage, which is said to have contained 500,000 books and manuscripts, including many on science, astronomy, mathematics, history, and geography. It was during the second Punic War (there were three in all) that the great Carthaginian general HANNIBAL led an army, complete with elephants, across the Alps.

Carver, George Washington (ca. 1861–1943) *botanist*

Born to slave parents living on the Carver plantation near Diamond Grove, Missouri, George Washington Carver and his mother were kidnapped and taken to Arkansas when Carver was a baby. His mother was never found, but the boy was returned to the Carver plantation in exchange for a racehorse. Because he was a sickly child, Carver was unable to do much work and instead spent his time collecting flowers and plants. After the Civil War, he taught himself to read, then left home in search of further education. After enrolling in Minneapolis High School in Kansas, he won a scholarship to Highland University but lost it when the school learned he was black. In 1887, he enrolled at Simpson College in Iowa, then went on to Iowa State Agricultural College. He graduated in 1894 and became the first African American on the faculty. Along with teaching, Carver engaged in agricultural research, experimenting with plant chemistry and conducting investigations into several varieties of fungus.

George Washington Carver (*Library of Congress*)

In 1896, Carver left Iowa State to create a department of agriculture at Tuskegee Institute in Alabama. When he arrived at Tuskegee, he found no laboratory and was forced to make his own equipment. However, he not only created an agriculture department, he developed the idea of the "movable school," which involved crossing the countryside in a wagon to teach local farmers new agricultural techniques. This movable school concept was later adopted by countries as far away as China and India. Carver taught farmers to enrich the soil through crop rotation and developed over 24 products from peanuts and 118 products made from sweet potatoes. He became world famous and was asked to join the staffs of Thomas Edison and the Ford Motor Company. But he preferred to remain at Tuskegee. President Harry Truman proclaimed January 5, 1946, George Washington Carver Day, and Congress established the George Washington Carver National Monument near his birthplace in Missouri. The National Park Service maintains a Carver Museum at Tuskegee University.

Central African Republic

Country wedged between Democratic Republic of Congo, Chad, Congo, Sudan, and Cameroon. Capital: Bangui. Evidence indicates settlement in the area goes back to ancient times. The region, which was hit hard by both the European and East African slave trade, came under French control in the late 1800s. The French instituted a policy of forced labor that cost thousands of lives, and famines, epidemics, and military repression killed thousands more. A resistance movement (the Movement of Social Evolution in Black Africa) founded by Barthélemy Boganda helped bring about independence in 1960, although Boganda was killed in a mysterious plane crash a year earlier. The country's first president was David Dacko, whose repressive regime was overthrown in 1966 by Jean-Bedel Bokassa. Bokassa's government was even more brutal than Dacko's, but he retained the support of the French, who were interested in the Central African Republic's mineral deposits. In January 1979, Bokassa murdered at least 100 schoolchildren who were protesting the fact that they were required to buy expensive school uniforms produced by a company owned by Bokassa's wife. Later that year, he had himself crowned emperor in a ceremony whose cost equaled the entire annual income of the country. In September 1979, France cut off all aid to the Central African Republic and provided Dacko with 1,000 French troops to take over the country after Bokassa left for Libya. Dacko was overthrown in 1981 by André Kolingba. Riots in 1990 forced Kolingba to agree to institute a democratic government, and when the first multiparty elections were held in 1993, Félix-Ange Patasse was elected president. In May 1996, mutinous army troops attempted to seize power, and the French sent in French troops supported by helicopter gunships and jet fighters to help the government maintain control.

Chad, Republic of

Central African country. Capital: N'Djamena. With an area of 495,752 square miles, Chad is the fifth-largest country in Africa. However, its population is only about 6,500,000, in spite of the fact that people have lived in the area since ancient times. One reason for the lack of population is the change in climate. About 2,500 years ago, Lake Chad, which straddles the border between Chad and Niger, covered almost 149,000 square miles. Today it ranges from 3,800 to 9,900 square miles in area, depending upon the season, and continues to shrink as the region becomes drier. The earlier, wetter climate was favorable to wildlife, and the area attracted hunters, who left beautiful rock paintings in the Tibesti Mountains region. A Nubian people called the Sao also settled in the region and developed the lost wax technique of bronze casting.

Around the eighth century, other Nile peoples began moving into the area. They intermarried with the Sao, who eventually disappeared. One of these early migrant groups established the kingdom of Kanem, which lasted 1,000 years. The Kanem empire expanded and became KANEM-BORNU, reaching its height under King Idris Alooma, who took power in 1571. Kanem-Bornu, along with the competing kingdoms of the Baguirmi and the Ouadai, which arose in the 16th and 17th centuries, was a major slave trader, regularly raiding the black peoples in southern Chad for captives. In fact, the slave trade continued in Chad until the 20th century.

The Sudanese conquered the region in the late 19th century, and they, in turn, were defeated by the French in 1913. At that point, Chad became a part of French Equatorial Africa. The French put an end to the slave raids, but they exploited the country economically and were such poor administrators that when Chad became independent in 1960, there were only three high schools in the entire country. Tension between the Arab nomads in the northern desert region and the black population in the south escalated into civil war, which, in turn, developed into a 20-year war with Libya, Chad's neighbor to the north. Even after peace had been declared, Libya continued to aid rebel groups in Chad, and the country has been the scene of numerous coups. Former guerrilla leader Idriss Deby seized control of the government in 1990. A new constitution was drafted in 1996 and multiparty elections were held. The government has been guilty of the torture of prisoners, and various rebel groups have engaged in hostage-taking and the murder of civilians. Chad is an extremely poor nation, with the average person earning less than $100 a year. Its population consists of three distinct groups: Tuareg-Berber people who live in the Sahara, an Arab population that occupies the central area where the old Kanem-Bornu kingdom once held sway, and various black groups to the south, of which the largest is the Sara.

See also TUAREG; BERBERS.

chain gangs   See CRIMINAL JUSTICE RIGHTS.

Chaney, James (1943–1964) *civil rights activist*
James Chaney was a 21-year-old African American who was murdered with Andrew Goodman and Michael Schwerner after the three were arrested in Philadelphia, Mississippi. The men were members of the CONGRESS OF RACIAL EQUALITY (CORE) and were working to register black voters as part of the Mississippi Freedom Summer Project.

Chaney was a native of Mississippi and had lived in the state all his life. His mother, speaking at his memorial service, said, "They's gone. They was beat. They was dogged . . . They dead. We gonna let all of that die? No, I can't let it die. No sir, I never let my child's work go in vain."[1]

See also PHILADELPHIA, MISSISSIPPI, MURDERS.

Changamire
An empire situated in what is now southern Zimbabwe and Mozambique. Established by Chief Changa around 1485, Changamire lasted approximately three centuries. It developed as a result of a war between Changa and the ruler of MONOMOTAPA. The people, who lived in stone houses, were farmers, miners, and traders. The fact that they were far from the ocean and from the Zambezi River protected them from both European and Arab slavers. The Changamire Empire was destroyed around 1831 by Ngoni invaders from South Africa.

[1] Liner notes on the recording *Movement Soul* (Folkway Records).

Chesnutt, Charles Waddell (1858–1932) *writer, attorney*

Born in Cleveland, Ohio, Chesnutt moved with his family to North Carolina when he was eight years old. He began a career in education as principal of State Normal School in Fayetteville in 1881 but left after deciding he did not wish to remain in the segregated South. Returning to Ohio, he became a lawyer. His first published story appeared in 1887 in *The Atlantic Monthly*. *The Conjure Woman* (1899) is a group of dialect stories set prior to the Civil War. Another 1899 book of stories, *The Wife of His Youth*, centers on a freedman whose relationship with an educated black woman is complicated by his past slave marriage. During this same period, he also wrote a successful biography of Frederick Douglass. Chesnutt had a white grandfather, and his books often stress the problems of mixed-race characters. *The Marrow of Tradition* (1901) portrays two half-sisters classified as being of different races and comments with irony on the meaning of civilization. Other books include *The House Behind the Cedars* (1900) and *The Colonel's Dream* (1905). In 1928, the NAACP awarded Chesnutt its Spingarn Award for "highest achievement by a black American."

Chilembwe Uprising

Rebellion against British colonial powers that took place in 1915 in Nyasaland in what is now Malawi. It was led by an African Baptist preacher named John Chilembwe and was fed by widespread discontent with the treatment of African laborers on European-owned plantations. Chilembwe had been converted to Christianity by Joseph Booth, a British evangelist who preached that Africa should belong to Africans in a united African Christian nation. Chilembwe trained for the ministry in the United States, where he was impressed by the philosophy of BOOKER T. WASHINGTON. After returning to Nyasaland, Chilembwe founded the Providence Industrial Mission, which established seven schools with a total of 1,800 pupils. Chilembwe was angered when white plantation owners exploited Mozambican refugees who had fled to Nyasaland because of a famine. When he protested the drafting of Africans

into the British army during World War I, several of his schools were burned down. Calling on his followers to "strike a blow and die," Chilembwe led 200 followers in an attack on a plantation that resulted in the deaths of three plantation managers. The colonial government responded by killing a number of Africans, including Chilembwe. The Chilembwe uprising is regarded as a forerunner of later militant independence movements.

Christian, Charlie (1916–1942) *musician*

Christian's enormous talent forced the recognition of the electric guitar as a solo instrument. He became famous after joining Benny Goodman's band in 1939. Along with THELONIOUS MONK, CHARLIE PARKER, and DIZZY GILLESPIE, he was instrumental in the development of bebop. Christian's work is noted for its harmonic innovations, legato phrasing, and inimitable sound. Though he died of tuberculosis at age 26, he influenced hundreds of later guitarists, including B.B. King.

Christian Nubia

Christian civilization that developed in the sixth century A.D. in southern Egypt and Sudan. Initially, the Christian Nubians were divided into three kingdoms: Nobatia in the north, Makuria in the middle, and, to the south, Alodia (or Alwa), which was to become heavily involved in the slave trade. Sometime before 710, Makuria merged with Nobatia. After defeating Muslim attackers at the city of Dongola, Makuria entered into a peace agreement with Egypt that was to last for 600 years. These Christian kingdoms enjoyed several centuries of peace and prosperity. Their religious orientation arose largely through the efforts of a monk named Julian who did missionary work in the area. However, in 639–642, when Egypt came under Muslim rule, Nubia was cut off from the rest of the Christian world. Christianity continued in Nubia until the 15th century, when the area became Muslim. The Christian Nubians left behind a great number of churches made of stone and brick. They are especially noted for the beautiful murals they painted. Archaeological excavations indicate that at least one citizen of

Old Dongola enjoyed the luxury of a heated bathroom with piped-in hot water.

Cinqué, Joseph (ca. 1814–1879)
(SIN-Kay) *leader of slave ship rebellion*

Cinqué was captured in 1839 and shipped to Cuba aboard the *Tecora* under conditions so terrible that more than one-third of the 500 slaves aboard died. He and the surviving slaves were then transferred to BARRACOONS (slave pens). Two weeks later, Cinqué and 52 other captives were placed aboard the AMISTAD. It was on this ship that one of the most famous slave uprisings in U.S. history occurred. Cinqué managed to pry a nail out of the ship's hull and used it to free himself and the other captives. After taking over the ship, they instructed the helmsman to set sail for Africa. Each night, however, the helmsman changed course, hoping to land in the southern United States, where slavery was legal. Instead, the *Amistad* landed in New York. Cinqué and the other slaves were arrested by the U.S. Coast Guard and charged with mutiny and murder. American abolitionists came to their aid, and, after a sensational trial and several appeals, Cinqué and the others were freed and allowed to return to Africa. The name *Cinqué* is a corruption of the African name *Sing-gbe*.

Civil Rights Act of 1964

Legislation passed by Congress that outlawed discrimination on the basis of race, color, sex, religion, or national origin in public accommodations,

Civil rights demonstrators and policemen at a rally, Alabama, March 27, 1965 (*Archive Photos*)

including restaurants, motels, hotels, and theaters. Discrimination in employment was also prohibited. President John F. Kennedy proposed the legislation in response to the 1963 May demonstration in Birmingham, Alabama, and the June murder of MEDGAR EVERS. Kennedy was assassinated before the bill could be enacted, but President Lyndon Johnson pushed it through Congress and signed it into law on July 2, 1964. It is regarded as one of the major pieces of congressional legislation of the 20th century.

A bloodied demonstrator is helped by others after protesting for civil rights in Selma, Alabama, 1965. (*Archive Photos*)

Civil Rights movement

Social, legal, and political movement that took place in the 1950s and 1960s with the intent of ending discrimination against African Americans across the United States. The 1954 BROWN V. BOARD OF EDUCATION OF TOPEKA Supreme Court decision was an enormous victory for the old-line civil rights organizations like the NATIONAL ASSOCIATION FOR THE ADVANCEMENT OF COLORED PEOPLE and had a critical psychological impact on millions of Americans. A year later, Rosa Parks refused to give up her seat on a bus to a white man and triggered the MONTGOMERY BUS BOYCOTT, which thrust MARTIN LUTHER KING JR. into a leadership role and made him a national figure. In 1957, the LITTLE ROCK NINE captured the national spotlight in their effort to integrate Central High School in Arkansas, and the FREEDOM RIDERS and the SIT-IN MOVEMENT gained attention in 1960 and 1961. Thousands of Americans, white and black, were demonstrating across the South in an effort to end segregation in stores, restaurants, hotels, libraries, and all public places. Fair housing and equal employment opportunities were also a major concern. Voter registration drives, particularly in Mississippi, gained force through the efforts of the activities of volunteers working with the CONGRESS OF RACIAL EQUALITY and the STUDENT NON-VIOLENT COORDINATING COMMITTEE.

Tactics ranged from legal and judicial action to picketing, marches, demonstrations, voter registration, and various forms of civil disobedience. Thousands of civil rights demonstrators were arrested, and hundreds were beaten. Scores of churches and homes were dynamited, and a number of activists were murdered, among them Martin Luther King Jr., MEDGAR EVERS, JAMES CHANEY, Andrew Goodman, Michael Schwerner, Rev. George Lee, Lamar Smith, Herbert Lee, Jimmie Lee Jackson, Rev. James Reeb, Viola Liuzzo, and Vernon Dahmer.

One reason for the success of the Civil Rights movement was the presence of television cameras that captured the readiness of police to ignore and/or indulge in criminal behavior in order to suppress peaceful civil rights demonstrations. The televised brutality infuriated millions of Americans, who put tremendous pressure on Congress and the White House to pass civil rights legislation.

Although the movement's emphasis on nonviolent action drew on the sentiments of Mohandas Gandhi and Henry Thoreau, the idea of nonviolent, passive sacrifice, even to the point of martyrdom, is basic to Christian tradition and was readily accepted by movement leaders, most of whom were Christian ministers. This interweaving of civil rights strategy and Christian religious thought attracted the support of thousands of churches, white as well as black. The many Jews, nonpracticing Christians, and those of other faiths who were also deeply involved in the movement accepted the leadership requirement that they "go limp" and respond nonviolently even when beaten. The nonviolent tactics used by civil rights demonstrators not only attracted widespread religious support but also allowed television cameras to cast them in a heroic light and permitted a minority group (blacks were approximately 10 percent of the U.S. population) with little economic and political leverage to gain the moral high ground.

The movement was also helped by the fact that the country had only recently emerged from World War II and the Korean conflict, and patriotic feeling was strong. The black protesters were lawfully demanding basic rights already guaranteed them by the U.S. Constitution. They were asking for fair and equal treatment in a country that prided itself on its democratic traditions. This struck a resounding chord among millions of whites who viewed themselves as patriotic Americans. Moreover, because of the "cold war" with the Soviet Union, the U.S. government was under pressure to demonstrate its commitment to democracy. This was especially true in regard to new countries that had recently emerged from colonial status. The fact that the country was in a period of prosperity also encouraged a generosity of spirit.

The presidency of Lyndon Johnson was of critical importance. A Texan who had grown up in poverty and who was well aware of the cruelty of discrimination, Johnson used his considerable political skills to push through the CIVIL RIGHTS ACT OF 1964 and the Voting Rights Act of 1965. He also appointed a number of judges, including THURGOOD MARSHALL, who were supportive of civil rights demands.

Other factors in the movement's success included a strong belief in the integrity of the civil rights leadership and the ability of the leadership to put forth precise, obtainable demands that could be readily met through legal and/or political action. Also important was the leadership's ability to provide a framework, in terms of marches, petitions, demonstrations, etc., through which thousands of ordinary people could make their concerns felt. While thousands of whites supported civil rights, the movement grew out of, and was solidly anchored in, black institutions and organizations, particularly the black churches, the black colleges, and the black civil rights organizations.

See also RALPH ABERNATHY, ELLA BAKER, DAISY BATES, STOKELY CARMICHAEL, EDUCATION, JESSE JACKSON, AUTHERINE LUCY, MARCH ON WASHINGTON, JAMES MEREDITH, MISSISSIPPI FREEDOM DEMOCRATIC PARTY, ROBERT MOSES, NATIONAL ASSOCIATION FOR THE ADVANCEMENT OF COLORED PEOPLE, SOUTHERN CHRISTIAN LEADERSHIP CONFERENCE, VOTING RIGHTS STRUGGLE.

Recommended Viewing: PBS television series *Eyes on the Prize* by Juan Williams.

Clark, Kenneth Bancroft (1914–   ) *psychologist*
Born in the Panama Canal Zone, Clark left there with his mother at age five and moved to Harlem. He earned a Ph.D. in experimental psychology from Columbia after graduating from Howard University. In the late 1930s, Clark became interested in the effect of segregation on the self-image of African-American children. In one experiment, black youngsters were given crayons and asked to color pictures of girls and boys and pretend that the pictures were pictures of themselves. Fourteen percent of the dark-skinned children colored the pictures white, yellow, or a color like blue or green, indicating a refusal to accept their own color. In other experiments, Clark found that the majority of African-American children picked white dolls rather than brown dolls as being "good" and most like themselves. Some children actually cried when forced to accept the dark-colored dolls as being most like themselves. Clark's groundbreaking research was used by THURGOOD MARSHALL to help win the 1954 *Brown v. Board of Education* case outlawing school segregation. Clark's publications include *Desegregation: An Appraisal of the Evidence* (1953), *Prejudice and Your Child* (1953), *Dark Ghetto* (1965), and *King, Malcolm, Baldwin* (1984).

Code Noir
Legal code issued by the French government in 1685 to regulate the treatment of slaves in French colonies.

See also SLAVERY.

coffle
Word describing a procession of slaves being marched to the African coast for shipment to the

Coffle (*Library of Congress*)

Americas. The word comes from the Arabic word *qafila,* meaning "caravan." Slaves captured in raids on inland villages were tied together with vines, chains, and wooden yokes and marched to the coast or to "slave fairs" for sale. Death rates in the initial raids often reached 50 percent, especially since the very old, the very young, and any wounded were generally killed immediately as worthless in terms of sale. Another 40 percent to 65 percent of the remaining captives usually died on the way to the coast. Coffle journeys generally lasted several months, and those too weak to keep up were murdered. Most deaths, however, were due to exhaustion combined with extreme malnutrition and dehydration. Dysentery, typhus, typhoid, and smallpox also took a large toll. Once coffles reached major rivers, captives were transferred to fleets of canoes, each of which generally held 20 to 30 slaves. Upon reaching the coast, slaves were held in slave pens, or BARRACOONS, until they could be loaded aboard ship. Some captives managed to escape the coffles and barracoons. Many of these runaways established MAROON colonies and survived by attacking slave-trader caravans carrying goods to exchange for slaves. The best-known of these African Maroon colonies was KISAMA in Angola. Coffles of slaves being transported for sale

were also seen in the Americas, but the death rates were generally considerably less.

Coffy's Rebellion

A major slave uprising that took place in the Dutch colony of Berbice (now Guyana) in February 1763. Coffy (or Cuffy) was an African-born Ashanti slave who intended either to create an independent black state or else set up a protected black-run region in the interior of the colony. The uprising began on a plantation in the Canje River region but soon spread to the estates on the Berbice River. Six hundred slaves attacked Peerboom Plantation, where a number of whites had taken refuge. The whites, who were rapidly running out of food, agreed to surrender the plantation in return for a guarantee of safe conduct. Their request was granted by a slave leader named Cosala, but many whites were killed anyway.

Many of the colony's remaining whites were then ready to abandon the colony, but the governor, a man named van Hoogenheim, was able to delay acting until a British ship carrying 100 soldiers arrived. This enabled the whites to occupy a key plantation on the Berbice River. Coffy's forces attacked but were beaten back. Coffy then offered to divide the colony, leaving the whites on the coast and the blacks in control of the interior. Again van Hoogenheim stalled, saying he needed authorization from Holland.

While Coffy waited, van Hoogenheim received help in the form of three warships and 250 soldiers and an Indian force from a neighboring colony. Hoping to save the deteriorating situation, Coffy launched an all-out attack on May 13 with 2,000 slave followers. After five hours of heavy fighting, he and his men were pushed back. Coffy committed suicide after a slave named Atta took over leadership. However, Atta was unable to hold onto the territory Coffy had won, and most of the rebelling slaves were forced into the forests, where many of them were hunted down and killed. The revolt lasted 10 months and came close to driving the whites out of Berbice. Coffy is regarded as a national hero in Guyana, and the day his revolt began—February 23—was selected as the day Guyana officially became a republic in 1970.

Coleman, Elizabeth ("Bessie") (1896–1926)
aviator

Inspired by the exploits of pilots in World War I, Bessie Coleman got her pilot's license in France after being barred from aviation schools in the United States. She was nicknamed "Queen Bess" because of the spectacular stunts she performed in air shows. She refused to perform before segregated audiences and once delayed her appearance in an Orlando, Florida, show until other aviators dropped notices on the city saying blacks were welcome to attend. She also lectured African-American groups on the need to support black aviators. Coleman was killed when the controls on her plane jammed while she was rehearsing for a Negro Welfare League benefit show in Jacksonville, Florida. She is one of the few women featured in the Black Heritage postage stamp series.

Coleridge-Taylor, Samuel (1875–1912)
musician, composer

Coleridge-Taylor was raised by his English mother after his father, a medical doctor, returned home to Sierra Leone in West Africa. He studied at the Royal College of Music in London and was aided by composer Sir Edward Elgar, who recommended him for commissions by choral societies.

As part of a deliberate effort to enhance the dignity of blacks, Coleridge-Taylor created compositions like *24 Negro Melodies*. He also wrote incidental music to accompany Shakespeare's *Othello*. However, his most successful compositions were inspired by Native Americans. The romantic appeal of Longfellow's poem *The Song of Hiawatha* led to a trilogy of choral works: *Hiawatha's Wedding Feast*, *The Death of Minnehaha*, and *Hiawatha's Departure*. The composer even named his son Hiawatha.

Coleridge-Taylor's interest in the music of different cultures also produced *Moorish Tone-Pictures*, *Toussaint L'Ouverture*, *La Bamboula*, and an American frontier rhapsody, *From the Prairie*. He made three tours of the United States, leading the Coleridge-Taylor Choral Society of black singers. His daughter, Avril Coleridge-Taylor, was one of the first women of African descent to be a classical music composer. Her works include a piano concerto and *In Memoriam R.A.F.*, a tribute to Britain's Royal Air Force.

Colfax

Louisiana town; the scene of a massacre of African Americans in 1873. Former slaves who supported the Republican Party had taken control of the government after winning the local elections. Fearing that the white Democrats would try to drive them out by force, they barricaded the town. Three weeks later, a large group of whites, armed with a cannon and other firearms, overpowered them. The resulting massacre convinced blacks across the South that they could not protect their rights against whites in major confrontations. "The organization against them is too strong," remarked one black man. "They attempted [armed self-defense] in Colfax. The result was that on Easter Sunday of 1873, when the sun went down that night, it went down on the corpses of 280 Negroes."[1] In response, the federal government indicted 97 whites, of whom nine stood trial. Three were convicted, but their convictions were overturned (*United States v. Cruikshank*). More than anything else, the kind of violence seen at Colfax kept African Americans from voting and effectively wiped out many of the gains they had made during Reconstruction.

Coltrane, John W. ("Trane") (1926–1967)
musician

Born in Hamlet, North Carolina, John Coltrane was raised in an atmosphere of southern church music. His father was an amateur musician, and Coltrane himself played clarinet, the E-flat horn, and the alto saxophone in his high school band. Afterward, he studied at the Ornstein School of Music in Philadelphia. After service in the navy, he played with several rhythm-and-blues groups, during which time he switched from alto sax and clarinet to tenor sax. He performed with DIZZY GILLESPIE in 1949 and in 1952 began working first with Earl Bostic and then with Johnny Hodges, who was an important early influ-

[1]Eric Foner, *Reconstruction*. New York: Harper & Row, 1988.

John Coltrane, playing the saxophone (*Archive Photos*)

as *A Love Supreme* (1964). He was famous for playing long solos, often lasting over 30 minutes. When asked why, he explained that it took that long to get all the music in. He is considered the leader in avant-garde, or free, jazz.

Comoros, Federal Islamic Republic of the

Indian Ocean archipelago located between Madagascar and Mozambique. Capital: Moroni. The archipelago is composed of four main islands, Grande Comore, Anjouan, Mayotte, and Moheli, and various islets and reefs. The first inhabitants probably arrived around the first century and were of Polynesian-Malay origin. They were followed by Arabs and Shirazi Persians, who established a number of rival sultanates and a trade in spices and slaves imported from Africa. Constant civil strife allowed the French to gain control of Mayotte in 1841. Control of the other islands was completed by 1912, when Comoros was declared a French colony. The French ruled the islands from Madagascar until 1946, when Comoros was granted administrative autonomy status within the French Union. In 1974, the Comoros islands, with the exception of Mayotte, voted to become independent. Mayotte remains a French dependency. After a coup in 1989, democratic elections were held in 1990. In 1999, a coup took place and Colonel Azaly Assoumani ousted President Tadjiddine Ben Said Massounde. The name *Comoros* is a corruption of the ancient Arabic description, *Djazair al Qamar*, "Islands of the Moon."

Congo, Democratic Republic of

African country. Capital: Kinshasa. The third-largest country in Africa (after Sudan and Algeria), Congo is dominated by the Congo River, the second-longest river in Africa. Once the site of the KONGO kingdom, certain sections of the country suffered greatly from the slave trade. Explorer/journalist Sir Henry Stanley helped King Leopold II of Belgium establish a claim to the region that later became the CONGO FREE STATE. Public exposure of atrocities in conjunction with forced labor practices led to the area being turned over to the Belgian government,

ence. Coltrane gained public recognition for his intense sound and virtuoso technique while working with MILES DAVIS from 1955 to 1957. He left Davis briefly to work with THELONIOUS MONK but returned and recorded *Kind of Blue* in 1959 and the highly original and musically intricate *Giant Steps* in 1959. His incredible technique enabled him to play notes so fast that he was described as hanging "sheets of sound" before listeners. He investigated African pentatonic scales, Indian ragas, and the polyphonic music of the Pygmies. In 1960, Coltrane recorded *My Favorite Things* with his own newly formed group, which included McCoy Tyner, Steve Davis, and Elvin Jones (and later Reggie Workman and Jimmy Garrison). Many of the group's recordings at Birdland and the Village Vanguard became classics. Coltrane's deeply spiritual side continued to find expression in his music, including such albums

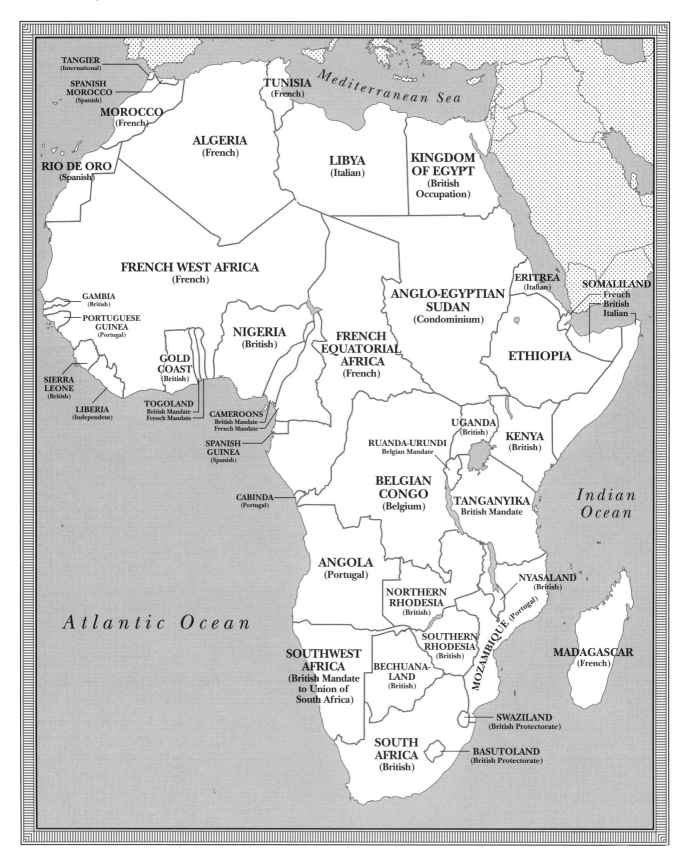

European influence in Africa, late 19th century (*Facts On File*)

which created a colony called the BELGIAN CONGO. The worst abuses were ended, but almost no preparations for decolonization were made, and when independence was granted in 1960, the country (renamed Zaire 1971–1997) had only 14 college graduates, none of them with any training in government.

Prior to independence, tension had developed between three rival political groups: the Mouvement National Congolais (MNC), led by PATRICE LUMUMBA; the Alliance des Ba-Kongo (ABAKO), led by Joseph Kasavubu and the Confederation des Associations Tribales du Katanga (CONAKAT), led by Moise Tshombe. Elections were held in May 1960, and a government was formed with Lumumba as prime minister and Kasavubu as head of state. Though Congo enjoyed one of the highest per capita income levels in Africa, its 200 tribal groups had little sense of national identity. Tribal disorders erupted a week after independence was declared, and mutinous soldiers killed a number of Europeans. Katanga province, under the leadership of Moise Tshombe, seceded—a major blow, since the province was responsible for half of Congo's income. An exceptionally vicious civil war marked by numerous atrocities broke out. The United Nations sent in a peacekeeping force, but Lumumba was murdered in January 1961, in Katanga Province while in the custody of Tshombe. Many accused the United States of being behind the assassination, as Congo had become the center of a cold war power struggle between the United States and the Soviet Union. Eventually Katanga Province rejoined Congo and the U.N. troops departed (1964)—though not before U.N. secretary general Dag Hammarskjöld was killed when his plane was shot down as he flew to meet with Tshombe to discuss a cease-fire (1961). A communist-backed rebellion continued in Oriental Province, however, and was not ended until a brutal battle for Staneyville (now Kisangani) in 1964. It is estimated that over 200,000 Congolese lost their lives in the five years of fighting following independence.

In 1965, General Joseph Mobutu (he later renamed himself Mobutu Sese Seko) took control following a coup supported by the U.S. Central Intelligence Agency. Mobutu eliminated his political opposition, nationalized many industries, and

defeated military attempts to overthrow him led by Congolese invaders based in Angola.

In spite of Congo's mineral wealth, extensive corruption led to economic crisis. The government was also severely criticized for its poor human rights record, which included torture, murder, and imprisonment without trial.

Following the Hutu massacres of Tutsis and subsequent Tutsi takeover in RWANDA in 1994, many Hutu murderers mingled with the thousands of Hutu refugees who flooded into Congo. There they became a target of Congolese Tutsi groups who revolted against the Mobutu government. Mobutu was overthrown in 1997 and the country, which had been called Zaire, was renamed Democratic Republic of Congo. Rebel leader Laurent Kabila, who had received backing from Hutu forces, named himself president but almost immediately was faced with an insurrection involving troops from Rwanda and Uganda backing different rebel groups. Angola, Namibia and Zimbabwe supported Kabila. Peace talks began in 1999 and were still going on in early 2000, but fighting continues.

In addition to its stunning geography and diverse peoples, Congo is famous for its music, its artwork, and its mountain gorillas.

Congo, Republic of the

Central African country located on the Atlantic Ocean between Gabon and the Democratic Republic of the Congo. Capital: Brazzaville. The equator divides the country almost in half, and most of the southeastern border is formed by the Congo River. During the years when the slave trade was at its height, the coastal area was dotted with small independent chiefdoms that were often little more than trading posts servicing the slavers. The exceptionally difficult terrain made it almost impossible for Europeans to travel up the Congo River beyond Livingstone Falls, and this kept the interior of the region free of colonization until the 1880s.

At that point, a French explorer named Pierre Savorgnan de Brazza signed treaties with a number of local chiefs placing their territories under the protection of France. In 1886, de Brazza (whose name was given to the capital) was named commissioner general of the colony. Thousands of Congolese were forced into labor for French companies attempting to exploit the natural resources of the area. Those who refused were often shot, and many others died of disease and ill-treatment. Food production fell dramatically, resulting in several widespread famines. In 1910, Congo (then known as Middle Congo), Gabon, Chad, and the Central African Republic (then called Ubangi-Shari) were consolidated into French Equatorial Africa.

In 1924, France began construction of the Congo-Ocean Railroad linking Brazzaville to Pointe-Noire, an Atlantic coast city 318 miles away. The railroad, completed in 1934, features 90 bridges and 12 tunnels, including the longest tunnel in Africa. All African men over 15 were required to provide a certain amount of free service on the railroad each year. Gallows were set up in each work camp, and those who tried to escape or failed to work hard enough were whipped or hanged. Though many fatalities were caused by disease, a sizable number were the result of executions or of men worked to death. In all, 30,000 workers are estimated to have died before the railroad was finally completed. An anticolonial movement began in the 1920s. Independence was finally achieved in 1960, and a series of procommunist governments gained power. Denis Sassou-Nguesso, who took power in 1979, backed away from Marxist ideology and brought in Western oil companies to develop the Congo's oil resources. Pascal Lissouba was elected president in 1992, but Sassou-Nguesso overthrew him in 1997 with help from Angola. The resulting civil war has resulted in more than 10,000 deaths and starvation conditions for thousands of people. A cease-fire was signed in January 2000, but fighting continued.

Congo Free State

Enormous private colony established by King Leopold II of Belgium in 1885. Leopold first set up a private, supposedly antislavery, philanthropic organization called the International Association of the Congo, through which he succeeded in having his claims in the Congo basin recognized at the Berlin Conference of 1884–85. The conference, which was attended by the United States and 13 European countries, but no African nations, divided most of Africa into European colonies and protectorates. Armed with this official endorsement, Leopold created the Congo Free State to exploit the rubber, ivory, and other resources in what is now the Democratic Republic of Congo. None of the 15 million Congolese who were living in the area was consulted.

An unsuccessful resistance was raised by an African king named Msiri, whom the Belgians managed to murder. Another problem developed around Tippu Tip, the notorious slave trader whose followers had established a state within the Congo area during the 1870s. Leopold arranged to appoint Tippu Tip governor of the Stanley Falls district, but the alliance soon fell apart. Tippu Tip's followers would not take orders from Leopold's officials, and the slave trader's livelihood made a mockery of Leopold's philanthropic claims. A brutal war, marked by numerous atrocities, flared, but by 1894 Tippu Tip had been driven out and the conflict was over.

More than 500,000 square miles (one-half the total land area) was designated state land, and private companies, in which the Free State was a major stockholder, were licensed to develop the region. This created tremendous hardship for thousands of African villagers who were cut off from lands they had farmed for generations. Every village and tribal group was required to produce a given amount of ivory and rubber that was to be sold to state-controlled companies at prices set by the state. A system of forced labor was also imposed, and discipline was established by the frequent use of the *chicotte,* a whip made of hippopotamus hide. Fifty lashes was a common punishment—for children as well as adults. One hundred lashes usually proved fatal. To ensure that the ivory and rubber quotas were met, African women and children were held hostage—often under near-starvation conditions—until their men produced a sufficient amount of rubber. Villages were looted and burned; murder and rape by state soldiers and company guards were common. In order to meet the quotas, both men and women had to give up time spent on food production, resulting in severe malnutrition and starvation. And because it was quicker and easier to burn down a village than cut down forest growth, the state often ordered villages destroyed to facilitate the planting of new rubber trees.

The unrelenting brutality sparked numerous rebellions. The Boa, Budja, and Yaka fought for years before being subdued, and the Chokwe staged a 20-year revolt. A Sanga chief named Mulume Niama barricaded himself and 178 warriors in a cave after another failed revolt. All chose death over surrender. The Africans' inability to protect themselves was due primarily to their lack of modern weaponry, especially the machine gun and breech-loading rifle. Moreover, the use of quinine and other drugs had begun to reduce European death rates in the tropics, and finally, the use of the steamboat made interior travel in the Congo much more feasible. Revolts were put down by Leopold's private army, the Force Publique. Established in 1888, it soon became the most powerful army in the region, with almost 20,000 men under arms. The soldiers of the Force Publique were black, though their officers were white. Many of the soldiers were misfits or criminals, but thousands of others were required to serve as part of their forced labor requirement. Children's "colonies"—made up of orphans whose parents had been murdered by Leopold's troops and others kidnapped from their villages—were set up to provide a source of future soldiers for the Force Publique. The treatment of children was brutal and the death rate in these "colonies" often reached 50 percent. Force Publique soldiers were required to kill those who failed to meet their quotas or be killed themselves. As proof that they were doing their job, the soldiers were expected to cut off the hands (or heads) of those executed and present them to their white commanders. Baskets of smoked hands, often taken from living victims, including children, became a symbol of the Congo Free State, as soldiers received bonuses according to how many hands they collected. One white officer used severed African heads as a border around his flower garden and another freely admitted that "To gather rubber one must cut off hands, noses and ears."[1] In 1896, a German newspaper reported that 1,308 severed hands had been turned over to one district commis-

sioner in a single day. Though civilians suffered the most, the black soldiers of the Force Publique were also treated with incredible cruelty, and many attempted to desert. Mutiny was a frequent occurrence. One, begun by a black sergeant named Kandolo, lasted 13 years and resulted in the deaths of several hundred soldiers and a number of white officers. Another mutiny, involving 3,000 troops, broke out in 1897 and lasted for three years, until 2,000 of the mutineers agreed to cease fighting in return for the right to settle in what is now Rwanda and Burundi. The population in the area experienced a sharp drop, and it is estimated between 5 and 10 million people—approximately 50 percent of the population—lost their lives in the Congo Free State in the years 1880–1908.

But Leopold's profits were enormous, and he became famous for creating public parks and monuments that he donated to the Belgian people. Nonetheless, word of the horrors occurring in the Congo began to emerge. The credit for this goes chiefly to four men. GEORGE WASHINGTON WILLIAMS was a black American historian and writer who traveled to the Congo in 1890 in hopes of finding new opportunities for American blacks and returned to lead a crusade against Leopold and the Congo Free State regime. Though several thousand whites had seen what was happening to blacks there, Williams was the first to condemn Leopold's Congo Free State publicly and describe the atrocities as "crimes against humanity."[2] An African-American missionary named William Shepard wrote about severed heads and hands in a number of articles for missionary magazines, which were widely quoted. An Englishman named Edmund Dene Morel worked as a clerk for a shipping company that transported goods to and from the Congo. He soon realized that Belgium's major exports were not materials that could be used for commerce but rather guns and ammunition. From this and company records, he concluded—correctly—that the thousands of dollars worth of ivory and rubber regularly passing through Belgium's ports were being obtained, not through trade, but through slavery. He then began a long campaign to bring Leopold's Congo venture to an end. In this he was greatly aided by Roger Casement, a British consular agent in the Congo who

[1]Adam Hochschild, *King Leopold's Ghost*. New York: Houghton Mifflin Co., 1998, p. 165.

provided Morel with details of what was happening there in addition to lodging angry reports with the British government. Writer Joseph Conrad also visited the Congo and based his famous novel *Heart of Darkness* on what he had seen there. As evidence of atrocities began to emerge, there was a public outcry. Leopold responded by turning the Congo Free State over to the Belgian government, which in 1908 turned the Congo Free State into the BELGIAN CONGO.

Recommended Reading: Hochschild, Adam. *King Leopold's Ghost.* New York: Houghton Mifflin Co., 1998. Nelson, Samuel H. *Colonialism in the Congo Basin 1880–1940.* Athens, Ohio: Ohio University Press, 1994.

Congo River

The major river of central Africa. The river begins more than 1,000 miles from Africa's west coast. In the course of its winding 2,720-mile east-west sweep to the Atlantic, it crosses the equator twice—the only major river in the world to do so. This means that there is always a rainy season somewhere along the river so that its flow is constant year-round. The Congo discharges 1.5 million cubic feet of water into the Atlantic every second, the second most powerful flow after the Amazon. Together with its tributaries, the Congo drains an area of 1,450,000 square miles, one-tenth of the African continent. Called the Lualaba at its head, it weaves down through the Gates of Hell, a 75-mile stretch of impassible rapids. From there it flows past Nyangwe, once a staging area for Arab slave traders. It flows through an impenetrable rain forest, where the river widens and is dotted with numerous islands. Just above Kisangani, a series of seven cataracts called Stanley Falls begins. From Kisangani, the Congo is navigable for 1,000 miles as far as Kinshasa. Beyond Kinshasa are the Livingstone Falls, a 220-mile-long complex of rapids and 32 waterfalls, which contain potential hydroelectric power equal to that of all the rivers of the United States. From there the river runs 100 miles to the Atlantic. The Congo's rapids and waterfalls, along with brutal terrain and dense rain forest, pre-vented extensive long-distance commerce from developing in Central Africa. However, it also limited both the Arab and the European slave trade in the area.

Congress of Racial Equality (CORE)

Civil rights organization founded by James Farmer in 1942 to integrate restaurants and other public places in the North. Farmer established CORE as a nonviolent organization that would fight racial segregation through direct action and civil disobedience. As the student SIT-IN MOVEMENT gathered strength in the South, CORE was called in to provide training in nonviolent techniques. In 1961, CORE took the lead in sponsoring FREEDOM RIDERS in an effort to integrate interstate bus terminals in the South. Tragedy struck when three CORE members were killed during the 1964 Mississippi FREEDOM SUMMER PROJECT to promote voter registration. (See also PHILADELPHIA, MISSISSIPPI, MURDERS.) After Farmer resigned in 1966, CORE rejected its multiracial orientation in favor of becoming an all-black organization.

Copeland, John Anthony, Jr. (1836–1859)
African-American revolutionary

Copeland grew up in Ohio, where he was jailed for helping free a runaway slave who had been caught and was about to be returned to his owner. In 1859, Copeland and his uncle, Lewis Sheridan Leary, joined John Brown shortly before Brown's attack on the federal arsenal at Harpers Ferry was scheduled to take place. Along with Copeland and Leary, there were three other black men—SHIELDS GREEN, a runaway slave; Dangerfield Newby, a free black man hoping to free his slave wife and children; and OSBORNE PERRY ANDERSON, a college student. John Copeland was hanged along with Green on December 16, 1859. In a letter to his family he wrote, "I am not terrified by the gallows . . . upon which I am soon to stand and suffer death for doing what George Washington was made a hero for doing." His last words were, "I am dying for freedom. I could not die for a better cause."

Coromantees (Coramantines)

European name for ASHANTI Africans from Ghana or any skilled fighter from the Gold Coast section of Africa. The name comes from an African town. Coromantee slaves were regarded as extremely rebellious and warlike. Jamaican MAROON leaders CUDJOE and Tacky were both Coromantee.

Cosby, William Henry, Jr. ("Bill") (1937–)
comedian, actor, author, philanthropist

Born in Germantown, Pennsylvania, Cosby used stories about his early life in his first comic routines. After a stint in the navy, he entered Temple University on an athletic scholarship and also began appearing in local nightclubs. In 1965, he won one of the lead roles in *I Spy*, becoming the first African American to star in a prime-time

Actor and comedian Bill Cosby, January 17, 1997
(*Popperfoto/Archive Photos*)

weekly television show. After *I Spy* ended its run in 1968, he continued his nightclub and TV appearances while earning a doctorate in education from the University of Massachusetts (1977). He also starred in several TV series. From 1984 till 1992, he played Dr. Heathcliff Huxtable on *The Cosby Show*, one of the most popular network shows of all time. It was followed by another hit show, *Cosby*, on the CBS network. However, in 1997, Cosby suffered a great tragedy when his only son, Ennis, was murdered in a robbery. During his long and varied career, Cosby has produced more than 20 comedy albums, starred in several movies, and won a number of Grammy and Emmy awards. He is the author of several best-selling books, including *Fatherhood* (1986) and *Time Flies* (1987). He is also famous as a commercial spokesman. His many philanthropies include a $20 million gift to Spelman College made in 1988.

Council of Federated Organizations (COFO)

A group founded in 1961 to coordinate the efforts of civil rights organizations operating in Mississippi. NATIONAL ASSOCIATION FOR THE ADVANCEMENT OF COLORED PEOPLE leader Aaron Henry was elected president, with STUDENT NON-VIOLENT COORDINATING COMMITTEE (SNCC) leader ROBERT MOSES as program director. In 1963, COFO began its Freedom Ballot Campaign that included a mock election intended to educate African Americans about the voting process, demonstrate their desire to vote, and convince the federal government to provide protection for civil rights workers. In the three weeks before the mock election, over 200 incidents of harassment were reported by COFO staff. In spite of this, the voter turnout was 83,000. Intraorganizational rivalries and the emergence of the MISSISSIPPI FREEDOM DEMOCRATIC PARTY led to the dismantling of COFO in 1964.

Craft, William (1824–1900)
and Ellen (1826–1897) *fugitive slave couple*

Ellen Craft, who was light-skinned, disguised herself as an elderly white man traveling with a servant when she and her husband made their escape in 1848. Since she was illiterate, she wore a sling on her arm to explain why she was unable to sign hotel registers. Once the Crafts reached freedom, they became involved in abolitionist work in the United States and later in England. After the Civil War, they moved to Georgia, where they established a combination school/farm for former slaves. It was burned by the Ku Klux Klan but was later rebuilt.

Recommended Reading: Freedman, Florence B. *Two Tickets to Freedom: The True Story of Ellen and William Craft, Fugitive Slaves.* Illus. by Ezra Jack Keats. New York: Simon & Schuster, 1971. Reprint, New York: P. Bedrick Books, 1989.

After club-swinging, steel-helmeted New York State Troopers crush race riots in Rochester, New York, African-American prisoners are led off in chains, July 29, 1964. (*Express Newspapers/A 161/Archive Photos*)

Creole Mutiny

Mutiny that occurred on the slave ship *Creole* during a voyage from Hampton Roads, Virginia, to New Orleans. The uprising, which involved 135 slaves under the leadership of Madison Washington and Ben Blacksmith, took place in November 1841. Washington had escaped once before but had returned to Virginia in an attempt to rescue his wife, Susan. For that reason, he had sewn miniature files, saws, and other tools into the lining of his clothes. Before he could reach his wife, he was caught and placed aboard the *Creole* to be sold in Louisiana. On the ninth day of the voyage, rough weather kept the crew occupied and Washington took the opportunity to free himself and the other slaves. The slaves killed owner Henry Hewell and wounded Captain Enson but spared the lives of the crew on the condition that they change course for the Bahamas, where slavery was illegal. On November 9, the *Creole* dropped anchor at Nassau, and the slaves went ashore and asked for asylum.

Southern newspapers in the United States demanded that the British return the *Creole* and its slave cargo. In response, Congressman Joshua Giddings of Ohio stated that past southern arguments that "the Federal government has no Constitutional right to interfere with slavery" meant that the federal government had no constitutional responsibility to support it either, that Virginia slave law did not apply once the *Creole* was at sea, and that the slaves

had the right to seek their freedom through violent means if necessary. When southern politicians had Giddings censured, he resigned in protest but was immediately reelected. British authorities decided to allow the slaves of the *Creole* to remain free but agreed to pay an indemnity for failing to return the slave cargo. Madison Washington was reunited with his wife. Unbeknownst to him, she was one of the slaves aboard the *Creole.*

criminal justice system, U.S.

The U.S. Constitution prohibits unreasonable search and seizure, double jeopardy, cruel and unusual punishment, and coerced self-incrimination. It specifically grants defendants the right to a speedy and impartial jury trial, the right to confront an accuser, and the right to counsel. None of these rights was enjoyed by slaves or free blacks prior to 1865. And while these rights were initially considered federal rights, and not necessarily applicable in state cases, it was not until after the Civil War that blacks enjoyed the same criminal justice rights as whites, even in theory.

Slaves were governed by slave codes, and their convictions and punishments were not subject to appeal. Those accused of crime were usually dealt with by their owners. Others might be tried by special slave tribunals, and some, particularly those accused of rebellion, received court trials. In any case, slaves were not protected by constitutional dictates governing the rights of the accused, and the emphasis was on protecting the property rights of the slave owner rather than any individual rights of the slave.

Whipping was the most common punishment, although there were many crimes (73 in Virginia) for which a slave might be executed. In 1814, a slave named Jack in Lincoln County, Georgia, was executed after being convicted of a $10 theft. Although masters could be penalized for maiming or killing a slave, the slaying was legal if the death occurred while the master was attempting to enforce discipline or maintain control. In practice, this meant that the murder of a slave was almost never prosecuted if the killer was white. The rape of slave women was not regarded as a crime and was a frequent occurrence.

Free blacks also suffered significant restrictions. They were subject to many laws limiting their right to earn a living, own property or firearms, meet with other blacks, enter a state, or acquire an education. Those who violated such laws might be imprisoned, whipped, or even sold into slavery. In addition, they were subjected to more severe punishments than were whites convicted of the same crimes.

Use of the Criminal Justice System to Maintain Political and Economic Control

Immediately after the Civil War, the southern state governments, which were still under white control, passed a series of laws known as the BLACK CODES. Designed to prevent a loss of white political and economic control, the Black Codes attempted to use criminal penalties to reestablish the labor and social conditions that had existed during slavery. In an effort to force blacks to accept jobs they might otherwise have rejected, special vagrancy laws were enacted that provided for the imprisonment of African Americans who could not provide written proof of employment. Florida made "disrespect" a crime, and in many places, black laborers who left their jobs before their work contracts had expired were subject to arrest.

The first major breakthrough in providing blacks with fair treatment came during RECON-STRUCTION with the passage of the Civil Rights Act of 1866, the Reconstruction Act of 1867, the Thirteenth Amendment outlawing slavery, and the Fourteenth Amendment, which gave all African Americans full citizenship rights, "equal protection" under the law, and the right to "due process" in government proceedings (including criminal proceedings). The Fifteenth Amendment gave black men the vote, thus putting them in a position to better protect their rights. (See RECONSTRUCTION AMENDMENTS.) While the amendments provided critical protections and invalidated laws that specifically targeted African Americans, they did not prevent whites from using supposedly race-neutral criminal statutes to achieve their political and economic goals. African Americans were routinely arrested for minor offenses, with the deliberate intent of forcing them into the convict lease system, whereby convicts were leased out to work for free for white individuals or companies. A variation of this involved arresting blacks in order to force them into "debt peonage"—the practice of coercing people to labor for years to pay off minor debts, such as court-instituted fines that had been paid for black defendants by white individuals. It was not uncommon for sheriffs to arrest black men (100 in one 1911 case) whenever additional laborers were needed by local employers who were unwilling to pay higher wages in order to attract them. To prevent workers from leaving their jobs, "false pretense" laws were passed, stating that anyone who failed to pay a debt was guilty of obtaining money under "false pretenses" or fraud. An important legal challenge to false pretense laws was successful in the case of Alonzo Bailey, who had been sentenced to 136 days of hard labor for quitting his job and failing to pay back a $15 loan from his employer. The U.S. Supreme Court overturned Bailey's conviction, ruling that the Alabama statute under which he had been convicted violated the federal Anti-Peonage Act, which had been passed to implement the Thirteenth Amendment's prohibition against involuntary servitude (*Bailey v. Alabama*, 1911). However, the legal victory, while important, was not absolute. A similar Georgia statute remained in effect until the 1940s.

The use of criminal sanctions to harass African-American leaders and maintain the political status

Chain gang, Newport News, Virginia, ca. 1898
(*Library of Congress*)

quo was a continuing phenomenon. FBI director J. Edgar Hoover, calling black nationalist MARCUS GARVEY "the foremost radical of his race," assigned at least four FBI agents to investigate him. Garvey was eventually convicted of mail fraud, sent to prison, and then deported. NATIONAL ASSOCIATION FOR THE ADVANCEMENT OF COLORED PEOPLE (NAACP) leader W. E. B. DUBOIS was indicted as a foreign agent in an attempt to silence him, though the charges were later thrown out. In an effort to limit political activity by blacks, some states instituted permanent disenfranchisement as an additional penalty for crimes, such as theft, wife-beating, and burglary, that whites assumed African Americans were more likely to commit.

Local opposition to the political and economic goals of the CIVIL RIGHTS MOVEMENT of the 1950s and 1960s resulted in numerous mass arrests of peaceful protesters. Three civil rights activists in Americus, Georgia, were charged with "seditious conspiracy," a crime that carried the death penalty, and spent three months in jail before being released. During this period, the FBI developed an extensive counterintelligence program referred to as COINTELPRO to infiltrate, spy on, and disrupt organizations the bureau had designated as "New Left," "espionage," "Black Nationalist," "white hate groups," or "Communist Party." Tactics included illegal electronic eavesdropping, the use of agents provocateurs to encourage illegal activities and disrupt lawful demonstrations, mail interception, bank account monitoring and various procedures aimed at undermining, destabilizing, and destroying such groups. In the process, the FBI targeted many civil rights activists engaged in lawful but politically explosive activities. In the case of MARTIN LUTHER KING JR., the FBI tapped his phone and placed recording devices in his hotel rooms. When the bureau found evidence that King had engaged in indiscreet sexual behavior, it sent him an anonymous letter along with an incriminating tape, and suggested that he commit suicide. In speaking of the FBI, King said, "They are out to get me, harass me, break my spirit."[1] This kind of illegal police activity was challenged by a COINTELPRO target named Julius Hobson. Hobson was a black leader who had led the fight to desegregate housing, department stores, and public schools in Washington, D.C., and was active in the anti–Vietnam War movement. He successfully sued the FBI in the case of *Hobson v. Wilson* (1984). (Wilson was the chief of police in Washington, D.C.) Hobson's victory was upheld by the U.S. Court of Appeals for the D.C. Circuit, which stated that ". . . it is never permissible to impede or deter lawful civil rights/political organization, expression or protest. . . ." and that "government action, taken with the intent to disrupt or destroy lawful organizations, or to deter membership in those groups is absolutely unconstitutional."

Chain Gangs/Convict Leasing

Thanks to the temporary political power blacks were able to acquire during Reconstruction, many brutal punishments such as branding were permanently outlawed. But prison conditions remained harsh. Chain gangs became a widespread phenomenon throughout the South after the Civil War as a means of obtaining free labor—mostly black— for state construction projects. As many as 300 men might be chained together for up to 16 hours a day building roads, breaking rocks in stone quarries, or working on land reclamation projects. Vicious beatings by guards were common. At night, the prisoners were locked in cold, damp

[1] David J. Garrow, *Bearing The Cross*. New York: William Morrow & Co., 1986, p. 374.

dormitories where they were sometimes chained to their beds. Even worse was the convict-lease system whereby convicts were rented out by the prisons to work for white individuals and private companies. Such prisoners lived in filthy degrading, conditions; were fed rotten, vermin-infested food; and suffered frequent beatings and whippings. In one privately owned Georgia work camp for men convicted of misdemeanors, 25 percent of the prisoners died before their sentences were up; in another, 17 percent died.[2] In 1880, author George Washington Cable wrote that "Ten years is the utmost length of time a convict can be expected to remain alive" in a convict-lease camp.[3] Women convicts in the camps were often forced to engage in sex with camp guards and were whipped if they did not. Even children convicted of minor offenses were forced to work in the camps. The *New York Freeman* reported that in 1886 there were boys and girls as young as six years old working on convict-lease gangs, and the *Atlanta Defiance* reported "The feet of a colored boy rotted off a few days ago. This was caused by his being worked in the county chain gang all winter without shoes."[4] The extreme brutality and corruption caused most states to do away with their convict-lease systems by the 1920s, although the use of chain gangs remained widespread until the 1960s.

Police Failure to Protect Blacks

The various constitutional amendments and civil rights acts have tried to guarantee that blacks and whites will be treated equally under the law, but local statutes have often been enforced differently depending on the race of the criminal and/or victim. In 1920, a southern police chief stated, "We have three classes of homicide. If a nigger kills a white man, that's murder. If a white man kills a nigger, that's justifiable homicide. If a nigger kills another

A portrait of a white police officer pinning a black man to the hood of a car, while holding a gun to his temple during a race riot, Newark, New Jersey, July 29, 1967 (*Express Newspapers/Archive Photos*)

nigger, that's one less nigger."[5] Antiblack violence by whites was often directed at black leaders who challenged white authority, and at African Americans whose success threatened white assumptions of black inferiority or whose growing prosperity created envy in the white community. Jim Hutchinson, a South Carolina man who had helped his black neighbors gain clear title to their land, was murdered because ". . . He helped them get straightened out and get their own homes. . . . Then one day they killed him . . . He was leading the Colored people too much."[6] Such crimes were sometimes ignored by white officials.

For more than 60 years following the Civil War, LYNCHING was a widely accepted means of extrajudicial control, with little or no effort made to stop the practice. At one lynching, police were seen directing traffic. State anti-lynching laws were almost never enforced, and although more than 200 anti-lynching bills were proposed in Congress, not one was enacted. The legislation was repeatedly blocked, even though the number of lynch victims was in the thousands.

---

[2] Donald L. Grant, *The Way It Was In The South.* New York: Birch Lane Press, 1993, p. 156.

[3] Donald L. Grant, *The Way It Was In The South.* New York: Birch Lane Press, 1993, p. 156.

[4] Donald L. Grant, *The Way It Was In The South.* New York: Birch Lane Press, 1993, p. 156.

[5] Lawrence M. Friedman, *Crime and Punishment in American History.* New York: Basic Books, a Division of HarperCollins, 1993, p. 375.

[6] Leon F. Litwack, *Trouble In Mind.* New York: Vantage Books, 1999, p. 151.

During the Civil Rights movement of the 1950s and 1960s, police not only arrested peaceful demonstrators, they also sometimes stood by as civil rights activists were beaten by Klan members and others. The refusal of police to protect the freedom riders in Montgomery, Alabama, in 1961 caused U.S. Attorney General Robert F. Kennedy to send in federal marshals and necessitated the calling up of the National Guard.

Police Brutality

Given that police repeatedly failed to protect African Americans from crime, it is not surprising that blacks have frequently been the victims of police brutality and that the courts have ignored the matter. A judicial break with this pattern occurred after three black defendants in Mississippi were viciously beaten until they confessed to the murder of a white farmer in 1934. Although they later repudiated their confessions, and the police admitted torturing them until they confessed, the Mississippi Supreme Court upheld the convictions, ruling that the Fifth Amendment privilege against self-incrimination was a federal right and did not apply in state cases. However, the U.S. Supreme Court, while agreeing that the protection against self-incrimination was a federal and not a state right, overturned the convictions, stating that "The rack and torture chamber may not be substituted for the witness stand" and that the convictions violated the Fourteenth Amendment's due process clause (*Brown v. Mississippi, 1936*).[7] Coerced confessions in several later cases were also thrown out on those grounds, and in 1964, the Court ruled that the right against self-incrimination applied in state cases as well as federal (*Malloy v. Hogan*). Two years later, in 1966, the Supreme Court, in another landmark decision, ruled that police officers must warn a person of his/her right to remain silent and that should a suspect decide to confess, he must do so willingly and with a clear understanding as to what he is doing (*Miranda v. Arizona*).

However, police brutality was not and is not employed simply to extract confessions. As various

[7] Randall Kennedy, *Race, Crime, and the Law*. New York: Pantheon, 1997, p. 106.

police sources—including Detective Mark Fuhrman, whose testimony was a turning point in the O. J. SIMPSON trial—have admitted it is also used to intimidate. Fear that black veterans returning from World Wars I and II would demand better treatment resulted in a number of violent incidents, many of them involving police officers. One especially shocking case occurred in 1946 when Isaac Woodard, an army sergeant who had just been discharged after spending three years in the South Pacific, angered a Georgia bus driver by taking too long to use a rest room. The driver called the police and when Woodard protested, the chief of police beat him severely and deliberately blinded him. Woodard was denied medical attention until the next day, when a judge noticed his condition after first fining him 50 dollars. President Harry S Truman ordered an FBI investigation, but the police chief was acquitted at trial.

During the Civil Rights movement, police in the South often led the violence directed against protesters. "BLOODY SUNDAY," the notorious attack on civil rights demonstrators that occurred in Selma, Alabama, in 1963 (see VOTING) has been termed a "police riot." In Birmingham, police turned high-power fire hoses and police dogs on peaceful demonstrators, including children. In fact, the civil rights leadership invited hundreds of white students to participate in the 1964 MISSISSIPPI FREEDOM SUMMER PROJECT partly because they expected police attacks and knew that assaults on white students were much more likely to generate nationwide protests and trigger federal intervention than would attacks on blacks. More recent cases of police brutality include the Rodney King beating (Los Angeles, 1991) and the assault on Haitian immigrant Abner Louima (New York City, 1997). The police shooting of Guinean immigrant Amadou Diallo (New York City, 1999) also sparked protest and outrage by the community, although the police officers involved were acquitted. Court sensitivity to police brutality; the requirement that defendants be represented by attorneys who can challenge police conduct; citizen review boards; better police training; and greater professionalism among police officers have had a major impact on this problem. Court rulings making it easier to sue individual police officers for misconduct has also had a significant effect.

Police Harassment

While law enforcement officials condemn police brutality, they often defend the harassment of "suspicious" persons as an effective way of discouraging crime. Unfortunately, there has been a historic tendency to equate crime with blacks, and this in turn has resulted in blacks being especially targeted for harassment. Dragnets—the practice whereby police routinely arrested scores of people in response to any given crime—have been ruled illegal. The Supreme Court also took decisive action to end illegal searches in two landmark cases: *Monroe v. Pape* (1961), which permitted federal damage suits against local police officers for violations of federal rights, and *Mapp v. Ohio* (1961), which ruled that evidence seized in violation of the prohibition on unreasonable searches could not be admitted in evidence in state criminal cases. But other controversial police tactics are still used. These involve "stop-and-frisk" practices on the basis of vague suspicions, "consent searches," where the consent given is under police pressure even though the person is not under arrest, and "profiling," whereby people, usually minority males, are stopped, questioned, and sometimes searched because they fit a police-determined "profile" of a "typical" drug dealer or other criminal. While the courts have ruled that it is illegal to stop a person solely on the basis of race, they have not ruled out race as a legitimate factor that police can take into account in deciding whether or not to stop an individual.

Although African Americans have often been singled out for police harassment under the guise of legitimate, albeit aggressive, law enforcement, this increased police attention has rarely resulted in a reduction of crime in black communities. Blacks are much more likely to be robbed, raped, and murdered than are whites.

Malicious Prosecution

The historic failure of police to protect African Americans victimized by criminal activity went hand-in-hand with an eagerness to prosecute them

when they were the ones accused. The result was the frequent conviction and incarceration of innocent blacks. In 1923, the U.S. Supreme Court overturned the convictions of six men sentenced to death in ELAINE, ARKANSAS, on the grounds that the presence of a lynch mob in the courtroom had prevented the men from receiving a fair trial (*Moore v. Dempsey*). One of the most outrageous, and notorious, miscarriages of justice involved nine young African Americans known as the SCOTTSBORO BOYS. Arrested and charged with the rape of two white women in 1931, the nine were convicted and sentenced to death after a series of sham trials. The case resulted in two precedent-setting Supreme Court decisions: *Powell v. Alabama* (1932), which reversed the initial convictions, ruling that the state must provide adequate counsel to indigent defendants in capital cases, and *Norris v. Alabama* (1934), which set aside the convictions obtained in a third trial on the grounds that blacks had been illegally excluded from the jury. The insistence on prosecuting blacks accused of assaults on white women, even where the evidence was extremely weak, was a widespread phenomenon. In the Scottsboro case, Ruby Bates, one of the two women who were supposedly raped, withdrew her original charges and later testified for the defense. It made no difference to the prosecution or to the community. Bates' companion, Victoria Price, was a known prostitute and, given the sexist culture of the time, her accusations ordinarily would never have been taken seriously. But racism was more important than sexism. Price insisted the rape charges were true, and according to one spectator, Victoria Price "might be a fallen woman, but by God she is a white woman."[8]

The Right to Testify and Serve on Juries

The jury system is designed to review evidence of crimes and determine guilt or innocence on the basis of it. To accomplish this objective, the Sixth Amendment to the U.S. Constitution guarantees defendants the right to an impartial, and the right to call favorable witnesses during trial, and the right to confront

[8] Dan T. Carter, *Scottsboro.* Baton Rouge: Louisiana State University Press, 1969, p. 295.

and cross-examine the witnesses against them. Prior to the Civil War, neither slaves nor free blacks could serve on juries (except in Massachusetts), and in many states, they could not testify against whites. This meant that white criminals who victimized blacks generally were not prosecuted because neither black victims nor black witnesses could testify against them. Even worse, free blacks who were kidnapped and sold into slavery (and there were hundreds of such victims) often were unable to prove their free status since they could not testify against their kidnappers. The ability of free blacks to overturn these discriminatory laws was extremely limited, since in most places they could not vote. In 1864, U.S. Senator Charles Sumner, after two years of effort, was finally able to get Congress to enact a law enabling African Americans to testify in federal courts. After the passage of the Fourteenth Amendment prohibiting discrimination on the basis of race or color, the U.S. Supreme Court ruled in *Strauder v. West Virginia* (1879) that a West Virginia statute limiting jury service to white males was unconstitutional. A year later in *Neal v. Delaware*, it reaffirmed its decision. In later decisions, the prohibition against discrimination was extended to grand juries as well. In spite of this, blacks continued to be routinely—and illegally—excluded from jury service in many areas. A related problem involved the use of peremptory challenges that allowed both prosecutors and defense attorneys to remove a given number of potential jurors without explanation. As a result, jurors were frequently removed for racial reasons. The practice was outlawed in 1986, when the Supreme Court ruled in *Batson v. Kentucky* that the Fourteenth Amendment's equal protection clause prohibits racially discriminatory peremptory challenges. Nonetheless, the evidence suggests that both prosecutors and defense attorneys continue to exempt jurors for racial reasons. Some have argued that defendants should be allowed to remove jurors for racial reasons to ensure fairness.

Jury Nullification

The term *jury nullification* refers to the practice whereby a jury refuses to convict a defendant in spite of overwhelming proof of guilt. Prior to the Civil War, juries in the North sometimes refused to convict abolitionists such as LEWIS HAYDEN, who illegally helped slaves escape. After the Civil War and continuing into the 1960s, southern juries routinely refused to convict whites accused of crimes against blacks, even when the criminals admitted their guilt. The 1955 lynching of 14-year-old EMMETT TILL created headlines across the country, but his murderers were not only acquitted by an all-white jury in spite of strong evidence but felt secure enough in their local community to brag about their guilt. Charges were dropped against Byron de la Beckwith, the man who murdered civil rights activist MEDGAR EVERS in 1963, after two trials ended in hung juries. He was retried and convicted in 1994.

Beginning with the 1964 case involving the murders of civil rights workers JAMES CHANEY, Andrew Goodman, and Michael Schwerner (see PHILADELPHIA, MISSISSIPPI, MURDERS), federal authorities have sometimes attempted to circumvent acquittals of this type by charging defendants in federal court with violating the victim's civil rights. They do this by invoking the Reconstruction-era Civil Rights Act of 1866, which makes it unlawful to conspire to interfere with an individual's rights "under the color of law"—that is, by government officials. Since some of the defendants in the Chaney/Schwerner/Goodman case were law enforcement officers, federal prosecutors decided to bring the charges under the 1866 law, even though the previous successful criminal prosecution brought under the act had been in 1945—and the decision in that case was later overturned on appeal (*Screws v. United States*). In the 1964 civil rights murder case, seven men were convicted of the charges and sent to prison. Charging defendants with violating an individual's civil rights has been attacked as constituting double jeopardy, since the defendant has already been tried and acquitted in state courts on different charges (such as murder), although arising from the same underlying facts; however, the practice has been upheld by the Supreme Court. A more recent case in which the possibility of jury nullification has been raised involved the acquittal by a largely white jury of the white police officers charged with assaulting Rodney King. (They were later convicted of civil rights violations in a federal trial.)

Military Justice

The military justice system differs substantially from the civilian judicial system. Even when they are off duty, soldiers remain under military command and they are held accountable not only for common crimes but also for a wide variety of military offenses, such as desertion or failure to obey a superior officer. Penalties may be imposed for offenses—such as sexual liaisons between men and women of different rank—that would not be subject to criminal sanction in civilian life. Punishments can range from reduction in rank and forfeiture of pay to dishonorable discharge and imprisonment. Fifteen offenses carry the death penalty. In 1951, the services instituted the Uniform Code of Military Justice (UCMJ) to systematize criminal proceedings and move away from command-directed rule to a more standardized system. Military defendants—unlike those in the civilian judicial system—have always been provided with free defense counsel, though they can hire their own attorneys from outside the system if they wish.

As in the civilian sector, criminal charges were sometimes brought to harass or force out blacks who were thought to undermine white authority, especially those blacks who sought to become officers. Of the 20 African-American men admitted to West Point in the 19th century, only three graduated. One—Cadet Johnson Whittaker—was found tied to his bed with his ears cut. When he claimed that he had been attacked, he was court-martialed, accused of self-mutilation and lying, and dismissed from the academy. West Point's first black graduate, Henry O. Flipper, was later accused of embezzling and conduct unbecoming an officer. Though the charges were unfounded, he was forced out of the army. According to him, the fact that he had gone riding with a young white woman was a major factor in accusations being placed against him.

Black enlisted men were often judged more by their color than their actions. In the BROWNSVILLE, TEXAS, AFFAIR, President Theodore Roosevelt dishonorably discharged an entire battalion of 167 black men after nine of them got into a fight with some townspeople in 1906, killing one white man and wounding two others.

The largest court-martial in American military history took place in 1917, when 110 black soldiers were convicted of murder and mutiny in the Houston Affair (see HOUSTON MUTINY). The first group of 63 defendants was represented by a single defense attorney. One hundred ninety-six witnesses were heard over a period of 22 days. Thirteen men were sentenced to death and secretly executed the day before the verdict was publically announced. There were widespread protests, and in response the War Department issued General Order # 7 mandating that any death sentence imposed in the continental United States must be reviewed by the judge advocate general and the president before it can be carried out.

During World War II, the NAACP received scores of complaints from black military personnel recounting serious racial incidents, including race riots and lynchings, that took place on military bases and for which white assailants, many of them military policemen, went unpunished. Rather than take legal action, the War Department tried to cover up the problem by listing the deaths that occurred in these incidents as combat fatalities or motor vehicle accidents. The black press, particularly the *Chicago Defender,* gave extensive publicity to these incidents, and as a result, black editors were threatened by War and Justice Departments with sedition and "interference with the war effort." The editors refused to back down, and the government took no further action against them.

While white soldiers who engaged in antiblack violence were ignored, black military personnel who protested poor working conditions were often prosecuted. In 1944, in Port Chicago, California, 258 black sailors were charged with refusing to obey orders when they refused to continue loading live ammunition under unsafe conditions after an explosion killed 320 men, including 202 black sailors. Two hundred and eight of the men were sentenced to bad conduct discharges. The other 50 black men were charged with mutiny, a crime that carried a death penalty. The 50 were defended by THURGOOD MARSHALL, who stated that "these men are being tried for mutiny solely because of their race and color."[9] They were convicted and sentenced to eight

[9] Howard Ball, *A Defiant Life.* New York: Crown Publishers, 1998, p. 104.

to 15 years of hard labor, but Secretary of the Navy James Forrestal commuted their sentences and ordered them freed in 1946.

In spite of President Truman's efforts to end segregation in the military and improve the circumstances of African-American personnel, dozens of cases of malicious prosecution for cowardice, desertion, failure to perform assigned duties, and similar offenses brought Thurgood Marshall to Korea in 1951. According to Marshall, "justice in Korea may have been blind, but (it was) not color blind."[10] "There were records of trials, so-called trials, in the middle of the night where men were sentenced to life imprisonment, in hearings that lasted less than ten minutes."[11] Thanks to Marshall's efforts, many of those convicted had their convictions overturned or their sentences reduced.

The military justice system has improved significantly since that time, and while the percentage of African Americans arrested and/or court-martialed continues to be higher than the percentage of black soldiers in the armed forces, the discrepancy is much lower than the corresponding percentages of black civilians incarcerated to those in the general population. By the late 1990s, black civilians were 24 times more likely to be incarcerated than were black military personnel.

Juvenile Justice

Historically, slave children were subject to the same punishments and the same mistreatment as adults. After slavery ended, black children were frequently arrested to force them into debt peonage. Others were incarcerated for long periods for minor offenses. One nine-year-old child, Ryder Hillard, received a life sentence in 1884 and spent 20 years working in coal mines as a convict laborer. At age 12, musician LOUIS ARMSTRONG was sent to the Colored Waif's Home for a year and a half for firing a gun into the air on New Year's Day. And baseball great SATCHEL PAIGE was approximately the same age when he was sentenced to the Industrial School for

Negro Children for five years for shoplifting. More serious offenses often resulted in children being sentenced as adults. In the case of 12-year-old Roy Wright, one of the nine defendants in the Scottsboro case, the judge declared a mistrial when the jury could not decide between the death penalty and life imprisonment. Fourteen-year-old George Stinney was electrocuted in South Carolina in 1944 three months after being arrested for the murder of an 11-year-old girl. A number of individuals are currently on death row for crimes committed when they were under 18 years of age.

Today, black children continue to be treated more harshly than whites by the juvenile justice system. According to a study sponsored by the U.S. Department of Justice and released in April 2000, black youths are more likely than whites to be arrested and more likely to be jailed rather than released to parental supervision. First-time black offenders are nine times more likely than whites to be sent to prison, and African-American teens convicted of drug offenses are 48 times more likely than whites to be incarcerated. Other major problems—which affect children of all races—involve the failure of many juvenile facilities to provide incarcerated youngsters with educational training, and the excessive use of powerful behavioral drugs to prevent conflict and to create docile, easily controlled inmates. However, thanks to the Supreme Court decision *In re Gault* (1967), juveniles—like adults—now have due process rights.

Treatment of Prisoners/Sentencing/Death Penalty

In general, incarcerated African Americans have felt the combined weight of racism and the brutality that has historically been a part of prison life. Although the Supreme Court outlawed segregation in public schools in 1954, it was not until the late 1960s that federal courts began to extend this prohibition to prisons.

Studies have shown that defendants, especially black defendants, who are convicted of crimes against whites tend to receive longer sentences than those (black or white) who victimize blacks. According to year 2000 government figures, nearly 11 percent of all young black males are incarcerated. One out of every three young black men nationally

[10] Howard Ball, *A Defiant Life*. New York: Crown Publishers, 1998, p. 112.

[11] Howard Ball, *A Defiant Life*. New York: Crown Publishers, 1998, p. 112.

is under some type of supervision by a sector of the criminal justice system. In some areas, 50 percent of African-American men between ages 18 to 35 are under such supervision. Although African Americans compose only 13 percent of the population, they constitute roughly 50 percent of those in prison. In 12 states, African Americans are imprisoned at a rate 10 times that of whites. A major reason for this situation is the ongoing attempt to control illegal drugs. Possession of a small amount of crack cocaine—an offense more prevalent among blacks—is punishable by extremely long jail terms. But possession of cocaine in its powder form—an offense frequently committed by whites—merits a much shorter sentence. As of 2000, this discrepancy was under legislative review. African Americans make up 35 percent of all drug arrests, 55 percent of all drug convictions, and 74 percent of all sentences for drug offenses.[12]

Another area of concern is the death penalty. Historically, the death penalty was much more likely to be sought—and imposed—on black defendants, and much more likely to be imposed on any defendant, black or white, in cases where the victim was white. In 1972, the U.S. Supreme Court ruled in *Furman v. Georgia* that the death penalty as administered at that time was capricious and arbitrary and therefore violated the Eighth Amendment's prohibition against "cruel and unusual punishment." The various state legislatures scurried to rewrite their death penalty statutes to conform with Supreme Court restrictions, but defendants have continued to argue that imposition of the death penalty is racially discriminatory. However, in 1987 the Supreme Court ruled that for a death sentence to be unconstitutional, a defendant must prove that the sentence imposed in his or her *particular* case (as opposed to generally) was racially motivated (*McCleskey v. Kemp I*).

Overview

Not surprisingly, a concern for the rights of criminal defendants has coincided with the three periods in

American history when the rights of individuals generally has been a major issue: the early years of the Republic when the Bill of Rights was passed; the period following the Civil War that saw the end of slavery and passage of the Reconstruction amendments and several important civil rights acts; and the 1950s and 1960s when the Civil Rights movement was at its height. Of these three periods in U.S. history, two were dominated by a concern for African-American rights.

The Civil Rights movement benefited from the fact that it became a dominant force during the tenure of U.S. Supreme Court Chief Justice Earl Warren (1953–69). While Warren is best known for obtaining a unanimous ruling in the *Brown v. Board of Education* school desegregation decision, it was during his term as chief justice that the Supreme Court greatly strengthened the rights of defendants in criminal trials. In addition to a number of the cases mentioned above, the Warren Court issued a landmark decision in *Gideon v. Wainwright* (1963), which ruled that all persons charged with a felony were entitled to counsel appointed and paid for by the state. The Warren Court also extended federal judicial supervision over state courts in many aspects of criminal justice. The Warren Court decisions marked a turning point in protecting the rights of criminal defendants.

Ideally, the criminal justice system operates free from the biases, prejudices, and political considerations that continually ruffle society. In practice, it often does not. For this reason, extensive protections for defendants are written into criminal justice law because the possible penalties upon conviction—incarceration and even death—are the harshest society can impose. Defendants in criminal cases frequently come from the most vulnerable groups in society: the poor, the uneducated, the mentally ill, members of minority groups, and those with little or no family support. And in spite of the presumption of innocence to which defendants are legally entitled, they often face a hostile press that assumes guilt and encourages the anger of the community at large.

Unfairness in law enforcement is extremely corrosive in terms of popular attitudes toward government and society. Prior to the 1950s, going to jail was often not considered a disgrace in the black

[12] David Cole, *No Equal Justice*. New York: 1999, p. 144 quoting Marc Mauer, Tracy Huling, The Sentencing Project, "Young Black Americans and the Criminal Justice System: Five Years Later" 12 (1995).

community since so many black inmates were innocent of the charges against them. And, in addition to the injustice individual defendants face, discrimination in law enforcement has resulted in resentment and distrust in the black community and a corresponding unwillingness to cooperate with police.

Recommended Reading: Alderman, Ellen, and Caroline Kennedy. *In Our Defense.* New York: Avon Books, 1991; Butler, Paul. *The Yale Law Journal; Racially Based Jury Nullification: Black Power in the Criminal Justice System*; Volume 105, December 1993; Cole, David. *NO Equal Justice.* New York: The New Press, 1999; Grant, Donald. *The Way It Was In The South: The Black Experience in Georgia.* New York: Carol Publishing Group, 1993; Kennedy, Randall. *Race, Crime, and the Law.* New York: Pantheon Books, 1997; Mann, Coramae Richey. *Unequal Justice: A Question of Color.* Bloomington & Indianapolis: Indiana University Press, 1993.

Crite, Allan Rohan (1910–) *artist, illustrator*
Born in Plainfield, New Jersey, Crite moved as a child to Boston, where he has lived most of his life. He received degrees in art from Harvard and the Boston Museum of Fine Arts. During the 1930s and 1940s, he painted scenes of his Roxbury, Massachusetts, neighborhood, capturing everyday black life in oil paintings that are displayed in some of the country's major museums. In his later years, Crite, a devout Episcopalian, has concentrated on religious themes, completing murals and other paintings for a number of churches. He has written and illustrated several books, including *Three Spirituals from Earth to Heaven* (1948) in which he uses a series of drawings to interpret three favorite SPIRITUALS. He has taught liturgical art at several universities and has won awards from such institutions as Harvard, the Massachusetts Institute of Technology, and the Museum of African-American History.

Cudjoe (unknown–unknown) *Jamaican slave insurrection leader*
From his base in the northwest part of Jamaica, Cudjoe succeeded in uniting several MAROON (run-

Countee Cullen (*Library of Congress*)

away slave) bands. He then joined forces with several other maroon leaders, including his brothers, Accompong and Johnny, and engaged in raids on plantations in the area, triggering what became known as the first Maroon War (1732–39). In 1732, the British militia managed to capture three maroon settlements but was forced to abandon them a year later. Two hundred British sailors sent to support the militia were ambushed by the maroons and forced to retreat with heavy casualties. The Jamaican colonial government then voted to hire 200 Moskito Indians along with several companies of free blacks to serve as mercenaries. Using guerrilla warfare methods, Cudjoe succeeded in holding out against these troops as well as against special tracking dogs brought in from Cuba and two regiments of soldiers shipped in from Gibraltar. In 1739, the British government was forced to agree to a peace treaty that guaranteed Cudjoe's followers their freedom and provided them with land in return for a promise to cease raiding white plantations and to assist in returning runaway slaves in the future. Cudjoe is believed to have been a COROMANTEE, a term used to identify skilled fighters from the Gold Coast section of Africa. He was described as short and heavy-set and as suffering from a hunchback condition.

Cuffe, Paul (1759–1817) *shipbuilder, merchant, civil rights activist*

Born in Massachusetts to an Indian woman and a former slave, Cuffe became rich through fishing and whaling. He refused to pay taxes in 1780 after the Massachusetts state constitution denied the vote to African Americans and Indians. Although blacks were required to pay school taxes, black children were not allowed to attend the public school, and the town of Westport refused to build another school for them. Consequently, Cuffe built one on his property and donated it to the community. Con- tinued slavery and racial discrimination in the United States convinced Cuffe that all blacks should return to Africa. He petitioned the U.S. Congress to resettle blacks in Africa but was unsuccessful. In 1815, he paid for the settlement of 38 African Americans in Sierra Leone. Though he visited Africa, Cuffe himself did not move there and died two years after bringing his group of settlers there.

Cullen, Countee Porter (1903–1946) *poet*

Countee Cullen was one of the leading figures of the HARLEM RENAISSANCE. He began writing poetry while still in elementary school and had achieved a national reputation by the time he had graduated from New York University. He also won numerous prizes for poems like *The Ballad of the Brown Girl*. In 1925, Cullen published *Color,* his first book of poetry. Two years later, his second book, *Copper Sun,* appeared. In addition to writing poetry, Countee Cullen worked as an editor for the magazine *Opportunity* and taught French and English at Frederick Douglass Junior High School in New York. It was there that he met and encouraged JAMES BALDWIN. Among Cullen's other poetry collections are *The Black Christ and Other Poems* (1929), *The Medea and Some Poems* (1935), and *On These I Stand: An Anthology.* He also wrote the novel *One Way to Heaven.* Cullen was briefly married to Nina Yolande DuBois, the daughter of W.E.B. DUBOIS.

Cush See KUSH.

D

Dahomey

A kingdom established in the 17th century in what is now Benin, Dahomey was created by the Aja to free themselves from the YORUBA of OYO and to provide protection against slave raiders operating from the city-states on the coast. The capital was at Abomey. All citizens were expected to provide service to the king, and there were several elite companies of women soldiers, whom the Europeans called Amazons. In fact, women alone formed the king's personal bodyguard. The king regularly dispensed money to various sections of society and regulated the economy by controlling key industries such as honey, ginger, and slave trading. Dahomey's first ruler was Dako, who came to power in 1625, but the kingdom did not become a centralized state until about 1650 under King Wegbaja.

Under King Agaja, who took the throne in 1708, Dahomey became strong enough to conquer the coastal cities. Alarmed at Dahomey's increasing military strength, Oyo invaded Dahomey in 1726, 1729, and 1730. Though Agaja's armies were defeated, Dahomey was still able to maintain control of the coastal cities. Dahomey kings were forced to provide the Oyo rulers with 1,681 guns a year, which they obtained through slave trading with the Europeans. In fact, the coastal area produced so many captives that it was known as the Slave Coast. Dahomey's later kings were extremely cruel, and human sacrifice, sometimes involving hundreds of victims at a time, was a long-term custom that grew more pronounced as the kingdom grew weaker. Villages of neighboring tribes were routinely attacked in order to obtain slaves, and the old, the young, the sick, and any others considered unfit for sale were either massacred or used as sacrificial victims. Dahomey came under attack from the French in 1892 and became a French colony in 1894.

Davis, Benjamin Oliver, Sr. (1877–1970) and Benjamin Oliver, Jr. (1912–) *U.S. Army and Air Force generals*

Benjamin Davis Sr. was denied admission to West Point, but served as a lieutenant in the Spanish-American War, then enlisted in the famous Ninth Cavalry in 1899. In 1901, he became a second lieutenant, but even as he rose in rank, the War Department kept him from postings where he might command white units or outrank white officers. In 1915, he was sent to historically black Wilberforce University to teach military science; other race-related billets included leading a national guard unit in Harlem and serving as army attaché in LIBERIA. In spite of racial prejudice, Davis was appointed the first black brigadier general in the U.S. Army in 1940. He remained the only African-American U.S. general during World War II.

Unlike his father, Benjamin O. Davis Jr. was able to enter West Point (1932) but was shunned by most of his fellow cadets. Nevertheless, he graduated 35th in in his class of 276 but was denied a commission in the Army Air Corps, being assigned instead to the infantry. In 1941, U.S. entry into

World War II gave him the opportunity to pilot military aircraft. He led the all-black 99th Pursuit Squadron (see TUSKEGEE AIRMEN) in Tunisia and Italy and the 332nd Fighter Group. In 1954, Benjamin Davis Jr. became the first African-American general in the Air Force. He retired in 1970 with three stars. In 1998, President Bill Clinton awarded Davis a fourth star, making him the first African American to receive this honor after retiring.

Davis, Miles Dewey III (1926–1991) *jazz trumpet musician, composer, arranger*

Born into a middle-class family, Miles Davis would, like JOHN COLTRANE who was born the same year, become a leading figure in the JAZZ world. He met DIZZY GILLESPIE and CHARLIE PARKER in 1944 when

Miles Davis (*Schomburg Center for Research in Black Culture*)

he filled in for three weeks with the Billy Eckstine orchestra in St. Louis. After graduating from high school, he went to New York, where he renewed his acquaintanceship with Parker and Gillespie, spending hundreds of hours listening to them play at Minton's Playhouse. He was invited to sit in with Coleman Hawkins' band and later took Dizzy Gillespie's place in Charlie Parker's group.

In 1949, Davis and Gil Evans released *Birth of the Cool*, which quickly become a jazz classic. After watching the Ballet Africaine, he became interested in modal music, which would find expression on the *Milestones* album. His association with John Coltrane led to the release of *Kind of Blue* in 1959. Davis frequently changed the musicians in his group, combining and recombining musical personalities in an effort to create just the right sound. In spite of criticism, he often refused to introduce his songs or talk to the audience, believing that the music spoke for itself. He refused to include liner notes in some albums for the same reason.

In the late 1960s, Davis turned to electric jazz. The result was the tremendously successful and innovative *Bitches Brew*. Recorded in 1969, it sold more copies than any other jazz album in history. The next year, Davis played before 350,000 people at the Isle of Wight concert in England. In 1984, he became the first jazz musician and the first African American to win the Sonning Music Award, which is usually awarded to classical musicians. Always sensitive to social and racial issues, Davis' 1985 album, *You're Under Arrest*, reflected the problems black men have with police and the threat of nuclear holocaust. *Tutu*, which won a Grammy in 1987, was named for South African bishop Desmond Tutu and included the song *Full Nelson*, named for Nelson Mandela.

Recommended Listening: *Birth of the Cool* (Capital); *Walkin'* (Prestige); *Milestones* (Columbia); *Kind of Blue* (Columbia); *Bitches Brew* (Columbia); and *Decoy* (Columbia).

Davis Bend

An area of Mississippi where Confederate president Jefferson Davis and his brother, Joseph, owned huge plantations. Before the Civil War (1861–65), the Davis brothers had established a model slave community where African Americans enjoyed a certain amount of self-government, including a slave jury system. After Union troops occupied the area, General Ulysses S. Grant set aside Davis Bend for freed slaves, who were assigned farmland of their own. By 1865, these freed slaves had set up an elected government and earned profits of $160,000 on cotton. Later, this land was ordered returned to Joseph Davis, the original white owner. He agreed to sell it on long-term credit to Benjamin Montgomery, a leader in the black community, and ordered his heirs to grant Montgomery liberal extensions if necessary in regard to payments. His heirs ignored Davis' orders and regained ownership of the land in 1878 when Montgomery was unable to meet his payment obligation.

Delany, Martin Robinson (1812–1885)
abolitionist, explorer, black nationalist, author, newspaper publisher, doctor, educator

Born in West Virginia, Martin Delany was the son of a free black woman who moved her children to Pennsylvania so they could acquire an education. A year later, his slave father managed to purchase his own freedom and join them there. At age 19, Delany crossed the Allegheny Mountains on foot and settled in Pittsburgh, where he studied medicine and became active in the UNDERGROUND RAILROAD. In 1843, he began publishing *The Mystery*, the first black newspaper west of the Alleghenies. When *The Mystery* failed for lack of financial support in 1847, Delany briefly became coeditor with Frederick Douglass of the *North Star*, then resumed his medical studies at Harvard in 1848. He was forced to leave after students protested his presence because he was black and spent the next few years helping runaway slaves, serving as a school principal and practicing medicine.

During this time, he wrote *The Condition, Elevation, Emigration and Destiny of the Colored People of the United States, Politically Considered*. In 1859, he left for Africa, where he signed a treaty with a local king allowing him to establish a settlement of American-born blacks in what is now NIGERIA. On his return, Dr. Delany spent two years attempting to sign up settlers for his African colony. He also lectured on AFRICA, taking care to dress in beautiful African robes in order to overcome the stereotype of the African savage.

After 1863, Delany became a recruiter for the Union army and came up with a plan to arm slaves still behind Confederate lines. He was promoted to major, the first African American to hold that military rank. Delany is remembered primarily for his work as a black nationalist and the great pride he took in his race. Frederick Douglass once said of him, "I thank God for making me a man, but Delany thanks Him for making him a **Black** man."[1]

Dessalines, Jean-Jacques (DES-ah-lean) (The Tiger) (ca. 1752–1806) *revolutionary and emperor of Haiti*

The slave of a free black man, Dessalines' back bore the scars of numerous whippings. He hated whites and mulattos (free persons of mixed race who constituted a distinct class in Haiti) and was brutal in his treatment of them. Though illiterate, Dessalines was a military genius who rose to prominence during the Haitian Revolution. He is especially noted for his brilliant defense of Crête-à-Pierrot (1802), where he held off 12,000 French soldiers with only 1,200 men. Forced to abandon the fortress, his losses totalled approximately 500 men, while the French dead numbered 2,000, with many more wounded.

In hopes of bringing the fighting under control sooner, French Commissioner Léger Félicité Sonthonax had abolished slavery in Haiti in 1793, but Napoleon later attempted to reinstate it by sending in 20,000 French troops under the command of his brother-in-law, General Charles Leclerc. Leclerc and his successor, General Donatien Rochambeau, acted with great cruelty. Rochambeau drowned so many people in the bay at Le Cap François that local residents refused to eat fish. He also imported 1,500 attack dogs to hunt down rebellious blacks and

[1] Rayford Logan and Michael Winston, *Dictionary of American Negro Biography*. New York: W. W. Norton & Co., 1982, p. 172.

chained 16 black military leaders to a rock and left them to starve to death. After revolutionary leader Toussaint Louverture was captured in 1802, Dessalines resurrected the scattered black army and drove the French out in 1803. On January 1, 1804, independence was declared, and the colony of Saint-Domingue was renamed Haiti. Dessalines was crowned Emperor Jacques I in October. In 1805, he ordered a massacre of the remaining white population. He was assassinated in 1806.

Dinka

An African tribal group living in the southern Nile region. The Dinka live in mud and wattle (sticks, twigs, and branches woven together) huts, wear few if any clothes, and possess only a few knives and fishhooks. The Dinka's life revolves around his cattle. During the rainy season, he drives his herd to higher ground where he builds a *wut,* or cattle camp, on the same piece of ground his family has used for generations. Each group of *wuts* constitutes a *gel,* around which Dinka society revolves. As the area dries out, Dinka herd their cattle closer to the river where there is pasture. Dinka society looks primitive to Westerners since the Dinka possess few material things and have no kings or any kind of formal ruling structure. However, Dinka society is actually very complex and highly organized. It revolves around kinship, and everyone has his or her specific obligations and responsibilities, which are passed down through each family. The simple homes and lack of all but essential material possessions work well for people who live in hot, swampy land and must move regularly to care for their cattle.

Currently, the Dinka in Sudan are the targets of government-backed Sudanese Arab militias who are encouraged to raid the black African villages in the southern part of the country and take slaves—particularly women and children—along with cattle and other property. These slaves are used as agricultural and domestic workers and are forced to become Muslims. A number are brought back to be ransomed by their families or clans. The price is usually five cows or one automatic rifle per person. The number of slaves now being held in northern Sudan is believed to be in the tens of thousands.

Diop, Cheikh Anta (1923–1986) *Senegalese historian*

An African nationalist, Cheikh Anta Diop attacked commonly held Western historical theories that denied that Africans had produced any advanced civilization or culture. Instead, Diop offered evidence that (1) the "classical" cultures of ancient Greece and Rome were greatly influenced by Egypt, and (2) the ancient Egyptians were themselves descended from black Africans.

Born in the village of Diourbel, Diop moved to Paris in the early 1950s. There he studied at the Sorbonne and was prominent in the anticolonial NEGRITUDE literary movement, which emphasized ethnic and cultural integrity. Shortly after Senegal gained its independence from France, Diop returned home (1961) and organized three opposition political parties, which were suppressed by Senegal's president, Leopold Senghor. He also set up Africa's first carbon-14 dating laboratory at Dakar's Institut Fondamental d'Afrique Noire to better analyze ancient African artifacts.

Among Diop's writings are *Cultural Unity of Black Africa* (1959), *Black Africa: Economic & Cultural Basis for a Federal State* (1960), and his best-known work, *The African Origin of Civilization* (1967), which contends that civilization developed first in sub-Saharan Africa. Current research supports Diop's arguments regarding black influence in ancient Egypt.

Dioulas (Dyulas) (DEE-OOH-lahs)

West African tribe related to the MANDINKA. They are noted for their religious zeal and business skills. In fact, they are such exceptional traders that the word *dioula* has come to mean "merchant" among many tribes. The Dioula maintained a network of market-towns linking the forest and the savannah and specialized in long-distance trade in gold, salt, cloth, kola nuts, dried fish, and slaves. Although fervent Muslims, they lived peacefully among their animist neighbors for several hundred years. In the 19th century, they established several small city-states, the most important being Kong and Odienne.

Djenne   See JENNE.

Djibouti, Republic of (je-BOOTĒ)

Northeast African country. Capital: Djibouti. Located on the Gulf of Aden at the entrance to the Red Sea and bordered by Ethiopia and Somalia, Djibouti is a stony, desert country of approximately 8,490 square miles. The nation is home to Issa and Afar (or Danakil) tribespeople. Many Ehtiopian refugees fleeing the Ethiopian civil war settled there after 1975. Djibouti's ethnic groups are divided into small clans whose leaders meet regularly. The people raise goats, sheep, cattle, and camels, and the importance of livestock is demonstrated by the fact that traditionally every newborn Afar child is given a female animal of each species that becomes the basis of a new herd.

The French arrived in the area in 1843 and over the years gained control of the region through a series of treaties with Somali sultans. Originally known as French Somaliland, Djibouti was renamed the French Territory of the Afars and the Issas in 1967. The country became independent in 1977 under the presidency of Hassan Gouled Aptidon, who remained in power until April 1999, when Ismail Omar Guelle was elected. The French maintain a large naval base in Djibouti, and the last African outpost of the French Foreign Legion is located there. The Addis Ababa-Djibouti railroad is of critical strategic and economic importance. In February 2000, rebels signed a peace accord ending a 10-year uprising by Afar tribesmen.

Dogon

possibly the oldest West African tribe. The Dogon live in Mali in the great bend of the Niger River. They are famous for their pointed thatched-roof homes and granaries built closely together on cliffs in terraced clusters. The configuration is important for defense and for land conservation. The Dogon are also noted for their carved doors and masks. Their mythological and religious beliefs are unusually complex, particularly in regard to twins. This concern with twins and twinship is related to the ancient Dogon realization that the star known as Sirius is actually two stars—something that was later hypothesized by astronomer F. W. Bissel in 1844 and confirmed in 1862 when Sirius was discovered to be orbited by a dwarf star. The Dogon

Dogon village, Mali (*United Nations*)

concept of twinship is related to sharing, equality, friendship, and all human relationships, as well as duality and balance.

Douglas, Aaron (1899–1979) *artist*

After attending the University of Nebraska and teaching art in a Kansas City high school, Douglas moved to New York. There he studied with German illustrator Winold Reiss and began to incorporate African design elements into his otherwise realistic approach to painting. His work came to the attention of ALAIN LOCKE, who incorporated six pages of Douglas' artwork into his pioneering book *The New Negro.*

His talent led to a commission to create a mural for Club Ebony, a popular Harlem nightclub. Later, he created murals for Fisk University, the ballroom of Chicago's Sherman Hotel, and the Countee Cullen Branch of the New York Public Library. The library murals, called *Aspects of Negro Life,* are a vibrant historic depiction of African-American life that are among Douglas' best-known work.

He created another critically acclaimed series of illustrations for JAMES WELDON JOHNSON'S 1925 book *God's Trombones: Seven Negro Sermons in Verse.* Often called "The Father of Black American Art," Douglas broke away from a traditional realistic approach to create a more geometric style, incorporating circles, squares, and triangles. His depiction of African and African-American figures through silhouettes

Aaron Douglas' *Jazz at Home,* reproduced in Alain Locke's *The New Negro,* 1925 (*Library of Congress*)

recalled the classical black silhouettes on Greek vases. Douglas often combined such figures with muted earth tones in order to create the presence of spirituality and celebrate the many facets of black life. Considered a "pioneering Africanist," Douglas was one of the most influential artists of the HARLEM RENAISSANCE.

Douglass, Frederick (1817–1895) *African-American leader, abolitionist, journalist, diplomat*

He is often called the "father of the Civil Rights movement." Born a slave, Frederick Douglass never knew his father. Nor did Douglass know the exact date of his birth. He picked February 14 as his birthday because his mother, who died when he was seven, used to refer to him as her "little valentine." When Douglass was eight, his master, Thomas Auld, lent him out to work for a family in Baltimore. There he learned to read and write and was relatively well treated. In 1833, Douglass was returned to Auld. When he resisted Auld's cruel treatment, he was hired out to a "Negro-breaker" named Covey, who whipped Douglass repeatedly and forced him to labor in the fields 12 to 14 hours a day. Later Douglass was hired out to another farmer, William Freeland, but after an attempted escape, he was sent back to Baltimore. There he was hired out to work in the shipyards, where he was attacked and almost blinded in one eye.

With the help of Anna Murray, a freeborn African-American woman whom he later married,

Douglass escaped to New York. From there, he made his way to New Bedford, Massachusetts, where he dropped the name he had carried since birth—Frederick Augustus Washington Bailey—and took the name Frederick Douglass. He became a lecturer for the Massachusetts Anti-Slavery Society and was so effective a speaker that some people questioned whether he had ever really been a slave. In response, Douglass wrote his autobiography, in which he provided so much detailed information that he jeopardized his own safety and was forced to flee to England. There he continued to speak out against slavery and to argue in favor of Irish freedom, women's rights, and world peace. His growing fame made it impossible for him to return to the United States while still a fugitive, so a group of supporters arranged to purchase his freedom.

Arriving back in the United States in 1847, Douglass settled in Rochester, New York, where he began publication of the *North Star* newspaper. Financially,

Frederick Douglass (*Library of Congress*)

Frederick Douglass resisting an Indiana mob (*Library of Congress*)

it was an extremely risky venture, but Douglass believed he could not continue to filter his thoughts through the white abolitionist press. The difficulty he had anticipated proved correct. Within six months, he was forced to mortgage his home to keep the paper going. He continued to lecture against slavery and suffered a broken arm after being attacked by a proslavery mob in Indiana. He also arranged for his printing shop to be used as a station on the UNDERGROUND RAILROAD. Over the course of 10 years, more than 400 escaped slaves found help there.

In 1848, Douglass met with John Brown, who later led the unsuccessful raid on HARPERS FERRY. In fact, Brown spent three weeks at Douglass' house shortly before the 1859 raid. Douglass thought Brown's plan suicidal but could not convince him to change it. Even though Douglass did not join the attempted uprising, he was forced to flee to Canada when the governor of Virginia swore out a warrant for his arrest as an accomplice. He returned to the United States in 1860.

When the Civil War broke out, Douglass pressed President Lincoln to free all slaves immediately and to allow African Americans to enlist in the Union forces. It was not until 1863, however, that Lincoln issued the Emancipation Proclamation freeing slaves in Confederate territory and allowing blacks to enlist. Douglass moved immediately to recruit black soldiers. His own two sons were among the first to enlist, but the outrageous treatment of black Union soldiers caused Douglass to halt his recruitment efforts. The unequal pay, inferior equipment, segregated units, and lack of black officers was infuriating enough. Even worse were the reports of Confederate atrocities against African-American soldiers. He met with Lincoln concerning these matters but was unable to get a satisfactory response.

Douglass feared that the North might agree to end the war should the Southern states offer to return to the Union provided they could keep their slaves. People were tired of fighting, dismayed by the ever-lengthening lists of dead and wounded, and apprehensive of the mounting financial cost. To block any attempt to end the war by selling out African-American rights, he embarked on a speaking tour. Again and again, Douglass repeated his four main points: that the aim of the war should be the abolition of slavery; that there could be no peace that did not include an end to slavery; that everyone was entitled to the same rights; and that black men should have the vote.

Once the war was over, Douglass began pressing for black voting and economic rights. Ironically, this forced a serious break between him and a group whose cause he had always championed—women. The Fifteenth Amendment gave the vote to black men. It said nothing about women, and, as a result, it was opposed by leaders in the women's movement. Douglass had always been a strong supporter of women's suffrage, but he was not willing to jeopardize the black male vote for it. The break with the women's movement was painful for Douglass, but he saw no alternative.

Douglass also became entangled in an unsuccessful effort to save the FREEDMAN'S SAVINGS AND TRUST COMPANY, a bank started in 1865 for newly freed slaves. Knowing that the bank's collapse would cost thousands of former slaves their life savings, Douglass took over the presidency of the institution and even invested his own money in it. However, in 1874, the Freedman's Bank was forced to close, and many depositors lost all or most of their money.

In 1877, President Hayes appointed Douglass marshal of the District of Columbia. Four years later, President Garfield made him recorder of deeds, a post Douglass held for five years. In 1889, President Benjamin Harrison named him minister-resident and consul-general to Haiti and the Dominican Republic. In each of these posts, Douglass served with distinction.

On February 20, 1895, Frederick Douglass died of a heart attack. "Save the Negro and you save the Nation," he said. "Destroy the Negro and you destroy the Nation, and to save both you must have but one great law of Liberty, Equality, and Fraternity for all Americans without respect to color . . . What I ask for the Negro is not benevolence, not pity, not sympathy, but simple justice."

draft riots

Antiblack riots that occurred in New York July 13–17, 1863. Many white workers resented competition from African Americans and feared that an end to slavery would result in the movement of thousands of former slaves to Northern cities. There was also anger concerning the Civil War, which was seen as being fought for the benefit of blacks. Tension began to build when 3,000 longshoremen went on strike for higher wages and African Americans were hired in their place. The riot was triggered by the passage of the Union Conscription Act, which made all able-bodied white men between the ages of 20 and 45 eligible for military service but allowed individuals to buy their way out of serving by paying a fee of $300. At least 400 African Americans were beaten or killed (some accounts say 1,000), and thousands of black homes and businesses were burned. The services of a number of military units were required before the white rampage was brought under control. The atrocities included the burning of the Colored Orphan Asylum, an act that left several hundred children homeless.

Drew, Charles Richard (1904–1950) *doctor and medical researcher*

Dr. Drew was born in Washington, D.C., and graduated from Amherst College. After working as a biology teacher and director of athletics at Morgan State College, he entered McGill University Medical School in Montreal, Canada. It was there that he became interested in the study of blood. After leaving McGill, Drew interned at Montreal General Hospital and then worked at Howard University Medical School in Washington, D.C., and Presbyterian Hospital in New York City. There he resumed his research in blood chemistry that led him to significant advances in the storage of blood and plasma.

In 1940, Drew was asked to arrange for 10,000 pints of plasma to be shipped to Britain, which was then under regular attack from Nazi bombers. Soon afterward, he became medical supervisor for the Blood for Britain program, where he standardized procedures for the collection, storing, and shipping of plasma. A year later, he became director of the American Red Cross Blood Bank in New York and assistant director of the National Research Council, which collected blood for the military. However, he resigned in protest when the armed forces first refused "colored blood," then agreed to accept it provided it was kept separate from "white" blood. Drew was killed in an automobile accident while on his way to a medical conference at Tuskegee Institute.

DuBois, William Edward Burghardt (du-boyse) (1868–1963) *author, editor, scholar, teacher, Pan-Africanist*

Born in Massachusetts, DuBois graduated from Fisk University, then entered Harvard, where he became the first African American to receive a Ph.D. from the school. His thesis, *The Suppression of the African Slave Trade to the United States of America,*

1638–1870, published in 1896, was only one of dozens of scholarly papers he was to produce. After receiving his doctorate, DuBois became a teacher at Wilberforce University in Ohio, where he taught Greek, Latin, German, and English.

In 1896, the University of Pennsylvania asked him to conduct a sociological study of African Americans living in Philadelphia. DuBois accepted and moved into a one-room apartment in Philadelphia's black ghetto, where he spent more than a year working on the project. It was later published under the title *The Philadelphia Negro*. In 1897, DuBois accepted a position as professor of history and economics at Atlanta University. There, under the Atlanta University conference program, he arranged to continue studies of African Americans.

In 1903, DuBois published the work for which he is most famous, a series of 14 essays called *The Souls of Black Folk*. In it, he stressed the need to protect African-American voting rights and made his famous prediction that "the problem of the Twentieth Century is the problem of the color line." He also attacked Booker T. Washington for submitting to the destruction of black political and civil rights and for opposing higher education for African Americans. It was in this book that DuBois discussed the need for educated African Americans, whom he called the "TALENTED TENTH," to take the lead in helping the black race advance. According to James Weldon Johnson, *The Souls of Black Folk* had a stronger impact on the African-American community than any book since *Uncle Tom's Cabin*.

Two years after its publication, DuBois organized the NIAGARA MOVEMENT, which led to the formation in 1909 of the NATIONAL ASSOCIATION FOR THE ADVANCEMENT OF COLORED PEOPLE (NAACP), the leading U.S. civil rights organization of the 20th century. DuBois also created and edited the NAACP magazine *The Crisis* for 24 years. During that time, he continued to write essays, books, papers, and articles.

Beginning in 1900, DuBois participated in a series of Pan-African conferences, where he demanded an end to colonialism in Africa. In 1934, differences with Walter White, the NAACP's chief executive, caused DuBois to resign from *The Crisis* and the board of the NAACP and return to Atlanta University as chairman of the sociology department.

W. E. B. DuBois, 1918 (*Library of Congress*)

He returned to the NAACP 10 years later as director of special research.

DuBois' continuing efforts to promote world peace through socialism caused the U.S. government to indict him as a foreign agent in an attempt to silence him. However, Judge James McGuire, a political conservative, threw out the charges. The government retaliated by revoking DuBois' passport (1951–58), tampering with his mail, and attempting, often successfully, to intimidate his friends and supporters. This treatment, combined with the government's failure to end racial discrimination, caused DuBois to turn to communism in 1961. Two years later he became a citizen of Ghana, where he died on August 27, 1963, one day before the historic March on Washington.

Dumas, Alexandre (Dumas Père [Sr.])
(1802–1870) *novelist, dramatist*

The author of *The Three Musketeers* and *The Count of Monte Cristo*, Alexandre Dumas also wrote 20 volumes of memoirs. Many of his historical novels were written with the aid of a group of collaborators, whom Dumas called his "factory." Since he wrote almost 300 volumes, it is not surprising he believed he needed help in developing plots, though the actual manuscripts are in Dumas' handwriting.

Dumas' father, Alexandre Davy de la Pailleterie, was the son of a French marquis and Marie Cessette Dumas, a black woman from Haiti. Davy took his mother's surname, served in France's Revolutionary army, and rose to the rank of general. After leading French cavalry in Napoleon's Egyptian campaign, he fell out of favor and died in poverty.

Dumas' son (1824–1895), Alexandre Dumas fils (Jr.), is the author of *The Lady of the Camellias*, which was the source of Giuseppe Verdi's opera *La Traviata*.

Dunbar, Paul Laurence (1872–1906) *poet, novelist, short-story writer*

Dunbar published his first collection of poetry, *Oak and Ivy*, in 1893, while employed as an elevator operator. Two years later, he published his second book, *Majors and Minors*, which contained a number of poems written in black dialect. The book was successful and led to the publication of his most famous work, *Lyrics of Lowly Life*, in 1896. In 1898, Dunbar published his first novel, *The Uncalled*, and a collection of short stories called *Folks From Dixie*. The last years of his life saw the publication of *Lyrics of the Hearthside* (1899), *The Love of Landry* (1900), *The Strength of Gideon and Other Stories* (1900), *The Fanatics* (1900), *The Sport of the Gods* (1901), *Lyrics of Love and Laughter* (1903), *The Heart of Happy Hollow* (1904), and *Lyrics of Sunshine and Shadow* (1905). Though Paul Laurence Dunbar's work took many forms, he is best known as a master of dialect verse. He was considered the most important African-American poet of his time.

Dunham, Katherine (1909–) *dancer, choreographer*

Katherine Dunham, who studied anthropology at the University of Chicago, is noted for incorporating African and Caribbean patterns and movements into her dance performances. In 1940, she danced in the musical *Cabin in the Sky*, which she choreographed with George Balanchine, and appeared in the movie *Stormy Weather*. She choreographed various other films and musicals and created her own shows, including *Bal Nègre* and *Tropical Review*. In 1943, she opened the Katherine Dunham School of Arts and Research, whose students included Marlon Brando and ARTHUR MITCHELL. Her troupe, The Katherine Dunham Dance Company, has toured in more than 60 countries. In 1964, she became the first African American to work with New York's Metropolitan Opera when she choreographed Verdi's *Aida*. She has written many books and articles on dance and has established schools of dance in the United States, Europe, and the Caribbean.

DuSable, Jean-Baptiste Pointe (ca. 1745–1818) *pioneer, founder of Chicago*

It is believed that DuSable was born in HAITI to a slave woman and a French sailor and was educated in Paris. Afterward, he journeyed to New Orleans and from there to St. Louis while working as a trapper and fur trader. In 1769, he traveled to Canada, stopping along the way at a place Native Americans called *Eschikagou*, a word that means "stinking onions." However, DuSable smelled not stinking onions but financial success and set up a trading post there. Though DuSable came under suspicion by the British because of his French background, he so impressed the British governor that he was asked to take charge of a settlement on the St. Clair River. He did so, and at the same time acquired considerable property in Peoria. In 1800, DuSable moved to St. Charles, Missouri, where he died. Eschikagou, where he built his trading post, would later become known as Chicago, one of the greatest commercial centers in the world.

E

education

In Africa

Educational opportunity in Africa prior to the colonial period varied tremendously from place to place. The ancient city of Alexandria was famous for its university, as was medieval TIMBUKTU, and an extensive school system had been established in the West African Songhai kingdom in the 16th century. As elsewhere in the world, education followed commercial development, since it was necessary that merchants be able to maintain written accounts and keep track of inventory. In areas where trade was relatively nonexistent, or purely local in character, the demand for education was much less. In spite of the fact that European colonialism was often excused as necessary in order to bring Western civilization to African natives, many of the European colonial powers paid no attention to education and did little or nothing to develop it. Many of the schools that were established during the colonial period were mission schools built by various religious orders. Following independence, educational opportunity expanded dramatically in many African nations. However, many African countries are poor and are limited in the resources they can allot to education.

In the United States

PRE–CIVIL WAR

Among whites, the idea of education for blacks met a mixed reception. From a practical point of view, educated slaves often acquired special skills that enabled them to earn money that was then shared with their owners. Also, slavery was often justified on the grounds that it made it possible to bring Christianity to "heathen" Africans. This resulted in pressure from religious whites who wanted slaves educated so they could read the Bible. Abolitionists favored black education as a way of preparing slaves for freedom, and a number of free African Americans opened schools for black children when the towns in which they lived failed to do so. Although most of the Northern states provided some sort of basic public education, African-American children usually were required to attend segregated schools, when they were allowed to attend at all. In spite of the difficulties they faced, a number of African Americans were not only literate but managed to acquire college educations. However, the idea of African-American education met with great hostility in the South. A slave who could read was a slave who might be influenced by abolitionist literature or who might forge a pass in order to run away. After the Nat Turner revolt of 1831, efforts to stamp out black literacy were intensified. Slaves who attempted to secretly acquire an education faced brutal punishment. But in spite of the danger they faced, some slaves did learn to read and write. Some were taught by sympathetic owners. Others, like Frederick Douglass, were taught by white children who enjoyed passing on what they themselves had learned in school. But while the desire to learn was strong, opposition was usually stronger. By the time

Catholic mission school in Buniam, Democratic Republic of Congo (*National Museum of African Art, Washington D.C.*)

ucated individual could be easily defrauded. But the main force driving this craving for learning was the feeling that freedom and education were indivisible.

African Americans were not the only ones to link education with freedom. In their frantic attempts to maintain control, the KU KLUX KLAN made African-American schools and teachers a special target. In fact, the Klan began its criminal activities with an attack on a black student who was regarded as too friendly with his white teacher. But despite the beatings and the violence, the African-American drive for education continued. According to an estimate by W. E. B. DuBois, freed slaves, in spite of their poverty, provided $785,000 for black education between 1865 and 1870.

With the passage of the Reconstruction Act of 1867, African Americans gained enough political power to insist that education be made a priority in the new Southern state constitutions that were being written. Prior to the RECONSTRUCTION period, not a single Southern state had maintained a free, statewide, tax-supported public school system—not even for white children. Now, for the first time, free public schools, supported by tax dollars and open to all children, were established in Virginia, North and

of the Civil War, only about 5 percent of the slave population was literate.

POST–CIVIL WAR

Following the Civil War, a massive effort was made to provide millions of freed slaves with an education. The FREEDMEN'S BUREAU, which was established to help the newly liberated slaves, made education a primary consideration. In five years, it spent $5,000,000 building 4,329 schools and hiring 10,000 teachers. Over 247,333 African Americans rushed to take advantage of the educational opportunities being offered them. Part of this hunger to learn stemmed from the desire to be able to read the Bible. Part was due to the recognition that an uned-

Black children studying their lessons on a southern street in 1867 (*Library of Congress*)

South Carolina, Georgia, Florida, Alabama, Arkansas, Mississippi, Louisiana, and Texas. Funding was, of course, a major problem. The African-American community and its white allies were attempting to create statewide educational systems from scratch in a region whose economy had been wrecked by war and where virulent racism prevailed. But by 1872, Texas had 1,500 schools in operation. Within 10 years of Robert E. Lee's surrender, approximately half the children in Florida, Mississippi, and South Carolina were attending class.

Advanced education also became much more attainable. Freedmen's Bureau funds made possible the establishment of Howard, Fisk, Atlanta, Storer, and Hampton Universities. With the end of Recon-struction, funding for education was drastically cut. Black students were forced to make do with out-of-date books, broken equipment, and class-rooms of 50 and 60 pupils. Poverty frequently caused African-American youngsters to drop out of school, and those who did finish were often unable to find work as anything other than labor-ers. But the educational legacy left by those African Americans of the Reconstruction period survived. The requirement for free, tax-supported public schools—a requirement determined ex-slaves had insisted be written into the constitutions of every Southern state—remained in effect and, with it, at least the promise of educational opportunity for all children.

History class, 1902 (*Library of Congress*)

COURT BATTLE TO END SEGREGATION

Legal challenges to school segregation can be traced as far back as 1849 when a lawsuit was filed on behalf of a six-year-old Boston child named Sarah Roberts who had been forced to walk past five white schools to attend a poor black one. She was represented by white abolitionist Charles Sumner and black attorney Robert Morris. Though they lost the case, mounting pressure caused the Massachusetts legislature to abolish segregated schools in 1855. However, racial segregation remained the rule in much of the North, while in the South at that time, there were no statewide public school systems at all. Though ex-slaves had forced all the former Confederate states to institute public school systems after the Civil War, in the late 1870s, African Americans lost much of what little economic and political power they had managed to acquire. Though the Southern states continued to maintain public school systems, racial segregation became the law throughout the region, and the segregation statutes were upheld in a series of Supreme Court cases, the most important being *Plessy v. Ferguson.*

Plessy v. Ferguson (1896) The Supreme Court decision in *Plessy v. Ferguson* firmly established racial segregation as legal. The case had to do with segregated railway cars. Homer Plessy, a black man from New Orleans, was convicted of riding in a railroad car set aside for whites. He appealed, but the Supreme Court upheld his conviction, ruling that the creation of "separate but equal" accommodations was "reasonable." The vote was seven to one with one abstention. Justice John Marshall Harlan, the lone dissenter, predicted—correctly—that the Supreme Court's decision would be used to limit the gains African Americans had made following the Civil War and that "the thin disguise of equal accommodations will not mislead anyone nor atone for the wrong this day done." As Justice Harlan predicted, the "separate but equal" ruling was soon used to buttress hundreds of laws and ordinances that extended racial segregation to almost every aspect of American life.

The NAACP Campaign to Overturn School Segregation: The Margold Strategy In 1931, the NATIONAL ASSOCIATION FOR THE ADVANCEMENT OF COLORED PEOPLE (NAACP) hired Nathan Ross Margold to analyze the legal situation and develop a comprehensive plan for fighting discrimination. His ideas became known as the "Margold Strategy." Although an end to school segregation was the ultimate goal, Margold advised against attacking the practice directly. His reasons were clear. The question of school segregation had been raised in more than 100 separate lawsuits, and each time the courts had upheld the practice. In view of this history, Margold recommended that the NAACP lawyers attack such unfair practices as paying white teachers more than black teachers or spending more to educate white children than African-American youngsters. But Margold did not want to bring hundreds of lawsuits in different jurisdictions. To do so would require endless time and money. Instead, his idea was to bring a succession of cases that would take advantage of weaknesses in state laws and produce wide-ranging results. The NAACP lawyers took the first step in implementing the Margold Strategy with the 1934 case *Murray v. Pearson,* which challenged the failure of the state of Maryland to provide equal educational opportunities at the graduate school level. Other cases involved unequal pay for teachers and unequal spending on black students. After a number of legal victories in matters such as these, the time came to challenge the concept of school segregation itself.

Brown v. Board of Education of Topeka (1954) The case, *Brown v. Board of Education of Topeka,* would be one of the most important in Supreme Court history. It began when Oliver Brown was refused permission to enroll his eight-year-old child, Linda, in a white school in Topeka, Kansas. The case was filed on February 28, 1951, in the U.S. District Court for Kansas. The district court noted that the Supreme Court had not yet overruled Plessy and proceeded to rule in favor of the defendant and against Mr. Brown and the NAACP. However, it agreed with the NAACP that segregation did indeed appear to constitute unequal treatment and cited an earlier NAACP case as evidence. In doing so, it provided the NAACP with an opportunity to persuade the Supreme Court to once again deal with the segregation issue. Did segregation, in and of itself, constitute unequal treatment under the Fourteenth Amendment to the Constitution, even if everything else, in terms of facilities, curriculum, and per-pupil expenditures, were equal?

The lawyers of the NAACP Legal Defense Fund and the black leadership in general were sharply divided as to the best approach to take in arguing Brown and similar cases. Slow progress was indeed being made in opening white schools to African Americans, and recent court decisions had caused several state legislatures to rapidly upgrade black schools. The Supreme Court had already had plenty of opportunity to overturn *Plessy v. Ferguson* and had shown no interest in doing so. Should the NAACP attack Plessy and lose, it would not only strengthen Plessy, but possibly undo some of what had already been accomplished.

Another source of contention was the decision to use evidence developed by Dr. KENNETH CLARK, a noted psychologist. Clark had determined that African-American children suffered emotional damage as a direct result of segregation. Using a technique that was to become famous, Clark had presented African-American children with a set of black dolls and white dolls. The children were then asked which dolls were "nice" and which were "bad," which dolls they preferred, and which dolls looked most like themselves. In a frightening display of low self-esteem, child after child linked the black dolls to negative characteristics and the white dolls to positive ones. Even more dismaying, close to half the African-American children selected the white dolls as being most like themselves—indicating a shocking refusal to accept their own color. Some children even cried when forced to accept the black dolls as being most like themselves. However, the doll tests did not prove that low self-esteem among African-American children resulted entirely or directly from school segregation. And the tests were open to different interpretations. Besides, this psychological approach did not rest on the kind of hard legal and historical arguments the judges were accustomed to hearing. It might be regarded as a gimmick and weaken the NAACP's case.

The question of whether or not to attack segregation directly was decided for the lawyers when the Supreme Court indicated that the time had indeed come to deal with the issue. It accepted the Brown case and ordered that it be argued in conjunction with four similar cases—*Briggs v. Elliott,* a South Carolina case; *Davis v. County School Board of Prince Edward County, Virginia; Bolling v. Sharpe* from Washington, D.C.; and *Gebhart v. Belton* from Delaware. Thurgood Marshall argued the case for the NAACP. On May 17, 1954, the United States Supreme Court, under Chief Justice Earl Warren, handed down a unanimous decision in *Brown v. Board of Education of Topeka*. In doing so, it firmly rejected *Plessy v. Ferguson,* stating:

> We come then to the question presented: Does segregation of children in the public schools solely on the basis of race, even though the physical facilities and other "tangible" factors may be equal, deprive the children of the minority group of equal education opportunities? We believe that it does . . . We conclude that in the field of public education the doctrine of "separate but equal" has no place. Separate educational facilities are inherently unequal.

AFTER THE BROWN DECISION

The Supreme Court's *Brown* decision told schools systems across the nation that they would have to integrate. But it did not say how and it did not say when. Fifty-four weeks after its initial decision, the Court issued a decree (generally referred to as "*Brown* II") indicating just how school desegregation should proceed. Some school districts did not wait for instructions. Washington, D.C., moved to integrate its system completely at the beginning of the new fall term. Baltimore, Louisville, and St. Louis began total integration programs, as did 25 counties in West Virginia and one school district in Arkansas. But most of the country waited for the Court to make its wishes clear. On May 31, 1955, it did so.

Noting the existence of local problems involving such things as scheduling, bus transportation, and revision of school districts, it ordered communities to proceed "at all deliberate speed." The Court's failure to set a definite date for compliance had its consequences. In 1958, four years after the *Brown* decision had been announced, integration efforts had begun in only 764 out of 2,889 southern school

Fifth-grade class at the Eli Terry School, Hartford, Conn., 1966 (*Library of Congress*)

districts. Virginia, Georgia, Mississippi, South Carolina, Florida, Louisiana, and Alabama remained completely segregated.

Rioting broke out in 1957 when attempts were made to integrate Central High School in Little Rock, Arkansas. After continued threats and violence, the U.S. Army's 101st Airborne was sent in and spent the rest of the year accompanying nine black students to school. (See LITTLE ROCK NINE.) Elsewhere, in Prince Edward County, Virginia, all public schools were closed to avoid integration and remained closed until reopened by Supreme Court order five years later in 1964. (See *GRIFFIN V. PRINCE EDWARD COUNTY, VIRGINIA.*) Nor was resistance limited to the public school system. In 1956, violence broke out when AUTHERINE LUCY attempted to attend the University of Alabama, and a major confrontation erupted in 1962 at the University of Mis-

sissippi when JAMES MEREDITH attempted to enroll there. Five hundred U.S. Army troops were sent in to back up almost 600 federal officers who were under attack by a mob of 2,000 people. By the time order had been restored, 28 marshals had been shot, and two people had been murdered.

The CIVIL RIGHTS ACT OF 1964 gave the Justice Department authority to intervene in school integration disputes. Over the next 10 years, the department would charge over 500 school districts with continuing segregation. In addition, several court decisions forced many school systems to institute busing to achieve integration. For many years, thousands of children across the country had ridden buses to school. But the use of busing to achieve integration drew a furious response, especially in Boston, Massachusetts, where fighting broke out. Even where there was no violence, school integration followed a twisting, bumpy road. African-American principals and teachers in the South sometimes lost their jobs when black schools were closed and students transferred to white schools. Arguments broke out over having to combine previously all-white or all-black cheerleading squads, bands, and other groups. The rapidly expanding Civil Rights movement generated new interests in black culture and history, and African-American students began demanding black studies programs, which later led to demands for Afrocentric education.

In its landmark decision, *Brown v. Board of Education of Topeka,* the Supreme Court set the stage for the termination of segregation everywhere. After all, if a city or state could not require segregation in public schools, why should it be able to insist on segregation in parks, libraries, swimming pools, and other public areas? The answer was, it couldn't. The *Brown* decision was critical in placing the nation firmly on the path to racial integration in all areas of American life.

Recommended Reading: Kluger, Richard. *Simple Justice.* New York: Vintage Books, 1977; Martin, Waldo E. *Brown vs. Board of Education: A Brief History with Documents.* New York: St. Martin's Press, 1998; Tackach, James. *Brown vs. Board of Education.* San Diego, Calif.: Lucent, 1997; Tushnet, Mark V. *Brown vs. Board of Education: Battle for Integration.* Danbury, Conn.: Franklin Watts, 1995.

Egypt, Arab Republic of

North African country. Capital: Cairo. Egypt was home to one of the most ancient and advanced civilizations on Earth. Its unique position on both the Mediterranean and Red Seas made it an early commercial and cultural focal point, linking the city-states of the Aegean, the kingdoms of the Middle East, and the African trade centers to the south. The Nile River provides transportation and is critical to Egypt's agriculture. Because the Nile runs from south to north, southern Egypt is known as Upper Egypt, and northern Egypt is referred to as Lower Egypt. The area was settled over 5,700 years ago by seminomadic blacks who moved into the

Nile Valley as the Sahara became drier and less suited to human habitation and by groups from Asia Minor.

Toward the end of the third millennium B.C., King Menes unified Upper and Lower Egypt and began the country's 3,000-year-long tradition of rule through pharaohs. These pharaohs are classified according to dynasty. Thirty dynasties, which ended with Egypt's conquest by Alexander the Great, are grouped as belonging to the Early Dynastic Period, the Old Kingdom, the First Intermediate Period, the Middle Kingdom, the Second Intermediate Period, the New Kingdom, the Third Intermediate Period, and the Late Period. (See chart.) The pharaohs who built the Great PYRAMIDS belonged to the Fourth Dynasty; Sixth Dynasty rulers oversaw the construction of canals around the first Nile cataract to facilitate trade with NUBIA and the sending of exploratory expeditions as far south as KERMA. The Eleventh through Fourteenth Dynasties developed a stronger central government and encouraged the arts and sciences.

In the 18th century B.C., Egypt was invaded by the Hyksos, a Canaanite people whose rulers promoted commerce with the Middle East. The Hyksos were overthrown by Amenhotep I, founder of

Carved relief of Horus, Egypt (*National Museum of African Art, Washington, D.C.*)

the Eighteenth Dynasty, whose pharaohs extended Egypt's control over Nubia and KUSH. It is the Egypt of the Eighteenth and Nineteenth Dynasties that is described in the Old Testament of the Bible.

Eventually, Egypt's government became weak and corrupt, allowing kings from Kush to extend their authority over Upper Egypt. At the end of the eighth century B.C., Kushite armies conquered all of Egypt and established the Twenty-fifth, or Kushite Dynasty. The Kushite rulers were driven out of Egypt by Assyrian forces (671–660 B.C.), who themselves were pushed out a short time later.

In 525 B.C., King Cambyses of Persia conquered Egypt but continued the observance of pharaonic traditions and religious observance. Persian rule continued until the Persian Empire was conquered by Alexander the Great. Following the death of Alexander in 323 B.C., the Macedonian general Ptolemy took control of Egypt, and for the next three centuries, his descendants ruled from the port city of Alexandria. Nectanebo II is considered to be the last pharaoh who was actually of Egyptian descent.

The last pharaoh in the Ptolemaic line was Cleopatra. With her suicide in 30 B.C., Egypt was absorbed into the Roman Empire. Culturally, the most significant change under Roman rule was the gradual replacement of Egypt's ancient religion by Christianity. This transition took place over a period of several hundred years marked by persecutions, schisms, and occasional civil disorder. The era of Christian dominance lasted about 350 years, until the Arab invasions in the seventh century A.D.

Arab administration of Egypt was marked by four ruling groups. The Umayyad caliphate, which was based in Damascus, ruled from around 640 to A.D. 750. They were followed by the Abassids (750–1258), who were based in Baghdad. Abassid rule was interrupted by the rival Fatimid Dynasty, which gained power between 968–1169. When Fatimid authority weakened, the Abassids sent the great Moslem warrior Saladin (who would later defeat the Crusaders at Jerusalem in 1187), to take control. Saladin established himself as sultan of Egypt (1169) and conquered Syria, rewarding his followers with fiefs in the Nile Delta. His successors came to depend on the Mamelukes, a warrior caste descended from non-African slaves who had been brought to Egypt in the 10th century from Greece, the Balkans, and Asia Minor. (*Mameluke* means "bought white man.") As these Mamelukes converted to Islam, they were freed. Their descendants achieved considerable success and power, which they retained even after Turkey's Ottoman Empire gained control of Egypt after 1258.

Though still nominally a part of the Ottoman Empire, Egypt was occupied by French and British troops during the Napoleonic Wars, a period that saw the rise of a Turkish soldier named Muhammad Ali, who established the last Egyptian royal line. Ali's successors were increasingly dominated by the British, and with the disintegration of the Ottoman Empire during World War I, Egypt became a British protectorate. The country regained partial sovereignty in 1923, becoming completely independent in 1936.

After World War II, Egypt's political life was dominated by conflict between Israel and the Arab states. Egyptian losses in the 1948 Arab-Israeli War led to the 1952 overthrow of Egypt's King Farouk by Gamal Abdel Nasser, who nationalized the Suez Canal and built the Aswan High Dam. Nasser's successor, Anwar El-Sadat, shocked the Arab world by visiting Israel and signing the Camp David peace accords. He was murdered by Islamic fundamentalists in 1981, and Hosni Mubarak became president. Terrorism by fundamentalist Islamic groups has been a problem in recent years. In an effort to destabilize Egypt's government by destroying the country's tourist industry, Islamic militants have staged a series of murderous attacks against Christians and Westerners. In 1997, 58 tourists were slaughtered in the ancient city of Luxor. In spite of a constitutional ban against religious political parties, Mubarak's government faces strong opposition from the Muslim Brotherhood. Political parties must be approved by the government. The Egyptian government has engaged in various human rights abuses, including torture of prisoners, secret trials, persecution of defense attorneys, and the harassment and intimidation of journalists. In return for Mubarak's support during the 1991 Persian Gulf War, the United States cancelled $7 billion of Egypt's debt to the United States.

EGYPTIAN DYNASTIC HISTORY

SELECTED DYNASTIES	NOTABLE RULERS	EVENTS/CHARACTERISTICS
Early Dynastic Period: Dynasties 1–3; ca. 3100–2575 B.C. First Dynasty ca. 2920–2770 B.C.	Menes	Unification of Upper and Lower Egypt
Old Kingdom: Dynasties 4–8; ca. 2575–2134 B.C. Fourth Dynasty ca. 2575–2465 B.C. Sixth Dynasty ca. 2325–2150 B.C.	Khufu Pepi I	Great Pyramids built at Giza Smaller-scale architecture; civil disorder; unfavorable Nile floods
First Intermediate Period: Dynasties 9–11 (Theban); ca. 2134–2040 B.C. Early Eleventh Dynasty ca. 2134–2040 B.C.	Mentuhotep II	Thebes becomes capital; return to large-scale building projects
Middle Kingdom: Dynasties Late 11th (All of Egypt)–14; ca. 2040–1640 B.C. Twelfth Dynasty ca. 1991–1783 B.C.	Amenemhet I	Feudal system established
Second Intermediate Period: Dynasties 15–17; ca. 1640–1550 B.C. Fifteenth–Seventeenth Dynasties	Hyksos rulers	Canaanite or Amorite people; introduction of the horse-drawn chariot
New Kingdom: Dynasties 18–20; ca. 1550–1070 B.C. Eighteenth Dynasty ca. 1550–1307 B.C. Nineteenth Dynasty ca. 1307–1196 B.C.	Amenhotep I, Hatshepsut, Tuthmosis III, Ikhnaton, Tutankhamon Ramses II	Egypt at its height; huge temple projects; Ikhnaton attempts to impose monotheistic cult Hebrew exodus

Third Intermediate Period:
Dynasties 21–25; ca. 1070–657 B.C.
Twenty-second Dynasty
ca. 945–712 B.C.
Twenty-third Dynasty
  several contemporary
  lines of kings
  established
ca. 828–712 B.C.
Twenty-fifth Dynasty
ca. 770–657 B.C.
	Shoshenq I
	
	Osorkon IV
	
	Shabaka, Taharqa
		Libyan dynasty in rivalry with Thebes; capture of
		Jerusalem, 930 B.C.
		Nubian dynasty in Upper Egypt
		
		Nubian dynasty

(continued)

EGYPTIAN DYNASTIC HISTORY (continued)

Selected Dynasties	Notable Rulers	Events/Characteristics
Late Period: Dynasties 26–30; ca. 657–332 B.C.		
Twenty-sixth Dynasty ca. 657–525 B.C.	Necho II	Expedition sails around Africa
Twenty-seventh Dynasty 525–404 B.C.	Cambyses, Darius I, Xerxes I	Persian Empire conquers Egypt but retains pharaonic rule
Greek Period: Macedonian/Ptolemaic Dynasties; ca. 332–30 B.C.		
Macedonian Dynasty ca. 332–304 B.C.	Alexander the Great	City of Alexandria founded
Ptolemaic Dynasty ca. 304–30 B.C.	Ptolemy I, Cleopatra VII	

Elaine, Arkansas, incident

A 1919 confrontation involving African-American sharecroppers who were attempting to organize a union. Called the Progressive Farmers and Household Union of America, the organization had been formed under the leadership of a black farmer named Robert L. Hill. The members were fired on by a group of whites while meeting at a church in Hoop Spur near the town of Elaine in Phillips County. After they returned the fire, killing several whites, antiblack riots broke out, hundreds of African Americans were arrested, and at least 20 were killed while "resisting arrest." The NATIONAL ASSOCIATION FOR THE ADVANCEMENT OF COLORED PEOPLE estimated that 60 to 70 black men were killed, and other reports put the number at close to 200. Seventy-three black men were indicted on charges of insurrection, and 12 were charged with murder. Many men confessed after being subjected to electric shock torture. Defense witnesses were whipped and forced to testify for the prosecution. The trials often lasted less than an hour, and in the cases of the twelve men charged with murder, the jury returned guilty verdicts after deliberating for eight minutes. The twelve men were condemned to death, and the rest sentenced to long prison terms. The Arkansas Supreme Court threw out six of the convictions of those sentenced to death; the con-

victions of the other six were overturned when the U.S. Supreme Court ruled that the presence of a lynch mob in the courtroom, which had refrained from acting only because it was assured a guilty verdict, had prevented the men from getting a fair trial (*Moore v. Dempsey,* 1923). The governor commuted the sentences of the others, and the last of the 73 men convicted was released in 1925. Robert Hill escaped to Kansas, where Governor Henry Allen refused to extradite him. One white man, O. S. Bratton, a lawyer who had been hired by the union, was also jailed and was held without charges for a month before being released.

Recommended Reading: Waskow, Arthur I. *From Race Riot to Sit-In, 1919 and the 1960's.* New York: Doubleday, 1966.

Ellington, Edward Kennedy ("Duke")

(1899–1974) *composer, jazz musician, bandleader*
Born in Washington, D.C., Ellington was nicknamed "Duke" because of his elegant way of dressing. He began playing professionally while still in high school, then left for New York in 1922. Unsuccessful, he returned to Washington and, after having expanded his band, tried New York again. This time well-received, the group was hired by the Kentucky

Club. In 1927, the group, which would eventually become a 15-piece orchestra, began a five-year engagement at Harlem's legendary Cotton Club, and it was there that Ellington developed his sophisticated "swing" style.

Ellington's musicians commonly stayed with him for years, and he kept his band together even during the 1950s, when financial difficulties stemming from the demise of the Big Band era forced many groups to break up. This was partly due to loyalty—Ellington was famous for never firing anyone—but also to Ellington's desire always to have a band available so that he could hear his compositions immediately. For 29 years, Ellington worked closely with writer-arranger-pianist Billy Strayhorn, who created the band's theme song, "Take the 'A' Train," and who cowrote "Satin Doll."

The Ellington band recorded more albums than any other JAZZ group; copyrights cover 952 compositions; 21 suites; three sacred concerts, including one that premiered at Westminster Abbey; three movie scores; and *The River,* a ballet choreographed by Alvin Ailey. His orchestra was voted the number one jazz group 76 times by various magazines. He was awarded the Presidential Medal of Freedom by President Nixon in 1969. During his last illness, Ellington insisted that his hospital room have a piano so that he could continue working on his opera *Queenie Pie.* Among his most popular compositions are *Sophisticated Lady; Mood Indigo; Black, Brown and Beige; Solitude;* and *Diminuendo and Crescendo in Blue.*

Duke Ellington, photographed by Gordon Parks, at the Hurricane Cabaret, New York, May 1943 (*Library of Congress*)

Ellison, Ralph Waldo (1914–1994) *novelist*
Ralph Waldo Ellison is the author of *Invisible Man,* a book considered one of the best novels of the 20th century and which won the National Book Award for Fiction in 1952. *Invisible Man* is the story of an unnamed African American who is unable to force the white world to see him as an individual human being apart from his ethnic background. Ellison, who was born in Oklahoma City, was named for the writer Ralph Waldo Emerson. His father was an ice and coal vendor who died when Ellison was three years old. His mother supported the family by working as a maid. *Invisible Man* was written over a five-year period and finally published in 1952. It immediately became a best-seller and continues to be recommended reading in many schools and colleges. Ellison also wrote many essays, reviews, and short stories, some of which were collected in the books *Shadow and Act* and *Going to the Territory.* In spite of the recognition he received, Ellison was bitter over criticism leveled at him in the 1960s and 1970s by black radicals who claimed he was not "black enough" because he focused on character and individuality in his writing, rather than political doctrine. Progress on a second novel was halted temporarily in 1967 when a fire destroyed much of the manuscript. Though Ellison resumed work on it, it was still unfinished

at the time of his death. Called *Juneteenth*, the novel was published in 1999 thanks to the efforts of John Callahan, who was Ellison's literary executor. Three years earlier, six unpublished stories by Ellison were discovered in an old briefcase.

Elmina Castle

Fort erected by the Portuguese in 1482 on the GOLD COAST. Its original name was São Jorge de Mina, and it was built to facilitate the Portuguese-African gold trade. The name "Elmina" means "the mine." The Portuguese would buy slaves at BENIN and then transport them to Elmina to sell to local Africans in exchange for gold dust. The slaves were often used to work the gold mines of the interior. Later, Elmina became a major shipping point for slaves headed for the Americas. Elmina Castle was protected by 400 cannons, mounted on walls 30 feet thick, and had space to hold up to 1,000 slaves. It was seized by the Dutch in 1637. Elmina Castle was one of approximately 40 African forts built by Europeans for the purpose of holding slaves and other goods.

Emancipation Proclamation

Order issued by President Abraham Lincoln on January 1, 1863, freeing all slaves in Confederate-held territory. The proclamation did not apply to the approximately 800,000 slaves held in the four border states that had not joined the Confederacy or to those in territory under Union control.

Shortly after Lincoln won the presidency, 11 slave states seceded to form the Confederate States of America. Four other slave states—Maryland, Delaware, Kentucky, and Missouri—remained in the Union, and Lincoln moved cautiously on the slavery issue in order to keep their allegiance. To calm white fears, he refused to let African Americans serve in the Union army. When the war began, many Northerners believed that the main goal of the Civil War was to hold the Union together, not to end slavery. But as the fighting continued, white attitudes began to change.

On September 22, 1862, Lincoln announced that on January 1, he would free all slaves in those areas still in rebellion against the Union. Hoping to

F. Pezzicar's sculpture, *The Abolition of Slavery in the United States,* displayed at the Centennial Exposition of 1876 in Philadelphia (*Library of Congress*)

attract Southern support, he promised to try to arrange payment for slave owners who freed their slaves. But the South ignored Lincoln's offer, and the war continued. On January 1, 1863, Lincoln issued the Emancipation Proclamation. In addition to freeing slaves in Confederate territory, it stated that African Americans would now be eligible to join the Union army. FREDERICK DOUGLASS moved at once to encourage black soldiers to enlist. His famous editorial "Men of Color to Arms" was reprinted in newspapers across the nation. "Who would be free themselves must strike the blow," he wrote. "I am authorized to assure you that you will receive the same wages, the same rations, the same equipment, the same protection, the same treatment, and the same bounty, secured to white soldiers."[1] In this, Douglass was deceived. Black soldiers did not

[1] Joanne Grout, ed., *Black Protest, History, Documents, and Analyses, 1619 to the Present.* New York: Fawcett, 1968, p. 113.

receive the same treatment as whites. Their pay was less, their equipment was inferior, and they were forced to serve in segregated units under white officers. Nevertheless, thousands of African Americans rushed to enlist, and within six months, over 30 black regiments had begun training.

Although the Emancipation Proclamation did not apply to the slaves in the four border states, it had an effect there as well. Army recruiters, promising freedom, persuaded thousands of slaves to run away and enlist. Others attempted revolt. For more and more whites, the war to save the Union became the war to end slavery. Of course, issuing the Emancipation Proclamation and enforcing it were two different things. Slavery in Confederate territory did not end until Union troops arrived on the scene, and it took the Thirteenth Amendment to abolish slavery throughout the United States. But the Proclamation was of major importance. More American soldiers lost their lives in the Civil War than in all other U.S. wars combined. The thousands of Union dead and wounded weakened Northern resolve and encouraged antiwar hysteria. For all its limitations, the Emancipation Proclamation gave the Civil War a critical moral dimension that was vital in maintaining Northern support.

Equatorial Guinea, Republic of

Country consisting of five islands (Bioko, on which the capital, Malabo, is located; Pagalu; Corisco; Elobey Grande; and Elobey Chico) and a mainland province called Rio Muni on Africa's Atlantic coast. The earliest inhabitants of the area were the Bubi people, who were pushed onto Bioko by invading Bantu tribes in the 13th century. The Portuguese arrived in 1472 but ceded their claim to the area to Spain in 1778. The Spanish settlers who attempted to colonize the area died of yellow fever, and in 1827, the Spanish agreed to allow the British, who had already outlawed the slave trade, to use Bioko (then known as Fernando Po) both as a base for antislaving patrols and as a site for the resettlement of freed slaves.

The Spanish established cocoa plantations on Bioko, and, in 1900, the five islands were united with Rio Muni as the colony of Spanish Guinea.

Laborers were brought over from the mainland to work the cocoa plantations, but they were treated so badly that the League of Nations sent a delegation to study the situation in 1920. A nationalist movement developed after World War II, and the country gained full independence in 1968 under President Francisco Macias Nguema.

Macias was a brutal dictator during whose reign approximately 50,000 people, including most political leaders, were murdered, the economy was destroyed, and up to 100,000 people were forced to flee the country. He was overthrown and executed in 1979 by Theodoro Obiang Nguema Mbasogo. The economy is slowly improving. The population numbers approximately 390,000, with most people living either on Bioko or in Rio Muni. Elections were held in 1993 and Obiang was reelected president. Equatorial Guinea has a weak human rights record; torture of political prisoners is common.

Eritrea (air-eh-TREE-uh)

modern African state. Capital: Asmara. A little over 36,000 square miles in area, the country has a population of approximately 3,317,000, 80 percent of whom are either farmers or herders of goats and camels. Located in the Sahel region, Eritrea has serious problems with drought and soil erosion, caused partly by deforestation. However, its ports on the Red Sea offer the possibility of expanded trade.

In ancient times, Eritrean territory formed part of the kingdom of Axum. In the 16th century the region came under the control of the Ottoman Empire, and in the 1800s, ETHIOPIA, EGYPT, and Italy all struggled for control of the area. Italy established the colony of Eritrea in 1890 and later used it as a base for its invasion of Ethiopia in 1935. The British captured Eritrea in 1941, and the United Nations established it as a federated part of Ethiopia in 1952. Ethiopia established its own Amharic-speaking regime in Tigrinya-speaking Eritrea. Eritreans seeking total independence formed the Eritrean Liberation Front after 1962 and began a guerrilla war. Following a United Nations referendum, Eritrea became a separate state in 1993, after 30 years of civil war. Though Eritrea is split between Christians, Muslims, and animists and is home to nine separate ethnic and tribal groups, it achieved a considerable sense of unity during its rebellion against Ethiopia, with both men and women playing major roles. In 1998, fighting again broke out between Eritrea and Ethiopia over disputed territory. The name *Eritrea* is from the Latin name (Mare erythraeum) for the Red Sea.

Estevanico (Esteban, Estevanillo)
(ca. 1500–1539) *explorer*

Estevanico (Little Steven) was born in Azemmour, Morocco. He was captured and sold into slavery around 1513 and at some point became the property of Andres Dorantes, a Spanish adventurer. He accompanied Dorantes on the 1528 expedition led by Pánfilo de Narváez to the New World.

The group started out with 600 men, but a year later, only four, including Estevanico were still alive. They were taken prisoner and spent six years enslaved by Native Americans. During this time, Estevanico learned five Indian languages and acquired knowledge of various medicines and herbs. He also heard many Indian stories about the Seven Cities of Cibola, which supposedly were made of gold.

After managing to escape, Estevanico and the others spent two years wandering through the Southwest before reaching Mexico City in 1536. There they met with the Spanish viceroy, who was fascinated by the tales of the seven cities filled with treasure and sent out an expedition led by Father Narcos de Niza (1539). Estevanico was chosen to go ahead of the group and send back crosses to indicate his findings. The larger the cross, the more important his discoveries. Posing as a powerful medicine man, he dressed in feathers and bells and traveled with an Indian entourage and two greyhounds. The journey took the group into Arizona, and Estevanico sent back larger and larger crosses. Then all communication stopped. Eventually two wounded Indians appeared and said Estevanico had been killed by a hostile tribe. Though the Seven Cities of Gold were never found, Estevanico's stories led to the later explorations of Coronado and other explorers. He is credited as the man who guided the first white explorers through the American Southwest.

Ethiopia, Federal Democratic Republic of

East African country. Capital: Addis Ababa. According to tradition, Ethiopia, then known as Habashat or Abyssinia, was founded in the 10th century B.C. by Menelik I, the son of the biblical King Solomon and the Queen of Sheba. The ancient kingdom's position on the Red Sea made it a center for trade. The powerful kingdom of AXUM arose in what is now northern Ethiopia in the first century A.D. and remained in existence for 1,000 years.

The 12th century saw the rise of the Zagwe dynasty, which established a feudalistic state and encouraged the spread of Christianity. Among the Zagwe rulers was King LALIBELA, who reigned between 1200 and 1250 and who oversaw the construction of an amazing group of churches hewn out of solid rock.

The Solomonid dynasty, which claimed descent back to Solomon and Sheba, came to power in 1270 and governed from a series of temporary courts set up in different parts of the kingdom. Their efforts to expand southward brought Ethiopia into conflict with the Muslim kingdom of Adal, which was located in present-day Djibouti and western Somalia. In 1526, a Muslim leader, Ahmad ibn Ibrahim—also known as Ahmad Gran (Ahmad the left-handed)—came to power in Adal and in 1530–31, brought much of Ethiopia under his control. Ethiopia's Christian emperor, Leban Dengel, appealed to the Portuguese for help, citing Islam as a common threat. A joint Portuguese-Ethiopian force managed to defeat Ahmad in 1543, but the weakened Ethiopian state proved attractive to Oromo tribespeople, who gradually occupied the southern third of the kingdom to provide pasture for their cattle. The Christian Ethiopian kings based in the north were more concerned with their trade arrangements with the Ottoman Turks, and the period was marked by frequent civil war as local Christian princes took control of various provinces. Southern Ethiopia was viewed primarily as a source of slaves, and approximately 10,000 captives, mostly women, were sold to Egyptian and Middle Eastern traders each year.

In the mid-19th century, Lij Kassa Haylu (ca. 1818–1868) put together an army, had himself crowned emperor in 1855 under the name Tewodros

(Theodore) II, and attempted to reform the government and bring the nobility under control. In 1867, Tewodros had several Englishmen, including the British consul, arrested, and England sent in a 30,000-man army to rescue the hostages. Tewodros' army deserted him, and he committed suicide. Britain's real interest in Ethiopia stemmed from the fact that the nearby Suez Canal was to open in 1869.

In 1889, MENELIK II came to power and signed a friendship treaty with Italy. Italy then claimed the treaty gave it protectorate status over Ethiopia. Menelik rejected the claim, and Italy invaded Ethiopia in 1895. The Italians were defeated at the famous battle of Adowa in 1896, and a new treaty confirmed the "absolute independence" of Ethiopia. When HAILE SELASSIE was crowned emperor in 1930, he abolished slavery and attempted to modernize the country. However, five years later, Italy invaded the country, and Ethiopia's army was unable to cope with air strikes, poison gas warfare, and modern, mechanized assault tactics. Addis Ababa was captured in 1936, and Ethiopia, Eritrea, and Italian Somaliland were combined to form Italian East Africa. Haile Selassie was forced to flee but returned in 1941 when the British, with the aid of Ethiopian guerrillas, recaptured the country.

In 1945, Ethiopia became a charter member of the new United Nations. Eritrea became an Ethiopian province. It seceded and became an independent country in 1993 after a long, bloody civil war. In 1973, Ethiopia was hit by drought, and the resulting widespread famine was a factor in Haile Selassie's overthrow in 1974. A leftist, military government took over with Soviet support and rapidly became a murderous communist dictatorship (1984) under Lt. Col. Mengisu Haile Mariam, who initially took power in 1977. War with Eritrea and Somalia, coupled with the regime's brutal and economically disastrous domestic policies, led to internal fighting and widespread starvation, but the Mengisu government refused famine relief to the rebel provinces of Tigre and Eritrea. In 1991, Mengisu was forced out by the Ethiopian People's Revolutionary Democratic Front (EPRDF), which promised democratic reforms. Fighting continues between the government and the Oromo Liberation Front (OLF), and the jailing of political opponents is common. In 1998, fighting again broke out between Eritrea and Ethiopia. Elections are planned for 2000.

Evers, Medgar Wiley (1925–1963) *civil rights activist*

Evers' family had a history of defiance against white domination. His great-grandfather, for whom Medgar Evers was named, was considered an extremely troublesome slave, and his grandfather had had to leave town after shooting at a white man who had insulted him. Evers' mother stressed the importance of education, although his Mississippi school was a stove-heated, one-room shack that was only open four months of the year.

Headshot of Medgar Evers, a vocal proponent of civil rights who was shot and killed in front of his home in 1963 for his social activism, becoming a martyr and inspiring other activists (*Archive Photos*)

After serving in the army during World War II, Medgar Evers and his brother Charles enrolled at Alcorn Agricultural and Mechanical College. In 1946, the two brothers managed, with some difficulty, to register to vote. On election day, they arrived at the polling booth accompanied by several armed friends. They were met by 200 whites, who threatened them, but who were unwilling to risk further action. Although the Evers brothers were prevented from voting in 1946, they did manage to cast their ballots the next year.

In 1954, Evers applied for entrance to the law school at the University of Mississippi. After his application was rejected because of race, Evers became the first field secretary of the Mississippi NATIONAL ASSOCIATION FOR THE ADVANCEMENT OF COLORED PEOPLE (NAACP). He worked to end school segregation, eliminate job discrimination, and promote the integration of parks, buses, and all public places. He also investigated racially inspired crimes, including the murders of EMMETT TILL and the Rev. George Lee, and helped JAMES MEREDITH enter the University of Mississippi. However, his main concern was voter registration. Death threats were frequent, and Evers' wife Myrlie (who later became president of the national NAACP) and his children learned to drop to the floor in case of shooting.

In 1963, the NAACP and the STUDENT NON-VIO-LENT COORDINATING COMMITTEE (SNCC) began a sit-in campaign in Jackson. On May 28, a Molotov cocktail was thrown at Medgar Evers' house. On June 12, he was shot in the back as he walked to the door of his home. Charges against his killer, Byron de la Beckwith, were dropped after two trials ended in hung juries in spite of strong evidence. Years later it was learned that prospective jury members had been secretly screened by the state Sovereignty Commission, an official government agency set up in 1956 to protect Mississippi's "sovereign" rights. The commission had investigated hundreds of people believed involved in or sympathetic to civil rights activities, spread rumors aimed at discrediting civil rights leaders, and worked to block new federal programs aimed at helping poor and minority groups. When the commission's efforts at jury tampering became known,

Beckwith was retried. He was convicted on February 5, 1994, and was sentenced to life in prison.

Ewuare the Great (Eh-WOO-ah-ray) (reigned ca. 1440–1473) *king, or oba, of medieval Benin*
Ewuare extended BENIN'S empire, establishing a standing army that conquered more than 200 towns and villages. He fortified Benin City, building defensive walls and ditches along with a network of roads. During his reign, a state council was formed, and various government reforms were instituted. Ewuare presided over a period of great artistic growth known for carved ivory and bronzes.

Exodusters
name given to thousands of ex-slaves who fled the South in 1879. With the end of RECONSTRUCTION, southern blacks were subjected to repression so severe it has been referred to as a second slavery. In response, about 150 African-American ex-soldiers, part of a group of 500 known as "the Committee," traveled undercover throughout the South to collect information on the situation. Armed with the reports of their investigators, the Committee requested help from the federal government. When its requests were ignored, black leaders recommended that African Americans leave the South. In 1879, between 20,000 and 40,000 former slaves migrated to Kansas, seeking a new life on land made available by the 1862 Homestead Act. Most came from Mississippi, Alabama, Louisiana, and Georgia. When the white South realized it was in danger of losing its labor force, it reacted violently. Klansmen in Mississippi threatened to sink any boat on which black migrants were found. Other Exodusters were beaten, and some were murdered for attempting to leave. The Democrats in Congress demanded an investigation, claiming the Exodus of 1879 was a Republican plot to wreck the southern economy. The huge numbers of ragged refugees often met a hostile reception, although more than $100,000 was collected for relief purposes. Among those who encouraged the Exodus of 1879 were BENJAMIN "PAP" SINGLETON and Henry Adams.

African-American people in the West after the Civil War: black Union Corpsmen guarding the Wright Surveying Party in 1867 (*Archive Photos*)

extended family

family that, according to African tradition, includes parents, children, numerous relatives, and the spirits of dead ancestors. Traditionally men had two or more wives, each of whom usually lived in her own hut with her children. Marriages were usually arranged between families, and the husband might be required to pay the woman's family a bride-price to compensate them for the loss of her services. Christian missionaries often had difficulty making converts in Africa because they usually insisted that men give up their additional wives.

The oldest man was usually the head of the family, and it was his responsibility to offer sacrifices to ancestors, mediate disputes, and maintain harmony within the group. The concept of extended family remains strong, although the tradition of multiple wives, while common in many areas, is no longer as widespread.

Ezana (fourth-century A.D.) *king of Axum*

Ezana was known for his military expeditions aimed at protecting caravan routes and for his successful campaign against KUSH in A.D. 325 that culminated with the sack of Meroe. At the urging of his tutor, Frumentius, Ezana converted to Christianity, which then became AXUM's state religion. His conversion had political ramifications since it helped solidify good relations with the Roman emperor Constantine.

F

Fanon, Frantz Omar (1925–1961) *writer, social and political theorist, psychiatrist*

Born on the French-ruled island of Martinique, Fanon volunteered to fight in Europe in 1944 during World War II. Afterward, he remained in France, where he became interested in the philosophy of existentialist writer Jean-Paul Sartre. He qualified as a psychiatrist in 1951 and became interested in the psychology of racism, the subject of his first book, *Black Skin, White Masks*. Shortly afterward, he traveled to the French colony of ALGERIA, where he viewed the Algerian war for independence (1954–1962) as an intertwining of racism and violence. In 1956, Fanon joined the Front de Libération Nationale (FLN) and moved to Tunis to promote FLN interests. He was injured when his car hit a land mine in 1959.

Fanon argued that only those with nothing to lose could be the true instruments of social revolution, since they alone were not corrupted by Western materialism. All others, he believed, benefited from racism and economic colonialism. His great gifts as a writer, which come across even in translation, gave his social theories compelling force and helped make his last and best-known book, *The Wretched of the Earth*, highly influential in Third World political movements.

Fante

Akan group who established a series of small states along the West African coast between the Pra and Volta Rivers in the late 17th century. A few years later they formed a league with a representative parliament headed by the ruler of Mankessim, which was designated the capital. The Fante acted both in response to population pressures and the growing power of the ASHANTI. Their role as middlemen in the trade with Europeans led to several wars with the Ashanti in which the Fante were aided by the British. In 1868, the Fante formed the Fante Confederation in an effort to create a single strong independent state. However, the British opposed this and in 1874 forced the Fante to become a part of the Gold Coast colony.

Farmer, James Leonard (1920–1999) *civil rights activist*

At age 14, Farmer entered Wiley College in Marshall, Texas. Later he earned a degree from Howard University, where he studied the teachings of Mahatma Gandhi. In 1942, he founded the CONGRESS OF RACIAL EQUALITY (CORE) to integrate restaurants and other public places, using direct action and civil disobedience. As the SIT-IN MOVEMENT took hold in the South in 1960, CORE was called in to provide training in nonviolent techniques.

In 1961, Farmer and his staff decided to attain integration on interstate buses through Freedom Rides, on which integrated groups of volunteers rode buses through the South and refused to accept separate seating or separate facilities in bus

James Farmer, executive director of CORE (Congress for Racial Equity), in a police wagon, following his arrest at a demonstration at the World's Fair, New York City, 1964 (*Archive Photos*)

terminals. The FREEDOM RIDERS met with substantial violence, and Farmer himself narrowly missed attack when the death of his father caused him to discontinue a trip into Alabama, where the freedom riders were viciously assaulted.

In addition to promoting freedom rides, CORE became deeply involved in the Mississippi Freedom Summer Project promoting voter registration. It was during this voter registration drive that three CORE members, JAMES CHANEY, Michael Schwerner, and Andrew Goodman, were murdered in 1964 (see PHILADELPHIA, MISSISSIPPI, MURDERS).

Farmer resigned as national director of CORE in 1966. He later ran for Congress and served in the Nixon administration and taught at Mary Washington College.

In 1998, he was awarded the Presidential Medal of Freedom, the nation's highest civilian award. He died in 1999. His autobiography is *Lay Bare the Heart.*

Farrakhan, Louis Abdul (Louis Eugene Walcott)

(1933–) *minister and leader of the Nation of Islam*
Originally named Louis Eugene Walcott, Farrakhan was raised in Boston, where he attended integrated schools and was a member of the Episcopal Church. As a young man, he studied at Winston-Salem Teachers College in North Carolina, and worked as a calypso singer. A gifted violinist, he appeared on TV's *Ted Mack's Original Amateur Hour* in 1949.

At the urging of MALCOLM X, Farrakhan joined the NATION OF ISLAM in 1955 and changed his name to Louis X. At that time, Malcolm X was leader of Temple No. 11 in Boston. Farrakhan became his assistant and took his place when Malcolm left to take over Temple No. 7 in Harlem. He became head of the Harlem mosque when Malcolm was removed from the post. When Malcolm X left the Nation of Islam, Farrakhan denounced him bitterly and later accepted responsibility for helping create the climate that led to Malcolm's murder. After Nation of Islam leader ELIJAH MUHAMMAD died in 1975, the Nation split into two camps, one of which was headed by Louis Farrakhan.

Nation of Islam leader Louis Farrakhan gestures with his hand during a speech delivered at Howard University, Washington, D.C., September 19, 1995. (*Reuters/Ron Thomas/Archive Photos*)

Over the years, Farrakhan built a reputation as a powerful and articulate speaker. He also ran into severe criticism for his frequent expressions of hostility toward whites and Jews. His religious philosophy includes aspects of numerology, Muslim mysticism, and Masonic symbolism. Under Farrakhan's direction, the Nation of Islam continued its efforts to develop black economic independence through its business ventures in publishing, restaurants, real estate, and the Fruit of Islam security force. He departed from the Nation of Islam's former antipolitical stance and registered to vote, throwing his support behind JESSE JACKSON'S 1984 presidential campaign. Farrakhan's leadership of the hugely successful 1995 MILLION MAN MARCH catapulted him to national prominence.

Fifteenth Amendment   See RECONSTRUCTION AMENDMENTS.

Fifty-fourth Massachusetts Regiment

Civil War all-black volunteer regiment. Organized in 1863, the Fifty-fourth was sent to Georgia's Sea Islands, where it was limited to raiding rebel towns for the purpose of demoralizing the civilian population. Thinking this dishonorable work for soldiers, the Fifty-fourth's commander, Col. Robert Gould

Fifty-fourth Massachusetts Regiment storming Fort Wagner, South Carolina, July 18, 1863 (*Library of Congress*)

Shaw, asked that the regiment be deployed against regular military targets. In July 1863, the Fifty-fourth received orders to charge Fort Wagner, a Confederate installation on Morris Island near Charleston, South Carolina. The Fifty-fourth attacked on July 18, immediately following a day-long forced march. Overwhelming artillery fire resulted in a 40 percent casualty rate, including Colonel Shaw, who was killed. Sgt. William Carney, who picked up the regimental colors and tried to rally the troops despite his own wounds, was later awarded the Congressional Medal of Honor—the first African-American soldier to receive this highest U.S. decoration. Although the Fifty-fourth Massachusetts was an all-black unit, its officers, including Colonel Shaw, were white, as it was believed that black men lacked the ability to command.

The fact that black soldiers were paid less than whites caused the men of the Fifty-fourth to refuse all pay as a protest; the situation was not corrected by Congress until 1864. The story of the Fifty-fourth Massachusetts was depicted in the 1989 movie *Glory*, whose script was based on the letters of Colonel Shaw and on two books: *One Gallant Rush* (Peter Burchard) and *Lay This Laurel* (Lincoln Kirstein).

Fisk Jubilee Singers

Originally, a group of nine young singers and a pianist who began training in 1866 under the leadership of a FREEDMEN'S BUREAU official named George White. Eight were former slaves. In 1871, the group, singing spirituals learned in slavery, began touring the United States and Europe in an effort to save Fisk School in Nashville, Tennessee. They raised $25,000, which was used to pay debts owed by Fisk School and to buy the land on which Fisk University would be situated. The next year, the singers were invited to perform before President Grant, and while touring England in 1873–74, they sang before Queen Victoria, who commissioned a life-size portrait of the group. The money raised on these and subsequent tours was used to establish Fisk University. The Fisk Jubilee Singers, who still exist as a musical group, were the first to popularize spirituals among whites.

Fisk Jubilee Singers (*Fisk University Library, Special Collections*)

Fitzgerald, Ella (1918–1996) *singer*

Known as the First Lady of JAZZ, Ella Fitzgerald got her start when she won the amateur contest at Harlem's Apollo Theater in 1934. Her prize was an opportunity to work with William "Chick" Webb's Orchestra. Webb asked her to join his group, which she took over after he died in 1939. Three years later, she began working with other groups and toured with Norman Granz's *Jazz at the Philharmonic*. In 1956, she signed with Verve Records, recording songs by Johnny Mercer, Rodgers and Hart, and George and Ira Gershwin. Famous for her scat singing, melodic improvisation, and musical flexibility fusing jazz and pop, Ella Fitzgerald worked with musicians such as Oscar Peterson, DUKE ELLINGTON, LOUIS ARMSTRONG, and Count BASIE.

Recommended Listening: *The Duke Ellington Songbook* (Verve Records); *From Spirituals to Swing* (Vanguard).

Fon

Tribal group whose ancestors, together with the Adjas to whom they are closely related, founded the

17th-century kingdom of DAHOMEY in present-day BENIN. Dahomey was established to provide protection from slave raiders and from Yoruba control, and it had a strong military tradition. As a result, the Fon were regarded as fierce warriors before being defeated by the French in 1893. Though some have been converted to Christianity, many Fon continue to practice traditional African religions.

Fort Negro

A fort on the Apalachicola River in Florida, about 60 miles from the Georgia border. The stockade had been built by the British. It acquired the name Fort Negro after the British withdrew following the War of 1812, and the stockade was taken over by about 300 runaway slaves and 30 Seminole Indians who used it as a base to raid Georgia plantations. After numerous complaints from slaveholders, Andrew Jackson sent a U.S. army force to destroy the fort, even though it was located in Spanish territory. After a 10-day siege, the runaway slaves, who were led by a man named Garcia, were forced to surrender when a heated cannon ball scored a direct hit on the fort's ammunition supply, causing a huge explosion and killing or wounding more than 250 of the fort's defenders. Garcia was shot by a firing squad, and the remaining 63 survivors were returned to slavery. The July 27, 1816, attack on Fort Negro marked the beginning of the Seminole Wars, which were to stretch over 40 years and cost the U.S. government more than 30 million dollars.

Fort Pillow

Tennessee fort that, on April 12, 1864, was the site of a massacre of black Union soldiers by Confederate troops led by General Nathan Bedford Forrest. The Union garrison was composed of 577 men, of whom 262 were African American. Though the official report stated that 300 Union soldiers had been murdered after they had surrendered, it is believed that the actual total was closer to 200. The majority of these were African Americans, who were slaughtered amid cries of "Kill them, God damn them; it is General Forrest's orders." Eyewitnesses stated that Confederate soldiers deliberately murdered scores of unarmed men, some of whom were on their knees, asking for mercy. There were also numerous— though disputed—reports of wounded soldiers being shot and of others being burned or buried alive. Forrest himself bragged that the Mississippi River "was dyed with the blood of the slaughtered for 200 yards." Six days after the fall of Fort Pillow, the First Kansas Colored regiment lost 117 dead and 65 wounded at the battle of Poison Spring in Arkansas. Again, Confederate troops murdered wounded soldiers and those attempting to surrender. The Second Kansas Colored Regiment took revenge for their sister unit on April 30, at the battle of Jenkins Ferry. Over 150 Confederate troops were killed or mortally wounded; Second Kansas Colored suffered 15 killed and 55 wounded. In response to the Fort Pillow and Poison Spring massacres, African-American soldiers fought furiously, often refusing to take prisoners or to submit to surrender themselves. General Forrest became Grand Wizard of the KU KLUX KLAN after the war.

Forten, James (1766–1842) *abolitionist, businessman*

Born free in Philadelphia, Forten enlisted as a powder boy on the ship *Royal Louis*, during the American Revolution. He became a prisoner of war (POW) when the *Royal Louis* was captured by the British ship *Amphyon*. Though the British usually sold black POWs as slaves in the West Indies, Forten was spared when he became friendly with the teenage son of the captain of the *Amphyon*. Instead of being sold, Forten was transferred to the prison ship *Jersey*, where the boy spent seven months under conditions so bad that several thousand other American prisoners died there during the course of the war. When he was finally freed, Forten returned to Philadelphia, where he became an apprentice to Robert Bridges, a sail maker. After Bridges retired, Forten took over the business and eventually became quite wealthy. An active abolitionist, Forten was a major contributor to William Lloyd Garrison's *Liberator* and an opponent of proposals to resettle African Americans abroad. He supported women's rights and was founder and president of the American Moral Reform Society, a group of African-American men active in promoting education, temperance, and the abolition of slavery.

40 acres and a mule

Slogan that originated as a result of U.S. Army general William T. Sherman's Special Field Order #15 (January 16, 1865) providing that every ex-slave family receive 40 acres of farmland. Former slaves were later lent army mules to facilitate plowing.

Fourteenth Amendment   See RECONSTRUCTION AMENDMENTS.

Franklin, Aretha (1942–) *singer*

Aretha Franklin grew up singing GOSPEL at the New Bethel Baptist Church in Detroit, where her father was pastor. She left home at age 18 to begin a singing career but found only limited success until she signed with Atlantic Records in 1966 and released "I Ain't Never Loved a Man (the Way I Love You)." This was followed by a string of hits, includ-

Close-up of vocalist Aretha Franklin, "Queen of Soul" (*Frank Driggs/Archive Photos*)

ing "Respect" and "Chain of Fools." She is noted for her powerful delivery and control, an extensive voice range, and her ability to create a searing emotional climate. In 1987, Aretha Franklin became the first woman inducted into the Rock and Roll Hall of Fame.

Recommended Listening: *Aretha* (Arista); *One Lord, One Faith, One Baptism* (Arista).

Franklin, John Hope (1915–) *historian, educator, author*

Franklin graduated from Fisk University in 1935 and obtained a master's degree (1936) and Ph.D. (1941) from Harvard. He taught history at Fisk, Howard, and Duke Universities, St. Augustine's College, North Carolina Central University at Durham, and the University of Chicago. He has also been a visiting professor at Harvard, Cornell, Wisconsin, the University of California, and Cambridge University in England. His careful, scholarly, yet very readable books have provided thousands of students with enormous insight into American and African-American history. His most famous work is the authoritative *From Slavery to Freedom: A History of Negro Americans*, first published in 1947. Other books include *Reconstruction After the Civil War; A Southern Odyssey: Travelers in the Antebellum North; The Free Negro in North Carolina, 1790–1860; The Militant South, 1800–1860; The Emancipation Proclamation; Racial Equality in America; Race and History: Selected Essays;* and *George Washington Williams*. In 1997, Franklin was appointed chair of President Bill Clinton's advisory board on race relations.

Frazier, E. Franklin (1894–1962) *sociologist, educator*

After graduating with honors from Howard University, Frazier received a master of arts degree from Clark University and a Ph.D. from the University of Chicago, where he first began his formal study of the African-American family. He then taught at a number of universities, including Morehouse, Fisk, Johns Hopkins, and Howard. One of his early essays, a 1927 article titled "The Pathology of Race

Prejudice," provoked such a negative reaction from the white community in Atlanta that he was forced to leave the city. In 1939, he published *The Negro Family in the United States,* a groundbreaking study on black families moving from the rural South to the urban North. In 1957, Frazier published his most controversial work, *The Black Bourgeoisie,* a study that criticized the values of the black middle class as too materialistic. Frazier stressed the need to replace the old sociological theories that invoked genetic rather than social factors to explain African-American problems and served to encourage prejudice. In 1948, Frazier became the first African American to head the American Sociological Society.

Freedman's Savings and Trust Company

Bank established by Congress in 1865 for the benefit of ex-slaves. The bank's headquarters was in New York, though all but two branches were in the South. Most accounts held less than $50, but in thousands of cases, this represented the total lifesavings of the former slaves. Unfortunately, the bank's directors speculated heavily in real estate and made unsecured loans to numerous companies. The Panic of 1873 caused many of these companies to default, resulting in a run on the bank. In an effort to save the bank, FREDERICK DOUGLASS was persuaded to take over its presidency. Though he invested $10,000 of his own money, it was too late, and the Freedman's Bank closed on June 28, 1874. The bank was a private corporation, but it had often shared office space with the Freedmen's Bureau, and most people were led to believe that it was backed by the federal government. Congress refused to reimburse the thousands who had lost their savings, although eventually about half the depositors received some money back, thanks in part to the efforts of Senator BLANCHE BRUCE. The failure of the Freedman's Bank destroyed black confidence in banks for years to come.

Freedmen's Bureau

Federal agency set up near the end of the Civil War to assist the 4,000,000 newly freed slaves making the transition from bondage to freedom. The full title of the agency was the Bureau of Refugees, Freedmen and Abandoned Lands. One of the most idealistic and far-reaching programs ever attempted by the federal government, the bureau was established in March 1865 under the administration of General Oliver Howard. It was conceived as a temporary agency, lasting one year, that would provide protection for former slaves, help them find jobs and homes, care for orphans and the aged, distribute relief to blacks and whites alike, devise fair labor contracts, set up a court system for cases involving African Americans, and establish schools and hospitals. Knowing they would not receive a fair hearing in Southern state courts, African Americans by the thousands turned to bureau tribunals for justice, particularly in contract disputes with whites. By 1867, however, many bureau courts had been disbanded in the belief that state courts would exercise equal justice regardless of race. General Howard made a strong effort to establish thousands of free blacks on abandoned lands under the bureau's jurisdiction but was thwarted by President Andrew Johnson's order to return such lands to their original owners. The Freedmen's Bureau had its strongest impact in the area of education. In five years, it spent $5,000,000 building 4,329 schools and hiring 10,000 teachers. More than 247,333 African Americans were able to take advantage of these educational opportunities. A bill extending the bureau's life and expanding its powers was passed over President Andrew Johnson's veto in 1866. Except for some of its educational programs, the Freedmen's Bureau was dismantled in 1869, since it was believed African Americans could fend for themselves, having gained voting rights under the Reconstruction Act of 1867.

freedom riders

Civil rights activists who attempted to force the integration of interstate buses and bus terminals. Although the Supreme Court in 1946 and 1960 had ruled that segregation was illegal on interstate buses and the terminals that served them, in much of the South, African Americans were still forced to use separate waiting rooms, ticket counters, and rest rooms. They were required to sit in the back of the bus and were forced to stand if all the back seats were taken—even if there were empty seats in the front.

On May 4, 1961, 13 members of the CONGRESS OF RACIAL EQUALITY (CORE), seven black and six white, left Washington, D.C., on two buses on their way south. In Anniston, Alabama, they were met by a white mob that slashed the tires of one bus, set the vehicle aflame, and at first refused to let the freedom riders off. The driver of the other bus allowed hoodlums to board the bus and beat the freedom riders with chains and baseball bats. After continuing on to Birmingham, the riders were again attacked, with the blessing of Public Safety Commissioner Eugene "Bull" Conner, who deliberately prevented the city police from protecting them.

The original freedom riders were forced to stop, but volunteers from the STUDENT NON-VIOLENT COORDINATING COMMITTEE (SNCC) decided to continue the freedom ride into Montgomery, where they were brutally attacked after arriving there on May 20. A protest rally at the First Baptist Church was planned in response, and MARTIN LUTHER KING JR. flew to Montgomery to address the meeting. U.S. Attorney General Robert Kennedy had received promises from Alabama governor John Patterson that the students would be protected. Infuriated by the violence, Kennedy ordered 600 federal marshals into Montgomery to protect the freedom riders. A mob gathered outside the church where King and the others were meeting. The marshals stepped in, but the situation remained extremely dangerous. Sometime after midnight, Governor Patterson ordered the National Guard under Gen. Henry Graham to the church to support the marshals. In a telephone conversation with Kennedy, however, Patterson said that Graham couldn't guarantee Dr. King's safety. "Have the general call me," said Kennedy angrily. "I want him to say it to me. I want to hear a general of the U.S. Army say he can't protect Martin Luther King." The guard and the marshals finally dispersed the mob, and the civil rights activists were able to leave in safety.

The freedom rides continued throughout the summer and resulted in the arrests of hundreds of volunteers on charges of trespassing and disorderly conduct. On December 1, 1961, the Interstate Commerce Commission banned racial discrimination in interstate travel.

Freeman, Elizabeth (Mum Bett or Mumbet)
(ca. 1742–1829) *slave*

Elizabeth Freeman's lawsuit helped bring an end to slavery in Massachusetts. Freeman and her sister were slaves owned by Col. John Ashley of Massachusetts. Though information is limited regarding her early life, it is known that Ashley's wife once became angry and attempted to hit Elizabeth's sister with a shovel. Elizabeth Freeman jumped to her sister's defense and was hit instead. The resulting injury left a permanent scar. After the adoption of a new state constitution in Massachusetts in 1780, Freeman left the Ashley household and convinced a young white lawyer named Theodore Sedgwick to represent her in an attempt to gain her freedom. Her case was heard by the County Court in Great Barrington, Massachusetts, in 1781. There she argued that slavery was illegal in Massachusetts under the new state constitution. The jury agreed, and Colonel Ashley was ordered to pay her 30 shillings in damages. After her victory, Freeman went to work for the Sedgwick family.

French West African Federation

A federation formed in 1904 that included five and later eight French colonies or territories. These were GUINEA, IVORY COAST, SENEGAL, MAURITANIA, Niger, Soudan (Mali), Upper Volta (BURKINA FASO), and DAHOMEY (BENIN). The federation is generally known as French West Africa (F.W.A.). It covered an area of 1,831,272 square miles. It was administered by French officials along with a small number of Africans who, because of their education, outlook, and position, were considered "black Frenchmen." The judicial system was divided between French and native law, with most people under the jurisdiction of native courts. Though the French outlawed slavery, they instituted a brutal forced labor system that was bitterly resented. The forced labor fell into three categories. The main one involved work on public service projects, and African men were required to work on these for a given number of days each year without pay. Another was military service, though much of this involved working on railroad construction. The third type of forced labor involved prisoners, many of whom had been jailed for minor offenses. In 1958, the people of the territories were asked to vote on whether or not they wanted to remain affiliated with France in a Franco-African community. Guinea voted no, and became independent. The others voted yes and remained closely tied to France economically and politically until they gained total independence by 1960.

Fugitive Slave Law

Part of the Compromise of 1850. In return for allowing California to enter the Union as a free state, northern congressmen agreed to pass a tough Fugitive Slave Law that provided for six months imprisonment and a $1,000 fine for anyone found guilty of helping a slave to escape, and required northern law officials to assist in the recapture of runaways. Prior to the law's passage, the recapture of escaped slaves was up to masters and bounty hunters. The new law created tremendous resentment, especially since eight years earlier, the Supreme Court had ruled that state officials did not have to assist in the return of fugitive slaves.

Fugitive Slave Law poster (*Library of Congress*)

Fulani (Foo-LAHN-ee) (Foulas, Foulbe)

A West African tribe living mainly in GUINEA, NIGERIA, and CAMEROON. A tall, light-skinned people, they are a branch of the Peul tribe. Some authorities believe they migrated to West Africa from Egypt many centuries ago, but others think they are related to the MAASAI of East Africa. Still others think the Fulani are the descendants of the early rock-painting people of the Sahara. In 1203, under their leader Sumanguru, they seized Kumbi Saleh, the capital of the medieval empire of Ghana, but were later defeated by MANDINKA armies under the command of SUNDIATA KEITA. During the 18th century, the Fulani waged successful jihads—Islamic holy wars—in Fouta Djalon in what is now Guinea and Fouta Toro in Senegal, where new Fulani states were established under Islamic law. Soon after, in the early 19th century, a charismatic Fulani religious leader named Usman dan Fodio called for a jihad against the leaders in several Hausa states. He and his followers conquered Kebbi in 1805, Zaria in 1806, Kano and Katsina in 1807, and Gobir in 1808. Usman died in 1817, and the Islamic empire he had established—the SOKOTO CALIPHATE—was taken over by his brother. By 1837, the Sokoto Caliphate was the largest state in West Africa with a population of over 10 million people. Today, the Fulani live as farmers and cattle herders. The women are noted for their elaborate hairdos and large, gold earrings.

Fuller, Charles (1939–   ) *playwright*

Fuller became interested in the theater as a teenager when he saw a Yiddish play in Philadelphia. In 1974, New York's famous Negro Ensemble Company produced his *In the Deepest Part of Sleep*. Two years later, Fuller wrote *The Brownsville Raid*, about the BROWNSVILLE, TEXAS, AFFAIR, an event that resulted in the dishonorable discharge of 167 African-American soldiers after nine had been involved in a shooting incident in Brownsville, Texas. In 1980, Fuller wrote a moving play about contemporary street violence called *Zooman and the Sign*. It won two Obie awards and was later made into the movie *Zooman*. His drama *A Soldier's Play*, a 1982 Pulitzer Prize winner, dealt with racial self-hatred and murder on a World War II army base. Two years later, it was released as

Meta Warrick Fuller's Talking Skull, 1937 (*Museum of Afro American History, Boston, Massachusetts*)

the critically acclaimed film *A Soldier's Story*. Other plays include *Sally, Prince Under the Umbrella, We,* and *Jonquiel*. Fuller is a cofounder of the Afro-American Arts Theatre in Philadelphia.

Fuller, Meta Vaux Warrick (1877–1968)
sculptor

After graduating from the Pennsylvania Museum School for the Industrial Arts, Fuller studied in France, where she attracted the attention of sculptor Auguste Rodin. Her preoccupation with the grotesque and her utilization of grim imagery caused the French press to nickname her "the delicate sculptor of horrors." After returning to the

United States in 1902, she focused more on African-American subjects.

A warehouse fire in 1910 destroyed much of her work, but in 1913 she created an eight-foot-tall piece called *Spirit of Emancipation*. Other works included two antilynching pieces and the 1921 *Ethiopia Awakening*, which illustrated her concern that black Americans recognize their inherent connection with Africa. This work creates a dark, moody effect while effectively capturing the emergence of a vital, thriving Africa after centuries of oppression. Forty-two years later, Fuller sculpted *The Crucifixion* in memory of the four young girls killed in the 1963 Birmingham church bombing. Another work, *The Good Shepard,* honored the clergymen who marched with Martin Luther King Jr. in Selma, Alabama (see VOTING RIGHTS STRUGGLE).

Though Meta Fuller's work reflected the realistic influences of the French sculpture of the late 19th century, the overall effect was an expressionistic one. She was among the first to address the condition of the African American, predating the concepts of Pan-Africanism explored by ALAIN LOCKE.

G

Gabon, Republic of

West African country situated on the equator. Portuguese explorers first explored Gabon's coast in the 15th century, and the area later became a major slave-trading center supplying French, Dutch, and British ships. France officially outlawed slavery in 1848, signed treaties with local Gabonese chiefs, and began to export ivory, sandalwood, gum, rubber, and ebony. In 1849, the French freed 53 captives from a slave ship bound for Senegal, and the ex-slaves established Libreville, now Gabon's capital. The area became attractive to American and French missionaries, though there was little exploration of the interior because of the extensive rain forests, which are still largely intact. In 1910, Gabon (then known as French Congo), along with Chad, Middle Congo (now Republic of Congo) and Ubangi-Shari (now Central African Republic), was incorporated into French Equatorial Africa. Though the French ended slavery, they instituted a forced labor system involving private French companies, which led to several unsuccessful revolts.

In 1913, Lambarene, an island in Gabon's Ogooue River, became the site of Dr. Albert Schweitzer's hospital. Care was provided to anyone free of charge in return for help with work around the hospital. Schweitzer was awarded the Nobel Peace Prize in 1952 for his work there.

Gabon attained its independence in 1960, under Leon M'Ba, who became its first president until he was ousted in a coup in 1964. He was succeeded by Albert-Bernard Bongo, who, with the help of French mercenaries, established a one-party state. (After converting to Islam, he changed his name to El Hadj Omar Bongo.)

After riots broke out in 1989, opposition parties were legalized in 1990. Elections were held in 1993 but the losing (opposition) candidate refused to accept the result. More rioting in 1994 led to the establishment of a coalition government.

Revenues from oil have made Gabon relatively well-off, though much money has gone into the construction of the Transgabonais Railroad. Among Gabon's population groups are PYGMIES and various BANTU peoples, the largest being the Fang, who are noted for their beautiful wood carvings.

Gaines, Ernest J. (1933–) *writer*

Ernest Gaines was born on a plantation in Louisiana, where, as a child, he once worked in the fields for 50 cents a day. His best-known book is *The Autobiography of Miss Jane Pittman* (1971), a novel presented as the tape-recorded reminiscing of a woman who was born into slavery and who lived to take part in the great Civil Rights movement of the 1960s. It was later made into a TV movie with Cicely Tyson. Other works include *Catherine Carmier, Of Love and Dust, Bloodline, In My Father's House, A Gathering of Old Men,* and *A Lesson Before Dying.* He is currently a writer-in-residence at the University of Southwestern Louisiana.

The Gambia, Republic of

West African country. The area was visited by Hanno, the great Carthaginian admiral who arrived in the region around 500 B.C. The country is dominated by the Gambia River, which was used to transport slaves and other goods. Growing trade encouraged the spread of Islam, which remains the dominant religion in the area. Most of the people are MANDINKA, WOLOF, or FULANI. The first Europeans to arrive were the Portuguese, who explored the mouth of the Gambia River in 1465. The British built Fort James there in 1661 to facilitate the slave trade. Control of the fort changed hands numerous times, though the British acquired all rights to Gambia in 1783, at least as far as the European powers were concerned. After the British abolished the slave trade in 1807, they based antislaving patrol ships at the mouth of the Gambia River, leased Banjul Island from a local chief, and founded the town of Bathhurst, which would later become Banjul, the capital. In 1888, Gambia was made a British crown colony.

In 1959, the People's Progressive Party was founded by Dawda Jawara. Six years later, the country became independent with Jawara as president, and Gambia formally changed its name to The Gambia. In 1981, a coup was attempted but was put down with help from Senegal, and the two countries formed the federation of Senegambia a year later. It was dissolved in 1989. After a military coup in 1994, all political parties were banned. In 1996, Gambians voted to return to democratic government. The leader of the coup, Yahya Jammeh, was elected president, although there were serious allegations that the election was characterized by fraud and violence.

The Gambia is the site of Alex Haley's ancestral village, Juffure, which he described in *Roots* and which is a major tourist attraction. Also of interest are the Senegambian Stone Circles located 150 to 300 miles up the Gambia River. Consisting of 40 clusters of 10 to 24 large cylindrical boulders, each rock approximately 9 feet tall and over 3 feet in diameter, these groupings are at least 1,200 years old and may have served as burial sites for a lost civilization. Similar Stone Circles are found in Senegal and Guinea.

Gao

West African city, once a major trading center and destination point for caravans crossing the Sahara. It is located on the Niger River southeast of Timbuktu. One tradition says Gao was established by Serko tribesmen sometime after A.D. 800. It was captured in A.D. 1010 by Kossoi, a TUAREG king, who established Gao as capital of the Empire of Songhai. Leo Africanus, writing in the 15th century, described Gao as a city to which "blacks come . . . bringing quantities of gold with which to purchase goods imported from the Berber country and from Europe, but they never find enough goods on which to spend all their gold and always take half or two-thirds of it home." This was also the report of the scholar Mahmud al-Kati, who stated that gold was so plentiful in Gao that African traders were "frequently forced to return with their gold because there was too much available at the time." Gao was captured by Moroccan armies in 1591 and lost much of its wealth and influence. It is now part of the modern country of MALI.

Garcia, Jose Mauricio Nunes (1767–1830)
Brazilian composer and conductor

The son of a Portuguese lieutenant and a woman of Guinean descent, Garcia is generally known in Brazil as Jose Mauricio (the Moor). By age 17, he was active with the Brotherhood of St. Cecilia, the most important group of professional musicians in Rio de Janiero. Ordained a priest in 1792, he became musical director of Rio's cathedral six years later.

Garcia mainly composed sacred works in 18th-century European classical style. In 1808, King John VI of Portugal moved his royal court to Brazil to escape an invasion by France. Garcia was appointed court composer, and in that capacity, he both composed music for the royal chapel and displayed his exceptional improvisational skills at the keyboard during aristocrats' parties.

In 1816, Garcia led an orchestra and chorus in what is considered his masterpiece, a requiem mass for the funeral of Queen Maria I. *Grove's Dictionary of Music* calls this "one of the most successful masses ever written in the Americas." For almost 30 years, Garcia also offered instruction, without charge, to many young musicians. One of his students, Francisco Manoel de Silva, later composed Brazil's national hymn.

Garifunas (Garinagus, Black Caribs)

Tribal group in Belize made up of descendants of African survivors from a slave ship wrecked off the Caribbean island of St. Vincent in 1675. The Africans intermarried with Carib and Arawak Indians and developed a distinct culture drawing on both African and Indian traditions. British troops occupied St. Vincent in 1763, and, after a failed Garifuna uprising in 1796, deported the community to the island of Roatan off Honduras. The Garifunas migrated from there to islands off what is now Belize, where they established isolated villages, accessible only by boat. Their language is derived from a mix of African, Carib, and Arawak words, and their music shows the influence of African-style drum rhythm patterns. Settlement Day, a national holiday throughout Belize, commemorates the landing of 200 Garifunas there in 1832. Today, Garifunas live by fishing, farming, and trading, although many have moved to more urban areas.

Garnet, Henry Highland (1815–1882)
abolitionist, minister, diplomat

Born a slave in Kent County, Maryland, Garnet escaped at age nine with his father and fled to New York City. There he attended African Free School #1 and later became a minister. Tall and possessed of a commanding manner, Garnet was known as the Thomas Paine of the abolitionist movement. At the National Negro Convention of 1843, he delivered his famous Call to Rebellion speech, in which he demanded an end to slavery through a slave strike and, if necessary, through armed rebellion. His words, "Brethren, arise, arise! Strike for your lives and liberties. Rather die freemen than live to be slaves. Let your motto be resistance! Resistance! Resistance!" shocked the more conservative black community. He also spoke out on the need for a national black press, strong black organizations,

and a free and independent Africa. Unlike many black leaders, Garnet supported black colonization of Africa. In response to criticism, he argued that black settlers in Africa could plant cotton and provide competition to plantations in the United States. After the Civil War, he worked with the FREEDMEN'S BUREAU. Twelve days after Congress passed the Thirteenth Amendment to the Constitution outlawing slavery, Henry Highland Garnet became the first black man ever invited to speak in the U.S. capital when he delivered a sermon to senators and congressmen. "We ask no special favors," he said, "but we plead for justice . . . in the name of God, the Universal Father, we demand the right to live, and labor, and to enjoy the fruits of our toil." Garnet continued to work for black equality as well as for land reform, women's rights, and world peace. In 1881, he was appointed consul-general and minister to Liberia. He died shortly afterward and is buried there.

Garvey, Marcus (1887–1940) *black nationalist leader*

Marcus Garvey was born in Jamaica, where he was forced to leave school at age 14 because of poverty. He became a printer but was fired after helping organize a strike. Leaving Jamaica, he worked in Costa Rica and Panama before traveling to London, where he became interested in African independence. Upon his return to Jamaica, Garvey established the Universal Negro Improvement and Conservation Association and African Communities League (generally referred to as UNIA) on August 1, 1914. Its purpose was to unite the black peoples of the world.

Two years later, he left to seek support for his organization in the United States. In 1918, Garvey began publication of the *Negro World,* which rapidly became one of the most popular African-American newspapers in the United States. This was followed by the establishment of the Black Star Line steamship company, the Negro Factories Corporation, the African Legion, the Black Cross Nurses, and the Black Eagle Flying Corps. Money was raised through the sale of stock to African Americans at $5.00 a share.

Marcus Garvey, New York, 1926 (*Library of Congress*)

In 1920, Garvey staged a month-long convention in Harlem that was attended by thousands of black people from all over the world. The delegates voted to create a free African republic with Garvey as president, and Garvey sent a delegation to Liberia to determine the possibility of establishing UNIA projects there. Pressure from the British and the French caused Liberia to expel the UNIA delegation, and the failure of the Black Star Line resulted in Garvey's indictment for mail fraud in connection with the sale of Black Star stock. In 1923, he was convicted, fined $1,000, and sentenced to five years in prison. Court appeals failed, and he entered Atlanta Penitentiary in 1925. In 1927, his sentence was commuted by President Calvin Coolidge, and Garvey was deported to Jamaica. His popularity among African Americans remained high, but his absence, combined with the coming of the Great Depression, made it impossible for him to revive his movement. In 1935, Garvey moved to London, where he died. He is notable for creating the first black nationalist mass movement in the United States.

Gates, Henry Louis, Jr. (1950–) *scholar, educator, author*

Gates was raised in a small segregated town in West Virginia called Piedmont. He graduated from Yale University in 1973 and received an M.A. (1974) and Ph.D. degree (1979) in English languages and literature from the University of Cambridge. He taught English literature and Afro-American studies at Yale from 1975 to 1985, and at Cornell University from 1985 to 1990. In 1991, he joined the faculty at Harvard, where he became director of the W. E. B. DuBois Institute for Afro-American research and chairman of the Afro-American Studies Department. In 1983, he arranged for the republication of Harriet Wilson's 1859 book *Our Nig,* the earliest novel by an African American. He had found an original copy two years earlier in a rare-book store and bought it for $50. In the process, he proved that Wilson was black, a fact that had been in question. He has written several books, including *Thirteen Ways of Looking at a Black Man* (1997), *Colored People: A Memoir* (1994), *Loose Canons: Notes on the Culture Wars* (1992), *The Signifying Monkey: A Theory of Afro-American Literary Criticism* (1988), and *Figures in Black: Words, Signs & the 'Racial' Self* (1987). He collaborated with Cornel West on a book entitled *The Future of the Race* (1996), and was editor of the Norton Anthology of African-American Literature and the Oxford-Schomburg Library of Nineteenth Century Black Women Writers. Gates writes frequently for the *New Yorker* magazine and *The New York Times Book Review* and is the author of dozens of essays, reviews, and articles. He is the recipient of many awards, including a 1981 MacArthur Foundation "genius" grant. He and Kwame Anthony Appiah edit *Transitions* magazine, an international journal whose contributors include WOLE SOYINKA and Carlos Fuentes. In 1999, he hosted a three-part documentary, *Wonders of the African World,* for the Public Broadcasting Service. Professor Gates was one of the primary editors of *Africana: The Encyclopedia of the African and African American Experience,* published in 1999. He is considered one of the United States' leading intellectuals.

Gaye, Marvin (1939–1984) *singer, songwriter*

Born in Washington, D.C., Marvin Gaye began singing in church at the age of three. After serving in the U.S. Air Force, Gaye sang with the Marquees and the Moonglows, and he toured with Smokey Robinson as a backup singer. In 1960, he signed with Motown Records as a solo artist. After recording several hits as a solo vocalist, Gaye teamed with Mary Wells, and the two enjoyed several hits, including the 1965 best-selling album *How Sweet It Is (To Be Loved By You)*. In 1967, Gaye teamed with Tammi Terrell, and the two recorded a number of songs that regularly entered the top 20 on the charts. Unfortunately, Terrell died of a brain tumor soon afterward. In 1968, Gaye recorded one of his most famous songs, *I Heard It Through the Grapevine*, to be followed with *What's Going On; Mercy, Mercy, Me;* and *Inner City Blues*. His career slipped in the late 1970s and he left Motown, but in 1982, he had a huge hit in *Sexual Healing*. His private life, however, was increasingly plagued by financial, drug, and family problems. In 1984, Gaye was shot and killed by his father during an argument.

Recommended Reading: David Ritz. *Divided Soul: The Life of Marvin Gaye*. New York: DaCapo Press, 1991.

Ge'ez

Written language used in ancient AXUM. It was the ancestor of the modern Ethiopian languages Amharic, Tigre, and Tigrinya.

Ghana, Kingdom of

A medieval trading empire that arose in what is now eastern Mauritania and western Mali. The kingdom was founded in the fourth century by the BERBER tribe known as the Zenagas, whose use of camels had given them a major military advantage. By A.D. 700, medieval Ghana had grown rich from trade and had come under control of kings from the Soninke tribe. These kings controlled a network of lesser kings, who, in return for paying tribute, were allowed to conduct their own affairs without interference. According to the historian al-Bakri, gold was so plentiful in Ghana that the king's horse was hitched to a huge gold nugget weighing 40 pounds. Along with gold and salt, traders in Ghana sold horses, honey, jewelry, metalwork, slaves, and textiles.

The military was of crucial importance in protecting the trade caravans, and Ghana's army was well trained and well equipped. Every man was required to serve in the army for one month each year, and one king claimed the ability to field a force of up to 200,000 soldiers. The capital of the kingdom at Kumbi-Saleh (in what is now Mauritania) was divided into two sections and was inhabited by 15,000 to 20,000 people. The king and his court inhabited one section, which contained a palace and a number of buildings and was surrounded by a wall. The other section, which was situated about six miles away, was a gathering point for Muslim merchants. It contained 12 mosques that were staffed by salaried employees and students of the Koran. Though Islam had been introduced into Ghana by Muslim traders, the majority of the people were farmers who continued to practice ANIMIST religions. Because of this, and because of its wealth, Ghana came under attack from a Muslim group called the ALMORAVIDS, who were intent on spreading Islam as far as possible. They captured Kumbi-Saleh in 1076 and forced the king to become a Muslim. But their attention was focused primarily on Almoravid conquests in Morocco and Spain, and they soon lost control of the kingdom. However, the Almoravid attacks weakened Ghana, and MANDINKAS from the Kingdom of Mali attacked and destroyed Kumbi-Saleh in A.D. 1240. The area was hit by drought and famine, and the Kingdom of Ghana fell apart and disappeared in the 13th century.

Ghana, Republic of

West African country. Capital: Accra. Ghana, which was formerly Britain's Gold Coast colony, became independent in 1957 and took the name of the ancient kingdom of Ghana, although it is not located in the same area. KWAME NKRUMAH led Ghana's independence movement and became the country's first president. He established a socialist regime that was marked by extensive and expensive building projects, the jailing of political opponents, and a deteriorating economy. He was overthrown in 1966. After a succession of corrupt governments, a military coup was staged in 1979 under the leadership of Flight Lieutenant Jerry John Rawlings. Rawlings completely revised Ghana's economic structure, which resulted in a drop in inflation and expanded production. A new constitution providing for a multiparty system of government was approved in 1992. A year later, ethnic clashes killed over 1,000 people. Ghana is one of Africa's most densely populated countries, with most of the people of Akan descent. The country is noted for its KENTE CLOTH. Ghanian diplomat Kofi Annan became secretary general of the United Nations in 1997.

Gillespie, John Birks ("Dizzy") (1917–1993)
jazz musician

Dizzy Gillespie is closely associated with the development of bebop. Born in Cheraw, South Carolina, the youngest of nine children, Gillespie began playing the piano at the age of four and later received a music scholarship to Laurinburg Institute in North Carolina. He admired trumpet-player Roy Eldridge and copied his style, which enabled him to obtain a job with the Teddy Hill band after Eldridge left. In 1937, Gillespie made his first record. Eventually, he began to create his own style. In 1939, he joined the Cab Calloway orchestra but was fired two years later in a famous incident in which Gillespie nicked Calloway's buttock with a knife after Calloway accused him of throwing spitballs at him. The two men later reconciled. Afterward, Gillespie worked with numerous bands, including several of his own, and led State Department–sponsored tours to Latin America and the Middle East. In the process, Dizzy Gillespie put his own distinctive stamp on American diplomacy, inviting a snake charmer to play with him in Pakistan and refusing to play at the American Embassy in Turkey until a group of street children waiting outside the fence were allowed in to listen. Gillespie was very conscious of his black heritage and greatly admired PAUL ROBESON for refusing to be intimidated by racism. He also admired CHAR-

American musician and composer Dizzy Gillespie performing in Paris, France (*Archive Photos*)

LIE PARKER, crediting him with the birth of modern jazz. His autobiography is entitled *to BE or not to BOP.*

Recommended Listening: *Jazz at Massey Hall* (Fantasy/Original Jazz Classics).

Gilliam, Sam (1933–) *painter*

Born in Tupelo, Mississippi, Gilliam grew up in Louisville, Kentucky. His early work reflected his interest in constructivism, a style characterized by abstract and geometric designs and structural forms. He is noted for his "draped" paintings in which paint is applied to canvases that are hung, drapery-like, on iron rods. Important elements in his work include his sense of color and his willingness to experiment with new styles and concepts. His paintings are found in the permanent collections of over 45 museums, and he has had numerous one-man and group shows in major galleries around the country. Along with several other artists, Gilliam designed art for the Georgia Airport Terminal in Atlanta. Among his well-known creations are *Plantagenets Golden* and

Mazda. Gilliam has had exceptional individual success and has worked to improve the position of other African-American artists.

Giovanni, Nikki (1943–   ) *poet, teacher*

Noted originally for her militant poems, Nikki Giovanni is a best-selling writer who has received numerous awards. She has published close to 20 volumes, including *Black Feeling, Black Talk; Black Judgment; My House; The Women and The Men: Poems; Cotton Candy on a Rainy Day; Vacation Time, Sacred Cows . . . and Other Edibles;* and *Re-Creation.* Many of her poems appear in anthologies of African-American literature. She is a professor of English at Virginia Polytechnic University.

Gold Coast

Term once used to describe the coast of modern-day GHANA and the British colony established there. Portuguese traders first arrived in the area in the 15th century and began a trade involving the exchange of guns and other manufactured goods for gold. Other European nations were soon attracted to the area, and the rapidly expanding trade was a major factor in the later rise of the ASHANTI state. In 1637, the Dutch captured the Portuguese fortress São Jorge de Mina and renamed it ELMINA CASTLE. The British purchased Elmina in 1872 but became involved in a war with the powerful Ashanti state the following year that resulted in the burning of the Ashanti capital at Kumasi in 1874. The British again invaded the Ashanti realm in 1895 and declared a protectorate over the region in 1896. Four years later, after putting down another Ashanti uprising, the British established the Gold Coast colony. The British built railroads and encouraged the export of cocoa, timber, manganese, diamonds, and bauxite. Africans were included in the government as both appointed and elected representatives, but a growing independence movement under the leadership of KWAME NKRUMAH developed after World War II. In 1948, riots occurred when police fired on peaceful demonstrators protesting economic problems. Nkrumah was imprisoned in 1950, but was released after his Convention People's Party swept the elections in 1951. Six years later, in 1957, the Gold Coast colony became the independent country of Ghana.

Gordone, Charles (1925–1995) *playwright, actor*

Gordone was the first African American to receive a Pulitzer Prize for Drama, presented in 1970 for *No Place To Be Somebody.* Born in Cleveland, Ohio, he served in the U.S. Air Force before earning a B.A. degree from California State University–Chico. Moving to New York, Gordone appeared in several off-Broadway plays, winning an Obie award for best actor. His experiences in both symbolic and realist drama are reflected in *No Place To Be Somebody,* on which he worked for almost 10 years before it was staged in 1969 by Joseph Papp's Public Theatre. Set in a neighborhood bar, the play's characters share their dreams and illusions, sometimes in monologues reflecting the pain and absurdity of racial conflict. Gordone's other works include a pair of one-act plays, *Willy Bignigga* and *Chumpanzee* (1970), and *The Last Chord* (1976).

Gordy, Berry, Jr. (1929–   ) *businessman, songwriter, record producer*

Born in Detroit, Gordy began his career as a professional boxer and songwriter. In 1959, he borrowed $700, set up a recording studio in an apartment, and established Motown Records. In the next few years, he signed contracts with Smokey Robinson and the Miracles, the Supremes, the Temptations, Marvin Gaye, Stevie Wonder, and other groups who turned out hit after hit. Rather than sign established stars, Gordy sought out unknown artists and worked to develop their talent. He insisted on quality of production, with the result that by the 1970s, Motown sales exceeded 10 million dollars a year. By 1988, when the company was sold to MCA Records for $61 million, Motown was one of the most successful black-owned businesses in America, and the "Motown Sound" had become legendary in the music business.

His autobiography is titled *To Be Loved: The Music, The Magic, The Memories of Motown.*

Gorée (Île de Gorée)

Island off SENEGAL where the Dutch built a fort in 1617 to hold slaves. Its name, a corruption of the Dutch words *goede reede,* meaning "good harbor," refers to Gorée's location, which made it an excellent shipping point for the transatlantic slave trade. While awaiting transport to a slave ship, the captives were put to work breaking up rocks and unloading goods to be used for trade. The French gained control of the island in 1677, and unsuccessful slave revolts took place there in 1724 and 1755. Approximately 60,000 slaves passed through the dungeons of Gorée until the French, in 1815, outlawed the international slave trade—though slavery itself remained legal in French colonies until 1848.

gospel music

African-American religious music that grew out of the SPIRITUALS sung by slaves. Gospel singers expand on the original melodies of their songs with screams, moans, and shouts, in addition to regular interjected comments such as "Lord, have mercy." The music is also accompanied by clapping, dancing, and stomping. Early gospel songwriters include Charles Tindley, whose composition "I'll Overcome Someday" may have been the foundation for "We Shall Overcome," the anthem of the Civil Rights movement. Tindley also wrote "Stand By Me." In the 1930s, a blues pianist named Thomas A. Dorsey wrote what he called "Gospel Songs," in which he linked hymns and spirituals to blues and jazz. He also established the first gospel choir. Dorsey's work became extremely popular thanks in part to singers like MAHALIA JACKSON, who toured with him. Another singer, Rev. James Cleveland, who is known as the "Godfather of Gospel," founded the annual Gospel Music Workshop of America, which helped trigger the popularity of the gospel mass and community choirs. Gospel quartets, another critical element in gospel music, developed out of the male jubilee groups of the late 1800s, and gained enormous popularity with the availability of phonograph records. Many major recording artists got their start in gospel music, and many more have been influenced by it. Singers like Sam Cooke and Wilson Pickett began in gospel quartets. Famous Gospel performers include The Staple Singers, The Sensational Nightingales, ARETHA FRANKLIN, Shirley Caesar, Five Blind Boys of Mississippi, Blind Willie Johnson, The Mighty Clouds of Joy, Al Green, and The Winans.

grandfather clauses

Statutes enacted in a number of Southern states to prevent African Americans from voting. The first grandfather clause was a part of the Louisiana state constitution passed in 1898. It added to the permanent voter registration list the names of all men whose fathers and grandfathers had been qualified to vote on January 1, 1867, a time when only whites had the vote. The grandfather clause meant that thousands of illiterate white voters could be added to the registration rolls without having to pass the literacy requirement. Blacks, on the other hand, were often required to read and interpret—to the satisfaction of hostile registrars—complicated sections of the state constitution. Other states soon followed Louisiana's example. Grandfather clauses were declared unconstitutional by the Supreme Court in 1915 in cases involving Oklahoma and Maryland (*Guinn v. United States*). However, the Oklahoma legislature responded by passing a law automatically qualifying voters who had voted in 1914 (all of whom were white) and permanently disqualifying those (all blacks and a few whites) who failed to register within a 12-day period in 1916 between April 30 and May 11. The situation remained this way for the next 20 years until a black man named Robert Lane decided to sue. In 1939, the Supreme Court ruled the Oklahoma statute illegal.

See also POLL TAX; VOTING RIGHTS STRUGGLE; WHITE PRIMARIES.

Great Migration See NORTHERN MIGRATION.

Great Zimbabwe (Great Enclosure)

Archaeological site found in Zimbabwe. The broad-based stone ruins were once at the center of a large Shona community of perhaps 18,000 people. They

Great Zimbabwe (*National Museum of African Art, Washington, D.C.*)

were built sometime between A.D. 1200 and 1450 and probably served as political and religious centers as well as enclosures for cattle and for the courts of Shona kings. Over 30 feet high in some places, the circular walls were built of granite using drystone masonry (without mortar). The longest of the walls is 244 meters and encloses a space 89 meters in diameter. The Shona kingdom provided much of the gold and ivory that fed the development of KILWA and its Indian Ocean trade. Shona kings wore gold and copper jewelry and enjoyed the porcelain, textiles, and other luxuries of Persia, India, and China. Great Zimbabwe was abandoned around the middle of the 15th century, as local resources gave out and trade shifts led to the development of the Mwene Mutapa kingdom to the

north. Archaeological sites similar to Great Zimbabwe have been found in Mozambique and at other locations within the modern state of Zimbabwe.

Green, Shields (ca. 1825–1859) *revolutionary*

Born a South Carolina slave, Green escaped and stayed for a time at the home of Frederick Douglass, where he met John Brown. Green decided to join Brown's HARPERS FERRY RAID, even though he was aware that Douglass opposed the plan as suicidal. He survived the rebellion but was captured with Brown, convicted of murder and leading a revolt, and hanged on December 16, 1859.

Griffin v. Prince Edward County, Virginia

Legal case in which the Supreme Court, in 1964, ordered the public schools reopened in Prince Edward County, Va., after they had been closed in 1959 to avoid integration. Segregated private schools, paid for with tax-deductible contributions, were set up for the county's 1,304 white students, but the majority of the county's 1,646 African-American youngsters were forced to go without schooling for five years.

Guinea, Republic of

West African country. Capital: Conakry. Once a part of the great MALI Empire, Guinea is a tiny country on the Atlantic coast. FULANI tribespeople began migrating into the area in the 15th century and in 1725–1750 engaged in an Islamic jihad (holy war) that gave them control over the Fouta Djalon highlands region. In the process, they took a large number of captives who were then sold into slavery. In the 19th century, conflict between two branches of the Fulani led to the rise of SAMORI TOURÉ, who managed to play the British and the French off against each other until 1898, when the French exiled him to Gabon and established a French protectorate. Declaring that Guineans preferred freedom in poverty to prosperity in chains, Samori Touré's grandson, Sekou Touré, led the country to independence in 1958 and rejected participation in a French-African commonwealth. The French were furious and pulled their people out immediately, taking everything with them, including phones and light bulbs. More importantly, Guinea lost all French financial assistance and faced economic collapse. Sekou Touré turned to the Soviet Union for help and set up a dictatorial socialist state, which caused hundreds of thousands of Guineans to seek work in other countries. Torture and the murder of opponents became common. In 1977, a revolt led by market women caused Sekou Touré to reverse certain economic policies. The military took over following his death in 1984. A new constitution providing for a multiparty-elected government was approved in 1990. Elections have been held several times since, but they have been marred by violence and fraud. The government has a poor human rights record. Lansana Conte has been president since 1984. Liberia has accused Guinea of sheltering rebel groups attempting to overthrow the Liberian government. In 1998–99, Guinea was flooded with refugees fleeing the civil war in Sierra Leone. Although the economic situation has improved considerably, Guinea remains one of the poorer countries in Africa.

Guinea-Bissau, Republic of

Tiny West African country. Capital. Bissau. The Portuguese first arrived in Guinea-Bissau in 1446 and established a slave trade shortly afterward. The region's many rivers made it easy to transport captives by canoe from the interior to slave ships waiting at the coast. The colony of Portuguese Guinea was formally established in 1879, although a long series of wars with the local people prevented the Portuguese from gaining control of the interior until 1915. Portuguese rule was brutal, and in 1956 the African Party for Independence in Guinea and Cape Verde (PAIGC) was formed. In 1961, the PAIGC began a guerrilla war with help from the Soviet Union and Cuba. Though many leaders, including Amilcar Cabral, the head of PAIGC, were from Cape Verde, the people of Guinea-Bissau were strongly supportive of the rebel effort, and within five years, half of the country had been liberated. Although Cabral was assassinated in 1973, the PAIGC declared Guinea-Bissau independent, and a settlement was reached with Portugal in 1974. Amilcar Cabral's brother, Luis de Almeida Cabral, became the first president. He was overthrown in 1980 by Joao Bernardo Vieira, and the organization of other political parties was approved in 1991. In 1999, Vieira was ousted by the military and a new president, Malan Bacai Sanha, was inaugurated.

See also CAPE VERDE ISLANDS.

Gullah (Gulla)

A language spoken by African-American slaves and their descendants in the Sea Islands of South Carolina and some parts of Georgia. The word also refers to people who speak it. The language is basically a mix of African and English words, with African-influenced intonation, cadence, pronunciation, and grammar. It has no gender or tense. The name *Gullah* is thought to come either from the word *Angola* or from *Gola,* the name of a tribe in Liberia.

H

Haile Selassie I (Ras Tafari Makonnen)

(1892–1975) *Ethiopian emperor from 1930 to 1974*
Haile Selassie was originally called Ras (Prince) Tafari Makonnen. He took the name Haile Selassie, meaning "instrument in the power of the Trinity," when he became emperor. His early life was marked by tragedy. His 10 brothers and sisters were killed in a boating accident when he was a child, and his father died when he was 15. Ras Tafari was crowned emperor on November 2, 1930, after the death of Empress Zauditu. He took the title Haile Selassie I, King of Kings, Conquering Lion of Judea and Elect of God, and immediately moved to establish ETHIOPIA as a modern state. He abolished slavery, instituted a constitution, and set up an appointed, advisory parliament and a more modern judiciary.

In 1935, Italy, which already controlled Eritrea and Italian Somaliland, invaded Ethiopia. Though Ethiopia was able to field an army of 1,000,000 men, it was not able to cope with air strikes, poison gas warfare, and modern, mechanized assault tactics. Haile Selassie was forced to flee in 1936 but returned in 1941 when the British, with the aid of Ethiopian guerrillas, recaptured the country.

Under Haile Selassie, Ethiopia became one of the charter members of the United Nations, and a leader in the establishment of the Organization of African Unity. When he first came to power, there were fewer than 10 schools throughout the country. Twenty-five years later there were over 10,000. His autocratic rule, combined with famine in the Horn of Africa, resulted in unrest in the 1960s. He was overthrown by a military coup in 1974 and murdered the following year. In addition to his legacy in Ethiopia, Haile Selassie became one focus of RASTAFARIANISM, a religion in Jamaica that derives its name from Haile Selassie's original name, Ras Tafari.

Haile Selassie, chatting with Franklin D. Roosevelt, on board ship, February 1945 (*Library of Congress*)

Haiti, Republic of

Caribbean nation located on Hispaniola, the second-largest island in the West Indies. Capital: Port-au-Prince. At the time Columbus landed there in 1492, the island was occupied by about 300,000 Arawak Indians. Within 58 years, all but 500 had been killed or had died from European-introduced diseases and forced labor, and Africans were being imported as slave labor to work on sugar plantations. In 1697, the western portion of the island, which would later become Haiti, was ceded by Spain to France under the Treaty of Ryswick and became the French colony of Saint-Domingue. The colony comprised four antagonistic groups: the rich planters and colonial administrators (*grands blancs*); the poor whites (called *petits blancs*); the black slaves; and the mulattoes, a free group of mixed black/white ancestry who could and did own slaves themselves but who lacked political rights. (The mulattoes were legally subdivided into numerous subgroups based on color and ancestry.)

In 1791, a slave named Boukman led a revolt in which more than 2,000 whites were killed. The BOUKMAN REVOLT overlapped the French Revolution, which had begun in 1789, and the new French government was not sympathetic to the problems of Saint-Domingue's wealthy planters. However, Saint-Domingue was the richest colony in the Western Hemisphere, and France was not willing to lose it. In 1792, French troops under the command of Commissioner Léger Félicité Sonthonax were sent to restore order. By that time, more than 100,000 slaves were in revolt. The next 12 years were filled with bloodshed as alliances shifted, towns and plantations were burned, and thousands of people were either killed or died of hunger or disease.

The French Revolution intensified the tendency of Saint-Domingue's inhabitants to split along class and racial lines. The rich planters supported the monarchy and slavery. The *petits blancs* supported both slavery and the revolution, even though the revolutionary left wing in France favored the abolition of slavery. The mulattoes supported slavery but hoped the new revolutionary government would provide them with voting rights. The rebelling slaves opposed whites and mulattoes but sometimes formed alliances with the prorevolutionary poor whites and/or the mulattoes in the hope that a successful French Revolution would mean an end to slavery and white domination.

TOUSSAINT LOUVERTURE, one of Boukman's followers, rapidly became a leader in the Haitian uprising. After Boukman's death in 1791, Toussaint joined forces with the Spanish in Santo Domingo,

the neighboring Spanish colony on the island, in his effort to overthrow the French colonial government.

The British, appalled at the violence of the French Revolution and fearing an end to slavery in Haiti would jeopardize slavery in their own colonies, invaded Saint-Domingue in 1793. In 1794, after the French abolished slavery on the island (1793), Toussaint left the Spanish to join the French forces against the invading British troops. Rallying an army of 20,000 black soldiers, Toussaint drove the British out in 1798, then massacred the mulattoes when they revolted against black rule. In 1801, he conquered Spanish Santo Domingo and took control of the entire island. He reorganized the government and issued a constitution without waiting for approval from France.

Although Toussaint continued to profess loyalty to France, his power angered French emperor Napoleon Bonaparte, who was determined to regain control of the island and reestablish slavery. In 1801, Napoleon sent a 20,000-man army and managed through treachery to capture Toussaint and confine him in a French prison, where he died of cold and malnutrition in 1803. Many blacks and mulattoes previously had joined the French forces, not knowing of Napoleon's plans to strip them of their rights and freedom. Toussaint's imprisonment reignited bitter fighting, and the French were driven out in 1803 by JEAN-JACQUES DESSALINES.

Independence was declared on January 1, 1804, and Saint-Domingue was renamed Haiti. Between 1791, when the fighting began, and 1803, an estimated 160,000 to 200,000 blacks died. Twenty thousand whites were either killed or driven into exile. Approximately 10,000 mulattoes and free blacks, 40,000 British troops, and 50,000 French soldiers also died—many from yellow fever.

Dessalines was crowned emperor of the new nation in October 1804. In 1805, he ordered a massacre of the remaining white population. He was assassinated in 1806 and replaced by Alexandre Pétion, a mulatto, in the south and ex-slave Henry Christophe* (later King Henry I) in the north. After

---

* Christophe, born in British Grenada (or St. Christopher, per some sources), used the English spelling of his first name.

their deaths in 1818 and 1820 respectively, Haiti was united by Jean-Pierre Boyer. However, Haiti's economy never recovered from the war for independence and the huge indemnity it had to pay France for formal recognition, and succeeding governments maintained a pattern of political repression resulting in economic destitution.

In 1915, Woodrow Wilson responded to riots in Port-au-Prince by sending a U.S. military force that occupied Haiti until 1934. In 1957, Francois "Papa Doc" Duvalier was elected president and instituted a despotic regime whose stability was guaranteed by a brutal secret police force known as the Tonton Macoutes. Duvalier was succeeded by his son, Jean-Claude ("Baby Doc"), who was finally forced out of power in 1986.

Jean-Bertrand Aristide, a former Catholic priest, was elected president in 1990, but was overthrown by the Haitian army the following year. Brutal army rule, coupled with a U.N. economic embargo against what was already the poorest nation in the Western Hemisphere, led to an exodus of thousands of "boat people" seeking asylum in the United States. In 1994, a threatened U.S. invasion of Haiti forced the military rulers into exile and restored the elected government. In 1996, René Préval was elected president. However, in 1999, after two years of political gridlock in parliament, Préval announced he would rule by decree. Elections have been postponed several times but were held May 21, 2000, preceded by a wave of politically motivated violence.

Overpopulation and depletion of Haiti's forests have made much of the country arid. The name "Haiti," which the country received at independence, was the original Arawak Indian name for Hispaniola. It means "mountainous country."

Haley, Alex Palmer (1921–1992) *writer*

Born in Ithaca, New York, Haley spent two years in college before joining the Coast Guard at age 17. During World War II, he spent many long hours aboard ship writing stories. After retiring from the Coast Guard at age 37, he became a full-time writer. An interview with Malcolm X for *Playboy* magazine led to a collaboration with the Muslim leader that resulted in the book *The Autobiography of Malcolm X*

(1965). Drawing on the stories passed down through his family, Haley began the extensive research that would finally result in his famous book, ROOTS. The book, which was published in 1976, traced Haley's family history back to a man named Kunta Kinte, who was born in a small West African village in 1750. The book sold millions of copies and was made into a 12-hour TV miniseries (1977). *Roots* won the National Book Award for 1976 and a special Pulitzer Prize in 1977. A second TV miniseries, *Roots: The Next Generation*, appeared in 1979. Two other writers accused Haley of plagiarism in connection with *Roots*. One case was dismissed and the other was settled out of court.

Hall, Prince (1735–1807) *founder of the Black Masons*

Accounts differ as to whether Prince Hall was born free in Barbados or was an American slave who managed to gain his freedom. On July 3, 1775, he and 14 other black men formed African Lodge No. 1. Following the Revolutionary War, their application was approved by the Freemasons of London, and in 1787, Prince Hall became the head of African Lodge No. 459 in Boston. Five years later, a second American Negro Masonic Lodge was established in Providence. These lodges and other black self-help organizations set high standards of personal behavior and worked to abolish slavery and to acquire equal rights for blacks. When three black men from Boston were kidnapped in 1788 to be sold as slaves in the Caribbean, Hall petitioned the legislature, protesting the kidnapping and denouncing slavery. The Massachusetts legislature responded by outlawing the slave trade, and Governor John Hancock was able to negotiate the release of the three kidnapped men. Hall also started a school for African-American children in his own home in 1800 when the Boston city government failed to provide one. Though Hall had strong doubts that black people would ever find acceptance in America—at one point, he backed efforts to establish a black colony in Africa—he insisted that members of his Masonic lodge treat everyone alike. In his famous "Charge Delivered to the African Lodge," he wrote, ". . . give the right hand of affection and fellowship to whom it justly belongs (and) let their color and complexion be what it will . . . for they are your brethren."

Hamer, Fannie Lou Townsend (1917–1977)
civil rights activist

The youngest of 20 children, Fannie Lou Townsend was born in Mississippi and began working in the cotton fields at age six. As an infant, she suffered a serious leg injury, but her family could not afford medical care, and she limped for the rest of her life. At one point, her father managed to save enough money to buy three mules that would allow him to work his own land, but the animals were poisoned by whites angry at the family's success. In 1944, she married Perry "Pap" Hamer, a sharecropper, living in Ruleville, Sunflower County.

On August 31, 1962, a day after attending a voter registration meeting, Mrs. Hamer and 17 other African Americans rented a bus to go to Indianola, the county seat, to try to register to vote. At that time, only 155 black people out of an eligible black population of 13,524 in Sunflower County were registered. Mrs. Hamer's group was rejected, and on the way home, the driver of the bus was arrested on the charge that the yellow bus looked too much like a school bus. When Mrs. Hamer finally returned home, she was ordered to leave the plantation where she had lived and worked for 18 years. Several nights later, shots were fired into the home of the woman with whom she had gone to stay.

In 1963, while returning from a voter education training session, Mrs. Hamer and several others, including 15-year-old June Johnson and STUDENT NON-VIOLENT COORDINATING COMMITTEE (SNCC) leader Lawrence Guyot, were arrested in Winona and jailed. All were beaten, and Mrs. Hamer sustained permanent kidney damage. While they were in jail, MEDGAR EVERS was murdered, and the publicity surrounding his death persuaded officials to free Mrs. Hamer and the others. In speaking of the beating later, Mrs. Hamer said, "We're tired of all this beating, we're tired of taking this. It's been a hundred years and we're still being beaten and shot at, crosses are still being burned, because we want to vote. But I'm going to stay in Mississippi, and if they shoot me down, I'll be buried here."

Mrs. Hamer became a leader in SNCC voter registration efforts, a position that cost her husband his job. No one would hire him, and the family was forced to live on the $10 a week Mrs. Hamer received from SNCC. In 1964, Mrs. Hamer helped form the new MISSISSIPPI FREEDOM DEMOCRATIC PARTY, which challenged the right of the regular all-white Mississippi delegation to be seated at the Democratic Party presidential convention being held in New Jersey. In 1966, she took in her two grandchildren after their mother bled to death when local hospitals would not accept her. She also helped care for her son who had been disabled in Vietnam.

Mrs. Hamer's effectiveness stemmed from her oratory (some say her skills were second only to those of MARTIN LUTHER KING JR.), her inspirational singing, and her tireless devotion to the cause of poor blacks. She is famous for saying, "I'm sick and tired of being sick and tired."

Hancock, Herbie (1940–   ) *pianist, composer*

A child prodigy, Hancock performed Mozart's *Piano Concerto in D Major* with the Chicago Symphony when he was only 11. However, he was primarily interested in JAZZ and later experimented with a variety of electronic instruments. His first album, *Taking Off* (1962), included the hit "Watermelon Man," which showed considerable GOSPEL influence. While touring with MILES DAVIS' quintet (1963–68), he developed a personal style combining jazz and rock. In 1971, Hancock formed a sextet that combined electronic instruments, Indian and African elements, jazz, and rock. A number of his compositions—"The Sorcerer," "Speak Like a Child," "Cantaloupe Island" and "Dolphin Dance"—have become jazz standards. In 1983, his single "Rockit" reached the top of the pop charts and demonstrated his skill in using electronic technology. He appeared in the 1986 film *Round Midnight,* and won an Oscar for his score.

Suggested Listening: *Headhunters* (Columbia); *Empyrean Isles* (Blue Note); *Maiden Voyage* (Blue Note); and *Mwandishi* (Warner Bros.).

Handy, William Christopher (1873–1958)
composer, collector, and publisher of blues music

Though trained in classical music, W. C. Handy became interested in BLUES music while listening to a local band perform in Mississippi. After that, he began composing and collecting blues songs while traveling across the country with his own bands, the best known being the Mahara Minstrels. His first big hit was "Memphis Blues," which started as a 1909 political campaign song for Edward "Boss" Crump of Memphis. Though cheated out of the profits of "Memphis Blues," Handy went on to write the even more popular "St. Louis Blues" in 1914 and "Beale Street Blues" in 1917.

During the labor shortage created by World War I, many African Americans, to the dismay of white plantation owners, traveled north in search of better working conditions. When the Chicago *Defender* newspaper encouraged this northern migration, the paper was banned in many southern towns, but while he was on tour, Handy would secretly distribute copies of the *Defender* to southern black leaders.

In 1918, Handy and Harry Pace established the Pace and Handy Music Company. Though he later became blind, Handy continued to collect and compose music. Other well-known songs include "Aunt Hagar's Blues," "A Good Man Is Hard to Find," and "Careless Love." He is known as the "Father of the Blues."

Hannibal (249 or 247–183 B.C.) *Carthaginian general*

A North African military genius who almost conquered Rome, Hannibal was born during the First Punic War (264–241 B.C.), when CARTHAGE, the dominant commercial power in the western Mediterranean, was seeking control of the Iberian Peninsula. When continuing tension with Rome led to the Second Punic War (218–201 B.C.), Hannibal led a 30,000-man army, along with several elephants, across the Pyrenees, through the Rhône valley, and over the Alps into Italy.

In 217 B.C., he defeated the main Roman army at Lake Trasimene, but lacked the necessary equipment to attack Rome itself. Instead he tried to foment rebellion against Rome elsewhere in Italy. The following year, Hannibal utilized brilliant cavalry tactics to encircle and destroy another Roman army at the Battle of Cannae. Although he remained in Italy a total of 15 years and won other battlefield encounters, he received little support from the rulers of Carthage.

In 203 B.C., Hannibal was summoned to defend Carthage from a Roman invasion but was defeated by Scipio Africanus at the Battle of Zama in 202 B.C. After the peace terms were determined, Hannibal became a Carthaginian minister and reformed the government. However, he aroused Rome's anger with his successful efforts to rebuild Carthage's influence and prosperity. He fled to Syria but poisoned himself when it looked as though he would be surrendered to the Romans.

Hannibal's military tactics were admired and adapted by later generals, including Napoleon Bonaparte. As a commander, Hannibal's innovations included removing himself from the center of combat. Earlier generals, such as Alexander the Great, led the charge themselves, a practice that often led to their armies' defeat if they were killed or wounded. By observing the course of battle from nearby high ground, Hannibal was better able to change tactics and preserve his limited forces. Hannibal was the son of Hamilcar Barca, a hero of the First Punic War. The family name "Barca" is the basis of the name of the Spanish city of Barcelona.

Hanno (fl. 520–470 B.C.) *admiral*

Hanno was an admiral from the North African city of CARTHAGE. Sometime between 520 and 470 B.C. Hanno undertook an expedition involving a fleet of 60 ships and 3,000 colonists. His task was to establish a series of settlements along the West African coast. According to his account of the voyage, Hanno established six settlements between what are now MOROCCO and SENEGAL. He then continued his journey, reaching as far south as Mt. Cameroon, which he named "Chariot of the Gods," before turning back. The entire voyage covered approximately 6,250 miles.

Hansberry, Lorraine Vivian (1930–1965)
playwright

Author of the prize-winning drama *A Raisin in the Sun*, Lorraine Hansberry was the first black woman ever to have a play produced on Broadway and the winner of the New York Drama Critics Circle Award for best play of the 1958–59 season. She was the first black, the fifth woman, and the youngest person ever to win the award. The drama focuses on an African-American family that is attempting to move into an all-white neighborhood. In writing the play, Hansberry drew on personal experience. When she was eight, her family had attempted to do the same thing in Chicago. They were threatened and then evicted under a court order. Though the decision was finally overturned in 1940 by the U.S. Supreme Court, the struggle had taken a toll physically and psychologically, as well as financially, and Hansberry's father died five years later.

In spite of the obvious emotional appeal of *A Raisin in the Sun*, the fact that Hansberry was an unknown African-American woman made it difficult to get producers to even read her work. There was also concern that there would be no audience for a serious, black-oriented play. So Hansberry decided to raise the $100,000 needed to produce the play herself. In the end, more people invested in *Raisin* than in any previous Broadway production. The show ran for 19 months on Broadway and was made into an award-winning movie starring Sidney Poitier. It was translated into 30 languages, and a 1974 musical version won a Tony Award.

In 1964, Hansberry's second play, *The Sign in Sidney Brustein's Window*, opened. That same year she wrote the text for *The Movement*, a collection of photographs documenting the Civil Rights movement. By this time, Lorraine Hansberry was seriously ill with cancer. After her death, autobiographical information taken from her stories, letters, and other writings was incorporated into a play called *To Be Young, Gifted and Black*.

Harlem

Predominantly African-American section of New York City located in upper Manhattan. Founded by Peter Stuyvesant in 1658, Harlem was originally the Dutch settlement of Nieuw Haarlem. Large numbers of blacks began moving into the area around 1910, and the section was the focal point of the famed HARLEM RENAISSANCE, which produced a huge outpouring of art and literature. Harlem has been one of the leading centers of jazz innovation, and the home of some of America's best-known writers, artists, and musicians. The APOLLO THEATER and the Schomburg Center for Research in Black Culture are both located there.

Harlem Renaissance

The period in HARLEM between 1919 and 1930 that was marked by an outpouring of African-American literature, music, art, and political and philosophical thought. During and after World War I, thousands of southern blacks (along with some immigrants from the West Indies and elsewhere) moved to Harlem as part of the NORTHERN MIGRATION to seek economic and creative opportunity. The resulting mix brought together not only writers, but hundreds of artists and performers, among them bibliophile ARTHUR SCHOMBURG; actor PAUL ROBESON; entertainers Roland Hayes, Bill "Bojangles" Robinson, and Ethel Waters; artists AARON DOUGLAS, Palmer Hayden, and WILLIAM JOHNSON; sculptors META WARRICK FULLER, SELMA BURKE, AUGUSTA SAVAGE, and RICHMOND BARTHE; photographer JAMES VANDERZEE; writers LANGSTON HUGHES and ZORA NEALE HURSTON; musicians Fletcher; Henderson, DUKE ELLINGTON, and Cab Calloway, and many others.

The success of the Harlem Renaissance was due not only to the presence of hundreds of talented African Americans, but also to the fact that Harlem's civil rights establishment actively sought to promote black talent as a way of eliminating prejudice and "advancing the race." Charles Johnson, editor of the NATIONAL URBAN LEAGUE journal *Opportunity*, is credited by Langston Hughes, Zora Hurston, and Aaron Douglas of almost single-handedly creating the renaissance by going to extraordinary lengths to seek out writers and artists from around the country. Jessie Fauset, the literary editor of the NATIONAL ASSOCIATION FOR THE ADVANCEMENT OF COLORED

PEOPLE (NAACP) magazine *The Crisis,* also played a major role in singling out and publishing the work of African-American writers. In addition to publishing the work of COUNTEE CULLEN, ARNA BONTEMPS, CLAUDE MCKAY, Hughes, JEAN TOOMER, and dozens of other black poets, essayists, and authors, *The Crisis* and *Opportunity* offered cash prizes to encourage literary excellence. NAACP leaders JAMES WELDON JOHNSON and Walter White, and Howard University professor ALAIN LOCKE, regularly used their connections with white philanthropists, publishers, and producers to obtain grants and contracts benefiting scores of black artists, writers, and performers. While the approach of many of these whites was paternalistic, and a number endorsed "Negro art" because they thought it primitive, sensual, and exotic, their money nonetheless helped many artists pursue their careers.

The period was also a time of political turmoil that saw the rise of MARCUS GARVEY, PAN-AFRICAN MOVEMENTS, unionization work by A. PHILIP RANDOLPH, and the growth of the NAACP and NATIONAL URBAN LEAGUE. This political activity contributed to a feeling of black progress and encouraged community pride in the accomplishments of black artists. Efforts by upper-class blacks to promote the work of African-American artists also reflected a belief in W. E. B. DuBois' theory of the TALENTED TENTH, the idea that the black race would advance through the efforts of its educated and cultured elite. The Harlem Renaissance ended with the coming of the Great Depression of the 1930s, when money for the arts became limited and attention focused more on political and social issues.

Recommended Reading: Bruce Keller, *The Harlem Renaissance.* Westport, Conn.: Greenwood, 1995. David Levering Lewis, *When Harlem Was in Vogue.* New York: Oxford University Press, 1981.

Harper, Frances Ellen Watkins (1825–1911)
writer, abolitionist, lecturer, social reformer
Born to a free black family in Baltimore, Maryland, Harper was orphaned at age three. After graduating from the William Watkins Academy for Negro Youth, she became the first female instructor at Ohio's Union Seminary, the school that would later become Wilberforce University. Moving to Pennsylvania, she became active in the Underground Railroad and lived for a while at the home of abolitionist William Still. A talented orator, Harper began touring the country, speaking against slavery. In 1854, she published *Poems on Miscellaneous Subjects,* which sold over 10,000 copies. Though a strong supporter of the women's suffrage movement, Harper broke with its white leaders when they refused to support the Fifteenth Amendment giving black men the vote because it did not include women. A board member of the Women's Christian Temperance Union and a founding member of the American Woman Suffrage Association and the National Association of Colored Women, Harper continued to write poems, essays, stories, and novels. Among her best-known writings are the novel *Iola Leroy* (1892) and several collections of poetry. Although her works sold well, they were often printed as inexpensive booklets, and few copies remain today.

Harpers Ferry Raid
Raid engineered by John Brown on the federal weapons arsenal at Harpers Ferry, West Virginia. Brown, who was white, had a long history of involvement with the UNDERGROUND RAILROAD, and was responsible for the 1856 attack at Pottawatomie Creek, Kansas, in which five proslavery settlers were killed. He planned to set up a biracial, independent republic in the Appalachian Mountains, which would serve as a base for a guerrilla war against slaveholders. He had discussed his plans with a number of African-American leaders but had received limited support. Frederick Douglass warned Brown that his plan was suicidal, but on October 16, 1859, Brown and 21 followers, including five African Americans, succeeded in seizing the armory. However, word had leaked out, and that night Brown's men were surrounded by marines led by Colonel Robert E. Lee. Ten of his followers were killed, and Brown himself was captured. Eight days later he was tried, found guilty, and sentenced to death. He was hanged on December 2, 1859. Unlike other whites who had participated in slave upris-

Bringing the Prisoners Out, an illustration depicting the aftermath of the raid on Harpers Ferry, from Frank Leslie's *Illustrated Newspaper*, November 5, 1859 (*Library of Congress*)

ings, Brown was unusual in that he was actually the initiating force. However, he was not unique. In 1815, a Virginia man named George Boxley engineered a slave revolt that involved attacking Fredericksburg and Richmond. Boxley was captured but managed to escape. Of the 30 slaves arrested with him, six were hanged.

See also OSBORNE PERRY ANDERSON; JOHN ANTHONY COPELAND JR.; SHIELDS GREEN.

Hausa (HOW-sah)

A group of West African tribes linked by a common language. At the end of the 11th century, the Hausa began establishing communities in northern NIGERIA, the main one being at Kano. By 1350, the communities had become seven separate states, which formed an important link in the trade between the YORUBA tribespeople to the south and the traders of North Africa. In the 1440s, Hausa kings began extensive use of slave labor, forcing captives to become soldiers, laborers, and developers of new settlements. Long-distance trade continued to expand, along with the growth in cloth and shoe manufacturing and the use of credit and currency. Growing wealth required protection, and Hausa kings were able to field large armies and a cavalry with horses and men protected by quilted cloth armor. Even so, Kano was eventually captured by the SONGHAI emperor Askia MUHAMMAD TOURÉ, and

several other states fell to other conquerers. Today, most Hausa are Muslims, though many still practice ANIMIST traditions as well. They number more than 20 million and are centered primarily in Nigeria and southern Niger. As in the past, they are known for their trading and business skills, though many also live as farmers.

Hawkins, Coleman Randolph (1904–1969)
jazz musician

Hawkins began playing piano at age five and soon moved on to the cello and then the tenor saxophone. In 1921, he was offered a job touring with blues singer Mamie Smith's Jazz Hounds. Two years later, he moved to New York, where he joined a band formed by Fletcher Henderson in 1924. He remained with Henderson for 10 years, leaving in 1934 to tour Europe with various local groups. In 1939, he returned to New York, where he formed his own band. Shortly thereafter, he recorded the highly successful *Body and Soul* that established his appeal with a mass audience. Hawkins' musical style is characterized by emotional intensity, rich tone, and harmonic patterns. He is regarded as one of the leading tenor saxophone players in jazz.

Suggested Listening: *Picasso* (Giants of Jazz); *Body and Soul* (Bluebird); *Coleman Hawkins and Roy Eldridge at the Opera House* (Verve); *Duke Ellington Meets Coleman Hawkins* (Impulse); *The Hawk Flies* (Fantasy/Original Jazz Classics)

Hayden, Lewis (ca. 1815–1889) *Underground Railroad activist*

Hayden's slave mother was so badly treated that she became insane, and his other brothers and sister were sold at auction. Hayden himself, while still a child, was traded for a pair of carriage horses. Though anxious to escape slavery, Hayden was unwilling to leave his wife and child behind and was forced to wait until 1844, when the entire family was able to get away to Canada with the help of two white teachers, Calvin Fairbank and Delia Webster. When Fairbank and Webster were arrested in Kentucky and charged with slave stealing, Fairbank pleaded guilty on condition that Webster be freed; he was sentenced to 15 years imprisonment. Hayden then arranged to pay his old owner $650 in return for which the owner petitioned the governor for Fairbank's release. Fairbank was freed in 1849, after spending four years in prison.

Leaving Canada, the Hayden family settled in Detroit, where Hayden established a school for African-American children. Moving to Boston around 1849, he became a leader in the black community and a major participant in UNDERGROUND RAILROAD activities. Among the scores of runaways who found shelter at his home were WILLIAM and ELLEN CRAFT. When their owner sent slave catchers after them, Hayden barricaded his house and threatened to blow it up rather than surrender the Crafts. He also led a group of men in the rescue of a runaway named Shadrach, who was being held pending his return to slavery. Arrested and brought to trial, Hayden was acquitted when the jury, ignoring the evidence, refused to convict.

During the Civil War, Hayden helped recruit black troops. His own son was killed in action. Following the war, Hayden was elected to the Massachusetts state legislature, where he arranged that a monument be erected in memory of African-American Revolutionary War hero CRISPUS ATTUCKS.

Hayden, Robert Earl (1913–1980) *poet*

Hayden was born in Detroit, Michigan. After his parents' divorce, his mother turned him over to foster parents who changed his original name, Asa Bundy Sheffey, to Robert Hayden. Much of his poetry centered on the black experience, an outgrowth of his work doing historical research in the 1930s for the Federal Writers' Project. A series of poems on slavery and the Civil War won him his second Avery Hopwood Award, and later work focused on such figures as NAT TURNER, MALCOLM X, FREDERICK DOUGLASS, and HARRIET TUBMAN. However, his insistence on being judged as an American poet rather than a black poet caused him to be harshly criticized in the 1960s. After graduating from Detroit City College (now Wayne State University), Hayden received a master's degree from the University of Michigan in 1944, then spent 23 years teaching at Fisk University before returning to teach at Michigan. In 1966, he gained widespread attention with the publication of *Selected Poems*. Ten years later, he was appointed consultant in poetry to the Library of Congress. His Baha'i religion was also a strong influence. Hayden is noted for his vivid portraits, diversity, and technical range. Other work includes *A Ballad of Remembrance, The Lion and the Archer, Heart-Shape in the Dust, Words in the Mourning Time, Angle of Ascent: New and Selected Poems, American Journal,* and *Robert Hayden: Collected Poems,* as well as the play *Go Down, Moses.*

Healy, Patrick Francis (1834–1910) *African-American Jesuit, president of Georgetown University from 1873 to 1882*

Born to an Irish father and a slave mother, Healy and his brothers attended a Quaker school in New York. From there, he entered Holy Cross College in Massachusetts, where he received his degree in 1850. After becoming a Jesuit, he taught at St. Joseph's College in Philadelphia and at Holy Cross. In 1858, Healy left the United States to study in Belgium, then returned to become a professor at Georgetown University in Washington, D.C., in 1866. He became a dean in 1868 and was made acting president in 1873. In 1894, Healy was confirmed as president. During his tenure, Healy modernized the curriculum and engaged in a major building program.

Healy's brother, James Augustine Healy, was the first African-American priest (1854) and bishop (1875) in the United States. A friend of Popes Pius IX and Leo XIII, Father James Healy was known as the "children's bishop" because of his work in building orphanages and opposing abusive child labor practices. Another Healy brother, Michael Augustine Healy, was a captain in what later became the Coast Guard. Famous for his arctic rescue missions, Captain Michael "Hell-Roaring Mike" Healy is believed to be one of the sea captains used as a model for Captain Larsen in Jack London's famous novel *The Sea Wolf.* A sister, Eliza Healy (Sister Mary Magdalen), was a teacher and mother superior of Villa Barlow of St. Albans in Vermont.

Hemings, Sally (1773–1835) *slave belonging to the family of Thomas Jefferson*

It is believed by many that Sally Hemings was Thomas Jefferson's mistress and the mother of at least one, and possibly several, of his children. She was the daughter of her master, John Wayles, Jefferson's father-in-law, and an enslaved woman named Elizabeth Hemings. With the death of John Wayles, Sally became the property of Martha Wayles Jefferson and went to live in the Jefferson household. Extremely pretty, she was nicknamed "Dashing Sally" as a teenager. In 1785, Jefferson was sent to France on a diplomatic mission and was accompanied by his eldest daughter, Martha. The two were joined by Jefferson's daughter Mary (or Polly) in 1787, and she brought Sally with her to France. There are indications in Jefferson's writings that he, then a 45-year-old widower, fell in love with the 14-year-old slave girl and that she became pregnant by him. After returning to the Jefferson estate at Monticello, Hemings gave birth to a son and later bore six more children, two of whom died in infancy. Jefferson's alleged relationship with Sally Hemings was publicized by a tabloid journalist named James Thomson Callender but did not have much affect politically. According to Hemings' son Madison, Sally Hemings and her children were treated well, and Jefferson was concerned about their welfare. Madison and his brother Eston were freed at Jefferson's death. Sally Hemings was freed in 1828 and went to live with a son near Monticello. Some historians believe that some of Hemings' children were fathered by Samuel Carr, Jefferson's nephew, rather than Jefferson himself. DNA tests, conducted in 1998, indicated that her children were related to Jefferson but did not prove conclusively that he was the father. More important, perhaps, is that Hemings' status as a slave made her exceptionally vulnerable to unwelcome and/or inappropriate sexual advances by white men.

Hendrix, Jimi (1942–1970) *guitarist, songwriter*

Born in Seattle, Washington, Hendrix learned to play by listening to blues artists like B. B. King, MUDDY WATERS, and ROBERT JOHNSON. Traveling to London in 1965, he founded a trio with Mitch Mitchell and Noel Redding called the Jimi Hendrix Experience. The group disbanded in 1969 but not before recording the highly successful *Are You Experienced?*, *Axis—Bold as Love*, and *Electric Ladyland*. Hendrix was noted for his unique guitar style that incorporated new electronic effects such as the inclusion of feedback and the use of the wah-wah pedal to vary the level of distortion and volume from the amplifier. His triumphant appearance at the Woodstock festival was marked by his performance of "The Star Spangled Banner" using feedback. Hendrix died at age 28 of barbiturate and alcohol poisoning, but he remains one of the greatest guitarists of the 1960s. His powerful, inventive approach helped shape contemporary rock and JAZZ.

Henson, Josiah (1789–1883) *runaway slave, abolitionist, minister, businessman*

Born a slave in Charles County, Maryland, Henson was considered hardworking and trustworthy and was made a manager on the Isaac Riley plantation. A devout Christian, he became a preacher, ministering to the other slaves. In an effort to protect his drunken master, he once suffered a beating so severe that afterward he was unable to raise his hands above his head. In 1830, he escaped to Canada with his wife and four children and became a conductor on the UNDERGROUND RAILROAD. He also built a sawmill and founded a school. He twice traveled to England, where he and his wife were presented to Queen Victoria. On his return he met with U.S. president Rutherford B. Hayes. Harriet Beecher Stowe met with Henson after reading his autobiography, *The Life of Josiah Henson, Formerly a Slave, Now an Inhabitant of Canada, as Narrated by Himself*, and used him as the model for Uncle Tom in her book *Uncle Tom's Cabin*. Stowe's depiction of Uncle Tom as pious and servile led to the current use of the term *Uncle Tom* to mean an obsequious, self-effacing black man, concerned primarily with the good opinion of whites. Henson was religious, and as a young man he was considered obedient and loyal enough to be made a manager or overseer. However, the fact that he not only escaped from slavery but became involved with the Underground Railroad is a clear indication that he was not the fawning character devoted to whites that the term *Uncle Tom* implies.

Henson, Matthew Alexander (1866–1955)
explorer

Born in Charles County, Maryland, Matthew Henson was orphaned by age eight. At 12, he signed on as a cabin boy on the merchant ship *Katie Hinds* and spent the next six years sailing around the world. He then settled in Washington, D.C., where he met Robert E. Peary, who was in the process of planning an expedition to explore the possibility of building a canal through Nicaragua to link the Atlantic and Pacific Oceans. Peary hired Henson to accompany him on the expedition. It was the beginning of a long association, as Henson came to share Peary's dream of being the first to reach the North Pole. Together, he and Peary made six trips to the Arctic, each time being driven back by storms and subzero temperatures.

Their seventh journey began in 1908, when they left Crane City, Greenland, for Cape Columbia on Ellesmere Island and waited for the sea to freeze

Matthew Henson (*Library of Congress*)

over. From there, they set off for the North Pole. According to Henson, "We [traveled] 18 to 20 hours out of every 24 . . . Forced marches all the time [because] . . . we couldn't carry food for more than 50 days." Henson's dog team moved out in front, covering 35 miles on the first day. Peary, whose toes had been amputated because of frostbite, followed. On April 6, 1909, Henson, along with two Eskimo assistants, reached the Pole, built an igloo, and waited for Peary to arrive and confirm his calculations. Afterward, he and Peary planted the American flag at the North Pole and spent approximately 30 hours making observations before beginning the long, cold trip home. Henson's participation in the enterprise was initially ignored because of his race, but he was later honored by Congress and by Presidents Truman and Eisenhower. In the 1990s, questions arose as to whether Henson and Peary's calculations were correct and whether their claim to have reached the Pole was valid.

hieroglyphics

Pictographic writing of ancient Egypt. The symbols represented objects, actions, and ideas. The direction of hieroglyphic writing was not fixed—it could be vertical or horizontal. Humans and animals were drawn to face the beginning of a line, and floral imagery was important. The lotus represented Lower Egypt, since its shape was thought to correspond to the shape of the Nile Delta. The development of hieroglyphics paralleled the development of papyrus, made from the pressed stalks of reeds growing along the Nile. The last hieroglyphic inscription dates from A.D. 394. The art of reading hieroglyphics was lost when the ancient Egyptian language was replaced by Arabic. Hieroglyphics remained untranslatable until 1799, when soldiers from Napoleon's army digging trenches near the city of Rosetta found a stone inscribed with identical messages in hieroglyphics, demotic Egyptian (a kind of ancient Egyptian shorthand), and Greek. Using this Rosetta Stone, a Frenchman named Jean Champollion (1790–1832) deciphered hieroglyphics in 1821. Later Egyptologists interpreted more than 600 symbols.

Hieroglyphics on pylon, Temple of Horus, Edfu
(*National Museum of African Art, Washington, D.C.*)

Himes, Chester Bomar (1909–1984) *writer*

Born in Jefferson City, Missouri, Himes began writing while in prison after being sentenced at age 19 to 20 years for armed robbery. While incarcerated, he witnessed murders, beatings, riots, and a fire that killed over 300 inmates. His first novel, *If He Hollers, Let Him Go,* published in 1945, was followed by *Lonely Crusade* in 1947. *Cast the First Stone* (1952) is considered a classic among prison novels. Though Himes' early novels are now regarded as among the best African-American writing, they did not sell well, and his prison record kept him from getting any but menial jobs. In 1953, he moved to Paris, where he lived most of his life. In 1956, Himes was asked by a French publisher to produce a crime novel set in Harlem as part as a series. The book, *For Love of Imabelle,* was highly successful, and Himes eventually did 10 novels for the series featuring black detectives "Coffin" Ed Jones and "Grave Digger" Johnson. These books, which Himes referred to as his "Harlem Domestic" series, were popular in the United States, and two, *Cotton Comes to Harlem,* and *The Heat's On* (retitled *Come Back, Charleston Blue*), were made into

movies. In all of his books—crime thrillers, social protest novels, an autobiography, and various short stories—the subject of racial oppression is a major theme. Himes also focused on tensions between light-skinned and dark-skinned blacks—something that had been a problem in his home. Among his other books are *A Rage in Harlem, The Real Cool Killers,* and *The Primitive.*

Holiday, Billie (1915–1959) *jazz singer*

Although her voice lacked resonance and her range was limited, Billie Holiday was able to imbue her songs with an emotional content that gave even banal lyrics emotional power. After cutting her first record with Benny Goodman in 1933, she became

Billie Holiday (*Library of Congress*)

famous recording with Teddy Wilson. In 1937, she joined Count Basie's band, where she met her close friend Lester Young, who nicknamed her "Lady Day." (She nicknamed him "the President" or "Prez.") With her debut with Artie Shaw in 1938, she became the first black vocalist to sing regularly with a white orchestra, and although Shaw and other white musicians tried to protect her while on tour, she experienced infuriating brushes with racial discrimination. Some of her most famous songs reflected social and personal problems. "Strange Fruit," a song recorded in 1939, referred to lynch victims hanging from trees. She wrote "God Bless the Child" after a quarrel with her mother and "Don't Explain" after finding evidence of her husband's infidelity. Drug and alcohol abuse eventually destroyed her voice. Her autobiography, *Lady Sings the Blues,* was later made into a movie starring Diana Ross.

Horse, John (Juan Caballo) (ca. 1812–1882)
black Seminole chief, warrior, negotiator, interpreter
Horse's mother was black; his father was a Seminole Indian. He was noted for his marksmanship and his diplomatic skills and was one of the men who signed the Treaty of Fort Dade in 1837. When the United States violated the treaty, John Horse joined with Osceola and other Seminole leaders in a renewal of hostilities. He was later captured, along with Osceola, Wild Cat, and others, when they arrived at a meeting with U.S. Army officers under a flag of truce. Together with Wild Cat, he led a daring mass escape from the military prison in St. Augustine. They were pursued by a force of nearly 1,000 men but managed to evade recapture and defeated American army forces at the Battle of Lake Okeechobee. Later forced to surrender, he agreed to work with U.S. forces in persuading the last Seminole holdouts to move west to Oklahoma. He later worked with Wild Cat and other Seminole leaders in efforts to protect Seminole and black Seminole interests. In 1849, he led black Seminoles into Mexico, where they were allowed to settle in return for a promise to provide military assistance against outlaws and hostile Indian tribes.

See also ABRAHAM and BLACK SEMINOLES.

Houphouët-Boigny, Félix (1905–1993)
(WHO-foo-ette BWAH-knee) *president of the Ivory Coast, leader in the fight for Ivorian independence*
In his youth, Félix Houphouët-Boigny was both a farmer and a doctor. A member of the Baoule tribe, he became chief of his village when his brother died. In the 1940s, he organized the African Agricultural Union and became a leader in the Ivory Coast anticolonial movement seeking independence from France. However, he advocated maintaining close ties with France after independence in order to strengthen his country's economy. He even served in the French cabinet for 13 years. After independence in 1960, Houphouët-Boigny ruled the Ivory Coast for 33 years. A Roman Catholic, Houphouët-Boigny arranged for the building of a huge gold-domed Catholic basilica in his home village of Yamoussoukro. Estimated to cost $200 million, it is the largest Christian church in the world. Though Houphouët-Boigny maintained a one-party rule, he remained popular until his death. In 1993, after suffering a long illness, he requested that his life support systems be turned off soon after dawn on December 7, Ivorian Independence Day.

Houston, Charles Hamilton (1895–1950)
lawyer, educator
Born in Washington, D.C., Houston graduated Phi Beta Kappa from Amherst, taught English for several years, then entered the army, where he was commissioned a first lieutenant. When his tour of duty ended, he entered Harvard Law School, where he became the first African American elected to *Law Review.* After graduating, Houston opened a law practice in the District of Columbia and began teaching at Howard Law School. After becoming dean at age 34, he closed the night school, raised admission requirements, brought in new faculty, and created a law school whose avowed mission was to train black lawyers dedicated to winning equal rights for African Americans. Among his students was THURGOOD MARSHALL. In 1935, Houston took a leave of absence from Howard to work for the NATIONAL ASSOCIATION FOR THE ADVANCEMENT OF COLORED PEOPLE (NAACP). Even before that, he had convinced the NAACP to hire Nathan Margold, who

had been instrumental in devising the strategy that finally ended school segregation. Houston played a critical role in determining and implementing legal action in a number of key civil rights cases, including the unlawful exclusion of blacks from juries, school integration, fair housing practices, and union discrimination. His influence on Howard University Law School, and on many of the lawyers who would determine the civil rights legal agenda during much of the 20th century, is immeasurable.

Houston Mutiny

Incident that took place on August 23, 1917, in Houston, Texas, involving men of the U.S. Army's all-black Third Battalion, Twenty-fourth Infantry. Twenty people were killed. Escalating tension between black soldiers and white civilians had been a nationwide problem, but particularly in Texas. The men of the Twenty-fourth Infantry were aware that two brutal lynchings had occurred in Texas in 1915 and 1916, as the cases had received extensive coverage in the black press. The East St. Louis, Illinois, riot in which at least 40 blacks lost their lives, had occurred just a few weeks earlier, and the soldiers of the Twenty-fourth Infantry had donated $150 (then a considerable sum of money) to help blacks there. The hostile racial climate in Texas was threatening enough that Colonel William Newman, the Third Battalion commander, tried unsuccessfully to have the order transferring his men to guard duty at Camp Logan, Texas, revoked. The soldiers arrived on July 28, 1917. On August 18, two black soldiers were pistol-whipped by white civilian police officers after they protested police harassment of a black teenager. Two other soldiers were beaten when they objected to police officers calling them "nigger." On August 23, police beat and arrested Private Alonzo Edwards for alleged interference in the arrest of a black woman. When a black military policeman, Corporal Charles Baltimore, asked city police about the arrest, a white police officer beat him brutally and threw him in jail. The new camp commander, Major Kneeland Snow, obtained the release of Baltimore. However, the black soldiers at Camp Logan were both angry and fearful. When Private Frank Johnson yelled that a white mob was approaching,

men raced to grab guns and ammunition. That night approximately 75 to 100 black soldiers began marching on the city, killing four policemen and wounding three others (one of whom later died). Ten other whites and one Mexican American were also killed, as were two black soldiers who were accidently shot by other black soldiers. Two other soldiers later died of wounds.

Following the incident, the Third Battalion was transferred to New Mexico. One hundred eighteen men were charged with murder and mutiny in the biggest court-martial in U.S. military history. The defendants were tried in three groups. The first 63 defendants were represented by a single defense attorney. One hundred ninety-six witnesses testified in a 22-day period. The trial lasted just under a month. Five men were acquitted. Thirteen received the death penalty and were secretly executed a day before the verdict was publically announced, before their cases could be reviewed or their families notified. The condemned were notified of their fate two days before the executions were carried out on December 11.

Though the Twenty-fourth Infantry was an all-black unit, its officers were white, and the prosecution seemed most concerned with ensuring that none of them could be blamed for what had happened. The incident had occurred after 9:00 P.M. on a rainy night, and the white officers stated they could not identify any individual defendants. Instead, the prosecution relied on the sometimes conflicting testimony of seven black soldiers who were promised leniency in return for their cooperation. In all, 110 men were convicted, seven were acquitted, and 28 received the death penalty. After the first 13 men were executed, there were widespread protests led by JAMES WELDON JOHNSON of the NATIONAL ASSOCIATION FOR THE ADVANCEMENT OF COLORED PEOPLE. President Woodrow Wilson reluctantly commuted the death penalty to life imprisonment in 10 of the cases. Black newspapers bitterly attacked the military judicial system and declared the executed soldiers "martyrs." Because of the protests regarding the secret hanging of the first 13 men, the War Department issued General Order # 7, mandating that any death sentence imposed in the continental United States must be reviewed by the judge advocate general and the president. The Houston army mutiny is often considered a prelude to the so-called RED SUMMER of 1919, during which there were 25 race riots and other violence.

Hughes, James Mercer Langston (1902–1967)
poet, writer

Until age 12, Hughes lived with his grandmother, Mary Langston, whose first husband, Lewis Sheridan Leary, had been killed fighting with JOHN BROWN at Harpers Ferry, West Virginia. At night, she would tell the boy stories of African-American heroes, then wrap Leary's bloodstained, bullet-riddled shawl around him while he slept. Hughes began composing poetry as a teenager after becom-

Langston Hughes (*Library of Congress*)

ing acquainted with the work of Walt Whitman and other American poets.

Hughes always resented the fact that his father had for the most part deserted him early in life and that his mother had turned him over to others to raise; this feeling is reflected in much of his writing. In 1921, the NATIONAL ASSOCIATION FOR THE ADVANCEMENT OF COLORED PEOPLE magazine *The Crisis* published Hughes' "The Negro Speaks of Rivers," in which Hughes affirms his link to Africa. Scribbled originally on the back of an old envelope, it was to become one of his most famous poems. After working as a sailor and traveling to Africa and Europe, Hughes moved to Washington, D.C., where he got a job as a busboy at a hotel. There he met the poet Vachel Lindsay, who was scheduled to give a reading of his own work. After reading some of Hughes' poems, Lindsay was so impressed that he read Hughes' work to his audience. The response was overwhelming, and Hughes soon began to give readings of his own.

In 1926, Hughes published his first book of poetry, *The Weary Blues*. His second book, *Fine Clothes to the Jew*, was published a year later, followed by his first novel, *Not Without Laughter* (1930). The year 1931 saw a bitter break between Hughes and Zora Neale Hurston, whom Hughes accused of stealing the play *Mule Bone*, which they had once worked on jointly, and presenting it as her own work. In 1934, Hughes published a collection of short stories called *The Ways of White Folk*. Three years later, he became a war correspondent covering the Spanish Civil War. Afterward he established the Harlem Suitcase Theatre in New York and later founded two other theaters in Los Angeles and Chicago.

In 1943, Hughes began writing a column for the Chicago *Defender* in which he presented the shrewd, humorous views of a black man named Jesse B. Semple, or "Simple." Later collected into five books, the Simple stories are among his best work. In addition to poetry, Hughes wrote plays, novels, children's books, short stories, articles, histories, biographies, anthologies, radio and TV scripts, and his autobiography. Often humorous, sometimes militant, occasionally subdued, Hughes celebrated ordinary black working people. He was known as the poet-laureate of Harlem.

Recommended Reading: Hill, Christine M. *Langston Hughes: Poet of the Harlem Renaissance.* Springfield, N.J.: Enslow, 1997; Meltzer, Milton. *Langston Hughes: An Illustrated Edition.* Brookfield, Conn.: Millbrook Press, 1997; Rampersad Arnold, *The Life of Langston Hughes.* New York: Oxford University Press, 1986.

Hurston, Zora Neale (ca. 1901–1960) *author, anthropologist*

Hurston was born in the all-black Florida town of Eatonville, steeped in the folk tales that influenced much of her later work. On her own from an early age, Hurston attended Howard University and won a scholarship to study anthropology at Barnard College. She first gained literary prominence with "Spunk," a short story published in 1925 and followed by numerous novels, stories, essays, and articles. She collaborated with Wallace Thurman on a short-lived magazine, *Fire!* (1926), and with LANGSTON HUGHES on the play *Mule Bone* (1930). When Hurston tried to produce the play under her own name, however, Hughes accused her of taking credit for his work. Hurston denied the charge, but their friendship was destroyed. She published several studies of African-American and Caribbean folklore, including *Mules and Men* (1935) and *Tell My Horse* (1938). Her novel *Their Eyes Were Watching God* (1937) has been rediscovered by a new generation of readers and appears on many high school and college reading lists. Hurston's autobiography, *Dust Tracks on the Road,* was published in 1942. Always a center of controversy, both for her work and her independent lifestyle, Hurston objected to

Zora Neale Hurston (*Library of Congress*)

the 1954 *Brown* school desegregation decision, because she believed it implied that black children could not learn properly from black teachers in an all-black environment. Despite the magnitude of her work, Hurston died penniless in 1960. She was a major figure of the HARLEM RENAISSANCE.

Ibn Battuta (Muhammad ibn Abdullah)

(1304–ca. 1377) *Muslim scholar, traveler*

Born in Tangier, Morocco, Ibn Battuta was a BERBER who studied Islamic theology and set out for Mecca when he was 21 years old. He spent the next 24 years traveling through Asia and Africa. He spent eight years in India (1334–1341) and was made ambassador to China by the sultan of Delhi. Later he made two trips to Africa, traveling down the east coast and across the Sahara throughout the MALI Empire. Ibn Battuta is one of the most widely traveled medieval Muslims known to us today. His writings constitute the only eyewitness accounts of Mali and East Africa. All other accounts of that period are secondhand reports gleaned from merchants. Modern historians consider Battuta's extensive notes concerning geography, local customs, and Islamic culture to be highly reliable. He died in Marrakesh in 1377.

Ife

Powerful YORUBA religious center established in the 11th century in modern-day Nigeria. According to Yoruba myth, Ife was established by Oduduwa, who was lowered to Earth at that extremely fertile location by the Yoruba god Olorun. Ife was noted for its fine artifacts, including ivory and wood carvings, terra-cotta, brass and copper castings, and bronze sculpture. Most of these were created between the 12th and 15th centuries, and some of the bronze portraits of Ife rulers are considered among the best naturalistic sculpture in the world. Ife's importance

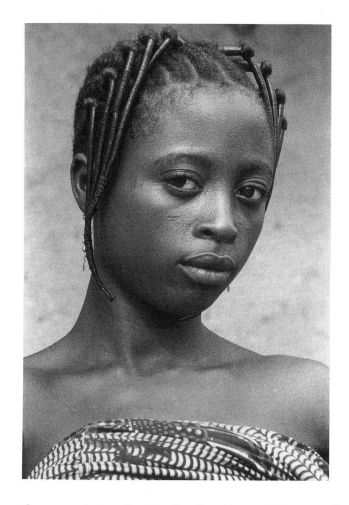

Ife woman (*photo by Eliot Elisofon, National Museum of African Art, Washington, D.C.*)

was somewhat eclipsed by the rise of OYO, a northern Yoruba kingdom that was established in the 14th century. The rulers of BENIN, a neighboring

146

state, also based their claims to the throne on descent from Oduduwa.

Imhotep (active ca. 2650–2610 B.C.) *ancient Egyptian architect, physician, priest, sculptor, writer of proverbs*

Imhotep was chief counselor to the Third Dynasty pharaoh Djoser (Zoser), and his name is still synonymous with profound learning. It was he who designed the famous 197-foot step pyramid near Memphis. Although no specific medical advances are credited to him, he was revered as a healer, and after his death, ailing Egyptians made offerings at shrines dedicated to him. The Greeks identified him with Asclepius, the god of medicine who was once (according to Homer) a human physician.

Indian Ocean trade

Highly lucrative long-term trade that existed between a number of East African coastal cities and the commercial centers of the Arabian Peninsula, India, China, and Indonesia. Although this trade goes back to ancient times, it reached its height between the 10th and 15th centuries, with the involvement of more than 40 East African cities. The inhabitants of these cities were primarily Swahili-speaking people of BANTU origin, although many were of Arab descent. Islam was widely practiced, and Swahili, though Bantu-based, includes many Arabic words, particularly in regard to government, commerce, and religion.

The wealth of these East African cities is referred to in the Sinbad stories of the *One Thousand and One Arabian Nights*. Some, such as KILWA, Mogadishu, and ZANZIBAR, even minted their own coins. These cities exported gold, ivory, rhinoceros horn, tortoiseshell, copper, frankincense, myrrh, resins, ebony, iron, slaves, sandalwood, hides, ambergris, and wild animals. Their imports included Persian glassware, Chinese porcelain, and Indian cottons. To this day, Swahili women place imported Chinese porcelain in wall niches to absorb evil spirits. The trade was made possible by the fact that Indian Ocean currents and winds shift direction twice a year, making round-trips between East

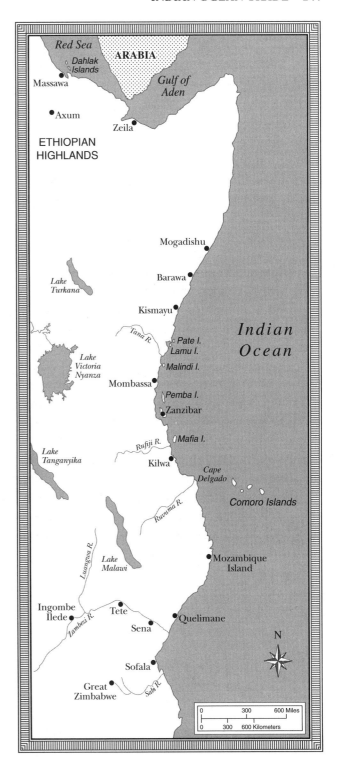

Above: Cities along the Indian Ocean Trade Routes (*Facts On File*)

Africa and the Persian Gulf, Arabian peninsula, India, Sri Lanka, Indonesia, and/or China feasible on a yearly basis.

The Indian Ocean trade was seriously disrupted by Portuguese attacks on East African cities in the early 1500s, and it never recovered. Attacks by inland tribes and the salt-water contamination or lack of fresh water supplies also led to the abandonment of some of these settlements. In addition to those listed above, East African cities and regions involved in the Indian Ocean trade included Pemba, Quelimane, Brava, MALINDI, the Comoro Islands, Sofala, MOMBASA, Pate, Lamu, MADAGASCAR, and MOZAMBIQUE.

Ivory Coast, Republic of (Côte d'Ivoire)

West African country, once a French colony. Its official capital is Yamoussoukro, which was the native village of FÉLIX HOUPHOUËT-BOIGNY, the Ivory Coast's first president. The leading city, however, is Abidjan, which is sometimes called the "Paris of West Africa" because of its beauty and its 30,000 French inhabitants. The area was originally settled by the Krou, Senoufo, and Lubi peoples. Baoule tribespeople migrated there from Ghana in the 18th and 19th centuries. The Portuguese arrived in the 1460s, but the slave trade was not as destructive in this area as in others because of a lack of good harbors for slave ships. The French became interested in the region in the 1840s, but they were unable to establish control until after an 1890s war with MANDINKA forces led by the famous Samori Touré. The French saw the area as a rich producer of coffee, cocoa, bananas, and palm oil. But in order to open up the interior of the country, they had to build a railroad, which they did through a brutal forced labor system using workers from the area and BURKINA FASO. The Ivory Coast achieved its independence in 1960 under the leadership of FÉLIX HOUPHOUËT-BOIGNY, who served as president for 33 years. However, the country faces a major environmental threat as its extensive rain forests are being destroyed at a rapid rate. In the 10 years between 1977 and 1987, the Ivory Coast lost 42 percent of its forest—a greater percentage than in any other country in the world. In 1999, the government ordered the closure of all schools in the two biggest cities in an effort to stem student unrest. However, on Christmas Eve 1999, President Henri Konan Bedie was overthrown by General Robert Guei and a military government was established.

In October 2000, Guei was ousted from office after he shut down the presidential election and declared himself the winner. Laurent Gbagbo, who was leading in votes, was declared president despite the absence of several popular candidates in the election. Violent outbursts and demonstrations plagued the country following the election, causing many deaths and injuries.

J

Jackson, Jesse Louis (1941–) *civil rights activist, minister*

Born in Greenville, South Carolina, Jackson became involved in the SIT-IN MOVEMENT while a student at North Carolina Agricultural and Technical College at Greensboro. After graduation, he entered Chicago Theological Seminary but remained deeply involved in the Civil Rights movement. He met DR. MARTIN LUTHER KING JR. at the Selma, Alabama, march and soon afterward joined the SOUTHERN CHRISTIAN LEADERSHIP CONFERENCE (SCLC). In 1965, Jackson was named head of the SCLC's Operation Breadbasket program in Chicago and was successful in convincing numerous corporations to hire black workers, contract with black-owned service companies, and utilize black-owned banks. He also remained involved in civil rights activities elsewhere and was with King at the Lorraine Motel in Memphis, Tennessee, when King was assassinated in 1968. In 1971, Jackson resigned from Operation Breadbasket and the SCLC to establish Operation PUSH (People United to Save Humanity), which aimed at improving the economic status of African Americans.

Believing that black political power was crucial to continued black economic growth, Jackson spent months traveling across the country urging people to register to vote. He traveled to the Middle East in 1979, and the personal contact he established with Syrian leader Hafez al-Assad proved helpful later when navy pilot Robert Goodman was taken prisoner by the Syrians after being shot down during U.S. military operations in Lebanon in 1984. That same year, Jackson ran for the Democratic nomination for president, putting together a "National Rainbow Coalition" to address the concerns of various groups that felt ignored by the other candidates. Although black congresswoman Shirley Chisholm had sought the Democratic nomination for president 12 years earlier, Jackson was the first African American to mount a major challenge. He made another strong run for the nomination in 1988. During the 1990s, Jackson worked to win statehood for the District of Columbia. In 1998, Jackson was invited to accompany President Bill Clinton to Africa. A year later, he arranged for the release of three American soldiers who had been taken prisoner during the conflict in Kosovo in the Balkans.

Jackson, Mahalia (1911–1972) *gospel singer*

Born in a three-room shotgun shack in New Orleans, Mahalia Jackson lost her mother at the age of four. She grew up singing in the choir of the Moriah Baptist Church and later said that when she was baptized at age 12 she promised God that she would dedicate her life to Him in song. Forced to leave school in the eighth grade, she went to work as a laundress, cook, and maid. In 1927, she moved to Chicago, where she joined the Johnson Singers quintet at Greater Salem Baptist Church. After coming to the attention of Thomas Dorsey, the "Father of Gospel Music," she began performing at Baptist conventions and churches around the country. In

1946, she released a recording of "Move on Up a Little Higher," which sold over eight million copies. Other multimillion sellers include "Upper Room," "Even Me," "Didn't It Rain," and "Silent Night." She also made several films, but turned down thousands of dollars in bookings at Las Vegas and New York clubs rather than abandon gospel for blues or pop music. A supporter of the Civil Rights movement, she sang "I Been 'Buked and I Been Scorned" at the historic 1963 MARCH ON WASHINGTON, minutes before Dr. MARTIN LUTHER KING JR. delivered his "I Have A Dream" speech. Over 6,000 people attended memorial services for her in Chicago, and over 50,000 filed past her casket in quiet tribute to both her voice and her faith.

Jackson, Michael (1958–) *singer, songwriter*

Michael Jackson began his career as a child singing star with his brothers in a group called the Jackson Five. In 1969, the group signed with Motown Records, becoming one of the company's most successful acts with 13 top 20 hits within a six-year period. Jackson also scored several successes as a solo act. With producer QUINCY JONES, he released his 1979 masterpiece album *Off the Wall,* followed in 1982 with *Thriller,* the biggest-selling album of all time. His dancing, as seen on videos and on tour, drew praise from Fred Astaire and Bob Fosse. In 1985, Jackson coauthored "We Are the World," with Lionel Richie for African famine relief and scored another musical success in 1987 with *Bad.* Other albums include *Victory, Dangerous* and *HIStory.* His autobiography, *Moonwalk,* is named for a dance step he created. In 1994, he faced serious accusations of sexual misconduct but was not formally charged.

Jackson, the "King of Pop," married Lisa Marie Presley, daughter of entertainer Elvis Presley, in 1994. The couple divorced two years later.

James, Daniel, Jr. ("Chappie") (1920–1978)

first African-American four-star general in the history of the American military

James learned to fly while a student at Tuskegee Institute, where he was a member of the all-black Army Air Corps advanced flying program. After graduation, he was assigned to the 477th Bombardment Group. The officers of the 477th found themselves subjected to racial discrimination at Freedman Field in Indiana and several staged a nonviolent sit-in at a segregated officers' club. When they were arrested, James and over 100 other African-American officers protested and were themselves arrested and threatened with court-martial. The charges were later dropped. On July 26, 1948, President Harry S. Truman issued Executive Order 9981 ending segregation in the armed forces. While assigned to Clark Air Force Base in the Philippines, James suffered serious injuries when he rescued another pilot who had crashed. During the Korean War, he won the Distinguished Flying Cross. He also fought in the Vietnam War, where he almost lost his life. In 1975, Daniel James became the head of the North American Air Defense (NORAD), which was crucial to America's nuclear defense.

jazz

Unique musical form developed by African Americans. The foundation of jazz is BLUES music. Ragtime, which was also created by African Americans, was another important influence. Jazz emerged as a distinct style around 1890 in New Orleans among the large black bands that often played for funeral processions and Mardi Gras celebrations and the smaller groups that entertained in the bars of the city's notorious Storyville district. This early jazz, called "Dixieland" by northern white musicians, emphasized collective improvisation during which cornet, trumpet, clarinet, and trombone players would add related melodies to a basic melody. When the navy placed much of Storyville off-limits to its personnel, scores of jazz musicians lost their jobs, and many, including LOUIS ARMSTRONG and Joe "King" Oliver, moved to Chicago. New Orleans Dixieland gave way to Chicago jazz that utilized a 2/4 jazz beat, added the saxophone and piano, and included more individual solos.

Swing, which was played by large bands such as those of COUNT BASIE, Fletcher Henderson, and DUKE ELLINGTON, developed in the 1930s. Swing involves playing two notes of equal value within a beat but lengthening the duration of the first beat, creating a danceable, swinging feeling. Swing limited improvisation and created a more structured form of jazz.

Bebop, which developed as a reaction to swing, was a sophisticated, virtuoso jazz style involving irregular melodies, exceptional speed, and complex chord structures. It developed in the early 1940s and appealed to exceptionally talented musicians seeking the kind of improvisational freedom that the big bands could not accommodate. Bebop utilized melodic extensions involving the use of dissonant notes (so-called because they are not the primary notes of the chords), polyrhythms in which two or more contrasting rhythms were played at the same time, and extended, improvised solos. The fact that the music patterns frequently ended with a two-note figure led to the adoption of the onomatopoeic term "re-bop" or "be-bop." CHARLIE PARKER, DIZZY GILLESPIE, and THELONIOUS MONK are closely linked to its development.

Cool or West Coast jazz emerged in reaction to bop, with slower melodies and more emphasis on ensemble playing. MILES DAVIS was associated with cool jazz before turning to modal jazz, which involved fewer chords. "Third stream," which was later connected with "avant-garde" or "free" jazz, refers to the merging of jazz with classical music and often incorporates orchestral instruments, as in the music of the Modern Jazz Quartet. CHARLIE MINGUS and Ornette Coleman are examples of avant-garde musicians. Electric jazz, so-called because musicians play electric instruments, ushered in another major change. Fusion jazz links jazz and rock.

In addition to those mentioned above, a partial list of black musicians who have made major contributions to jazz include ART BLAKEY, CLIFFORD BROWN, COLEMAN HAWKINS, Nat King Cole, "Jelly Roll" Morton, SONNY ROLLINS, ART TATUM, CHARLIE CHRISTIAN, JOHN COLTRANE, ELLA FITZGERALD, HERBIE HANCOCK, BILLIE HOLIDAY, SARAH VAUGHN, Fats Waller, Lionel Hampton, and Wynton and Bradford Marsalis.

Recommended Reading: Megill, Donald D., and Richard S. Demory. *Introduction to Jazz History.* Englewood Cliffs, N.J.: Prentice-Hall, 1993.

Jefferson, Lemon ("Blind") (1897–1929) *blues singer*

Believed to have been blind since birth, "Blind" Lemon Jefferson grew up in Texas amid the sounds of GOSPEL music. Probably self-taught, he played for dimes and quarters while in his early teens. Around 1912, he and HUDDIE "Leadbelly" LEDBETTER began performing together. Jefferson began making records in 1925, and eventually released 89 titles, becoming the most famous BLUES singer of the 1920s. His singing is noted for its expressive, often lonely, bitter quality, and LOUIS ARMSTRONG cited it as a major influence on his own work. Jefferson's guitar work often involved long improvisational passages as a way of emphasizing a line or a word. By the late 1920s, Jefferson was the most successful "country" blues singer in the country. It is believed that his death in Chicago occurred after a recording session when he became lost and collapsed during a blizzard.

Jenne (Djenne)

West African city located in what is now MALI, on the Bari River on the edge of the Sahel. Jenne was a major link in the caravan trade between North Africa, TIMBUKTU, and the gold merchants further to the south. Radiocarbon dating indicates settlement began in the area in the third century B.C. According to archaeological evidence, the region was originally much wetter and able to support a much denser population 1,000 years ago than today. This early population supplied much of the rice and other foodstuffs that made the development of Timbuktu and GAO possible. Jenne's earliest occupants were iron-using, an indication that trade in the area goes back 2,000 years. The city began to take shape during the 13th century, when it underwent extensive construction by members of the Soninke tribe, and it became a center for the trade in gold, salt, and slaves. Jenne was captured by Sunni Ali of the SONGHAI EMPIRE in 1473, and it was attacked by the BAMBARA in the late 16th century. The city became an important center for Islamic learning in the 17th century. It was overrun by Seku Ahmadu Bari of the Macina Empire in the early 19th century, only to come under French control in the 1890s. Jenne, as part of what was then Soudan (French Sudan), was later incorporated into the FRENCH WEST AFRICA federation.

Jemison, Mae Carol (1956–) *astronaut, physician*

Born in Decatur, Alabama, Mae Jemison graduated from Stanford University in 1977 with a degree in chemical engineering. She then entered Cornell Medical School, earning her M.D. in 1981. She joined the Peace Corps in 1983 and served as a medical officer in Sierra Leone and Liberia. In addition to English, she speaks Swahili, Japanese, and Russian. In 1987, Jemison was accepted into NASA's astronaut training program and, in 1992, became the first African-American woman in space as part of the crew aboard the space shuttle *Endeavor*. In 1993 she left NASA to establish The Jemison Group,

Mae Jemison (*NASA*)

Inc., a company that designs programs utilizing advanced technology to solve social problems in developing nations. She is also the director of The Jemison Institute for Advancing Technology in Developing Countries.

Jim Crow

A slang expression dating from the 1890s. It indicates a segregationist law, custom, or atmosphere targeting African Americans. The expression was taken from the name of a comic character created by a white actor who painted his face black (an offensive practice known as wearing blackface) and pretended to be a foolish black man. This type of comic routine proved popular among prejudiced whites and became a regular part of so-called minstrel shows that involved jokes, songs, and comic skits making fun of African Americans.

Johnson, Henry (ca. 1897–1929) *soldier*

Born in North Carolina, Johnson grew up in Albany, New York, and joined the army in 1917. He was assigned to the all-black 369th Infantry and promoted to sergeant. The 369th was sent to France and assigned a position at a bridge on the Aisne River. In the early morning hours of May 14, Johnson and Pvt. Needham Roberts were on sentry duty when a unit of 32 Germans attempted unsuccessfully to overrun their position. Roberts was taken prisoner, but Johnson freed him using the butt of his empty gun and a knife. In vicious hand-to-hand fighting, Johnson killed four Germans and wounded 10. In the struggle, he suffered bayonet wounds to his back, arm, feet, and face. Both men were awarded the Croix de Guerre by the French government and were cited by Generals Foch and Pershing. Johnson was given a hero's welcome on his return to the United States, but he received no medals, not even a Purple Heart (the medal awarded to any member of the U.S. armed forces who has been wounded or killed in action). He was denied disability pay and was unable to find a job due to his injuries. The fight at the bridge became known as the "Battle of Henry Johnson."

Johnson, James Weldon (1871–1938) *writer, lyricist, civil rights leader, diplomat*

Born in Jacksonville, Florida, James Weldon Johnson attended Atlanta University, became a high school principal, and in 1898 was the first African-American lawyer admitted to the Florida Bar Association. In 1895, he founded and edited the first African-American daily newspaper in the United States. Moving to New York City in 1901, he attended classes at Columbia University and collaborated with his brother, John Rosamond Johnson, in writing more than 200 songs, including what is often referred to as the Negro national anthem, "Lift Every Voice and Sing" (1900). After writing the song "You're All Right, Teddy" for Teddy Roosevelt's 1904 presidential campaign, he was appointed to consular posts in Venezuela (1906–1908) and Nicaragua (1909–1913). During this period, he wrote his only novel, *The Autobiography of an Ex-Colored Man* (1912), an indictment of racial injustice.

After the election of Democrat Woodrow Wilson, Johnson returned to the United States, where he became editor of the *New York Age*. He also worked as a speechwriter for presidential candidate Charles Evans Hughes in 1916 and finished his first book of poetry, *Fifty Years and Other Poems* (1917). He joined the NATIONAL ASSOCIATION FOR THE ADVANCEMENT OF COLORED PEOPLE in 1915, becoming a field secretary a year later and executive secretary in 1920. He increased the organization's membership, denounced the occupation of Haiti by U.S. Marines, and organized the famous Silent March against lynching, which took place in New York in 1917.

A major leader of the HARLEM RENAISSANCE, Johnson regularly used his position with the NAACP *Crisis* magazine and his connections with white publishers and producers to promote African-American artists, writers, and performers. His own work includes *God's Trombones: Seven Negro Sermons in Verse* (1927). He also completed a 1930 history book, *Black Manhattan*. From 1930, he was a professor at Fisk University in Tennessee, where he wrote his autobiography *Along This Way*. His faculty residence at Fisk is now a National Historic Landmark.

James Weldon Johnson (*Library of Congress*)

Johnson, John Arthur (Jack) (1878–1946) *first black heavyweight boxing champion*

Born in Galveston, Texas, Jack Johnson stowed away on a boat when he was 12 in an effort to get to New York so that he could meet Steve Brodie, the man who had jumped off the Brooklyn Bridge and survived. He got as far as Florida, where he got work as a fisherman before continuing to New York where he finally met Brodie.

Johnson's first professional boxing match (in 1897) was a winner-take-all contest with five men in the ring. Johnson won, knocking out the other four. In 1908, he took the heavyweight crown from Tommy Burns even though he had been forced to allow Burns' manager to serve as referee. The public immediately demanded a "great white hope"—a white boxer who could take back the title. Johnson

Jack Johnson, 1909 (*Library of Congress*)

defeated all comers, including Jim Jeffries, a former champion who came out of retirement to fight him in 1910. Jeffries' defeat triggered race riots across the country as white mobs attacked African Americans. Nineteen people were killed and 251 injured. In response, laws were passed in several states forbidding interracial boxing matches. Though such laws were clearly unconstitutional, many white fighters, among them Jack Dempsey, agreed to honor the ban.

Johnson further infuriated whites by marrying a white woman in 1912. Shortly afterward, he was convicted of transporting a woman across a state line for sexual purposes (even though the acts with which he had been charged had occurred before the law had been passed) and he fled the country rather than go to jail. He continued to fight overseas, including a bout with American Jim Johnson whom

he fought to a 10th-round draw in spite of having suffered a broken left arm in the third round. Johnson's desire to return to the United States affected his decision to fight Jess Willard in Cuba in 1915. Willard won in what looked suspiciously like a fix, but having lost the championship, Johnson felt political opposition to his return would fade away. He returned to the United States in 1920 and served 10 months in Leavenworth prison. He died in an automobile accident. Johnson's life was the subject of the play and film *The Great White Hope,* starring James Earl Jones.

Johnson, John Harold (1918–   ) *publisher*

Johnson began his publishing career in 1942 when he borrowed $500 to launch the *Negro Digest.* The first printing of 5,000 copies sold out within a week. Circulation reached 150,000 within a few years, and one magazine column, "If I Were a Negro," included contributions from various public figures, including First Lady Eleanor Roosevelt. Johnson's next magazine, *Ebony,* begun in 1945, featured glossy photo-articles showcasing successful African Americans, in-depth historical/civil rights stories, and general interest material. With over 2 million subscribers, it is the best-selling black magazine in the world.

In 1950, Johnson introduced *Tan* magazine and in 1951 began publishing the enormously successful *Jet,* which shocked the world in 1955 with its exclusive, close-up photographs of EMMETT TILL's battered face. In addition to these, Johnson Publishing now includes *EM:Ebony Man.* Johnson also created Fashion Fair Cosmetics and developed the nationally syndicated TV show *Ebony/Jet Showcase.* He is chairman of Supreme Life Insurance Company and WJPC-AM in Chicago. He is known for the expression, "Failure is a word I don't accept."

Johnson, Robert (1911–1938) *blues singer, guitarist*

Johnson's fame derives in part from his early death at age 26, probably from poison, and the brooding, tormented quality of his music. "I got to keep movin'/Blues falling down like hail/And the day keeps on worryin' me/There's a hellhound on my trail" ("Hellhound On My Trail"). An illegitimate Mississippi child, Johnson was rejected by his stepfather. He married while still in his teens, but his wife died in childbirth along with their baby. He was described as moody and unstable and had a tendency to become involved with married women. Johnson was heavily influenced by Delta bluesmen Eddie "Son" House and Willie Brown, but often incorporated various other styles into his music. His songs "Dust My Broom" and "Terraplane Blues" are considered classics, and he had enormous influence on both BLUES and rock musicians. Versions of over 30 songs associated with him have been recorded by singers ranging from Muddy Waters to Jimi Hendrix to Eric Clapton to Keith Richards.

Recommended Listening: *Robert Johnson: The Complete Recordings* (CBS/Sony).

Johnson, William Henry (1901–1970) *artist*

Born in Florence, South Carolina, Johnson spent five years studying at the National Academy of Design in New York. In 1926, he traveled to Europe, where he was influenced by the work of Cezanne, Rouault, van Gogh, and Soutine. In 1932, he visited North Africa and decided to adapt the "primitive" lifestyle of Arabs and BERBERS to his work. Johnson returned to America in 1938 and began to focus on subjects related to African Americans. He created hundreds of paintings, many of them centered on the HARLEM community. Others had religious themes but portrayed African Americans as holy figures. Still others reflected historical and social justice themes. His work is noted for its strong colors, clear lines, and geometric forms. Among his best-known works are *Chain Gang, Going to Church, Li'l Sis,* and *Young Man in a Vest.*

Jones, Absalom (1746–1818) *Episcopal priest, abolitionist*

Born a slave, Jones worked in his master's store in Philadelphia during the day and worked for himself and attended school at night. He managed to purchase his freedom and that of his wife by 1784. Two years later, he met RICHARD ALLEN and became a lay preacher at St. George's Methodist Episcopal Church. When the congregation decided to become segregated, Jones, Allen, and the other black members walked out and formed the Free African Society, an abolitionist, benevolent, religious group. In 1793, Jones and Allen arranged for nurses and undertakers from the black community to help fight a severe yellow fever epidemic. Along with JAMES FORTEN, they also organized 2,500 men to defend Philadelphia during the War of 1812. The three worked closely to promote abolition and various African-American interests. Jones eventually established the St. Thomas African Episcopal Church and became the first African-American Episcopal priest in the United States.

Jones, Frederick McKinley (1893–1961) *inventor*

Orphaned at age nine, Jones had little formal education. He taught himself electronics and auto mechanics. After serving in the army during World War I, he moved to Hallock, Minnesota, where he became interested in radio and built the first radio station transmitter in Hallock. He also developed a soundtrack device for motion pictures. Word of his work reached Joseph Numero, the owner of Cinema Supplies, a movie equipment company in Minneapolis, and Numero hired Jones in 1930. Seven years later, Jones received his first patent for a movie-ticket dispenser.

After hearing Numero discuss the problems of developing a workable unit for truck refrigeration that could operate in limited space and withstand the vibrations of road travel, Jones designed a small, shock-proof refrigeration unit that could be mounted on top of trucks. He and Numero then formed the U.S. Thermo Control Company (later called Thermo King Corp.) to manufacture and market his device. Jones' refrigeration unit revolutionized the food industry by making it possible to ship fruit, vegetables, meat, and dairy products across the country without fear of spoilage. It was also critically important in the transport of blood and medicine during World War II. Jones was eventually awarded over 60 patents, of which 40 were for refrigeration equipment.

Jones, Lois Mailou (1905–1998) *artist, teacher*

Born in Boston, Jones began painting during summers spent at Martha's Vineyard in Massachusetts. Her interest in African art began when, as a teenager, she designed masks for dancers at a local school. She studied at the Boston Museum of Fine Arts, established an art department at Palmer Memorial Institute in North Carolina, then taught for 47 years at Howard University. After her marriage to Haitian graphic artist Louis Vergniaud Pierre-Noel, she began working Haitian motifs into her painting. She was also strongly influenced by African artistic tradition. Her work is noted for its vivid color and energy. Her artwork is exhibited in the Metropolitan Museum of Art in New York; the National Portrait Gallery and Hirshhorn Museum in Washington, D.C.; and the Museum of Fine Arts in Boston. Lois Jones died on June 9, 1998.

Jones, Quincy Delight, Jr. (1933–) *composer, arranger, producer, musician*

Jones grew up in Seattle, Washington, where he began playing the trumpet while still in grade school. He met Count BASIE and worked with Ray Charles while in his early teens. He won a scholarship to Boston's Berklee School of Music and earned money by playing in strip clubs at night. At age 17, he was invited to New York to do some arrangements for JAZZ musician Oscar Pettiford. There he met CHARLIE PARKER, MILES DAVIS, and THELONIOUS MONK. He toured Europe with DIZZY GILLESPIE in 1956–57. He remained in Paris where he studied classical composition with Nadia Boulanger.

Returning to New York, Jones became vice president at Mercury Records (1961–68). In 1965, he scored his first film, *The Pawnbroker*. Other film scores include *In Cold Blood, In The Heat of the Night, The Color Purple,* and *The Wiz.* He has also scored many TV shows, including *Roots, The Bill Cosby Show, Ironside,* and *Sanford and Son.* Jones has won over two dozen Grammy awards and has pro-

Composer, conductor, producer, and arranger Quincy Jones (*Frank Driggs/Archive Photos*)

duced and arranged material for many of the biggest stars in the music business, including MICHAEL JACKSON'S *Off the Wall* and *Thriller* albums and the *E.T.* storybook album with Steven Spielberg.

In 1974, he suffered a near-fatal cerebral aneurysm, but he recovered and six years later founded his own label, Quest Records. In 1985 he organized the "We Are the World" famine relief project to help people in Africa. In 1995, Jones produced the film *The Color Purple* from the book by ALICE WALKER. He went on to produce the hit television show *The Fresh Prince of Bel Air* in 1990. Two years later, Jones became the publisher of *Vibe,* a glossy rap magazine. In 1994, he established Quest Broadcasting, with television stations in New Orleans and Atlanta. He is the subject of a documentary: *Listen Up: The Lives of Quincy Jones.*

Recommended Listening: *The Dude; Walking in Space; Body Heat; Gula Matari;* and *Smackwater Jack* (all on the A&M label).

Joplin, Scott (1868–1917) *musician, composer*

After leaving home while still in his midteens, Scott Joplin became one of hundreds of black musicians who traveled the country after the Civil War and developed new musical forms. One of these was ragtime, a musical style that drew on African traditions and combined syncopated or varied rhythm patterns with the melody. This was known as "ragging" the melody. Joplin began composing his own music and, in 1899, published some of his work in *Original Rags*. With the help of a white man named John Stark, Joplin published "Maple Leaf Rag," which was named for a club where he worked at night. Considered by many experts to be the best-written rag ever, "Maple Leaf Rag" became the first piece of sheet music to sell 1,000,000 copies. It also created a worldwide demand for ragtime music.

Joplin's later work included the opera *Treemonisha,* which he wrote in tribute to his mother. Unable to find backers, he unsuccessfully tried to produce it himself; it was revived on Broadway in the 1970s and became a hit. Joplin's "The Entertainer" was chosen as the theme for the 1973 Academy Award–winning movie *The Sting.*

Jordan, George (1847–1904) *soldier*

Born in Kentucky, Jordan joined the Ninth Cavalry in 1866 and served in the Victorio Indian War (1879–80). It was during this campaign that Jordan led a group of 25 black soldiers in rescuing a small white settlement in New Mexico that was being threatened by Apaches from the nearby Mescalero Reservation. After riding through the night, Jordan and his men erected a stockade and positioned themselves for combat. At sunset, they were attacked, and though outnumbered four to one, twice drove off the Indian forces. For his courage and leadership, Jordan was awarded the Congressional Medal of Honor. He served with the U.S. Army for 30 years.

Jordan, Michael Jeffrey (1963–) *basketball player*

Though he did not make the varsity basketball team in high school, Michael Jordan later became one of the most spectacular players in the history of professional basketball. He gained national renown at the University of North Carolina and was a member of the winning U.S. basketball squad at the 1984 Seoul Olympics. He then joined the Chicago Bulls, where he led his team to six national championships, won 10 NBA scoring titles, and was named MVP five times. He won a second Olympic gold medal in 1992 as a member of the U.S. "Dream Team." In October 1993, two months after his father was murdered by car thieves, Jordan retired from basketball to attempt a career in professional baseball, but he returned to basketball in 1995. He retired again in January 1999 after achieving 29,277 career points and a career scoring average of 31.5. In addition to his basketball success, Jordan became one of the most recognizable and sought-after personalities for product endorsements. In January 2000, Jordan became president of basketball operations for the Washington Wizards.

Juba II (unknown–A.D. 25) *Berber king, writer, geographer, explorer*

Born in Numidia (what is now coastal Algeria and Libya), Juba was taken by Julius Caesar to Rome, where he received an education. His interest in geography caused him to read everything he could find on sailing and navigation. He also spent many hours interviewing sailors and ship captains about their travels. In 25 B.C., after Augustus became emperor of Rome, he made Juba king of Mauretania, the ancient name for what is now northern Morocco and Algeria.

Juba discovered, and wrote a description of, the Canary Islands, a group of several islands situated in the Atlantic Ocean off the coast of North Africa. In Juba's time, the Canaries were uninhabited, but his men found large dogs on one of the islands, so Juba named it Canaria from the Latin word *canis,* meaning "dog." Whether King Juba left colonists on the Canaries is unknown, but a BERBER-like North African people, known as Guanches, did settle the islands shortly before the time of Christ. King Juba also wrote several books, including a detailed history of Africa, that discussed the geography of the continent and provided information about many of its animals.

Julian, Percy Lavon (1899–1975) *chemist*
Julian graduated with honors from DePauw University. When racial prejudice prevented his acceptance at leading graduate schools, he began teaching chemistry at Fisk University. Later, while studying for his Ph.D. in Austria, he accomplished the first successful synthesis of physostigmine, a drug used in fighting glaucoma. His work saved millions of glaucoma victims from blindness. Returning to the United States, he became chief chemist at Glidden Paint Company, where his research caused Glidden to go from a $35,000 loss to a $135,000 profit in one year. Dr. Julian also developed Aero-Foam, a substance for putting out oil and gas fires, and found a way to manufacture hormones for medical use and to synthesize cortisone. In 1954, Dr. Julian founded Julian Laboratories. In its first year, the company earned $71.70. Six years later, due to Dr. Julian's research, Julian Laboratories commanded a selling price of $2,338,000.

Just, Ernest Everett (1883–1941) *scientist*
Just was born in Charleston, South Carolina. His father died when Just was four, and his mother supported the family as a teacher. In 1903, he enrolled at Dartmouth College, where he studied zoology. He was elected to Phi Beta Kappa in his junior year and graduated magna cum laude in 1907. He then became an English instructor at Howard University, where he organized the college's first drama club.

In the summer of 1909, Just began graduate work at the Marine Biological Laboratories at Woods Hole, Massachusetts, where he specialized in the study of marine invertebrates and embryology. From then on, he spent his winters teaching and his summers doing research. In 1912, Just became head of the department of physiology at Howard University Medical School, a post he held until 1920.

Percy Julian (*Schomburg Center for Research in Black Culture*)

In later years, Just spent much of his time in Europe, where there was less racial prejudice. In 1929, he became the first American scientist invited to do research at the highly respected Kaiser Wilhelm Institut für Biologie, Berlin-Dahlem. He later worked at the Stazione Zoologica in Naples and at the Sorbonne at the University of Paris. Just's findings on fertilization, on the role of ectoplasm in cellular development and evolution, and on hydration and dehydration had a critical impact on medicine. His books are *The Biology of the Cell Surface* and *Basic Methods for Experiments in Eggs of Marine Animals*.

K

Kanem-Bornu

Feudal West African kingdom near Lake Chad that existed for about 1,000 years. Kanem was founded in the ninth century by Kanuri and Zaghawa tribespeople who displaced the So people who had originally settled in the area. The royal house became Islamic in the 11th century in response to growing trade with Muslim states in the north and east, and the kingdom was ruled through an extensive bureaucracy. Women maintained a high status and enjoyed significant political power.

During the 13th century, Kanem absorbed the Bornu kingdom to the west, then underwent a period of relative weakness that lasted approximately 100 years. Kanem-Bornu was revitalized under Ali Ghaji and his son, Idris Katakarmabi, who ended years of political intrigue and strengthened the army. The empire reached its height under King Idris Alooma, who reigned from 1571 to 1603 and oversaw victorious military campaigns against the TUAREG and the HAUSA, thanks partly to the use of firearms. Idris also established a number of mosques and set up a judicial system based on the Koran. Kanem-Bornu continued its traditional practice of raiding southern tribes for slaves—especially women—who were traded in the north for horses or used as agricultural laborers.

The kingdom became weaker during the 1700s and in the early 19th century suffered a revolt by FULANI subjects who were encouraged by attacks on Bornu by the Fulani of the Sokoto Caliphate. Though Sokoto was initially successful, most of Bornu's territory was salvaged by Al-Kanemi, an Islamic scholar and leader who was called in to repel the invaders. The empire fell apart after Al-Kanemi's death in 1835, as Bornu was torn by civil war and Kanem came under the control of the eastern kingdom of Wadai.

Kanissa'ai (CAN-ee-sa-Eye-ee) *legendary king of medieval Ghana*

Kanissa'ai supposedly owned 1,000 horses, each of which had its own mattress and copper urinal and was cared for by three servants. Each evening, in the light of a huge bonfire, he would set forth food for 10,000 people. It is thought that the legend of King Kanissa'ai is based on the life of an actual 11th-century Ghanaian king who held nightly audiences where disputes were heard and settled. In addition to numerous princes and courtiers, this king was often accompanied by dogs and horses draped in gold and silver decorations.

Kay, Ulysses (1917–1995) *composer, teacher*

The nephew of JAZZ cornetist Joe "King" Oliver, Ulysses Kay was a prolific composer of opera and symphonic music. A graduate of the University of Arizona, he received a master's degree in music at the University of Rochester and also studied at Yale and Columbia. Following World War II service in the navy, he studied music as a Fulbright Fellow in Rome. He also taught at Boston University, UCLA, and Lehman College in New York. His work, such as his opera *Frederick Douglass,* often drew on African-American themes. Other works include *Jubilee, The Juggler of Our Lady, Choral Triptych, Six Dances, Fantasy Variations,* and *Sinfonia in E.*

kente cloth

Brightly colored cloth that comes in many beautiful geometric designs. Kente cloth originally came from Ghana in West Africa, where it was first made for 16th-century Ashanti kings and members of the royal court. The name *kente* means "basket," and refers to the cloth's basket-weave appearance, the result of four-inch strips that are woven and then sewn together. Traditional Africans wear kente only on important occasions.

Kenya, Republic of

East African country. Capital: Nairobi. At an early date, the area attracted migrants from the Horn of Africa, and these were followed by BANTU-speaking peoples from the interior. Arabs, Shirazis from what is now Iran, and Indian settlers were attracted to Kenya's coastal region, which has been a center of long-distance trade since approximately A.D. 1000. The lucrative Indian Ocean trade and the possibility of access to gold deposits in the interior also made the coastal area attractive to European and Middle Eastern rulers, and after 1500, the area was subjected to military conquest by Portugal and Oman.

In the late 19th century, a British colony was established in Kenya, although the Omani Sultan, who was then based in Zanzibar, maintained sovereignty over the coastal area under a British protectorate. After coming to terms with MAASAI tribal leaders, the British built the Mombasa-Uganda railroad, which facilitated the movement of white settlers into the area. The whites eventually pushed the Maasai and the KIKUYU off much of their land, although certain tribes, such as the Luo, were barely affected.

Opposition developed among the Kikuyu, which resulted in the shooting of between 21 and 100 protesters by police in 1922. The independence movement was led by Kikuyu leader JOMO KENYATTA,

who later became Kenya's first president. Part of the drive for independence involved the MAU MAU, a violent resistance organization that operated in Kenya between 1952 and 1960. Kenya became an independent nation in 1963. After Kenyatta died in 1978, he was succeeded by Daniel arap Moi, who has come under increasing criticism for his economic policies, one-party rule, imprisonment and reported torture of political opponents, and the elimination of the secret ballot. Harassment of journalists and the elimination of independent radio stations are also problems. In 1998, the U.S. embassy in Nairobi was the target of a terrorist bomb that killed 215 people, most of them Kenyan nationals. Kenya is famous for its game reserves and national parks.

Kenyatta, Jomo (1892–1978) *African independence leader*

Kenyatta was born near Nairobi, Kenya. His father was a KIKUYU farmer, and, until age 10, Kenyatta spent his days tending sheep. At that point, he ran away to a Christian mission, where he received treatment for a spinal disease and learned to read and write. In 1921, he traveled to Nairobi and found work as a water-meter reader. His father had named him Kamau wa Ngengi, but in Nairobi, he took the MAASAI name Jomo Kenyatta, meaning "burning spear."

Kenyatta's concern for African rights led him to become involved with the Kikuyu Central Association (KCA), a group challenging the British colonial occupation of Kenya. In 1928, he became its general secretary, and three years later he left for England to represent the interests of the KCA there. He returned to Kenya following World War II and, in 1947, became head of the Kenya African Union, an organization seeking political and economic reform. Opposition from British settlers caused the British government to ignore African demands. As a result, many Africans turned to the MAU MAU, a violent resistance organization that came into being in 1952. Accused of being a Mau Mau leader, Kenyatta was arrested on October 20, 1952, a day that is now a national holiday in Kenya. After a five-month trial, he was convicted on the basis of perjured testimony and sentenced to seven years of hard labor.

The Mau Mau resistance was eventually defeated, but the British were forced to institute land reform and give Africans the vote in 1956. In 1961, the Kenya African National Union party, which had won the election, refused to take office until Kenyatta, out of prison but under house arrest, had been freed. He was released in August 1963 and shortly thereafter became Kenya's first prime minister. A year later, he became president. While in office, Kenyatta established close ties with the West and worked to develop a sense of national pride, reduce tribal rivalry, and strengthen Kenya economically. He remained president until his death in 1978.

Kerma

An ancient kingdom that came into existence sometime before 2000 B.C. in what is now Sudan. Fortifications found in the area, and containers with Egyptian seals, indicate the kingdom was a major distribution and possibly manufacturing center. The people of Kerma produced exceptionally fine pottery, a tradition that continued long after the kingdom ceased to exist. Kerma was a forerunner of the KUSH kingdom, which arose around 750 B.C.

Khoi (Khoisan, Khoikhoi)
(COY)

A branch of the BUSHMEN people of southern Africa. The term also refers to the "click" languages spoken by various Bushmen tribes. These languages are distinguished by frequent pops and clicks that are made by placing the tongue against the roof or sides of the mouth while sucking the breath in sharply. It is very difficult to learn, especially since the slightest mispronunciation will often completely change the meaning of a word.

Kikuyu

East African BANTU tribal group. An agricultural people, the Kikuyu settled near Mt. Kenya, apparently after migrating there from Somalia in the 13th century. A highly cohesive community, the Kikuyu maintain close ties through elaborately defined family, clan, and age group obligations. Leadership is

Young Kikuyu woman and child, Nairobi, Kenya, 1921 (*Osa & Martin Johnson Safari Museum/Archive Photos*)

provided through village councils made up of family heads, district councils, and national councils composed of Kikuyu elders. Trade among themselves as well as with other tribes such as the MAASAI is a long-standing tradition. Cattle are extremely important in Kikuyu society, representing both wealth and social position. Under the leadership of JOMO KENYATTA, the Kikuyu opposed British colonial rule in Kenya and were deeply involved in the MAU MAU insurgency.

Kilwa (Kilwa Kisiwani)

An African city-state located in what is now Tanzania. Thanks to its harbor, which could accommodate large ships, Kilwa became the most important trading center in East Africa between A.D. 1100 and

1500. It was visited in 1331 by IBN BATTUTA, a Moroccan scholar, who described it as "elegantly built" and "one of the most beautiful and well-constructed towns in the world." The royal palace had more than 100 rooms and a freshwater bathing pool. Kilwa's BANTU merchants had long engaged in trade with the cities of the Arabian peninsula, India, China, Thailand, and Indonesia. The city was rich enough to mint its own coins, and by the end of the 12th century, Kilwa had gained control of Sofala, a major trading port to the south. Long-term trade with Arab countries resulted in strong Arab influence, but the culture retained its dominant African flavor. Kilwa's immensely profitable trade with India and the Far East was seriously disrupted when the Portuguese sacked the city in 1505 and much of the population fled. Though the Portuguese tried to resurrect Kilwa's Indian Ocean trade, they were unsuccessful and instead instituted a large-scale slave trade. In 1587, Kilwa was attacked by ZIMBA raiders, and over 3,000 of its inhabitants were slain. In the late 1600s, the Portuguese were defeated by Arab forces, but by this time, the slave trade was strongly established in the area, and Kilwa soon deteriorated into a poverty-striken ruin.

King, Martin Luther, Jr. (1929–1968) *civil rights leader*

The son of an Atlanta, Georgia, minister, King graduated from Morehouse College, then enrolled at Crozer Theological Seminary in Pennsylvania, where he was deeply influenced by Mohandas Gandhi's belief in nonviolent action to achieve social change. In 1954, he became pastor of the Dexter Avenue Baptist Church in Montgomery, Alabama.

King came to prominence in 1955 when he took over the leadership of the Montgomery Improvement Association. The organization was established to coordinate the MONTGOMERY BUS BOYCOTT that began when ROSA PARKS was arrested for refusing to give up her seat on a bus to a white man. The boycott's successful conclusion made King a hero throughout the country. Afterward, he and the other black leaders formed the SOUTHERN CHRISTIAN LEADERSHIP CONFERENCE (SCLC), with King as president, to promote other civil rights activities.

Martin Luther King Jr. (*Library of Congress*)

In 1958, King was the victim of an assassination attempt by a mentally disturbed black woman. After he was released from the hospital, he and his wife, Coretta Scott King, traveled to India, then moved to Atlanta, where King joined his father as pastor of the Ebenezer Baptist Church.

On May 19, 1961, a group of FREEDOM RIDERS trying to integrate interstate buses was brutally attacked after arriving in Montgomery, Alabama, and a protest rally at the First Baptist Church was planned in response. King flew there to address the meeting, which attracted more than 1,000 people. A mob gathered outside the church where King and the others were meeting. Infuriated by the earlier violence, U.S. attorney general Robert Kennedy had ordered 600 federal marshals into Montgomery to protect the freedom riders. In the early morning hours, the National Guard also arrived at the church to support the marshals. The guard and the marshals finally dispersed the mob and the civil rights activists were able to leave in safety.

In December 1961, King attempted to help activists in Albany, Georgia, who were working to increase voter registration. But after a pregnant woman was beaten by police when she tried to bring food to demonstrators jailed in a nearby town, blacks in Albany rioted. Many thought King's nonviolent policy was finished. Resentment and rivalry among local black groups was a continuing problem, and in August, King returned to Atlanta.

King went on the offensive in 1963 with a campaign in Birmingham, Alabama, a city that had closed its parks, libraries, and swimming pools rather than integrate. The Birmingham police commissioner was Eugene "Bull" Conner, who had earlier encouraged violence against Freedom Riders. After three days of demonstrations, the police, using dogs, moved against the protesters. King was arrested and placed in solitary confinement. Eight white clergymen signed a statement denouncing the demonstrations and urging blacks to show restraint. King responded with his LETTER FROM BIRMINGHAM JAIL, which became one of the most famous statements of the Civil Rights movement.

After his release, the civil rights leadership planned a children's march for May 2 to dramatize the situation. Nine hundred fifty-nine children, ages 6 to 16, were arrested. On May 3, when the children continued their protest, they were knocked to the ground by fire hoses while police dogs were turned on them. The black community was furious, as were thousands of whites who had watched the attacks on television. Protests poured into Congress and the White House, and Birmingham's city leaders finally agreed to King's demands to desegregate downtown stores, hire blacks as clerks, and release all demonstrators. On May 11, the Ku Klux Klan bombed the home of King's brother and the Gaston Motel in Birmingham, where the SCLC had its headquarters, but King's victory remained intact.

Martin Luther King Jr. delivering his memorable "I Have a Dream . . ." speech at the Lincoln Memorial during the March on Washington, D.C., 1963 (*Archive Photos*)

King mesmerized the country with his "I Have a Dream" speech at the MARCH ON WASHINGTON on August 28, 1963. He then turned his attention to the violence and harassment plaguing civil rights protesters in St. Augustine, Florida, where Judge Bryan Simpson threatened to throw St. Augustine city officials in jail if they continued to interfere with the demonstrators. That same year, Dr. King was awarded the 1964 Nobel Peace Prize.

A few months later, King traveled to Selma, Alabama, to help the STUDENT NON-VIOLENT COOR-DINATING COMMITTEE (SNCC) in its voter registration drive, and the violence that erupted there helped persuade Congress to pass the Voting Rights Act of 1965. (See VOTING RIGHTS STRUGGLE: "Selma.")

The passage of the CIVIL RIGHTS ACT OF 1964 and the Voting Rights Act of 1965 provided a framework for civil rights progress in the South, and Dr. King decided to concentrate on northern poverty. He announced his intention of leading a rent strike in Chicago in an effort to force landlords to improve housing conditions. His efforts were unsuccessful, and he alienated President Lyndon Johnson by denouncing the war in Vietnam. He next began working on a Poor People's Campaign, but he interrupted his efforts to travel to Memphis, Tennessee, to provide support for striking sanitation workers. On April 4, 1968, he was assassinated by James Earl Ray while standing on the balcony of the Lorraine Motel in Memphis. When news of his death was announced, riots broke out in over 100 cities around the country. Dr. King's birthday is now a national holiday.

King, Riley Ben ("B. B." King) (1925–   ) *blues singer*

Nicknamed "B. B." for "Blues Boy," King is also called "King of the Blues." Born in Mississippi, King was left on his own at age nine when his mother died. Afterward, he worked as a farmhand for $15 a month and attended school sporadically. He began playing the guitar after being reunited with his father at age 14. Major influences were "BLIND" LEMON JEFFERSON, Lonnie Johnson, and

B. B. King playing his guitar (*Camera Press Ltd./ Archive Photos*)

ROBERT JOHNSON. Since his relatives did not approve of BLUES music, King would travel to small towns where he would play on street corners for tips. Two years after moving to Memphis in 1947, he made his first records, which were unusual in that they included a small horn section, reflecting the impact of JAZZ musicians like CHARLIE CHRISTIAN, Benny Goodman, and Django Reinhardt. He was later influenced by the electric guitar of bluesman T-BONE WALKER. Phonograph records and movies brought many diverse strands of music to King's attention, and he incorporated many of them into his own unique blues style. He is the most successful and popular of all blues performers and a major influence on all blues musicians who followed him.

Kisama

A huge fugitive slave settlement in Angola. Thousands of runaway slaves found safety there after escaping the slave pens, or barracoons, where they had been held until they could be loaded aboard slave ships. The local African chiefs in Kisama welcomed these fugitive slaves, who would regularly attack Portuguese traders heading for slave markets in the interior.

kola nuts

Edible fleshy seeds of the kola tree, a relative of chocolate. These trees are native to the tropical rain forests of West Africa, where they are called *guru, goora,* or *bissey.* The nuts are a source of caffeine and other stimulants, and for centuries Africans chewed them, despite their bitter taste, to ward off hunger and fatigue. Extensive cultivation began at the end of the 19th century. The trees were imported to the New World in the 17th and 18th centuries and are now grown in Jamaica and Brazil. The United States currently imports tons of kola nuts each year, mostly from Nigeria. Used in medicines and soft drinks, kola nuts (along with the coca leaves used in the original formula) gave Coca-Cola its name.

Kongo, Kingdom of

A feudal kingdom created by a BANTU people (the Bakongo), possibly in the early 14th century, along the Congo River in central Africa. By the time the Portuguese first learned of it in 1482, the Kongo Kingdom stretched across 200,000 square miles and had a population of 4 to 5 million. It was divided into six ministates, each of which had its own feudal chief, who governed at the pleasure of the king, or "ManiKongo." Kongo was basically an agricultural society, though the people were skilled in ironwork and in the lost-wax technique of copper casting. They were such excellent weavers that the Portuguese mistook the cloth they produced for satin, velvet, taffeta, damask, and brocade.

The Portuguese were anxious to establish diplomatic relations with Kongo, both for trading purposes and because they thought the ManiKongo

might have knowledge of the legendary Prester John. Prester John was actually a hoax, concocted in 1144, about a king who supposedly ruled a rich and powerful Christian kingdom that would help deliver the Holy Land from its Moslem conquerors. Though no one had been able to locate Prester John for 200 years, many Europeans still believed in his existence.

When the Portuguese met with the ManiKongo in 1491, they offered him gifts and asked him to accept Christianity. Impressed with the Portuguese guns more than anything else, the ManiKongo agreed, in return for an alliance with Portugal. Since the ManiKongo was facing a rebellion, the alliance was put to the test almost immediately. Though relatively few in number, the Portuguese soldiers proved helpful, and the grateful ManiKongo set aside a portion of the royal court for them.

However, the Europeans' religious demands alienated many Bakongo people, and the ManiKongo expelled the Portuguese four years later. At the same time, he exiled his son, Affonso, who had refused to give up his new Catholic faith. When the ManiKongo died, around 1506, Affonso returned and claimed the throne. Reversing his father's policies, Affonso moved to establish close relations with Portugal, partly out of religious belief and partly in an attempt to convert Kongo into a technically advanced state. He established a number of schools and asked the Portuguese to send teachers, priests, and technicians to his country. By 1516, more than 1,000 Bakongo people, including women, were in school, and a number had been sent to Portugal to study at the university at Santo Eloi. Affonso also encouraged the cultivation of Portuguese-introduced crops such as oranges, maize, and manioc.

But once it became clear that the Americas could generate enormous wealth through sugar production, the Kongo kingdom became of interest to the Portuguese primarily as a source of slaves. Many of the whites who had been sent to Kongo to promote development could not resist the money to be made from slaving and not only became corrupt themselves but also corrupted Kongo government officials. To bring slave trading back within tolerable limits, Affonso repeatedly and unsuccessfully sought the help of Portuguese King Manuel.

In frustration, Affonso outlawed all slave trading in 1526. However, the situation had already deteriorated to the point where he was forced to revoke his order after only four months. He was obliged to settle for creating an inspection agency that was to ensure that all captives were criminals who had been enslaved according to African custom and were not innocent people who had been kidnapped. Corruption prevented this agency from operating honestly, and the slave trade continued to intensify. In 1539, eight Portuguese slave traders, led by a corrupt priest, unsuccessfully attempted to assassinate Affonso while he was at Mass. Affonso died three or four years later. In 1568, Kongo was seriously weakened by attacks by Jaga tribesmen, and the kingdom eventually disintegrated into violence and ruin.

Ku Klux Klan (KKK)

criminal white supremacist organization. The Klan began as a social club in Pulaski, Tennessee, in 1866, but soon degenerated into a loosely knit terrorist group whose goal was to maintain white supremacy. Blacks who voted, ran for office, supported education, were community leaders, owned land, and/or refused to work for whites were favorite targets for Klansmen, who murdered, whipped, branded, raped, and burned those who represented a threat to their authority. A tidal wave of terrorism swept over southern black communities between 1866 and 1871, as local law enforcement officials either were

Ku Klux Klan meeting, 1923 (*Library of Congress*)

afraid to interfere or were themselves Klansmen. In 1868, Arkansas governor Powell Clayton, after 200 Klan murders, established a predominantly black militia, placed 10 counties under martial law, arrested dozens of Klansmen, and temporarily crippled the organization in that state. Governor Edmund Davis of Texas set up a special police force, 40 percent black, that arrested more than 6,000 Klansmen and greatly limited violence there. Throughout much of the South, however, the Klan operated almost without restraint, murdering thousands of blacks and subjecting millions more to what has been described as a second slavery.

In response to Klan violence, Congress passed four anti-Klan laws, including the Ku Klux Klan Act of 1871, which made it possible to prosecute certain crimes under federal law. Hundreds of Klansmen were indicted, but thousands more escaped federal prosecutors, and many of those who were convicted served short jail terms or received suspended sentences. Nonetheless, the level of violence declined dramatically.

The decades that followed RECONSTRUCTION saw white supremacist governments established throughout the South. The Klan and such organizations as the Knights of the White Camellia, the White Brotherhood, and the Invisible Empire continued to operate, but the number of lynchings dropped from a high of 231 in 1892.

The original Klan had operated primarily in the South; after World War I, it spread throughout the country and added Jews, Catholics, unions, and immigrants to its list of enemies. Movies like the 1914 *Birth of a Nation,* which portrayed the Klan as honorable, courageous, and patriotic, helped the organization attract millions of new members and become politically powerful. Many Klansmen were leading citizens in their communities. But after reaching a high of 5 million members in 1925, the Klan began to lose support, dropping to approximately 100,000 members in 1929.

A Klan revival occurred in the 1950s in response to the CIVIL RIGHTS MOVEMENT, but by this time, many segregationists viewed the Klan as a disreputable organization and instead joined White Citizens Councils to fight integration. The late 20th century saw the development of white separatist

militias and gangs of racist "skinheads." Unlike the Klan, which prided itself on its patriotism and often acted as an unofficial enforcer for the white community, these groups are often violently antigovernment and see themselves as underdogs rather than the saviors of society.

Recommended Reading: Foner, Eric. *Reconstruction: America's Unfinished Revolution: 1863–1877.* New York: Harper & Row, 1988; Katz, William Loren. *The Invisible Empire.* Seattle, Wash.: Open Hand, 1986.

!Kung San

Branch of the BUSHMEN people of southern Africa. Like other Bushmen, !Kung San are a shy, gentle people who live in the Kalahari Desert. They divide the year into six seasons rather than four. The !Kung San live in groups of 10 to 30 persons and, like other nomadic peoples, have little in the way of possessions. In fact, the average individual owns less than 25 pounds worth of personal property. However, reciprocal gift-giving is a cultural tradition, and this provides for the frequent exchange of those possessions that are available. It also encourages the development of relationships that can be depended upon in time of sickness or need. !Kung camps are built around a core group of older people who have lived together most or all of their lives. Other !Kung individuals often visit for days or months before moving on to another camp. Of great importance is the ancient !Kung trance dance, which is designed to encourage sickness to leave an individual's body. It is performed several times a month and is traditional with all !Kung groups.

The !Kung stand approximately five feet tall and hunt with poisoned arrows. Women are highly regarded and generally are involved in all major decisions. The !Kung enjoy an extremely nutritious diet and little stress. They rarely suffer from high blood pressure, arteriosclerosis, ulcers, deafness, or senility. However, almost 50 percent of !Kung children die before age 15 from gastrointestinal infections, with 20 percent dying in their first year. Those who survive childhood have a life expectancy of approximately 55 years. Unless they are working for BANTU or white farmers, !Kung wear very little clothing, but they often decorate themselves with beads made from ostrich eggshells. !Kung San speak a Khoisan, or "click," language, and the exclamation point preceding their name indicates a click sound on the first letter.

Kush

An ancient African kingdom based in what is now SUDAN. Its influence lasted approximately 1,000 years, from 750 B.C., when it was founded, until A.D. 300, when it was overthrown by AXUM. During its early history, Kush was under Egyptian control and was often referred to as NUBIA. Its people utilized at least two different irrigation techniques, allowing them to produce enough food to encourage the growth of towns. They were also excellent sailors. The Kushites were able to throw off Egyptian rule in the 11th century B.C., and the Kushite Empire, with its capital at Napata, began to take form in the 8th century B.C. At that point, its king, Kashta, seized southern Egypt. This territorial expansion continued under Kings Piankhi and Shabako. Kushite pharaohs ruled southern Egypt for about 100 years and all of Egypt for more than 50 years. The Kush-held Egyptian territory was invaded by iron-armored Assyrian troops around 660 B.C., and the Kush, who had only bronze weapons, were forced to withdraw. Though heavily influenced by Egypt during this period, Kush retained its basic Nubian culture. About a century after the Assyrian invasion, Kush kings established a new capital at MEROE, which would become one of the richest and most important commercial centers of the ancient world. In 450 B.C., the Greek historian Herodotus visited Kush and described it, saying, "Here gold is found in great abundance, and huge elephants, and ebony, and all sorts of trees growing wild. The men, too, are the tallest in the world, the best looking, and the longest-lived." Kush began to decline around A.D. 200 for reasons that are still unclear, and an invasion from the Ethiopian-based kingdom of Axum in A.D. 300 brought its power to an end.

Kwanzaa

A secular, seven-day African-American holiday created by Maulana Ron Karenga in the 1960s to cele-

Kwanzaa display in Germantown, Pa. (*Temple University Libraries Urban Archives*)

brate and encourage African values among black American families. The word *kwanzaa* is of East African origin and refers to the "first fruits" of harvest. The seven principles of Kwanzaa are Umoja (unity), Kujichaguilia (self-determination), Ujima (collective work and responsibility), Ujamma (economic cooperation), Nia (purpose), Kuumba (creativity), and Imani (faith). Kwanzaa is celebrated from December 26 to January 1.

kwosso (QUO-so)

A fast-moving game played in the Horn of Africa among the Afar or Danakil people. *Kwosso* involves two teams, each of which may be composed of as many as 100 warriors. These attempt to keep a ball made of tightly rolled goatskins away from each other. The game is played all day without a break in the hot desert sun and frequently results in serious injuries and even deaths. This indifference to physical safety parallels an Afar belief that violence is a virtue. An Afar warrior who has killed one enemy wins the right to adorn himself with a feather or comb in his hair. After his second kill, he will split his ears. After 10 kills, he is allowed to wear a special iron bracelet.

labor and property rights of African Americans in the United States

Before the Civil War, African Americans were divided into two groups: slave and free. Slaves were considered property, and all proceeds from their work belonged to their owners. In addition to agricultural and domestic labor, slaves did much of the skilled work in the community, such as carpentry, iron work, ship caulking, brick and stone masonry, lumberjacking, mining, and all manner of crafts. They also provided most of the labor in mills and factories. Those with special skills were frequently allowed to "contract out" for their services, splitting the money they earned with their owners.

Free blacks, including those in the North, were subjected to extensive discrimination, barred from engaging in many occupations and professions, and restricted for the most part to low-paying menial and dangerous jobs. Those attempting to combat these restrictions ran into two roadblocks. First, they were unable to use the political process to attain their economic goals because most blacks, in both North and South, were not allowed to vote. Second, white workers feared black competition. Blacks who worked at jobs that whites also sought were frequent targets of hostility.

In 1834, white rioters in Philadelphia attacked blacks, accusing them of working for such low wages that employers were tempted to hire them instead of whites. FREDERICK DOUGLASS, who, as a slave, had been hired out to work on the Baltimore docks, was attacked by resentful white dock workers and almost lost an eye. Competition from black workers resulted in white rioting in Cincinnati and Brooklyn in 1862. More rioting broke out in 1863, culminating in the New York City DRAFT RIOT, which began in July 1863 and continued for five days. Hundreds of African Americans were killed or injured, and a black orphanage was burned, leaving hundreds of children homeless. The rioting began when the federal government passed a law that required whites to serve in the army but allowed individuals to buy their way out of serving by paying a fee of $300. However, a major underlying cause of the riot was the fear that after the Civil War, freed slaves would flood the job market, resulting in white unemployment.

The end of the Civil War in 1865 brought extensive social and economic upheaval in the South. Former slaves gained the right to own property, sign contracts, and demand a say in the terms and conditions of their employment. This infuriated whites who wanted what they called "a disciplined labor force"—meaning one that they could easily control. They reacted by passing the notorious BLACK CODES, which included strict vagrancy laws that provided for imprisonment for those who could not provide written proof of employment, forced blacks to forfeit wages already earned if they left their jobs before their contracts ended, and limited their right to engage in various skilled professions. An angry northern reaction resulted in the passage of the 1866 Civil Rights Act, and later the Fourteenth

Amendment (1868), which forced the repeal of many of these laws. However, KU KLUX KLAN violence often succeeded where repressive laws were not enough. As part of a so-called apprentice program, judges appointed white "guardians" for thousands of orphaned black children, the purpose of which was really to provide a continuation of free, forced child labor. In a number of cases, children were placed in these apprentice programs after their fathers were killed or forced to leave the area and their mothers then declared unable to support them.

Prison Labor

The RECONSTRUCTION period saw the emergence of prison CHAIN GANGS, which were instituted for the purpose of obtaining free—mostly black—labor for state construction projects. A variation of this involved the convict leasing programs whereby convicts, mostly black, were forced to work years without pay under terrible conditions for white individuals or companies. Unlike slaves, leased convicts did not represent a financial investment on the part of the company or individual leasing them. If a convict died, the company or individual simply leased another one from the prison system. As a result, leased convicts regularly endured whippings, serious malnutrition, chronic exhaustion, and exposure to harsh weather conditions. Of the 285 convicts leased to a railroad construction company in South Carolina in the 1870s, 44.9 percent died.

Land Acquisition

Although some efforts had been made during and after the Civil War to seize the land of Confederate planters and distribute it to former slaves (see DAVIS BEND), the famous slogan "40 acres and a mule" remained pretty much an empty promise. The Southern Homestead Act of 1866 did make 80-acre plots in Alabama, Arkansas, Louisiana, Florida, and Mississippi available free of cost to heads of households, black and white, and several thousand black men were able to take advantage of this program. Under the urging of a black activist named PAP SINGLETON, 20,000 to 40,000 so-called EXODUSTERS (from the biblical book of Exodus) migrated to Kansas in 1879 seeking land made available under the 1862 Homestead Act. Thousands of other blacks

moved west to establish farms and settlements. But most blacks who sought to own their own farms were thwarted, not only by a lack of government help, but also by hostile whites who refused to sell them land even if they were able to meet the purchase price.

Sharecropping and Debt Peonage

Because most blacks were unable to acquire their own property, the majority of the approximately 4 million ex-slaves in the South at the end of the Civil War were forced to continue working for their former owners in order to survive. The result was the establishment of the SHARECROPPING system. White planters agreed to provide the land, seed, and equipment, and the former slaves provided their labor. They usually lived on the land in shacks provided by the planters. At the end of the year, when the crop was sold, the former slaves were supposed to receive one-quarter to one-half the profits. However, most of the ex-slaves were illiterate and therefore easily cheated. An extension of sharecropping was the "crop lien" system whereby tenant farmers were forced to use an anticipated future crop as collateral to get credit to buy food or supplies at stores that charged exorbitant prices. The interest they were charged was sufficiently high to ensure that they would remain permanently in debt and unable to better themselves economically. Special lien laws made financial independence almost impossible. White-controlled local governments and the threat of Klan violence made protest dangerous. In 1876, two black sharecroppers in Georgia who went to court to file a grievance because of their treatment were murdered when they tried to claim their settlement.

Blacks were also victimized by a labor system known as debt peonage. Under this system, people were forced to labor for years to pay off debts. Often people were arrested on minor or fraudulent charges and were unable to pay their fines. The fine would then be paid by a white person, and the convicted person would be required to work for that person for free until the cost of the fine (including interest) was paid. In this way, even a small fine of 10 or 20 dollars could force someone into debt peonage for years. If an individual died, the debt would be passed on to his or her children. Those who attempted to leave before the debt was paid were arrested, charged with obtaining money under false pretenses, and jailed. Congress outlawed peonage in 1867, and the Supreme Court ruled against it in *Bailey v. Alabama* (1911) and *U.S. v. Reynolds* (1914), but peonage continued until the 1950s, when mechanization made sharecropping unprofitable.

Low wages, inability to obtain loans, the refusal of whites to sell land to blacks, and fraud all combined to prevent African Americans from advancing economically. But the underlying cause of the grinding black poverty that was pervasive throughout the South prior to the 1960s was the determination of many in the white community to keep blacks financially dependent, in what has been termed a "second slavery."

Black Entrepreneurs and Professionals

Although it was difficult, some African Americans did manage to acquire the education and skills that allowed them to enter professional occupations. Many entered the ministry. Others became teachers. A few managed to acquire the specialized training that allowed them to become lawyers, doctors, or scientists. Still others established small stores and businesses that catered to the black community. However, success could be extremely dangerous. In 1912, a prosperous black farmer named Ben Pettigrew was shot as he drove a wagonload of cotton to market. His two young daughters who were with him at the time were hanged and the cotton was burned. IDA WELLS BARNETT began her antilynching crusade in 1892 after three of her friends were murdered in Memphis because they owned a grocery store that competed with a nearby white-owned store. Nevertheless, a number of black entrepreneurs were successful, particularly in journalism, insurance, and businesses that served the black community such as beauty and barber shops. MADAME C. J. WALKER, who founded a million-dollar cosmetics empire, is a well-known example, and many others enjoyed more limited success. Even today, however, when the threat of physical violence has disappeared black businesspeople frequently run into problems when they attempt to obtain loans and insurance, and profes-

The storefront and shared sign of a black-owned music store and restaurant—the Manhattan Music Shop and Sky Rocket Grill, owned by Rufus "Sonnyman" Jackson, co-owner with Cum Posey of the Homestead Grays baseball team, Homestead, Pennsylvania, 1948. (The Homestead Grays won the final National Negro League pennant that year.) (*Pittsburgh Courier Archives/Archive Photos*)

sionals often complain of the so-called glass-ceiling syndrome, limiting their advancement in corporations, law firms, and other businesses. Approximately 95 percent of chief executive officers of major corporations are still white males.

Unionization

Although there were a few exceptions, such as the short-lived but egalitarian National Labor Union formed in 1866 and the Knights of Labor organized in 1869, unions initially refused to admit black members. However, this did not stop white union members from complaining bitterly when blacks accepted jobs below union wages or when they took jobs as strikebreakers. Blacks sometimes formed their own unions, such as the Baltimore Colored Caulkers Trade Union Society (1865) formed by black labor leader ISAAC MYERS, after white workers successfully went on strike to have hundreds of black caulkers and dockworkers dismissed from their jobs. Under Myers' leadership, the ousted black workers raised enough money to purchase a shipyard and railway company. He also established the Colored National Labor Union, a confederation of black labor organizations. But their attempts to form links with white labor organizations ran into serious problems. Not only were the white unions segregated, white union leaders did not support equal pay for blacks. Also, the white union leaders strongly opposed the Republican Party, which they regarded as capitalist and antilabor. In the black community, the Republican Party was revered as the "party of Lincoln" that had freed the slaves and supported civil rights. In view of the racist history of the white labor movement, black workers had little faith that the Socialist and Labor Reform Parties, which the white labor leaders favored, could be trusted to look out for black interests. The refusal of most unions to accept black members, and the spreading segregationist practices that kept African Americans out of many trades, prevented many blacks from acquiring needed job skills. This was one reason BOOKER T. WASHINGTON favored vocational training for blacks, even at the expense of liberal arts education.

Black workers continued to try to unionize, but even when they had white support the results were often discouraging. In 1886 the Knights of Labor began organizing both black and white sugar workers in Louisiana. A year later, 10,000 workers—9,000 black and 1,000 white—went on strike. The emergence of an integrated local union caused Louisiana governor Thomas McEnery to call in the militia, which began its activities by firing on the strikers, killing four men and wounding five. Arrests, beatings, and the reported murder of at least 20 blacks in a nearby shantytown caused the national Knights of Labor to abandon the local union workers; the strike failed.

The American Federation of Labor (AFL), a group of white unions headed by Samuel Gompers, also made an effort to unionize black workers, partly to prevent their use as strikebreakers. And the United Mine Workers included many African Americans among its members. Even here there were problems, as blacks complained that white union officials ignored their problems and discriminated against them when it came to jobs and promotions. More important was the continuing practice by companies to use nonunionized blacks as strikebreakers. During an 1897 mine workers strike in

Illinois, poor black strikebreakers imported from Alabama were fired on by union workers. Company guards fired back, killing 14 white workers. Governor John Tanner called in the National Guard, this time in support of the union, drawing approval from white mine workers, but antagonizing the black community, including many black miners. Many blacks believed that even integrated unions could not be trusted; they might push out their black members once they became strong enough. It was not an unreasonable fear. As time went on, the AFL turned a blind eye to discrimination when faced with pressure from white union members.

In 1905, a group of white revolutionary activists, including Eugene Debs and "Mother" Mary Jones, formed the Industrial Workers of the World (IWW). The so-called Wobblies sought to advance the employment interests of all workers, including blacks, and successfully organized farmworkers in several states. But during World War I, the IWW was attacked as anti-American and lost most of its political and economic clout.

Other efforts to unionize agricultural workers met similar resistance. In ELAINE, ARKANSAS, in 1919, African-American sharecroppers attempting to organize a union got into a gunfight with local whites. Hundreds of blacks were arrested, and scores were killed. Seventy-three were indicted on charges of staging an insurrection and 12 were sentenced to death. Though the convictions were later

Two black migrant farmworkers pick okra, Alabama, 1968. (*Shel Hershorn, UT Austin/Archive Photos*)

overturned, the union was finished. In 1934, 18 Arkansas sharecroppers, black and white, formed the Southern Tenant Farmers' Union (STFU). A year later, the STFU had 10,000 members, but it had run into so much antagonism that its headquarters was moved to Memphis. The STFU fell apart several years later but not before it established a dramatic encampment of 1,700 evicted sharecroppers and their families along Highway 61 in Missouri. The state soon declared the encampment a health hazard and had it disbanded, but the STFU did succeed in bringing the problems of sharecroppers to the attention of the nation.

A. PHILIP RANDOLPH was more successful in his efforts to organize the Brotherhood of Sleeping Car Porters. The Pullman Company was the country's largest employer of black workers, and while it took 10 years, in 1935 the Pullman Company finally agreed to recognize the Brotherhood as the porters' official representative.

The Great Depression of the 1930s was devastating to black workers. In many areas, more than half the black workforce was unemployed. Black women were particularly hard hit as they were pushed out of factory jobs back into domestic service, when they could find work at all. In 1935 an AFL faction formed the Committee for Industrial Organization (CIO), which supported the unionization of workers in the mass-production industries, such as steel, rubber, auto, and meatpacking. Blacks held many of the jobs in these industries, and the continuing refusal of the AFL to demand nondiscrimination among its member unions made the CIO, which strongly opposed racial discrimination, attractive to black workers. By 1938, the newly independent (and renamed) Congress of Industrial Organizations counted 210,000 black members. Four years later, the Supreme Court ruled in *Steele v. Louisville & Nashville R.R.* (1944) that unions, including all-white unions, had a "duty of fair representation," meaning that any benefits they acquired for their members must be available to other nonunion members. This greatly improved the position of black workers.

However, after World War II, the CIO became a strong supporter of the government's anticommunist cold war policies. It expelled 11 unions as "communist-dominated." Unfortunately, these unions were the strongest advocates of African-American rights. In 1955, the AFL and the CIO reunited. Even though a number of trade unions continued to exclude African Americans, the AFL-CIO leadership was generally supportive of the Civil Rights Act of 1964, which prohibited all race and gender discrimination by employers and unions. The act forced all unions to admit black members, and it ultimately forced trade unions to admit African Americans into their apprenticeship programs, which trained people to become skilled artisans.

Property Acquisition

Interference with African-American efforts to acquire property extended to housing. For years, African Americans had been segregated in ghettos and had faced substantial discrimination when attempting to buy or rent in predominantly white areas. "Restrictive covenants," forbidding the sale of houses to blacks (and Jews) were common in sales agreements until ruled illegal in *Shelley v. Kraemer* (1948). Those blacks who did move into all-white areas sometimes faced threats and vandalism. Many were forced to deal with unreasonable demands when they attempted to obtain mortgages and financing. The Civil Rights Act of 1968 dealt with housing discrimination, and, although the problem has lessened in recent years, it has still not disappeared entirely.

Even with the end of sharecropping and debt peonage, black farmers faced significant discrimination in their efforts to obtain credit and loans. Often this resulted in the forced sale of black-owned farmland. In 1900 black farmers owned approximately 15 million acres of land. By 1999, they owned 2.3 million. Between 1982 and 1992, the number of African-American farmers dropped by 43 percent, and they now make up less than 1 percent of all farmers. In 1997, a class-action lawsuit (*Pigford v. Glickman*) was filed against the U.S. Department of Agriculture because of alleged discriminatory practices. Two years later, the Department of Agriculture agreed to settle the suit and to pay hundreds of millions of dollars to black farmers.

Ending Segregation in the Workplace

In 1941, A. Philip Randolph threatened to lead 100,000 African Americans in a March on Washington to protest racial discrimination in defense industries. In response, President Franklin D. Roosevelt issued Executive Order 8802, banning discrimination in industries with government contracts. Although black men had served with distinction in the armed forces in all wars fought by the United States, the U.S. military remained strictly segregated and hostile to African-American progress. This situation began to change after World War II, in 1948, when President Harry S Truman issued Executive Order 9981, ending segregation in the military. In the following years, the military and the federal government became increasingly attractive to African Americans looking for career opportunities.

Pressure generated by the Civil Rights movement, together with AFFIRMATIVE ACTION programs and legal decisions, brought thousands of African Americans into corporations and many government agencies, such as police and fire departments. The Civil Rights Act of 1964 established the Equal Employment Opportunity Commission (EEOC), whose purpose was to investigate charges of discrimination. In 1972, Congress amended the Civil Rights Act to give the EEOC the authority to bring

In the years after World War II, more employment opportunities opened up for blacks. (*Lambert/Archive Photos*)

suit in federal court to remedy discriminatory practices. Today, discrimination in employment based on race or color is illegal, and most government agencies have Equal Employment Opportunity (EEO) divisions that oversee and enforce anti-discrimination regulations. Affirmative-action policies in both the private and public sector have succeeded in opening millions of jobs to African Americans, and discrimination is less of a problem than in the past. However, competition from overseas has meant the disappearance of thousands of traditional, well-paid factory jobs. The shift to a technology-driven, communications/service economy, with its demand for special skills and education, is intensifying, and black economic progress is likely to depend on the ability of African Americans to meet these challenges.

Recommended Reading: Foner, Philip S., and Ronald L. Lewis. *Black Workers.* Philadelphia, Pa.: Temple University Press, 1989; Gould, William B., IV. *Black Workers in White Unions: Job Discrimination in the United States.* Ithaca, N.Y.: Cornell University Press, 1977; Litwack, Leon F. *Trouble in Mind.* New York, Vintage Books, 1999.

Lalibela (reigned ca. 1200–1250) *Ethiopian king*
Lalibela was a ruler of a feudalistic Christian state that rose following the fall of Axum. According to legend, sometime in the late 12th century, a boy was born into the Zagwe royal family, rulers of northern Ethiopia. Shortly after his birth, his mother saw him surrounded by a swarm of bees and, taking it as a sign from God, named him Lalibela, meaning "the bees recognize his sovereignty." When he grew older, the reigning king, fearful of being overthrown, had Lalibela poisoned, and the boy fell into a coma. While the child lay unconscious, God brought him into heaven and promised him that he, Lalibela, would become king in return for building 11 churches that God Himself would design. Lalibela recovered and became king and ordered the construction of the promised churches. According to the legend, angels of God worked with the laborers during the day and continued by themselves throughout each night to ensure that

the churches were constructed exactly according to God's plan. Once the churches were complete, King Lalibela gave up his throne to become a holy man, sleeping on rocks and eating only roots and berries. He is now regarded as a saint by the Ethiopian people. Whatever the exact truth of the religious story, the town of Lalibela (named for the boy-king) and the 11 churches do, in fact, exist. Carved directly out of the rock on which they stand, the churches were created between the 10th and early 16th centuries. They are connected by an intricate network of underground tunnels and passageways and represent an amazing feat of architectural skill. Four of the churches are, except for their bases, cut completely away from the surrounding rock. While the rock-hewn churches of Lalibela are the best known, similar structures can be found at other Ethiopian sites.

Latimer, Lewis Howard (1848–1928) *inventor*

Latimer is creator and inventor of the Latimer Lamp, which greatly improved light bulbs by revising the manufacturing of the carbon filaments that actually give off the light. Latimer was born in Chelsea, Massachusetts, and, as a child, sold the *Liberator,* the abolitionist newspaper published by William Lloyd Garrison. When he was 10, his father deserted the family, and young Lewis was forced to quit school and go to work. Six years later, he enlisted in the Union navy and served aboard the U.S.S. *Massasoit* during the Civil War. Afterward, he returned to Boston and became an office clerk at Crosby and Gould, a law firm specializing in patent work.

At that time, inventors trying to acquire patents were required to submit detailed drawings, or drafts, of their inventions, as well as written descriptions.

Latimer (second from right) with the staff of the Legal Department, General Electric Company, 1894 (*Photographs and Prints Division, Schomburg Center for Research in Black Culture, The New York Public Library, Astor, Lenox and Tilden Foundations*)

Crosby and Gould employed a number of artists, or draftsmen, and Latimer soon became an expert in the work. His drawings were so well done that Alexander Graham Bell asked him to do the illustrations for his newly invented telephone. In 1880, Latimer began work at the United States Electric Company in Bridgeport, Connecticut. By that time, he had also begun working on his own inventions. The year before, Thomas Edison had invented the incandescent light bulb. Latimer, always fascinated by scientific breakthroughs, studied the new light process and, in 1881, along with Joseph V. Nichols, created the Latimer Lamp. Soon afterward, he was asked to supervise the installation of electric light plants in New York City and was hired to create an incandescent light department for the Maxim-Weston Electric Co. of London. In 1884, Latimer began working with Thomas Edison and became a leading member of an elite group of scientists known as the Edison Pioneers.

Lawrence, Jacob Armstead, Jr. (1917–2000) *artist*

Born in New Jersey, Lawrence spent his teen years in HARLEM, where he became involved in an after-school arts program and became fascinated with patterns and the use of color. He also developed a strong interest in black history, which resulted in a series of 41 narrative paintings focusing on the life of TOUSSAINT LOUVERTURE. At age 21, Lawrence joined the government's Work Progress Administration (WPA) and later won three Rosenwald fellowships, which led to the creation of a series of paintings on John Brown. During the 1940s, he created the *And the Migrants Kept Coming* series, 60 panels depicting the migration of poor Southern blacks to Northern cities in search of better job opportunities. During World War II, Lawrence served with the Coast Guard and created a pictorial record of the service that was later exhibited in New York's Museum of Modern Art.

After the war, his work focused on ordinary African Americans and the theatrical world. During the 1950s, Lawrence created a huge historical series called *Struggle: From the History of the American People,* which attracted much praise. In 1964, he moved to Nigeria, where he spent eight months painting scenes from African life. He also did several civil rights–oriented paintings, including *The Ordeal of Alice* and *Praying Ministers.* Other Lawrence work in this period included a 40-panel series on HARRIET TUBMAN, collected in the volume *Harriet and the Promised Land.* Jacob Lawrence's work stresses strong line and color patterns that emphasize emotional content rather than natural detail. In 1983, he became the second African American (RALPH ELLISON was the first) to be elected to the elite American Academy of Arts and Letters.

Recommended Reading: Bearden, Romare, and Harry Henderson. *A History of African-American Artists: From 1792 to the Present.* New York: Pantheon Books, 1993.

Ledbetter, Huddie ("Leadbelly") (1885–1949) *blues singer, composer*

Born in Louisiana, Huddie (pronounced "Hue-dee") Ledbetter grew up on a cotton farm and began his career singing in the bars of Shreveport. Arrested repeatedly for assault and murder, he spent much of his life in Texas and Louisiana penitentiaries. One story said he received his nickname "Leadbelly" after being shot in the stomach. Twice, in 1925 and in 1934, he won release from prison because of his singing ability. His second pardon was due to the influence of folk music historians John and Alan Lomax. Ledbetter was known for his extensive repertoire of BLUES, chain gang songs, folk songs, spirituals, work songs, and ballads. A charismatic performer with a powerful delivery, he influenced Paul McCartney, Pete Seeger, and Bob Dylan. He himself was greatly influenced by "Blind" Lemon Jefferson. His best-known compositions include "Midnight Special," "Goodnight, Irene," and "Rock Island Line."

Lee, Shelton ("Spike") (1957–) *film director, actor, producer*

After graduating from Morehouse College, Spike Lee entered New York University's Institute of Film and Television, where he won the 1982 Student Academy award for his film *Joe's Bed-Sty Barbershop: We Cut*

Heads. He went on to win the Los Angeles Film Critics New Generation award and the Prix de Jeuness at the Cannes Film Festival for his 1986 hit film *She's Gotta Have It.* Produced on a $175,000 budget, the film, about a woman with three lovers, went on to earn over $8 million. Lee followed this with *School Daze,* a musical comedy about color and class consciousness among African-American college students. Other films include *Mo' Better Blues, Jungle Fever, Do the Right Thing, Malcolm X, Crooklyn, He Got Game, Clockers,* and *Girl 6.* His documentary *4 Little Girls* was based on the bombing of the 16th Street Church in Birmingham during the CIVIL RIGHTS MOVEMENT (See SIXTEENTH STREET BAPTIST CHURCH BOMBING) and was nominated for an Academy Award. *Get On the Bus* dealt with men going to Washington, D.C., to attend the MILLION MAN MARCH. In 1999, Lee released *Summer of Sam,* a film that used the murders committed by serial killer David Berkowitz as a backdrop, and in 2000, *The Original Kings of Comedy.* Lee has also directed and/or appeared in commercials for a number of leading companies. In addition to his willingness to take on controversial subjects, such as female sexuality, interracial romance, and color consciousness among blacks, Lee is known for his insistence on maintaining control of his projects. He named his production company 40 Acres and a Mule in reference to government promises made to freed slaves following the Civil War.

Leo Africanus (Al-Hassan ibn Muhammad el-wazzan el Zayyati) (1485–1554) *Moorish merchant and writer who traveled widely in Africa*

Born in Grenada, Spain, Leo Afircanus' original name was Al-Hassan ibn Muhammad el-wazzan el Zayyati. His parents sent him to Morocco to escape discrimination against Muslims. In 1518, he was captured by Christian pirates while sailing to Tunisia from Egypt. Impressed with his knowledge of AFRICA, the pirates, instead of selling him into slavery along with their other captives, carried him to Rome and presented him to Pope Leo X. Pope Leo freed him, and he converted to Christianity and took the name Johannes Leo de'Medici (Giovanni Leone, Leo Africanus). His written account of his travels was published in 1550

and became a best-seller in Europe. He is still considered an excellent source of information about the kingdoms of medieval Africa.

Lesotho, Kingdom of (le-SO-to)

South African country. Capital: Maseru. A small, mountainous country with an area of only 11,720 square miles, Lesotho is surrounded by the Republic of South Africa. Formerly known as Basutoland, Lesotho was designated a state under British protection in 1868 under the rule of Chief Moshesh. Early in the 19th century, Moshesh had recognized the defensive possibilities of the mountainous Basuto homeland, and, as the Basuto were being threatened by the Tlokwa and several other tribes, he established a base at a site called Thaba Bosiu. Aware that ultimate security lay in diplomacy, Moshesh managed to come to terms with the Zulus and the Ndebele and persuaded other groups to attack the Tlokwa. He successfully adopted guerrilla tactics against the Boer settlers of South Africa and gained British support by allowing missionaries to settle among his people—making sure, however, that they did not gain political power. In the process, Moshesh created a Basuto nation that absorbed and sheltered various smaller groups in return for military assistance. Continuing conflict with the Boers forced Moshesh to agree to accept British High Commission Territory status in 1868. Along with Bechuanaland and SWAZILAND, Basutoland was for years regarded as little more than a source of labor for the mines of South Africa. Originally, the British planned to absorb the three territories into the Union of South Africa, but this plan was abandoned after the 1960 South Africa Sharpeville Massacre (see REPUBLIC OF SOUTH AFRICA). Basutoland became an independent state named Lesotho in 1966. It is a constitutional monarchy. Its king is Letsie III.

Letter from Birmingham Jail

9,000-word letter written by Dr. MARTIN LUTHER KING JR. in 1963 in response to a request by eight white religious leaders in Birmingham, Alabama, that the civil rights demonstrators there cease their protests. Birmingham was widely viewed as one of the most violent and intransigent cities in the South in terms of granting civil rights. It had closed its parks, libraries, and swimming pools rather than integrate, and its police commissioner, Eugene "Bull" Conner, had earlier encouraged violence against FREEDOM RIDERS. Dr. King and the SOUTHERN CHRISTIAN LEADERSHIP CONFERENCE (SCLC) launched a major campaign there in 1963, demanding desegregation of lunch counters, rest rooms and drinking fountains and the hiring of African Americans by local businesses and the city government. After three days of protests, the police, using dogs, moved against the demonstrators. King was arrested and placed in solitary confinement. Instead of protesting the brutal police attack on the demonstrators, the eight clergymen issued a formal statement questioning King's presence and calling the protests and the boycott of white-owned stores "unwise and untimely." Dr. King's response, written on scraps of toilet paper and a small notepad, said, ". . . I am in Birmingham because injustice is here . . . For years now I have heard the word 'Wait!' . . . This 'Wait' has almost always meant 'Never' . . . We have waited for more than 340 years for our constitutional and God-given rights . . . If the inexpressible cruelties of slavery could not stop us, the opposition we now face will surely fail. We will win our freedom because the sacred heritage of our nation and the eternal will of God are embodied in our echoing demands." Shortly afterward, King was released. The letter became one of the most famous statements of the CIVIL RIGHTS MOVEMENT.

Representative John Lewis in Atlanta, Georgia, 1994 (*Chris Folver/Archive Photos*)

Lewis, John Robert (1940–   ) *civil rights leader, U.S. Congressman*

John Robert Lewis was born in 1940 in Pike County, Alabama, the third oldest of 10 children. He grew up in a small house with no electricity or running water. As a young child, he took care of the family's chickens and developed his speaking skills during the many hours he spent "preaching" to them. The lynching of 14-year-old EMMITT TILL made a strong impression on him, as did the actions of ROSA PARKS, which triggered the 1955 MONTGOMERY BUS BOYCOTT. In 1957, Lewis entered the American Baptist Theological (ABT) Seminary in Nashville, where he

first encountered the nonviolent philosophies of Henry David Thoreau and Mohandas Gandhi that were to influence his involvement in the CIVIL RIGHTS MOVEMENT. He took part in sit-ins and boycotts and was one of the young founders of the STUDENT NON-VIOLENT COORDINATING COMMITTEE (SNCC). In 1961, Lewis participated in the violence-plagued freedom rides that resulted in a bus burned out in Anniston, Alabama, and was subject to brutal attacks in Montgomery. Over the next few years, Lewis suffered numerous beatings and 40 arrests—one of which resulted in imprisonment at the notorious Parchman penitentiary in Mississippi. Lewis' commitment to the cause of civil rights led to his being elected chairman of SNCC in 1963. One week after being elected chairman, Lewis and five other black leaders met with President John F.

Kennedy to discuss the proposed civil rights bill and the upcoming MARCH ON WASHINGTON, during which Lewis would later deliver a fiery speech. The increasingly brutal antiblack activity of the next few years, the murder of President John F. Kennedy, and the rejection of the Mississippi Freedom Democratic Party delegates at the Atlantic City Democratic presidential convention in 1964 caused many civil rights activists to rethink their commitment to nonviolence. The breaking point for many came after the violence in Selma, Alabama, in 1965. (See VOTING.) Although Lewis had been classified by the U.S. armed services as a conscientious objector, he was suddenly reclassified 4-F as "morally unfit" (supposedly because of his many arrests) after he and other SNCC leaders released a strong statement denouncing the Vietnam War. In 1966, Lewis was replaced as SNCC chairman by STOKELY CARMICHAEL amid bitter infighting over nonviolence and the role (if any) of whites in the organization. Lewis was still strongly committed the nonviolent principles of Gandhi and DR. MARTIN LUTHER KING JR., and he refused to turn against those whites with whom he had worked for years. He resigned from SNCC on July 22, 1966. The next year, he joined the Southern Regional Council (SRC) in Atlanta, where he worked to establish cooperatives, credit unions, and community development groups. He became involved in the Robert Kennedy presidential campaign and was with Kennedy shortly before he was assassinated. In 1978, Lewis became associate director of ACTION, the federal agency that oversaw both the Peace Corps and the VISTA (Volunteers in Service to America) programs. He was elected to the Atlanta city council in 1982 and to the U.S. Congress in 1986. Reelected on a regular basis, Lewis continues to support antipoverty programs and to back efforts to extend and protect civil liberties. His autobiography is entitled *Walking with the Wind.*

Lewis, Mary Edmonia (1845–ca. 1909) *sculptor*
Edmonia Lewis was born in New York to an African-American father and Chippewa Indian mother. In 1859, she entered Oberlin College, where she was subjected to the bizarre accusation that she had caused two girls to become sick by feeding them an aphrodisiac. Though she denied the accusation and the girls offered no evidence of their charges, Lewis was not allowed to complete her final term. The scandal and humiliation haunted her for the rest of her life.

She moved to Boston, where she began her sculpting career with a bust of John Brown. She also sculpted a bust of Col. Robert Shaw, the leader of the Union Army's famous all-black Fifty-fourth Massachusetts Regiment. With the money she earned, Lewis was able to finance a trip to Rome in 1865. There, she developed a neoclassical style, though she broke away from it to create *Forever Free,* a work celebrating the EMANCIPATION PROCLAMATION.

Other famous pieces include a bust of Longfellow, whom Lewis respected because of his poem *Song of Hiawatha,* and *Hagar,* the biblical woman who had been cast out into the wilderness—a situation Lewis identified with because of her Oberlin experience. Other important Lewis works include *The Death of Cleopatra, The Old Indian Arrowmaker,* and *Hygieia.* Lewis spent much of her life trying to gain acceptance as a female African-American artist. Her work reflects her concerns regarding the position of women, African Americans, and Native Americans.

Liberia, Republic of
West African country. Capital: Monrovia. Liberia was founded in 1822 by American ex-slaves who migrated there under the sponsorship of the AMERICAN COLONIZATION SOCIETY, which had bought the land from local tribespeople a year earlier. The colony became independent in 1847 under the control of the *Americo-Liberians* (local term for the freed American slaves and their descendants), and approximately 15,000 blacks migrated there during the 19th century. Serious economic and constitutional problems led to the overthrow of the government in 1871, and Liberia lost sizable portions of its land to France and Britain in 1885, 1892, and 1919. In 1930, there was an international scandal over government involvement in forced labor practices, and the president resigned. In 1944, newly elected President William V. S. Tubman instituted numerous

reforms and attracted substantial foreign investment. However, the 16 indigenous tribal groups continued to lack basic political rights. In 1972, William Tolbert was elected president, but he was assassinated in a brutal coup led by Master Sergeant Samuel K. Doe in 1980. The Doe government was corrupt and brutal, forcing thousands of Liberians to flee to Guinea and the Ivory Coast. In 1990, Charles Taylor, leader of the National Patriotic Front of Liberia (NPFL) invaded the country. Doe was assassinated by another rebel group led by Prince Yormie Johnson, and the country was engulfed in civil war. A cease-fire was signed in August 1995, but fighting broke out briefly in 1996 and 1998. The various warring groups frequently used teen and preteen soldiers whom they controlled by supplying them with drugs. Approximately 150,000 people were killed in the war, and more than 1 million became refugees. In 1997 Charles Ghankay Taylor became president. Some rebel activity continues, and Liberia has accused Guinea of sheltering rebel groups. Liberia itself has been accused of aiding the exceptionally vicious insurrectionists fighting in SIERRA LEONE in the 1990s.

Libya (The Socialist People's Libyan Arab Jamahiriya)

North African nation. Capital: Tripoli. Located on the Mediterranean, the mostly desert country is divided into three provinces: Tripolitania, Fezzan, and Cyrenaica. The original inhabitants were probably BERBERS. In the seventh century B.C., the PHOENICIANS established a colony at what is now Tripoli. Various groups, including the Greeks, Carthaginians, Romans, and Vandals, later extended their authority over the area. In A.D. 666, the Fezzan region, which has long been important in the trans-Saharan trade, was conquered by ARABS who retained their sovereignty until the 10th century, when much of northern Africa came under the control of the ALMORAVIDS and later the Almohads. Various competing Arab and Berber tribal groups also established small fiefdoms during this period.

The Ottoman Turks took control of the region in the 16th century and drew financial support from the region's Barbary Coast pirates, a situation that led to a war between the United States and Tripoli in 1801. (A line in the "Marine Corps Hymn"—"the shores of Tripoli"—is a reference to this.) Italy captured Tripoli during the Turko-Italian War of 1911–12 and, by 1914 had conquered much of the country, although there was continuing resistance from a religious brotherhood founded in 1837 by Muhammad bin Ali Sanusi. In 1934, Italy formally designated Libya as a colony, and the country became a major African battleground during World War II.

The United Nations arranged for Libya's independence in December 1951 under King Idris I, the leader of the Sanusi brotherhood. The discovery of oil in 1958 made Libya politically important. In 1967, a successful coup was staged by a group of army officers led by Col. Muammar al-Qaddafi, who established an anti-Western, Islamic/Socialist state. In 1986, the United States bombed Tripoli and Bengasi in an unsuccessful attempt to kill Qaddafi after a Libyan-sponsored terrorist attack resulted in the deaths of two American servicemen. U.N. sanctions were imposed after Libya refused to surrender terrorists believed to be involved in the 1988 Pan-American airline bombing at Lockerbie, Scotland. The sanctions were lifted in 1999 after Libya turned two suspects over to authorities for trial in Scotland.

literacy requirements

Legal method used to prevent African Americans from voting in elections. The first literacy requirement was written into the Mississippi state constitution in 1890. It denied the vote to anyone who could not read and be able to explain any section of the state constitution. Other Southern states soon followed Mississippi's lead. In spite of massive efforts to make education available to black people after the Civil War, thousands of African Americans were still unable to read. However, the literacy requirements were designed to disqualify all blacks. The decision as to whether or not any given section of the state constitution had been read and interpreted correctly rested with local election officials, who would frequently rule against well-educated African Americans while helping semiliterate whites pass. The Voting Rights Act of 1965 suspended all literacy tests in areas where fewer than 50 percent of the adults had voted in 1964. Federal registrars were also sent into a number of states to ensure that those attempting to register would not be discriminated against.

See also VOTING RIGHTS STRUGGLE.

Little Rock Nine

A term referring to the nine high school students who successfully integrated Central High School in Little Rock, Arkansas, in 1957. The Little Rock school board had decided to begin the integration process at Central High School. Initially, 75 African-American students signed up to attend the school. The board of education cut this number to 25. In the end, only nine enrolled. Opposition surfaced immediately, much of it directed against DAISY BATES, president of the Arkansas NATIONAL ASSOCIATION FOR THE ADVANCEMENT OF COLORED PEOPLE (NAACP).

On September 2, the day before school was scheduled to open, Arkansas governor Orval Faubus announced that "blood will run in the streets" if Central High were integrated and that he would use National Guard troops "to protect lives and property." The next day, 250 National Guardsmen were stationed around the school to prevent the nine black students from entering. Faced with this situation, the NAACP turned to the federal district court, where Judge Ronald Davies ordered that the integration of Central High proceed as planned.

On September 4, Daisy Bates made arrangements to have the nine students driven to school in two police cars. Eight of them got the message.

National Guard troops line the streets to enforce desegregation at Central High School in Little Rock, Arkansas, 1957. (*Archive Photos*)

Fifteen-year-old Elizabeth Eckford, who had no phone, did not. When she arrived at school, she was met by a National Guardsman, who refused to let her pass. She was forced to walk 100 yards, alone, to a bus stop while a vicious mob followed, cursing and threatening to kill her. The other black students had also been refused admittance but had returned home safely.

Three weeks later, the Little Rock Nine, armed with a federal court order, tried again. As word that they had arrived spread, a mob of about 1,000 people formed outside the school. Police managed to get the students home safely, but mob violence was evident elsewhere, as rioters attacked news reporters and various African-American adults. Harry Ashmore, editor of the *Arkansas Gazette,* when asked to describe the situation, said, "I'll give it to you in one sentence. The police have been routed, the mob is in the streets, and we're close to a reign of terror." That night, police stopped a motorcade of approximately 100 cars filled with dynamite, guns, and other weapons two blocks from the Bates house.

The next day, Little Rock mayor Woodrow Mann requested that federal troops be sent in. President Eisenhower agreed, and, on September 25, the nine students were escorted from Bates' house to the school in a convoy that included armed soldiers and jeeps with machine gun mounts. A helicopter and 350 paratroopers from the U.S. Army's 101st Airborne Division met them at the school. For the rest of the year, the nine attended school under military protection. But while army troops protected them from outside mobs, they were repeatedly attacked, both physically and verbally, by other students. One of them, Minnijean Brown, was expelled after she dumped a bowl of chili on some boys who had harassed her. Finally, two soldiers from the 101st Airborne were assigned to each of the students.

That spring, the Little Rock school board, citing continuing tension, petitioned the courts, asking that all further integration be delayed until 1961. The Eighth U.S. Circuit Court refused the request, and its decision was upheld by the U.S. Supreme Court. Several months later, Governor Faubus ordered all four public high schools in Little Rock closed. They remained closed for a year, until the U.S. Supreme Court ruled the action unconstitutional.

The nine students were Minnijean Brown, Elizabeth Eckford, Ernest Green, Jefferson Thomas, Carlotta Walls, Thelma Mothershed, Terrance Roberts, Melba Pattillo, and Gloria Ray.

Recommended Reading: Bates, Daisy. *The Long Shadow of Little Rock.* Fayetteville: University of Arkansas Press, 1987; Beals, Melba Patillo. *Warriors Don't Cry.* New York: Simon & Schuster, 1994; Lucas, Eileen. *Cracking the Wall: The Story of the Little Rock Nine.* Minneapolis, Minn.: Lerner, 1997.

Locke, Alain Leroy (1885–1954) *philosopher, educator, author*

Born in Philadelphia, Alain Locke graduated magna cum laude from Harvard after three years and became the first African-American Rhodes Scholar. While studying in Europe, he developed a strong interest in Africa and was a founder of the African Union Society, which was established to promote communication among prospective black leaders and to improve the situation of blacks in Africa, the Caribbean, and the United States. Returning to the United States in 1912, Locke spent six months touring the South, then accepted a position as assistant professor of English at Howard University. In 1915, he initiated a pioneering series of lectures there on race and race relations.

After receiving his Ph.D. from Harvard following World War I, Locke became one of the intellectual leaders of the emerging HARLEM RENAISSANCE. Upon returning from a trip to Africa in 1925, he came into conflict with Howard's white president and was fired, an action that resulted in widespread protests from students and alumni. That same year, he published *The New Negro,* a collection of essays, poems, artwork, and stories that argued that a "New Negro" now existed who rejected past stereotypes and embraced a proud consciousness of race. *The New Negro* made Locke the leader and principal spokesman of the "New Negro Movement," which he encouraged through numerous essays and art and literary reviews. He also was deeply involved in efforts to help African-American artists and writers—including LANGSTON HUGHES, ZORA NEALE HURSTON, AARON DOUGLAS, and RICHMOND BARTHE—find financial support.

Returning to Howard in 1928, Locke worked closely with Howard's first black president to promote the university as a focal point for African and African-American studies and the development of black cultural and social leadership. He organized Howard's Division of Social Sciences, which included a department of philosophy, an area of study that Locke considered crucial. Though he was unable to create an African Studies program during his lifetime, the Social Sciences Division at Howard sponsored a series of conferences on racial issues for over 40 years. Locke was also instrumental in reforming the liberal arts curriculum and was deeply involved in efforts to promote adult education. At the time of his death, Alain Leroy Locke was perhaps the most famous African-American scholar in the country. Among his most famous publications are *The New Negro, Plays of Negro Life: A Source-Book of Native American Drama, The Negro in Art: A Pictorial Record of the Negro Artist and the Negro Theme in Art*, and *When Peoples Meet: A Study in Race and Culture Contacts*.

Loguen, Jermain Wesley (1813–1872) *conductor on the Underground Railroad, educator, religious leader*
Loguen is known to have helped 1,500 people, including HARRIET TUBMAN, escape from slavery. His mother, Cherry, a free, black woman, was kidnapped and sold to David Logue, who became Loguen's father. Brutal treatment, the sale of his sister, and the vicious murder of another slave caused Loguen to run away when he was 21. Making his way to Canada, he got an education and then returned to the United States, where he continued his studies at New York's Oneida Institute. He then opened a school for black children, moved to Syracuse, where he opened a second school, and, in 1842, became a Methodist minister. Loguen changed his original name, Jarm Logue, to Jermain Loguen around this time to make it more difficult for slave catchers to locate him. He took his middle name Wesley from the great Methodist minister John Wesley.

In addition to the two schools, Loguen established the Abolition Church, as well as five smaller churches. As the name Abolition Church implies, Loguen was a strong supporter of the movement to end slavery. He frequently wrote articles for FREDERICK DOUGLASS' *North Star* newspaper and was a major conductor on the UNDERGROUND RAILROAD. When Congress passed the Fugitive Slave Act in 1850 requiring Northern law officers to arrest and return runaway slaves, it became especially dangerous for Loguen to continue his abolitionist activities since he himself was a runaway. In 1851, he was indicted for helping free another runaway slave who had been caught and imprisoned. At that point, Loguen left for Canada but later returned to continue his Underground Railroad work. With the end of the Civil War and the passage of the Thirteenth Amendment outlawing slavery, Loguen focused his attention on the African Methodist Episcopal Zion Church.

Louis, Joe (1914–1981) *heavyweight boxing champion*
Born in a tiny shack in Alabama, Joe Louis was the fifth child of Lillie and Monroe Barrow. (He dropped his last name after he began boxing.) When Louis was only two, his father was placed in a mental hospital, and the family never saw him again. Because of poverty, Louis was able to attend school only sporadically and consequently did not learn to read and write until he was about nine years old. After his mother remarried, the family moved to Detroit, and it was there that Louis began his boxing career. In his two years as an amateur light heavyweight, he won 48 of 54 fights by knockouts. In 1934, when Louis turned professional under the management of Julian Black and John Roxborough, the boxing world was hostile to African-American fighters. White titleholders often refused to accept a challenge from a black contender, and riots sometimes broke out when white boxers were defeated by blacks.

In 1935, Louis stopped Primo Carnera in a sixth-round technical knockout. Thousands of African Americans jammed the streets of Harlem in celebration. A year later, Louis was defeated by Max Schmeling. In 1937, Louis took the heavyweight crown after defeating James Braddock. The following year, he had a rematch with Schmeling and knocked him out in the first two minutes of the

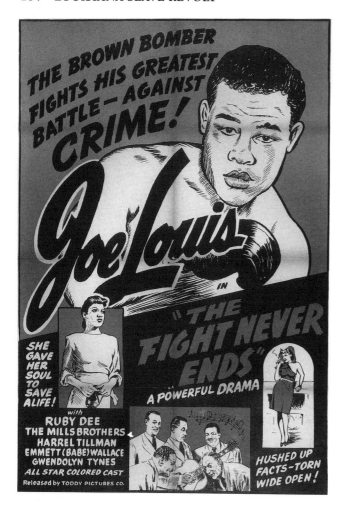

Poster advertising Joe Louis' appearance in the film *The Fight Never Ends* (*Library of Congress*)

fight. Louis spent four years in the army during World War II and was instrumental in helping JACKIE ROBINSON gain admission to Officer Candidate School. He retired from boxing in 1949, having held the heavyweight crown for a record 11 years and eight months. In 71 professional bouts, he was defeated only three times.

Louisiana Slave Revolt

The biggest slave revolt ever carried out in U.S. territory. Other plots, such as the GABRIEL PROSSER and DENMARK VESEY conspiracies, although involving larger numbers, were stopped before they could actually get under way. The 1811 Louisiana uprising took place in St. Charles and St. John the Baptist Parishes and involved an estimated 500 slaves armed with axes, knives, and clubs. They marched with flags flying on the city of New Orleans. Four hundred and sixty soldiers under the command of General Wade Hampton, along with 200 additional troops from Baton Rouge, located and attacked the rebelling slaves on January 10, killing at least 66. Sixteen others were executed later, their heads cut off and placed on pikes along the road leading to the André plantation, where the revolt had begun. An additional number of slaves are believed to have been murdered later in revenge. The leader of the revolt was a free black man named Charles Deslondes, who had worked as a driver on the André plantation. Eastern newspapers paid little attention to the revolt, partly because the United States had only recently acquired Louisiana (in 1803) and partly because the territory was regarded as the "wild West," where violence was expected. An earlier uprising had taken place in Louisiana 16 years before, in 1795, in Point Coupée Parish. At that time, Louisiana was still under French control, and the rebelling slaves hoped to take advantage of existing tensions between France and Spain. Approximately 25 slaves died resisting capture, and another 25 were executed later. In an unsuccessful attempt to discourage future uprisings, the French governor ordered slaves be given more food and clothing, shorter work hours, and 30 cents a day when working on Sunday.

Love, Nat (Deadwood Dick) (1854–1921)
cowboy, rodeo star

Born a slave in Davidson County, Tennessee, Nat Love was 11 years old when the Civil War ended in 1865. Four years later, he won a horse in a raffle. He sold it, gave part of the money to his widowed mother, and then left for Dodge City, Kansas, where he found employment at the Duval Ranch. He became known as a gunfighter and scout and claimed to have survived outlaw attacks, capture by Indians, and being shot 14 times. In 1876, a huge centennial Fourth of July celebration and rodeo was held at Deadwood, South Dakota. After winning the rifle and handgun contests and setting records in other events, Love was nicknamed "Deadwood Dick." A book based on his life introduced him to

Nat Love (*Library of Congress*)

thousands of readers. While his life was more color-ful than most, Nat Love was only one of the thousands of black people who traveled west after the Civil War. It is estimated that between 20 percent and 25 percent of America's cowboys were black men.

Lucy, Autherine Juanita (Autherine Lucy Foster) (1929–) *civil rights activist*

In 1952, Lucy requested legal help from the NATIONAL ASSOCIATION FOR THE ADVANCEMENT OF COLORED PEOPLE (NAACP) in gaining admittance to graduate school at the University of Alabama, which, like the state universities of Florida, Georgia, Mississippi, and South Carolina, refused to admit blacks. On June 29, 1955, she obtained a court order forbidding the school to reject her on the basis of race. She enrolled on Friday, February 1, 1956. That night 1,200 students and townspeople rioted outside her dormitory. The following Monday, 3,000 white supremacists roamed the campus threatening her life as she attended class under police protection. That evening, the university, citing the growing violence, suspended her. The NAACP filed suit, and the court ordered Lucy reinstated. Instead, the university expelled her, charging her with making "outrageous" statements accusing the administration of conspiring with the mob. Thirty-two years later, the University of Alabama overturned the expulsion, and in 1989, Autherine Lucy Foster and her daughter enrolled. They received degrees in 1992.

Lumumba, Patrice Emery (1925–1961) *political leader in Democratic Republic of Congo*

Born in the village of OnaLua in what was then the Belgian Congo, Lumumba was educated in French-speaking schools and worked as a postal employee as a young man. His 1956 book *Congo My Country* helped to consolidate his position as a leader of the Congolese National Movement Party. Fluent in Swahili, French, and Lingala, Lumumba was a powerful and charismatic public speaker.

In 1958, Lumumba defied the government to attend a pan-African conference in Ghana, where he met Kwame Nkrumah and other African leaders. When he returned, he gave a major speech demanding independence. Six days later, government repression led to a riot in which 42 Congolese were killed.

Lumumba became prime minister after the Democratic Republic of the Congo (renamed Zaire 1971–1997) achieved its independence in 1960, but the country was almost immediately immersed in civil war. Katanga Province seceded under the leadership of Moise Tshombe, and Belgian troops, which had been sent in to protect whites, were involved in massacres of blacks. Lumumba appealed for help from the United Nations, which sent in troops to restore order. The UN troops failed to pacify the country, and Lumumba then turned to the Soviet Union for help, a move which infuriated the United States. The U.S. Central Intelligence Agency plotted to have him poisoned, but before this could occur, Lumumba was murdered by followers of Tshombe. Lumumba's memory has been invoked by various factions contending for power in central Africa. His anticolonialism made him a martyr for African independence, while his opposition to ethnic rivalries was cited to justify authoritarian rule. He is regarded as a national hero in Democratic Republic of the Congo.

lynching

willful murder for racial or religious reasons. Most victims were black or whites who supported civil rights; others were targeted because they were Asian, especially Chinese, or, as in the notorious 1915 case of Leo Frank, Jewish. Lynching became widespread after the Civil War as former supporters of the Confederacy struggled to maintain social, economic, and political control of the South. Lynch mobs directed their fury at blacks who voted, ran for office, owned land, were successful in business, or were leaders in the community. Initially, the killers defended lynching as necessary to maintain white authority. After the 1880s, when it was clear whites were in control, killers started accusing black lynch victims of criminal activities, usually the murder of a white man or the rape of a white woman.

Victims were tortured, hanged, burned alive, and shot, sometimes before crowds numbering in the thousands. A number of lynchings were preannounced in newspapers. Tuskegee Institute listed 4,743 lynch victims between 1882 and 1968. Of these, 3,446 were black and at least 80 were women. Many were not guilty of any crime, let alone a serious felony. Among other things, blacks were lynched for "insolence," testifying against a white in court, economic success that threatened white competition, organizing workers, and "disrespect." After World War I, several black soldiers were lynched for wearing their uniforms, an indication of segregationists' fears that returning black soldiers would resist continued discrimination. Ten thousand blacks left Yazoo City, Mississippi, in 1923 following a lynching there, and thousands of other African

Lynching in Duluth, Minnesota (*Library of Congress*)

Americans fled the South for the same reason. Antilynching activists like IDA WELLS-BARNETT and Walter White of the NATIONAL ASSOCIATION FOR THE ADVANCEMENT OF COLORED PEOPLE (NAACP) faced the problem of dealing with a white community that often regarded lynch victims as criminals who "deserved" their fate. The first antilynching bill was introduced by African-American congressman George White of North Carolina in 1901. It failed to pass, as did more than 200 other bills on the subject. Other antilynching legislation was passed by the U.S. House of Representatives in 1922, 1937, and 1940, but was defeated in the Senate. Well-known lynch victims include EMMETT TILL (1955), Mack Parker (1959), Lemuel Penn (1964), and JAMES CHANEY, Andrew Goodman, and Michael Schwerner (1964). Richard Wright described the psychological effects of lynching in his autobiography *Black Boy*.

Maasai (ma-SIGH)

Nomadic tribal group that migrated to what is now Kenya and Tanzania during the 16th century. The Maasai govern themselves through councils of village elders. They measure wealth by the size of their herds and own approximately 3 million cattle, more than any other tribe in Africa. However, the Kenyan and Tanzanian governments have taken part of their

Maasai warriors (*National Museum of African Art, Washington, D.C.*)

land for national parks, and many Maasai have sold their land to KIKUYU farmers. This loss of grazing land threatens their cattle, especially in times of drought.

Most people live in *bomas,* camps of about 12–14 huts enclosed by a thorny fence. Duties and privileges are determined by AGE GROUPS, and both boys and girls undergo circumcision without anesthesia shortly after puberty. Boys are expected to endure the operation in silence, and those who cry out are regarded as cowards. The circumcision must be performed before a boy can join the *moran,* the name for the famed Maasai warriors who live together in separate camps. To prove their courage, young *moran* are sent out alone armed only with a spear to kill a lion. The Maasai believe that all cattle belong to them, and *moran* warriors are often in trouble with authorities for raiding the cattle of other tribespeople. Their legendary fighting ability, which involved the use of the phalanx formation, kept both Arab slave traders and European colonists out of Maasailand for years.

In the early 20th century, the British forced the Maasai, along with 175,000 cattle and 1,000,000 sheep, onto a single large reserve. The trek to the reserve resulted in a number of Maasai fatalities and disease outbreaks among their herds. Although a few hundred Maasai now work in Nairobi, most continue to live with the tribe. Alcoholism, tuberculosis, eye infections, and malaria are serious problems among Maasai, and many children die before the age of five. The name *Nairobi* is the Maasai word for "cold," and the word *kenya* may derive from the Maasai word *e-rukenya,* meaning "mist." The current Maasai population is estimated at approximately 300,000.

Recommended Reading: Bentsen, Cheryl. *Maasai Days.* New York: Doubleday, Anchor Books, 1989.

McCoy, Elijah (1843–1929) *inventor*

McCoy was born in Canada to slaves who had escaped via the UNDERGROUND RAILROAD. He was sent to Scotland to study mechanical engineering, then settled in Detroit. When racial prejudice prevented him from being hired as an engineer, McCoy was forced to take a job as a fireman on the Michigan Central Railroad. At that time, all trains had to be stopped periodically so they could be oiled by hand. McCoy developed a device that lubricated machinery automatically while it was still in operation. He received a patent for it in 1872. McCoy developed numerous variations of his device for use with other machinery, as well as other inventions, acquiring 42 patents in all. His inventions were soon in use around the world and resulted in the saving of millions of dollars. Others tried to copy his work, but many people refused to accept substitutions. In a phrase that has become a part of the American language, they said they wanted "the real McCoy."

McKay, Festus Claudius (Claude) (1890–1948) *poet*

Born in Jamaica, McKay published his first two books of poetry, *Songs of Jamaica* and *Constab Ballads,* in 1912. Written in dialect, they describe the lives of poor island blacks. Moving to the United States, McKay studied agriculture briefly at Tuskegee, transferred to Kansas State College for two years, then left for New York, where he became coeditor of *The Liberator,* an avant-garde literary journal. In 1922, he published *Harlem Shadows,* which made him a leading figure in the HARLEM RENAISSANCE. His poetry influenced the work of LANGSTON HUGHES, Senegalese poet Léopold Senghor, Aimé Cesaire from Martinique, and J. J. Rabearivelo from Madagascar. His 1919 poem "If We Must Die," which attacked lynchings and mob violence, was quoted by British prime minister Winston Churchill during World War II to bolster English morale.

A socialist and a supporter of MARCUS GARVEY, McKay championed independence movements in Africa and elsewhere and emphasized the superiority of black rural culture. Always a subject of controversy, McKay's work was dismissed by philosopher ALAIN LOCKE but defended by JAMES WELDON JOHNSON. Among his books are three novels, *Home to Harlem, Banjo: A Story Without a Plot,* and *Banana Bottom;* several books of poetry and short stories, including *Spring in New Hampshire, Gingertown,* and *Selected Poems;* and two memoirs, *A*

Long Way from Home and an autobiography, *My Green Hills of Jamaica.*

Madagascar, Republic of

island country located 250 miles off the coast of East Africa. Capital: Antananarivo. The people and language are known as Malagasy. Madagascar is the fourth-largest island in the world after Greenland, Borneo, and New Guinea. It is sometimes called the Great Red Island because erosion has caused its red soil to flow into the sea, staining the surrounding water red. The country is home to hundreds of plants and animals found nowhere else in the world. Among these are more than 1,000 varieties of orchids, 150 species of frogs and toads, 30 kinds of lemurs, 28 species of bats, and most of the world's chameleons. Many of these plants and animals are close to extinction, and conservation efforts have met with only limited success.

Though some Stone Age relics have been found, Madagascar was apparently uninhabited when settlers arrived from Indonesia and Malaysia 1,500 to 2,000 years ago. Later arrivals included African slaves, Arabs, Indians, and Europeans. Descendants of these groups formed 18 tribes or ethnic groups, which make up Madagascar's population today. The people support themselves primarily through agriculture, fishing, and the raising of livestock. They are noted for their construction of tombs that are often larger and more ornate than houses. These tombs may be decorated with cattle skulls and with sculptures depicting birds, airplanes, and police in the act of arresting cattle thieves.

Although Madagascar was known to Marco Polo, the first Europeans to arrive were the Portuguese, who landed there in 1500. A growing trade in slaves and guns led to the development of three small kingdoms, one of which, the Menabe, became dominant in the late 16th century. Madagascar became an important base for pirates in the 18th century, and one, an Englishman named Thomas White, married a Malagasy princess, who gave birth to a son named Ratsimilaho. Ratsimilaho unified the island's mulattoes into a new state called Betsimisaraka, but the kingdom fell apart during his grandson's reign. In the 1790s, a Merina tribal chief named Andrianampoinimerina, using guns obtained from the Europeans, gained control of half the island. His son, Radama I, conquered the rest and convinced Britain to recognize Madagascar as an independent state.

Missionaries arrived in the late 1700s and converted much of the country to Christianity. It was around this time that the Malagasy language was first written down. After Radama I's death in 1828, his widow forced the missionaries out and declared Christianity illegal. Her son, Radama II, reversed his mother's anti-European policies when he became king in 1861. But he was assassinated a year later after the country was struck by a deadly plague that many believed was retribution for his pro-European policies.

In 1890, the British agreed to recognize French domination over Madagascar in return for French recognition of British rule in Zanzibar. Several years later, the French demanded the Malagasy government step down. When it refused, the French attacked, occupying the capital in 1895 and setting up a colonial administration. They abolished slavery but instituted high taxes and a forced labor system for anyone unable to pay. A bloody uprising in which thousands died occurred in 1947, but Madagascar did not become independent until 1958.

A number of coups took place following independence, leading to a 17-year dictatorship under Didier Ratsiraka, which began in 1975. In 1985, Bruce Lee–inspired kung fu clubs fought with each other and the police in battles in which scores of people died. The widespread popularity of Bruce Lee was due in part to the popular Malagasy sport of *moraingy* fighting, in which the objective is to knock your opponent out. Riots followed the kung fu club battles, and the government banned martial arts. Ratsiraka was forced out after a strike in 1991 led to the formation of an interim government and elections that brought Albert Zafy to power in 1993. Ratsiraka was elected president in 1997.

Malawi, Republic of

Landlocked East African country. Capital: Lilongwe. Malawi was originally settled by BANTU-speaking people sometime between the first and fourth centuries. During the 15th century, three groups—the Kalonga, the Lundu, and the Undi—formed the Maravi (people of the fire) kingdom, which developed a long-distance trade in ivory with KILWA and MOZAMBIQUE. Portuguese efforts to control the ivory trade in East Africa led to conflict with Maravi and may have triggered attacks by the ZIMBA, believed to be a Lundu mercenary group, on Portuguese-controlled coastal cities in 1580.

In the 18th century, internal problems and attacks by Yao tribesmen led to the Maravi kingdom's disintegration. Additional disruption was caused by NGONI invasions in the 1840s. In 1883, partly in response to British businessman Cecil Rhodes' land acquisition and diamond mining activities in southern Africa, the British sent a consul to the area and declared a protectorate—later known as Nyasaland—in the region in 1889. The British ended the slave trade, but their labor and taxation policies led to the unsuccessful CHILEMBWE UPRISING in 1915.

The Nyasaland African Congress Party was formed in 1944, and the first African was admitted to the Nyasaland legislature in 1949. In 1953, the British formed the Federation of Rhodesia and Nyasaland, linking what would eventually become Zimbabwe, Malawi, and Zambia. The efforts of the Congress Party (renamed Malawi Congress Party in 1959) led to Malawi independence in 1964 under Prime Minister and later President Hastings Banda. Banda's efforts to maintain good relations with the white-ruled government of South Africa for economic reasons created resentment with other African countries. Support for rebels in Mozambique led to tension with that nation, especially after Malawi accepted over 600,000 refugees from Mozambique's civil war. Banda's one-party rule was overturned in 1993, and elections were held in 1994, leading to the election of Bakili Muluzi.

Malcolm X (Malcom Little, El-Hajj Malik El-Shabazz) (1925–1965) militant African-American leader, Nation of Islam minister

Born Malcolm Little in Omaha, Nebraska, Malcolm X was the son of a Baptist minister. He stated that his father's support for MARCUS GARVEY and insis-

Malcolm X (Library of Congress)

tence on black equality led to an arson attack on the family home by white supremacists, and that his father was murdered by racists after the family moved to Lansing, Michigan. However, others in his family have claimed that the fire and death were accidental. Poverty and stress led to his mother's mental breakdown. Malcolm dropped out of school after the eighth grade and moved to Boston and then to HARLEM, where he became involved in crime and was arrested and sentenced to eight to ten years in prison for burglary. While in jail, he became a member of the NATION OF ISLAM and took the name Malcolm X. After his release, he became the Nation of Islam's best-known minister, attracting numerous new members. He was appointed head of Boston's Temple # 11 and later Temple # 7 in Harlem.

His growing popularity caused jealousy within the movement, and he became disillusioned when he learned of sexual misbehavior on the part of Nation of Islam leader Elijah Muhammad. When President John F. Kennedy was murdered in 1963, Malcolm X commented that the assassination was a case of "chickens coming home to roost," meaning that the hatred and violence that for years had been unleashed against black people had now been turned against the chief executive. Nevertheless, Elijah Muhammad ordered Malcolm X suspended, ostensibly to counter any negative publicity his remark might attract.

In March 1964, Malcolm X left the Nation of Islam. He made a pilgrimage (hajj) to Mecca, and traveled through Africa and the Middle East. He then returned to the United States, where he established the Muslim Mosque in Harlem and the Organization of Afro-American Unity. Now an orthodox Muslim, he denounced Elijah Muhammad as a "racist" and a "religious faker." The hierarchy in the Nation of Islam reacted angrily, and the Nation's newspaper, *Muhammad Speaks,* stated that Malcolm was "worthy of death." On February 14, 1965, his house was firebombed. One week later, Malcolm X was shot to death as he spoke at the Audubon Ballroom in New York. The killers were three members of the Nation of Islam.

Recommended Reading: X, Malcolm, and Haley, Alex. *The Autobiography of Malcolm X.* New York: Grove Press, 1965; Meyers, Walter Dean. *Malcolm X: By Any Means Necessary.* New York: Scholastic, 1994; Sagan, Miriam. *Malcolm X.* San Diego, Calif.: Lucent, 1997.

Mali, Empire of (Melle)

West African empire established by the Malinke leader SUNDIATA KEITA, who defeated the Soso king Sumanguru in 1235. The capital was at Niani. Sundiata went on to conquer the remnants of the Ghana Empire in 1240 and acquired the gold-rich area of Wangara. Sundiata ruled through the traditional allegiances of clans and families, maintaining their support by shifting his headquarters among the various villages. Although Mali was still a predominately agricultural nation, there was a growing trans-Saharan trade in gold, salt, and copper.

Within 100 years of Sundiata's reign, Mali had become one of the greatest empires of its time. Its ruler sat on an ebony throne placed between two huge elephant tusks. Around him stood his official spokesman, musicians, the royal executioner, and various courtiers and military personnel. Among its major cities were TIMBUKTU and Jenne, both famous throughout the Muslim world as centers of commerce, religion, and learning.

The Mali people had converted to Islam in the 11th century, and boys were expected to memorize the Koran. Those who did not were often put in chains. However, many native African religious customs remained, particularly in regard to women. The most famous of all Mali rulers was the great MANSA KANKAN MUSA, who took power in 1312. Following Mansa Musa's death in 1337, Mali grew weaker, and its major cities, including Timbuktu, eventually came under the control of the SONGHAI Empire.

Mali, Republic of

modern West African state. Capital: Bamako. The Niger and Senegal Rivers provide water and transportation. Several ancient kingdoms, including Mali, SONGHAI, and GHANA, once occupied what is now Mali territory, and the country is the site of several historically important cities, including TIMBUKTU and JENNE.

When the Songhai Empire fell to the Moroccans in 1591, the area entered a period of disruption. After 1851, the French attempted to gain control of the area, which they called Soudan (French Sudan), but ran into great opposition from various tribal groups, particularly the Tukulors, whom they fought from 1881 to 1893. They also had to contend with the forces of a Soninke leader named SAMORI TOURÉ who battled the French intermittently form 1882 until his defeat in 1898. His grandson Sékou Touré was the first president of Guinea.

After finally gaining control of the region, the French established the FRENCH WEST AFRICA FEDERATION, of which Mali (or French Sudan) was a part, along with areas of Benin, Burkina Faso, Senegal, Guinea, and the Ivory Coast. A nationalist movement developed, and Mali, under the leadership of Modibo Keita, became fully independent in 1960. Keita's autocratic rule led to his imprisonment following a military coup under Lt. Moussa Traoré in 1968. Severe droughts in 1973–74 and 1983–84 caused great hardship and famine, and the country continues to face serious economic problems. Keita died in prison in 1977, and Traoré was elected president in 1979. In 1991, the country was torn by demonstrations that led to three days of violence

Dogon women pounding millet in central Mali (*National Museum of African Art, Washington, D.C.*)

during which government troops killed almost 150 people. A bloody coup followed, Traoré was overthrown, and the army promised to institute a multiparty democracy. Elections were held in 1992, and Alpha Oumar Konare was elected president. Although slavery is illegal in Mali, there are reports that it continues to exist in the salt-mining area of Taoudeni.

Malindi

City in Kenya, possibly dating back to the 10th century A.D. In medieval times, Malindi was a major trading port that exported ivory, iron, gold, tortoiseshell, and other goods. It was a city of stone houses surrounded by fields of rice, wheat, and millet. In 1414, the sultan of Malindi sent the emperor of China a gift of a giraffe. The Chinese emperor was so impressed that he had the famous Chinese naval commander Cheng Ho personally accompany the Malindi ambassadors home to ensure their safety.

See also INDIAN OCEAN TRADE.

Mandela, Nelson Rolihlahla (1918–) *South African statesman*

Mandela was born in the village of Mvezo in what is now Transkei. His father was an adviser to the king of the Thembu people, who are part of the XHOSA nation. Mandela's original name, Rolihlahla, can mean troublemaker; he was renamed Nelson by an African teacher when he was seven. When Mandela was nine, his father died, and he became a ward of the Thembu regent. In 1943, he received his bachelor of arts degree from the University of South Africa and Fort Hare College and began the study of law at the University of the Witwatersrand. During this time, he met Walter Sisulu and other leaders in the AFRICAN NATIONAL CONGRESS (ANC), which he joined in 1944. Mandela organized the ANC's youth league and led nonviolent protests against APARTHEID laws. After receiving his law degree in 1951, he and his friend Oliver Tambo opened South Africa's first black law practice. Shortly afterward, he, along with 8,500 other blacks, was arrested under the Suppression of Communism Act. Mandela was banned (forbidden to attend meetings and restricted to Johannesburg). After the 1960 Sharpeville Massacre, in which 69 unarmed black protesters were slain by police and more than 400 wounded, Mandela agreed to coordinate an ANC paramilitary group to carry out sabotage against government targets. He and other ANC leaders had previously been acquitted of treason charges in a trial that had lasted from 1957 until 1961. Fearing re-arrest on new charges, Mandela went "underground." He visited England, Algeria, and Ethiopia seeking support for the ANC's guerrilla campaign. After returning to South Africa in 1962, he was convicted of conspiracy to overthrow the government and sentenced to life in prison.

Nelson Mandela receiving the Medal of Freedom, Philadelphia (© 1997 Michael Brown/National Parks Service)

Mandela and other ANC leaders were originally held under harsh conditions on Robben Island. Prisoners' contacts with the outside world were limited to supervised family visits, and they were not allowed to see newspapers or TV from 1964 to 1980. Mandela, prisoner #466/64, worked in the stone quarry and later gathered seaweed that the government sold for fertilizer. While still in prison, he learned of his mother's death from a heart attack and of a car crash that killed his son. In 1982, he was moved from Robben Island to Pollsmoor Prison, where conditions were better. He was released in 1990. Mandela was awarded the 1993 Nobel Peace Prize for his efforts in ending apartheid and moving the South African government toward democratic rule. In 1994, he was elected president of South Africa. In 1998, he married Grace Machel, the widow of Mozambican president Samora Machel. Mandela stepped down as president in 1999 after the election of Thabo Mbeki.

Mandinka (Mandingo, Mandes)

Ethnic group, originally from the Sahara. The Mandinka were pushed southwest by increasing dryness into West Africa, finally settling in the upper reaches of the Niger River. An extremely productive agricultural people, they soon developed a special deep-plowing technique and were one of the few peoples to utilize irrigation. They are credited with developing many basic African foods, including pearl millet, sorghum, watermelons, and yams.

According to the stories of the griots (native historian-storytellers), the Mandinka people were originally divided into 12 groups, each of which specialized in a particular skill or profession, such as artisans, hunters, or farmers. At age 12, Mandinka boys became apprentices in the profession of their family or clan. With the development of cities, some were sent to Niani, TIMBUKTU, or GAO to study at the university or with a master craftsman.

Early in their history, the 12 Mandinka groups united under a Mansa, or sultan. The people converted to Islam sometime in the 11th century when the reigning Mansa, whose name was Barmandana, became a Muslim in hopes of ending a drought.

The Mandinka were well-known as merchants and developed an extensive trade in salt, kola nuts, and slaves. They were also famous for their weaving and pottery-making skills. Storytelling was used to pass on the history of the people to each generation and to explain various natural phenomena. Mandinka poets would also recite poems on feast days to encourage good deeds. A short-lived Mandinka state was established by SAMORI TOURÉ in the 18th century.

Mandinka people are found today throughout Senegal, Gambia, Guinea-Bissau, Guinea, Ivory Coast, and Mali. Subgroups include the Malinke, the Soninke, the DIOULA, and the BAMBARA.

Mansa Kankan Musa (unknown–1337) *Mali king*

Musa came to power in 1312 (*Mansa* means "sultan.") During Mansa Musa's reign, MALI became the strongest, richest state in Africa with an army of 100,000 men. In 1324–25, Mansa Musa undertook a pilgrimage to Mecca, which spread Mali's fame throughout Europe and the Middle East. His entourage numbered in the thousands, including 500 slaves, each of whom carried a golden staff weighing four pounds. One hundred camels, each loaded with 300 pounds of gold, completed the caravan. When Musa reached Egypt, he spent so lavishly and gave away so much money, that the value of gold in Cairo became seriously depreciated and remained so for at least 12 years. His fame was such that a picture of Mansa Musa holding a huge gold nugget was used to decorate the famous 1375 map drawn by Abraham Cresques, the leading European cartographer of the age.

Mansa Musa arranged for a poet and architect named as-Sahili to return to West Africa with him in order to introduce Arabian styles and brick construction to Mali architecture. To encourage the spread of Islam, he also brought back Muslim scholars and established several mosques. However, he continued to rely on traditional African rituals and customs for the administration of his empire. During Mansa Musa's rule, Mali expanded until it stretched from the Atlantic Ocean east to what is now the country of Niger. The empire enjoyed a golden age of peace and prosperity. There was almost no crime, and it was during this time that TIMBUKTU and JENNE developed as centers of learning and culture.

Mansa Musa stated that he had ascended to the throne after his predecessor, King Abubakari II, had sent forth 400 ships to determine what lay beyond the Atlantic. Only one ship returned, and so the king himself had set sail with 2,000 ships—1,000 for himself and his men, and 1,000 loaded with gold and provisions. When none of these ships returned, Mansa Musa became king.

March on Washington

Massive civil rights demonstration that took place in Washington, D.C., on August 28, 1963. The idea for the march originated with BAYARD RUSTIN, close friend and adviser to A. PHILIP RANDOLPH.

March on Washington, August 18, 1963—the view from the Lincoln Memorial (*Library of Congress*)

Randolph believed that the various sit-ins and protests being held throughout the South needed the backing of a huge national demonstration. Rustin suggested a march that would involve all the civil rights organizations and that would demand jobs, a higher minimum wage, and a guaranteed income. After adding a demand for full civil rights, Randolph approved the idea and met with other civil rights leaders. They agreed, and Randolph was designated national director of the project, with Rustin his deputy director.

Working out of a small office on New York's West 130th Street, Rustin, together with a few volunteers, secured the participation of hundreds of organizations, including churches, labor unions, businesses, sororities, fraternities, and civic groups. The march was opposed by President John F. Kennedy, who feared it would create a backlash in Congress and make it harder to pass the civil rights legislation he had proposed. But the leaders of the various civil rights organizations, fearing the legislation might fail to pass anyway, refused to call off the march, and Kennedy reluctantly endorsed it at a press conference on July 17.

The march attracted 250,000 participants, making it the biggest civil rights demonstration ever held up to that time. It was there that Dr. MARTIN LUTHER KING JR. gave his famous "I Have a Dream" speech. Other speakers included JOHN LEWIS of the STUDENT NON-VIOLENT COORDINATING COMMITTEE (SNCC), ROY WILKINS of the NATIONAL ASSOCIATION FOR THE ADVANCEMENT OF COLORED PEOPLE (NAACP), and Whitney Young of the NATIONAL URBAN LEAGUE. Fifteen senators, including future vice-president Hubert Humphrey, took part, along with scores of celebrities, including Sidney Poitier, Marlon Brando, Burt Lancaster, Harry Belafonte, and Charlton Heston. Among the entertainers were MAHALIA JACKSON, Joan Baez, Bob Dylan, and Odetta. The 1963 March on Washington marked one of the major turning points in the civil rights movement.

Marley, Robert (Nesta Bob Marley)
(1945–1981) *reggae singer, composer, guitarist*

Born in Nine Miles, Jamaica, Bob Marley grew up in Kingston's tough Trenchtown district. His first group, the Rudeboys, later became known as the Wailers. In 1964, they released their first hit, "Simmer Down," which was written in response to gang violence. In 1972, the Wailers were signed by Island Records, and Bob Marley began to gain a worldwide following, especially in Africa. His songs spoke of crime, revolution, RASTAFARIANISM, strength through unity, and human rights. In 1976, seven men broke into his home in an assassination attempt the night before he was to sing at a concert supporting Jamaican prime minister Michael Manley. Wounded in the arm, he nevertheless appeared at the concert. Two years later, he gave a historic concert emphasizing political conciliation with the song "One Love." In 1980, he gave another historic performance celebrating independence in Zimbabwe. A heavy smoker of marijuana, Marley died of lung cancer at age 36.

Recommended Listening: *Catch a Fire* (Island); *Burnin'* (Island); *Natty Dread* (Island); *Songs of Freedom* (Island).

Maroons (Outlayers)

Fugitive slaves who formed settlements in forests, swamps, or mountain areas rather than try to escape to free territory like Canada. The word *Maroon* comes from the Spanish word *cimarron,* meaning "one who lives on a mountaintop." Maroons were considered extremely dangerous, since they often raided nearby plantations to free friends and family and to obtain food and supplies. An 1856 letter to North Carolina's governor told of slaveholders who attacked a Maroon colony only to be driven off amid threats and curses after seeing one of their party killed.

The largest Maroon colony on the North American continent was Florida's FORT NEGRO, which sheltered about 300 runaway slaves and Seminole Indians. Maroon groups in the United States, however, tended to be small. In Jamaica, Haiti, Venezuela, Suriname, and Brazil, Maroon settlements often had several thousand members. PALMARES, a Maroon colony in Brazil, sheltered as many as 20,000 fugitive slaves.

In addition to raiding plantations, Maroons frequently were involved in slave revolts. By 1730,

Maroons in Jamaica had united under a man named CUDJOE and become so strong that England sent two additional regiments to the colony to protect local slaveholders. The Haitian colonial government granted recognition to a large Maroon colony in 1784 in a vain attempt to head off the coming revolution there. Several Maroon colonies also existed in Africa, where slaves who managed to escape from slave pens, or barracoons, sought safety. The best known was KISAMA in Angola.

Marshall, Thurgood (1908–1993) *first African-American U.S. Supreme Court justice*

Born in Baltimore, Maryland, Thurgood Marshall graduated from Lincoln University, was rejected from the University of Maryland Law School on racial grounds, and then enrolled at Howard University Law School. After graduating from Howard in 1933, Marshall went into private practice in Baltimore, where he agreed to serve as local counsel for the NATIONAL ASSOCIATION FOR THE ADVANCEMENT OF COLORED PEOPLE (NAACP). The organization paid Marshall $25 a year for stationery and postage and $5 a day for research, investigations, and court

Thurgood Marshall with Lyndon Baines Johnson (*Library of Congress*)

appearances. One of Marshall's first projects was to help organize a picketing campaign to force white shop owners to hire African-American salespeople. He also led a drive to get Maryland congressmen to back a federal antilynching bill and tried to organize black schoolteachers in an attempt to bring their salaries into line with those of whites. In 1936, Marshall began working full-time for the NAACP. At that point, he had already begun work on the series of cases that would lead to a successful conclusion in his most important case: *BROWN V. BOARD OF EDUCATION OF TOPEKA* (1954), which outlawed school segregation.

But school integration was only one of several concerns. In 1938, Marshall was instrumental in getting the governor of Texas to provide protection to African Americans serving on jury duty. Later, when 25 African-American men in Tennessee were charged with attempted murder because they had defended themselves when white mobs stormed through the black section of town, shooting into homes and beating people, Marshall succeeded in getting 23 of the 25 acquitted.

In 1940, Marshall became director-counsel of the NAACP Legal Defense and Educational Fund. Four years later, he won a major victory for black voting rights when the Supreme Court voted 8-1 to outlaw white primary elections (*Smith v. Allwright*). His success in *Morgan v. Virginia* (1946) marked the NAACP's first victory in cases involving segregated seating arrangements in interstate public transportation. Another landmark case involved a court ruling that housing agreements that prevented the sale of a house to an African American (known as restrictive covenants) were not legally enforceable (*Shelley v. Kraemer,* 1948).

In 1951, Marshall left for Japan and Korea to investigate court-martial proceedings involving 32 African-American soldiers. By the time he arrived, 16 men had already been sentenced to death or life imprisonment, and the rest to between 10 and 50 years at hard labor. Marshall's investigation turned up evidence that one man had actually been in a hospital and that others had been on duty when they were accused of deserting. His work enabled the NAACP to win reversals in many of these convictions and to achieve reduced sentences in others.

Of the 32 major cases Marshall argued for the NAACP, he won 29. In 1960, he was asked to help draft the constitution for the new Republic of Kenya. A year later, President John F. Kennedy nominated him to be a judge on the Second Circuit Court of Appeals. He was confirmed on September 11, 1962. Of the more than 150 opinions he handed down, none was ever reversed by a higher court. In 1965, President Lyndon Johnson appointed Marshall solicitor general of the Department of Justice. Of the 19 cases Marshall argued for the Justice Department, he won 14. In 1967, Johnson appointed Marshall associate justice of the Supreme Court of the United States. During his tenure, he took particular interest in cases involving discrimination, the rights of the poor, and persons accused of crimes. He retired in 1991 after 24 years of service.

Matabele   See NDEBELE.

Matzeliger, Jan Ernst (1852–1889) *inventor*
Born in Paramaribo, Dutch Guiana (now SURINAME), Jan Matzeliger went to work at age 10 in a machine shop. At 19, he became a sailor, and two years later he moved to the United States, finally settling in Lynn, Massachusetts, in 1877. There he got a job with a shoe manufacturing company. He also began studying English and physics, painted, and gave lessons in art.

However, his main interest was mechanics. Using wood, wire, and cigar boxes, he designed a machine to speed the manufacture of shoes. Though crude, his design was impressive enough to attract a $50 offer, which Metzeliger turned down. By 1880, he had built a more advanced model, which attracted a $1,500 offer, which Metzeliger again rejected. On March 20, 1883, he received a patent for a "Lasting Machine," which cut the cost of manufacturing shoes in half while greatly increasing production. He went into business, but later sold his five patents to another company in return for stock.

Years of poverty and self-sacrifice had left Matzeliger in poor health, and he contracted tuberculosis and died at age 37. He left his stock to the North Congregational Church, the one church in Lynn that had not rejected him on account of race. The company that had bought Matzeliger's patents later became the United Shoe Machinery Corporation. Within 65 years of acquiring the patents, it was worth over $1 billion

Mau Mau
A violent resistance movement based in Kenya between 1952 and 1960. Made up primarily of KIKUYU tribesmen, the Mau Mau fought the British colonists in a war of national liberation. Ninety-five whites (mostly police and soldiers) and approximately 13,500 Africans were killed. Though many Africans were killed by the British, several thousand were killed by Mau Mau guerrillas for refusing to take an oath of loyalty or for refusing to turn against white employers. The British jailed JOMO KENYATTA as a suspected Mau Mau leader in 1952. The Mau Mau were not put down until 1956; its formal end was declared in 1960. Even though the uprising ended in defeat, it had a strong psychological impact throughout Africa.

Mauretania and Numidia
Latin names for two ancient regions of North Africa. Although the Phoenicians and Hellenistic peoples established colonies along the coast, various BERBER kingdoms remained in control of much of the desert and mountain region, thanks to superior horsemanship and mobile cavalry. Numidia, which was located in what is now eastern Algeria, became a province of the Roman Empire after the Second Punic War (218–201 B.C.) It later merged with Mauretania ("land of Moors"), which occupied the area that is now modern Morocco. The people of coastal Mauretania traded extensively with southern Europe. Berber horsemen were recruited for the Roman army and Numidian soldiers were deployed as far east as the Euphrates River. During the centuries of Roman rule, there were frequent rebellions, some of which saw multi-ethnic alliances among city dwellers and desert tribes. The Vandals hastened the end of Roman rule early in the fifth century, and the region was controlled by local Berber tribes until the Arab invasions in the seventh century.

Mauritania, Islamic Republic of

West African country located on the Atlantic Ocean. Capital: Nouakchott. BERBERS began moving into Mauritania in the first century, pushing the local tribes further south. They founded the kingdom of Ghana and its capital, Kumbi-Saleh, in eastern Mauritania and established a strong trade in gold and salt across the SAHARA.

The 1076 capture of Kumbi-Saleh by the Muslim ALMORAVIDS permanently established Islam in the region. In the 19th century, the French gained control of southern Mauritania and declared the country a protectorate in 1903, but it took the French 30 years to pacify the Moors in the north. Originally ruled in conjunction with SENEGAL, Mauritania was made a separate colony of French West Africa in 1920 and became independent in 1960.

France abolished slavery in Mauritania in 1905, and the Mauritanian constitution of 1961 outlawed it as well. It was again made illegal in 1980. However, slavery is a continuing problem, with an estimated 90,000 to 300,000 people still in bondage, and the government has made little attempt to correct the situation. To this day, slaves who attempt to escape are subjected to brutal tortures that often handicap them for life.

Tension continues among Beydanes ("white" or light-skinned Moors [or Maurs]), who control the government; black slaves known as the Abd; black ex-slaves known as Haratines who have accepted Arab culture and who, though technically free, remain subservient to their former Beydane masters; and free black ethnic groups such as the Halpulaar, Soninke, WOLOF, and BAMBARA. Severe droughts in the 1970s and 1980s killed approximately 80 percent of Mauritania's livestock, and forced northern Beydane nomads into the Senegal river valley, which had been settled by black farmers. The Beydane-controlled government sided with the Beydane nomads in their efforts to drive the blacks out. In 1989, a border dispute between Mauritania and Senegal led to violence, and more than 70,000 blacks were accused of being Senegalese and expelled from Mauritania. In 1990–91, 500 blacks were massacred and hundreds more arrested and tortured. Col. Maaouya Ould Sid Ahmed Taya has been president since 1984.

Though Mauritania's economy is primarily agricultural, there is fishing along the Atlantic coast. Fishermen pound the water with sticks in the evening, then wait until dolphins appear, driving thousands of fish toward the shore where the fishermen wait with nets. Fish that escape the nets are caught by the dolphins. This interaction between humans and wild dolphins may be unique in the world.

Mauritius   See SAINT MAURICE.

Mauritius, Republic of

East African island republic located in the Indian Ocean east of Madagascar; part of the Mascarene island group. Capital: Port Louis. The majority of the population is of Indian descent, with the rest being of French-African or French ancestry. Mauritius was visited by Arab, Malay, and Portuguese ships in the Middle Ages and was the site of a Dutch colony in 1638. (The name Mauritius is from Prince Maurice of Nassau of the Netherlands.) The Dutch introduced the cultivation of sugarcane but found life on the island too difficult and abandoned Mauritius in 1710—not, however, before wiping the dodo bird out of existence. In 1722, French settlers from the nearby island of Réunion arrived. They renamed Mauritius "Île de France" and imported large numbers of African slaves to work on sugarcane plantations.

Mauritius came under British control in 1810 and was formally ceded to England after the Napoleonic wars. The British outlawed slavery there in 1835, then brought in indentured laborers from India to replace the slaves. At one time, Mauritius was an important way station for ships making the long voyage around Africa to India, but it became less important after the opening of the Suez Canal in 1869. Clashes between the nation's various ethnic groups have been a frequent problem. Mauritius became independent in 1968 and is now a democratic republic within the British Commonwealth.

Melanesia

South Pacific region that includes Fiji, New Guinea, Vanuatu, New Caledonia, Tuvalu, the Solomon

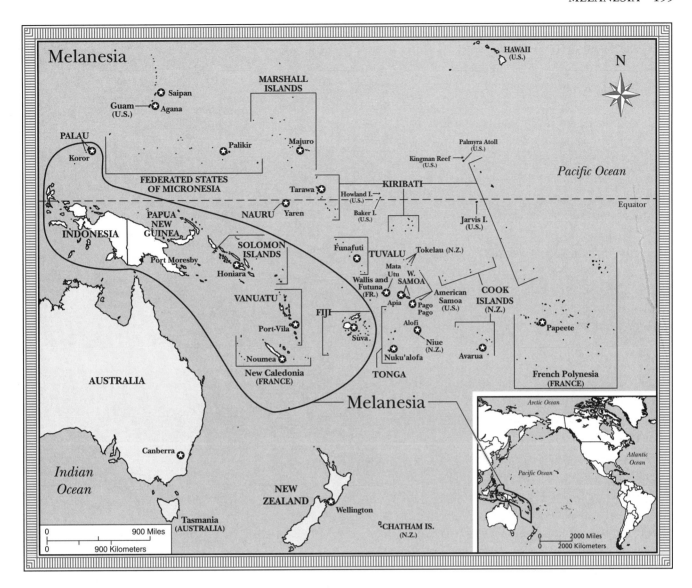

Melanesia (*Facts On File*)

Islands, the Bismarck Archipelago, and the Admiralty Islands. The word *Melanesia* means "black islands," and Melanesians are characterized by their dark skin, hair texture, and Negroid appearance. In fact, New Guinea received its name because 16th-century Spanish explorers thought the inhabitants resembled the natives of West Africa, which was then known as Guinea.

The people of these islands were originally divided into three main groups: NEGRITOES, Papuans (the Malay term for "wooly hair"), and Melanesians. The Negritoes, who stand about five feet tall and who are also found in the Philippines and the Malay Peninsula, probably arrived in the islands first— possibly as much as 30,000 years ago. Like many Africans, they used cowrie shells as money. They were followed by the Papuans, a taller, brown-skinned people who were once known as head-hunters. The Melanesians, a dark-skinned people who arrived somewhat later, are famous for their seamanship and their use of large outrigger and composite canoes, some with cabin and sails. All these groups are noted for their emphasis on kinship and clan responsibilities.

Various island groups were colonized by the Spanish, Dutch, Germans, French, and English, who became involved in the production of copra (from coconuts), coffee, and spices. After 1830, workers from the Solomon Islands, Vanuatu, and later, New Guinea, were often tricked into signing labor contracts by recruiters known as "blackbirders" and forced to work under conditions so bad the practice was referred to as the "disguised slave trade." This led to clashes with whites, and some, including a number of white missionaries, were killed in the Solomons in 1845. Forced labor practices also resulted in an insurrection in New Caledonia in 1878 and the death of 200 French settlers. Australia became involved in the disguised slave trade after 1868, importing Melanesians from New Guinea to replace convict slave labor, which was declared illegal. An Australian court ended the practice in 1884.

Menelik II (1844–1913) *emperor of Ethiopia (Abyssinia)*

Menelik seized the throne in 1889 after the death of Emperor Johannes IV. After first agreeing to the 1889 Treaty of Uccialli with Italy, Menelik rejected it when Italy used it to claim Ethiopia as an Italian protectorate. When Italy responded by invading (1895–96), Menelik defeated the Italian army at Adowa, in the greatest modern victory of an African army over European troops. A new treaty confirmed the "absolute independence" of Ethiopia. Menelik extended Ethiopia's territory, made Addis Ababa the capital, encouraged the development of roads, improved communications, instituted a postal service, and encouraged agricultural, industrial, and commercial development. He also attempted to end the slave trade and bring Ethiopia's feudalistic nobility under control. In March 1910, ill health forced Menelik to yield power to a regency council that ruled in the name of his 13-year-old grandson, Lij Yasu.

Meredith, James (1933–   ) *civil rights activist*

In April 1961, Air Force veteran James Meredith applied for admission to the University of Mississippi, but his application was rejected because of his race. Sixteen months later, in September 1962, a

James Meredith, escorted by federal marshals, enters the all-white University of Mississippi, 1962. (*Archive Photos*)

federal court ordered him admitted. Mississippi Governor Ross Barnett appeared on television stating that the Caucasion race could not survive integration and personally blocked Meredith's attempt to register. Surrounded by over 300 federal marshals, border patrolmen, and guards, Meredith arrived on the Mississippi campus on September 30. Almost immediately after his arrival, a mob of over 2,000 people attacked the federal force with bricks, guns, and Molotov cocktails. The marshals, under orders not to shoot, fought back with tear gas. Army reinforcements began arriving at 4:00 A.M. By the time order had been restored, 28 marshals had been shot, and over 300 people had been injured. Two people, a French journalist and a bystander, had been killed. The next day Meredith took his seat in a class on American history. He remained under federal protection for the rest of the year. Those few white students and professors friendly to him were subjected to severe harassment. In 1966, Meredith was shot and wounded near Hernando, Mississippi, while on a solitary March Against Fear to dramatize the voter registration drive. The march was continued by MARTIN LUTHER KING JR. and other civil rights leaders.

Meroe

Second capital of the KUSH empire. It is located on the Nile River, about 100 miles from Khartoum, and is over 2,500 years old. Though most of its ruins have yet to be investigated, it is clear Meroe was once a thriving metropolis with temples, palaces, royal pyramids, and bathhouses. Situated near several major caravan routes, Meroe was also one of the largest African centers for smelting and iron manufacture. In ancient warfare, iron weapons could mean the difference between victory and defeat, and iron production technology probably spread to much of western Africa through contact with the Kushite Empire and Meroe.

Knowledge of day-to-day life in Meroe is still limited, although it is clear Meroitic citizens engaged in trade with many nations and had a major impact on surrounding civilizations. Evidence of their work has been found as far south as Uganda and as far west as Lake Chad. In addition to iron manufacture, they were also known for domesticating elephants, which they used in war and for ceremonial purposes. Women played an important role in Meroitic royalty and sometimes ruled in their own right. In the beginning, the Meroitic people used a kind of writing that combined Egyptian hieroglyphics with their own pictographic symbols. By about 200 B.C., however, they had developed their own alphabet—which has yet to be deciphered. With the fall of the Kushite Empire around A.D. 300, Meroe became isolated and fell into obscurity.

Middle Passage

term used during the years of the transatlantic slave trade to refer to the shipping of slaves from Africa to the New World. A round-trip would include a voyage from England to Africa, a second or "middle" voyage from Africa to the Americas, and a third voyage from the Americas back to England.

See also SLAVERY; TRIANGULAR TRADE.

Military See BLACK SOLDIERS.

Miller, Doris ("Dorie") (1919–1943) *World War II naval hero*

The son of Texas sharecroppers, Miller joined the navy at age 19. He was assigned to the battleship *Arizona* as a mess attendant and was aboard when it came under attack at Pearl Harbor on Dec. 7, 1941. Seeing the ship's captain severely wounded, Miller moved him to safety, then manned a machine gun and brought down four Japanese planes before being ordered to abandon ship. He was awarded the Navy Cross and asked to address the graduating class at the U.S. Navy's Great Lakes Training School—a school Miller himself was not eligible to attend because he was an African American. He was killed along with 644 shipmates, when his ship, the *Liscome Bay*, was sunk on Thanksgiving Day by a Japanese submarine while sailing to Makin Island in the Pacific. A destroyer escort ship was named in his honor.

Million Man March

March that took place in Washington, D.C., on October 16, 1995, to promote unity and responsibility among African Americans. Called by Nation of Islam leader LOUIS FARRAKHAN, the black, all-male march was billed a "Day of Atonement" during which African-American men were to express remorse for mistreatment of women and behavior detrimental to the black community. Those who were unable to attend were asked to stay home from work and school as a gesture of support. African-American women were not invited to march, though many provided behind-the-scenes support for the event, and several, including civil rights activists Dorothy Height and ROSA PARKS, writer MAYA ANGELOU, and Betty Shabazz, the widow of MALCOLM X, addressed the gathering.

Other speakers included JESSE JACKSON, singer Stevie Wonder, and Democratic congressmen John Conyers of Michigan and Kweisi Mfume of Maryland. Criticism of the event centered on whether endorsement of the march automatically meant support for the highly controversial Farrakhan and the Nation of Islam. A majority of the marchers insisted that it did not, arguing that "the march is bigger than Farrakhan." In a two-and-one-half-hour speech addressing the gathering, Farrakhan denounced white supremacy and asked that the marchers refrain from referring to black women in disparaging terms, support black business, register to vote, and join black organizations concerned with the African-American community. The prevailing mood was one of hope, pride, encouragement, and brotherhood. Boston University's Center for Remote Sensing, which provides expertise in aerial reconaissance, estimated the number of men who attended the march at 870,000.

Mingus, Charles ("Charlie") (1922–1979) *bass player, jazz composer*

Born in Arizona, Mingus grew up in Los Angeles, where he used to listen to GOSPEL and BLUES at church. He was also influenced by the music of DUKE ELLINGTON and Béla Bartók. Mingus learned to play the trombone and cello while in school but switched to bass in order to join a JAZZ band. He received instruction from Red Callender and also studied the work of Andres Segovia and jazz musician Jimmy Blanton. He later worked closely with Kid Ory, Lionel Hampton, Fats Navarro, DIZZY GILLESPIE, Max Roach, and CHARLIE PARKER. Mingus was known to stop and lecture audiences on their conduct and was famous for criticizing and/or firing musicians in the middle of a performance if they failed to meet his standards. He was incensed by racial prejudice, and the pressures of segregation in the South in the 1940s forced him to stop touring with LOUIS ARMSTRONG. Though he was popular, club owners sometimes hesitated to book Mingus, fearing he would lecture the audience on racial discrimination. Among his compositions were *Mediations on Integration* and *Fables of Faubus*, this last in reference to the segregationist Arkansas governor.

Highly innovative, Mingus was a leader in third stream or avant-garde jazz.

Recommended Listening: *Mirage, Avant-Garde and Third Stream* (New World Records), *Money Jungle* (United Artists).

Mississippi Freedom Democratic Party (MFDP)

Rival Democratic party established in 1964 in Mississippi. At that time, fewer than 7 percent of the eligible African Americans in the state were registered to vote. Those who did attempt to register frequently faced economic and physical harassment. In a five-month period in 1964, 21 homes and churches linked to voting rights activists were either burned or dynamited in McComb, Mississippi, alone.

Since African Americans had been illegally frozen out of regular Democratic Party politics, civil rights workers established the Mississippi Freedom Democratic Party and sent a rival slate of delegates to the 1964 Democratic Party presidential convention that was meeting in Atlantic City. Sixty-eight MFDP delegates, including ROBERT P. MOSES, FANNIE LOU HAMER, and NATIONAL ASSOCIATION FOR THE ADVANCEMENT OF COLORED PEOPLE (NAACP) activist AARON HENRY, arrived in New Jersey and challenged the right of the regular all-white Mississippi delegation to be seated. A compromise was offered whereby the MFDP would be given two seats (to be occupied by MFDP delegates selected by the regular Democratic Party leadership), 66 honorary seats, and a promise that party rules would be revised to eliminate segregated delegations in the future. The compromise was rejected, with many of the MFDP delegates bitterly accusing Democratic liberals of betrayal for failing to support the challenge. Still, the MFDP gained a major victory in the backing it had received from thousands of African Americans across Mississippi who had voted—most for the first time—to establish the party, in the attention it focused on segregated delegations, and in the promise that future delegations would be elected on a nondiscriminatory basis. The MFDP later challenged the seating of Mississippi's five white congressmen, arguing that blacks had not been allowed to vote.

Mississippi Freedom Summer Project

a special voter registration drive that took place in 1964 during the CIVIL RIGHTS MOVEMENT.

See also VOTING RIGHTS STRUGGLE.

Mitchell, Arthur (1934–   ) *dancer, founder of the Dance Theater of Harlem*

Mitchell was born in New York City, where he received his training in ballet. From 1956 to 1971, he was a principal dancer with the New York City Ballet, becoming the first African American featured in a major ballet company. His grace and technique belied the common prejudice that blacks were physically unsuited for classical dance. In the 1960s, Mitchell established the National Ballet Company of Brazil. Deeply affected by the death of MARTIN LUTHER KING JR. in 1968, Mitchell set up ballet classes in a church basement in HARLEM, welcoming any neighborhood child who wanted to study with him. From this small beginning, Mitchell created, as a living memorial to King, the Dance Theater of Harlem, now acclaimed as one of the world's premier ballet companies. Mitchell has choreographed a number of works for his company, including *Rhythmetron,* which successfully combines jazz dance techniques and classical ballet.

Mombasa

African city located in what is now Kenya. Mombasa was first settled around A.D. 1000 by BANTU people who later intermarried with Arab settlers. The Portuguese sacked the city in 1505 in an effort to gain control of the INDIAN OCEAN TRADE and take over the gold trade routes to the interior. Mombasa's native population rebuilt the city, but the Portuguese burned it again in 1528. In 1589, Mombasa was overrun by cannibalistic ZIMBA raiders, and many of the city's people ran into the sea to avoid capture. Four years later, the Portuguese chose Mombasa as a site for Fort Jesus, a fortification they constructed to defend their East African conquests against threats from Egypt's Ottoman rulers. The fort's walls were built at angles so that any attackers would themselves be exposed to assault from the fort's defenders. However, by 1728, the Portuguese had been pushed out by the Omani Arabs. In the late 19th century, the English reached an agreement with the Omani and set up a British East Africa protectorate with Mombasa as its capital. Today, Mombasa is the largest port on the East African coast.

Monk, Thelonious Sphere (1917–1982) *jazz pianist*

When Monk was four years old, his family moved from his native North Carolina to New York, where he began taking piano lessons at age 11. He won several amateur-night competitions at the APOLLO THEATER, but left New York at age 16 to travel across the country with a woman evangelist. Returning to

Thelonious Monk, 1965 (*Bernard Gotfryd/Archive Photos*)

New York a year later, he worked with small groups, becoming closely involved with musicians DIZZY GILLESPIE, CHARLIE PARKER, Kenny Clarke, and CHARLIE CHRISTIAN in the development of behop.

Monk was known for his unusual melodic lines and rhythmic ideas. Though he led the first bebop group at the Village Vanguard in 1948, he began drifting away from mainstream bebop and had difficulty finding steady work. His career revived in 1957 when he opened at the Five Spot with JOHN COLTRANE. In the early 1970s he toured with Dizzy Gillespie in a group known as the Giants of Jazz. Monk's unique compositional ability is apparent in such works as "Round Midnight"; "Evidence"; "Well You Needn't"; "Ruby, My Dear"; and "Blue Monk." (See also JAZZ.)

Monomotapa

Medieval African empire established in 1440 by a BANTU group known as the Rozwi. Based in what is now ZIMBABWE, Monomotapa, under its two original kings, Mutota and Matope, expanded its borders from the Kalahari Desert in the west to the Indian Ocean in the east and from the Zambezi River in the north to the Limpopo River in the south. Its kings, like the gold-rich empire itself, were called Monomotapa, a word that means "lord of the mines." Architecture flourished in the kingdom, which controlled the region's extensive gold mines and the trade routes linking the interior to the Indian Ocean seaports. A Portuguese writer described the king's palace as draped in expensive tapestries, with floors and ceilings covered in gold plate and gilt. Around 1485, a successful revolt under Chief Changa resulted in the establishment of the CHANGAMIRE Empire in what had been the southern portion of the empire. Monomotapa came under Portuguese domination in 1629 and was finally conquered by Changamire toward the end of the 17th century.

Montgomery Bus Boycott

Boycott that took place in Montgomery, Alabama, in 1955 after ROSA PARKS was arrested there for refusing to give up her seat on a bus to a white man. Following the arrest, Edgar Daniel (E. D.) Nixon, former president of the local NATIONAL ASSOCIATION FOR THE ADVANCEMENT OF COLORED PEOPLE, called a meeting, and the black community leaders decided to hold a one-day bus boycott on Monday, December 5, in protest. African Americans made up 75 percent of the bus company's passengers, and almost all of them supported the boycott. The leaders established the Montgomery Improvement Association (MIA) to continue the boycott and negotiate demands regarding the hiring of black bus drivers, courtesy toward black riders, and equal seating on a first-come, first-served basis. Since Nixon's job as a railroad porter often kept him out of town, a young minister, Dr. MARTIN LUTHER KING JR., was chosen to head the new organization. The Montgomery Bus Boycott lasted 381 days and cost the bus company over $750,000. Hundreds of boycotters, including Rosa Parks, lost their jobs, and many were jailed for their actions. King's home was dynamited, as was Nixon's and RALPH ABERNATHY's. On November 13, 1956, the United States Supreme Court affirmed a U.S. district court's decision that segregation on public buses was unconstitutional.

Moors

Historically, the name applied to dark-skinned Berbers in West Africa. The word *Moor* comes from the Greek and Roman words *maures* and *maurus,* meaning dark or black. In the eighth century, many Moors converted to Islam, spreading the religion throughout West Africa and then into Spain, which they overran in A.D. 711 under the leadership of TARIQ IBN ZIYAD. From there, they crossed the Pyrenees into France but were defeated by Charles Martel at the Battle of Tours (732). Under Abd ar-Rahman I's Umayyad dynasty, which was established at Córdoba, Spain, in 756, and was known as the Caliphate of Córdoba, the Moors established an advanced civilization that eventually became the leading agricultural, industrial, cultural and educational center of Europe.

Another Moorish group, the ALMORAVIDS, invaded Spain in 1086, and they, in turn, were supplanted in 1174 by the Moorish Almohads. All of these groups, particularly the Almohads, brought thousands of skilled workers and artists into Spain.

The cultivation of silk, rice, cotton, sugarcane, ginger, dates, and lemons was introduced, and the cities of Córdoba, Toledo, and Seville were celebrated for their universities and their architecture. Toledo was internationally famous for its production of swords, and other Moorish cities were known for the manufacture of shields, leather, carpets, woolens, glass, and pottery. The streets of Córdoba were both paved and lighted, and the city boasted many schools, colleges, universities, libraries, and public baths. The Moors built tunnels, aqueducts, dams, and reservoirs, along with numerous mosques and the magnificant Alhambra complex at Granada. Almohad rule ended in the early 13th century, and the Moors were driven out of Spain at the end of the 15th century.

Most Moors now live in Mauritania, Mali, and Senegal. In fact the word *Senegal* comes from the name of a Moorish clan, the Zenaga, and *Mauritania* means "land of Moors." Extensive intermarriage between Moorish Berbers, Arabs, and Spanish women resulted in light-skinned descendants who are today referred to as "white Moors."

Morgan, Garrett A. (1875–1963) *inventor*

Morgan grew up in Cincinnati, then moved to Cleveland, where he got a job as a sewing machine adjuster. In 1907, he opened a successful repair shop. Two years later he also began a tailoring business, and in 1913, he established a company to sell a hair-straightening process he had developed. Morgan received a patent in 1914 for a "breathing device," or gas mask, he had developed earlier. Two years later an explosion ripped through the Cleveland Water Works' Tunnel # 5, 250 feet beneath Lake Erie. Many workers were trapped, and when heavy smoke prevented rescue workers from entering the tunnel, officials contacted Morgan and asked for his help. Using his gas masks, Morgan and others entered the tunnel and brought 32 workmen to safety. The rescue created great interest in the gas mask, and Morgan was asked to demonstrate it in cities across the country. However, when prospective buyers learned that Morgan was black, orders for the apparatus dropped off. When Morgan demonstrated the gas mask in the South, he was forced to do so with the help of a white man while

he pretended to be an American Indian. During World War I, the gas mask proved of critical importance in protecting American soldiers from poison gas attacks. Morgan became wealthy and is said to have been the first African American in Cleveland to own his own car. That in turn led to another Morgan invention—the three-way traffic light. Morgan sold the rights to his traffic light to General Electric for $40,000. Morgan also founded the *Cleveland Call*, a weekly newspaper, and was active in protecting African-American civil rights.

Morocco, Kingdom of

North African nation. Capital: Rabat. Tools dating back to 800,000 B.C. have been found in Morocco, an indication that the country was home to some of Africa's earliest inhabitants. Rock carvings created around 1600 B.C. by BERBER tribesmen have also been found in the Atlas Mountains.

In 25 B.C., the Roman emperor Augustus installed JUBA II as king of the region, which was then known as MAURETANIA, meaning "land of MOORS." The Vandals forced the Romans out in the fifth century A.D., and the region was ruled by local Berber tribes until Arabs, under the command of Musa-ibn-Nusair, conquered the area around 708. In 711, thousands of tribesmen joined TARIK IBN ZIYAD, a Moorish general in Musa-ibn-Nusair's army, when he invaded Spain and established a great civilization there.

Regional conflicts divided Morocco into small kingdoms and principalities. In 1063, the ALMORAVIDS, a fanatical Islamic Berber group from Senegal, overran the country before continuing on to Spain. The Almoravids were succeeded in Morocco by the Almohad dynasty (ca. 1174), which in turn was ousted by the Merinids, who ruled from 1259–1550.

After the Christians recaptured the Iberian Peninsula and drove the Moors into exile, Spain attacked Morocco and occupied several cities, but most of the country remained under the control of local rulers. In the 19th century, there were clashes with France and Spain, and in 1912, Morocco was divided into a French-Spanish protectorate. During World War II, French Morocco remained loyal to France's German-controlled Vichy government and was invaded by Allied forces in 1942. A major conference between Franklin Roosevelt and Winston Churchill was held in Casablanca in 1943. A nationalist movement resulted in independence in 1956 under King Muhammad V. Today Morocco is a constitutional monarchy under King Muhammad VI, who took power in 1999. It is an economically stable country with extensive trade with the United States, Europe, and West Africa.

Morrison, Toni (1931–) *writer, editor, winner of the 1993 Nobel Prize in Literature*

Originally named Chloe Anthony Wofford, Toni Morrison graduated from Howard University in 1953 and earned a master's degree in English from Cornell. In 1966, she became a textbook editor with Random House. Later, as senior editor, she used her position to help young African-American writers and to encourage the publication of books on black history. In 1970, she published her first novel, *The Bluest Eye,* about a young black girl destroyed partly by society's rejection of nonwhite standards of beauty. Her second novel, *Sula,* was published in 1973. *Song of Solomon,* which was published in 1977, won the National Book Critics' Circle Award and was a Book-of-the-Month Club selection. After the release of *Tar Baby* in 1981, Morrison began teaching at State University of New York at Albany, where she wrote *Dreaming Emmett,* a play about EMMETT TILL, the 14-year-old black boy who was murdered in 1954 because he whistled at a white woman. She also finished her 1988 Pulitzer Prize–winning novel *Beloved,* a book based on the true story of a slave named Margaret Garner who killed her own daughter rather than see her live as a slave. *Beloved* was made into a movie starring OPRAH WINFREY. In addition to these books, Morrison has written numerous essays and the novels *Jazz* and *Paradise.* In 1996, she received the National Book Foundation Medal for Distinguished Contribution to American Letters. Morrison is currently a professor at Princeton University.

Moses, Robert Parris (1935–) *leading figure in the Student Non-violent Coordinating Committee.*

Moses was born in New York City, graduated from Hamilton College, and received a master's degree

from Harvard in 1957. Family problems forced him to discontinue his studies, and Moses returned to New York, where he became a high school math teacher. In 1961, he became a field secretary with the STUDENT NON-VIOLENT COORDINATING COMMITTEE (SNCC) in McComb, Mississippi. A quiet, self-effacing man, Moses identified strongly with the philosophy expressed by French writer Albert Camus that people should work for change, refusing to be "victims" while avoiding becoming "executioners"—that is, becoming violent themselves. He believed strongly that local people must develop their own leadership rather than depend on civil rights workers. He played a major role in organizing the 1964 Mississippi Freedom Summer Project, which brought over 1,000 volunteers—mostly white college students—to Mississippi to help register black voters. He also was a founder of the MISSISSIPPI FREEDOM DEMOCRATIC PARTY (MFDP), which challenged the regular Mississippi delegation to the 1964 Democratic Party presidential convention.

The refusal of the federal government to take more forceful action to protect local blacks who were attempting to vote left Moses disillusioned. A turning point was the 1961 death of Herbert Lee, a local farmer and SNCC supporter, who was killed by Mississippi state representative E. H. Hurst. Louis Allen, a black witness to the incident, agreed to testify and asked Moses to arrange for federal protection. Moses' request to the Justice Department was rejected, but the FBI was informed of Allen's statements that Lee had been murdered in cold blood. The FBI informed the local police, who harassed Allen repeatedly, jailing him on trumped-up charges and breaking his jaw. In 1964, Allen was shot to death by an unknown assailant. Hurst was never charged in Lee's murder.

Moses was also bitter at the failure of many Democratic liberals to support the challenge of the MFDP to unseat the regular Mississippi delegation at the 1964 Democratic Party presidential convention. Disillusioned, he traveled to Africa, then returned to the United States where, in an effort to avoid the press, he dropped his last name and refused for a while to associate with whites. In 1966, the government rejected Moses' application for conscientious objector status and ordered him to report for military service. Moses was then 31 years old. He fled to Canada, then moved to Africa, where he remained until granted amnesty under President Jimmy Carter's 1977 amnesty program. After winning a five-year "genius" award from the MacArthur Foundation, he established the Algebra Project in Boston to improve math skills of inner-city youngsters.

Recommended Reading: Burner, Eric R. *and gently he shall lead them*. New York: New York University Press, 1994.

Mossi (Moro)

Tribe centered in BURKINA FASO. Beginning in the 11th century, the Mossi formed several kingdoms: the Ouagadougou, Yatenga, Fada-n-Gourma, Mamprussi, Dagomba, and Tenkodogo. These were noted for their stable political, economic, and military structure. The Mossi boast the longest continuous royal dynasty in West Africa, and a Mossi emperor, though lacking in political power, still presides regularly at weekly ceremonies in Burkina Faso. Mossi horsemen captured TIMBUKTU in 1338 and for years remained a concern to the Mali and Songhai Empires. Mossi attempts to expand westward ended when Yatenga suffered a major defeat by Songhai emperor MUHAMMAD TOURÉ in 1497–98. Since then, the Mossi have remained at peace, while holding fast to their own cultural and religious traditions. Efforts to convert them to Islam have largely failed. Poor land resources in Burkina Faso have driven many Mossi men to seek work in Ghana and the Ivory Coast.

Mozambique, Republic of

East African country. Capital: Maputo. Mozambique's earliest inhabitants were BANTU-speaking people who settled in the area around A.D. 700. The region is the site of Sofala and Quelimane, two cities important in the INDIAN OCEAN TRADE. Portugal occupied coastal Mozambique in 1505 in hopes of gaining control of the gold trade then under the dominion of the inland kingdom of MONOMOTAPA in Zimbabwe. In the late 1500s, Portuguese settlers

along the coast established plantations using slave labor and Portugal, after several unsuccessful attempts, eventually gained a limited control of the interior. A large-scale slave trade developed in the 18th century with thousands of captives shipped to the Mascarene Islands (now Mauritius and Réunion) and Brazil. In spite of strong African resistance, Portugal was able to establish a colony in Mozambique in 1910. Rule was largely through privately chartered companies, and Africans were required to perform forced labor on European-owned plantations. Fierce guerrilla warfare under the leadership of the Mozambique Liberation Front (Frelimo) broke out in the 1960s, and Mozambique was granted independence under Frelimo leader Samora Moises Machel in 1975. White settlers fled the country, destroying property in an effort to destabilize the economy. Though buffeted by internal infighting, murders, and disappearances, Frelimo established a Marxist government, forced almost 2 million people into communal villages, and instituted major health and education reforms in a country that had a 90 percent illiteracy rate. Civil war broke out in 1977 between Frelimo and an exceptionally vicious opposition group called the Mozambique National Resistance Movement (Renamo), which received considerable support from South Africa. By 1988, Renamo forces had killed at least 100,000 people, mutilated hundreds of others, including many children, and established slave labor camps in territory they controlled. Thousands of refugees fled to Malawi, Zambia, and Zimbabwe. Drought and famine in the early 1990s made guerrilla operations increasingly difficult, and a cease-fire was signed in 1992. Widespread planting of landmines during the war has resulted in 10,000–15,000 casualties, including an estimated 8,000 amputees. In February 2000, Cyclone Eline slammed into Mozambique, causing massive floods. More than 300,000 people lost their homes and at least 800 people drowned. At least 30,000 cattle were also lost along with other livestock. Also, the flood water washed many land mines into areas that had been cleared and were believed safe. Mozambique is one of the world's poorest countries, with the average citizen earning only $90 a year. The destruction of Mozambique's transportation system has made economic progress difficult.

mud cloth

A distinctive textile originally made by the Bamana people of central and western Mali. The African word for mud cloth is *bogolanfini*, which means "mudded cloth." Traditionally, men wove five-inch strips of cotton, which were then loosely sewn together. The women then would take the cloth and create various designs in yellow, brown, black, and white. To create black and white mud cloth, a woman would soak the cloth in black river mud and then bleach out her designs with a caustic solution. Yellow and brown designs are made with dyes from various trees and plants that are then dried with mud. The symbol *X* stands for nobility. Other marks indicate wealth or various objects. Traditionally used for clothing, mud cloth patterns with their dashes, dots, *X*s, squares, and jagged lines are now used on furniture, plates, wallpaper, and other household items.

Muhammad, Elijah (1897–1975) *leader of the Nation of Islam*

The son of an ex-slave and a Baptist preacher, Elijah Muhammad (originally Elijah Poole) moved his wife and children from Georgia to Detroit in 1923. There, in 1930, he became a follower of Fard Muhammad, the founder of a religious group called the Lost-Found NATION OF ISLAM, or BLACK MUSLIMS. Two years later, he established Temple No. 2 in Chicago, which would later become the Nation of Islam's headquarters. When Fard Muhammad disappeared in 1934, Elijah Muhammad took over the organization. Fard became identified with Allah, and Elijah Muhammad became known as both the prophet and the messenger of Allah. During World War II, Muhammad was jailed for sedition after expressing support for Japan and urging his followers not to register for the draft. The Nation's most famous convert was MALCOLM X, who accused Elijah Muhammad of sexual misbehavior in 1963 and left the movement in 1964. When Malcolm was murdered a year later by three members of the Nation of

Elijah Muhammad, leader of the Black Muslims, wearing a black cap printed with the star and crescent symbol of Islam, 1960 (*Archive Photos*)

Islam, Elijah Muhammad was suspected of involvement, but nothing was ever proved.

Muhammad Touré (Muhammad ibn Abu-Bakr) (1443–1538) *West African Songhai emperor*

Touré overthrew the son of SUNNI ALI and assumed the throne in 1493. When a daughter of Ali called him *askia*, meaning "usurper," Muhammad took the word as his title and established his dynasty under that name. He continued Sunni Ali's work in expanding SONGHAI territory through military conquest. He also centralized and consolidated the government, established a professional army, standardized weights and measures, and engaged in trade with regions as far as Baghdad and Portugal. A Muslim, Askia Muhammad made a pilgrimage to Mecca in 1496, accompanied by an entourage that numbered well over 1,000 persons. He encouraged the spread of Islam and appointed many Muslim ministers, though he continued to tolerate traditional African religious practices, which were still common in rural areas. During his reign, schools and universities were established in Jenne, Gao, and Timbuktu. He was overthrown by his son in 1528 and exiled to an island in the Niger River.

Murphy, Isaac Burns (1861–1896) *jockey, Kentucky Derby winner (1884, 1890, 1891)*

Murphy was born in Kentucky. His father was a Union soldier who died in a Confederate POW camp. Murphy won his first race at age 14, nine years after Oliver Lewis, another African American, won the first Kentucky Derby. Murphy won three Kentucky Derbies: 1884, 1890, and 1891. The winner in 44 percent of his races, Isaac Murphy is considered the most successful professional African-American athlete of the 19th century.

Issac Myers (1835–1891) *pioneer labor leader*

Born in Baltimore, Maryland, to free parents, Issac Myers became an apprentice at age 16 to James Jackson, a black man well-known in the ship-caulking business. By age 20 he had been made a superintendent and placed in charge of the caulking of clean-line clipper ships. In 1860, he became chief porter and clerk in the Woods, Bridges & Co. grocery business. Four years later, in 1864, he took over the management of another grocery store. In 1865 he resigned and returned to ship caulking. That same year the white caulkers and ship carpenters went on strike, demanding that all black caulkers and longshoremen be fired. More than 1,000 black men lost their jobs. Myers reacted by proposing that the black workers band together and buy a shipyard and rail-

way. Within six months, Baltimore African Americans had raised $10,000, and the project, known as the Chesapeake Marine Railway and Dry Dock Company, was under way. It employed 300 African-American men at a wage of $3 a day. Myers also organized a black union known as the Colored Caulkers' Trade Union Society. According to W. E. B. DUBOIS, Myers' organizations "saved the colored caulkers" and ended white efforts to "drive colored labor out of other fields." Five years later, Myers accepted a position with the Customs Department. In 1870, he was appointed a special agent of the Post Office Department. In 1871, Myers arranged for what at that time was the biggest convention of African-American men in U.S. history. After five days of intense debate, the participants established the Colored National Union, with Myers as president. In 1869, Myers was a delegate to a convention of the white National Labor Union (NLU), where he made an electrifying speech in support of President Ulysses Grant and the Republican Party. The white union leaders, who had met to form the Labor Reform Party, reacted with anger and came close to assaulting Myers. In 1879, Myers opened a coal yard and later became the editor of the *Colored Citizen,* a weekly newspaper. In 1888, he became secretary of the Republican Campaign Committee, and he also organized the Maryland Colored State Industrial Fair Association. Other posts he held included president of the Colored Business Men's Association, head of the first Baltimore Building and Loan Association, superintendent of the Bethel A.M.E. [African Methodist Episcopal] School in Baltimore, and a grand master of the Masons. He was the author of the play *The Missionary.* Myers died in 1891.

Recommended Reading: Foner, Philip S., and Ronald L. Lewis. *Black Workers.* Philadelphia, Pa.: Temple University Press, 1989.

N

NAACP See NATIONAL ASSOCIATION FOR THE ADVANCEMENT OF COLORED PEOPLE.

Namibia, Republic of

Country in southern Africa. Capital: Windhoek. The earliest inhabitants were !Kung San BUSHMEN and KHOI nomads, who left cave paintings dating back to A.D. 500. The Herero and the Ovambo settled in the area between 1500 and 1800. The coastal area was explored by several European groups, and English and German missionaries began work in the region in the early 19th century.

The Germans established the South-West Africa colony in the area in 1884 and began a campaign, regularly punctuated by violence, to gain control of the land from the native population. A Nama/Herero revolt from 1903 to 1908 resulted in the deaths of 84,000 people, including approximately 54,000 Herero men, women, and children, many of whom were deliberately driven into the Kalahari Desert to die of thirst. Thousands of others died in concentration camps.

Namibia was occupied by South African forces in 1915, and in 1920, South Africa received a mandate from the League of Nations to administer the area. A revolt by Khoi tribesmen in 1921–22 was crushed by South Africans using air power. In 1960, the South-West African People's Organization (SWAPO) began a guerrilla campaign to free Namibia from South African control. Pressure from SWAPO, the United Nations, and the international community resulted in elections in 1989, which ended in a SWAPO victory and the election of Sam Nujoma as president. The country became independent in 1990 and is now a multiparty democracy. A state of emergency was declared briefly in Namibia's Caprivi region following attacks by members of the Lozi tribe, who are demanding independence. There have been allegations of abuse by state security forces. Young men from the region have also been lured into service by members of Angola's rebel forces, and then beaten when they try to return to Namibia.

Nanny ("Granny Nanny") (unknown–1750)
Jamaican Maroon leader in the 1730s

Nanny was an ASHANTI woman and the sister of Maroon leaders CUDJOE and Accompong. She founded Nanny Town, a settlement for MAROONS (runaway slaves) in the Blue Mountains in the eastern part of the island. Nanny Town was destroyed in a raid in 1734 during the First Maroon War, and Maroon ghosts are still said to haunt the site. When the war ended in 1739, Nanny initially refused to sign the peace treaty, though a settlement was finally arranged giving her Maroon followers 600 hectares and the right to hunt anywhere outside a three-mile limit of towns and plantations. She is a national hero in Jamaica, where there is a statue of her in the main square in Montego Bay.

Nascimento, Edson Arantes do   (Pele)

(1940–   ) *Brazilian soccer player*

Pele (a nickname) was taught to play soccer by his father, who was once a minor league player. A poor child, Pele's first soccer ball was a lumpy sphere made from old socks. At 15, he was signed by the pro team in the seacoast city of Santos. A brilliant defensive and offensive player, Pele was known for his tactical flexibility and field sense. Hailed as Brazil's "black pearl," he retired from the Santos team in 1974, then joined the New York Cosmos club in the North American Soccer League from 1975 to 1977. During his career, he scored 1,281 goals and led Brazil's national soccer team to three World Cup victories (1958, 1962, 1970). In great demand as one of the most popular athletes in the world, Pele refused to do advertisements for cigarettes or liquor companies, wishing to set an example for young Brazilians. His 1977 autobiography is entitled *The Beautiful Game*.

Nation of Islam   (The Lost-Found Nation of Islam)

Religious group founded in Detroit in 1930 by W. D. Fard, also known as Fard Muhammad as well as several other pseudonyms. Its members were known during the 1960s as the Black Muslims. Fard established a temple, a newspaper, a University of Islam, the Muslim Girls Training Class, and the Fruit of Islam (FOI), a men's group that enforces internal discipline and provides security. He disappeared in 1934, and his place was taken by ELIJAH MUHAMMAD. Fard was designated Allah, and Elijah Muhammad is believed to be his prophet and messenger.

Traditionally, Nation of Islam (NOI) followers believed that all people were originally black and divine but that a rebellious scientist named Yacub created an evil white race whose 6,000-year rule is now coming to an end. Nation of Islam leaders rejected the idea of integration and expressed their belief in the need to establish a separate black state in America. People who join the faith give up their "slave," or surnames, and are assigned African or Arabic names. (Formerly, they took the letter *X* as their last name.) Members are expected to dress modestly, live frugally, support black-owned businesses, and refrain from using tobacco, drugs, or alcohol. There are strict rules regarding worship, diet, personal morality, and religious obligations, and those who break them are subject to suspension and/or expulsion. In its effort to promote black economic self-sufficiency, the Nation of Islam has invested in real estate and owns restaurants, publishing houses, bakeries, barbershops, a FOI security force, and various other businesses.

The Nation was shaken when MALCOLM X left the organization in 1964 after a rift developed between him and Elijah Muhammad. Malcolm was assassinated a year later by three Nation of Islam members. After Elijah Muhammad died in 1975, the Nation of Islam split into several groups, with the most prominent one under the leadership of LOUIS FARRAKHAN.

National Association for the Advancement of Colored People   (NAACP)

Premier civil rights group in the United States. It was founded in 1909 by a group of whites and African Americans in reaction to bloody rioting in Springfield, Illinois, during which eight blacks were killed and over 2,000 others were forced to flee the city. Many of the NAACP founders, including W. E. B. DUBOIS, had been involved in the NIAGARA MOVEMENT, which is generally considered the precursor to the NAACP. Early leaders included JAMES WELDON JOHNSON and Walter White, whose light skin color allowed him to pass for white in order to investigate lynchings and antiblack riots, including the ELAINE, ARKANSAS, INCIDENT in which at least 20 blacks were killed and many more injured. ROY WILKINS, who joined the organization while in college, became White's assistant in 1931 and led the organization during the CIVIL RIGHTS MOVEMENT of the 1950s and 1960s. Though active in many areas, the NAACP focused primarily on litigation and legal challenges to discrimination. Its lawyers, including CHARLES HOUSTON and THURGOOD MARSHALL, were responsible for such successes as an end to the WHITE PRIMARY and the BROWN V. BOARD OF EDUCATION OF TOPEKA Supreme Court decision ending school segregation. The importance of the NAACP was underscored by the fact that during the civil rights movement, several southern states attempted to ban it and/or force teachers and other civil servants to quit the organization. Efforts were made by segregationist forces to obtain NAACP membership lists for purposes of harassment. The NAACP magazine *The Crisis,* which was edited by W. E. B. DuBois for 24 years, was of critical importance as a forum for political and philosophical thought and as a means of promoting the work of black writers and artists during the HARLEM RENAISSANCE.

National Urban League

An interracial organization established in 1911 through the merger of three other groups: the National League for the Protection of Colored Women, the Committee for Improving Industrial Conditions in New York, and the Committee on Urban Conditions Among Negroes. Working at the local level, the league attempted to improve economic opportunities for African Americans and provide housing assistance and educational programs, with particular emphasis on aiding migrants from the South. The league played a major role in helping southern blacks find jobs in northern cities during the NORTHERN MIGRATION during and following World War I and in promoting the work of black artists during the HARLEM RENAISSANCE. Substantial gains also were made during the 1960s under the leadership of Whitney Young Jr.

Ndebele (Matabele) (En-de-BE-lee)

a BANTU-speaking South African tribe founded by Mzilikazi Khumalo (whose name means "the great trail"), once a protégé of Zulu chief SHAKA. When Mzilikazi enlisted in Shaka's army, he brought with him a number of his Khumalo clansmen, who became a part of the growing Zulu nation. In 1822, Mzilikazi was sent on a successful military expedition but deserted with his men to form his own nation. Shaka's fondness for Mzilikazi caused him to respond halfheartedly, and he seemed pleased when Mzilikazi escaped the force that had been sent after him. Mzilikazi's men moved northward, raiding other tribes along the way and, following Shaka's example, incorporated their people into the Ndebele. In 1837, the Ndebele were pushed farther north by the Zulus and Boers and finally settled in what is now southwestern Zimbabwe where Mzilikazi, like Shaka, named his capital Bulawayo.

Chief Lobengula, who succeeded Mzilikazi in 1870, was tricked into turning much of his land over to British businessman Cecil Rhodes in 1888. The British government closed its eyes to the fraud and approved the colonization of the region by Rhodes' British South Africa Company (BSAC). In 1893, BSAC mercenaries attacked the Ndebele, invading Bulawayo and killing Lobengula. Ndebele cattle and land were confiscated by white settlers. An Ndebele/Shona revolt in 1896 ended in defeat. The Ndebele now live as farmers and cattle herders.

Neco (Neche) (NECK-oo) (reigned 616–600 B.C.)
Egyptian pharaoh

According to the Greek historian Herodotus, Neco sent a fleet of Phoenician sailors to circle the African continent. The ships set sail from the Red Sea down the East African coast. At one point, the sailors went ashore and planted grain. After the harvest, they continued their journey around the Cape of Good Hope and up the West African coast. They returned to Egypt after three years. Assuming the story is correct, this exploration would have taken place more than 2,000 years before Vasco da Gama became the first European to travel around Africa. Neco also attempted to dig a canal between the Red Sea and the Nile River but was eventually forced to give up the project.

Ned (ca. 1800s) *inventor*

A slave living on a plantation owned by Oscar Stuart in Pike County, Mississippi, Ned's last name and birth and death dates are unknown. He invented a machine to harvest cotton. With it, one person and two horses were able to do the work of four people and four horses. Stuart attempted to gain a patent for the cotton harvester in his own name, arguing that, as Ned's owner, he had a right to anything Ned had invented. Stuart's demand for a patent was rejected. What happened to Ned is unknown.

Negritos (Aeta)

The dark-skinned original inhabitants of the Philippines. Negritos usually live in small bands deep in the mountains on various Filipino islands. Because they generally stand a little under five feet tall, they are sometimes thought to be related to the PYGMIES of central Africa, but this is by no means certain. They are known for their exceptional stamina and unusually keen sense of hearing and smell. They are skilled hunters, using poisoned arrows to kill both land animals and fish. When hunting game, they often tie the arrowhead to the shaft with string. When the arrow strikes its target, the shaft comes loose, but because it is tied to the arrowhead, it trails along behind the wounded animal and becomes entangled in the underbrush. This forces the animal to stop and allows the hunters to catch up to it and kill it.

Negritos believe that a person's physical and mental well-being are closely related. For that reason, it is usually taboo to quarrel while in the home of a pregnant woman. Religious ideas relating to creation of the universe and origin of human beings vary, but most Negritos believe that all living things possess souls, and are concerned with pleasing the spirits of dead ancestors. Because they believe that dreams reflect the activities of souls that have left the body temporarily, it is taboo to awaken someone from sleep, because his or her soul may be absent. During World War II, Negritos were hired to guard Clark Air Force Base, but were later replaced by Filipino guards. To prove their superiority, several Negritos sneaked into the bedroom of the commanding officer while he slept and painted an "X" on the bottom of his foot.

Negritos live on various Philippine islands and are thought to number about 30,000 to 40,000. They are also found in Malaysia, Indonesia, and MELANESIA. Some Negritos practice SCARIFICATION, tooth-chipping, tatooing, face-painting, and other forms of physical decoration. One unusual practice involves smoking cigarettes with the lighted end inside the mouth so that no glow can be seen by enemies at night. As Negritos come into contact and intermarry with their more urban neighbors, and as their children attend school, they generally give up many of their traditional customs and habits.

Negritude

A literary movement that flowered in Paris during the 1930s, 1940s and 1950s. Its leaders were LÉOPOLD SENGHOR, Léon Damas, and Aimé Cesaire. It emphasized the richness of African culture and history and condemned European exploitation of Africa.

Negro baseball leagues

Leagues formed by all-black teams prior to the integration of professional baseball in 1947. The first salaried African-American ballplayer was John "Bud" Fowler, hired in 1872 by an all-white club in New Castle, Pennsylvania. But after touring with a black team, he was not allowed to rejoin the white club.

The first African-American professional team— the Cuban Giants—made its debut in 1885. By pretending to be foreign, the players were able to tour Florida and the Southwest at a time when native Hispanics were also unwelcome in major league ball. In an unsuccessful attempt to undermine baseball's color line in 1901, Baltimore Orioles manager

A Negro League baseball team, 1931 (*American Stock/Archive Photos*)

John McGraw put black player Charlie Grant on his roster under the name Charlie Tokahama and tried to claim he was a Cherokee Indian.

Nationwide black baseball leagues were organized following World War I, thanks partly to the efforts of star pitcher Rube Foster, who was co-owner and manager of the Chicago American Giants. The pay was low, traveling accommodations were poor, and the players, who usually played in rented stadiums when the resident white teams were on the road, often were not allowed to use "white" dressing rooms. Teams regularly played schedules of 60 to 70 games. During the off-season, they often played – and beat – major league white players in exhibition games.

The Negro leagues produced some of baseball's finest players, among them Josh Gibson, whose career statistics include over 900 home runs and a lifetime batting average of .423. Even better known was pitcher SATCHEL PAIGE. Other legendary players included Leon Day, Chet Brewer, Oscar Charleston, Ray Dandridge, John Henry "Pop" Lloyd, James "Cool Papa" Bell, Walter "Buck" Leonard, and William "Judy" Johnson. Among the major teams were the Pittsburgh Crawfords, the Kansas City Monarchs, the Leland Giants, and the St. Louis Stars.

In 1947, the Brooklyn Dodgers under Branch Rickey signed JACKIE ROBINSON to a major league contract. It signified a turning point in U.S. racial history and an end to the Negro leagues, even though some white teams were slow to sign black players. The Red Sox did not integrate until 1959. In 1971, the Baseball Hall of Fame began to induct players from the Negro leagues.

Newton, Huey P. (1942–1989) *cofounder of the Black Panther Party for Self-Defense*

A handsome and charismatic figure, Newton became a favorite of white radicals as well as many in the black community who were attracted to his defiant, militant stance. In 1966, he and Bobby Seale founded the BLACK PANTHER PARTY FOR SELF-DEFENSE in Oakland, California. Both Newton and the party became the focus of hostile police attention that intensified after Newton was convicted of voluntary manslaughter in the 1967 shooting of police officer John Frey. His conviction was overturned by the California Court of Appeals. He fled to Cuba in 1974 after being charged with the murder of a 17-year-old prostitute. In 1978, he returned to the United States, where charges were dropped after two trials resulted in hung juries. He was killed while participating in a drug deal in 1989.

New York Slave Rebellion of 1712

Uprising involving 25 to 30 slaves. Nine whites were killed, and six others were wounded. The rebelling slaves planned to take advantage of fighting between the British and the French, as well as increased tension between the colonists and the Iroquois Indians. Soldiers were called out and the revolt was brought to a halt. In the aftermath, more than 70 African Americans were jailed, and 21 were executed. The fear generated by the uprising was a major factor in the passage of legislation the next year in Massachusetts that forbade the further importation of more slaves into that state. The New York Rebellion of 1712 is considered one of the six major slave revolts that took place in U.S. territory. The others were the STONO, SOUTH CAROLINA REBELLION, 1739; the GABRIEL PROSSER Conspiracy, 1800; the LOUISIANA SLAVE REVOLT, 1811; the DENMARK VESEY uprising, 1822; and the NAT TURNER rebellion, 1831.

Ngoni

Southern Africa tribal group. Following defeat by SHAKA's Zulu forces, the Ngoni fled into Mozambique and southern Zimbabwe, where they destroyed the CHANGAMIRE empire. Continuing northward, the Ngoni utilized Zulu fighting tactics to subdue local peoples. These peoples were then absorbed into the Ngoni nation. Prisoners of war, instead of being sold into slavery or killed, were made members of Ngoni families and inducted into Ngoni fighting units. There they were allowed to advance on the basis of merit alone. Eventually, the Ngoni divided into six kingdoms, which disappeared during the European colonial period. Ngoni culture had, by that time, however, spread through much of south-central Africa, along with the idea that different peoples speaking different languages could be successfully united into one state.

Ngũgĩ, Wa Thiong'o (James Ngũgĩ) (EN-googee) (1938–) *Kenyan novelist*

Ngũgĩ Wa Thiong'o's literary career reflects his life as an English-speaking youth educated at mission schools who becomes a KIKUYU advocate at odds with his national government. Like his West African contemporary Wole Soyinka, Ngũgĩ studied at Leeds University in England before returning to Kenya to write and teach. His first and best-known novel, *Weep Not, Child* (1964), deals with Africans caught in the middle of the MAU MAU uprising. It was written in English, as were *The River Between, A Grain of Wheat,* and *Petals of Blood,* and his plays, *The Black Hermit* and *The Trial of Dedan Kimathi.* However, Ngũgĩ later opposed the teaching of English at East African universities and began to write under his tribal name. In 1977, he decided to write his novels, plays, and short stories in Kikuyu so that ordinary Africans could understand his work. That same year, he was imprisoned without charge in Kamiti Maximum Security Prison under the Public Security Act because of his critical play *I Will Marry When I Want.* He was released after a year. His prison diary, *Detained,* was published in 1981. Though he had continued to write nonfiction in English, he announced his decision to discontinue this practice in his 1986 book *Decolonising the Mind.* He left Kenya in 1982 and is now a professor at New York University.

Niagara Movement

Civil rights group formed in 1905. It was named for its initial meeting place at Niagara Falls, Canada— selected after the group's organizers, under the leadership of W. E. B. DUBOIS, were refused admittance to hotels on the U.S. side of the border. The Niagara Movement strongly condemned racial discrimination and demanded a vote for black men, equal economic and educational opportunity, freedom of speech, and an end to segregation. Members met annually until 1908, when bloody riots erupted in Springfield, Illinois, resulting in the deaths of eight blacks, two by LYNCHING, and the flight from that city of over 2,000 African Americans. In reaction to the riot, plans were made to form a new, permanent organization. The NATIONAL ASSOCIATION FOR THE ADVANCEMENT OF COLORED PEOPLE (NAACP), of which the Niagara Movement is considered the precursor, was formally incorporated in 1909.

Niger, Republic of

West African country. Capital: Niamey. In medieval times, Niger was crossed by several trans-Sahara caravan routes, and small city-states were established there by the TUAREG and the HAUSA to facilitate the trade. Sections of the country were once part of the KANEM-BORNU and SONGHAI empires, and the Hausa of southern Niger were the target of FULANI jihads (holy wars) in the 19th century. France gained official control of Niger at the 1884 Conference of Berlin but ran into considerable resistance from Tuareg tribespeople and was not able to occupy the city of Agades until 1904. In 1922, Niger became a colony within French West Africa. Pressure to end colonial status began after World War II, and Niger became independent in 1960. Niger's first multiparty elections were held in 1993. The following year a rebellion broke out in the north but ended when the region was granted a limited autonomy. The country was badly hit by drought from 1968 to 1974 and lost thousands of head of livestock. Much of the nation is covered by the Sahara Desert, and efforts to prevent its expansion are being made through reforestation. In 1996, the civilian government was overthrown by the military. In 1999, Niger's president Ibrahim Bare Mainassara was assassinated by members of his presidential guard shortly after Niger's Supreme Court annulled voting results and ordered new elections. Maj. Daouda Mallam Wanke assumed the presidency.

Nigeria, Federal Republic of

The most populous country on the African continent. Capital: Abuja. Lagos is the largest city. Settlement in the area began around 2000 B.C., and today Nigeria is home to approximately 250 ethnic groups, including the HAUSA, FULANI, and YORUBA.

Its territory was the site of the ancient NOK civilization (800 B.C.–A.D. 200), which produced some of Africa's earliest sculpture. Sections of Nigeria were once part of the KANEM-BORNU Empire, and various Hausa city-states were also located there. The kingdoms of IFE, OYO, and BENIN arose there in the 14th and 15th centuries.

The transatlantic slave trade led to the development of several Nigerian city-states based on the sale of captives. The coastal town of Bonny was the leading slave-trading kingdom in the 19th century. Another major slave trader was the SOKOTO CALIPHATE. Regional conflict made it possible for England to annex Lagos in 1861 and establish formal claim to the entire area at the 1884 Conference of Berlin. Total British control was achieved through treaties with local chiefs and/or the use of force. Sokoto was conquered in 1903, and two Nigerian protectorates were established in 1906. They were combined into a single colony in 1914.

The British appointed African rulers, but all important decisions were made by the British governor. Internal self-government was granted in the 1950s, and Nigeria became independent in 1960. In 1966, the Ibos attempted to seize power but were pushed out by a Hausa-led military regime under Col. Yakubu Gowon. Between 10,000 and 30,000 Ibos were massacred, causing the Ibos to secede and form the Republic of Biafra in 1967. The resulting civil war ended in the death by starvation of approximately one million Ibos. The country was reunited in 1970. Its oil supplies are an important source of revenue. From 1983 to 1998, Nigeria was ruled by a military dictatorship that had been guilty of many human rights violations. These included the torture of prisoners and the 1995 execution of writer Ken Saro-Wiwa and eight other men on murder charges in spite of overwhelming evidence of innocence. Civilian rule was reestablished in 1999 with the election of President Olusegun Obasanjo. In the fall of 1999, violence broke out between members of the Yoruba and Hausa tribespeople.

Nile River

world's longest river (ca. 4,160 miles). The Nile is one of the few major rivers whose waters flow south

The Nile River in the 1880s (*Library of Congress*)

to north. Its chief branches, the White Nile and the Blue Nile, come together at Khartoum in Sudan, just above the Shabluka Gorge. From the gorge, the Nile formerly descended over six cataracts (waterfalls) into Egypt. Some of these valleys are now submerged by Lake Nasser, formed by the Aswan High Dam.

The source of the Nile had been a mystery since ancient times, since the Sudd, an enormous swamp stretching thousands of square miles, made it impossible simply to follow the river south to its source. In A.D. 150, the Greek scholar Ptolemy (TOL-ah-mee) drew a map of the world and depicted the source of the Nile as two lakes situated high in an African mountain range that he called Lunae Montes (Moon Mountains). How Ptolemy came to this decision regarding the Nile's source is unknown, but the Ruwenzori range in Uganda does feed Lake Edward and Lake Albert, where one strand of the Nile begins. When the English explorer Henry Stanley reached the Ruwenzoris, he named them the Mountains of the Moon. Among the explorers who searched for the source of the Nile were Samuel Baker, Sir Richard Burton, and John Speke. In addition to Egypt and Sudan, the Nile drains parts of Zaire, Ethiopia, Rwanda, Burundi, Uganda, and Kenya.

Nkrumah, Kwame (EN-crew-mah, QWAH-may) (1909–1972) *African political leader, former president of Ghana*

The son of a goldsmith, Nkrumah became the first African teacher in a Catholic seminary in Ghana.

After spending 10 years (1935–45) studying and teaching at Lincoln University and the University of Pennsylvania in the United States, he moved to England, where he studied at the London School of Economics, became involved in Pan-African organizations, and edited *New African* magazine. He returned to Britain's Gold Coast colony (as Ghana was then called) in 1947, joined the United Gold Coast Convention Party, and led a series of strikes and boycotts protesting colonization. Two years later he formed the Convention People's Party (CPP). Nkrumah was imprisoned in 1950 but was released after the CPP swept the elections in 1951. He became prime minister in 1952, and then president when Ghana became independent in 1957. He established a socialist regime that was marked by extensive and expensive building projects, the jailing of political opponents, and a deteriorating economy. Overthrown in 1966, Nkrumah remained in exile in Guinea until his death in 1972. Among his books are *Education and Nationalism in West Africa* (1943), *Towards Colonial Freedom* (1946), and *Ghana: The Autobiography of Kwame Nkrumah* (1957).

Nok

Term referring to an iron-using people who lived in Nigeria between 900 B.C. and A.D. 200 and also to the terra-cotta sculptures they produced. The first sculptures were discovered as a result of tin mining in the 1880s. The name comes from other sculptures that were found in the village of Nok in the 1920s and turned over to the Jos museum. Nok artwork influenced the later art of Ife and Benin.

northern migration (Great Migration)

The migration of thousands of southern African Americans who moved north during and after World War I and during World War II. At least 450,000 blacks moved to Chicago and other northern cities between 1916 and 1918, and thousands more arrived during the 1920s. Blacks had begun leaving the south following the Civil War, and the process accelerated with the end of RECONSTRUCTION.

World War I created a huge demand for labor in northern factories as almost 5 million men left to serve in the armed forces and foreign immigration dropped from 1,218,480 in 1914 to 110,618 in 1918. The Pennsylvania Railroad was so desperate for workers that it paid the travel expenses of 12,000 blacks; the Illinois Central Railroad and numerous steel mills, factories, and tanneries also provided blacks with free railroad passes. To discourage the northern labor agents who fanned out across the South encouraging blacks to leave, the city of Birmingham and the state of Alabama each required such agents to pay a $2,500 tax, and other cities and counties imposed their own fees.

Aside from better job opportunities, blacks moved north to escape segregation, local government refusal to provide services such as sanitation, roads, and educational opportunities, and in reaction to LYNCHING. Moreover, the boll weevil infestation of the cotton crop in 1915 and 1916 combined with heavy rains and flooding to ruin harvests across the South and threaten thousands of blacks with starvation. Unlike the PAP SINGLETON–led EXODUSTERS of 1879, the World War I and II migrations were not organized by any one individual. People often decided to leave after receiving letters from friends and relatives and in response to frequent Chicago *Defender* editorials urging southern blacks to move north.

Nuba (Nubians)

African people living today in the Nuba Mountains of Sudan. The Nuba, who are divided into several tribes, are descendants of the ancient Meroitic people. They live in silo-shaped houses, and their languages differ substantially from those of other Africans. They raise sorghum, wear colorful beadwork and gold jewelry, and often paint themselves with white, geometric designs. Every boy at about age 13 is sent to a special camp where he is trained as a wrestler. Until he marries, he will spend six months of every year in the wrestling camp, leaving only to help with the harvest or to fight in exhibition matches. Once he marries, he leaves the camp, builds a home for himself and his bride, and begins farming. Wrestlers preparing to compete shave their heads and smear ashes mixed with milk over their bodies. The ashes are supposed to improve a wrestler's grip, and according to tradition, the milk provides strength. When a champion wrestler dies, thousands of tribesmen from neighboring villages will attend the funeral. A funeral feast is prepared, and a wrestling tournament is held to honor the deceased.

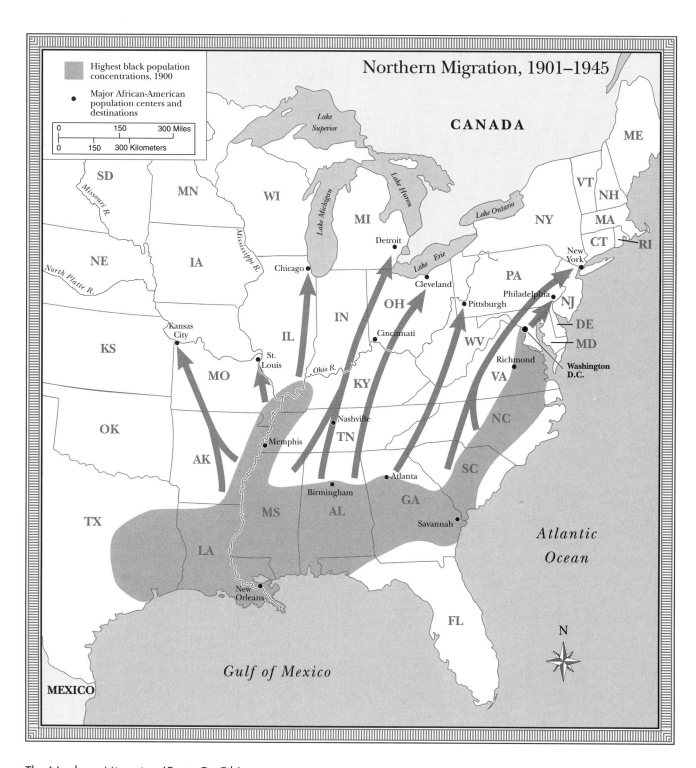

The Northern Migration (*Facts On File*)

The Nuba are a frequent target of government-backed Arab militias that raid their villages for slaves—primarily women and children—as well as cattle and other property. The captives are taken north and used for agricultural and domestic labor. Some are ransomed by their families or clans—typical prices are five cows or one automatic rifle.

Nubia

The name for the ancient region that is now southern Egypt and northern Sudan and for the sophisticated civilizations that flourished there ca. 3100 B.C. to A.D. 400. Nubia was once an important commercial corridor between Egypt and the towns to the south, but much of it is now covered by Lake Nasser, which was created by the Aswan Dam. In addition to serving as a trade route, Nubia was a source of ivory, ostrich eggs, and feathers. Gold, copper, and iron were also found there. Information about Nubia is far from complete, although we do know that Egyptian political and cultural influence was strong. Egypt built a number of fortress towns in the area to protect Nile valley commerce, and Egyptian art was heavily influenced by Nubian art. The people of the area were said to be exceptionally handsome, and Egyptian pharaohs often married Nubian queens. Among the civilizations that developed in Nubia were KERMA, KUSH, and CHRISTIAN NUBIA.

Nuer

A seminomadic people living in the swampy Sudd area of Sudan. The Nuer are extremely independent, and decisions affecting the group are made by consensus rather than by a tribal chief. During the rainy season they live, with their cattle, in family compounds above the floodplain. When the dry season begins, all but the very old, infants, and nursing mothers move to the pastureland left behind by the receding water. The Nuer live on milk, meat, fish, and sorghum. Like other neighboring peoples, they decorate their bodies with scars. At age 14, boys go through a ceremony whereby six parallel lines are cut across their foreheads. (See SCARIFICATION.) Each boy is then given a spear and presented with an ox. From then on, he will sleep in his father's hut and help tend the herd. The importance of cattle is indicated by the fact that the Nuer have hundreds of words to describe the color, markings, shapes, horns, and patterns of the animals. Once a year, the Nuer gather at a sacred site called Duar, where a single fig tree grows. The tree, which is hung with bracelets and pouches of tobacco, marks the spot where Dja-gay, the first man, came up out of the earth. Nearby are two small holes that supposedly were made by the knees of the first woman when she gave birth to the first child. The tobacco is a present to the ancestors who like to smoke. The Nuer people feast, dance, and sleep near the fig tree at this time to ward off sickness and bad luck.

Nyerere, Julius Kambarage (1920–1999)
African leader, former president of Tanzania
Nyerere was known as the "Conscience of Black Africa" and as *Mwalimu*, a Swahili word for "teacher." He was the son of a Zanaki chief and was one of the few children in his village to attend school. He graduated from Makerere University in Uganda and Edinburgh University in Scotland. After acquiring his master's degree from Edinburgh, he returned to Tanzania (then Tanganyika) in 1952 and became involved with the Tanganyika African National Union (TANU) in its effort to guide Tanganyika's transition from colonialism to independence. Tanganyika became independent from Britain in 1961, and Nyerere became its president with 97 percent of the vote. As president, he sought to promote African unity and establish a socialist economy. Tanganyika joined with the island of Zanzibar in 1964 to become Tanzania. Nyerere retired from the presidency on November 5, 1985.

Nzinga Mbande (EN-zin-ga EM-bahn-day)
(1582–1663) *queen of the Mbundu kingdoms of Ndongo and Matamba in what is now Angola*
Nzinga murdered her nephew and succeeded to the Ndongo throne after her brother died in 1624. Attacks on Ndongo by Imbangala slave raiders caused her to turn to the Portuguese for help. Instead, the Portuguese arranged to place her sister

on the throne as a puppet ruler, and Nzinga retreated to the mountains and established the kingdom of Matamba. She also put together a powerful guerrilla army and conducted several successful military campaigns against the Portuguese in the 1640s. In 1656, she forced them to accept Matamba as a major intermediary in the slave trade. Nzinga was famous for her use of women warriors. Though she never married, she kept approximately 30 male concubines, executing those who ceased to please her. She abolished polygamy and the practice of sacrificing prisoners of war. She accepted Christianity during the years she sought Portuguese help but rejected it once the Portuguese became her enemy. However, she returned to Christianity again toward the end of her life.

Owens, James Cleveland (Jesse) (1913–1980)
track and field athlete, winner of four gold medals at the 1936 Berlin Olympics

Owens was born to a poor family in Alabama, the seventh of 11 children. He took up track after the family moved to Cleveland. While in college, he competed in the Big Ten Track and Field Championships at Ann Arbor, Michigan, and within 45 minutes broke three records and tied a fourth. At the 1936 Berlin Olympics, he won four gold medals in the 100- and 200-meter events, broad jump, and 400-meter relay. The victory was particulary significant because Germany at that time was under the control of the Nazis, who regarded blacks (and also Jews, Gypsies, Asians, homosexuals, and others) as subhuman. When Jesse Owens won, Nazi leader Adolf Hitler refused to shake his hand and left the stadium in anger. Owen's was a record that stood for 40 years. Though he returned home to a parade and a gala reception at a New York hotel, he was forced to take the freight elevator to the reception hall because of the hotel's segregationist policies. He was unable to get a well-paying job, and dishonest business partners left him deeply in debt. In 1976, Jesse Owens was awarded the Medal of Freedom by President Gerald Ford. Owens died in 1980.

Jesse Owens (*Library of Congress*)

Oyo

Powerful YORUBA state established in the late 14th century. According to tradition, Oyo and various other Yoruba states were founded by the offspring of Oduduwa, a prince of Mecca who was lowered to Earth by the god Olorun at IFE. Old Oyo, which rapidly eclipsed Ife as the leading Yoruba state, reached its height during the 18th century when its influence extended from the Niger River to the Atlantic Ocean and from the Kingdom of DAHOMEY to the Kingdom of BENIN. Oyo was administered by the *alafin* (king), though outlying provinces retained much local autonomy under ruling *obas* (kings). Captured states retained their independence but were required to pay tribute. The *alafin* was elected by a council of elders, the Oyo Mesi, who could condemn him to death by suicide if they felt he abused his authority. However, there was also a secret religious and political group known as the Ogboni that could override the decisions of the Oyo Mesi. Oyo was noted for its cavalry and its efficient army—not surprising, perhaps, since defeated generals were condemned to death. Oyo defeated Dahomey in 1726, 1729, and 1730 and demanded slaves as part of its tribute. Slaves not used to work the royal farms were sold to Europeans, and as its successful military expeditions continued, Oyo became a major slave trader. When the French and the British ceased trading in slaves in the 19th century, the *alafin* lost considerable revenue and authority. Internal power struggles and civil war followed. Oyo was overrun by the FULANI and disintegrated as the *alafin* lost power, the capital at Old Oyo was destroyed, and the population shifted to the south.

Paige, Leroy Robert ("Satchel") (1906–1982)
baseball pitcher

As a young boy in Mobile, Alabama, Paige developed his pitching skills by throwing rocks at chickens in order to kill them for the family's dinner.

Satchel Paige pitches for Kansas City, September 25, 1965. (*Sporting News/Archive Photos*)

Arrested for shoplifting in 1918, he was sentenced to five years at the Industrial School for Negro Children at Mount Meigs. After his release at age 17, he joined a semiprofessional team called the Mobile Tigers, earning a dollar a game, or, if the owners could not afford cash, a keg of lemonade. As word of his pitching ability spread, Paige frequently pitched for other teams as well as his own in order to earn extra money. In 1926, he became a baseball legend when, with a 1–0 lead, and angry at his infield for committing three errors, he ordered the outfield to sit down and then struck out the last batter, winning the game without any help. He became a full-time professional when he joined the Chattanooga Black Lookouts at $50 a month. He later played for the Birmingham Black Barons, the Pittsburgh Crawfords (for whom he won 100 games in three years), and the Kansas City Monarchs. He also continued playing for other teams in the off-season. His showmanship—and his fastball—enabled Paige to draw thousands of fans into the ballparks and ensured the financial success of the team for which he played.

Paige was famous for his fastball, but he also had a "bee ball" ("because it be where I want it to be"), "trouble ball," "hesitation pitch" (which was banned when no one could hit it), "four-day rider," "bat dodger," "midnight creeper," and "jump ball." From 1929 until 1958, he played year-round, pitching almost every day. In addition to playing in the United States, Paige played in Puerto Rico, Venezuela, and the Dominican Republic and won numerous all-star exhibition games against white major leaguers. After one exhibition game, a young Joe DiMaggio said, "Now I know I can make it with the Yankees. I finally got a hit off Ol' Satch."

Paige was bitter about racial prejudice, which kept him out of the major leagues until the very end of his career, and he once refused to sign autographs for white fans in a southern town after he had been refused service in a restaurant. He also would not return to Mobile, Alabama, after he was arrested there in 1928 by a police officer who assumed that because Paige was black, the new car he was driving must be stolen. His willingness to stand up for principle was also evident during World War II when he refused to participate in the popular East-West all-star game after the team owners rejected his request to contribute $10,000 from the gate to wounded soldiers.

Satchel Paige played in over 2,500 Negro league games before he was signed by the Cleveland Indians in 1948 as a 42-year-old major league "rookie." In that year, his 6–1 winning record helped Cleveland get to the World Series for the first time in 28 years. After retiring in 1953, Paige briefly returned to pitching in 1965, the oldest man ever to play in the majors. He was elected to the Hall of Fame at Cooperstown in 1971.

He was famous for his advice "Don't look back. Something might be gaining on you." He appears as a character in William Brashler's novel *The Bingo Long Traveling All-Stars and Motor Kings* (1973). Paige's own autobiography is called *Maybe I'll Pitch Forever* (1962).

Palmares, Republic of (Quilombo dos Palmares)

Brazilian settlement established by runaway slaves and their children that lasted from about 1605 to 1695. Located in the Serra da Barriga (Belly Mountains), the African-style community, which was protected by three formidable walls, sheltered as many as 320,000 runaways. Over the years, Portuguese and Dutch soldiers attacked Palmares between 14 and 25 times, but its mountain site made it accessible from only one direction, and attackers were unable to capture it. Its last leader

was a man named Zumbi (1655–1695). Born a slave, Zumbi was taken from his mother when he was only a few weeks old and given to a local priest, who taught him Latin. At age 15, he ran away to Palmares, where he eventually became the leader, thanks to his exceptional talent for guerrilla warfare and his administrative skills.

Zumbi's military genius made him a legendary figure, and his plans to free all the slaves in the region terrified white planters. In 1694, soldiers caught and tortured a trusted aide, who finally revealed Zumbi's whereabouts. Though he escaped initially, Zumbi was caught and killed on November 20, 1695. A statue of him is located in a clearing in the Serra da Barriga range, and the tricentennial of his death was observed as a municipal holiday in Rio de Janeiro. According to one tradition, when Palmares was finally overrun, its leaders jumped off a cliff rather than be taken prisoner. Slavery in Brazil was so brutal that the average slave lived only seven years after arriving from Africa. Palmares was only one of a number of *quilombos* (slave settlements) built in the mountains and forests along the Brazilian coast.

Pan-Africanism

An intellectual movement promoting African culture, black unity, and the establishment of black African republics free of white control or influence. Early Pan-Africanists such as MARTIN DELANY and PAUL CUFFE believed blacks would never experience true equality in the United States and supported the return of all black people to Africa. Later Pan-African advocates such as W. E. B. DUBOIS were primarily concerned with an end to European colonialism in Africa. The Pan-African movement is a recurrent phenomenon. It was most popular during MARCUS GARVEY's crusade to attain economic independence for black people and unite them in an independent republic in Africa. Other well-known Pan-Africanists include Henry McNeal Turner, West Indian scholar and diplomat Edward W. Blyden, JOMO KENYATTA, FRANTZ FANON, JULIUS NYERERE, MALCOLM X, and KWAME NKRUMAH, who wanted to unite the newly independent African countries into some form of political union.

The first Pan-African Conference was organized by DuBois and H. Sylvester Williams of Trinidad in London in 1900 and included black intellectuals from the Caribbean, Africa, Europe, Canada, and the United States. Later conferences were held in 1919, 1921, 1923, and 1927. After World War II, the establishment of the Pan-African Federation and the Pan-African Congress of 1945 coincided with the growing independence movements in African colonies.

Black nationalism constitutes a strand within the Pan-African movement. Black nationalists emphasize black political and cultural autonomy and the unity of all black peoples, but they do not necessarily advocate a back-to-Africa goal. Today, certain Pan-African concepts find expression in writings about the African diaspora, that is, people of African descent who live elsewhere in the world.

Parker, Charles Christopher, Jr. ("Charlie," "Yardbird," "Bird") (1920–1955) *jazz musician*

Parker is closely linked to the development of bebop. His mother bought him an alto saxophone when he was 13 and he carried it with him constantly, even sleeping with it under his pillow. Parker grew up in Kansas City, Missouri, where he spent his nights listening to jazz musicians playing in local clubs.

At age 15, despite poor technique, he got a job playing professionally. Two years later, when some of Count BASIE'S musicians allowed him to sit in during a jam session, his playing was so bad drummer Jo Jones threw a cymbal at him. But his technique improved markedly after he spent hours memorizing tenor saxophonist Lester Young's solos.

In 1941, he settled in New York, where he began working with DIZZY GILLESPIE, THELONIOUS MONK, and other musicians experimenting with bebop. In 1945, he recorded the celebrated *KoKo,* which has been described as a condensed history of bop. A year later, however, his long-term heroin habit led to his commitment to California's Camarillo State Hospital. Released after six months, he made several recordings, including *Relaxin' at Camarillo.* Though the years 1947 to 1950 were productive, Parker's

health declined; he began drinking heavily and died at age 34. He is considered jazz's greatest saxophonist and one of its strongest improvisers. He is frequently described as an artist who changed the whole concept of jazz. Dizzy Gillespie said of his work, "That's how our music should be played."[1]

Recommended Listening: *The Bird You Never Heard* (Stash); *Bird's Night* (Savoy Jazz).

Parks, Gordon (1912–) *photographer, composer, writer, movie director*

Gordon Parks grew up in Fort Scott, Kansas, the youngest of 15 children. After his mother's death when he was a teenager, Parks supported himself by working as a dish washer, waiter, and piano player in Minnesota. He began working as a freelance photo journalist after buying a used camera in 1938 for $7.50. In 1941 he won the first Julius Rosenwald Fellowship for photography, and in 1942 went to work taking pictures of the poor in Washington, D.C., for the Farm Security Administration (FSA), an agency established to document poverty in the United States. In 1943 the FSA became a part of the Office of War Information, and Parks was assigned to cover the famous 332nd Fighter Group, an all-black unit of fighter pilots. From there, he moved to New York, where he began photographing fashions for *Vogue* magazine. In 1948 he received an assignment from *Life* magazine to do a photo documentary of gang life in HARLEM. Its success earned him a staff job with *Life* and an assignment to cover the fashion industry in Paris. While in France, he became friendly with the author RICHARD WRIGHT and composed a piano concerto. In 1961, Parks took an assignment in Brazil, where he discovered the plight of 12-year-old Falvio da Silva and his family. His photographs depicting their poverty and misery shocked the nation. Other work centered on crime in Chicago, poverty in Harlem, the Civil Rights movement, Dr. MARTIN LUTHER KING JR., the BLACK PANTHER

[1] *San Francisco Chronicle,* May 25, 1991, as quoted in Nat Hentoff, *Listen to the Stories.* New York: Harper-Collins, 1995.

American director Gordon Parks, whose films include *Shaft*, looks through a camera lens while on the set of a film. (*Archive Photos*)

movement, and MUHAMMAD ALI. In 1963, Parks published his first book, *The Learning Tree,* which is still recommended reading for many high school and college students. It was made into a movie, which Parks directed. The first African American to direct full-length films, Parks also directed *Shaft, Shaft's Big Score, Leadbelly,* and several other movies. He also wrote a number of other books, including *Born Black, The Choice of Weapons, Gordon Parks: Whispers of Intimate Things, Moments Without Proper Names, To Smile in Autumn, Voices in the Mirror, Arias in Silence,* and *Glimpes Toward Infinity.* A Gordon Parks exhibition, entitled "Half Past Autumn: The Art of Gordon Parks," began a tour of the United States set to continue to 2003.

Recommended Reading: Parks, Gordon. *Gordon Parks: Half Past Autumn, A Retrospective.* New York: Little, Brown, in association with the Corcoran Gallery of Art, 1997.

Parks, Rosa Louise McCauley (1913–) *civil rights activist*

On December 1, 1955, Rosa Parks set off one of the most famous actions of the CIVIL RIGHTS MOVEMENT when she refused to give up her seat on a bus to a white man and triggered the famous MONTGOMERY BUS BOYCOTT. Born in Tuskegee, Alabama, Parks attended Alabama State College. She and her husband, Raymond Parks, took an early interest in civil rights activities, working to free the SCOTTSBORO BOYS in the 1930s and joining the NATIONAL ASSOCIATION FOR THE ADVANCEMENT OF COLORED PEOPLE (NAACP). In 1955, she was earning 75 cents an hour as a seamstress at the Fair Department Store.

Rosa Parks (*Schomburg Center for Research in Black Culture*)

At that time, blacks who wanted to ride a city bus were required to board, pay the fare, and then exit and reenter the bus by the rear door. Bus drivers frequently pulled away before such riders could reboard. If all seats in the white section were taken, blacks were required to move so white passengers could have their seats.

After Rosa Parks refused to give up her seat on the bus, she was arrested and jailed. Her mother called E. D. Nixon, the local NAACP head, who arranged to have Parks released. The NAACP had been hoping to test the bus segregation laws in court but needed a defendant of impeccable reputation who could stand up to any attempted intimidation. Nixon immediately recognized that Rosa Parks was such a person.

The boycott lasted 381 days and ended only when the U.S. Supreme Court ruled segregation on city buses was unconstitutional. Rosa Parks lost her job because of her actions but was hired as a staff assistant to Congressman John Conyers of Detroit. She is known as the "Mother of the Civil Rights Movement."

Pele

See EDSON ARANTES DO NASCIEMENTO.

Philadelphia, Mississippi, Murders (1964)

murders of JAMES CHANEY, Michael Schwerner, and Andrew Goodman, three civil rights workers who were a part of the Mississippi Freedom Summer Project to encourage voter registration. The three men left the Congress of Racial Equality (CORE) office in Meridian, Mississippi, on June 21 to drive to a small town called Philadelphia in Neshoba County in order to look over the ruins of a burned-out church where CORE had been holding voter registration classes. Before leaving, Schwerner, a 24-year-old white social worker from New York, told a coworker that the three would be back before 4:00 P.M. When they did not return, experienced civil rights workers feared the worst. Philadelphia Sheriff Lawrence Rainey and Deputy Cecil Price came under immediate suspicion when Price admitted having arrested the three for speeding. Later he

released them on a road where a group of men was waiting to abduct them. The three were beaten and murdered, and their bodies were buried in an earthen dam on a nearby farm. A massive search was undertaken, and their remains were finally discovered by FBI agents on August 4. Sheriff Rainey and Deputy Price, along with 17 other men, were eventually charged with conspiracy in connection with the murders. Seven later went to prison. James Chaney was a 21-year-old African-American native of Mississippi. Goodman was a white college student who had been the state only a few days.

Phoenicians

Ancient people who invented the alphabet. Although the Phoenicians were based in the cities of Tyre and Sidon in what is now Lebanon, there are strong indications that they may have been partly of African descent. The Phoenicians were a Semitic people, but the term *Semitic* properly refers to languages, not race. There is linguistic evidence that Semitic-speaking peoples originated in western Europe and northwestern African and that the African groups later migrated across the continent, settling in North Africa, Egypt, and western Asia. (See Wolfram vol Soden. *The Ancient Orient*. Grand Rapids, Mich.: Eerdmans Publishing, 1994.) Additional evidence of African descent comes from the Bible, which states that Noah's son, Ham, the biblical ancestor of the black race, had four sons, Egypt, Cush, Put (believed to refer to either Libya or PUNT), and Canaan (Genesis 10:6). The Phoenicians commonly referred to themselves as "Canaanites" and they are regarded as the Canaanites' ethnic descendants.

Known for their exceptional navigational skills, the Phoenicians were asked by King Solomon for assistance in building the Israelite fleet. They also were commissioned by the Egyptian pharaoh NECO to circle the African continent, a task they completed some 2,000 years before Vasco da Gama became the first European to do the same thing. They established a number of settlements along the North African coast, including Utica (1100 B.C.) and Carthage (814 B.C.), and regularly traveled through the Straits of Gibraltar down the Moroccan coast.

They also obtained silver from Spain and may have sailed as far north as Britain and Ireland.

The earliest form of the Phoenician alphabet—today known as proto-Canaanite—came into existence during the 16th–17th centuries B.C. By 1000 B.C., it had developed into the 22-letter Phoenician alphabet, which was adopted by the Greeks around 800 B.C. The word *phonics,* referring to the practice of sounding out letters when learning to read, comes from the word *Phoenician.* The word *Phoenician* itself comes from the Greek *phoinikes,* "dark red," which refers to the Phoenicians' ability to create beautiful red and purple dyes from the *Murex* sea snail.

Pickett, Bill (1870–1932) *rodeo performer, originator of bulldogging*

Born and raised in Texas, Pickett left school after the fifth grade and became a ranch hand. While in his early teens, he developed the skill of bulldogging, which involves jumping onto a steer's back, grabbing its horns, twisting its head, and wrestling it to the ground. To accomplish this goal, Pickett would also sink his teeth into the animal's lip or nose. Pickett became an international star with the 101 Ranch Rodeo, with bulldogging one of the most popular events. At one performance in New York's Madison Square Garden, a frightened steer ran into the grandstand but was brought under control by Pickett, who rode his horse into the audience. His assistants included Will Rogers, who later became a famous comedian. Pickett was the first African American admitted to the National Rodeo Hall of Fame.

Pinchback, Pinckney Benton Stewart (1837–1921) *political leader, newspaper publisher*

The eighth of 10 children, Pinchback was the son of a white planter and Eliza Stewart, a slave woman who was freed shortly before the boy's birth. During the Civil War, he volunteered for service with the Union army and was given the assignment of recruiting African-American volunteers. He later resigned in protest against the discriminatory treatment they received. He demanded political rights for blacks, arguing that they should not be drafted if they were not allowed to vote.

After the war, Pinchback became a leader in the Republican Party in Louisiana. In 1867, he was selected as a delegate to the Louisiana state constitutional convention, where he emphasized the need for universal suffrage, civil rights, and a free tax-supported public school system. The following year, he was elected to the Louisiana state senate and was a delegate to the Republican National Convention. Pinchback established a newspaper, *New Orleans Louisianian,* which remained in existence from 1870 until 1881. A year later, he became lieutenant governor of Louisiana when Oscar Dunn, another black legislator, died. When the governor, Henry Warmoth, was impeached, Pinchback served as acting governor for a period of 43 days, beginning December 9, 1872.

In 1872, Pinchback was elected both U.S. congressman and U.S. senator from Louisiana. Both elections were contested, and Pinchback was prevented from taking a seat in either body, though he was later awarded $16,666 to cover part of the salary he would have received. Several other African Americans were also prevented from taking their seats at that time for racial reasons. In a speech defending his election, Pinchback stated, "If I cannot enter the Senate except with bated breath and on bended knees, I prefer not to enter at all . . ." He remained active in Louisiana politics and was instrumental in the establishment of Southern University in New Orleans.

Plessy v. Ferguson

1896 Supreme Court case that established the principle of "separate but equal" in regard to racial segregation. Homer Plessy, a black man from New Orleans, was convicted of attempting to ride in a railroad car set aside for whites. He appealed, but the Supreme Court, by a vote of 7–1, upheld his conviction, ruling that the concept of "separate but equal" accommodations was reasonable and that the Fourteenth Amendment was not meant "to abolish distinction based on color." The Court went on to say that "the assumption that the enforced separation of the two races stamps the colored race with a badge of inferiority . . . is not by reason of anything found in the act, but solely because the colored race chooses to put that construction upon it." Justice John Marshall Harlan, the lone dissenter, predicted—correctly—that the Supreme Court's decision would be used to limit the gains African Americans had made following the Civil War.

See also EDUCATION: "Court Battle to End Segregation."

Poison Spring

Massacre of African-American Union army troops that took place in Arkansas on April 18, 1864.

See also FORT PILLOW.

poll tax

Legal device used to prevent African Americans from voting. The first poll tax was instituted in 1890 by Mississippi. Though it was only $2, it was sufficient to keep many African Americans from voting, since many earned less than $30 a month. Other southern states followed Mississippi's example, instituting poll taxes, LITERACY REQUIREMENTS, GRANDFATHER CLAUSES, and residence requirements. These legal restrictions led to thousands of African Americans being dropped from the voting rolls. Opposition to poll taxes grew during World War II. The idea of forcing soldiers who were risking their lives for their country to pay a poll tax for the privilege of voting was hard to justify, and Congress passed the Soldier Vote Act in 1942, which eliminated the poll tax in federal elections for all military personnel. In 1962, Congress passed the Twenty-fourth Amendment to the Constitution banning poll taxes in national elections. It was ratified by the states in August 1964. In 1966, the Supreme Court cited the Fourteenth Amendment in outlawing poll taxes in all elections.

Powell, Adam Clayton, Jr. (1908–1972) *U.S. congressman, minister, civil rights leader*

Born in New Haven, Connecticut, Powell grew up in New York City, graduated from Colgate University, and received a master's degree from Columbia University. In 1937, he succeeded his father as pastor of the 14,000-member Abyssinian Baptist Church in HARLEM, where he led demonstrations against job discrimination and pressured the previously all-white city transit company to hire black bus drivers.

In 1941, Powell became the first African American elected to the New York City Council. Three years later, he won the first of 11 terms to Congress, where he challenged tradition by refusing to accept second-class treatment for himself or his staff. He was instrumental in seeing that African-American cadets were admitted to the Naval Academy at Annapolis and that blacks were included in the U.S. delegation to the United Nations. He supported legislation that assured fairer treatment of African Americans and prevented discrimination in the allocation of funds.

In 1961, his congressional seniority earned him the chairmanship of the House Committee on Education and Labor. However, Powell's frequent absenteeism and his flamboyant, confrontational style earned him many enemies. He was expelled from Congress in 1967 on charges of misusing public funds. Reelected by his district, he was readmitted in 1969 but stripped of his seniority and his committee chairmanship. That same year, the U.S. Supreme Court declared that his expulsion had been unconstitutional. He remained in Congress until he was defeated by Charles Rangel in the 1970 primary election. His writings include his 1971 autobiography, *Adam by Adam,* and a 1964 work titled with a phrase that was his personal trademark, *Keep the Faith, Baby!*

Powell, Colin Luther (1937–) *U.S. Army general*

The son of Jamaican immigrants, Powell was born in New York City and graduated from City College, where he majored in geology. Commissioned a second lieutenant in the U.S. Army, Powell was sent to Vietnam in 1962 and was injured by a punji stick the following year. On his second tour of duty (1968–69), he was injured in a helicopter crash but was able to rescue others from the burning aircraft.

In 1971, as an army major, Powell received a political appointment as a White House Fellow in the Office of Management and Budget in the Nixon

U.S. general Colin Powell, Chairman of the Joint Chiefs of Staff, talks to reporters in the National Press Club in Washington, D.C., September 28, 1993. (*Reuters/Stephen Jaffee/Archive Photos*)

administration. In 1983, he became military assistant to Defense Secretary Caspar Weinberger and helped coordinate the U.S. invasion of Grenada and later the planning of air raids against Libya. After a six-month stint commanding U.S. troops in Germany, Powell was assigned to the National Security Council, where he advised an increased military presence in the Persian Gulf. He also worked on the summit meetings with Soviet leader Mikhail Gorbachev that led to major arms control pacts.

Powell reached the apex of his military career in 1989 during the presidential term of George Bush, who promoted him over more senior generals to become chairman of the Joint Chiefs of Staff. He usually advocated caution in applying military pressure but, when military intervention was required, recommended the use of overwhelming force in campaigns of limited duration with well-defined goals. This strategy was seen in both the U.S. invasion of Panama (1989) and the Persian Gulf War (1991). Powell retired from active service in 1993. In 1997 he became the chairman of America's Promise—The Alliance for Youth, a new organization dedicated to building character and opportunities for young people. His best-selling memoir is entitled *My American Journey.*

Recommended Reading: Powell, Colin. *My American Journey.* New York: Random House, 1995.

Price, Mary Violet Leontyne (1927–) *soprano*
Born in Laurel, Mississippi, Leontyne Price began her singing career as a child in a church choir. An accomplished pianist as well as a singer, she earned a scholarship to the renowned Julliard School of Music in New York. In 1952, she won the coveted role of Bess in a Broadway production of George Gershwin's *Porgy and Bess.* Three years later she became the first African American to sing opera on television, performing the title role in Puccini's *Tosca.* When the Metropolitan Opera opened its new opera house at Lincoln Center in New York in 1966, Leontyne Price was chosen to star in the opening night performance. She gave her final performance there in 1985 in her signature role of Verdi's *Aida.* She is considered one of the foremost opera and concert singers of the 20th century.

Prince, Lucy Terry (1730–1821) *poet*
At age five, Lucy Terry was kidnapped from her African home and sold to a family in Deerfield, a small settlement on the western border of the Massachusetts colony. It was there, in 1746, during the French and Indian War, that she witnessed the famous Indian attack on Deerfield. Her poem about the attack, *The Bar's Fight,* was frequently read at town meetings and various social occasions and is still regarded as the best account of the attack. In writing it, Lucy Terry became America's first

African-American poet. (PHILLIS WHEATLEY, who wrote later, was the first to have a poem published.) Lucy Terry married Abijah Prince, a former slave, who purchased her freedom and moved with her to Vermont. Two of their sons served in the American Revolution. After Abijah Prince's death, a neighbor tried to claim Lucy Prince's property. When she took her case to the Vermont Supreme Court, the judge, ruling in her favor, said she had made one of the best arguments he had ever heard.

Prosser, Gabriel (ca. 1776–1800) *slave revolt leader*

Called "The Great Gabriel Conspiracy," the 1800 insurrection Prosser led is believed to have involved well over 1,000 slaves from Henrico County, Virginia, and the surrounding area. Prosser, who worked as a coachman and blacksmith, planned the revolt with the aid of his brothers, Martin and Solomon, and a trusted lieutenant, Jack Bowler. The slaves planned to rendezvous shortly before midnight on Saturday, August 30, at Old Brook Swamp just six miles outside of Richmond. There, under a Haitian-inspired flag reading "Death or Liberty," they intended to take over Richmond after dividing into three groups. One unit would attack the powder house, another the armory, and the third would set fires to create alarm and divert attention from the others.

Prosser was clearly influenced by the revolt in HAITI, and hoped to take advantage of deteriorating relations between France and the United States. In an effort to encourage possible French assistance, he had ordered his followers to spare all Frenchmen as well as all Quakers and Methodists (religious groups that opposed slavery). There were also indications that the slaves hoped for support from poor whites and Catawba Indians.

Though vague rumors of an uprising had been circulating for several months, no concrete information about the plan surfaced until the afternoon of August 30, when Tom and Pharoah, two slaves belonging to Mosby Sheppard, apparently lost their nerve and betrayed the plot. Governor James Monroe acted immediately, fortifying Richmond and mobilizing over 650 men. Prosser might still have prevailed had not an enormous rainstorm flooded the area, destroying roads and bridges and drowning all chance of success. Even so, approximately 1,000 slaves managed to gather at the assigned rendezvous point.

Over the next few days, dozens of slaves were arrested. Gabriel attempted to escape but was apprehended in Norfolk on September 25 aboard the schooner *Mary*. At least 35 to 40 slaves were hanged. Others were ordered sold out of state. Owners of executed slaves were routinely compensated for their losses by the state. In the case of the Gabriel Conspiracy, fees paid to owners of executed slaves amounted to $14,242.31. Additional expenses involving guards, militia, and the like raised the price tag on the revolt to approximately $25,000. The Virginia legislature arranged to purchase Tom and Pharoah, the two slaves who had betrayed the revolt, for $500 apiece and awarded them their freedom. As for Gabriel Prosser, he was returned to Richmond in chains, tried, and condemned to hang. The execution was put off briefly so Governor Monroe could personally interview him, but Prosser refused to talk. He went to his death in silence on October 7, 1800.

Pryor, Richard Franklin Lennox Thomas III (1940–) *comedian, actor*

Pryor was born in Peoria, Illinois, and raised in a family-owned brothel. His comedy career began when his sixth-grade teacher allowed him 10 minutes performance time in exchange for good conduct. After spending two years with the U.S. Army in Germany, he returned to Peoria and began work as a stand-up comic. He gained recognition after moving to New York in 1963 and appeared on *The Ed Sullivan Show* in 1965. Though his idol was Bill Cosby, Pryor's comedy was strikingly different. Much of his act revolved around sex and racism, and his angrily accurate, barbed comedy influenced a generation of comedians. Profane yet at the same time sensitive, he etched classic neighborhood characters such as "Mudbone" into comic history.

Pryor released 23 best-selling albums, five of which won Grammy awards, including *That Nigger's*

Crazy and *Bicentennial Nigger.* He has appeared in over 40 films and won an Academy Award nomination for his performance in *Lady Sings the Blues.* Plagued by a life-long drug problem, Pryor accidently set fire to himself in 1980 while freebasing cocaine. He later chronicled his life in the film *Jo Jo Dancer, Your Life is Calling* (1986). Other hit movies include *Silver Streak, Stir Crazy,* and *Car Wash.* He was diagnosed with multiple sclerosis in 1986. His autobiography, published in 1995, is called *Pryor Convictions.*

Punt

The ancient name for what is now Somalia, Djibouti, and Eritrea. Trade between Punt and Egypt goes back at least as far as 2500 B.C. Exports included gold, wood, incense, slaves, ivory, cattle, and exotic animals. Queen Hatshepsut of Egypt sent a major expedition there in the 15th century B.C.

Puryear, Martin (1941–) *artist*

Martin Puryear was born in Washington, D.C., and graduated from Catholic University of America. He joined the Peace Corps in 1964 and lived in Sierra Leone, where he investigated African pottery and weaving and learned woodworking techniques from tribal carpenters. Even before going to Africa, Puryear had built furniture, canoes, and musical instruments. After leaving the Peace Corps, he moved to Sweden to study printmaking, sculpture, and Scandinavian crafts. Returning to the United States, Puryear received a master's of fine arts degree from Yale, then went to Nashville in 1971 to teach at Fisk University. During this period, he began to exhibit his sculpture and, in 1973, opened a studio in Brooklyn, New York. In 1984, Puryear designed a poster for the Olympic Games in Los Angeles. New York's Museum of Modern Art included him in its exhibit Primitivism in 20th Century Art: Affinity of the Tribal and the Modern. He was the recipient of a MacArthur Foundation Fellowship "genius" award in 1989.

Pushkin, Alexander Sergeyevitch (1799–1837) *Russian writer*

That Russia's most important literary figure was partly of African descent was a fact proudly acknowledged by the author himself. His maternal great-grandfather was from Ethiopia and had been a favorite courtier of Czar Peter the Great. This family background provided the basis for Pushkin's unfinished novel *The Moor of Peter the Great.*

Pushkin gained early recognition as a poet and is credited with creating a new language for Russian poetry by gracefully blending three elements: the elevated tone of Church Slavonic; the spoken language of the people; and the various examples of foreign writers such as Shakespeare and Lord Byron. Though his first poems were published when Pushkin was 15, most of his lyric poetry was written between 1820 and 1830, a period that also produced his verse novel *Eugene Onegin.* Many of his verses were later set to music, beginning with Glinka's opera *Ruslan and Ludmilla.* Pushkin's prose narratives were the basis of Mussorgsky's opera *Boris Godunov* and Tchaikovsky's operas *The Queen of Spades* and *Eugene Onegin.*

Although employed by the czarist government, Pushkin was exiled from St. Petersburg in 1820 for writing "revolutionary epigrams." Four years later, he was fired for "atheistic writings." In 1832, he married a beautiful woman named Natalia Goncharova. The story of his death in a duel over her is widely known throughout Russia, and it remains true that many Russians can recite poetry written by Alexander Pushkin.

Pygmies

A people believed to be distantly related to the KHOI of southern Africa. They are mentioned in ancient Egyptian records dating back 4,000 years. Pygmies originally lived throughout much of central Africa until pushed into the equatorial rain forests hundreds of years ago by migrating BANTU peoples. Divided into the Mbuti, Twa, Tswa, Bagesra, and Binga subgroups, forest Pygmies have generally maintained their distinct culture. They stand about four-and-a-half-feet high, travel in small bands, and survive through hunting and the gathering of roots, berries, nuts, fruits, grubs, and various plants. What little clothing they wear is made of pounded bark.

Pygmy: Mbuti dancing (*National Museum of African Art, Washington, D.C.*)

Excellent hunters, Pygmies often hang nets between trees and then stampede game into them where the prey can be killed. They also are known to kill elephants with poisoned bananas and then set up their camps around the body. This allows them to preserve the meat, most of which would go bad if it had to be transported to a distant village. Though Pygmies use spears and machetes, they favor poisoned arrows or blowguns for hunting birds and small game, since larger weapons or bullets would tear the carcass apart, leaving nothing to eat.

Pygmies see the forest in an almost religious light. When a child is born, they will wrap it in a cloth made from pounded bark, wash it in water from vines, and decorate it with wooden beads. The idea is to provide the child with the protection of the forest spirits. Music and dancing are very impor-

tant in Pygmy life and are invoked for expressing all important events. Nowadays, forest Pygmies often collect latex from rubber trees and trade it for tools, tobacco, and lighters. Others have moved to the cities and intermarried with their BANTU neighbors. About 150,000 Pygmies remain, with the largest group, about 40,000, living in the Ituri Forest in Democratic Republic of Congo.

pyramids

Massive four-sided complexes built as tombs by Egyptian pharaohs of the Third through Thirteenth Dynasties. They varied in shape, with the earliest known being the step pyramid, which has a flat top and terraced sides. The best known are the three giant pyramids located near the city of Giza. The largest is the Great Pyramid, which was built for Khufu and which has a base area of 13 acres and an original height of 482 feet. The largest all-stone building ever erected in the history of the world, it required almost 6 million tons of stone. It is still not known how the Egyptians were able to move thousands of heavy stone blocks, some of which weighed 50 tons, into the precise positions required to create these geometric structures. Beginning in the 10th century A.D., Egyptian rulers began using the stones from the pyramids' outer surfaces for their own building projects. The Great Pyramids are referred to as one of the Seven Wonders of the World.

Late 19th-century photo of the Pyramid of Cheops (*Library of Congress*)

Quarles, Benjamin (1904–1996) *historian, teacher, scholar, author*

Born in Boston, Massachusetts, Benjamin Quarles graduated from Shaw University in Raleigh, North Carolina, in 1931 and received his master's and Ph.D. degrees from the University of Wisconsin. He taught at Shaw University, Dillard University in New Orleans, and Morgan State University in Maryland and wrote numerous books and articles on African-American history, the Civil War, and the Revolutionary War, including *Frederick Douglass* (1948), *The Negro in the American Revolution* (1961), *The Negro in the Making of America* (1964), and *Black Abolitionists* (1969). His work has been influential in promoting the importance of African-American historical studies.

R

race records

Early phonograph records recorded by African Americans and intended primarily for African-American buyers. White record companies originally refused to sign black artists, but in 1920, composer Perry Bradford managed to convince Fred Hagar of Okeh Records to record BLUES singer Mamie Smith doing pop songs with white musicians. The record, *That Thing Called Love,* was a hit. A few months later, Smith, this time backed by a black group called the Jazz Hounds, recorded *Crazy Blues,* which sold 75,000 records its first month and proved the commercial appeal of so-called "race music."

The years 1927–30 were a peak period for race records, with GOSPEL and blues records being released at a rate of 10 per week. Paramount, Columbia/Okeh, Vocalion/Brunswick, Gennett, and Victor, the five leading companies in the field, commissioned talent scouts throughout the South to look for new singers.

At first, race music was recorded only in northern studios, but in 1923, the first field recording was made. Though recording in the field, and particularly in the segregated South, had its problems, temporary studios using portable equipment were set up in hotel rooms, schools, and hired halls. Since microphones then in use were sensitive to heat, they were kept in ice to prevent crackling sounds. Engineers were often forced to put pillows under the feet of country musicians who were used to stomping their feet when they played. Scores of obscure musicians got once-in-a-lifetime chances to record and some of them went on to stardom.

However, the record industry was devastated by the Great Depression; sales in 1932 were only $6 million as compared to $104 million in 1927. The race record market was especially hard-hit, and field recording became a thing of the past as companies stuck to known stars. Some African Americans did continue to record, among them BESSIE SMITH, whose record sales are credited with keeping Columbia Records from bankruptcy.

Rainey, Gertrude Pridgett ("Ma") (1886–1939)
blues singer, songwriter

Born in Georgia, Ma Rainey began singing and dancing in traveling vaudeville shows while still a teenager. She quickly became popular throughout the South for her warm, serious style. Though the legend that she discovered Bessie Smith is not correct, she did advise her when Bessie joined the Moses Stokes traveling show in which Ma Rainey was then performing. Along with her singing, Ma Rainey was known for her mouthful of gold teeth, her love of jewelry—including a necklace of gold coins that she even wore to bed—and her suitcase full of money. She recorded with some of the outstanding musicians of the time, including LOUIS ARMSTRONG, Fletcher Henderson, and COLEMAN HAWKINS, but always retained her rural southern BLUES style. She retired in 1935 to run two theaters she owned in Georgia. She is known as the "Mother of the Blues."

Gertrude "Ma" Rainey and her Georgia Jazz Band, Chicago, Illinois, 1923 (*Frank Driggs/Archive Photos*)

There he attended classes at City College of New York while working at a series of menial jobs, a number of which he lost for agitating for better working conditions and for stirring up trouble among the other workers. In 1915, he met Chandler Owen, and the two men joined forces to promote socialism and labor unionization. They also began publication of *The Messenger,* through which Randolph argued that racism could be overcome by the integration of the growing American labor movement. Although *The Messenger* was primarily a political magazine, it also published the work of writers like COUNTEE CULLEN, LANGSTON HUGHES, and CLAUDE MCKAY. It regularly attacked the American Federation of Labor (AFL) for the racist policies of its member unions and the Republican Party for failing to run black candidates. It also attacked most

Ramses II (Ramses the Great, Ramesses)
Nineteenth Dynasty king of Egypt who reigned from 1290 to 1224 B.C.

Ramses II extended the empire of Egypt south beyond the fourth cataract of the Nile into Kush/Upper Nubia. He left many monuments to his own glory, including massive statues at Abu Simbal and the great hall of Karnak, along with countless inscriptions recounting military campaigns against Nubians, Libyans, and the Hittites of Asia Minor. His building projects required huge numbers of slaves, and he is believed to be the biblical pharaoh confronted by Moses, although it probably was his son, Merneptah, who was ruling at the time of the exodus of the Hebrews from Egypt. Ramses depleted Egypt's wealth with extravagant splendor and wars that required thousands of foreign mercenaries. He had at least seven queens, 79 sons, and 31 daughters. In 1995, archaeologists digging in the Valley of the Kings near Luxor found what is believed to be a tomb complex for 50 of his sons.

Randolph, Asa Philip (1889–1979) *labor leader, civil rights activist, publisher*

Born in Crescent City, Florida, A. Philip Randolph was the child of a minister who insisted his sons walk rather than ride a segregated streetcar. Randolph moved to New York City when he was 22.

Colossus of Ramses II (*National Museum of African Art, Washington, D.C.*)

of the black leadership for supporting American efforts in World War I, arguing that rather than "make the world safe for democracy," it would be preferable to "make Georgia safe for the Negro."

While speaking in Cleveland in 1918, Randolph and Owen were arrested and charged with violating the Espionage Act because of their *Messenger* editorials. The judge, after expressing his amazement that two black men could write so well, dismissed the charges and told them to leave town. The incident did not faze Randolph, who continued to call for forceful action. He wrote that "a bullet is sometimes more convincing than 100 prayers. . . ." in advocating blacks defend themselves after the RED SUMMER of 1919, in which at least 76 blacks were lynched and hundreds of others were shot and beaten during 25 race riots.

In 1925, Randolph began working with some Pullman porters in their attempt to organize what would become the Brotherhood of Sleeping Car Porters. Pullman cars were railroad cars with sleeping berths, and porter jobs were considered good positions. Pullman was the largest employer of blacks in the nation. Most unions had antiblack clauses in their constitutions, which members justified by accusing blacks of working as strikebreakers. The fact that Randolph was not a porter himself was an advantage since it meant that he—unlike hundreds of porters who joined the union—could not be fired by the Pullman Company. The union managed to hold together in the face of severe economic and political pressure. According to one story, the Pullman Company secretly offered Randolph a blank check and told him to fill in any amount up to $1 million if he would quit the union. Randolph handed it back in spite of the fact that *The Messenger* had folded in 1928 and he was forced to rely on his wife for support. During the Great Depression, half of the blacks in the country were unemployed, and union membership dropped drastically as many porters feared for their jobs. In 1935, 10 years after Randolph began his organization work, the Pullman Company finally recognized the Brotherhood of Sleeping Car Porters as the porters' official representative.

During World War II, Randolph threatened to lead 100,000 African Americans on a march on Washington to protest racial discrimination in

A. Philip Randolph speaking at the National Press Club, August 26, 1963 (*Library of Congress*)

defense industries. In response, President Franklin Roosevelt issued Executive Order 8802 banning discrimination in industries with government contracts. However, segregation was still the rule in the military, and in 1948, Randolph helped persuade President Harry S Truman to issue Executive Order 9981 integrating the armed forces. He continued to fight discrimination in the labor movement and in 1955 became a vice president in the AFL-CIO federation of labor unions. In 1963, Randolph, working with his deputy BAYARD RUSTIN, agreed to serve as director of the historic MARCH ON WASHINGTON.

Recommended Reading: Anderson, Jervis. *A. Philip Randolph.* Berkeley, Calif.: University of California Press, 1972; Cwiklik, Robert. *A. Philip Randolph and the Labor Movement.* Brookfield, Conn.: Millbrook Press, 1993.

rap

Musical form that combines speaking in rhymes and techniques such as manipulating turntables to move records back and forth to create a distinct sound. The 1960s group The Last Poets used raplike styles in their performances, but rap did not become widely popular until the 1980 release of *Rapper's Delight* by the Sugar Hill Gang. As interest in rap grew, groups like Public Enemy became prominent, and rap music became associated with black protest and the violent aspects of inner-city life. Much of it also was linked to lyrics that disparaged women and glorified guns and sexual conquest. It remains a popular branch of African-American music, with particular appeal to young people.

Rastafarianism

A religion that developed in Jamaica in the 1930s and that continues to have a widespread impact. Rastafarians believe that the Ethiopian emperor HAILE SELASSIE (1892–1975) was a direct descendant of the biblical King Solomon and the queen of Sheba and was a living god. The belief in the holiness of Haile Selassie derived from MARCUS GARVEY'S prophecy that an African king would arise who would unite all the black peoples in the world. The name "Rastafarian" comes from Haile Selassie's early title, Ras, and his original name, Tafari. Rastafarian men do not shave or cut their hair, which hangs in long twisted strands called dreadlocks. Rastafarians see themselves as the reincarnation of the ancient Hebrews of Israel, and their interpretation of biblical scriptures differs substantially from mainstream Christian and Jewish doctrine. Rastafarian beliefs focus on the oppression of black peoples around the world, the future overthrow of wicked, repressive governments (referred to symbolically as Babylon), and the eventual triumph of the poor and righteous. Though many Rastafarians are vegetarians and refrain from using alcoholic beverages, the use of marijuana, or ganja, is an important part of various Rasta rituals, especially "Groundation," during which Rastafarians reaffirm their beliefs. Among the most famous Rastafarians was BOB MARLEY.

Reconstruction

The period following the Civil War during which procedures were established to readmit the former Confederate states to the Union, help former slaves create new lives for themselves, and rebuild the wrecked southern economy. It began in 1865 with

Radical members of the reconstructed South Carolina legislature: 50 were black or biracial and 13 were white (*Library of Congress*)

passage of the Thirteenth Amendment to the Constitution, which abolished slavery. That same year, Congress established the FREEDMEN'S BUREAU to help former slaves become independent. But many whites opposed giving blacks the vote and supported President Andrew Johnson's program of "presidential reconstruction."

Presidential Reconstruction

Johnson was serving as U.S. senator from Tennessee when the South seceded from the Union. He rejected secession, however, and supported the Union, serving eventually as Lincoln's vice president after the 1864 election. At Lincoln's death, he became president. At the end of the Civil War, he took the position that the southern states had never legally seceded and therefore had never surrendered the right to govern their own affairs. Because of this, and because he himself held strong racist views,

Johnson dealt with the southern states very leniently in his presidential reconstruction plan. He opposed giving blacks the vote, stating that it would create "tyranny," and he remarked that blacks "have shown a constant tendency to relapse into barbarism."[1] He also suggested to a black delegation that African Americans leave the country. With Johnson expressing such views, it is not surprising that presidential reconstruction proved less than successful in securing African-American rights.

Under Johnson's program, most Confederates were granted amnesty and restoration of all property rights, except in regard to former slaves. New state governments were established throughout the South that denied African Americans the vote and kept the region under white control. The Freedmen's Bureau, which Johnson had opposed, did offer assistance to the ex-slaves, and Union troops, particularly the black regiments, provided some protection. However, the bureau faced enormous problems, and troops tended to be concentrated in the cities, leaving rural blacks extremely vulnerable to KU KLUX KLAN attacks. Moreover, Johnson actively sought to cripple the Freedmen's Bureau, and by 1867 he had removed most of the black troops from the South.

In an effort to maintain economic, political, and social control, the new white southern governments passed a series of laws known as BLACK CODES that severely limited African-American rights. Physical intimidation of blacks became widespread. In 1866, whites in New Orleans attacked a meeting of 25 black political leaders and approximately 200 supporters. Many were shot as they attempted to flee, and one Civil War veteran described the slaughter as worse than anything he had seen on the battlefield. That same year, a white mob in Pine Bluff, Arkansas, burned an African-American settlement to the ground and hanged the 24 men, women, and children living there.

Klan violence and the Black Codes drew a furious response in the North. Presidential reconstruction came under vigorous attack, as more and more people came to agree with so-called Radical Republicans that the federal government had to take a strong stand to protect blacks and pro-Union southerners. Congress responded by extending the life of the Freedmen's Bureau and by passing the Civil Rights Act of 1866 aimed at protecting black rights. To ensure that the protections offered by the Civil Rights Act could not be revoked at a later date, Congress passed the FOURTEENTH AMENDMENT to the Constitution guaranteeing black citizenship rights. Congress also passed the Reconstruction Act of 1867, which marked the beginning of Radical Reconstruction.

Radical Reconstruction

The Reconstruction Act of 1867 divided the confederacy into five military districts. In order to rejoin the Union every former Confederate state was required to hold a constitutional convention, elect new state governments, and allow black men to vote. The states were also required to ratify the Fourteenth Amendment. The situation was complicated by the fact that as commander in chief of the armed forces, President Johnson could—and did—try to thwart the aims of the Reconstruction Act by limiting the powers of the commanders of the military districts. Many in Congress were so angry at him that on February 24, 1868, the House of Representatives, using his firing of Secretary of War Edward Stanton as an excuse, voted 126 to 47 to impeach him under the Tenure of Office Act. Andrew Johnson became the first U.S. president ever to be impeached. Although he was not convicted and was able to serve out the rest of his term, his political power was greatly diminished.

Impact of Radical Reconstruction

The effects of the Reconstruction Act of 1867 reverberated across the South. Strikes broke out among African-American workers in Charleston, Mobile, Savannah, Richmond, and New Orleans. In several cities, black activists forced the integration of horse-drawn streetcars. The former slaves were quick to use their newly acquired voting rights. African Americans accounted for 265 of the delegates to the new state constitutional conventions, and many white delegates owed their election to black support. Together, these people created the most

---

[1] Eric Foner, *Reconstruction: America's Unfinished Revolution, 1863–1877.* New York: Harper & Row, 1988, p. 180.

progressive, democratic state constitutions the South had ever seen.

Equal rights were granted to all men regardless of race or color. For the first time, states were required to establish hospitals and asylums for the care of the sick, insane, orphaned, the poverty-stricken, and disabled. Whipping as a punishment for crime was outlawed, as was branding, and imprisonment for debt. New legislation sharply reduced the number of crimes punishable by death and eliminated property qualifications for serving on juries. Nine states expanded the rights of women, and the Florida constitution granted the Seminole Indians the right to two representatives in the state legislature. Every southern state was now required to establish a free, tax-supported public school system open to children of all races. New state governments were created, and over 600 African Americans were elected to the new legislatures. Hundreds of others were elected to other offices.

Faced with bankrupt state economies, a wrecked agricultural base, and thousands of families, white and black, crippled by the devastation of war, these men began the task of putting together modern representative governments. Alabama voted to provide free legal aid for poor defendants, and South Carolina set up free medical care for the indigent. Women and children received additional protection against abuse, and Nashville set up a limited welfare system. Roads were paved and, in some areas, modern sewer systems came into existence. Segregation was made illegal on railroads, steamships and streetcars. Mississippi, Florida, and Louisiana outlawed discrimination in hotels and theaters, and many of the oppressive laws passed under the Black Codes were revoked. The leasing of convicts was restricted in several states, and ended completely in South Carolina. All over the country, black political power was further enhanced by the 1868 passage of the FIFTEENTH AMENDMENT to the Constitution granting black men the vote.

White Terrorism

In spite of their newly acquired political power, African Americans in much of the South remained outnumbered and outgunned since the Confederate soldiers had been allowed to keep their weapons after the surrender. In order to regain control of the state and local governments, white Democrats turned to the Ku Klux Klan and similar white supremacist groups. These organizations began a vicious campaign of murder, rape, torture, arson, and assault. Thousands of African Americans who voted, ran for office, or took leading roles in the community were killed, and thousands more were brutally beaten. Those who did manage to fight off Klan attacks often had to leave the state for their own protection, and sometimes saw their families victimized in revenge. The most famous case of black resistance took place in COLFAX, Louisiana, in 1873, when whites attacked a town after a black government had been elected. Two hundred and eighty African Americans were killed. In an effort to curb the violence, Congress passed the Ku Klux Klan Act of 1871. As a result, thousands of Klansmen were arrested; 700 were indicted in Mississippi alone. Even though thousands more escaped arrest, and others usually received short jail terms or suspended sentences, the level of violence dropped dramatically.

However, northern commitment to African American rights was declining. In 1873, a major depression swept the country, idling thousands of workers. The voters responded by voting Republicans out of office, and this led to a backing away from the Reconstruction policies that had benefited African Americans. A series of Supreme Court decisions limiting protections offered by the Fourteenth Amendment added to the problem. The Klan again became active. In the disputed Hayes-Tilden presidential election of 1876, Democrats in South Carolina and Louisiana agreed to throw their support to the Republican Hayes in return for a withdrawal of federal troops and a policy of noninterference in state affairs. Hayes kept his word. Two months after he took office, federal troops surrounding the statehouses in Louisiana and South Carolina were withdrawn and Democratic governors installed. Reconstruction was over.

See EDUCATION; FREEDMEN'S BUREAU; RECONSTRUCTION AMENDMENTS; VOTING RIGHTS.

Recommended Reading: Foner, Eric. *Reconstruction: America's Unfinished Revolution, 1863–1877.*

New York: Harper & Row, 1988; Golay, Michael. *Reconstruction and Reaction: The Emancipation of Slaves, 1861–1913.* New York: Facts on File, 1996.

Reconstruction Amendments

Term used to describe the THIRTEENTH, FOURTEENTH, and FIFTEENTH AMENDMENTS to the U.S. Constitution. The Thirteenth Amendment abolished slavery. The 1863 EMANCIPATION PROCLAMATION had freed only those slaves in Confederate states, and further action was needed to permanently guarantee the elimination of slavery throughout the United States and its territories. Congress passed the Thirteenth Amendment by a vote of 119 to 56 on January 31, 1865. It was ratified by the states on December 18, 1865. The amendment reads: "Neither slavery or involuntary servitude, except as punishment for crime whereof the party shall have been duly convicted, shall exist within the United States, or any place subject to their jurisdiction. Congress shall have the power to enforce this article by appropriate legislation." The end of slavery in the United States did not mean the end of slavery in the Western Hemisphere, and the practice still continued in Brazil, Puerto Rico, and Cuba.

After slavery ended, southern states attempted to control African Americans through BLACK CODES, a series of laws which enforced segregation, limited black job opportunities, and kept African Americans from voting. In an effort to combat this, Congress passed the Civil Rights Act of 1866, which defined all persons (except Native Americans) born in the United States as full citizens with the right to bring lawsuits, make contracts, and enjoy equality under the law. The bill also overturned many discriminatory laws then in effect in the North. Although of major importance, the Civil Rights Act of 1866 had two important weaknesses. The first was political: Southern Democrats might vote to overturn it should they gain control of Congress. The second problem was a legal one. The U.S. Constitution did not specifically grant Congress the right to pass legislation protecting civil rights from abuse by the states.

The Fourteenth Amendment was adopted to answer these concerns. The first sentence of the amendment states that "all person born or naturalized in the United States, and subject to the jurisdiction thereof, are citizens of the United States and of the State wherein they reside." This means that anyone—no matter what race or color—who is born or naturalized in the United States is automatically a citizen, not only of the United States, but also of the state in which he or she lives, and is entitled to full citizenship rights. Thus the amendment overruled the U.S. Supreme Court DRED SCOTT decision of 1857, which stated that because Dred Scott was a black man, he was not a citizen and therefore did not have any of the rights of citizens. The second sentence of the Amendment says that "no state shall make or enforce any law which shall abridge [limit] the privileges or immunities [rights] of citizens of the United States." Originally, this meant that no state could pass laws limiting the rights of African Americans because African Americans were citizens. Over time, this clause has been broadened to mean that states cannot interfere with those rights associated with U.S. citizenship, and that such rights belong to all citizens regardless of race or color.

The first section of the Fourteenth Amendment also contains the famous "due process" and "equal protection" clauses. The equal protection clause meant that the states could not discriminate against African Americans and must grant them equal protection under the law. The equal protection clause refers to "any person," not just any citizen. This indicates that states may not discriminate against any person on account of race or color, whether or not the person is born in the United States or is a U.S. citizen. This clause was of crucial importance in the 1954 *Brown v. Board of Education of Topeka* decision outlawing school segregation. The equal protection clause was later expanded to mean that the government ordinarily cannot discriminate against anyone because of sex, national origin or circumstances of birth (i.e., whether or not a child's parents are married). There are some exceptions to this—for example, draft registration is required for males only.

The due process clause means that before the government can take anything of value away from a person—such as his life, freedom, or property—it must first notify him of the charges against him and allow him a fair trial or hearing. This applies to both criminal and noncriminal matters, although an individual has more procedural rights in criminal cases. The Bill of Rights (the first 10 amendments to the Constitution) protected citizens against actions by the federal government, not against actions by the states. The Fourteenth Amendment has been interpreted to ensure that all the rights and freedoms guaranteed by the Bill of Rights—such as freedom of speech, of the press, of assembly, the right to counsel, and the right to religious freedom—must be honored by the states as well as by the federal government (*Gitlow v. New York,* 1925).

The Fourteenth Amendment did not provide African Americans with the vote, but it tied congressional representation to the proportion of the population eligible to vote. Thus, if a state allowed its black population to vote, it would be entitled to more congressional representatives and to more electoral votes in presidential elections. The enactment of the Fifteenth Amendment in 1870 giving African-American men the vote made this section of the Fourteenth Amendment inoperative. The Fourteenth Amendment passed Congress on June 13, 1866, and was ratified by the states on July 21, 1868. All 10 southern states initially rejected it. The Reconstruction Act of 1867 required these states to ratify the amendment as one of the conditions for rejoining the Union.

The Fifteenth Amendment guaranteed the right to vote to all male citizens. It was passed by Congress on February 26, 1869, and ratified by the states on March 30, 1870. It states that the right of a citizen to vote shall not be denied or limited by the federal government, or by any state government, by reason of race, color, or previous condition of servitude (by the fact that a person had once been a slave). The amendment was necessary to ensure that the reforms put into place following the Civil War would not be overturned should Southern Democrats ever gain political control of Congress. The Reconstruction Act of 1867 had, among other things, required that black men be allowed to vote in the former Confederate states in order for the states to be readmitted to the Union. However, the act did not apply to northern states, and, in a number of them, African Americans still lacked the right

to vote. The Fifteenth Amendment corrected this. It did not, however, forbid the use of literacy, property, or educational tests that would later be used to keep blacks from voting. It also left the control of violence against black voters to the states rather than the federal government.

The amendment's failure to provide for women's suffrage brought on feminist attacks, and this led to a break between FREDERICK DOUGLASS and the women's rights organizations. Although Douglass had always been a strong supporter of women's suffrage, he was not about to jeopardize the black male vote for it. He argued that, while women should have the vote, their rights were to some extent protected by their fathers, husbands, sons, and brothers. Black people, on the other hand, had no protection at all. Feminist leaders refused to accept Douglass' reasoning, arguing that women's rights were just as important as those of African Americans. The high moral stand taken by the feminist leaders was undercut, however, by their own willingness to sacrifice black rights for women's suffrage. Several had attempted to appeal to racial prejudice by arguing that giving the vote to white women would offset any political power gained by blacks. In providing African Americans with the vote, the Fifteenth Amendment was a critical step toward obtaining full civil rights for all citizens. Its limited impact was due to the fact that, in much of the South, government officials would actively seek to circumvent it, and, failing that, would refuse to prosecute those who attempted forcibly to deny African Americans the vote.

Red Record

A comprehensive report on LYNCHING in the United States published by IDA WELLS-BARNETT in 1895. Titled *A Red Record: Tabulated Statistics and Alleged Causes of Lynching in the United States, 1892, 1893, 1894,* the 100-page-long report was part of Wells-Barnett's antilynching crusade that had been triggered by the 1892 murder of three of her friends, Thomas Moss, Calvin McDowell, and Henry Stewart. The men were killed because their grocery store competed successfully with a nearby white-owned store. In its first chapter, *A Red Record* stated, "Not all nor nearly all of the murders done by white men, during the past thirty years in the South, have come to light, but the statistics as gathered and preserved by white men, and which have not been questioned, show that during these years more than ten thousand Negroes have been killed in cold blood," and "the same record shows that during all these years, and for all these murders only three white men have been tried, convicted, and executed." Many of these murders were committed during RECONSTRUCTION, as southern whites struggled to maintain economic and political control; they were rationalized as necessary to prevent "insurrection" and "Negro domination." When these excuses lost their impact, black men were frequently accused of raping white women, even though in numerous cases, the relationship—if any—between the man and woman involved was known to be a voluntary one. To avoid charges of inaccuracy, Wells-Barnett limited her study to lynchings that had been reported in the *Chicago Tribune*. In her words, "Out of their own mouths shall the murderers be condemned."

Recommended Reading: Wells, Ida B., and Afreda M. Duster, ed. *Crusade for Justice: The Autobiography of Ida B. Wells*. Chicago: University of Chicago Press, 1970.

Red Summer of 1919

JAMES WELDON JOHNSON coined the term *Red Summer* (the reference is to blood, not communism) to describe the approximately 25 race riots and 76 lynchings that took place that year. The first major riot took place in July in Longview, Texas, when several white men were shot when they entered a black section of town in search of a black schoolteacher who had attempted to publicize a lynching that had occurred a month earlier. Whites retaliated by burning several black homes, flogging a black school principal, and forcing a number of black leaders to leave town. A week later, a riot broke out in Washington, D.C., that resulted in the deaths of several blacks and whites.

The best-known riot of Red Summer occurred in Chicago when an African-American teenager swim-ming in Lake Michigan drifted into the "white" section and was stoned. He drowned, and when black witnesses attempted to have a white stone thrower arrested, the police refused and arrested a black man instead. The riot that broke out lasted six days. Thirty-eight people were killed (15 whites and 23 blacks), and 537 were injured.

In addition to rioting, violence shook ELAINE, ARKANSAS, when a confrontation between whites and black sharecroppers attempting to form a union resulted in a gunfight. In the aftermath, between 20 and 200 African Americans were killed. Seventy-nine blacks were indicted; 12 were convicted of murder and sentenced to death, though the convictions were later overturned.

During World War I, almost 5 million men left to serve in the armed forces, and foreign migration was cut by close to 90 percent. As a result, there was a huge demand for labor in northern factories, and thousands of African Americans moved north to take advantage of the job situation there. Previously, many of these positions would have been filled by whites. Severely overcrowded black ghettoes forced some blacks to move into what had been all-white neighborhoods, creating additional tensions. After the war, competition for jobs intensified as whites attempted to reestablish the prewar racial situation. There was a dramatic increase in KU KLUX KLAN membership that was accompanied by numerous lynchings, floggings, and murders. Many African Americans, particularly those who were former soldiers, refused to accept a return to their prewar status. A foreshadowing of this resistance took place two years earlier, in 1917, when members of the army's famed Twenty-fourth Regiment became involved in a shoot-out with whites after white law enforcement officers threatened black military police. (See HOUSTON MUTINY/RIOT)

President Woodrow Wilson had called World War I the war "to make the world safe for democracy," and many in the black community had hoped that their contributions to the war effort would substantially improve the situation of African Americans. The postwar antiblack violence filled many with despair, though others reacted with fury. CLAUDE MCKAY spoke for many with his 1919 poem

If We Must Die, with its demand that blacks fight back.

As the Red Summer of 1919 drew to a close, racial violence tapered off. However, two years later the Tulsa riot of 1921 left 10,000 blacks homeless and between 70 and 300 dead.

reggae

music form developed in Jamaica. The term *reggae* was taken from a 1960s song, "Do the Reggay" by Toots Hibbert and the Maytals. Reggae developed from mento, an African musical traditional style brought to the Western Hemisphere by slaves. Mento later fused with CALYPSO, RHYTHM AND BLUES, and rock and roll to become an instrumental Jamaican musical style known as ska. The RASTAFARIAN religious emphasis on Africa influenced ska music, which developed into reggae around 1968. The most famous reggae musician was BOB MARLEY. Other well-known reggae artists include Jimmy Cliff, Peter Tosh, and Third World.

Renaissance Big Five

first professional black basketball team. Organized in 1923 by Robert Douglas, the team was named for the Renaissance Ballroom, which doubled as their home court. The Renaissance Big Five (or Rens) won their first game 28–22. They regularly crisscrossed the country, traveling approximately 38,000 miles a season and playing 140 to 150 games a year, sometimes three in a day. Since they were not allowed in segregated restaurants or white locker rooms, players often ate and changed clothes on the bus. Except for the Celtics and a few other good clubs, the Rens usually spotted their opponents 10 points and, to ensure they would be invited back, had a policy of holding the score down so that they never won by more than 10 points. Fans of opposing clubs who persisted in yelling racial slurs at the Rens were often "accidentally" hit by missed passes. The Renaissance Big Five folded in 1948 after winning 2,588 games and losing 529. Robert Douglas is considered the father of black professional basketball.

Revels, Hiram Rhoades (1822–1901) *U.S. senator*

Born free in North Carolina, Revels became an ordained minister in 1845 and served congregations in Maryland and several other states. During the Civil War, Revels helped recruit black soldiers and established a school for freed slaves in St. Louis. In 1868 he was elected to the Mississippi state senate and in 1870 was elected to the U.S. Senate by the Mississippi state legislature. The Senate agreed to seat him only after a bitter debate, and he served only one year. After his return to Mississippi, he became president of Alcorn University. Revels was the first African American elected to either house of Congress.

Rhodesia   See ZIMBABWE.

rhythm and blues

African-American music that fused JAZZ and BLUES. It became popular in the 1930s and heavily influenced the development of rock and roll as well as white stars like Elvis Presley. Outstanding rhythm and blues (R&B) artists include Esther Phillips; ARETHA FRANKLIN; Dinah Washington; Ray Charles; Chaka Khan; Otis Redding; Stevie Wonder; Sam and Dave; the Temptations; Earth, Wind and Fire; Ramsey Lewis; and Lou Rawls.

Rillieux, Norbert (1806–1894) *inventor, engineer, Egyptologist*

Rillieux was born in New Orleans, the son of a plantation owner. It is not known if his slave mother was freed before his birth or if he was born a slave and freed shortly afterward. His father sent him to France to be educated. He studied engineering at the Ecole Centrale, where, at age 24, he became an instructor in steam engine technology. While there, he developed the theories he would later rely on in New Orleans to develop his Multiple Effect Vacuum Pan Evaporator. This device not only improved the quality of sugar but allowed it to be produced at a much lower cost. Unfortunately, it also greatly increased the demand for slave labor to work the sugarcane fields. Rillieux also developed a plan for a sewer system for New Orleans. Though it would have greatly improved health conditions there, the city government rejected the plan because Rillieux was black. Years later, an almost identical plan was adopted. In 1854, Rillieux returned to Paris, where he began studying Egyptian HIEROGLYPHICS. Rillieux's work continues to have an impact in the sugar industry and in the manufacture of soap, glue, gelatin, condensed milk, and other products. Charles A. Brown, a chemist with the U.S. Department of Agriculture, described Rillieux's invention as "the greatest in the history of American chemical engineering."[1]

Robeson, Paul (1898–1976) *actor, singer, civil rights activist*

Robeson became the first black all-American in football while at Rutgers College, where he also won letters in baseball, basketball, and track, and was elected to Phi Beta Kappa, the national honors society. After graduation, he played professional football on weekends while attending Columbia Law School. He graduated in two years but decided to become an actor. He won rave reviews for his performances in Eugene O'Neill's plays *All God's Chillun Got Wings* and *The Emperor Jones* and the Jerome Kern musical *Showboat*. His greatest success was as the lead in *Othello*. In addition to his stage career, Robeson recorded more than 300 records and starred in several movies.

In the fight against discrimination, Robeson picketed the White House, protested against LYNCHING, and refused to sing before segregated audiences. Because of his political activities, the State Department revoked his passport, making it impossible for him to work abroad. Called to testify before Congress, he refused to say whether or not he was a communist. As a result, no one would hire him. Robeson's income, which in 1947 had been $104,000, dropped to $2,000 a year. Though a 1958 Supreme Court ruling in a related case forced the

Paul Robeson in *The Emperor Jones* (Museum of Modern Art Film Stills Archive)

government to return Robeson's passport to him, it was by then too late to revive his career, and illness forced him into retirement.

Robinson, Jack Roosevelt ("Jackie") (1919–1972) *first African American to play major league baseball*

At UCLA, Jackie Robinson became the first person to win letters in four different sports: baseball, basketball, football, and track. During World War II, he was stationed at Fort Riley in Kansas, where he was originally denied a chance to enter Officer Candidate School (OCS) because of his race. He was finally admitted with the help of heavyweight boxing champion JOE LOUIS, who was also stationed at Fort Riley. Robinson was later transferred to Fort

[1] Louis Haber, *Black Pioneers of Science and Inventions.* New York: Harcourt, Brace & World, 1970, p. 22.

Baseball player Jackie Robinson swings a bat while in uniform. (*Archive Photos*)

Hood, where he was court-martialed for refusing a bus driver's order to move to the black of the bus. The charges were dismissed.

After the war, Robinson joined the Kansas City Monarchs, one of the baseball teams playing in the NEGRO BASEBALL LEAGUES. His skills brought him to the attention of Brooklyn Dodgers president Branch Rickey, who was attempting to integrate the major leagues. Rickey arranged for Robinson to join the Montreal Royals, the Dodgers' farm club. The next year, in 1947, Robinson joined the Dodgers.

He was subjected to considerable abuse from opposing players. The president of the Philadelphia Phillies stated that his team would not play the Dodgers as long as Robinson remained on the roster, and the St. Louis Cardinals threatened a protest strike. Ford Frick, the president of the National League, reacted forcefully, telling the Cardinals, "If you do this, you will be suspended from the League . . . I do not care if half the League strikes. Those who do it will encounter quick retribution. They will be suspended, and I don't care if it wrecks the National League for five years. This is the United States of America, and one citizen has as much right to play as another. The National League will go down the line with Robinson whatever the consequence." In his first year with the Dodgers, Jackie Robinson helped the team win the National League pennant, and on Sept. 30, 1947, he became the first African American to compete in the World Series. (The Yankees won.) He also was named Rookie of the Year.

Recommended Reading: Tygiel, Jules. *Baseball's Great Experiment.* New York: Oxford University Press, 1983.

Robinson, Randall (1941–) *founder and executive director of TransAfrica*
Born in Richmond, Virginia, Robinson graduated from Harvard Law School and worked as an assistant for Congressman Charles Diggs (D-Mich.) He founded TransAfrica in 1977 as a political action group to promote human and civil rights for blacks, particularly those in Africa and the Caribbean. His initial efforts focused on bringing an end to white rule in Rhodesia, now Zimbabwe. Under Robinson's direction, TransAfrica took the lead in protesting apartheid in South Africa. TransAfrica also lobbies to increase U.S. aid to Africa. Randall Robinson has written two books: *Defending the Spirit* and *The Debt: What America Owes to Blacks.*

Rollins, Theodore Walter ("Sonny") (1930–) *jazz saxophonist*
Rollins was strongly influenced by COLEMAN HAWKINS. He worked with THELONIOUS MONK and performed frequently with MILES DAVIS. He also recorded with CHARLIE PARKER, ART BLAKEY, the Modern Jazz Quartet, J. J. Johnson, Bud Powell, and Fats Navarro. Among his recordings with Miles Davis were three of his own compositions—"Doxy,"

"Oleo," and "Airegin"—which are now considered classics. In 1955, he joined the Clifford Brown/Max Roach Quintet and a year later released *Saxophone Colossus,* making him one of the most innovative tenor saxophonists in hard bop. From 1959 to 1961, Rollins stopped performing, although he became famous for his habit of practicing on New York bridges. In 1962, he resumed his career, becoming famous for his "stream-of-consciousness" improvisations. He temporarily retired again from 1969 to 1971. Rollins is considered a leader in hard bop and avant-garde and was one of the first to incorporate Caribbean music into JAZZ.

Recommended Listening: *Saxophone Colossus* (Fantasy/Orig. Jazz Classics); *Tenor Madness* (Fantasy/Orig. Jazz Classics); *Sonny Rollins Plus 4* (Orig. Jazz Classics); *The Bridge* (RCA); *Our Man in Jazz* (RCA).

Roots

Best-selling ALEX HALEY book and dramatic TV miniseries. The 688-page book traced Haley's family history back to a man named Kunta Kinte, who was born in a small African village in 1750. Haley published *Roots* in 1976 after 12 years of writing and research. A dramatic miniseries based on the book aired on eight consecutive nights on ABC-TV in 1977 and attracted over 100,000,000 viewers for its final episode. A sequel called *Roots: The Next Generation* aired on ABC in 1979. Two authors accused Haley of plagiarism in conjunction with *Roots,* but one case was dismissed and the other was settled out of court.

Rosewood

A small Florida community of about 120 people that was the target of a week-long race riot in January 1923. At least six African Americans and two whites were killed and all the buildings were burned. Most of the men worked at a sawmill in the nearby town of Sumner, where many of Rosewood's women worked as domestics. The riot was triggered by the claim of Fannie Taylor, a white Sumner woman, that she had been assaulted by a black man who had bro-

ken into her house. This story was contradicted by a black laundress who stated that the attacker was white. However, whites blamed Jesse Hunter, an escaped black convict, whom bloodhounds tracked to Rosewood. White vigilantes attacked the small community the next day, killing several people and burning six buildings. Many were also wounded. After the Rosewood inhabitants had fled, the 12 remaining buildings were burned. Some reports stated that an additional 17 to 26 African Americans were murdered and buried in a mass grave, but this has never been verified. In May 1994, the Florida state legislature authorized the payment of $2 million in compensation to the survivors and the descendants of the victims.

Rudolph, Wilma Goldean (1940–1994) *track star*

Born in Saint Bethlehem, Tennessee, Wilma Rudolph was the 20th of 22 children. At age four, she contracted pneumonia, scarlet fever, and polio, and her family was told she would never walk again. Her parents refused to accept this prognosis, and the entire family took turns massaging her legs four times a day. By age six, she was walking with the aid of a leg brace. Later, a special orthopedic shoe allowed her to play basketball with her brothers. When she was 11, she began playing in her bare feet, and four years later she became an all-state high school basketball champion. She also began to compete in track. In 1956, when she was a high school senior, Wilma Rudolph qualified for the Olympics in Melbourne, where she won a bronze medal. Four years later, in Rome, she became the first American woman to win three gold medals in track in one Olympics, winning the 100-meter dash in 11 seconds, the 200-meter dash in 24 seconds, and the 400-meter relay. Called "La Gazelle" and "The Black Pearl," she later became a teacher, coach, and television host.

Russwurm, John Brown (1799–1851) *co-founder and coeditor of Freedom's Journal*

A graduate of Bowdoin College in Maine, Russwurm was one of the earliest black college graduates in the country. After finishing at Bowdoin, he moved to New York, where in 1827 he and Samuel Cornish published the first issue of *Freedom's Journal,* the first African-American newspaper published in the United States. DAVID WALKER's "Appeal" first appeared in the *Journal's* pages. In 1829, Russwurm moved to Liberia, where he spent the rest of his life working as an editor, superintendent of education, and government official.

Rustin, Bayard (1910–1987) *civil rights activist, principal organizer of the 1963 March on Washington*
Born in West Chester, Pennsylvania, Rustin was one of 12 children. While on a trip with his mostly white high school football team, he was thrown out of a restaurant because he was black. In 1936, he joined the Young Communist League but quit the organization five years later. However, his early communist association was later used in an attempt to discredit him with MARTIN LUTHER KING JR. and other civil rights leaders. (See also MARCH ON WASHINGTON.)

In 1942 Rustin was brutally beaten by Tennessee police when he refused to move to the back of a bus. He worked closely with A. PHILIP RANDOLPH and was a youth organizer for a proposed march protesting the failure of the U.S. government to force defense industries to end job discrimination. The march was canceled when President Roosevelt issued an executive order banning discrimination in industries with government contacts. During World War II, Rustin spent 28 months in prison as a conscientious objector and later helped found the CONGRESS OF RACIAL EQUALITY (CORE).

Arrested in 1947 in North Carolina for participating in a freedom ride, Rustin spent 22 days on a chain gang. Two years later, his published account of his treatment led to the abolition of chain gangs in North Carolina. He led protests against British colonialism in India and was one of the activists who helped persuade President Harry Truman to end segregation in the armed forces. He was also active in the fight against racial injustice in South Africa and in the nuclear disarmament campaign. He later became an adviser to Martin Luther King Jr. and helped organize the MONTGOMERY BUS BOYCOTT in Alabama and the

SOUTHERN CHRISTIAN LEADERSHIP CONFERENCE (SCLC).

Rwanda (Rwandese Republic)

African country located between Democratic Republic of Congo, Uganda, Tanzania, and Burundi. Capital: Kigali. The mountainous country includes the Virunga Range, which is home to endangered mountain gorillas. About 90 percent of Rwanda's inhabitants are Hutu, 9 percent are Tutsi, and 1 percent are Twa Pygmies. Most people are subsistence farmers. Like Burundi, Rwanda is dominated by the Tutsi, whose kingdom reached its height in the early 1800s. In 1890, Germany asserted sovereignty over Rwanda but had no real economic or local political influence in the region. Rwanda was invaded by Belgium during World War I, and the area became part of Belgium's Ruanda-Urundi League of Nations mandate in 1919. In 1946, the area became a United Nations trust territory, though the Belgians continued to rule through Tutsi leaders.

The Hutus began demanding reforms in 1957, and in 1959, after the death of Mwami (King) Matara III, fighting broke out between the Hutu and the Tutsi. The Tutsis' murder of a number of Hutu leaders resulted in a massive Hutu uprising and the slaughter of approximately 100,000 Tutsi. Thousands of others fled the country. The Belgians introduced political reforms and, under pressure from the United Nations, granted independence on July 1, 1962. The first president was a Hutu, Grégoire Kayibanda. Conflict with Tutsi-dominated Burundi in 1964 led to the deaths of many Tutsis in Rwanda and caused many others to leave the country. In 1972, a massacre of an estimated 100,000 Hutus in neighboring Burundi led to a resurgence of anti-Tutsi feeling in Rwanda. A year later, several hundred Rwanda Tutsis were forced to flee to Uganda after renewed fighting between the two tribal groups. Kayibanda was overthrown by Hutu general Juvenal Habyarimana in 1973. It was at this time that Tutsis were ejected from the universities. In 1990, a Tutsi organization called the Rwanda Patriotic Front invaded Rwanda from bases in Uganda. They were repulsed, and the Hutu responded by killing thousands of Tutsis.

In 1994, Habyarimana was killed in a plane crash along with Burundi president Cyprien Ntaryamira when their plane was hit by rocket fire while returning from peace talks in Tanzania. The deaths sparked genocidal massacres in Rwanda, as Hutus murdered between 500,000 and 1,000,000 Tutsis and moderate Hutus. Prior to the genocide Radio Mille Collines had called for all Tutsis to be put to death, and other news outlets regularly referred to Tutsis as *inyezi*, or "cockroaches." Habyarimana had authorized the buildup of an armed militia of extremist Hutus—known as the Interahamwe—which later led the rampage. The Tutsi Patriotic Front under Maj. General Paul Kagame managed to oust the Hutu regime, which caused approximately 2 million Hutus to flee the country. Thousands died of hunger and disease in refugee camps. Though bystanders, almost 20,000 of Rwanda's 30,000 Twa Pygmies also died in the conflict. Many of the refugees have now returned to Rwanda. The government is placing people who took a leading part in the genocide on trial. (Approximately 130,000 people are expected to be tried for murder and genocide.) The United States blocked the U.N. Security Council from intervening in Rwanda while the genocide was in progress, causing U.S. President Bill Clinton to later apologize to

A group of predominantly elderly Rwandan refugees, too weak to walk, sit and wait for the arrival of humanitarian aid some seven kilometers south of Kissanagani, Lula, Zaire, March 25, 1997. The refugees, part of a group of some 17,000, arrived in Kissangani after fleeing the Tingi Tingi camp three weeks before. (*Reuters/Corrine Dufka/Archive Photo*)

Rwanda. Troops from Rwanda provided support for rebels in Democratic Republic of Congo in 1998–99.

Recommended Reading: Keane, Fergal. *Season of Blood*. London: Penguin Books, 1996.

S

Sahara

The world's largest desert. More than 3.5 million square miles in area, the Sahara stretches across northern Africa from the Atlantic Ocean to the Red Sea. It covers most of Egypt, Libya, Algeria, Niger, Mauritania, and Western Sahara and substantial portions of Morocco, Tunisia, Chad, Sudan, Mali, and Senegal. Approximately 15 percent of the Sahara is sand dunes, with much of the rest being stony plateaus and gravel. The Atlas Mountains to the north block moisture-bearing winds from the Mediterranean from entering the region. Other mountain ranges are the Ahagger in southern Algeria, the Tibesti Massif in Chad, and the Air Mountains in Niger. Before 3000 B.C., the Sahara was much wetter and supported an extensive human and animal population, as evidenced by the rock painting found in the TASSILI-N-AJJER range in Algeria and the Tibesti Mountains in Chad. It is now home to approximately two million people, mostly TUAREG and nomads of Arab-Berber heritage. Once the camel was introduced sometime between 500 and 100 B.C., caravans crossed the Sahara regularly, traveling between the West African trade centers like TIMBUKTO and GAO and Egypt and the cities of the North African coast.

See also ARABS; BERBERS.

Sahel

An Arabic word meaning "shore," which is used to describe the semiarid land bordering the southern edge of the Sahara Desert. The Sahel extends across the continent through Senegal, Mauritania, Mali, Burkina Faso, Niger, Nigeria, Sudan, and Ethiopia. Soil depletion through overcultivation, overgrazing by cattle, and the widespread destruction of trees for firewood has contributed to increasing dryness in the area, which was hit by extensive drought in the 1960s, 1980s, and early 1990s. Thousands of people starved to death, and thousands more became refugees.

Saint-Georges, Joseph Boulogne, chevalier de
(ca. 1739–1799) *composer, violinist, soldier*

A noted athlete as well as a musician, Saint-Georges engaged in public fencing matches until he was past 50. His mother was a native of Guadeloupe, his father a Frenchman who moved the family from the West Indies to Paris while Saint-Georges was still a child. The details of Saint-Georges' musical education are unknown, but his first professional work was as a violinist in an orchestra led by composer François Gossec. Most of his instrumental music was written in the 1770s, including violin sonatas, string quartets, and two symphonies. He favored rapid-fire violin parts to demonstrate his own agility in fingering and bowing, but he was also noted for the emotional expression of his performances. He wrote at least six operas, including *Ernestine* (1777). During the French Revolution, Saint-Georges joined the National Guard and led a corps of black troops whose ranks included the father of writer ALEXANDRE

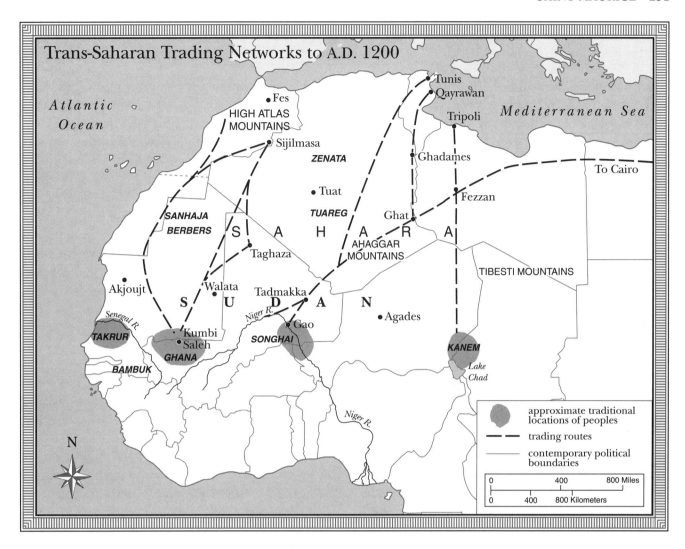

Trans-Saharan Trading Networks to A.D. 1200

Atlantic Ocean

Mediterranean Sea

Fes
HIGH ATLAS MOUNTAINS
Sijilmasa
ZENATA
Tunis
Qayrawan
Tripoli
Ghadames
To Cairo
Tuat
TUAREG
Fezzan
SANHAJA BERBERS
S A H A R A
Ghat
AHAGGAR MOUNTAINS
TIBESTI MOUNTAINS
Taghaza
Akjoujt
Walata
Tadmakka
S U D A N
Kumbi Saleh
SONGHAI
Gao
Agades
KANEM
Lake Chad
TAKRUR
GHANA
BAMBUK
Senegal R.
Niger R.
Niger R.

N

approximate traditional locations of peoples
trading routes
contemporary political boundaries

0 400 800 Miles
0 400 800 Kilometers

Trans-Saharan Trade Routes (*Facts On File*)

DUMAS. Saint-Georges' recorded works (on Columbia M 32781) include his String Quartet No. 1 in C Major; Symphony No. 1 in G Major; and a soprano aria from *Ernestine*.

Saint Maurice (Mauritius) (unknown–ca. A.D. 286) *Christian martyr, Roman soldier*

An African whose service in the Roman army brought him into conflict with his pagan commanders, Mauritius (his Latin name) belonged to a unit of Christian troops recruited from Thebaid, a region of Upper Egypt. The earliest known account of this Theban Legion, written around 450 by the Bishop Eucherius, tells how Mauritius and his companions, having been sent to put down a rebellion in what is now France, were executed by order of the general Maximian after they refused to offer sacrifices to the Roman gods. Later writers also claimed that Mauritius had refused to persecute fellow Christians living in the Rhône valley. The supposed site of the martyrdoms is Martigny, an area near Geneva, Switzerland.

During the Middle Ages, veneration of the Theban Legion became widespread in Europe. Relics of the martyrs were kept in a church built in their honor in the Swiss canton of Valais. Mauritius was designated a patron saint of foot soldiers and swordsmiths, and September 22 on the Gregorian calendar was celebrated as the feast day of St. Maurice and Companions.

Salem, Peter (1750–1816) *American Revolutionary War soldier*

Salem fought at Concord and fired the shot that killed Major John Pitcairn, the British commander at the Battle of Bunker Hill. A slave who had been freed so he could fight in the revolution, Salem served in the Revolutionary army until at least 1780 and possibly until 1782. According to one story, his fellow soldiers took up a collection for him as a reward for his actions at Bunker Hill, and he later met with General George Washington. The Sons of the American Revolution later erected a memorial to Peter Salem in Framingham, Massachusetts.

Samori Touré (ca. 1832–1900) *Mandinka slaver, military and political leader*

Born in Guinea, Samori had, by 1865, acquired a band of followers and declared himself king of Sanankoro, the village where he was born. He led numerous raids on villages in the Niger River region and expanded his territory until it covered several thousand square miles. In 1884, he declared it an official Muslim state and required all its inhabitants to accept Islam. He divided his kingdom into 10 administrative districts and required his troops to spend half of each year farming and half in military training. However, in 1882, his territorial designs brought him into conflict with the French. He attempted to join forces with Ahmadu, the FULANI king of the Macina region, and for a while he was able to play the French and the British off against each other. However, when a group of warriors commanded by his son massacred a British army unit, the British sent troops into the Ivory Coast to catch him. The French, alarmed by the British troop movements and anxious to forestall future British incursions, launched an offensive against Samori. He was finally captured in 1898 and died two years later while in exile in Gabon. His impressive military and administrative accomplishments have been overshadowed by his well-earned reputation for cruelty and his practice of selling all inhabitants of conquered villages into slavery in order to pay for the guns he needed to arm his followers. His grandson, Sekou Touré, later became president of Guinea.

Sao

A somewhat mysterious people who migrated from the Nile Valley to the Lake Chad region around the eighth century A.D. According to legend, the Sao were highly knowledgeable giants who possessed tremendous strength. They are famous for their pottery and also for developing the lost-wax technique of bronze casting. (In lost-wax casting, a clay model is coated with wax. The wax is then covered with perforated clay and heated. The wax melts and is "lost" through the holes in the clay, leaving a mold.) The Sao established a number of walled towns and developed a sophisticated political system in which women often played a major role. They intermarried with other groups moving into the area and eventually disappeared as a distinct people.

São Tomé e Príncipe

Tiny West African country consisting of two islands off GABON. Capital: São Tomé on the island of São Tomé. The islands were uninhabited in 1471 when the Portuguese arrived and turned them into a major supply center for slave ships traveling to the West Indies and a site for sugar plantations manned with slave labor. Although a successful slave revolt in 1530 caused many landowners to flee to Brazil, the islands remained an important port for slave ships. During the 18th and 19th centuries, the Portuguese established a number of large cocoa and coffee plantations and continued to utilize slave labor until the practice was abolished in 1875. Afterward, island landowners brought in contract laborers (*libertos*) from Angola but treated them so badly that England temporarily boycotted São Tomé cocoa in protest. After a temporary improvement, labor conditions again deteriorated, and in 1953 Portuguese troops fired on striking plantation workers, killing over 1,000 in the Batepa Massacre. A Movement for the Liberation of São Tomé and Príncipe (MLSTP) formed, and independence was finally achieved in 1974 after black troops mutinied. The new government nationalized most of the large plantations without compensation, resulting in a mass exodus of Portuguese. The country found political allies among the Communist bloc until the mid-1980s, when President Manuel Pinto da Costa sought better relations with the West. The population is made up of the descendants of slaves, the mixed-race descendants (mestizos) of slave laborers and Portuguese, migrant laborers, and Angolares, the descendants of slaves who survived a shipwreck in 1540.

Sara

A black tribal group living in southern CHAD. The Sara were a primary target of Arab slave traders and later of French colonialists who forced them to work on the Congo-Ocean railroad. The French also insisted the Sara grow cotton that could only be sold to a French company at an exceptionally low price. The practice of Sara women artificially stretching their lips grew out of a desire to make themselves unattractive to slave traders. Like many customs, the habit continued long after the need for it disappeared.

Savage, Augusta Christine Fells (1892–1962)
sculptor, teacher

The seventh of 14 children, Augusta Savage developed a lifelong interest in teaching when she was hired to teach sculpture for a dollar a day. After winning a $25 prize at a Florida county fair, she moved to New York. In 1923, Savage applied to a program in which American experts selected women for study in France. Savage was rejected because of race and remained bitter about the incident for the rest of her life. The resulting scandal brought her national attention and made Savage one of the first African-American artists to challenge the prejudices of the art establishment. That same year, she created a bust of W. E. B. DUBOIS that is considered the finest portrait of him ever made. She also sculpted a memorable portrait of MARCUS GARVEY. A few years later, Savage created what is probably her best-known work: a bust of a young boy titled *Gamin*. During the Great Depression, Savage successfully supervised a Works Progress Administration (WPA) arts project involving 1,500 students, but she repeatedly clashed with WPA bureaucrats over the ability of black artists to supervise white ones and white authority in regard to black art projects. In 1937, in a tribute to African-American music, Savage created one of her most famous works, *The Harp*, also known as *Lift Every Voice and Sing*. She is considered one of the leading artists of the HARLEM RENAISSANCE.

scarification

The procedure, prevalent in many African tribes, whereby people cut designs into their faces and bodies and pack the open wounds with ashes, juice from plants, or other materials in order to create scars. The custom is similar to the Western and Asian practice of tattooing and is generally done for the same reasons—decoration, initiation into various groups, and as an indication of status or position. Since tattoos do not show up well on dark skin, Africans often prefer scarification.

Scarification (*National Museum of African Art, Washington, D.C.*)

Schomburg, Arthur Alfonso (1874–1938)
bibliophile, curator, writer

Born and raised in Puerto Rico, Arthur Schomburg began collecting books and photographs on black history in the Caribbean while attending St. Thomas College in the Virgin Islands. After graduating, he became involved in political efforts to free Puerto Rico and Cuba from Spain. He moved to New York City in 1891 but continued his political work. Stating that "history must restore what slavery took away," Schomburg spent much of his life collecting thousands of books, manuscripts, pamphlets, prints, etchings, and photographs, some of which he described in "The Negro Digs Up His Past," which appeared in Alain Locke's *The New Negro*. His efforts were critical to the work of hundreds of historians. In 1940, the New York Public Library renamed its division of black history, literature, and prints after him.

Scott, Dred (ca. 1795–1858) *slave, subject of a major Supreme Court decision*

Dred Scott belonged to Dr. John Emerson, a U.S. army surgeon stationed in Missouri. Missouri was a slave state, but when Dr. Emerson was transferred to Illinois, a free state, and later to the free territory of Wisconsin, he took Scott with him. The Emerson family, along with Dred Scott, returned to Missouri in 1839, and Dr. Emerson died in 1843. At that point, Dred Scott tried to purchase his freedom, but Mrs. Emerson refused to allow it. So Scott sued, arguing that because he had lived in free territory, he should be free. (Bringing suit was not as easy as it sounds. Dred Scott got away with it because his owner supported him in his lawsuit but believed it was impossible simply to free him because Dr. Emerson had left him in trust for a minor child.) The case (*Scott v. Sandford** [sic]) went to the Supreme Court, which issued its decision on March 6, 1857. Ruling against Scott, the Court stated (1) that Scott was a black man and therefore was not a U.S. citizen and had no right to sue; (2) that he was a resident of Missouri and that the laws of Illinois

* The court misspelled Sanford's name.

Dred Scott, St. Louis, 1851 (*Library of Congress*)

did not apply to him; and (3) that people had the right to take their property (in this case, slaves) with them anywhere they went and Congress had no right to interfere. This third point meant that the 1820 Missouri Compromise, which stated that slavery was illegal north of 36°30' north latitude, was unconstitutional and that no state or territory could keep slavery out. The Dred Scott decision was of critical importance. It left many abolitionists with the feeling—accurate, as it turned out—that the political and judicial systems had failed and that only war could bring an end to slavery.

Scottsboro Boys

nine African-American youths, ages 12 through 20, who were falsely accused of rape in 1931. The nine youths had scrambled aboard a slow-moving freight train traveling through Alabama on March 25. Also hitching rides on the train were several other black men, a group of white boys, and two white women: Victoria Price and Ruby Bates. Several blacks got into a fight with the whites and forced them to jump from the train as it slowed down to pass a small town. The whites complained to the stationmaster, who wired ahead to have all African Americans on the train arrested at Scottsboro, the next stop. When the train was stopped, the women, who were both prostitutes, accused the nine black youths of rape.

Amid newspaper reports that described the nine youths as "savages" engaging in acts that "savored of the jungle," trial under Judge Alfred Hawkins began on April 6. The nine defendants were assigned an alcoholic lawyer who arrived at the courtroom drunk after having conferred with his nine clients for less than 30 minutes. In spite of the fact that a mob of several thousand people surrounded the courthouse and that the sheriff, fearing a lynching, had asked for National Guard protection, requests for a change of venue were denied. Charley Weems and Clarence Norris were the first defendants to be tried. The alleged victims offered contradictory stories, and the medical evidence did not indicate rape. Nonetheless, Weems and Norris were convicted after a trial that lasted less than two days. Both were sentenced to death. An hour after their case went to the jury, the trial of Haywood Patterson began. The state rested its case against Patterson the next morning, and the jury returned a guilty verdict 35 minutes later. Meanwhile, the trial of Ozie Powell, Willie Roberson, Andy Wright, Eugene Williams, and Olen Montgomery had already begun. Their case went to the jury at 4:30 that afternoon, and the trial of 12-year-old Roy Wright began. Judge Hawkins declared a mistrial in Roy Wright's case when the jury could not decide between the death penalty and life imprisonment. The verdicts in the Scottsboro Boys case resulted in nationwide protests, and the NATIONAL ASSOCIATION FOR THE ADVANCEMENT OF COLORED PEOPLE (NAACP) and the International Labor Defense (ILD) of the Communist Party became involved in a tug-of-war for the right to represent the nine during an appeal. On March 24, 1932, the Alabama Supreme Court upheld the convictions of all except Eugene Williams, who was granted a new trial since he was only 13, and therefore a juvenile. In November 1932, the U.S. Supreme Court, in a split decision, reversed the convictions of the other seven on grounds of inadequate counsel (*Powell v. Alabama*).

Haywood Patterson, one of the "Scottsboro Boys," who recounts the shameful story of his experiences in *Scottsboro Boy*, written with Earl Conrad (*Archive Photos*)

When Haywood Patterson was retried, Ruby Bates retracted her accusations and testified for the defense. However, the prosecutor, in reference to the new defense attorney, Samuel Leibowitz, demanded that the jury "show them that Alabama justice cannot be bought and sold with Jew money from New York." Patterson was again convicted and sentenced to death. The new judge, James Horton, convinced by the testimony that there had been no rape, later set the verdict aside and granted Patterson a new trial. He also transferred the case of Roy Wright to juvenile court and ordered the other cases postponed. Horton later was removed from the case and was defeated for reelection the next year.

In November 1933, seven of the nine (all except Eugene Williams and Roy Wright) were again placed on trial for their lives. Judge William Callahan made it clear he wanted convictions, and he got them. On April 1, 1934, the convictions were set aside by the U.S. Supreme Court on the grounds that blacks had been illegally excluded from the juries (*Norris v. Alabama*). Patterson, Weems, Norris, and Andy Wright (Roy's brother) were retried, convicted, and sentenced to terms ranging from 75 years to death (later commuted to life imprisonment–Norris). Ozie Powell pled guilty to assaulting a deputy and was sentenced to 20 years. Charges against the other four defendants were dropped. Roy Wright and Eugene Williams were juveniles, and the cases against the other two were even weaker than the rest. Olen Montgomery was almost completely blind, and Willie Roberson had been so severely afflicted with venereal disease that he could barely walk. Nonetheless, by the time they were released, they had each spent over six years in prison.

Weems was released on parole in 1943. Norris and Wright were released a year later, but were sent back to prison after leaving the state to seek work. Norris and Powell were released in 1946. Patterson escaped in 1948 and fled to Michigan, where Governor G. Mennen Williams refused to extradite him. Andrew Wright was paroled in 1950, 19 years and two months after he had been arrested.

Recommended Reading: Carter, Dan T. *Scottsboro: Tragedy of the American South.* Baton Rouge: Louisiana State University Press, 1979; Horne, Gerald. *Powell vs Alabama: The Scottsboro Boys and American Justice.* Danbury, Conn.: Franklin Watts, 1997.

segregation

The legal and social separation of whites and blacks in a wide range of situations in order to keep blacks

Segregated entrance of a movie theater, Michigan, October 1932. (*Library of Congress*)

Segregated restroom doors in the South, labeled "Ladies," "Men," and "Colored," 1960s (*Archive Photos*)

from advancing economically, socially, and politically and to prevent them from exercising their legal and political rights. In the South, segregation was "de jure," meaning it was defined by legislation. Hundreds of laws and local ordinances were enacted forcing African Americans to drink from separate water fountains, ride in separate railroad cars, attend separate schools, and sit in the back of buses. In many places, they were forbidden by law to borrow books from public libraries, swim in "white" pools, eat at "white" restaurants, use "white" restrooms, or try on clothes in department stores. Intermarriage between whites and blacks was subject to criminal penalties. On a federal level, African Americans were restricted to all-black units in the military and limited to certain duties. "De facto" segregation meant segregation based on custom rather than law and was often illegal. For example,

blacks in the North were often restricted to certain neighborhoods and denied the right to join unions.

Whites defended segregation as socially desirable and as part of the "natural order" of things, but its real purpose was political and economic. By isolating blacks socially from whites and by limiting much white-black interaction to employer-employee relationships, segregation reinforced ideas of white supremacy and usually prevented whites from working with blacks to end unjust and/or illegal practices. Segregation made it easier to deny blacks the vote and to prevent them from serving on juries or exercising other civil rights. It also made it almost impossible for blacks to join with working class whites to command better wages. Although individual whites (other than children) might enjoy a close personal relationship with an African American, the relationship was almost always one of employer-employee. In a society where whites held political and financial control, segregation made it difficult for blacks to find powerful white allies to help advance their concerns.

The practice of APARTHEID in SOUTH AFRICA was similar to segregation in the United States, but apartheid was much more extensive. The greater oppressiveness of the apartheid system stemmed from the fact that blacks in South Africa greatly outnumbered whites. In the United States, whites outnumbered blacks and felt less of a need for legal controls. The United States also differed from South Africa and other places in that U.S. laws and customs classified all persons as black who had any African ancestry, no matter how little. In South Africa and elsewhere, persons of mixed race were often subject to different laws and regulations. This racial fragmentation often leads to confusion. Many Africans regard CLARENCE THOMAS, who is dark-skinned, as the first African-American Supreme Court justice, rather than THURGOOD MARSHALL, who was light-skinned.

Selma

Alabama town where a major voting rights confrontation took place in 1963.

See also VOTING RIGHTS STRUGGLE; BLOODY SUNDAY.

Senegal, Republic of

West African country. Capital: Dakar. Early settlers included the Tukolor who established the Tekrur kingdom in the 10th century. During the 11th century the ALMORAVIDS, a Muslim group, rose to power and spread Islam throughout the area. The expansion of the MALI Empire in the 14th century led to the fall of the Tekrur state. Sometime after 1300, the Wolof in eastern Senegal established the kingdom of Jolof, which became powerful in the 15th century.

In 1444, Portuguese explorers reached the Senegal river and began a trade in gold dust and ivory. Several trading stations were established, including one at GORÉE Island that would later become a notorious holding pen for slaves. In the 17th century, the Senegal region became attractive to the Dutch and the French, who displaced the Portuguese. The second half of the 18th century witnessed a tug-of-war between the French and the British for control of Senegal. In the end, France retained its authority in Gorée and gradually extended its control into the interior of the region.

In 1895, Senegal was made a French colony and became a part of French West Africa. After World War II, all Senegalese were granted French citizenship, and LÉOPOLD SÉDAR SENGHOR became the dominant Senegalese political leader. In 1960, Senegal became an independent state within the French community. Economic problems and drought led to protests and civil unrest in the 1960s and early 1970s, and in 1982 and 1988 there were violent uprisings. In the 1990s, Senegal took in thousands of black Mauritanian refugees who were driven out of their country in a power struggle between tribal groups in the south and the ruling Arab-Berber class. Senegal enjoys a multiparty political system with a national assembly whose members are elected every five years. Violent clashes between government troops and the Mouvement des Forces Democratiques de Casamance (MFDC) have been a continuing problem in Senegal's Casamance region amid allegations of torture and murder by both MFDC and state security forces. Efforts to end the conflict are continuing.

Senghor, Léopold Sédar (1906–) *Senegalese statesman, poet*

Senghor was educated in Dakar, then the colonial capital of French West Africa, and later in Paris at the Sorbonne. During the 1930s, he was among the black intellectuals promoting the concept of NEGRITUDE, which emphasizes awareness of African-based culture and values. When World War II began, Senghor served in a French infantry battalion for colonial natives but was captured and imprisoned for three years. He was sent to a special punishment camp after he organized a resistance movement among the other African prisoners. After France's liberation, he served as a deputy from Senegal to the French national assembly, was elected mayor of Thies, Senegal, and was a member of the general council of Senegal.

As the best-known Senegalese outside his homeland, Senghor became a spokesman for those who wished to see France and her colonies united in a federation similar to the British Commonwealth. When Senegal became independent in 1960, Senghor, as president, tried to keep the French-speaking states together in the short-lived Mali Federation. This union quickly broke up, in part due to the opposition from Ivory Coast president FÉLIX HOUPHOUËT-BOIGNY.

Senghor was Senegal's president during its first 20 years of independence and encouraged close economic ties with France. He maintained his popularity until he retired in 1980, despite increasing agitation among Muslim factions (Senghor was Catholic) and the nation's largest ethnic group, the Wolofs.

Senghor wrote poetry in French but drew themes and imagery from his Serer tribal heritage. In 1984, Senghor became the first black man elected to the French Academy, the highest honor for French-speaking literary figures. His writings include *Chants d'Ombre* (1941), *Hosties Noires* (1948), *Chants pour Naett* (1949), *Ethiopiques* (1956), *Nocturnes* (1961), *Élégies majeures* (1979), and *The Poetry of Action* (1980).

Seychelles, Republic of

A 92-island archipelago located in the Indian Ocean about 600 miles north of Madagascar. The capital, Victoria, is located on Mahé Island, where most of the population lives. The islands were explored by Portuguese navigator Vasco da Gama in 1502 and claimed by France in 1756. Twelve years later, French settlers began bringing in slaves from Mauritius to work on the spice plantations. Following the Napoleonic Wars, England gained permanent control of the Seychelles through the 1814 Treaty of Paris. After Britain outlawed slavery in 1833, the British Navy often resettled slaves rescued from Indian Ocean slave ships in the Seychelles. In 1903, the Seychelles, which before had been administered in conjunction with Mauritius, was constituted a separate Crown colony. An elected legislative council was established in 1948, and independence was granted in 1976. Its first president, James Mancham, was overthrown in 1977 by France-Albert René,

who remains in power. In 1981, 50 South African mercenaries posing as rugby players tried to oust René in an unsuccessful coup. A new constitution authorizing a multiparty system was approved in 1993.

Shaka (Nodumehlezi or Sigidi) (1787–1828)
Zulu chief

Shaka was an illegitimate child. After his birth, his father, Chief Senzangakona, reluctantly took Nandi, Shaka's mother, as a third wife, but the marriage was unhappy. When Shaka was six, a dog killed one of the sheep he was tending, and the boy and his mother were sent away in disgrace. Other youngsters bullied him, and his childhood was unhappy.

In 1809, according to ZULU custom, Shaka's AGE GROUP was called up, and he became a soldier. He distinguished himself by utilizing the throwing spear as a stabbing weapon, which he redesigned as a shorter, heavy weapon with a massive blade (the *assagai*). He quickly came to the attention of Dingiswayo, chief of the Mtetwa, who began grooming Shaka to become Chief of the Zulu, then a small clan under Mtetwa domination. Dingiswayo also promoted him to regimental commander. Shaka forced his troops to go barefoot (as he did) to increase their running speed, developed new tactics for hand-to-hand combat, and instituted the famous Zulu battle formation mimicking the chest, horns, and loins of a cow. After a hugely successful campaign against Chief Zwide of the Ndwandwes, Shaka became commander in chief of all Dingiswayo's armies.

After the death of his father, Chief Senzangakona, in 1816, Shaka became chief of the Zulu clan. He established a capital at Kwa Bulaway, took steps to limit the power of the witch doctors, and immediately began building his own army. He also killed all those who had hurt or insulted him or his mother during his childhood and any who had opposed his chieftaincy. Shaka was popular with his troops due to his concern for their well-being, his willingness to reward those who fought well, and his policy of promoting men based on merit rather than tribal affiliation. As a result, many men from other tribes joined his army, even though discipline was extremely harsh and warriors were not allowed to marry until they reached senior status.

In 1818, the first Zulu-Ndwandwe war took place, ending with the famous battle of Qokli Hill in which about 7,500 Ndwandwe were killed within a 24-hour period. Dingiswayo was also killed during this period. After this battle, 1,000 warriors were allowed to marry and transfer from active duty to reserve status.

After a successful war against the Tembu, Shaka established a new capital and centralized his authority over the various clans. Contact with whites was limited, although Shaka made a point of demonstrating his power and his wealth (he had his 60,000 cattle—divided by color into herds of 5,000—driven past British emissaries). Although Shaka treated whites with deference, he and his counselors secretly assessed their military capabilities and determined the best methods of attacking them if necessary. When he was 38, Shaka was stabbed in an assassination attempt. Though he recovered, the assault triggered a brief war against the Ndwandwe, who were believed responsible.

In 1827, Nandi, Shaka's mother, died. More than 7,000 people were killed for failing to show sufficient remorse. Twelve thousand warriors were assigned to guard her grave for a year. The drinking of milk and the cultivation of crops was forbidden for a year, as was sex. Anyone found breaking these restrictions was executed. The food regulations were relaxed after two months, but pregnancy or failure to show remorse still rated a death penalty.

Shaka was assassinated by his stepbrothers Mhlangana and Dingane on September 22, 1828. When he first became chief, his domain stretched approximately 100 square miles, but within three years, Shaka had extended his control over a 7,000-square-mile area. At his death, his realm covered 200,000 square miles, and his influence was felt over a million-square-mile area.

Shange, Ntozake (N-toe-zaki SHONG-gay)
(1948–) *playwright, poet, novelist*
Born Paulette Williams, Shange grew up during the height of the civil rights movement in a family whose friends included W. E. B. DUBOIS, MILES DAVIS, and CHARLIE PARKER. She suffered from severe depression, which caused her to attempt suicide several times, but graduated with honors from Barnard College and earned a master's degree from the University of Southern California. She adopted her African name in 1971. Her play, *for colored girls who have considered suicide/when the rainbow is enuf,* opened on Broadway in 1976. Featuring 20 choreographed poems that depict women in various states, the show won an Obie Award and was nominated for Emmy, Grammy, and Tony awards. Other works include *Nappy Edges, Three Pieces, Sassafrass, Cypress and Indigo,* and *The Love Space Demands.*

sharecropping
System of tenant farming which arose in the South following the Civil War. Laborers agreed to work on a plantation or farm in return for one quarter to a half of the crop they raised. Initially, blacks who refused were sometimes arrested for vagrancy. Sharecroppers usually lived on the land they worked and might be provided with seed and tools. Poverty usually forced them to obtain credit from the

Sharecropper picking cotton in Pulaski County, Arkansas, 1935 (*Library of Congress*)

landowner, their share of the crop pledged in collateral. Even when the crop was good, tenants frequently were told their earnings did not equal the amount they had borrowed. Because of illiteracy, many sharecroppers were unable to challenge their landlords. Others were afraid to do so. In 1919, African-American sharecroppers in Arkansas attempted to form a union. After a gunfight with local whites, hundreds were arrested, 79 were indicted for murder, and scores were shot. More successful was the Sharecroppers Union established in 1931 in Tallapoosa, Alabama. By 1933, the union had 3,000 members, including some whites, in spite of harassment by vigilantes. Though it launched a semisuccessful strike in 1934, the union dissolved in 1936. Sharecropping declined in the 1950s and 1960s as mechanization on farms became prevalent.

See also ELAINE, ARKANSAS, INCIDENT; LABOR AND PROPERTY RIGHTS.

Sharpe, Samuel (unknown–1832) *slave leader in the Baptist War in Jamaica*

Sharpe had been a slave on the Croydon plantation near Montego Bay. He could read and write and was a deacon in the Baptist Church. He was aware that abolitionists in England were close to winning the battle to end slavery and urged slaves to hold a protest strike after the Christmas holidays and refuse to work without being paid. The strike began peacefully on December 27, 1831, but it soon turned into a violent rebellion that became known as the BAPTIST WAR. It was eventually put down with great brutality. Although Sam Sharpe had not advocated violence, he was executed in May 1832. His last words were, "I would rather die on yonder gallows than live in slavery." Two years later, slavery was ended in Jamaica. Sam Sharpe, often called "Daddy" Sharpe, is today regarded as a national hero in Jamaica, where the main square in Montego Bay is named for him.

sickle-cell anemia

inherited blood disorder in which a large number of red blood cells (erythrocytes) assume a sicklelike shape as opposed to a normal disclike shape. Sufferers of the disease are mainly blacks of West African ancestry. The abnormality offers some protection against malaria, although sickle-cell anemia is itself often fatal. Approximately one in 500 African Americans suffers from the disease, and an additional 8 percent to 13 percent carry the sickle-cell gene.

Sierra Leone, Republic of

West African country. Capital: Freetown. Portuguese explorers named the region Sierra Leone ("lion mountains") in 1460 and began a limited trade in ivory and slaves around 1500. In the mid-16th century, a number of small states were established in the area by Mande-speaking peoples, many of whom converted to Islam in the 18th century.

After the American Revolution (1775–1783), a number of freed slaves were resettled in Sierra Leone, but most of the colony died from disease, and Temne tribesmen killed the rest in a 1790 attack. A second settlement of 1,100 black soldiers who had supported the British during the American Revolution was established in 1787. After England outlawed the slave trade in 1807, it settled approximately 50,000 freed slaves in Freetown, which it used as a naval base for antislaving patrols. The descendants of these freed slaves are known as Creoles. In 1896, England established a protectorate in the area and instituted a special tax to pay administrative costs. Two years later, a Temne chief named Bai Bureh led an unsuccessful uprising called the Hut Tax War.

In the 1950s, Africans were given increased political rights, and the colony became independent in 1961. Since then, Sierra Leone has been torn by several coups and sporadic civil unrest. In 1971, Siaka Stevens took power with the help of troops from Guinea, but his handpicked successor, Joseph Saidu Momoh, was ousted during a military coup in 1992.

In 1997, noncommissioned army officers overthrew the government of Ahmad Tejan Kabbah, who had been elected the year before. The rebels were driven out by the Nigerian-led Economic Community of West African States Military Observer Group (ECOMOG), and Kabbah was returned to power in 1998. The rebels then joined another antigovernment guerrilla organization called the Revolutionary United Front (RUF), which was headed by Foday Sankoh, a former photographer and army corporal. With military support from Liberia's president Charles Taylor, the rebel groups greatly expanded the civil conflict that had been going on since 1991. In an effort to terrorize the civilian population into ending support for the government, RUF terrorists cut off the hands, feet, lips, ears, and/or genitals of thousands of people, including hundreds of small children. The aim of the RUF was to control the gold and diamond mines in Sierra Leone's western region. The failure of Western nations to extend much support to Sierra Leone's government, in spite of the incredible atrocities committed by rebel troops, forced President Kabbah to agree to peace talks in July 1999. An agreement was reached whereby the rebel forces were granted amnesty for all atrocities and given several government cabinet posts, including control of mining operations. After the peace agreement was signed, Johnny Paul Koroma, one of the rebel leaders, visited a camp sheltering about 500 mutilated refugees, broke down in tears, and asked for forgiveness. The amputees rejected his appeal. In October 1999, fighting broke out between the rebel groups. Several months later, in May 2000, four United Nations peacekeepers were killed and more than 500 taken hostage by RUF soldiers but later released. In May 2000, RUF leader Foday Sankeh was captured and turned over to authorities for trial.

Simpson, Orenthal James (O. J. Simpson)
(1947–) *athlete, television sports commentator, defendant in sensational murder trial*
Born in California, O. J. Simpson attended the University of Southern California, where he won the Heisman Trophy in 1968. He joined the Buffalo Bills football team in 1969, retiring in 1978 after a very successful career. He later appeared in several movies and became a popular sports commentator for ABC and NBC. In 1994, he was accused of brutally stabbing to death his white ex-wife, Nicole Brown Simpson, and her friend Ron Goldman. His trial lasted nine months and was televised daily to a worldwide audience. During the entire period the case was being investigated and tried, it was a con-

tinuing topic on hundreds of radio and television programs. More than fifty books were written about it.

The Simpson case revealed an enormous racial divide in America in regard to the fairness of the CRIMINAL JUSTICE SYSTEM. Two-thirds of the black community believed the prosecution had failed to meet its burden of proof and that Simpson should be found not guilty. Eighty percent of whites thought he should have been convicted. The readiness of much of the black community to believe that police would manufacture or manipulate evidence to ensure the conviction of a black defendant revealed a deeply held cynicism. When it was discovered that a key police officer had a history of racist behavior, whites argued that the officer's past was irrelevant, while blacks insisted it was of crucial importance in determining whether he had tampered with evidence. The case was also notable for the enormous anger it generated in much of the white community, along with a thinly disguised contempt for Simpson's defenders. After Simpson was acquitted by a predominantly black jury, whites bitterly accused defense attorneys of "playing the race card," and many stated that no prosecution could have succeeded given the jury's racial makeup. In fact, black juries have frequently convicted black defendants. While the evidence against Simpson was strong, a number of trial lawyers who believe Simpson was guilty attributed the acquittal, at least in part, to prosecution errors rather than racial bias.

Shortly after Simpson was acquitted, he was sued by the families of Nicole Brown Simpson and Ron Goldman. In 1997, he was found responsible for their deaths and ordered to pay damages of $33.5 million.

Singleton, Benjamin ("Pap") (1809–1892)
leader of the Exodusters
Born a slave in Tennessee, Singleton made several unsuccessful escape attempts before running away and settling in Detroit. After the Civil War, he returned to Nashville, where he began helping small groups of ex-slaves find land in Kansas under the 1862 Homestead Act. The numbers increased after 1874 when he formed the Edgefield Real Estate and

Homestead Association. When thousands of former slaves began fleeing the South in what was called the Exodus of 1879, Singleton took credit for the mass migration. He had, in fact, printed and circulated thousands of posters urging blacks to leave the South. Later he tried to arrange for the resettlement of African Americans in Cyprus and Africa. (See also EXODUSTERS.)

sit-in movement

Movement that began in Greensboro, North Carolina, on February 1, 1960, when Ezell Blair, Joseph McNeil, David Richmond, and Franklin McClain, four students from North Carolina Agricultural and Technical College, entered an F. W. Woolworth store, sat down at a lunch counter, ordered coffee, and then refused to leave when told the counter was for whites only. The following day, the four returned with 16 additional students. Again they were refused service, and again they refused to leave. On Wednesday, February 3, 70 students, including some whites, arrived to continue what was now known nationwide as a "sit-in." By the 10th day, the sit-in movement had spread to five other states. Students were now being arrested and charged with tresspassing and disorderly conduct. Over the next two years, more than 70,000 people, black and white, became involved in the sit-in movement, and

A policeman speaks with black protesters during a sit-in at Brown's Basement Luncheonette, Oklahoma, 1958. (*Shel Hershorn, UT Austin/Archive Photos*)

the tactic had spread to encompass kneel-ins at segregated churches, swim-ins at segregated pools, and read-ins at segregated libraries. People also protested segregated seating arrangements at theaters and the refusal of department stores to allow blacks to try on clothes before buying them. Thousands of protesters were arrested, and more than 100 students expelled from their schools. Many businesses succumbed to the pressure and integrated their facilities. Others were forced to integrate with the passage of the CIVIL RIGHTS ACT OF 1964. The sit-in movement led to the formation of the STUDENT NON-VIOLENT COORDINATING COMMITTEE (SNCC).

Sixteenth Street Baptist Church bombing

A bombing that occurred at the Sixteenth Street Baptist Church in Birmingham, Alabama, on Sunday morning, September 15, 1963, just 18 days after the historic MARCH ON WASHINGTON. Four young girls, Denise McNair, Addie Mae Collins, Cynthia Wesley, and Carole Robertson, were killed, and more than 20 people were injured. Another young boy was shot that same weekend while riding his bicycle, and one black man was killed by police as hundreds of angry African Americans roamed the streets. The church had been a rallying point for marches and other civil rights activities. On May 17, 2000, nearly 37 years after the bombing, Thomas E. Blanton Jr. and Bobby Frank Cherry, both of whom were affiliated with the Ku Klux Klan, were charged with the crime. They had allegedly been aided by Robert Chambliss, who was imprisoned for the crime in 1977, and Herman Cash, who died in 1994 and was never charged.

Recommended Viewing: *4 Little Girls*, a documentary by Spike Lee.

Slave Coast

European slave traders' name for the coastal area of present-day Benin, referring to the huge number of slaves offered for sale there. Major ports included Ouidah (Waydah), which as early as the 1680s was said to produce 1,000 slaves a month. Landing along the Slave Coast was dangerous because of the surf, and the canoes carrying slaves to the ships were often upset, resulting in much loss of life due to the shark-filled waters. Trading there required the payment of various fees and customs duties to the king of DAHOMEY, along with many presents to royal retainers and servants. Other expenses involved the leasing of canoes to take slaves to the ships, the hiring of a messenger to announce the ship's arrival to the king, a gong beater to announce the opening of trade, interpreters, guards, and porters to protect goods to be traded, and various servants to assist in entertaining officials. Ironically, the Slave Coast became less important as a trade center in the late 1700s, when the transatlantic slave trade reached its height.

slavery

condition of bondage in which one individual is considered the property of another. Until modern times, slavery was a common phenomenon, practiced by many peoples around the world. It was accepted in Africa as the fate of prisoners of war and as appropriate punishment for criminal activity. Unlike the captives brought to the Americas, however, such slaves frequently retained important rights and were often able to work off their obligations. Slaves in Africa were not looked upon as subhuman or racially inferior; rather, they were regarded as outside the tribal group or clan and therefore not subject to its protections. As a slave lived with a tribe or family, his or her status might change. For example, a slave who adopted the religion of his owner or a slave woman who had children by her master might gain the right not to be sold. In effect, they would become less a slave, and more an official member of the tribe.

Prior to A.D. 1500, the demand for African slaves was limited, since the economic systems of Africa, Europe, and the Middle East were not based on vast plantation systems requiring millions of slave laborers. For much of recorded time, the supply of black slaves was also limited by the impossibility of transporting huge numbers of people across oceans or deserts. After camels were introduced into the Sahara around 500–100 B.C., the traffic in

African slaves increased to about 2,000–3,000 a year, since camels could carry the food and water that made regular caravans, including slave caravans, possible. Most captives were women who were shipped from the seaports of North and East Africa to various Mediterranean, Indian, and Arabian markets for sale as concubines, domestic servants, or agricultural laborers. An exception to this occurred during the ninth century when thousands of captives were imported from East Africa to Iraq to clear marshland. (See also ZANJ REBELLION.)

Once ARABS began arriving in North Africa in large numbers in the seventh century, they enslaved thousands of African prisoners of war, who frequently were forced to become soldiers in Moslem armies. The Arabs also became heavily involved in the commercial slave trade that stretched from North Africa across the Sahara. After A.D. 900, the number of African slaves sold abroad rose to about 8,700 annually, as Europeans found it more difficult to acquire white slaves from the Balkans and Middle East, due to the disruptions caused by the Crusades, the rise of the Ottoman Empire, and the appearance of Tamerlane, a Mongol conqueror whose military campaigns spread terror through much of the Middle East. Another reason for the increased demand was the bubonic plague, which wiped out a quarter of the population of 14th-century Europe, killing thousands of white laborers. Moorish control of the Iberian Peninsula also contributed to the expanded trade, and Spain, Portugal, and Italy turned to sub-Saharan Africa for workers even before the discovery of the Americas. By the early 16th century, approximately 10 percent of Lisbon's population consisted of African slaves.

East Coast African Slave Trade

The East Coast slave trade is often referred to as the Arab slave trade; however, this phrase is somewhat misleading. Early travelers to the area generally referred to any Muslim who was not of pure black African ancestry as Arab. Although many slave traders were of Arab descent, many, including the notorious TIPPU TIP, were of mixed Afro-Arab ancestry. As the demand for slaves increased in the West, it increased in the East also, where it was closely linked to the trade in ivory. Slave traders made regular trips deep into the interior, buying ivory from various tribes and acquiring approximately 1,000 captives per trip through raids on villages. Captives carried the ivory on their heads. If a captive woman with a baby tied to her back became too weak to carry both child and ivory, the baby was killed or abandoned along the trail. After weeks or months of marching, the slave caravans arrived at East African seaports where the victims were often transferred to ships taking them to Zanzibar for sale and from there to Brazil, Mauritius, and Réunion (then known as Mascarenes) or the Arabian Peninsula. Those slaves who became sick on the voyage to Zanzibar were thrown overboard to avoid paying customs duties on them. The East African slave trade, although involving fewer victims, lasted longer than the West Coast trade. Slaves continued to be imported into Zanzibar until 1889.

Transatlantic Slave Trade

Once it became clear that huge fortunes could be made in the Americas from gold mining and sugar production, the demand for slaves escalated dramatically. Since the Europeans lacked the military strength to take African slaves by force, they went into partnership with local kings and village chiefs who received a commission on each slave sold. As far as the African rulers were concerned, their relationships with the Europeans were no different from those they had formed with other trading partners over the years. But the Europeans' constant demands for more slaves could only be met through the acquisition of prisoners captured in raids on neighboring tribes. As raiding to acquire captives became more frequent, defense became a primary concern, especially as firearms became more effective. To protect their own people from slave raiders, African rulers soon realized they had to have guns, which they could secure only from the Europeans in exchange for slaves. In short, the Africans faced the choice of either providing slaves to the European traders or risk being enslaved themselves. The result was an arms race, with huge quantities of weapons pouring into Africa. In the 1700s, when the slave trade was at its height, 100,000 to 150,000 muskets were exported to Africa each year from Birmingham, England, alone. Several African kings tried to limit

The Africans of the slave bark *Wildfire* (*Library of Congress*)

or halt the trade, but the corrupting influence of slave trade money often made them targets for rivals, who—with European help—were willing to overthrow them. (See KONGO.)

The demand for guns, combined with greed, resulted in the development of West African states dependent on slave trading for survival and led to a huge buildup of slavery within Africa itself. The armies of slave-trading states were often largely made up of slave warriors, who themselves might be given slaves as a reward after successful raids. Such states also needed slaves as agricultural workers to provide food for their armies and for the slave ships that brought provisions for the journey across the Atlantic. By the end of the 19th century, slavery was so widespread within parts of West Africa that when those territories became English colonies, the British, who had outlawed slavery elsewhere, feared that ending the practice in Africa would cause economic and agricultural disaster and outlawed only the sale of slaves.

Death Rates/Numbers of Victims

According to ships' records, bills of sale, and various tax and other documents, it is estimated that approximately 12 million slaves were legally imported into the New World between 1500 and 1880. Thousands of others were illegally smuggled into the Americas after the transatlantic slave trade was outlawed by Great Britain, the United States, and various other countries in the early 1800s.

Most slave deaths were due to severe dehydration. Ordinarily, a 150-pound man will take in over two quarts of water a day in food and liquid form. Slaves aboard ship were generally given one pint of water and two meals of boiled vegetables a day. Frequently, bad weather or lack of winds caused delays, and food and water ran short. On one voyage, slaves received only a teacup of water every three days. The results were disastrous. Temperatures in the holds of slave ships regularly reached 100° to 120°, with air quality so bad that candles sometimes would not burn. Between 400 and 700 sweat-drenched slaves were generally packed together, in spaces so small they could not stand. What food and water there was, was frequently contaminated, resulting in bacillary and amebic dysentery (the infamous "bloody flux" and "white flux"), both of which caused severe vomiting and diarrhea, and thus a further loss of water. Descriptions of the majority of slave deaths are consistent with shock due to extreme dehydration, with electrolyte loss and a resulting fall in blood pressure. Diseases such as smallpox were also a frequent and fatal problem. So many slaves arrived in the Americas in extremely poor condition that special recuperation farms had to be set up to rehabilitate them so they could be sold. In spite of this, approximately 40 percent of those sent to the farms died within a few days of landing.

Estimates of average death rates during the Atlantic crossing range from 9.5 percent to 25 percent. Records published by the British Royal African Company for the years 1680 to 1688 show shipments of 60,783 slaves, with a death rate of 23.6 percent. French data indicate 35,927 Africans died aboard French ships during the years 1715 to 1775, a rate of 14.9 percent. A Spanish frigate, the *Amistad,* lost 545 out of 733 captives—a death rate of 74.3 percent. While this was unusually high, it was far from being an isolated occurrence.

Another indication of slave death rates can be inferred from the number of crew members who died. A House of Commons report placed mortality rates among slave ship crew members during the 1780s at 21 percent. Though crew members were probably more susceptible to malaria than the Africans, they enjoyed better food and water and did not suffer the dehydration of those chained in the hold. Also, we can assume crew members were in reasonably good health when they boarded ship; the large number of slaves suffering from scurvy, whose symptoms take months to appear, indicates that many of them were severely malnourished to begin with. If the mortality rate for crew members was 21 percent, that of the slaves was undoubtly greater.

In addition, many estimates are based on the number of slaves who died aboard ships that actually reached their destinations. Shipwreck, with the loss of all aboard, was a real possibility, especially since a majority of vessels were headed for the Caribbean, a major hurricane center for several months of the year.

The main factors influencing the death rates were length of voyage, season of year, and "close" versus "loose" packing. The longer the voyage, the higher the mortality rate. Bad weather meant that slaves were kept below decks day and night, and that gratings and ventilation openings were closed, no matter how hot the holds became. As a result, death rates were higher during the rainy season. In the 19th century, newer slave ships were built to carry more water. However, this advantage was off-set by the increased tendency to pack slaves more closely together and by the increase in the slave trade from Mozambique to Brazil. "Close packing" meant more fatalities, and the greater distances involved in the Mozambique/Brazil trade meant longer voyages with an average death rate of 25.8 percent.

After the British and the United States outlawed the slave trade in 1807–08, ship captains caught with slaves on board forfeited their vessels. To avoid this, when escape from antislaving patrols was impossible, many slave ship captains would simply destroy the evidence. Captain Homans of the *Bril-*

lante tied 600 slaves to the anchor chain and threw them overboard when surrounded by British cruisers one evening. Even though the cries of the drowning slaves could be heard by British sailors and the *Brillante* still carried manacles and other evidence, Homans went free, since no slaves were found aboard his ship.

During the approximately 380 years the transatlantic slave trade was in operation, it is estimated that at least 12 million slaves were imported into the Americas and that an additional 1.3 to 4 million people died aboard ship. The 12 million figure represents those people who survived not only the slave ships but also the initial capture, forced marches to the African coast, and imprisonment in BARRACOONS; for every slave loaded aboard a slave ship, three or four others died before ever reaching the African coast. It is generally accepted that since they were easier to catch, many more women and children than men were seized. However, 65 percent to 70 percent of those loaded aboard the slave ships were men. While thousands of captured women and girls were kept in Africa to provide agricultural labor and as wives for soldiers, these cannot possibly account for the huge difference in numbers between those believed captured and those sold to the European slavers. Moreover, it is thought that the overall population of Africa in the area between Senegal and Angola fell or stagnated between 1730 and 1850. Part of this drop was due to the numbers shipped abroad (mostly men) and to population displacement, but a dramatic fall in population in such a broad area generally reflects a drop in the number of women of childbearing age. Given the fact that many African cultures were polygamous (each man had several wives), it is unlikely that millions of female captives could have remained alive in Africa and simply never married or had children.

Slave Ship Mutinies

Mutinies aboard slave ships were a constant threat, occurring most often when slaves were brought up on deck for exercise and meals. Capt. William Snelgrave, a British slaver, in an account published in 1754, described three attempted mutinies that he had personally witnessed, as well as the deaths of almost 80 Africans in an unsuccessful mutiny aboard the *Ferres Galley*. Several African survivors of the *Ferres* mutiny starved themselves to death afterward, and others twice more attempted to mutiny after the ship arrived in Jamaica. COROMANTEE Africans were exceptionally dangerous, according to Snelgrave, who referred to them, stating, "I knew of several Voyages had proved unsuccessful by Mutinies; as they occasioned either the total loss of the Ship and the white Men's Lives; or at least by rendering it absolutely necessary to kill or wound a great number of Slaves, in order to prevent a total Destruction."[1] Two slave ship mutinies in which U.S. officials became involved were the AMISTAD and the CREOLE mutinies.

Merchant Companies

From the 16th century, European countries granted monopolies and special privileges to associations of merchants. Queen Elizabeth I chartered the Levant Co. (1581) and the British East India Co. (1600). The Royal African Co., which later dominated slave-trade shipping from Liverpool, was chartered by King Charles II in 1664. The Dutch East India Co. (1602) and the Dutch West India Co. (1621) also reaped huge profits in the 17th-century slave trade. Slave-trading French companies included the Compagnie de Guinée and Compagnie du Sénégal, both of which were absorbed in 1721 by the Compagnie des Indes Orientales. These companies were not like modern monopolies: They did not control their "product" from enslavement in Africa to sale in the New World. Rather, they were investor-funded middlemen, controlling much of the shipping that made intercontinental trade possible.

Slave Life

Half of the slaves in the U.S. South lived on farms with 20 or fewer slaves. Their owners worked in the fields with them, ate the same food, and were more likely to be considerate. However, the close daily interaction between the two groups meant that

[1] George Francis Dow, *Slave Ships and Slaving*. Salem, Mass.: Marine Research Society; Brattleboro, Vt.: Hildreth, 1927, p. 123.

SOUTHERN SCENES IN 1846.

Murder of Slaves.

The Abbeville (S. C.) Banner states, that two of Gov. McDuffie's slaves were killed on Friday, Feb. 13th, by two other slaves, acting in the capacity of *drivers!* They were killed by what the law terms "moderate correction!"

A Slave Woman attempting Suicide at Baltimore.

In June, 1846, the Baltimore Sun gave an account of a woman who "jumped out of the window of the place in which her owner had confined her, and immediately took the nearest route to throw herself into the water." She was rescued. But, says the Sun, "Upon being taken upon the deck of the vessel, she begged the by-standers to let her drown herself, stating, that she would 'sooner be dead, than go back again *to be beaten as she had been!*'"

A Slave Suicide effected at Richmond, Va.

A correspondent of the Philadelphia Inquirer, July 25, 1846, wrote from Richmond, as follows:—"An unpleasant occurrence took place in this city yesterday. A man, who has a number of negroes in his employment, was proceeding, for a slight offence, to punish one of them by whipping, when the poor wretch, knowing his master's unmerciful nature, implored that he might be *hung* at once, instead of whipped. This of course would not answer, and on tying the negro's hands behind him in the usual manner, the employer went into another room to procure a cowhide, when the negro, taking advantage of his master's absence, rushed from the room, jumped into the river, and was drowned."

Slave Suicide and Slave Hunting in Louisiana.

In June, 1846, the New Orleans Commercial Times said—"We learn that a few days since a negro man, belonging to Captain Newport, of East Baton Rouge, while closely pursued by the dogs of Mr. Roark, of this Parish, ascended a tree and hung himself. Mr. Roark, with Captain Newport's son-in-law and overseer, were in pursuit of a runaway slave. They did not know that this negro was out, and were surprised upon their arrival, a few minutes in the rear of the dogs, to find him suspended by his neck, with his feet dangling only a foot or two from the earth. Every effort was made to restore animation, but without success, although on their coming up the body was still warm. The act was one, it would seem, of resolute predetermination, as the slave was well provided with cords, which he made use of to perpetrate his suicidal purpose."

More Murders of Slaves.

The Palmyra (Mo.) Courier, in August, 1846, says:—"We understand that a gentleman, living in Macon county, while out hunting with his rifle, last week, came suddenly upon two fugitive slaves, who gave him battle. He shot one, and split the other's skull with the barrel of his gun. He then started for home, but before reaching it he met a man in the road, who inquired if he had seen or heard of two runaway negroes—describing them. The gentleman replied, that he had just killed two, and related the circumstance. On proceeding to the spot, the stranger identified them as his slaves.

THE FUGITIVE SLAVE.

A Slave Hunter Killed.

The following is from the Washington (Pa.) Patriot of 1846: "We learn that a few days ago, a fugitive slave from Maryland was pursued and overtaken in Somerset county, in this State by a man named Holland, a wagoner from Ohio, who was tempted to the task by the reward offered, $150. When they reached McCarty's tavern the slave attempted to escape, but was caught by Holland while in the act of climbing a fence. The slave drew a long knife, which he had concealed about his person, and plunged it into Holland's heart, causing his death instantly. He made good his escape, immediately pursued by the people of the neighborhood, who at nightfall had surrounded him, but in the darkness of the night he eluded their vigilance, and is now beyond their reach."

The Rights of the Fugitive.

The Hon. J. R. Giddings, in a speech in the House of Representatives, at Washington, Feb. 18, 1846, said—"In regard to arresting slaves, we [of the free States] owe no duties to the master; on the contrary, all our sympathies, our feelings, and our moral duties, beyond what I have stated, are with the slave. We will neither arrest him for the master, nor will we assist the master in making such arrest. I am aware that the third clause of the second section of the first article of the Constitution was once believed, by some, to impose upon the people of these free States the duty of arresting fugitive slaves. But it is now judicially settled that no such obligation rests upon us. Indeed a proposition to impose upon us such a duty, at the time of framing the Constitution, was rejected, without a division, by the Convention. We, therefore, leave the master to arrest the slave if he can; and we leave the slave to defend himself against the master if he can. We do not interfere between them. The slave possesses as perfect a right to defend his person and his liberty against the master as any citizen of our State. Our laws protect him against every other person, except the master or his agent, but they leave him to protect himself against them. If he, while defending himself, slays the master, our laws do not interfere to punish him in any way, further than they would any other person who should slay a man in actual self-defence. The laws of the slave State cannot reach him, nor is there any law, of God or man, that condemns him. On the contrary, our reason, our judgment, our humanity approves the act; and we admire the courage and firmness with which he defends the "inalienable rights with which the God of Nature has endowed him. We regard him as a hero worthy of imitation; and we place his name in the same category with that of Madison Washington, who, on board the Creole, boldly maintained his God-given rights, against those inhuman pirates who were carrying him and his fellow-servants to a worse than savage slave-market."

ANOTHER SLAVE SUICIDE. "The slave of a farmer in an adjoining county, (Jefferson,) having been jumped upon and stamped by his master, *with spurs on,* so as to cruelly lacerate his face as well as his body, he was found, next morning, in an adjacent pond or stream of water—having tied a stone to his own neck, (as it is said,) and plunged in, for the successful purpose of drowning himself, under the feelings of desperation caused by the fiendish treatment of his master!"—*Balt. Sat. Visiter, Aug.,* 1846.

Southern scenes, 1846 (*Library of Congress*)

those slaves whose masters were cruel suffered to a much greater degree. Because small farmers were poorer, their slaves were often malnourished and were more likely to be sold in bad economic times. They were also more likely to be rented out, a practice that increased the risk of mistreatment. Slaves on large plantations were divided into three groups: field hands, house slaves, and those with particular skills, such as blacksmiths, drivers, or carpenters. Infants, toddlers, and young children were often turned over to older female slaves to care for while the mothers were at work. Poorly clothed, and sometimes fed in groups from a trough, many of these children died from neglect, sickness, and malnutrition.

Most of the larger plantations in the United States had resident owners. Although these plantations had overseers, the presence of a resident owner tended to restrict—though not eliminate—an overseer's harsh treatment. In the Caribbean, the majority of plantations had absentee owners. Treatment of slaves there was extremely harsh, and most slaves died within five years of arriving from Africa.

Slave Codes

These laws covered all aspects of slave life. The 20 Africans who arrived in Jamestown in 1619 were viewed more as indentured servants than slaves, but by 1640, some blacks in Virginia had become bondsmen for life. Slavery in Virginia was formally recognized by law in 1661, and the following year it was declared that children could be born into slavery according to the condition—slave or free—of their mother. Although slavery spread more rapidly in the South, it eventually became legal throughout the American colonies. In general, the slave codes focused on the ownership rights of whites and the safety of the white community. Slaves could not testify in court except in cases involving other blacks, and they could not contract for their services without the approval of their owners. They could not possess firearms or strike a white person, even in self-defense. They were not allowed to assemble, even for religious purposes, without a white person in attendance and were not allowed to learn to read and write. Slaves were required to have written permission to travel and could be branded or maimed for insolence or association with free blacks. Only two states actually forbade the breakup of slave families, and those laws referred only to the separation of children under 10 from their mothers. Slaves were sometimes tried in regular courts, but in general, owners enforced the laws and determined punishments. Most offenses were punishable by whipping, but more serious ones might result in branding, maiming, or death. Though some laws were enacted for the purpose of protecting slaves, they were rarely enforced. Murder, torture, assault, rape, and child neglect/abuse were common.

Where slaves were concentrated in large numbers, as in Jamaica, Cuba, or Peru, the laws were often exceptionally harsh. Slaves found on the streets of Lima, Peru, after dark were given 100 lashes for a first offense. But in the Spanish and Portuguese colonies, there was greater respect for slaves as persons. Intermarriage between blacks and whites was common, and masters were not allowed to work their slaves on Sundays or on approximately 30 Catholic feast days. Slaves in Brazil were allowed to read and write, and manu-

mission (the freeing of a slave by his/her owner) was encouraged.

Slaves in French colonies were governed under the 1685 Code Noir. The code required that slaves be instructed in Catholicism and that they not be required to work on Sundays and holy days. Punishments were limited to whipping and putting slaves in irons, and it was illegal to break up families through sale. Slaves had the right to complain to a legal officer if a master failed to carry out his legal responsibilities, and freed slaves were guaranteed the same rights as other Frenchmen. However, as the number of slaves grew, those aspects of the code dealing with owner responsibilities and slave rights were generally ignored.

Though free African Americans in the United States were not subject to the slave codes, their rights were greatly restricted. In several states, free blacks were required to register with state authorities, and some states insisted they have white guardians. Free African Americans were barred from entering many southern states, and laws limiting contact between slaves and free blacks were vigorously enforced. Other laws made it difficult for free African Americans to compete economically with whites. It was extremely difficult for African Americans to fight these restrictions, since in many states they were denied the vote.

Inherent in the slave codes, and clearly spelled out in several southern state court rulings, was the recognition that slaves were human beings and therefore not the same as other property. They could be held responsible for their actions, and they had certain, limited rights, which owners were supposed to respect. The acknowledgment that slaves were human was used by abolitionists to demand an end to slavery and by many who justified slavery as a way to bring "civilization" to blacks.

Slave Revolts

Over 250 organized slave revolts and conspiracies took place in what is now United States territory. Thousands of others occurred in the Caribbean and in Central and South America. The first slave revolt in the New World took place in 1522 on the island of Hispaniola; the first one to occur in what is now the United States took place in South Carolina in

1526. In the South Carolina rebellion, slaves in a Spanish settlement took advantage of trouble with local Indians to revolt and flee. One month later, the approximately 150 whites—all that remained of the Spanish settlers—packed up and returned to Hispaniola, leaving the ex-slaves the first permanent non-Indian residents north of the Rio Grande.

Major precipitating factors in slave revolts were cruelty and harsh living conditions, favorable black/white population ratios, the possibility of taking advantage of wars and conflicts, and the philosophical impact of the French, Haitian, and American Revolutions. Periods of economic depression were particularly likely to trigger slave uprisings, since living conditions generally worsened, food was usually scarce, and owners frequently sold slaves to pay debts, a practice that often broke up families. The poor economic situation in the late 1730s resulted in numerous plots, culminating in the STONO, SOUTH CAROLINA, REBELLION in 1739. In an effort to stem the unrest, the South Carolina colonial government passed laws requiring better food and clothing for slaves and that they not be worked more than 14 hours a day in winter and 15 hours a day in summer. However, the legislators also ordered that bounties be paid for the scalps of runaways, an indication that this typical carrot and stick system of control placed its main emphasis on the stick.

The ratio of blacks to whites influenced not only the frequency of revolts but also their probable success. At the time of the Haitian Revolution, Haiti's population figures indicate 30,000 whites 24,000 free blacks, and 452,000 slaves. In Jamaica and Guyana, slaves outnumbered whites ten to one. Both these areas averaged a major revolt every two years between 1731 and 1832. In the United States, where whites generally outnumbered blacks, there were many fewer revolts than in the Caribbean. The most successful U.S. revolt was that led by Nat Turner in Southhampton, Virginia, in 1831. There, the population figures read 6,574 whites and 9,501 blacks.

The American Revolution, with its explosive concept of a God-given right to freedom, liberty, and individual rights resounded with shattering force, and the period from 1776 to 1810 was marked by intense and widespread slave unrest. It was during this time that GABRIEL PROSSER attempted his 1,000-man uprising in Virginia. The reverberations of the Haitian Revolution, which ended slavery on the island, were felt for years throughout the Western Hemisphere. DENMARK VESEY was only one of several insurrectionists influenced by it. The psychological impact of the Haitian victory was magnified by the fact that it overlapped the French Revolution and followed directly on the heels of the American War for Independence.

Slaves often saw other conflicts as being to their advantage. Fighting between the British and the French and tension between colonists and Iroquois Indians helped trigger a serious uprising in 1712 in New York, and slaves in the Stono Rebellion were partially motivated by promises of freedom offered by Spanish leaders attempting to undermine British authority.

The U.S. conflict that generated the most slave unrest was the Civil War. Drafting white men for the Confederate army was often opposed on the grounds that it left the remaining white population vulnerable to slave revolts. More critical was the fact that over 200,000 African Americans, most of them runaway slaves, enlisted to fight for the Union. An additional 200,000 black men and women served the U.S. Army as scouts, guides, nurses, cooks, and laborers. As with the soldiers, most of these people were slaves who took advantage of Confederate retreats to escape to Union lines. The situation was summed up by a slave named Scipio who predicted shortly before hostilities broke out that, in case of war between the North and South, the South would lose because "they'll fight with only one hand. When they fight the North with the right hand, they'll have to hold the Negro with the left."[2] Rebelling slaves sometimes received help from Native Americans and/or MAROONS (runaway slaves), and white support for slave revolts was not uncommon. John Brown's HARPERS FERRY raid was the most famous instance of white encouragement of slave rebellion.

---

[2] Herbert Aptheker, *American Negro Slave Revolts.* New York: International, 1983, p. 358.

The slave revolts played a major role in efforts to outlaw the African slave trade, to limit the spread of slavery into new territories and, in some areas, end its existence entirely. As a result of the Stono Rebellion of 1739, James Oglethorpe outlawed slavery in Georgia, and the ban remained in place until 1750. The NEW YORK SLAVE REBELLION of 1712 led directly to Massachusetts and Pennsylvania laws that either forbade the importation of more slaves or made it unprofitable to do so. The picture of passive, docile slaves meekly accepting their fate is incorrect. In reality, smoldering resentment repeatedly erupted into violence, conspiracy, and revolt. The slave system survived through force, and force, much of it on the part of the slaves themselves (including the 200,000 who fought in the Civil War), finally destroyed it.

Other Slave Resistance

Although slave revolts constituted the most dramatic form of slave resistance, they were by no means the only method of reprisal. Arson proved to be an exceptionally effective and consequently frequent form of retaliation. In 1795, slave-set fires in Charleston, South Carolina, prompted the governor to declare a day of fasting. More arson there in 1804 resulted in the destruction of six ships and hundreds of homes. The problem of arson was so widespread that, in 1820, the American Fire Insurance Company of Philadelphia stopped issuing policies in the South.

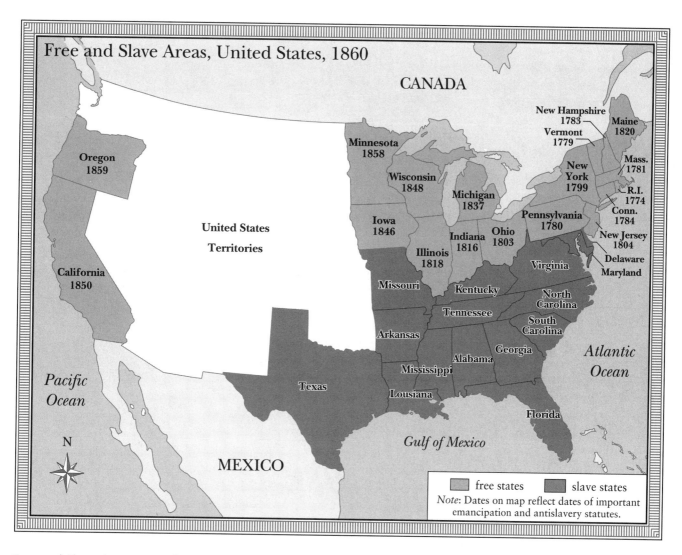

Free and Slave Areas, United States, 1860 (with Dates of Emancipation) (*Facts On File*)

Assaults and attempts at assassination were also common. In 1740, accusations that slaves were attempting to poison New York City's water supply resulted in widespread arrests and executions. Poison attempts were so frequent they were even referred to in the lyrics of at least one slave song. Vandalism and destruction of crops were also regular occurrences. Some slaves engaged in self-destructive behavior in order to lessen or destroy their economic value, and at least two shiploads of newly arrived Africans committed mass suicide in 1807 by starving themselves to death. Psychological and cultural resistance to slavery was expressed through songs, folktales, and jokes. In spite of the efforts of whites to portray slavery a part of the natural order of life, most slaves never accepted this ideology.

Impact

The transatlantic slave trade involved the biggest forced migration of people in history and had lasting consequences for Africa, Europe, North and South America, and the Caribbean. In Europe, and especially England, the slave trade helped usher in the Industrial Revolution. Whole industries sprang

Slaves left behind by James Hopkinson when he fled his Edisto Island, South Carolina, plantation in 1862 (*Library of Congress*)

up to build slave ships and create the guns, textiles, and other products needed to exchange for captives. With this increased industrial demand came scientific development. In the Americas, the consequences were even more far-reaching. The fortunes created through slave-grown sugar, cotton, and tobacco helped speed the development of both North and South America. The forced migration of millions of Africans to the New World permanently affected the racial composition of almost every country in the Western Hemisphere. By 1800, one-half of the population of Brazil was of African origin, and Cuba, Jamaica, Haiti, and many of the other countries of the Caribbean were predominantly black.

In the U.S. the issue of slavery gnawed at American society for over 250 years. It was a dominating factor in domestic, foreign, and economic policy, including the decision to go to war against Mexico in 1846, the major consideration in determining the admission of several states, and a crucial element in the creation of three political parties—Liberty, Free-Soilers, and Republican. It influenced the election of several presidents, came close to destroying the Union in the bloodiest war ever fought by American soldiers, and necessitated the passing of three constitutional amendments.

Slavery had its strongest impact in Africa, which lost millions of its most productive inhabitants. Major population shifts occurred as old kingdoms collapsed and new states based on the slave trade took their place. Huge areas were subjected to constant warfare and violence, leading to a breakdown in ancient traditions and customs. On the east coast, such legendary cities as KILWA, Quelimane, MOMBASA, Sofala, and Lamu were looted and burned, and their lucrative trade with India and the Middle East was wrecked. Economically, slavery prevented much of Africa from developing an industrial capacity. The production of fine cotton goods and metalware in Africa was undercut by the dumping of cheap imports designed to facilitate the slave trade. In the 1500s, West African textiles were exported to Europe. Later, the reverse was true. Trade in other African goods (except gold and ivory) was forgotten as the demand for slaves crowded other commerce out.

The slave trade also brought a halt to African scientific progress. Prior to the 18th century, many African societies had reached highly skilled levels in mining, metalworking, architecture, textile production, agriculture, and irrigation. In many places, education was highly regarded, and several medieval African states were equally or more democratic than their European counterparts. However, after 1750, Europe and North America, driven by the Industrial Revolution, rapidly began to outpace the African states technologically and scientifically. Frozen out of the kind of trade that would have helped them advance, and robbed of many of their most productive workers, African states remained outside the circle of industrially and economically developed countries. Moreover, the constant warfare and widespread violence weakened the states socially and politically, leaving them vulnerable, finally, to European colonization.

Slavery also spewed forth a virulent racism in both Europe and the Americas. To justify the vicious treatment of their black victims, whites convinced themselves that the Africans were inferior and in need of "civilization." As the Industrial Revolution, fueled in part by the slave trade, continued to provide whites with technical advantages, ideas of racial superiority took root. African skills and accomplishments were overlooked, ignored, or denied outright, a situation that has yet to be rectified. Slavery's human toll can never be calculated, but it clearly ranks among the worst crimes of humankind.

Recommended Reading: Aptheker, Herbert. *American Negro Slave Revolts.* New York: International Publishers, 1943; Curtin, Philip D. *The Atlantic Slave Trade.* Madison, Wisconsin: University of Wisconsin Press, 1969, 1970, 1975; Davidson, Basil. *The African Slave Trade.* Boston, Mass.: Little, Brown, 1988; Davis, David Brion. *Slavery and Human Progress.* New York, Oxford: Oxford University Press, 2000; Genovese, Eugene D. *Roll, Jordan, Roll.* New York: Vintage Books/Random House, 1976; Franklin, John Hope. *From Slavery to Freedom: A History of Negro Americans.* New York: Alfred A. Knopf, 1980; Inikori, Joseph, and Stanley Engerman, ed. *The Atlantic Slave Trade.* Durham and London:

Duke University Press, 1992; Stampp, Kenneth M. *The Peculiar Institution.* New York: Vintage Books/Random House, 1989; Walvin, James. *Black Ivory.* Washington, D.C.: Howard University Press, 1994.

Smalls, Robert (1839–1915) *Civil War hero, U.S. congressman*

When the Civil War began, Robert Smalls was assigned to the slave crew of a Confederate ship called the *Planter,* which was berthed in Charleston, South Carolina. On the night of May 13, 1862, while Captain Relyea and the white officers were ashore, Smalls smuggled his wife and five other people aboard, and then, together with the rest of the eight-man crew, weighed anchor and silently guided the *Planter* out of Charleston Harbor. Wearing clothes belonging to Captain Relyea, Smalls steered the vessel past Confederate forces holding Fort Sumter and Morris Island and became an instant hero when he turned the *Planter* over to the Union navy. Congress awarded Smalls and the rest of the crew one-half the appraised value of the *Planter.* Smalls was also made a captain in the Union navy and given command of the *Planter.* After the war, Smalls was elected to the South Carolina House of Representatives and state senate and, later, to the U.S. Congress. In 1913, at the age of 73, Robert Smalls singlehandedly saved two black men from a lynch mob.

Smith, Bessie (1894–1937) *blues singer*

Born to a poor family in Chattanooga, Tennessee, Bessie Smith was one of seven children. She was orphaned at an early age and was raised by her sister Viola. At age nine, she began singing on street corners for nickels and dimes, and at 18 she joined a traveling show, where she met BLUES legend GERTRUDE ("MA") RAINEY. She spent the following years singing in clubs, tents, and theaters, frequently doing several shows a day under difficult conditions. Though Bessie Smith attracted both black and white audiences and was one of the most popular blues singers in the country, segregation

Bessie Smith, 1936 (*Library of Congress*)

was the rule across the South and travel was often difficult and uncomfortable. Her first record, *Down-hearted Blues,* sold over two million copies, and her later albums were so popular they saved Columbia Records from bankruptcy. Bessie Smith drank heavily and was often referred to as "rough." However, she was also extremely generous, kind, and courageous. When a group of Ku Klux Klan thugs attempted to collapse the tent at one of her shows, she confronted them with curses and threats, telling them, "You just pick up them sheets and run!" Her sensitivity to the problems of poor blacks is clear in her lyrics to the song "Poor Man's Blues," which she wrote and recorded in 1928. Bessie Smith worked with many of the best musicians of her day and influenced later artists like BILLIE HOLIDAY and MAHALIA JACKSON. She died after an automobile accident near Clarksdale, Mississippi. The story that she died because white ambulance drivers refused to help her is untrue.

Sokoto Caliphate

empire established in northern Nigeria in the 19th century. The Sokoto Caliphate was founded by Usman dan Fodio (1754–1817), a FULANI Muslim teacher living in the HAUSA state of Gobir. In the 1770s, Usman began preaching to Fulani tribesmen, advocating an end to corruption and excessive taxation and adherence to Islamic law. He quickly gathered a large following among both Fulani and Hausa, infuriating the Hausa king, Nafata, who forbade Usman to preach and prohibited further converts to Islam. Nafata's successor, Yunfa, attacked Usman's supporters, who retaliated in 1804 with a jihad (holy war) against him. Uprisings broke out thoughout the region, leading to the capture of several Hausa city-states, including Gobir, and the death of Yunfa in 1808. Usman's brother Abdullahi and his son Muhammad Bello took over leadership of the jihad and built a capital at Sokoto. The Sokoto Caliphate (or empire) eventually became West Africa's largest state, with a population of over 10 million. It was made up of independent Muslim emirates that maintained considerable local autonomy but deferred to Sokoto in religious matters. Islam brought a certain amount of unity to the area and trade flourished, as did slavery, with many individuals owning over 1,000 slaves. In the 1890s, the British overran much of the area, eventually conquering the Sokoto Caliphate between 1900 and 1903.

Somali Democratic Republic

Country located on the Horn of Africa. Capital: Mogadishu. The people are largely nomadic pastoralists, although trade along the coast goes back to ancient times, and Mogadishu has been an important commercial center for centuries.

In 1871, Mogadishu came under the authority of the Sultan of Oman, who sold the city to the Italians in 1905. It then became the capital of the Italian Somaliland colony, which had been established in 1889. Britain had established a protectorate, known as British Somaliland, in the region in 1887. The British drove the Italians out during World War II and ruled Italian Somaliland in conjuction with British Somaliland.

In 1950, Italian Somaliland became a United Nations Trust Territory under Italian rule. Ten years later, it joined British Somaliland as the independent United Republic of Somalia. War between Somalia and Ethiopia broke out in 1964 over the disputed Ogaden region and continued, with brief interruptions, through much of the 1970s. Somalia received help from the Soviet Union until the Marxist regime of General Mengistu took power in Ethiopia in 1974. At that point, the Soviet Union switched sides and the Somalis were driven out of Ogaden in 1978.

The Somali people are divided into numerous competing clans, a situation that led to a disastrous civil war in 1988. The violence has continued to this day, resulting in the deaths of thousands of people, millions of refugees, and the destruction of Mogadishu and other cities. Thousands more have died of starvation or disease, and severe drought is a continuing problem. Major General Muhammad Siyad Barre came to power after a successful coup in 1969 but was overthrown in 1991. The country was plunged into anarchy with various warlords and guerrilla groups competing for control. All clan/militia leaders have encouraged wanton violations of basic human rights, including widespread rape, torture, and murder. Islamic courts have subjected prisoners to punishments that include floggings and amputations. United States troops were sent to Somalia in December 1992 to protect the delivery of emergency food relief to the population, and the United Nations took over the U.S. role in May 1992. The United States withdrew its forces in 1994 after a battle with Somalia gunmen resulted in 18 U.S. casualties. U.N. troops were evacuated in 1995. As of 2000, Somalia still did not have a unified government.

Songhai, Empire of

Medieval West African kingdom that arose in the Niger River region. Initially under the influence of the MALI empire, Songhai established its independence by the early 15th century. Its greatest expansion came under SUNNI ALI THE GREAT, who assumed the throne in 1464. Ali overran much of the Mali kingdom, conquering TIMBUKTU in 1468 and Jenne in 1473 and conducting raids deep into territory claimed by the independent MOSSI kingdoms. He died in 1492, and Askia MUHAMMAD TOURÉ took the throne after overthrowing Ali's son.

Askia Muhammad encouraged the acceptance of Islam while continuing Ali's military policies. He also centralized the government bureaucracy and created a professional army. He was overthrown by his son in 1528, and the Songhai Empire entered a period of political instability. By the late 1500s, the empire came under pressure from the sultanate of Morocco, who sought control of Songhai's gold supply. Incorrectly assuming the desert would provide protection, Songhai's soldiers were defeated in 1591 by a 3,000-man Moroccan army that included a number of European mercenaries armed with muskets. Political collapse followed, and the Songhai Empire fell apart as military defeat was followed by famine, plague, and attacks by FULANI, BAMBARA, and TUAREG tribesmen.

soul

African-American music that grew out of RHYTHM AND BLUES in the 1950s. Its early stars, like Sam Cooke, were often known for their GOSPEL singing as well. Many of soul music's original artists recorded at Stax Records in Tennessee, where a style known as the "Memphis sound" became popular. Soul music crossed over into mainstream pop with the 1966 release of Percy Sledge's "When a Man Loves a Woman." It rapidly became a multimillion dollar industry in the 1960s thanks in part to Motown Records (founded by BERRY GORDY) and artists like ARETHA FRANKLIN; MARVIN GAYE; Smokey Robinson; the Temptations; the Spinners; Gladys Knight; Patti LaBelle; Curtis Mayfield; Stevie Wonder; the O'Jays; Earth, Wind and Fire; MICHAEL JACKSON; and JAMES BROWN. Among those white artists strongly influenced by soul music were the Rolling Stones and Rod Stewart, as well as musicians throughout Africa, Europe, and the Caribbean. A popular blend between soul and CALYPSO is known as soca.

South Africa, Republic of

Nation at the southern tip of the African continent. Capital: Pretoria. During the 16th century, Dutch and English ships on their way to India began stopping regularly at the southern tip of South Africa to buy meat and vegetables from KHOI tribesmen. In 1652, the Dutch established a permanent settlement known as the Cape Colony there to supply ships of the Dutch East India Company. The Europeans acquired cattle from the local tribespeople and seized thousands of acres of grazing land. Slaves were brought in to work the land, and other whites soon settled in the area, especially after 1688 when the Huguenots arrived fleeing religious persecution in France. These white settlers eventually became known as Afrikaners. As more whites arrived, Afrikaner pioneers, known as Boers, moved further inland, where they came into conflict with the XHOSA.

Political events involving England and the Netherlands resulted in the extension of British authority over the Cape Colony in 1795, with England assuming permanent control in 1806. The British passed the "Hottentot Code" of 1809, which forced African blacks to carry passes and restricted their activities. However, they also required the Boers to sign written contracts with their servants and gave black workers access to courts to redress grievances against white employers. In 1828, the British revoked the Hottentot Code limiting the rights of free blacks, and in 1834, they abolished slavery. In an effort to rid themselves of British interference, approximately 4,000 Boers set out in the 1830s on what would become known as the Great Trek in an effort to obtain land further inland. This resulted in a clash with the ZULU nation in 1838, resulting in the deaths of about 70 Boers who thought the Zulu had agreed to a peace treaty. Ten months later, the Boers retaliated at the Battle of Blood River, killing 3,000 Zulus. The Boers then set up their own government in the Transvaal region. In 1868, diamonds were discovered along the Orange River, followed by gold in 1886. White treasure seekers flooded the area and the British decided to create a new colony that would include the Boer republic in the Transvaal. Local opposition resulted in the Boer War (1899), which ended with a Boer surrender in 1902. The terms of the treaty provided for Boer self-government and an agreement to deny the vote to blacks. With the establishment of the

Holding weapons and shields, members of the Inkatha Freedom Party (IFP) sing at a rally in the Thokoza township of South Africa, May 13, 1999. (*Reuters/Juda Ngwenya/Archive Photos*)

Union of South Africa (1910), white domination was assured. Strict racial segregation known as APARTHEID was hammered into place with a series of acts passed in the late 1940s and 1950s, culminating in the Group Areas Act of 1959, which reserved cities almost exclusively for whites and assigned blacks to BANTUSTANS, a situation which resulted in the forced relocation of 3.5 million Africans. All opposition was brutally repressed.

On March 26, 1960, in what became known as the Sharpeville Massacre, police fired into a crowd of unarmed Africans demonstrating against laws requiring that all blacks carry passes allowing them to move about. Sixty-nine people were killed and more than 400 were wounded, including many women and children. The event drove African opposition organizations such as the AFRICAN NATIONAL CONGRESS (ANC) underground and caused them to turn to terrorism and guerrilla warfare. The following year, South Africa left the British Commonwealth and became a republic. In 1962, ANC leader NELSON MANDELA was arrested and sentenced to life imprisonment. Apartheid was extended and South Africa did what it could to prevent black rule in Mozambique, Rhodesia, and Angola.

In the 1970s, black protests, capped by rioting in 1976 in the all-black Soweto township, resulted in the deaths of approximately 700 people. The next year, black leader STEPHEN BIKO was murdered while in police custody. A new constitution was instituted in 1984, but failed to provide political rights for blacks. The result was continuing attacks against government facilities and police and growing pressure on the international community to impose economic sanctions against South Africa.

In 1989, the South African government began dismantling the legal structure of apartheid. A year later, Nelson Mandela was freed and the ANC was recognized as legal. Constitutional reform granting racial equality occurred in 1992. After a triumphant 14-nation tour, Mandela was elected president in 1994, and remained in office until 1999 when Thabo Mbeki was elected. The government has established a Truth and Reconciliation Commission to conduct hearings on abuses that occurred during the apartheid era.

Southern Christian Leadership Conference (SCLC)

Civil rights organization founded on January 9, 1957 by MARTIN LUTHER KING JR. and more than 60 other ministers and civil rights activists. Its purpose was to help coordinate the growing CIVIL RIGHTS MOVEMENT throughout the South and to encourage nonviolent, direct-action operations directed toward ending discrimination and segregation. Among its most important activities was the 1962 Voter Education Project aimed at increasing black voter registration, the 1968 Poor People's Campaign, and Operation Breadbasket. Other leading figures in the SCLC in addition to King were BAYARD RUSTIN, RALPH ABERNATHY, ANDREW YOUNG, Wyatt T. Walker, Fred Shuttleworth, JESSE JACKSON, Hosea Williams, and Joseph Lowery.

Soyinka, Wole (Akinwande Oluwold Soyinka)

(1934–   ) *Nigerian writer, winner of the 1986 Nobel Prize in literature*

The Nobel selection committee honored Soyinka as a "dramatist, actor, producer, poet, novelist and teacher." This versatility enables him to evoke African society in a narrative mixture of folklore, modern theater technique, political satire, and poetic fantasy.

Born in western NIGERIA, Soyinka attended the University of Leeds in England before returning to Africa, where he marked Nigeria's independence with the drama *A Dance of the Forests* (1960). His first novel, *The Interpreters* (1965), promoted the ideal of a "New Africa," free of the institutions left by former colonial powers. Because of his support for the breakaway region of Biafra during Nigeria's civil war, Soyinka was arrested in 1967 and held in Kaduna Prison (1967–69), often in solitary confinement. His prison writings were later collected in the book *The Man Died* (1972). After his release, he headed a drama school at Ibadan University until political strife forced him to move to Ghana in 1972.

Soyinka's bold satire is evident in his play *Kongi's Harvest* (1967), in which a new-style African ruler is seen as a demagogue without the moral stature of the traditional tribal chiefs. Greater optimism is revealed in *Death and the King's Horseman* (1975), based on YORUBA communal beliefs. Other works include an early comedy, *The Swamp Dwellers*; a volume of verse and prose, *Madmen and Specialists*; *Myths, Literature and the African World*; the poem "Ogun Abibiman," which praises Yoruba gods and ZULU kings; the autobiographical *Ake: The Years of Childhood*; and a collection of essays on African, European, and American culture entitled *Art, Dialogue, and Outrage*. Soyinka was forced to flee Nigeria in 1994 for protesting human rights abuses. He was able to return in 1998, after four years in exile, with the end of military rule there.

Sphinx

Monumental statue with the body of a lion and the head of a man found in EGYPT near the city of Giza. Carved from a natural limestone foundation, the Sphinx is 240 feet long and 66 feet high. Recent geological studies have found that the Sphinx's lower body was eroded by water, not desert winds, an indication that it may have survived pre-dynastic floods, putting its age at over 5,000 years. Egyptologists say the lion's body represents physical strength, and the man's head reflects divine power.

spirituals

Music created by North American slaves, who combined West African rhythms and vocal patterns with the music—usually church hymns—of their

An 1893 photo of the Sphinx (*Library of Congress*)

owners. In addition to religion, the lyrics of many spirituals were used allegorically to express political ideas and to pass on escape information. Examples are "Let My People Go," "Stealin' Away to Jesus," and "Wade in the Water," which advised runaway slaves to wade in the water of rivers and streams so that dogs tracking them could not pick up their scent. North American slaves developed spirituals since they were generally forbidden to play African music. Caribbean and South American slaves faced fewer musical restrictions, and, as a result, more African sounds survive in Latin American music.

Still, William (1821–1902) *abolitionist, writer, conductor on the Underground Railroad*

William Still helped 649 people escape from slavery, one of them his own brother. His mother was a Maryland slave who managed to escape but was forced to leave two of her four children behind. One was the brother Still later rescued. William Still received little formal schooling and had to teach himself to read and write. In 1844, he traveled to Philadelphia, where he found employment with the Pennsylvania Society for the Abolition of Slavery. Shortly afterward he became a conductor (guide) on the UNDERGROUND RAILROAD.

For the next 14 years, Still maintained a safe house or "station" for runaways passing through Philadelphia. He also kept a record of their escapes. The purpose was to enable friends and relatives of runaway slaves to locate them. Moreover, Still was determined that a history be kept of their suffering. Such records were dangerous to keep. Not only could they be helpful in locating escaped slaves, they could also be used to send William Still to prison. "Slave stealing" was a serious crime, and the records provided proof of Still's activities. In 1872, William Still incorporated his records into a book called *The Underground Railroad*. The book provides one of the few antislavery histories written by an African American of that time. It showed runaway slaves as courageous and resourceful rather than as helpless victims relying exclusively on white help. Still also helped organize one of the first YMCAs for African Americans, established an orphanage for black children, and helped manage homes for black senior citizens.

Stono, South Carolina, Rebellion (Sept. 9, 1739)

A major slave uprising that took place in South Carolina at Stono, an area several miles southwest of Charleston. Approximately 20 slaves under the leadership of a man named Jemmy killed two guards at a warehouse, stole guns and ammunition, and proceeded southward toward Spanish Florida, killing all whites they met along the way. As the rebellion unfolded, the original group was joined by about 60 additional slaves, bringing the total number to about 80. The militia was called out, and the rebelling slaves were defeated in battle. Most of those not killed in the fighting were tracked down and jailed. Approximately 25 whites and 50 blacks died during the uprising and its aftermath. The revolt had been triggered in part by exceptionally bad economic conditions that had resulted in even more suffering than usual. Slaves were given less food, and there were more forced sales, making the breakup of families more frequent. The rebelling slaves had hoped to take advantage of the fact that the white population was facing a serious threat from hostile Indians. In addition, the Spanish had tried to undermine English control of the colony by

promising freedom to any slave who managed to escape to Spanish Florida or Puerto Rico, and those promises were a factor in the Stono uprising. A number of the rebelling slaves were "salt-water" slaves—that is, they were born in Africa—and their military tactics, which were similar to those used in Angola, reflected their African origin.

Student Non-Violent Coordinating Committee (SNCC) (pronounced "snick")

civil rights organization. Founded in 1960 largely through the efforts of ELLA BAKER, SNCC's original mission was to coordinate the student SIT-IN MOVEMENT. In 1961, the organization came to national attention when SNCC volunteers decided to continue the freedom ride campaign begun by the CONGRESS OF RACIAL EQUALITY (CORE).

SNCC emphasized participatory democracy and the need to develop local black leadership. In 1962, the organization targeted six rural Mississippi counties to promote the registration of black voters. Whites retaliated with bombings, beatings, jailings, and economic intimidation, which included preventing poor blacks from receiving surplus food from the U.S. Department of Agriculture. Two years later, frustrated at the lack of progress, SNCC and COFO (the COUNCIL OF FEDERATED ORGANIZATIONS) established the 1964 MISSISSIPPI FREEDOM SUMMER PROJECT, which brought more than 1,000 volunteers—mostly white college students—to Mississippi to help register black voters. The disappearance of two white volunteers and their black coworker focused national attention on Mississippi and forced the federal government to send in a federal task force to search for the missing men and to infiltrate the KU KLUX KLAN.

SNCC workers like ROBERT MOSES and FANNIE LOU HAMER also played a major role in the formation of the MISSISSIPPI FREEDOM DEMOCRATIC PARTY and in the establishment of 41 Freedom Schools that provided political training and literacy education. However, many SNCC workers were becoming more radical, and in 1966, whites were voted out of the organization. Other SNCC leaders included JOHN LEWIS, later a U.S. congressman, STOKELY CARMICHAEL, James Forman, Marion Barry, Lawrence Guyot,

Diane Nash, Brenda Travis, Victoria Grey, and Eleanor Holmes Norton.

See also VOTING RIGHTS STRUGGLE; PHILADELPHIA, MISSISSIPPI, MURDERS.

Sudan, Republic of the

Africa's largest country. Capital: Khartoum. The inhabitants of the north and west are largely Muslim; those in the south follow ANIMISM. Sudan has been the site of various kingdoms, including Kerma, Nubia, Kush, and Christian Nubia. The Muslim Funj Sultanate rose to power in the early 16th century. In 1821, Funj fell to Muhammad Ali, the Turkish ruler of Egypt who was interested in obtaining Sudanese slaves. Egypt's harsh rule caused a revolt that ended in the devastation of Sudan's southern villages and towns and the murder of many of its inhabitants. Heavy taxes were imposed with payment often made in slaves.

In 1881, Muhammad Ahmad (1844–85), the son of a boatbuilder, declared himself the Mahdi (an Islamic savior or holy man) and led a campaign to free Sudan from Egyptian rule.

The Egyptians had the support of the British, but the Mahdists defeated the Egyptian-British forces in 1885 and killed Charles Gordon, who had been sent to evacuate British and Egyptian troops from Sudan. The Mahdi also died in 1885, but his successor, the Khalifa Abdallahi, continued the effort to create an Islamic theocratic state. This period is known as the Mahdiya and is considered a central event in Sudanese history.

The British defeated Mahdists in 1898 at the Battle of Omdurman and set up a "Condominium" government whereby Sudan was ruled by a governor selected by Egypt with the approval of Great Britain. However, Sudan remained rebellious, particularly in the south, until the 1920s. The British concentrated their economic development efforts in north and central Sudan, which resulted in the political and economic isolation of the south. In 1953, three years before granting the country independence, the British "Sudanized" the government, turning over 800 administrative posts to Sudanese bureaucrats. Only four of these posts went to southerners, and in 1955, the southern garrison at Torit revolted, beginning a

civil war that continues today. Religious differences in the north and south contributed to the conflict.

In the north, the Sudanese government alternated between military and civilian rule. In an effort to speed development, the Sudanese government, under Colonel Jaafar al-Numeiri, ran up more than $8 billion in debts during the 1970s. Rising opposition led Numeiri to close the universities and arrest political dissidents. In 1983, he instituted strict Islamic Law (shari'a), which authorized punishments such as flogging, stoning, and amputation. Rebellion again broke out in the south, and drought and famine in 1984–85 led to the deaths of 250,000 people, partly because the Sudanese government refused to acknowledge the problem and seek aid. In 1985, Numeiri was overthrown.

A reformist Transitional Military Council (TMC) was followed by a civilian government under Sadiq el Mahdi (1986–89), but the southern rebellion continued. On June 30, 1989, Sadiq was overthrown in a military coup carried out by the Revolutionary Command Council for National Salvation (RCC) under General Omar Hassan Bashir. The RCC created the National Islamic Front (NIF), which now governs Sudan. The NIF has an extremely poor human rights record, and its actions have resulted in the deaths of thousands of people.

In 1998, the United States launched a missile strike against el Shifa, a Sudanese pharmaceutical plant, charging that the factory was producing chemical weapons for the terrorist Osana bin Laden. Subsequent investigation cast substantial doubt on those charges. A three-month state of emergency was declared by President Bashir in December 1999, in response to changes in U.S. law allowing the U.S. government to provide food aid to rebel fighters— not just civilians. The parliament was dissolved after members were involved in efforts to curb the powers of the president. U.S. efforts to isolate Sudan have been unsuccessful partly because France, Britain, Canada, Saudi Arabia, and China have oil investments in Sudan and do not want to offend the Sudanese government. Talisman Energy, Inc., a Canadian company, hopes to be able to deliver up to 1 million barrels of oil a day by the year 2005, and both the Sudanese government and the rebel forces (which favor secession or regional autonomy) want part of the profits. The civil war has resulted in 2 million dead and 4 million people displaced. A peace accord between Sudan and Uganda was signed in December 1999 thanks to efforts of former U.S. president Jimmy Carter. Carter became involved as a result of his campaign to eradicate Guinea worm disease in southern Sudan and northern Uganda. Though slavery is illegal, DINKA and NUBA children and women captured in military raids are frequently sold as slaves, and the government has made little or no effort to end the practice.

Recommended Reading: Petterson, Donald. *Inside Sudan*. Boulder, Colorado: Westview Press, 1999.

Sudd

A vast, hot, steamy swamp the size of Maine, located on the White Nile in southern Sudan. It is filled with grasses, papyrus, and floating vegetation packed into chunks up to 20 feet thick and stretching as far as the eye can see. Crocodiles, hippopotamuses, snakes by the thousand, and millions upon millions of disease-bearing insects, including 60 species of mosquito, make it a death trap for humans. In fact, the word *sudd* is Arabic for "barrier." Even so, the Sudd is inhabited by the NUER, a seminomadic tribe who camp above the floodplain and live on cattle, sorghum, and fish. Originally, there were three natural channels that wove through the Sudd and finally merged to form one main channel leading north. However, at any time, any or all of them might be blocked with floating vegetation. Since navigation through the Sudd was almost impossible, European explorers searching for the source of the Nile could not simply follow the river southward to locate its origin. An expedition attempting to cross the Sudd risked losing most of its men to disease and starvation. In 1899, British army engineers undertook a program to clear a channel through the Sudd. It was completed in 1904. Since then, several permanent channels have been hacked through the swamp and efforts are being made to turn the Sudd into a vast reservoir.

Sundiata Keita (KAY-ee-ta) (unknown–1255)
Malinke leader who established the Mali Empire
According to legend, Sundiata's father, Allakoi Keita, and his family had been killed by Soso raiders, but Sundiata was spared because of his crippled condition. Sundiata, whose name means "Hungering Lion," overcame his physical handicaps, put together an army, and defeated the Soso king, Sumanguru, in 1235. He then went on to conquer the remnants of the Ghana Empire in 1240 and became founder of the Empire of MALI.

Sunni Ali the Great (Ali Ber) (unknown–1492)
Songhai emperor, military leader
Sunni Ali came to the throne in 1464. He drove the TUAREG out of TIMBUKTU in 1468 and brought JENNE under SONGHAI control in 1473 after a seven-year siege. He divided his territory into provinces, set up an efficient administration, and created a large fleet that controlled the Niger River and maintained communications within his realm. When he died in an accident, the governor of Hombori province staged a coup against Sunni Ali's son and took over the throne as Askia MUHAMMED TOURÉ.

Swahili

Language and culture found throughout much of eastern Africa. The word *swahili* comes from an Arabic word meaning "of the coast," and though the Swahili language is BANTU-based, it exhibits a strong Arabic influence, particularly in regard to words linked to government, commerce, seamanship, and religion. Swahili lends itself to poetic expression, and Swahili poetry has a long tradition, with emphasis on *mashairi* (lyric songs) and *tendi* (epic poems). Swahili is spoken by 30 million people.

Swaziland, Kingdom of

South African country. Capital: Mbabane. Swaziland is a small, landlocked country (6,704 square miles) surrounded by South Africa and Mozambique. It was settled by BANTU people who migrated to southern Africa in the 16th century and occupied what is now Swaziland after being defeated by ZULU forces in 1820. Pressure from Europeans in the mid-19th century cost the Swazi people much of their land. The territory was annexed by the British in the mid-1890s and became independent in 1968 under King Sobhuza II. When he died in 1982, a mandatory 75 days of mourning was instituted during which no farming was allowed, no cattle were slaughtered, and all sex was banned. Sobhuza was succeeded by his 14-year-old son, although the Queen Mother, known as the "Great She Elephant," ruled as regent until the boy reached 18. Sobhuza had banned political parties, but his son, Mswati III, initiated limited political reform, and elections were held in 1993. Swaziland exports sugarcane, but its economy is heavily dependent on the tourist trade from South Africa. The country's name comes from that of an early Swazi king, Mswati II.

T

Tacky's Rebellion

A carefully planned slave uprising that took place in Jamaica in 1760. The leader, Tacky, had been an African chief in Ghana. Together with a small group of ASHANTI followers, he broke into the armory at Port Maria, killed the guard, and stole muskets, powder, and ammunition. As the rebels moved inland, attacking farms and plantations, they were joined by hundreds of other slaves. However, a slave from Esher, one of the plantations they had overrun, slipped away and gave the alarm. Two companies of regular army, along with 70 to 80 militia, were called out. These were joined by MAROONS (runaway slaves), who were obligated by treaty to support the government in the event of a slave uprising. A number of Tacky's followers believed that slave obeahmen (sorcerers) had made them immune from injury. Knowing this, the British made a special effort to capture an obeahman. After doing so, they hanged him dressed in his mask and obeah ornaments. At that point, a number of the slaves gave up and returned to their plantations. Tacky and about 25 followers continued to fight. A maroon sharpshooter named Davy managed to kill Tacky, and the other rebels committed suicide rather than surrender. Slave revolts in other parishes had broken out as news of Tacky's insurrection became known. They were put down with help from the Maroons. In the end, 60 whites and 400 blacks lost their lives. An additional 600 slaves were deported to Honduras. The fact that Maroons helped suppress the rebellion soured relations between them and the slave population for years to come.

Taghaza

City and salt-mining center in northwestern Africa. It was described by IBN BATTUTA in 1352 as a village whose "houses and mosques are built of blocks of salt, roofed with camel skins. There are no trees there, nothing but sand. In the sand is a salt mine; they dig for salt and find it in thick slabs, lying one on top of the other, as though they had been tool-squared and laid under the surface of the earth." Taghaza was abandoned in 1582 on orders of Askia Daoud, king of SONGHAI, in order to prevent the Moroccan sultan Mulay Ahmed from profiting from his anticipated capture of the city. Ahmed's army found Taghaza deserted, with no one left to work the mines. It marked the end of the slave-driven salt trade that had existed there for almost 1,000 years.

Taharqa (unknown–663 B.C.) *pharaoh*

Taharqa was a pharaoh of the Twenty-fifth (Kushite) Dynasty in EGYPT (ruled 688–663 B.C.). The son of the Kushite king Piankhi, Taharqa constructed monuments at Tanis, Thebes, and Karnak and rebuilt several temples in KUSH, including at least one graced with silver, gold, and bronze altars and surrounded by gardens and a lake. Invading Assyrian troops defeated Taharqa's Egyptian forces, and he was forced to retreat to Thebes. There he raised another army and moved into Lower Egypt when the Assyrians withdrew temporarily. He was forced out a second time when Assyrian forces reoccupied Egypt. The conflict between Taharqa and the Assyrians is referred to in the Bible (II Kings 19:9 and Isaiah 37:9), where Taharqa in some versions is referred to as "Tirhakah," king of Ethiopia.

Talented Tenth

Concept put forth by W.E.B. DUBOIS in 1903 in which he argued that the Talented Tenth—"the educated and intelligent of the Negro people"—was the critical factor in "elevating" the black race in America. Stating that "the Negro race, like all other races, is going to be saved by its exceptional men," DuBois urged the creation of a university-trained black elite to teach the African-American masses and be "leaders of thought and missionaries of culture among (black) people." The concept was quickly embraced by educated blacks, many of whom rejected the philosophy of BOOKER T. WASHINGTON, which emphasized vocational training.

Tanner, Henry Ossawa (1859–1937) artist

Tanner began his formal studies in 1879 at the Pennsylvania Academy of Fine Arts. Though he found acceptance among the faculty, Tanner met with prejudice from fellow students, which caused him to leave the academy. His painting *The Battle of Life* showing an elk being attacked by wolves is thought by some to be a metaphor for the racial attacks he suffered. Tanner moved to France in 1891, where he was able to escape the racism he had endured at home. There he studied at the Académie Julien in Paris, where he received strong encouragement from Jean-Jacques Benjamin-Constant, a leading French painter. Though Tanner did several paintings, such as *The Banjo Lesson* and *The Thankful Poor,* that featured African-American subjects, much of his work featured biblical themes and, as he gained international recognition, he was criticized for failing to produce more "Negro art."

He developed a unique style that is noted for his exceptional use of light and color, and mystic, symbolic figures.

Shocked by the brutality of World War I, he found it impossible to paint, but devised a successful gardening therapy program for wounded soldiers. This helped bring him out of his own depression so that he was able to paint again. He was awarded the Legion of Honor by the French government in 1924 for his work with wounded soldiers.

Tanner's work helped establish American painting as an important force in the international art world, and he is regarded as the dean of African-American art. Among his most famous paintings are *Daniel in the Lions' Den, The Annunciation, The Destruction of Sodom and Gomorrah,* and *The Raising of Lazarus.*

In 1995, Tanner became the first African-American artist to have a painting included in the White House art collection. The work is *Sand Dunes at Sunset, Atlantic City.*

Recommended Reading: Bearden, Romare, and Harry Henderson. *A History of African-American Artists.* New York: Pantheon Books, 1993.

Tanzania, United Republic of

East African nation formed in 1964 by the union of Tanganyika and Zanzibar. Capital: Dar-es-Salaam. Various tribal groups began to appear in the area during the first century A.D. Indian and Arab traders began settling in the region around A.D. 900, in response to an extensive trade that had developed between the city of KILWA and the port cities of India, Arabia, northeast Africa, Thailand, China, and Indonesia. In 1505, Kilwa was sacked by the Portuguese in their drive to gain control of East Africa's lucrative INDIAN OCEAN TRADE. In the late 1500s, Tanzanian territory was subjected to incursions by ZIMBA raiders. Kilwa was attacked in 1587 and more than 3,000 of its inhabitants slain. Although an extensive slave trade existed in East Africa, the northern section of Tanzania was spared because the presence there of the warlike MAASAI discouraged slave raiders. In 1698, the Portuguese were driven out by Omani Arabs based in Zanzibar, who established an extensive trading empire specializing in slaves and ivory. In the late 19th century, the British forced the Omanis to end their overseas slave trade, and the area was visited by various European explorers, among them David Livingstone, in their search for the source of the Nile River. Germany, through agreements with Britain and the Omanis, gained control of the area in 1886, a situation that lasted through World War I in spite of strong resistance from several African tribes. After World War I, the League of Nations made Tanganyika a British mandate. Great Britain granted Tanganyika its independence in 1962 under the leadership of JULIUS NYERERE; two years later, the new nation joined with the island of Zanzibar to become Tanzania. An invasion by Uganda in November 1978 led to full-scale war in 1979 as Tanzanian troops joined with rebel forces in Uganda in a successful effort to overthrow Uganda's president Idi Amin. Nyerere resigned in 1985, and Ali Hassan Mwinyi became president. Tanzania contains the famous Serengeti National Game Preserve and Mt. Kilimanjaro. The Olduvai Gorge, where Dr. Louis Leakey discovered 1.75-million-year-old *Homo habilis* fossil remains, runs through the country. The country has been hard-hit by the AIDS crisis.

In 1998, the U.S. embassy in Tanzania was bombed by terrorists. Eleven people were killed.

Tariq ibn Ziyad *Moorish general*

After being captured during the Arab conquest of Morocco, Tariq was released from prisoner-of-war status when he became a Muslim and joined the Arab forces. He rose to the rank of general in the army of Musa-ibn-Nusair, who also appointed Tariq governor of the ancient province of MAURETA-NIA on the North African coast. Political turmoil in Spain led the heirs of the Visigoth king Witiza to request military assistance from the Muslims of North Africa. Tariq responded, leading a 12,000-man army in a successful invasion of Spain in A.D. 711. He defeated Roderick, who had seized control, but instead of placing Witiza's heirs on the

throne, proceeded to conquer the country and establish a Moorish-Islamic regime. The point at which Tariq landed after crossing the Mediterranean from Africa was given the Arabic name *Jabal-al-Tariq*—"Tariq's Mountain"—which is the source of the name *Gibraltar.*

Tassili-n-Ajjer rock paintings

approximately 15,000 rock paintings, many of them prehistoric, found at Tassili-n-Ajjer, a rocky region in the SAHARA. The paintings feature people engaged in various occupations, as well as a number of different animals—many of which are no longer found in the Sahara. Among the drawings of animals are 15-foot-tall pictures of elephants and 25-foot-long drawings of rhinoceroses. These constitute the largest prehistoric drawings ever found. The drawings of people include pictures of warriors, men hunting and drawing water, and women gathering grain, tending cattle, caring for children, and preparing food. People are also shown dancing, playing music, and engaging in various community activities. The paintings of both animals and people show great detail and skill and indicate that the prehistoric peoples who created them lived in highly organized societies. The paintings have been divided into four groups: Hunter (8500–6000 B.C.); Herder (6000–1500 B.C.); Horse (1500–600 B.C.), and Camel (600 B.C. on).

Tatum, Art, Jr. (1909–1956) *jazz pianist*

Tatum suffered severe vision problems stemming from cataracts on both eyes from birth. Although he underwent a series of operations, he had only limited sight in his right eye and was completely blind in his left. He began playing the piano in his teens, often entertaining at local parties. In 1927, he was hired as a pianist by radio station WSPD in Toledo, Ohio, and given his own 15-minute show. Five years later he left for New York as the accompanist to singer Adelaide Hall. Once in New York, Tatum quickly developed a reputation as a virtuoso known for his phenomenal speed (his 1949 recording of "I Know That You Know" at times reached 1,000 notes per minute) and his mastery of every keyboard style. His skill was admired by classical musicians like Vladimir Horowitz as well as artists like Count BASIE, Oscar Peterson, and Herbie Hancock. He spent thousands of hours playing in the Manhattan after-hours clubs, where his exceptional improvisational ability caused him to be regarded as one of the finest musicians in JAZZ. In 1943, Tatum formed a trio with Slam Stewart on bass and Tiny Grimes (later Everett Barksdale) on guitar and performed with them for the rest of his career.

Recommended Listening: *Solos* (MCA); *Art Tatum: Piano Starts Here* (Columbia).

Temple, Lewis (1800–1854) *inventor of a harpoon called Temple's Toggle*

Temple's invention revolutionized the whaling industry. Whales often pulled free from the traditional barbed harpoons. Temple designed a harpoon whose head would turn, or toggle, when it struck the whale so the animal could not free itself. His invention is considered one of the most important in the entire history of whaling. Temple himself was born in Richmond, Virginia. Little is known of his early life, suggesting he may have been an escaped slave. New Bedford, Massachusetts, where he had a blacksmith shop and where he devised his harpoon, was an important stop on the UNDERGROUND RAILROAD, and many runaways found safety there. Temple never bothered to acquire a patent for his invention, an oversight that allowed other harpoon makers to profit extensively from his device. However, Temple's business was successful, and he was able to acquire a larger shop. He was also active in civic affairs and in the abolitionist movement. In 1853, he sued the city of New Bedford after being injured in a fall caused by a board left lying in the street by city workmen. He was awarded $2,000, but the money was never paid, and when Temple died the following year, his home and shop had to be sold to cover debts.

Terrell, Mary Eliza Church (1863–1954) *civil rights activist, feminist, writer*

Born in Memphis, Tennessee, to prosperous former slaves, Mary Church graduated from Oberlin College in 1884 and a year later began teaching at Wilberforce University, much to the displeasure of her father, who believed ladies should not work. "He disinherited me," she said, "[and] refused to write to me for a year . . . I was . . . told that no man would want to marry a woman who studied higher mathematics. I said I'd take a chance and run the risk." In 1887, she took a job teaching Latin in Washington, D.C. There she met and married attorney Robert Terrell, a decision that meant turning down an opportunity to become registrar at Oberlin in 1891.

The 1892 murder of three black men—one of them a close friend—led her to join FREDERICK DOUGLASS in an unsuccessful effort to persuade President Benjamin Harrison to publicly condemn LYNCHING. She was appointed to the Board of Education in Washington, D.C., in 1895, making her possibly the first African-American woman to hold this position. A year later she founded the National Association of Colored Women (NACW), an organization offering self-help programs, kindergartens, and education in parenting and home economics. While attending the 1904 International Congress of Women in Berlin, Terrell delivered a speech in German (she was fluent in three languages) in which she spoke of the numerous contributions of the black race. She wrote articles and stories about lynching and discrimination, and strongly protested the dismissal of African-American soldiers after the 1906 BROWNSVILLE, TEXAS, AFFAIR. She was also one of the founders of the NATIONAL ASSOCIATION FOR THE ADVANCEMENT OF COLORED PEOPLE in 1909.

Terrell worked closely with white feminist leaders like Susan B. Anthony and Jane Addams in an effort to win the vote for women. The alliance was sometimes a rocky one. Several leading white suffragettes indicated they would be willing to deny black rights in return for support on the Nineteenth Amendment guaranteeing women the vote.

In 1949, Terrell ended the discriminatory policies of the American Association of University

Women when she became a member of the organization after a three-year battle. She also fought to free Rosa Lee Ingram and her two sons, ages 14 and 17, who had all been sentenced to death in 1948 for killing a white farmer who had attempted to rape Mrs. Ingram. (The sentence was commuted to life imprisonment, and they were paroled in 1959.) At the age of 90, Mary Church Terrell walked with a cane at the head of a picket line in a successful campaign to force the integration of restaurants in Washington, D.C. Her autobiography is entitled *A Colored Woman in a White World.*

Thirteenth Amendment   See RECONSTRUCTION AMENDMENTS.

Thomas, Clarence (1948–   ) *associate U.S. Supreme Court justice*

Thomas began his life in poverty in Pinpoint, Georgia. He and his brother were raised by their grandparents when his father abandoned the family. Thomas planned to become a Catholic priest but left Conception Seminary in 1968 because of racial prejudice he suffered there. He graduated cum laude from Holy Cross College in 1971 and from Yale Law School in 1974.

After law school, Thomas became assistant attorney general of Missouri (1974–77) under Attorney General John Danforth and then worked for the Monsanto Corporation. When Danforth was elected to the U.S. Senate, Thomas became his legislative assistant (1979). President Ronald Reagan appointed Thomas assistant secretary of civil rights in the U.S. Department of Education in 1981. However, when it appeared the Reagan administration would grant tax-exempt status to the segregated Bob Jones University, Thomas told friends he planned to resign in protest. In 1982, Thomas was appointed Chairman of the Equal Employment Opportunity Commission (EEOC), where he substantially increased the number of cases accepted for litigation, and in 1990 President George Bush appointed him a federal judge for the U.S. Court of Appeals for the District of Columbia.

Thomas was vilified by the political left for his conservative views when Bush nominated him to the U.S. Supreme Court in July 1991. In September, Anita Hill, a law professor at the University of Oklahoma, accused Thomas of sexually harassing her when they were coworkers at the Department of Education and the EEOC. Thomas flatly denied the accusations, and questions were raised about Hill's credibility because she had arranged to continue working with Thomas when he left the Department of Education to go to the EEOC and had deliberately remained in contact with him long after the alleged harassment had taken place. Thomas was confirmed and became the second African-American Supreme Court Justice.

Till, Emmett (1941–1955) *murder victim*

Emmett Till was a 14-year-old boy murdered in Money, Mississippi, because he whistled at a white woman. Till, who lived in Chicago, had been visiting his uncle, Moses Wright. On August 24, while standing with friends outside a small store, Till boasted about having a white girlfriend in Chicago. His friends then dared him to ask the white woman inside the store for a date. According to the woman, Carolyn Bryant, Till entered the store, bought some gum, asked for a date, and then whistled at her as he left the store. When her husband, Roy Bryant, learned of the incident, he and his brother, J. W. Milam, went to Moses Wright's house shortly after midnight on August 28 and abducted Till. Three days later, the boy's body was found in the Tallahatchie River tied to a cotton gin fan. Bryant and Milam were tried for the crime but were found not guilty by an all-white jury in spite of the testimony of Moses Wright identifying them as the men who kidnapped Till. The following year, after being paid by a reporter, Bryant and Milam admitted that they had indeed murdered Till. Though the two men could not be retried because of constitutional protections against double jeopardy, the Emmett Till lynching shocked the country and motivated thousands of young people who later became involved in the Civil Rights movement.

Recommended Reading: Whitfield, Stephen J. *A Death in the Delta: The Story of Emmett Till*. Baltimore, Ma.: Johns Hopkins University Press, 1991.

Timbuktu (Timbuctoo)

Famous West African city on the Niger River. Timbuktu was located at a crossroads for several major trade routes and was a final destination point for many caravans. The city also served as the place where merchants, having crossed the Sahara with their loads of salt and other goods, could transfer their wares from camel to canoe in order to continue their journey further south to GAO, JENNE, and Kirina. Timbuktu was founded around A.D. 1100 by TUAREG nomads, and it expanded with the increasing trade in salt, gold, copper, silver, textiles, kola nuts, ivory, spices, ostrich feathers, slaves, and other goods. After being incorporated into the MALI Empire, the city became a major cultural center. Its Sankore University was famous throughout the Muslim world, and the city was noted for its many libraries. The historian LEO AFRICANUS described Timbuktu as a city where "there are numerous judges, doctors and clerics, all receiving good salaries from the king. There is a big demand for books in manuscript, imported from Barbary. More profit is made from the sale of books than from any other merchandise." MANSA KANKAN MUSA, who ruled the Mali Empire between 1312 and 1337, built a beautiful mosque and palace in Timbuktu, and by the early 16th century the city had become a leading Islamic cultural and intellectual center. At the time Leo Africanus visited the city in the early 16th century, its population probably approached 50,000. Timbuktu remained a cultural and commercial center even after being seized in 1468 by the Songhai king SUNNI ALI THE GREAT. The city went into decline after capture by Moroccans in 1591.

Tippu Tip (Hamidi bin Muhammad, Tippu Tib) (ca. 1830–1905) *slave trader*

Born in Zanzibar of Arab-Swahili-Nyamwezi ancestry, Tippu Tip began his career as a slave and ivory trader for his merchant father. In the 1860s he

Tippu Tip's captured slaves (*Library of Congress*)

established a base on the Lualaba River at a town called Nyangwe, and soon extended his control over the surrounding area. In 1866, he met and extended assistance to Dr. David Livingstone. Twelve years later, for a fee of $5,000, he briefly provided protection to explorer Henry Stanley, who described him as "a tall black-bearded man, of negroid complexion, . . . straight and quick in his movements, a picture of energy and strength . . . with the air of a well-bred Arab, and almost courtier-like in his manner . . . I came to the conclusion that this Arab was a remarkable man—the most remarkable man I had met . . ." By that time, Tippu Tip was the most successful slave trader in East-Central Africa and had created a loosely knit federation of several hundred bands of men who regularly raided villages for slaves and ivory. Within his territory, he built roads, established plantations, and regulated the hunting of elephants for ivory.

When King Leopold of Belgium set up the CONGO FREE STATE, he attempted to avoid a confrontation with Tippu Tip by appointing him governor of the Congo's Stanley Falls district in 1887. Tippu Tip was aware the alliance could not last, and in 1891, he returned to Zanzibar where he owned seven plantations and 10,000 slaves. A year later, a brutal war, marked by numerous atrocities, broke out between his men and Leopold's Force Publique. Tippu Tip's Arab-Swahili forces were driven out after 18 months of fighting, and he remained in Zanzibar until his death.

Togo, Republic of

West African country. Capital: Lomé. Prior to the late 1600s, Togo was the home of various tribes, particularly the Ewe, the Guin, and the Mina. Though many Mina tribesmen acted as agents for European slave traders based in what is now Ghana and Benin, Togo's coastline did not provide natural harbors that would attract slave ships. German missionaries arrived in what was then called Little Popo, or Togoland, around 1840, and the region became a German protectorate in 1884. After Germany's defeat in World War I, Togo was divided between the French and the British through a League of Nations mandate. The mandate prevented the French from instituting a forced labor policy similar to those in its other colonies. The country became independent in 1960 as the Republic of Togo under the leadership of Sylvanus Olympio, who became the country's first president. He was assassinated in a coup in 1963, and his brother-in-law, Nicolas Grunitzky, became president. He was overthrown in 1967 by Ghansimgbe Eyadema, who remains in power. Several critics of the government have died in prison. Hundreds of people were murdered during Togo's 1998 election. Togo is noted for its *Nanas-Benz*. These are elderly women who run the Togo's textile import business. *Nana* means "woman of means," and Benz refers to their habit of driving Mercedez Benz cars.

Toomer, Nathan Eugene ("Jean") (1894–1967)
novelist, dramatist, poet
Born into a middle-class family in Washington, D.C., Toomer was the grandson of P. B. S. PINCH-BACK, the former U.S. senator from Louisiana. His book *Cane* was published in 1923. Described as the most important novel of the HARLEM RENAISSANCE, *Cane* is an assortment of prose and poetry, including stories linked by verses and a short drama. The book is divided into three sections: The first part portrays southern blacks, many of them women; the central section is set in the North and suggests the social uncertainty of light-skinned African Americans; the last part, which Toomer claimed to identify with, is *Kabnis*, a story about a teacher from the North who encounters southern blacks. Although *Cane* was well received by literary critics, its first edition sold only 500 copies. Toomer's other books include a volume of social principles entitled *Essentials* (1931) and *Portage Potential* (1932). Other stories and essays were published after his death in *The Wayward and the Seeking: A Collection of Writings by Jean Toomer* (1980). This last volume shows the influence of the Russian mystic Georgei Gurdjieff, of whom Toomer became a devoted follower.

Toussaint Louverture, François Dominique (Toussaint Breda, L'Ouverture) (1744–1803)
leader of the Haitian Revolution, military genius
Originally known as Toussaint Breda, his military skills earned him the nickname L'Ouverture, meaning "the opening." Later, he dropped the apostrophe. Toussaint was born a slave in Saint-Domingue, the French colony that would later become HAITI, and acquired a knowledge of medicine and herbs from his African-born father. He also learned to read. He joined the BOUKMAN REVOLT one month after it began in 1791 and rapidly became a leader in the rebellion. Beginning with a few hundred handpicked men, he organized thousands of untrained slaves into an army that would eventually defeat the forces of France, Britain, and Spain.

Toussaint was motivated by the idea of freedom for all slaves, and he maintained this goal through more than 12 years of brutal warfare marked by shifting alliances, betrayals, numerous bloody massacres, and racial hatred. When the slave insurrection faltered in 1793, Toussaint and 600 of his men joined the Spanish forces in the neighboring Spanish colony of Santo Domingo with the idea of overthrowing the French colonial government in Saint-Domingue. In 1794, after the new revolutionary government in France abolished slavery, Tous-

Toussaint Louverture (*Library of Congress*)

saint deserted the Spanish to support the new French regime, bringing with him 4,000 troops. The French placed him in command of an army of 20,000 soldiers and turned him loose against the British who had invaded Saint-Domingue the year before. Toussaint defeated them, then put down a revolt by the mulattoes, who constituted a distinct class in Haiti and opposed black rule. In 1801, he drove the Spanish out of Santo Domingo, uniting the entire island.

In an effort to reestablish the colony's wrecked agricultural base, Toussaint insisted the ex-slaves return to work on the plantations where they were now to receive one-quarter of the produce they grew. Schools were established and the beating of laborers forbidden. He reorganized the local government and issued a new constitution. Though he distrusted the whites and the mulattoes, Toussaint worked closely with both in organizing and reforming Saint-Domingue's government. A master diplomat, he continued to profess loyalty to France but did not provide the French government with more than an advisory role in the colony's future. This was not acceptable to Napoleon, France's new leader, who secretly intended to reinstate slavery on the island. A French army under the command of General Charles Leclerc, Napoleon's brother-in-law, was sent to Saint-Domingue, and fighting again broke out. Toussaint was seized by treachery and died of cold and malnutrition in a French prison in 1803. A year later, JEAN-JACQUES DESSALINES declared Saint-Domingue an independent state and renamed the country Haiti.

Recommended Reading: James, C. L. R. *The Black Jacobins*. New York: Vintage Books/Random House Inc., 1989: Meyers, Walter Dean. *Toussaint L'Ouverture: The Fight for Haiti's Freedom*. New York: Simon Schuster Children, 1991; Santrey, Lawrence. *Toussaint L'Ouverture: Lover of Liberty*. Wahwah, N.J.: Troll, 1997.

triangular trade

Term used during slavery to describe trade between England, Africa, and the Americas. Guns and other goods were manufactured in England and shipped to Africa to exchange for slaves. The slaves were then transported to the Americas, and the ships would return to England loaded with sugar, cotton, and tobacco. A variation of this involved ships leaving New England loaded with rum to exchange for slaves in Africa. The slave cargo was sold in the West Indies, where the ships picked up molasses for transport back to New England to be made into rum. The England-Africa-Americas triangular trade was also known as the Great Circuit or the Triangle Trade Route.

Trotter, William Monroe (1872–1934) *civil rights activist, editor*

Trotter grew up in Massachusetts and graduated from Harvard University. In 1901, he began a news-

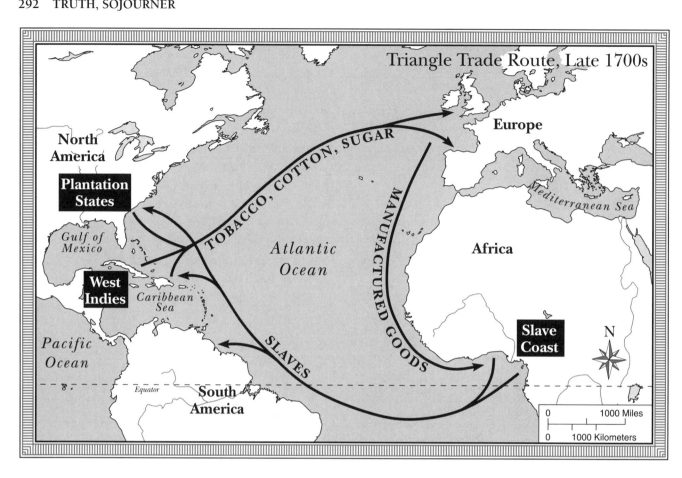

Triangular Trade Route (*Facts On File*)

paper called the *Guardian,* which he used to begin a crusade against BOOKER T. WASHINGTON. Trotter believed Washington was too accepting of an increasingly hostile racial climate, had failed to insist on black political rights, and was interested in promoting only the kind of education available at Tuskegee Institute. In 1903, Trotter spent a month in jail after disrupting a speech by Washington and causing a disturbance known as the "Boston Riot." After his release Trotter began working with W. E. B. DuBois to launch the NIAGARA MOVEMENT and, later, the NATIONAL ASSOCIATION FOR THE ADVANCEMENT OF COLORED PEOPLE. Trotter and DuBois eventually found it difficult to work together, and Trotter concentrated his energies on his own organization, The National Equal Rights League. He later campaigned against the racist movie *Birth of a Nation* and tried to have a racial equality clause included in the treaty ending World War I.

Truth, Sojourner (ca. 1797–1883) *abolitionist, crusader for women's rights*

Born a slave in New York State, her original name was Isabella Bomefree. Sojourner Truth's family was broken up while she was still a young child, and she suffered serious beatings at the hands of at least one master. Her last owner, John Dumont, promised to free her one year before slavery was to officially end in New York in 1827. However, he changed his mind and refused to let her go, claiming an injured hand had kept her from working. She ran away and, with the help of some Quakers, filed suit in court to successfully force the return of her young son who had been illegally sold out of state.

Deeply religious since childhood, Sojourner Truth joined a religious community led by a self-proclaimed prophet named Matthias from 1832 to 1835. In 1843, she made the religious decision to change her name to Sojourner Truth and began traveling through the North preaching at camp meetings. She also joined a utopian abolitionist/feminist commune in Massachusetts known as the Northampton Association, through which she met abolitionists David Ruggles and FREDERICK DOUGLASS.

Truth began addressing antislavery and women's rights groups and soon gained a reputation as a strong speaker. When challenged in 1851 by a minister who stated that since Jesus had been male, only men should have rights, she responded with her famous "And Ain't I a Woman" speech: "That man over there say that woman needs to be helped into carriages and lifted over ditches . . . Nobody ever helps me into carriages or over mud-puddles . . . And ain't I a woman? . . . I have ploughed and planted and gathered into barns . . . I could work as much . . . as a man . . . and bear the lash as well!

Abraham Lincoln presents Sojourner Truth with a Bible on behalf of the black people of Baltimore. (*Library of Congress*)

And ain't I a woman? . . . Then that little man in black there, he say women can't have as much rights as men 'cause Christ wasn't a woman! . . . Where did your Christ come from? From God and a woman! Man had nothin' to do with Him!"

During the Civil War, Sojourner Truth nursed African-American soldiers and moved to northern Virginia to help destitute former slaves. She established a job placement program in 1867 and petitioned Congress to set aside western land for ex-slaves. Though illiterate, she dictated her autobiography, which was published in the 1850s under the title *The Narrative of Sojourner Truth*.

Tuareg

A nomadic people of BERBER-Arab ancestry, the Tuareg were the dominate group inhabiting the Sahara and the West African SAHEL by A.D. 1000. A tall, graceful people known for keeping their word, they are tough, skillful fighters who traditionally demanded tribute from caravans that stopped at oases while traveling through the Sahara. They founded TIMBUKTU around A.D. 1100, but lost control of the city to the MALI Empire. In the late 18th century they regained control of the Niger River bend region, recovering Timbuktu, which was then held by the SONGHAI Empire.

The Tuareg traditionally maintained a feudal society composed of nobles and warriors (*imohagh*), vassels (*imrad*), serfs (*haratom*), craftsmen (*inaden*), and slaves (*iklan*). *Imohagh* and *imrad* were usually light-skinned, and the others were dark. However, evidence of racial mixture is evident in all classes of Tuareg society. Because of their willingness to resort to violence, the Tuareg tended to be left alone by European colonial powers, even with regard to their practice of slavery, which continued long after it had been made illegal. With the disappearance of the slave trade and the tribute-paying caravans, through which Tuareg nobles supported their vassels and serfs, the traditional Tuareg class structure was severely weakened.

Today, the Tuareg maintain herds of sheep, goats, and camels and move frequently—usually every three to five days—in search of water and pasture. According to ancient custom, the men wrap their heads with veils and never uncover their mouths even while eating. They also wear indigo-dyed robes that stain their skin and, as a result, are sometimes called the "Blue Men." Their alphabet is the only written form of Berber that still exists. Though the Tuareg were converted to Islam centuries ago, the Christian cross remains a favorite item of decoration. Unlike the men, the women, though Islamic, do not cover their faces.

Tubman, Harriet Ross (ca. 1821–1913)
Underground Railroad conductor

Born in Dorchester County, Maryland, to slave parents who named her Araminta, Tubman later took her mother's name, Harriet. She suffered recurrent seizures as a result of being struck on the head by an overseer when she went to the defense of another slave. She escaped in 1849 and made her way to Philadelphia after learning that she was destined to be sold. After saving enough money to finance her trip, she returned to rescue her sister and her two children. It was the first of 19 trips that would bring 300 slaves to freedom. Tubman planned her escapes for Saturday nights, knowing that slaveowners would not be able to have "wanted" posters made up before Monday. Her rules were simple: Be on time, follow instructions; tell no one of the escape; and be prepared to die rather than turn back. People who saw her walking along back southern roads saw what they thought was a harmless old woman wandering along singing songs. But the lyrics were a code alerting slaves to her presence, and Harriet Tubman was anything but harmless. She usually carried a gun. Slave owners considered her extremely dangerous and put a $40,000 price on her head. Called "The Moses of Her People," Tubman worked closely with WILLIAM STILL and was a friend of FREDERICK DOUGLASS. She conferred with John Brown, though sickness prevented her from participating in the 1859 raid at Harpers Ferry. That same year, she endured physical assault to rescue a runaway slave named Charles Nalle from police custody and helped him escape to Canada. During the Civil War, she planned and led a raid that freed 750 slaves. She also worked for the army as a spy, scout, and nurse. Afterward, Tubman attempted to establish schools

Harriet Tubman (*Library of Congress*)

for freedmen in North Carolina and later founded a home for destitute former slaves who were too old and feeble to work. In 1978, the U.S. Postal Service issued a stamp in her honor. (See also UNDERGROUND RAILROAD.)

Tunisia, Republic of

North African country located between Algeria and Libya. Capital: Tunis. The coastal area was settled in the 10th century B.C. by the PHOENICIANS, who founded the city of CARTHAGE there in 814 B.C. Tension with Rome in the third century B.C. resulted in the Punic Wars, which ended in a Carthaginian defeat and the destruction of the city in 146 B.C. The area later came under the control of the Vandals and the Byzantine Empire (fourth and sixth centuries A.D.), and the Arab invasions in 648–698 permanently established Islam in the region. Various BERBER and Arab dynasties controlled the area until 1574, when it came under the control of the Ottoman Empire. In the 19th century, the French invaded Tunisia and established a protectorate over the region. The country was the site of several battles during World War II, and a strong independence movement under Habib Bourguiba developed there once the hostilities ended. In spite of resistance from French settlers, Tunisia became independent in 1956. A year later, Tunisia declared itself a republic under President Bourguiba. Tunisia's support for a political settlement with Israel caused problems with other Arab countries. Opposition parties were legalized in 1986. Bourguiba was ousted in a bloodless coup in 1987 by Zine el Abidine Ben Ali, who won a general election (running unopposed) later that year and again in 1994. The government has engaged in the harassment and intimidation of persons critical of it, particularly members of the press and judiciary.

Turner, Nat (1800–1831) *slave revolt leader*

The Nat Turner uprising occurred in 1831 in Southampton County, Virginia. Turner was both charismatic and educated. A preacher, he had lived an ascetic life and was widely admired by both blacks and whites. He is even said to have baptized a white overseer and convinced him to change his ways. Though he rejected the conjuring of spirits, Turner was a mystic who saw visions and heard voices that called upon him to free his people. Other slaves called him "The Prophet" and believed he had special healing powers. At the age of 21, he ran away but returned voluntarily to his master after 30 days, convinced that he had another destiny.

In 1825, Turner had a vision in which he saw black and white spirits fighting. Three years later, he had another vision calling upon him to fight evil. In February 1831, there was an eclipse, which Turner took as another sign. At that point, he spoke to four friends, telling them of his plans to stage a revolt on the Fourth of July. But as the time approached, Turner became sick, and so another sign was sought. It came on August 13, when a bluish-green

Nat Turner (*Library of Congress*)

haze covered the Sun. In the early hours of August 22, Nat Turner met once more with his small group, which had now grown to include two additional men. Armed only with a hatchet and a broadax, they set forth. At this time, Turner was the slave of Joseph Travis, who was the first to die. After killing the Travis family, the group traveled from house to house, killing all whites, with the exception of one very poor white family. The revolt continued for 40 hours, during which the original insurgents were joined by approximately 60 additional slaves.

The day after the Travis killings, Turner's men were attacked by a group of armed whites, and within 24 hours, hundreds of soldiers had spread out across the countryside. Nat Turner managed to hide but was captured six weeks later. He pleaded not guilty, saying that he did not *feel* guilty. He was convicted and on November 5, the sentence was handed down by Judge Jeremiah Cobb who ordered that Turner "be hung by the neck until you are dead! dead! dead!"

Following the revolt, at least 12 states passed legislation tightening restrictions on slaves and limiting the rights of free African Americans and encouraging their migration to Africa. The issue of actually abolishing slavery was debated for weeks in the Virginia state legislature. Fifty-seven whites lost their lives to "General Nat's" army and many blacks with no connection to Turner's revolt were later murdered by vengeful whites.

Tuskegee Airmen

Term used to describe four all-black World War II squadrons—the Ninety-ninth, 100th, 301th, and 302d. Nine hundred twenty-six pilots earned their pilot's wings under the Army Air Force Aviation Cadet program, which began in 1941 at Tuskegee Institute in Alabama. Although the program's first students graduated three months after the bombing of Pearl Harbor, the army refused to deploy the Tuskegee pilots outside the United States until 1943, when the 99th was shipped to North Africa. Racial hostility in the military almost led to its recall, but the squadron was saved thanks to the testimony of its commander, BENJAMIN O. DAVIS JR., who later became the first African-American U.S. Air Force general. In 1944, the Ninety-ninth merged with the other three black squadrons to form the 332d Fighter Group. As a bomber escort group on 200 bomber missions, the 332d won fame for not losing a single U.S. bomber to enemy aircraft. In 1,578 combat missions, the Tuskegee Airmen shot down 111 enemy planes, destroyed 150 others on the ground, and sank a German destroyer. Tuskegee Airmen saw action in Africa, Sicily, Italy, France, Germany, and the Balkans; 66 were killed in action. Members of the 332d won more than 100 Distinguished Flying Crosses, and the group won three Distinguished Unit Citations.

Tuskegee syphilis experiment

Medical study undertaken in Macon County, Alabama, by the U.S. Public Health Service (PHS), which denied medical attention to 412 African-American men suffering from syphilis while pretending to treat them. The study, which received cooperation from the hospital at Tuskegee Institute and the medical community in Alabama, began in 1932. It was designed as a short-term project (six to eight months) whose purpose was to gain a greater scientific understanding of syphilis by studying the untreated progression of the disease. At that time, successful treatment for syphilis took a year to complete, sometimes had serious side effects, and was expensive. It was assumed that those black men who were syphilic would remain untreated anyway, there being no government medical program for poor people.

However, the African Americans being studied were never informed that they had syphilis (they were told they had "bad blood"), they were never told their illness could be sexually transmitted to others, and they were led to believe that they were, in fact, receiving treatment. In the event that any of them did seek other medical help, area doctors were told that they were not to be treated but were to be referred to the health service program workers. To acquire the cooperation of the Macon County Board of Health, the PHS had to agree to provide some treatment; however, they did not provide enough to effect a cure. They also provided the men with aspirin, iron supplements, and, beginning in 1935, $50 for burial expenses.

The study was continued after the first year because of the scientific information it generated. When the PHS began a nationwide venereal disease control program in the late 1930s, the men in the Tuskegee study were denied treatment. Treatment continued to be denied even after the therapeutic effectiveness of penicillin was determined in the early 1940s. The study, which was officially known as The Tuskegee Study of Untreated Syphilis in the Negro Male, was finally terminated in 1972 after it came to public attention. By that time, many of the men had died from syphilis, often after going blind or insane from the disease. Treatment was provided for survivors, approximately 50 surviving wives who had been infected, and 20 surviving children who had been born with congenital syphilis. The government also agreed to pay each survivor $37,500 and heirs $15,000. In 1997, President Bill Clinton formally apologized to those victimized by the experiment.

Recommended Reading: Jones, James H. *Bad Blood.* New York: The Free Press, 1981, 1993.

Tutu, Desmond Mpilo (1931–) *archbishop of Cape Town, Anglican primate of southern Africa*

Tutu grew up in the Transvaal region of South Africa, where he was subjected to the constant indignities of racial discrimination. His family moved to Johannesburg in 1943, and it was there that Tutu met Father Trevor Huddleston, who would later become a close friend and mentor. While a teenager, Tutu spent 20 months in a hospital recovering from tuberculosis. Afterward, he entered medical school but was forced to drop out for lack of money. He then became a teacher but resigned when the South African government introduced a discriminatory education plan for blacks. In 1961, Tutu was ordained an Anglican priest, and in 1972, he became associate director of the Theological Education Fund in England and traveled throughout Asia and Africa. When he returned to South Africa in 1975 he became deeply involved in the anti-APARTHEID cause. He became the first black secretary general of the 13-million-member South African Council of Churches in 1978 and used his position to intensify criticism of South Africa's racial policies. In 1984, Tutu won the Nobel Peace Prize for his efforts to bring racial justice to South Africa.

Bishop Desmond Tutu at the American Bookseller's Association Convention in the Los Angeles Convention Center, California (*Lee/Archive Photos*)

U

Uganda, Republic of

African country. Capital: Kampala. The area was first settled about 500 B.C. by BANTU-speaking people who eventually founded several small kingdoms known as the Chwezi states. The prosperous Bunyoro and Buganda states rose to power during the 16th and 17th centuries. Buganda raided neighboring tribes for slaves and ivory, which it sold to Muslim traders for guns. Buganda was visited by explorer Henry Stanley in 1875. Both Britain and Germany attempted to expand their influence in the area, and in 1890, the two European countries reached an agreement that allowed the Imperial British East Africa Company (IBEA) to bring in troops and take over most of southern Uganda. In 1894, Uganda became a British protectorate. The British replaced the Buganda king, who was not submissive enough, and established their authority over other tribes through treaty, though they were willing to use force if necessary. Buganda, which had always resisted British rule, was allowed considerable autonomy. The British built a railway from Lake Victoria to the East African coast and encouraged the cultivation of cotton, coffee, and sugar. Although a legislative council was established in 1921, it did not seat its first African member until 1945.

In 1962, Uganda became independent under Prime Minister Milton Obote. Nine years later, Obote was overthrown by Idi Amin, who began his regime by expelling over 60,000 Asians whose families had settled in Uganda decades before.

During his rule, Amin was responsible for the deaths of approximately 250,000 Ugandans. In 1976, Amin declared himself president for life. Two years later, he ordered the invasion of Tanzania. Tanzania successfully counterattacked, uniting Amin's opponents and forcing Amin to leave the country. Obote was returned to power, and murdered thousands of Amin supporters and drove 200,000 others into exile. Obote was overthrown in 1985. Uganda began rebuilding in 1986 under president Yoweri Museveni, but in addition to past misrule, the country has been hit hard by the current AIDS crisis.

Uganda's northern region has been the site of fighting by a vicious fanatical group called The Lord's Resistance Army, which has engaged in the kidnapping of children and other atrocities. Fighting among Karimojong tribes has also resulted in the deaths of several hundred people. In 2000, a religious cult called the Movement for the Restoration of the Ten Commandments of God was linked to the murders of more than 900 people. The emergence of extreme religious cults is believed to be an outgrowth of Uganda's violent past. President Museveni is rapidly emerging as a major leader in sub-Saharan Africa. He provided significant military support to Tutsi leader Paul Kagame in RWANDA, intervened militarily in CONGO, and sent aid to rebels trying to overthrow the government in SUDAN. His government has made a strong effort to bring the AIDS epidemic in Uganda under control.

Uncle Tom's Cabin

Antislavery novel written by white abolitionist Harriet Beecher Stowe. Subtitled *Life Among the Lowly,* it was published in 1852 and is credited with converting thousands of readers to the abolitionist cause. The book tells of the suffering of Uncle Tom, an elderly slave who dies as the result of a beating. His devotion to his white master led to the use of the term "Uncle Tom" in reference to African Americans who behave in an obsequious manner when dealing with whites. The character of Uncle Tom was based on JOSIAH HENSON, a runaway slave and conductor on the UNDERGROUND RAILROAD who wrote a book about his life that was read by Stowe.

Magee House, an Underground Railroad station during the Civil War (*Library of Congress*)

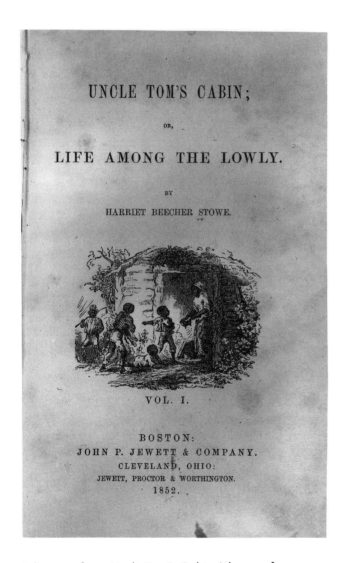

Title page from *Uncle Tom's Cabin* (*Library of Congress*)

Underground Railroad

A loosely organized escape system to help runaway slaves that was established in the United States around the time of the American Revolution. It was called the Underground Railroad because, as one man put it, escaping slaves seemed to vanish "as if on an underground track into the earth."

The runaways followed different paths—usually north to Canada, but sometimes south to Mexico and the Caribbean. Running away took considerable courage, as those who were recaptured faced brutal retaliation. The ingenuity demonstrated by escaping slaves was often considerable. Henry "Box" Brown sealed himself in a carton and had himself mailed from Richmond to Philadelphia. Twenty-eight other slaves formed a funeral procession and walked all the way from Kentucky to Ohio. Others traveled in wagons hidden under hay and straw, on trains disguised as nurses with white babies, by mule and horseback, and on boats, rafts, and even pine logs.

Underground Railroad people used a special code in discussing their work. A "station" or "depot" was a safe house were fugitive slaves could find food and shelter. "Tracks" were backcountry roads and trails that could be used safely. "Conductors" were people like HARRIET TUBMAN who were

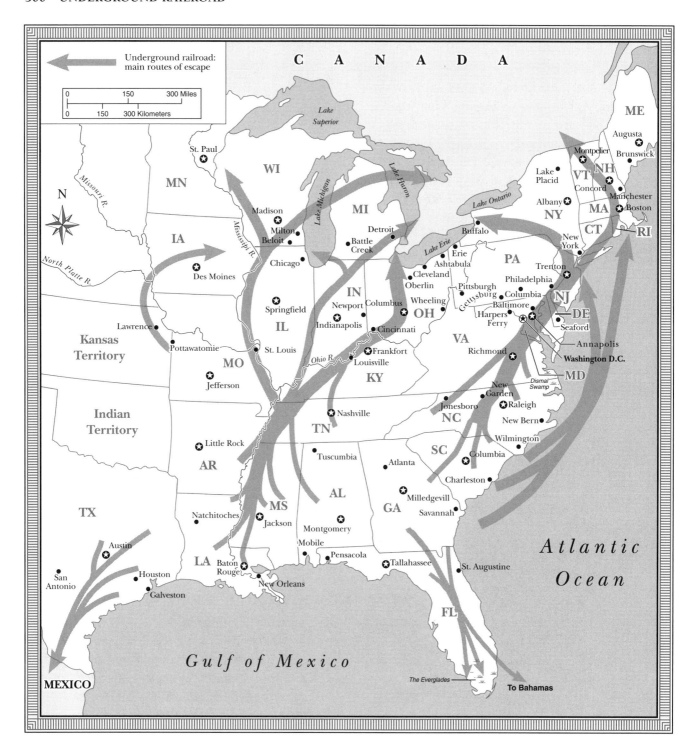

Routes of the Underground Railroad (*Facts On File*)

willing to slip deep into slave territory in order to lead runaways to freedom. And "parcels" or "passengers" were the runaway slaves themselves.

Slaves passed escape information along what was known as the grapevine telegraph. They also used song lyrics as a means of providing instruction. "Swing Low, Sweet Chariot, coming for to carry me home" meant a conductor of the railroad was in the area and that an escape was due soon. The spiritual "Wade in the Water" was a code instructing slaves to wade in rivers and streams so that dogs tracking them could not pick up their scent. And the lyrics to the hymn "Follow the Risen Lord" were changed to "Follow the Drinking Gourd," the drinking gourd being the Little Dipper constellation that contains the North Star pointing the way north.

Underground Railroad "agents" faced considerable danger, as "slave stealing" was a serious crime, punishable by fines, branding, and/or imprisonment. Calvin Fairbank, a white minister, spent a total of 17 years in prison because of his work on the Underground Railroad, and many others endured terrible beatings, sometimes resulting in death. A free African American named Samuel Burris was punished for his Underground Railroad activities by being sold into slavery himself. In his case, however, the highest bidder was secretly working for another Railroad agent named Thomas Garrett and had orders to purchase Burris and return him to freedom. Others were not so lucky.

"President" of the Underground Railroad was a Quaker named Levi Coffin. Based in southern Indiana, he helped more than 3,000 slaves escape. John Mason, a runaway slave himself, led 265 fugitives to safety during one 19-month period alone. Recaptured and sold back into slavery, he managed to escape a second time. Thousands of people favored abolition, and many were prepared to support the Underground Railroad in spite of the risks. In addition to those mentioned above, well-known agents of the Railroad included human-rights activists FREDERICK DOUGLASS and SOJOURNER TRUTH, women's-rights leaders Susan B. Anthony and Lucretia Mott, Congressman Thaddeus Stevens, writers Henry David Thoreau and Harriet Beecher Stowe, and poet John Greenleaf Whittier.

Exactly how many persons escaped via the Underground Railroad will never be known. During the American Revolution, more than 30,000 slaves ran away in Virginia alone. According to one Mississippi governor, 100,000 slaves valued at more than $30 million escaped between 1810 and 1850. Slaves who escaped but who remained in the area and established settlements in nearby swamps and forests were known as outlayers, or MAROONS. Maroon settlements in the United States tended to be small, with perhaps only a dozen or so escaped slaves. But those in Central and South America and the Caribbean sometimes sheltered thousands of runaways. The Underground Railroad continued in the United States until the Civil War brought slavery to an end.

Union League

a patriotic society that began in Philadelphia during the Civil War and became a primary supporter of the Republican Party in the South during Reconstruction. Meetings, which usually opened with a prayer and declarations of support for equal rights, were held in schools, churches, homes, and open fields and were often guarded by armed black men. Monies were collected for schools, churches, and the support of the old and sick. But the league's most important work involved political education. Issues were debated, and decisions were made regarding political support of various candidates. Since many members were illiterate ex-slaves, newspapers were regularly read aloud. Many African-American leaders gained their early political experience through Union League meetings where emphasis was placed on character rather than social status or education. As one former slave said, "You can teach me the law, but you cannot (teach) me what justice is."[1]

[1]Eric Foner, *Reconstruction: America's Unfinished Revolution, 1863–1877.* New York: Harper & Row, p. 288.

V

VanDerZee, James (1886–1983) *photographer*
VanDerZee's parents worked for a time as maid and butler to former president Ulysses S. Grant but in 1885 moved to Lenox, Massachusetts, where VanDerZee was born. As a child, he was encouraged to pursue art and music, and he became interested in photography while in his early teens. He moved to New York City in 1905, working at various jobs until he was able to open his own photographic studio in 1916. VanDerZee's thousands of photographs provide a unique history of this country's African-American community. His subjects ranged from celebrities like Joe Louis, Hazel Scott, and Romare Bearden to weddings, funerals, parades, group portraits, nudes, and photographic collages. In 1924, MARCUS GARVEY commissioned VanDerZee to do a series of photographs documenting the work of Garvey's UNIA organization. In 1969, VanDerZee's work was presented as part of the New York Metropolitan Museum of Art's *Harlem On My Mind* exhibition. Apart from its artistic value, VanDerZee's work was critically important at a time when African Americans were frequently depicted in advertisements, comic strips, and other media in highly racist, negative ways.

Vaughan, Sarah (1924–1990) *jazz singer*
In 1943, Sarah Vaughan won the amateur night contest at the APOLLO THEATER and was invited to join the Earl "Fatha" Hines band as a vocalist and second pianist. There she became close to DIZZY GILLESPIE and CHARLIE PARKER and, in 1944, left with them to join Billy Eckstine's band. The following year she began working as a solo artist. Called "The Divine Sarah," she appeared in a variety of groups ranging from trios to symphony orchestras. Her voice, which spanned two and one-half octaves, was regarded by many as the best in JAZZ, and her performances might include anything from scat singing to pop ballads.

Recommended Listening: *The George Gershwin Song Book* (EmArcy Jazz Series).

Vesey, Denmark (ca. 1767–1822) *slave insurrection leader*
Believed to have been born in Africa, Vesey was sold into slavery and spent at least two years as a slave member of the crew of a slave ship. In 1800, he won a $1,500 lottery ticket and used part of the money to obtain his freedom. He then opened a carpentry shop in Charleston, South Carolina, and became relatively wealthy.

But though free, Vesey became increasingly bitter about the treatment of blacks. His family remained in bondage, and the sight of his children growing older under slavery must have been extremely painful to him. There was also his pride. Even successful free black men such as himself were treated with disdain, a situation Vesey refused to accept. He frequently stated that all men were born equal and that any black man who lowered himself before whites was not much of a man. Vesey was also aware that, because of an economic depression, many whites had left the area, leaving Charleston with a population that was 57 percent black. The large black presence had resulted in laws outlawing manumission (the freeing of a slave by an owner) without the approval of the legislature. Free African Americans from elsewhere were barred from taking up residence in the state, and free blacks who left the state were not allowed to return. Especially infuriating to many blacks, slave and free, was the closing of the African Methodist Episcopal Church, which the authorities had shut down as subversive. In addition, the furious and prolonged antislavery debate engulfing the Missouri Compromise of 1820 had led many blacks to believe that abolitionist sentiment throughout the country was considerably stronger than it actually was.

Vesey began planning his revolt in 1818. He was aided by several other men: Peter Poyas, a man described in the official report as "intrepid and resolute"; Ned and Rolla Bennett, slaves belonging to the governor of the state; Gullah Jack Pritchard, a slave believed by many to possess magical powers; and Mingo Harth. Working with great caution, these men eventually enlisted as many as 9,000 others in their cause. The plan involved a five-pronged attack on the city, with a sixth force that would patrol the streets. Two hundred and fifty bayonets and pikes and more than 300 daggers were secretly forged. The location of all armories, powder houses, and stores containing weapons were noted. All slaves with access to horses and wagons were contacted and given instructions as to their roles. At least two letters were sent by Vesey to individuals in Haiti discussing the proposed revolt and asking for help.

The date for the uprising was set for the second Sunday in July 1822. The reasons were twofold. In the first place, it was a summer month when many whites would be away on vacation. Planning the attack for Sunday allowed the insurgents to take advantage of the fact that slaves routinely gathered in Charleston on the Sabbath, thus allowing the rebels to gather without drawing immediate attention.

Though great care was taken in selecting slaves to join the uprising, Peter Devany, a favorite slave of Colonel Prioleau, learned of the plot and revealed it

to a free black man named Pencell. Pencell advised Devany to inform his master, which he did, leading to the arrest of Peter Poyas and Mingo Harth. Vesey immediately decided to move up the date of the revolt, but he was unable to communicate this to many of his followers who lived in outlying areas. Meanwhile, another slave, William, broke down and confessed, resulting in more arrests. The whole conspiracy began to fall apart. One hundred thirty-one slaves were arrested. Vesey went into hiding but was apprehended on June 22. Five days later, he was tried and condemned to hang. Of the 131 others charged, 49 were sentenced to death. Twelve were later pardoned, but the rest were executed. Four white men were also fined and imprisoned for encouraging revolt.

Fear of a general uprising was so strong that federal troops were assigned to the courthouse and to the prison to prevent rebellious slaves from freeing Vesey and the other conspirators. Peter Devany, the slave who first betrayed the plot, was freed and given a yearly pension of $50. Pencell, the free black man who had advised Devany, was granted a $1,000 reward. On July 2, the date of Vesey's execution, the state militia broke up a large black demonstration, and federal troops were again called out. Although thousands of slaves were believed involved in the uprising, only Vesey and a few of the leaders knew their names. Their attitude toward confession was summed up in the words Peter Poyas spoke to his subordinates as he stood waiting to be hung. "Do not open your lips! Die silent as you shall see me do." It was left for their actions to speak for them.

Voodoo (Vodun)

Haitian religion combining Catholic, traditional African, and American Indian religious beliefs. As in many African religious traditions, Voodoo worshipers pray to hundreds of spirits, who may or may not be sympathetic. Believers also pray to Catholic saints like St. Patrick, St. Anthony, and the Virgin Mary. The African influence has resulted in attributing to individual saints special characteristics not found in orthodox Catholic tradition. For example, St. Peter—or Papa Pie—is said to have a martial appearance and to live at the bottom of rivers and

Bottles and chalk markings on the ground in a Voodoo ritual, either in Haiti or the Dominican Republic. Voodoo is practiced on many Caribbean islands. (*Archive Photos*)

streams, and St. John is believed to like champagne. Objects on Voodoo altars include Catholic crucifixes, rosaries, candles, and holy water, but there are also flowers, flags, special stones, and foods that the African Voodoo spirits are supposed to like. Services mix Catholic prayers and rituals with dancing, trances, and animal sacrifice.

HAITI's violent history has resulted in the development of different strands of Voodoo. Rada Voodoo developed among slaves and emphasized protective spirits. In contrast, the spirits of Petro nation Voodoo, which developed among runaway blacks, are generally regarded as much more aggressive, especially when faced with oppression. In the Rada tradition, the spirit Ogun is a chivalrous warrior. In Petro Voodoo, he is called Ogun Ge-Rouge, and is regarded as a vicious and ruthless fighter. Many of the leaders of Haitian slave revolts claimed to represent Voodoo spirits, and were sometimes Voodoo priests. They often claimed that the spirits of those who died in revolts would return to Africa. Efforts to suppress or exploit this militant religious streak were common, even after the Haitian Revolution, as rulers sought to maintain control. While Voodoo is associated with Haiti, it is also practiced elsewhere.

voting rights struggle

legal, political, and social effort to win voting rights for African-American citizens of the United States. Although black people were among the first non-native Americans to set foot on this continent, they were the last group in the United States to win voting rights on a truly permanent basis. Slaves were never allowed to vote, and, in most places, neither were women—black or white. Before the passage of the FIFTEENTH AMENDMENT, free black men in some areas did manage to gain voting privileges, but the right was often revoked. North and South Carolina had both disenfranchised (taken their vote away from) free blacks by 1715, although North Carolina reinstated black voting rights 15 years later. Virginia denied the ballot to African Americans in 1723, and Georgia did the same in 1761. Blacks in Washington, D.C., were denied the vote in a bill signed by President Thomas Jefferson in 1803, and Maryland restricted the ballot to white males in 1810. Except for Tennessee, no southern state entering the Union after 1789 allowed blacks to vote, and Tennessee revoked the right in 1834. North Carolina followed Tennessee and disenfranchised its free black citizens a year later. New York continued to allow free blacks to vote but instituted a property qualification of $250 and a three-year residence requirement. Pennsylvania restricted voting to white males in 1838, and Indiana did the same in 1851. Only Rhode Island, Massachusetts, New Hampshire, Maine, and

Voting in Alabama, late 1860s (*Library of Congress*)

Vermont allowed African-American men to vote on an equal basis with whites.

Many white abolitionists were divided on the subject of voting rights for blacks. A number regarded the majority of African Americans as too ignorant and uncivilized to be entrusted with the ballot. Others did not view voting rights as important. President Lincoln said he favored giving the vote to black soldiers and "the very intelligent." But during the Civil War, as Union troops pushed into Confederate territory, newly freed slaves often voted to establish their own local governments without waiting for white approval. The best-known examples of this occurred in the Sea Islands of South Carolina and in DAVIS BEND, Mississippi. When the Civil War ended, it was clear that black people were ready to take control of their own affairs. The whites, however, were not prepared to let them.

Part of the reason for white resistance to black voting was racial prejudice. But much of the opposition was due to economic concerns. Most former slaves did not want to work for whites, in white homes, or on white-owned plantations. They wanted their own farms where they could set their own hours, grow their own crops, and sell their products to whomever they pleased. They wanted their children to go to school, and black women wanted to stay home and care for their own infants—something they had not been able to do under slavery. Black laborers who were willing to work for whites refused to accept whipping as punishment, wanted a say in setting their wages, and resisted the idea of working under the old "gang" system with a white overseer. To the white planters, this meant disaster. They wanted a "disciplined labor force"—in other words, one that they could easily control. To add to their dilemma, labor was scarce. Almost 250,000 white men had died fighting for the Confederacy. Thousands more had been permanently disabled. Thousands of African-American men, many from the South, had been killed fighting for the Union. White political control meant the power to write laws regarding labor contracts, land ownership, and work enforcement regulations. And white political control depended upon control of the vote. African Americans realized this, of course, but they were faced with serious obstacles in securing their political rights. Many northern merchants and factory owners, whose businesses depended on southern cotton, also wanted a stable labor force in the South and were prepared to sacrifice black voting rights to get it.

Presidential Reconstruction

Those opposing black voting rights had the support of President Andrew Johnson. In May 1865, Johnson issued two proclamations requiring that the southern states hold constitutional conventions creating new state governments. The only people eligible to vote for delegates to these constitutional conventions were Confederates who had received amnesty and those who had been eligible to vote in 1860. In other words, no blacks. By 1866, new southern state governments created by these all-white conventions had been established. Almost none of the people elected to them favored black voting rights. Johnson also removed most of the black U.S. Army troops that had been stationed in the South. The combination of pro-white state governments and the withdrawal of black army troops left African Americans extremely vulnerable to repression, and it was not long in coming. All of the southern states, with the exception of North Carolina, passed a series of laws known as BLACK CODES that severely limited black rights. They also lent encouragement to terrorist groups like the KU KLUX KLAN.

Radical Reconstruction

Johnson's policies resulted in antiblack violence, which had an extremely negative effect on Northern public opinion and on Congress. Like the African Americans of the South, the North saw the Black Codes and the physical intimidation for what it was: an attempt to reestablish slavery in everything but name. There was a furious reaction, and in January 1867, Congress, over Andrew Johnson's veto, voted to enfranchise blacks in the District of Columbia. In March, again over the president's veto, Congress passed the Reconstruction Act of 1867, which marked the beginning of the period known as Radical Reconstruction. Among the provisions of the Reconstruction Act of 1867 was a demand that the southern states enact new constitutions that provided for African-American suffrage. Because of Radical Reconstruction, 16 African Americans were elected to Congress, and in 1870, Hiram Revels of Mississippi became the first black man to be elected to the U.S. Senate. More than 600 African Americans, mostly former slaves, served in the state legislatures and hundreds of others were elected to local offices.

The Fifteenth Amendment

The Reconstruction Act of 1867 gave African Americans the right to vote in the South. However, they still lacked the vote in most northern states. Also, there was concern that the gains they had made would be lost if the white Southern Democrats ever gained control of Congress. The Fifteenth Amendment to the Constitution, which states that the right to vote cannot be denied by reason of race, color, or previous condition of servitude, was passed in order to deal with these concerns. It was passed by Congress on February 26, 1869, and ratified by the states on March 30, 1870. Had the 15th Amendment been enforced, African Americans would have been able to protect their civil rights. But it was not enforced, and the Ku Klux Klan managed to destroy the black vote in the South by murdering thousands of African Americans who voted, ran for office, or took leading roles in the community. When the Civil War ended, General Grant had allowed Confederate soldiers to keep their weapons, with the result that the black community was not only outnumbered but outgunned. The most famous case of black resistance took place in COLFAX, Louisiana, in 1873 and ended with the deaths of 280 African Americans. The political impact of all this violence was unmistakable. In 1873, black-supported Republican Governor Adelbert Ames carried Yazoo, Mississippi, by 1,800 votes. Two years later, the Democrats won Yazoo with a vote of 4,044 to seven. Where blacks did win, they were often forced to resign under threat of death.

End of Reconstruction

The election of President Rutherford B. Hayes in 1876 brought Reconstruction to an end. Federal troops—who were often the only protection the blacks had—were withdrawn from the South, and the state governments were left in white Democratic hands. Since the Fifteenth Amendment had guaranteed African Americans the right to vote, the southern states could not simply deny them the ballot. They could, however, through fraud and legal technicalities, make it almost impossible for blacks to meet voting qualifications allowing them to register. This was achieved through such devices as GRANDFATHER CLAUSES, LITERACY REQUIREMENTS, the POLL TAX, the WHITE PRIMARY, and a denial of the vote to persons convicted of various crimes. Denying the vote to convicts enabled registrars to exclude thousands of African Americans who had been convicted of petty theft or other minor offenses. Sometimes, these people were, in fact, guilty. Often, however, they were innocent men who had been jailed as a result of a dispute with a white person. What the whites could not control through law, they accomplished through violence, economic pressure, vote manipulation, and outright fraud. The destruction of the democratic process affected whites as well. Constitutional rights do not exist in a vacuum— they are protected to a large extent by the fact that other people have the same rights. In order to uphold a racist system that denied basic rights to African Americans, the rights of all individuals had to suffer. Among those rights most damaged by racial prejudice were freedom of speech, freedom of the press, and freedom of assembly. Anyone, black or white, who spoke out against injustice and discrimination risked being beaten or killed. The NATIONAL ASSOCIATION FOR THE ADVANCEMENT OF COLORED PEOPLE, various black individuals, and other civil rights organizations continued to work through the political and judicial systems to overturn the legal obstacles, and some progress was made including the outlawing of grandfather clauses (1915) and the white primary (1944). However, the basic situation remained unchanged until the civil rights movement of the 1950s and 1960s.

Impact of the Civil Rights Movement

The civil rights leaders of the 1950s and 1960s were immediately aware that voting was the key to many of the needed reforms. However, they faced not only legal and criminal opposition but also the fact that many African Americans had long since given up the hope of regaining their voting rights. In 1957,

MARTIN LUTHER KING JR. and other leaders formed the SOUTHERN CHRISTIAN LEADERSHIP CONFERENCE (SCLC), with the declared goal of registering 3,000,000 black voters across the South. That fall President Eisenhower signed the first civil rights bill passed by Congress in 82 years. It expanded the federal government's authority to take action to protect voting rights. Three years later, in 1960, a second civil rights act also aimed at protecting voting rights was passed. However, the voter registration drive continued to face massive resistance. One of the groups leading the effort to register voters in Mississippi was the recently formed STUDENT NON-VIOLENT COORDINATING COMMITTEE (SNCC). A number of SNCC workers were beaten and several were killed for trying to register black voters. But it took police attacks on demonstrators in Birmingham, Alabama,

and the murder of NAACP organizer MEDGAR EVERS in 1963 to convince President John F. Kennedy that what was needed was a far-reaching civil rights bill that would not only strengthen voting rights but also ban segregation in stores, hotels, restaurants, and other public places. Kennedy was assassinated before the bill could be enacted, but President Lyndon Johnson pushed it through Congress and signed it into law on July 2, 1964. The CIVIL RIGHTS ACT OF 1964 now stands as one of the major pieces of congressional legislation of the 20th century. But though it helped in the fight for voting rights, it could not provide the whole answer.

The Mississippi Freedom Summer Project

In 1962, the various civil rights groups had begun the Voter Education Project. By 1964, 500,000

Police form a barrier to prevent voters from registering, in Selma, Alabama, March 1965. (*Archive Photos*)

African Americans had been registered across the South. But most of these gains had occurred in areas where physical intimidation was not a major problem. In Mississippi, which had a long history of violence, only 4,000 black voters out of a possible 394,000 had been added to the registration rolls. In an effort to deal with this, SNCC and the other civil rights groups put together the Mississippi Freedom Summer Project and asked student volunteers from all over the country to come to Mississippi to register voters. Nine hundred college students—mostly white—answered the appeal. The decision to appeal for white volunteers was the subject of much debate. Many SNCC workers feared well-educated whites would tend to dominate SNCC's organization and undercut their efforts to develop local black leadership. However, others led by ROBERT MOSES believed that only massive involvement of whites would focus the attention of the nation on the situation in Mississippi. Moses was proved correct when three members of the CONGRESS OF RACIAL EQUALITY (CORE)—JAMES CHANEY, a 21-year-old black man who had lived in Mississippi all his life, Michael Schwerner, a 24-year-old white social worker from New York, and

Andrew Goodman, a 20-year-old white college student also from New York—were murdered. (See PHILADELPHIA, MISSISSIPPI, MURDERS.) The FBI sent in a task force to investigate, and more than 200 sailors from a nearby naval base were assigned to search for the bodies of the missing men. During the course of the summer, at least 80 other volunteers were beaten, and 1,000 civil rights workers were arrested. Sixty-eight homes and churches were dynamited or firebombed. The Mississippi Freedom Summer Project also established Freedom Schools to educate blacks about their political rights and to teach those who were illiterate. That same summer the MISSISSIPPI FREEDOM DEMOCRATIC PARTY was formed and challenged Mississippi's segregated delegation to the Democratic Party presidential convention. The year 1964 also marked the radification of the Twenty-fourth Amendment to the Constitution banning poll taxes in federal elections.

Selma

Since 1963, SNCC organizers had been working in Selma, Alabama. Two years later, after numerous protests, they decided to ask Martin Luther King Jr.

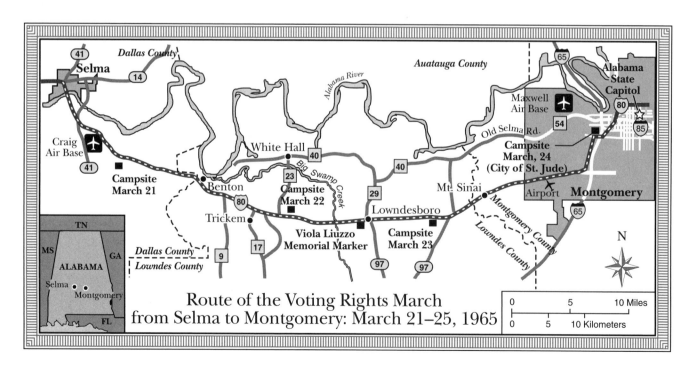

Route of the Voting Rights March from Selma to Montgomery: March 21–25, 1965

The Route from Selma to Montgomery (*Facts On File*)

Roy Wilkins and President Lyndon B. Johnson at the White House reviewing strategies for the passage of the Voting Rights Act, 1965 (*Library of Congress*)

for help. After several marches and hundreds of arrests, a young man named Jimmie Lee Jackson was shot down when he went to the defense of his mother who was being beaten by police. A protest march was scheduled for March 7, 1965. The date would later be known as BLOODY SUNDAY. Six hundred marchers gathered in Selma to begin the long march to Montgomery. When they reached the Edmund Pettus Bridge, they were met by state troopers who attacked them with clubs, whips, and tear gas. Millions of people watching TV saw what was, in effect, a police riot. Thousands of letters and phone calls poured into the White House and Congress, demanding that something be done. King announced another march for that coming Tuesday

and asked the nation's clergy to participate. Fifteen hundred people, including hundreds of priests, ministers, nuns, and rabbis responded to the call. Though the march itself went peacefully, four white ministers were assaulted that night as they left a restaurant. One, James Reeb, died from his injuries. President Lyndon Johnson had already planned to press for a strong voting rights bill. After watching the televised footage of Bloody Sunday, he decided to address a joint session of Congress, during which he endorsed the Civil Rights movement.

The Voting Rights Act of 1965

On March 19, 1965, President Johnson sent Congress a bill that would allow the Justice Department to send in federal examiners to take over voter registration in places where discrimination had occurred. On August 3, the Voting Rights Act of 1965 passed the U.S. House of Representatives with a vote of 328 to 74. The next day, the Senate passed it 79 to 18. It was signed into law by the president on August 6. The Voting Rights Act and the use of federal registrars led to the registration of thousands of African Americans across the South. In 1965, approximately 100 African Americans held elective office. By spring 2000, there were 39 black U.S. con-gressional representatives, hundreds of black may-ors, and thousands of other African-American elected officials throughout the country.

Recommended Reading: Burner, Eric R. *And Gently He Shall Lead Them*. New York: New York University Press, 1994; Foner, Eric. *Reconstruction: America's Unfinished Revolution, 1863–1877*. New York: Harper & Row, 1988; Franklin, John Hope. *From Slavery to Freedom: A History of Negro Americans*. New York: Knopf, 1980.

W

Walcott, Derek (1930–) *poet, dramatist*
Born on the Caribbean island of Saint Lucia, Derek Walcott is considered the leading poet of the West Indies. His family was English-speaking, but he grew up hearing the Creole-French patois of his home island. He attended Jamaica's University of the West Indies and worked as a journalist in Trinidad. Drawing on the history and traditions of the Caribbean, Walcott's early poems evoke such characters as Henri Christophe, Sir Francis Drake, and Robinson Crusoe. He also drew inspiration from the 1950s MAU MAU rebellion in Kenya.

Walcott's work incorporates many musical references, reflecting an interlinking between rhythmic language and physical movement. Caribbean dialects glint through even his most formal poetry, and he hints at an alienation from modern society in collections entitled *The Gulf* and *The Castaway*. Other well-known works include *In a Green Night* (1963), which draws on tropical imagery; a long, autobiographical poem, *Another Life* (1973); and *Omeros* (1990), which builds on Greek myth. His interest in art is reflected in the poem "The Polish Rider," which alludes to both Rembrandt and Durer. Among his plays are *The Dream on Monkey Mountain* (1967) and *Ti-Jean and His Brothers* (1971). In 1965, Walcott was invited to record a number of his poems for the Archive of Recorded Poetry and Literature of the Library of Congress in Washington, D.C. Other awards include a 1981 MacArthur "genius" fellowship award and the 1992 Nobel Prize in Literature. In 1997, he published another image-filled collection of poetry called *The Bounty*. In addition to writing, Walcott teaches at Boston University.

Walker, Aaron Thibeaux ("T-Bone") (1910–1975) *guitarist, singer*
Considered among the greatest of the BLUES guitarists, T-Bone Walker's playing strongly influenced B.B. KING and Albert Collins, among others. Walker himself grew up under the influence of "BLIND" LEMON JEFFERSON, and he passed Jefferson's tin cup in the days Jefferson played on street corners for tips. At age 10, he sang and danced in a family band and later practiced dance routines with JAZZ guitarist CHARLIE CHRISTIAN.

In 1929, Walker got a job with Cab Calloway's band after winning an amateur competition. Later that year, he recorded his first record, *Trinity River Blues*. After a racial incident in Oklahoma City, he left for Kansas City but returned home after a severe attack of stomach ulcers, a problem that plagued him all his life. In 1934, he moved to California where he joined a band featuring Zutty Singleton and quickly became a star attraction.

In addition to his considerable musical skills, Walker was a performer who would do splits, swing his guitar around his neck, and play one-handed while executing dance steps. One of the first musicians to master the electric guitar, Walker reached the height of his popularity during the 1940s when he became known as the father of the electric blues.

Recommended Listening: *The Complete T-Bone Walker, 1940–54* (Mosaic); *T-Bone Blues* (Atlantic); *Low Down Blues* (Charly); and *The Complete Imperial Recordings* (EMI).

Walker, Alice Malsenior (1944–) *writer*
The daughter of Eatonton, Georgia, sharecroppers, Alice Walker was blinded in one eye by her brother when she was eight years old. With a scholarship for the disabled and $75 for travel expenses raised by the black community in Eatonton, she was able to attend Spelman College. Two years later she transferred to Sarah Lawrence College in New York. Upon graduation, Walker moved south, where she worked in voter registration drives and later the

Alice Walker, an active participant in the Civil Rights movement and author of *The Color Purple*, in 1991. Walker won the Pulitzer Prize in 1983. (*Frank Capri/SAGA/Archive Photos*)

Head Start program. A gifted and prolific writer, Walker has written several novels, numerous essays, short stories, and poems and is a contributing editor to *Ms.* magazine. Her second book of poetry, *Revolutionary Petunias and Other Poems* (1973), won the Lillian Smith Award and was nominated for a National Book Award. Her third novel, *The Color Purple* (1982), won the Pulitzer Prize and became a hit movie. Walker's writings focus on the lives of black women and their ability to survive and triumph as strong, undiminished human beings. She has tackled several controversial topics, including the abuse of black women by black men and the practice of female circumcision in parts of Africa. In addition to civil rights, she is concerned with the antinuclear movement, women's issues, and animal rights. Walker's other novels include *Possessing the Secret of Joy, The Temple of My Familiar, Meridian, The Third Life of Grange Copeland,* and *By the Light of my Father's Smile.*

Walker, David (1785–1830) *pamphleteer*
Walker is the author of *David Walker's Appeal,* one of the strongest condemnations of slavery ever written in the United States. Walker was born in Wilmington, North Carolina, to a slave father and a free mother. Leaving home as a young man, he moved to Boston, where he became a regular supporter and occasional contributor to abolitionist journals and newspapers. In 1829, Walker published his famous *Appeal.* It was so inflammatory that the legislatures of Georgia and North Carolina were called into secret session to try to prevent Walker's message from being heard. Georgia also outlawed the teaching of reading to free blacks as well as slaves and instituted the death penalty for any African American involved in the distribution of Walker's *Appeal* or any other antislavery material. Since many copies of the *Appeal* were smuggled into the South by African-American seamen, both Georgia and North Carolina instituted quarantine laws restricting African-American seamen to their ships while in port. The governor of Georgia wrote the mayor of Boston, the city where Walker lived, asking that Walker be stopped from publishing. When the *Appeal* was blamed for a series of fires that had been

set in Savannah and Augusta and for a planned uprising that had been uncovered in South Carolina, a group of slave owners put a price on Walker's head—$1,000 dead, $10,000 alive.

The *Appeal* was divided into four sections. It condemned white Christians, charging that the sufferings of the Jews under Pharaoh were nothing compared to the sufferings of African-American slaves under Christians in America. Walker also attacked Thomas Jefferson for saying that blacks were inferior mentally and of an "unfortunate" color. He attacked blacks who were afraid to stand up to whites or, worse, who betrayed those who did. And he constantly emphasized the need for African Americans to gain skills and education. It was the duty, Walker said, for all free African Americans to strive for the freedom of enslaved blacks not only in the United States but all over the world. The furious reaction to the *Appeal* caused Walker's wife and friends to beg him to flee to Canada for safety. But he refused to leave. "I will stand my ground," he said. "Somebody must die in this cause. I may be doomed to the stake and the fire or the scaffold tree, but it is not in me to falter if I can promote the work of emancipation."[1] His words were prophetic. The *Appeal* was published in 1929. One year later, David Walker was dead, possibly a victim of poisoning, although no one could be sure.

Walker, Madam C. J. (Sarah Breedlove) (1867–1919) *businesswoman, inventor*

Walker's name was originally Sarah Breedlove. Orphaned at age five, she married at age 14, became a mother, and was widowed at 20. When her hair began to fall out, she tried various remedies without success. Then the recipe for a treatment came to her in a dream, and when she tried it, found it worked. Moving to Denver, she married Charles Walker and began selling her hair restorer door to door. Soon she began hiring other women to sell this and other beauty products. In 1908 she opened a second office in Pittsburgh. Two years later she opened her own

factory in Indianapolis. For the several thousand black women who worked for her, Madame Walker offered good pay and pleasant working conditions in jobs carrying considerably more prestige than most of those open to black women. More important, she linked loveliness to cleanliness rather than to race. In a society where white skin and Caucasian features set the standard for beauty, Madame Walker's insistence that African-American women were beautiful also was of critical importance. She was the first African-American woman to found a million-dollar empire. Her daughter A'Lelia Walker (1885–1931) promoted the work of many black artists during the HARLEM RENAISSANCE.

Washington, Booker Taliaferro (1856–1915) *educator, founder of Tuskegee Institute*

Washington was nine years old when the Civil War ended. He and his family moved to Malden, West Virginia, and Washington went to work in a salt furnace. After a workday that began at four in the morning, he would sit up at night teaching himself

Booker T. Washington with backers of the Tuskegee Institute at the 25th anniversary of the school in 1906 (*Library of Congress*)

[1] Herbert Aptheker, *One Continual Cry*. New York: Humanities Press, 1971, p. 43.

to read. At age 14, he left home on foot to attend Hampton Institute in Virginia. There, he came under the influence of General Samuel Armstrong, the school's founder. Armstrong believed in manual labor in order to promote honesty, discipline, and intelligence, and Washington took these concepts as the basis of his own educational philosophy.

In 1881, the Alabama state legislature decided to establish Tuskegee Institute to train African-American teachers, and Washington was chosen to head the new school. Two thousand dollars had been appropriated for Tuskegee, but this money was just for faculty salaries. Washington began by locating "a dilapidated shanty." Its condition was so bad that whenever it rained, one of the students would have to hold an umbrella over Washington's head as he taught. Since there were no funds for land, buildings, books, or supplies, Washington borrowed money to purchase an abandoned plantation. There his students built classrooms, dormitories, and a chapel. They also produced all their own food. By 1888, thanks to Washington's determination, Tuskegee owned 540 acres of land and had a student population of 400.

Following Armstrong's ideas, Washington focused on teaching vocational skills rather than traditional college subjects. In order to raise the living standards of black farmers, he promoted black land ownership, and in 1892, he established the annual Tuskegee Negro Conference to which thousands of African Americans were invited to learn better farming methods. He also managed to persuade Dr. GEORGE WASHINGTON CARVER to join the faculty at Tuskegee. Carver introduced concepts of fertilizer, crop rotation, and multicrop farming, and developed new products for farmers.

In an effort to encourage the development of more black-owned businesses, Washington established the National Negro Business League. His autobiography, *Up From Slavery,* became a best-seller and was translated into a dozen languages. He persuaded many white businessmen to make substantial contributions to Tuskegee and advised Presidents William Howard Taft and Theodore Roosevelt on political appointments of importance to the African-American community. But Washington ran into considerable criticism from several black leaders, especially W. E. B. DUBOIS. Although supportive of Washington's emphasis on work and thrift, DuBois attacked Washington's rejection of classical education and his failure to publicly criticize the steady erosion of black civil rights after the end of RECONSTRUCTION. Though he had written Washington a complimentary letter at the time, DuBois later attacked Washington's address at the 1895 Atlanta Exposition. In it, Washington seemed to accept both segregation and second-class citizenship with the words, "in all things that are purely social, we can be as separate as the fingers, yet one as the hand in all things essential to mutual progress . . . The wisest among my race understand that . . . social equality is the extremest folly." Washington greatly resented DuBois' criticisms. He had, in fact, secretly paid the legal fees of several lawyers working to overturn discriminatory laws, and had used his position to try and maintain black influence in the Republican Party.

Twice Washington had aroused the fury of the white community. Speaking in Chicago, he had charged that racial prejudice was "eating away the vitals of the South." On another occasion, he had lunch with President Roosevelt and thereby infuriated thousands of racists who felt blacks should never eat or socialize with whites. Faced with a vicious backlash that threatened support for Tuskegee, Washington retreated back into his old position of accommodation and conciliation.

Whether there was anything he could have done that would have slowed or stopped the continued chipping away at African-American civil rights is an open question. That Washington's public statements were always made with a possible white reaction in mind is clear; however, his primary concern was always the welfare of the black community. The vast majority of African Americans looked to him for leadership until his death in 1915. His accomplishments were long-enduring, and he remains the primary black leader of the post-Reconstruction period.

Washington, George (1817–1905) *founder of the city of Centralia in Washington State*

Washington was born to a black slave father and a white woman. When his father was sold, his mother

George Washington (*Oregon Historical Society; OrHi 11917*)

Unable to pay a bond, George Washington and his foster parents left for the Oregon Territory, part of which would later become Washington State. Once there, he staked out a plot. Since black men could not own property, he put his land in his foster parents' name. When plans were made in 1872 for the Northern Pacific Railroad to cross his property, Washington decided to establish a town on the location. Since it was to be located midway between the Columbia River and Puget Sound, he called it Centerville, though the name was later changed to Centralia. In 1875, Washington began selling lots for $5 each to anyone willing to build on them. He also donated land for the First Baptist Church, a cemetery, and a public square. When Centralia was hit by a serious economic depression from 1893–97, Washington gave away food and clothing, loaned money, and created jobs for townspeople.

He died at age 88 of severe injuries suffered in a buggy accident. On the day of George Washington's funeral, all businesses were closed. Services were held in the church that had been built on land he had provided, and he was buried in the cemetery he had donated, in Centralia, the city he had founded.

gave him to a white couple, James and Anna Cochran, to raise. The family moved to Missouri, where Washington grew up and later got into a legal dispute with a white man. When Washington took the case to court, the judge dismissed it, telling him that, as a black man, he had no right to sue. Washington then traveled to Illinois, where he learned that all black men had to post a bond guaranteeing their good behavior.

These restrictions of basic rights were not uncommon for African Americans. A number of "free" states denied blacks the right to vote, forbade them to testify in any trial involving whites, and required them to pay special taxes. (Occasionally, these policies backfired. One slave, who had been taken to California, refused to return east with his owner, claiming he should be free. In court, he admitted he was a slave, but the judge—citing the law forbidding black testimony—threw out his statement. He walked out of the courtroom a free man.)

Waters, Muddy (McKinley Morganfield)

(1915–1983) *blues singer, guitarist, harmonica player, songwriter*

Waters spent his early years working in the cotton fields in Clarksdale, Mississippi. He was nicknamed "Muddy Waters" while a child. He began playing the harmonica for 50 cents a night plus food at age 13, and became a "bottleneck" guitarist at age 17. (The term "bottleneck" refers to the practice of sliding the neck of a glass bottle over the little finger of the left hand so that when it touches the strings there is a special, "singing" sound.) Two musicians who influenced him were Eddie "Son" House and ROBERT JOHNSON. Waters left for Chicago in 1943 after a plantation overseer refused to raise his pay to 25 cents an hour on his daytime job.

In 1947, after signing with Aristocrat Records (later Chess), he had two hits with "I Can't Be Satisfied" and "I Feel Like Going Home." His career continued to grow with songs like "She Moves Me," "I'm Your Hoochie Coochie Man," "Close to You," "Baby

Please Don't Go," and "I Got My Mojo Workin'." One of Waters' most famous songs was "Rollin' Stone," which gave its name to the British rock group, *Rolling Stone Magazine,* and a Bob Dylan song. A central figure in creating what became known as Chicago Blues, Muddy Waters' music merged Mississippi blues with electrified instrumentation. His music has been recorded by Alan Lomax for the Library of Congress. He was a major influence in BLUES, RHYTHM AND BLUES, folk, pop, country, and rock music.

Recommended Listening: *They Call Me Muddy Waters* (Cadet); *The London Muddy Waters Sessions* (Cadet); *The Best of Muddy Waters* (Chess); *Folksinger* (Chess); *Fathers and Sons* (Chess); *Muddy "Mississippi" Waters Live* (Columbia).

Watts, Andre (1946–   ) *concert pianist*

Born in Nuremburg, Germany, to a Hungarian refugee woman and an African-American soldier, Andre Watts lived on military bases most of his early childhood. His mother introduced him to the piano, and his musical talent developed so rapidly that at age 10 he performed a Mendelssohn piano concerto with the Philadelphia Orchestra. He became nationally famous in 1963 when, at age 16, he appeared in televised concerts playing Liszt's first piano concerto with the New York Philharmonic Orchestra conducted by Leonard Bernstein. The Liszt concerto was also the first work he recorded, winning a Grammy Award as "best new classical artist" in 1964. In the 1960s, he became a box office attraction second only to Van Cliburn among U.S. pianists. He performed at Richard Nixon's 1969 presidential inaugural concert and toured Russia with the San Francisco orchestra in 1973. He is quoted as saying, "No one will ever get to know me better than by listening to me play."

Wells-Barnett, Ida Bell (1862–1931)
newspaperwoman, antilynching leader

Born of slave parents in Holly Springs, Mississippi, Ida Wells was orphaned at age 16 and left to care for her five younger brothers and sisters. She got a job as a teacher at $25 a month but left to take a better-

Ida B. Wells (*Library of Congress*)

paying job in Memphis, Tennessee, taking the two youngest children with her and leaving the other three with relatives.

Her civil rights activities began in 1888 when she was forced off a train after refusing to sit in a segregated car. She also began writing newspaper articles under the pen name Iola. In 1889 she bought a one-third interest in The Memphis *Free Speech and Headlight* and became an editor. For financial reasons she continued to teach. But in 1891, she lost her position with the Memphis public schools after writing an article protesting conditions in black schools. In 1892, three black men were lynched in Memphis because they owned a grocery that competed with a white-owned store nearby. Wells responded by writing an editorial that condemned the white leadership in Memphis and recommended that all African Americans leave the city. In response to the editorial, hundreds of blacks moved away, and thousands of others began boycotting white businesses. Shortly afterward, a mob destroyed the offices of the *Free Speech* and made it clear that Wells, who was in New York at the time, would be killed if she returned to Memphis.

After being hired by the *New York Age,* Wells began investigating lynchings and wrote a feature article, which charged that most lynch victims were not criminals but were killed primarily to maintain white domination. Ten thousand copies of the *New York Age* were printed and distributed across the country. One thousand issues were sold in Memphis alone. Soon afterward, Wells began lecturing on the subject, traveling to England and Scotland where she successfully gathered public support condemning the practice. In addition to her antilynching campaign, Wells helped publish *The Reason Why the Colored American Is Not in the Columbian Exposition,* a pamphlet attacking the 1893 Chicago World's Fair for its segregationist policies. She also set up the Negro Fellowship League to provide housing and employment help to black men, established the Alpha Suffrage Club to promote voting rights for black women, and was one of founders of the NATIONAL ASSOCIATION FORO THE ADVANCEMENT OF COLORED PEOPLE. In 1895 she married Ferdinand Barnett, publisher of the *Chicago Conservator.*

However, lynching remained her first concern. Her 1895 comprehensive report on the subject, *A RED RECORD,* provided a history of lynchings in the United States since the RECONSTRUCTION era. She also successfully prevented a man named Steve Green from being extradited to Arkansas where a mob had threatened to burn him, kept an innocent man from being executed in Illinois, and personally investigated the 1918 riot in East Saint Louis, Illinois, which killed 150 African Americans.

Recommended Reading: Klots, Steve. *Ida Wells-Barnett: Civil Rights Leader.* New York: Chelsea House, 1994; Mcmurry, Linda O. *To Keep the Waters Troubled: The Life of Ida B. Wells, Agitator.* New York: Oxford University Press, 1999; Wells, Ida B. *Crusade for Justice: The Autobiography of Ida B. Wells.* Chicago: University of Chicago Press, 1972.

Western Sahara

A phosphate-rich West African territory and former Spanish colony. Political pressure caused the Spanish to withdraw in 1975. The mostly desert territory, which was a subject of conflict between Morocco and Mauritania after the Spanish withdrawal, came under Moroccan control after Morocco's King Hassan organized a "Green March" of 350,000 settlers. Mauritania renounced its claims to the territory in 1979, but a locally formed guerrilla independence movement, the Polisario Front, continues to contest Moroccan rule. Morocco has invested heavily in the territory, building roads, schools, and hospitals. The capital of the territory is El Aaiun.

Wheatley, Phillis (ca. 1753–1784) *poet*

Kidnapped from Africa's SENEGAL region when she was about eight, Phillis Wheatley was bought by wealthy Bostonian John Wheatley as a maid for his wife Susannah. Wheatley quickly learned to speak English and began publishing poetry while still in her teens. Her poem "On the Death of the Reverend George Whitefield" was published in 1770 and attracted a good deal of attention. She was freed in 1773 and traveled to England, where her book *Poems on Various Subjects, Religious and Moral* was published. In 1775, she dedicated a poem to George Washington, who was so impressed that he invited her to visit him at his headquarters. Unfortunately, she married unhappily, and her husband spent much of the small inheritance she had received from John Wheatley. Two of her three children died, and she struggled to earn a meager living. She died on December 5, 1784, at age 31, and her last child died the same day. Her vivid poetry, which often gently rebuked whites for promoting slavery, provided proof, in a time of great prejudice, that blacks were equal to whites intellectually, emotionally, and spiritually.

white primary

A political procedure used to control the outcomes of local and state elections in the South. As RECONSTRUCTION drew to a close following the Civil War, the Republican Party was eliminated in the South as a political force. Its collapse meant that the winner of the Democratic primary would automatically win the election, since there was no real opposition. To make sure the Democratic Party remained under white control, the white primary was created.

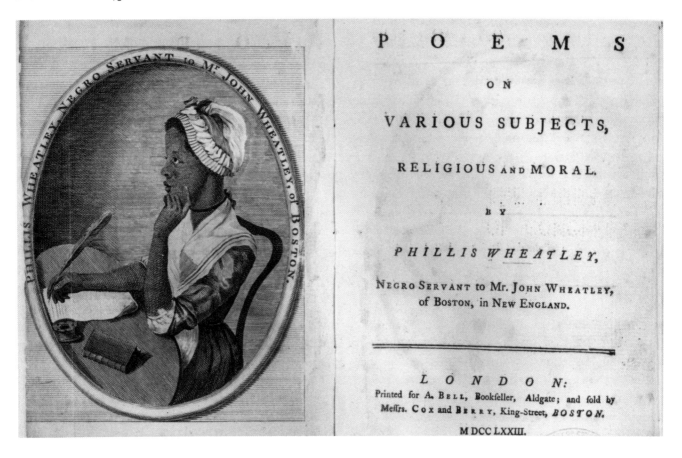

Title page of Phillis Wheatley's book of poetry (*Library of Congress*)

The FIFTEENTH AMENDMENT forbade government interference with voting in government elections on the basis of race or color, but supporters of white primaries argued that political parties were private, voluntary organizations and therefore could discriminate in the primary elections that determined the party candidates. From a racist point of view, the safest thing was to keep blacks from voting at all. Failing that, the next best thing was to keep blacks from voting in primaries so that no white candidate seeking a nomination would be tempted to appeal to black voters by agreeing to civil rights measures. This situation continued for more than 60 years until the Supreme Court ruled white primaries unconstitutional in 1944 in *Smith v. Allwright.*

See VOTING RIGHTS STRUGGLE.

Wideman, John Edgar (1941–) *writer*

Born in Washington, D.C., Wideman grew up in Pittsburgh, Pennsylvania, and became the second African American (ALAIN LOCKE was the first) to win a Rhodes Scholarship. Returning to the United States in 1966, Wideman taught writing at the University of Iowa and later at the University of Pennsylvania, where he developed and chaired the Afro-American studies program. Much of his writing focuses on the connection between the black intellectual and the black community, and on the historical ties linking African Americans to each other. He has also written forcefully about his family, especially his relationship with his imprisoned brother. Among his novels and books of short stories are *A Glance Away, The Lynchers, Fever,* and the autobiographical *Brothers and Keepers,* and *Fatheralong.* Wideman is a two-time winner of the PEN/Faulkner Award for *Sent for You Yesterday* (1984) and *Philadelphia Fire* (1991). In 1994, he received the MacArthur Prize Fellowship. He is currently a professor of English at the University of Massachusetts at Amherst. His latest novel is *The Cattle Killing.*

Wilkins, Roy (1901–1981) *executive director of the NAACP, civil rights leader, journalist*

Wilkins' mother died when he was three, and he and his younger brother and sister were sent to live with relatives in St. Paul. There he worked as a redcap, waiter, and stockyard laborer while attending the University of Minnesota. He also edited a black newspaper, the *Appeal,* as well as a school paper, the *Minnesota Daily.* After graduating in 1923, he joined the staff of the *Kansas City Call,* a black weekly newspaper, and soon became managing editor. As a member of the local NATIONAL ASSOCIATION FOR THE ADVANCEMENT OF COLORED PEOPLE (NAACP), he came to the attention of executive secretary Walter White and, in 1931, left for New York to become White's assistant. He became editor of the NAACP magazine *The Crisis* in 1934 and served in that post until 1949. In 1955, he became executive secretary (the title was later changed to executive director) of the organization. During his tenure, Wilkins made several trips south, where he posed as an ordinary black working man in order to gather evidence on racial discrimination. One such venture almost ended in disaster when a suspicious white storekeeper noted that Wilkins' hands appeared too soft for those of a workman. Wilkins was noted for his behind-the-scenes work with both Congress and the White House in promoting the civil rights agenda, and he had a particularly

close relationship with President Lyndon Johnson. He played a leading role in organizing the historic 1963 MARCH ON WASHINGTON and in the passage of critical civil rights legislation, including the CIVIL RIGHTS ACT OF 1964, the 1965 Voting Rights Act, and the 1968 Fair Housing Act.

Williams, Daniel Hale (1856–1931) *surgeon, educator*

Born in Pennsylvania, Williams went to work at age 12 as an apprentice to a shoemaker. Afterward, he worked at a variety of jobs, finally moving to Wisconsin, where he became an apprentice to Dr. Henry Palmer in 1878. Palmer helped him enter Chicago Medical College, from which Williams graduated in 1883. He set up an office in Chicago and joined the staff of the South Side Dispensary. He also became an instructor at Chicago Medical College and, in 1889, was appointed to the Illinois State Board of Health. In 1891, Williams established Provident Hospital, which was open to persons of all races and maintained an integrated medical staff and nurses' training program.

In 1893, "Dr. Dan," as he was affectionately known, became the first doctor in history to operate successfully on a human heart. The patient, a man named James Cornish, had been stabbed in the heart and left for dead. The operation made news all over the world, and the following year, Williams became chief surgeon at Freedman's Hospital in Washington, D.C. There, he reorganized the various medical departments and established new ones. However, frustration with hospital politics caused him to return to Chicago in 1898, where he was asked by the army to evaluate and select surgeons for service during the Spanish-American War. Over the next 20 years, Dr. Williams was instrumental in the establishment of 40 hospitals primarily serving African Americans.

Roy Wilkins in front of Attorney General Robert Kennedy during an NAACP march on the Justice Building in Washington, D.C., June 24, 1964 (*Archive Photos*)

Williams, George Washington (1849–1891) *historian, soldier, minister, lawyer, legislator, newspaperman*

Born free in Pennsylvania, Williams joined the Union army at 14 after lying about his age. When the army discovered the truth, it discharged him, but Williams pleaded to be allowed to serve and was finally allowed to reenlist. He was assigned to the staff of General N. P. Jackson and fought in several battles before being wounded. After the Civil War, he joined the Mexican army but resigned after a year to enlist in the U.S. Tenth Cavalry. He was discharged after being wounded in a battle against the Comanche Indians. Williams was then one month short of his 19th birthday and had enlisted four times in two different armies.

He then entered Howard University but dropped out to enroll in Newton Theological Institution in Massachusetts. He graduated in 1874, the first black man to do so at that school, and became a pastor at the 12th Street Church in Boston. Over the next few years, he founded a newspaper in Washington, D.C.; served as a minister at the Union Baptist Church in Cincinnati; became a lawyer; and won election as the first black member of the Ohio state legislature. There he infuriated people by attempting to repeal a law that banned interracial marriages. In 1882, he published his famous work *History of the Negro Race in America from 1619 to 1880.* Five years later, he published a second book, *History of the Negro Troops in the War of the Rebellion.* Both books were successful, and Williams became a popular lecturer and made several trips to Europe. On one of them he met King Leopold II of Belgium and became interested in recruiting African Americans to work in the CONGO FREE STATE, a private colony owned by Leopold. However, when Williams actually visited the Congo, he was shocked by the conditions he found. Africans were forced to work on rubber plantations in near-slavery conditions. Those who failed to produce enough suffered terrible punishments—often the loss of a hand or foot. Outraged, Williams began a personal crusade to expose conditions there. His first attack was contained in "An Open Letter to His Serene Majesty, Leopold II, King of the Belgians." In it, Williams denounced the king and the regime Leopold had established, accusing him of causing widespread hunger by forcing native people to supply soldiers with food and of the deliberate destruction of whole villages,

torture, rape, mutilation, murder, and the forcing of even young children to labor under slavelike conditions. He pointed out that Leopold's claim to provide schools, hospitals, and other public services was a lie. The letter received extensive publicity in Belgium, England, France, and the United States. But Williams did not stop there. He met with U.S. president Benjamin Harrison, and, in a letter to the U.S. secretary of state, accused Leopold of "crimes against humanity." Though Leopold tried to discredit Williams, a number of newspapers took his allegations seriously. Williams returned to Africa, then moved to England where he died at the age of 41. In 1975, the historian John Hope Franklin arranged for a tombstone to be placed over his grave. At the time of his death, hundreds of whites had visited the Congo Free State and had seen the atrocities being committed there. But George Washington Williams was the first person to report them and to attempt to destroy the system that produced them.

Recommended Reading: Franklin, John Hope. *George Washington Williams.* Chicago: University of Chicago Press, 1985.

Wilson, August (1945–) *playwright, poet*
Wilson began writing poetry while in seventh grade. He dropped out of school in the ninth grade but continued writing poetry as he worked at a series of menial jobs. He came of age during the BLACK POWER MOVEMENT, and this had a strong impact on his outlook. In 1968, he founded Black Horizon Theater. His play, *Ma Rainey's Black Bottom* opened on Broadway in 1984. It won the 1986 New York Drama Critics' Circle Award, as did *Fences, Joe Turner's Come and Gone, The Piano Lesson,* and *Two Trains Running. Fences* and *The Piano Lesson* also won Pulitzer Prizes. Wilson has described his writing as "a demonstration of the black culture's existence as well as its capacity to offer sustenance."[1] His most recent work is *Seven Guitars.*

[1] Rebecca Carroll, *Swing Low.* New York: Crown, 1994, p. 254.

Winfrey, Oprah (1954–) *television talk show host, actress*

After being sexually abused as a child, Winfrey developed behavioral problems and was sent to live with her father in Nashville, Tennessee. There she was hired as a reporter by a local radio station. While in college, she went to work for Nashville's local CBS television station and, in 1971, became the city's first TV anchorwoman. In 1976, Winfrey joined WJZ-TV in Baltimore, where she demonstrated strong appeal as the cohost of a morning show called *Baltimore Is Talking*. She left in 1984 to host *A.M. Chicago*. Within three months, she surpassed her competition, *The Phil Donahue Show,* in the ratings and proved so popular that her program was renamed *The Oprah Winfrey Show*. Widely syndicated, *The Oprah Winfrey Show* became one of the most successful shows in television history and made Winfrey one of the richest women in America. In 1985, she earned an Academy Award nomination for her role in the film version of ALICE WALKER's *The Color Purple*. Her company, Harpo Productions, ("Harpo" is "Oprah" spelled backwards), produced *The Women of Brewster Place,* a miniseries based on a novel by Gloria Naylor, and the 1997 TV movie *Before Women Had Wings.* The following year, she produced and starred in a film version of TONI MORRISON's *Beloved.* As part of her regular television program, Winfrey also instituted a book club that has resulted in millions of additional book sales. In 2000 Winfrey began publication of a magazine entitled *O.*

Wolof

One of the most important of the tribes in SENEGAL and THE GAMBIA. Tall and dark-skinned, the Wolof are generally regarded as intelligent and highly skilled. Sometime after A.D. 1300, the Wolof established the kingdom of Jolof in what is now eastern Senegal. Jolof extended its influence over a number of neighboring states, becoming a powerful empire during the 15th century. According to the Portuguese, in 1506, the Jolof king commanded an army of 100,000 soldiers and 10,000 cavalry. Growing European trade with Jolof's neighboring states allowed them to grow stronger until one, Cayor, rebelled in 1556. The various Wolof states continued to fight among themselves until they were conquered by the French in the late 19th century. Today, most Wolof are Muslim, although many continue to practice animist rituals. The Wolof are found in positions of authority in many West African countries.

Woods, Granville T. (1856–1910) *inventor*

Nicknamed "The Black Edison," Granville Woods held more than 60 patents, mostly in the field of electronics. Forced to quit school at age 10 to go to work in a machine shop, he became fascinated with electronics and spent hours studying it. After a few years working in different states, he returned to Ohio in 1881 and opened The Woods Electric Company in Cincinnati with his brother Lyates. In 1884, Woods received a patent for an improved telephone transmitter and sold the rights to it to the American Bell Telephone Company of Boston. Over the next six years, he acquired over a dozen more patents relating primarily to electric motors, telecommunications, railroad safety, and electromagnetic brakes. Among his most important inventions was a device that made it possible to transmit messages to moving trains warning of obstacles on the track ahead. In 1890, Woods moved to New York City where he continued his work. Many of his patents were sold to companies like General Electric, Westinghouse, and American Bell Telephone. He is responsible for developing the "third rail," an important element in subway systems.

Woods, Tiger (Eldrick Woods) (1975–) *champion golfer*

Tiger Woods was born in Cypress, California, in 1975, the same year that Lee Elder became the first African American to break the color barrier at the Masters Tournament in Augusta, Georgia. With the help and encouragement of his father, Earl, Woods began learning to handle a golf club as a toddler. At age three, he appeared on television in a putting exhibition with comedian Bob Hope. Woods attended Stanford University for two years, then turned pro in 1996 after winning three consecutive U.S. Amateur Championships (1994, 1995, and 1996). That same year he changed his given name, Eldrick, to Tiger, the nickname his father had given him in honor of a South Vietnamese army officer with whom he had served. In 1997, Tiger Woods won the Masters Golf Tournament by a 12-point margin and was named PGA Rookie of the Year. Two years later, he won the 81st PGA Championship, beating Sergio Garcia by one point. It was his 14th worldwide tournament victory. On July 23, 2000, Tiger Woods became the youngest player to complete the career Grand Slam, winning the British Open by a record-breaking 19 under par. (The other three tournaments in the career Grand Slam are the Masters, the PGA Championship, and U.S. Open.) On August 20, 2000, Woods won the PGA Champi-

Tiger Woods holds up the Wanamaker Trophy after winning the PGA Championship August 15, 1999. Woods bested Sergio Garcia by one stroke. (*Reuters/Sue Ogrocki/Archive Photos*)

onship, becoming the first player since Ben Hogan in 1953 to win three majors in one year. Golf has traditionally been a largely white sport, particularly at the professional level. Tiger Woods' dramatic play caused millions of young African Americans to regard golf as a sport at which they too might enjoy and excel. In addition to prize money, Woods has earned millions of dollars in endorsements.

Woodson, Carter Godwin (1875–1950)
historian, educator, author, intellectual

The son of former slaves, Carter G. Woodson left home in 1892 to work in the coal mines of West Virginia. There he entered high school, finishing after a year and a half. After graduating from Berea College in 1903, he was hired to teach in the Philippines, which the United States had acquired following the Spanish-American War. Later, he spent a year traveling throughout Asia, North Africa, and Europe, then returned to the United States where he became the only African American of slave parents to earn a Ph.D. in history (Harvard University, 1912).

In 1915, Woodson, along with George Hall, W. B. Hartgrove, Alexander Jackson, and J. E. Stamps, founded the Association for the Study of Negro Life and History (ASNLH), whose purpose was to educate the public, and especially blacks, about the history and achievements of African Americans. Four months after the association was founded, Woodson launched its *Journal of Negro History*. Although always teetering on the brink of financial disaster, Woodson refused to follow suggestions that he align the association with a black college, believing that the black schools were subject to too much white influence.

Convinced that education was the key to racial advancement, Woodson worked tirelessly, researching and writing hundreds of scholarly articles on slavery, black labor, and other aspects of African-American history and culture. Among the people he worked with, or who submitted articles for his publications, were ZORA NEALE HURSTON, W. E. B. DUBOIS, Charles Houston, ALAIN LOCKE, and MARY MCLEOD BETHUNE. To promote greater awareness of African-American achievements, Woodson inaugurated

Negro History Week in February 1926. Highly successful, it would eventually be superseded by Black History Month. He also offered black teachers correspondence courses in black history, literature, art, and philosophy so that they could better educate their students. In 1937, he began publication of the *Negro History Bulletin,* which was aimed at ordinary people rather than academics. Woodson not only filled the *Bulletin* with historical information and biographical data on black figures past and present, but he also used it to advocate the patronage of black businesses, condemn U.S. treatment of black soldiers, and later to argue that the United States should not be allowed to join the United Nations until it took action to solve its racial problems.

Though often difficult to work with, Carter G. Woodson succeeded in maintaining almost single-handedly for 35 years an organization that would prove invaluable in developing black historical material and in promoting recognition of the importance of such material to African-American historical research. Among his many books are *The Education of the Negro Prior to 1861, The Negro Church, A Century of Negro Migration, Negro Makers of History,* and *The Miseducation of the Negro.* He is known as the "Father of Black History."

Recommended Reading: Goggin, Jacqueline. *Carter G. Woodson: A Life in Black History.* Baton Rouge, La., and London: Louisiana State University Press, 1993.

Wright, Richard (1908–1960) *author*

At the age of four, Richard Wright accidentally set his home on fire; as punishment, he was beaten so badly he lost consciousness and almost died. His father deserted the family when Wright was very young, and poverty forced his mother to place Richard and his younger brother in an orphanage for a short time. Later the family moved to Arkansas to live with relatives but was forced to move after Wright's uncle was murdered by a white man who wanted to take over his business. When Wright's mother suffered a stroke, the family moved in with his grandmother in Jackson, Mississippi. Extreme

Richard Wright as Bigger Thomas in the movie version of his novel *Native Son* (*Museum of Modern Art Film Stills Archive*)

poverty continued to plague the family, and Wright did not get along with his grandmother.

At age 17, he left home, moving first to Memphis and then to Chicago, where he worked at a series of menial jobs while pursuing his dream of becoming a writer. He also joined the Communist Party but later became disillusioned and quit. In 1938, Wright published a collection of short stories called *Uncle Tom's Children,* reflecting the discrimination of the South. Two years later, he published his most famous novel, *Native Son,* which dealt with racism in the North. It sold 200,000 copies in less than three weeks and established Wright's reputation as a leading author. These were followed by a folk history called *Twelve Million Black Voices* (1941) and a painfully sensitive autobiography, *Black Boy.* In 1946, Wright moved to France, where he continued to publish novels, stories, articles, and essays. Other books include *The Outsider* (1953), *Savage Holiday* (1954), *The Long Dream* (1958), *Lawd Today* (1963) and *Eight Men* (1961), which includes his famous story "The Man Who Lived Underground." *American Hunger,* a sequel to his autobiographical *Black Boy,* was published in 1977.

Xhosa (co-sa)

South African tribe. During the 1760s, the Xhosa came into conflict with whites, who had established the Cape Colony there in 1652. Unlike the relatively small Khoisan clans that the Boers (whites of Dutch or French Huguenot descent) had previously wiped out, killing parents and enslaving children, the Xhosa were more populous and better organized. The result was a series of so-called "Frontier" or "Cape-Xhosa" Wars. The first began in 1779 and ended inconclusively in 1781. KHOI slaves began running away from their masters to join the Xhosa, triggering a second war in 1793 that ended with a Boer defeat. The third war began in 1799 and ended in 1803. The British, who had taken control of the Cape Colony in 1795, established a standing army in the area and pushed the Xhosa out in the fourth war of 1811–12. The conflicts were to continue for almost 100 years. The Xhosa formed the majority in the AFRICAN NATIONAL CONGRESS, although ZULU, NDEBELE, Sotho, and other groups were also represented. The best-known leader of Xhosa origin is NELSON MANDELA.

Y

Y

York (1770–ca. 1832) *member of the Lewis and Clark expedition*

The mission of the Lewis and Clark expedition was to explore the territory the United States had acquired from France through the Louisiana Purchase of 1803 and find a land route through it to the Pacific Ocean. The region for which the United States had paid $15 million covered 875,000 square miles. York, a slave belonging to William Clark, soon became one of the most important members of the expedition. Standing six feet tall and weighing 200 pounds, York was an experienced hunter, an expert in woodlore, and fluent in several languages. The expedition was guided by a French trapper named Toussaint Charbonneau who was married to a Shoshoni Indian woman named Sacagawea, or "Bird Woman." Sacagawea would translate what the Indians were saying into French for her husband, who would then repeat her information to York. York would translate Charbonneau's French into English for Lewis and Clark. The Flathead Indians, who customarily painted themselves black when they were victorious in battle, took York's black skin to mean he was exceptionally courageous. But all Indians were greatly interested in him and, as a result, York did most of the trading for the group. York used the Indians' curiosity about him and their admiration for his athletic ability to overcome their hostility and suspicion.

Following the expedition, York returned with Clark to Kentucky and was later freed. Some accounts say he established a freight line, others that he became a chief with the Crow Indians.

Yoruba

West African people who established several kingdoms, including IFE, OYO, and Ibadan, in what is now Nigeria. According to tradition, the Yoruba descended from Oduduwa, a prince of Mecca who was lowered to Earth by the god Olorun and

Yoruba palace door, Olowe of Ife (*National Museum of African Art, Washington, D.C.*)

325

founded Ife. This myth is an indication that the Yoruba probably arrived in a series of migrations from the north and intermarried with local people. The Yoruba were known for their shrewdness in business, their honesty, and their cleanliness. Being dirty was a sign of mourning.

Ife, which is still famous for its bronzes, gave way to Oyo as the leading Yoruba state. Oyo maintained its power until the 19th century, when it disintegrated in a period marked by widespread civil strife. It was during these "Yoruba wars" that Ibadan emerged as the most prominent Yoruba state. The conflict allowed the British to establish a protectorate over Yorubaland in 1893. The term *Yoruba* originated in the 19th century among outsiders to refer to those cities linked by similar language.

Young, Andrew Jackson, Jr. (1932–) *U.S. ambassador to the United Nations, mayor, civil rights activist, minister*

Born in New Orleans, Andrew Young became a minister in the United Church of Christ after graduating from Howard University and Hartford Theological Seminary. A close friend of Dr. MARTIN LUTHER KING JR., he became a leader within the SOUTHERN CHRISTIAN LEADERSHIP CONFERENCE. He was heavily involved in the Birmingham and Selma demonstrations and also participated in anti–Vietnam War protests. In 1972, he was elected to the U.S. House of Representatives from Georgia. A strong supporter of President Jimmy Carter, Young became U.S. ambassador to the United Nations in 1977, but was forced to resign after it was learned he had circumvented U.S. policy by meeting secretly with a representative from the Palestine Liberation Organization. He then ran for mayor of Atlanta, winning with 55 percent of the vote. Young was reelected in 1985 and served until 1989. He later became chairman of the committee coordinating Atlanta's role as host city for the 1996 Olympic Games.

Young, Charles (1864–1922) *army officer*

Young was the ninth African American to be appointed to West Point and the third to graduate. (Black men at that time were generally believed to be unfit to serve as military officers, and those few who were admitted to West Point faced tremendous hostility. Another black cadet, Johnson Whittaker, was found unconscious and tied to his bed with his earlobes slashed. When he said he had been attacked, he was accused of lying and self-mutilation and was expelled. Henry O. Flipper, the first black man to graduate from the academy, was later forced out of the army on fraudulent charges.)

After graduating, Young was assigned to the famous Ninth Cavalry at Fort Robinson, Nebraska. Later, he was transferred to Fort DuChesne, Utah, and then to Wilberforce University, where he taught French, mathematics, tactics, and military science. Young was placed in command of the Ninth Ohio Volunteer Infantry during the Spanish-American War and later served in the Philippines. In 1904, Young was assigned to HAITI and the Dominican Republic as the United States' first African-American military attaché. While there, he traveled throughout the island, charting many previously unmapped areas and writing detailed reports on the people and culture. He also compiled an English-French-Creole dictionary and wrote a play based on the life of TOUSSAINT LOUVERTURE and a book called *Military Morale of Nations and Races*.

In 1912, Young was assigned as a military attaché to LIBERIA, where he served for two years. Though he had hoped to serve in World War I, doctors discovered that he was suffering from nephritis and high blood pressure, and he was forced to retire. Believing he was a victim of racial discrimination, Young rode horseback from Ohio to Washington in an unsuccessful attempt to prove his physical fitness. In 1919, Young became a special adviser to the Liberian government. He died and was buried in Liberia.

Z

Zaire
See DEMOCRATIC REPUBLIC OF CONGO.

Zambia, Republic of
South-central African country Capital: Lusaka. Iron-using people who raised cattle and traded in copper and ivory occupied the area around A.D. 800 and appear to have spread throughout the region between A.D. 1000 and A.D. 1200. Their culture, in reference to their pottery, is generally known as the "Luangwa tradition." Other groups migrated to the area between the 16th and 18th centuries. Arab and other traders interested in acquiring slaves, ivory, copper, and wax began to move into the region in the late 18th century. In 1835, the NGONI occupied eastern Zambia, and the Kololo invaded the southwest and took control of the Lozi or Barotse kingdom from 1838 to 1864. Zambia was visited by explorer David Livingstone in 1851. He returned twice more, dying there in 1873.

In 1890 and 1900, the Lozi chief, Lewanika, signed treaties granting extensive mining rights to Cecil Rhodes' British South Africa Company (BSAC). Other tribal chiefs also signed treaties with BSAC; those who refused—principally the Ngoni and the Bemba—were subjected to attacks by BSAC mercenaries. In 1911, the region was unified into Northern Rhodesia under BSAC control, although local chiefs continued to exercise extensive authority.

Increased copper mining led to an increase in the number of white settlers, especially in the 1920s when additional massive copper deposits were discovered. Discrimination against African copper workers and the displacement of African farmers led to strikes in 1935, 1940, and 1956. Although they were not allowed to unionize, the Africans did form self-help groups, which brought people of various tribes together and led to political organization. In spite of African protests, the British, in 1953, established the Federation of Rhodesia and Nyasaland, which linked Northern Rhodesia with Southern Rhodesia (now Zimbabwe) and Nyasaland (now Malawi).

In 1959, Kenneth Kaunda, a former schoolteacher, formed the United National Independence Party (UNIP). After massive civil disobedience campaigns, Northern Rhodesia became the independent Republic of Zambia on October 24, 1964. Kaunda was elected president and attempted to diversify the economy in an effort to reduce European financial control. In the 1960s, Zambia joined Britain and other countries in promoting economic sanctions against the breakaway white regime in Rhodesia, causing its own economy to suffer greatly and making it the target of white terrorists.

Growing political opposition caused Kaunda to ban political parties other than the UNIP in 1972. The formation of rival political parties was legitimized in 1990, and in 1991, Frederick Chiluba of the Movement for Multiparty Democracy was elected president. Zambia is among the world's five leading producers of copper.

Zande (Azande)

A highly aggressive people living in the grassland area in the south SUDAN. They are famous for their throwing knives (*kpinga*), which are known for their aerodynamic qualities. These multibladed knives are highly prized, not only as weapons but as symbols of office, as dancing implements, and as payment for brides. When thrown, they fly in a circular motion, and if hurled with reasonable accuracy, at least one of the blades is likely to find its mark. Zande warriors traditionally hung up to four knives from iron disks that were attached to the backs of their shields and carried two to four spears in their hands. Zande battles were often small, but some kings could muster up to 20,000 warriors. In spite of their lethal weapons, the object of Zande battles was generally to force the withdrawal of the enemy, preferably with as little bloodshed as possible. For this reason, the Zande often would take care not to completely encircle their opponents but instead would leave a gap through which their enemies might retreat. Other rules included fighting only after four o'clock in the afternoon so that the losers would be able to sneak away as darkness approached.

Zanj

Name given East Africa and its black population by ARAB traders. It is thought to have derived from the Arabic word *zinj*, meaning "black." (The Arabic phrase *Zinj el Barr*, meaning "land of blacks," gave the island of ZANZIBAR its name.) At one point, the East African coast (or Zanj), as well as Zanzibar, were part of the biblical kingdom of Saba (Sheba) and engaged in trade with various Arabian cities. Trade continued to expand as migrating groups of BANTU peoples arrived in the area in the third and fourth centuries. Medieval writers describe the Zanj as being skilled metalworkers and eloquent speakers who held animist religious beliefs. They raised cattle, planted a variety of crops, and were considered shrewd merchants who traded gold, ivory, copper, hides, pearls, coral, and amber for silks, Indian beads, Chinese porcelain, and cotton cloth. The Abbasid Empire, which ruled Iraq from A.D. 750 to 1258, imported huge numbers of Zanj slaves, and a large-scale Zanj rebellion took place in Iraq in 869.

The word *Zanj* today is sometimes used in fiction to identify lost African civilizations of fabulous wealth.

Zanj Rebellion

Iraqi rebellion in A.D. 869 involving thousands of slaves from East Africa, which was then known as ZANJ. While most medieval states did not have economic systems that could absorb hundreds of thousands of slave laborers, an exception was the Abbasid Empire that ruled Iraq from 750 until 1258. There, the Abbasid rulers were involved in a major land reclamation project in the Tigris-Euphrates delta region and brought in thousands of African slaves to do the labor. The rebelling slaves, who repeatedly ambushed and defeated the forces sent against them, were joined by peasants, bedouins, and black deserters from Arab armies. They set up fortified communities from which they continued to raid Iraqi villages, finally capturing Basra in 871. Fighting continued until 883, when the main Zanj force was defeated, although isolated groups continued their resistance. The Zanj Rebellion was the biggest slave uprising since the Servile Wars of the Roman Empire 800 years earlier. Its success discouraged the further use of slave labor in the Middle East except as domestic servants and army recruits.

Zanzibar (Unguja)

Island located in the Indian Ocean and now a part of TANZANIA. The name ZANZIBAR is a corruption of the Arabic *Zinj el Barr*, meaning "land of black people." Zanzibar's earliest inhabitants were East Africans who arrived around 4000 B.C., and the island was later visited by the PHOENICIANS, Sabeans, and other traders. At that time, Zanzibar was primarily a way-station for ships sailing between East Africa and Arabia, Persia, India, and other commercial centers. BANTU immigrants arrived during the 11th century, along with Persians and ARABS, who intermarried with them and encouraged the spread of Islam. The growing INDIAN OCEAN TRADE made Zanzibar an important commercial center that imported Chinese porcelain, Persian carpets, silk, cotton, and copper.

In 1499 Zanzibar was visited by Portuguese navigator Vasco da Gama; within 10 years, the Portuguese had taken control of Zanzibar (1503) and much of the East African coast. In 1698, the Portuguese were pushed out by the Omani Arabs, who regularly imported African slaves to Oman to work on date plantations and to serve as domestic workers and concubines. By the mid-18th century, Zanzibar had become a major center of the ivory and slave trade, supplying captives to Brazil, Mauritius and Réunion, Oman, and the Dutch East Indies.

Britain had banned the overseas slave trade in 1807 and brought pressure on Omani sultan Sayyid Said (reigned 1804–56) to halt the East African slave trade also. In 1822, Said signed a treaty with Britain banning the sale of slaves to Christians and the transport of slaves from Zanzibar to Mauritius and Réunion (then under French control). However, the introduction of clove plantations (1812) had already led to a sharp increase in slavery in Zanzibar, which was rapidly becoming one of the world's leading clove producers. In 1840, Sayyid Said moved his capital to Zanzibar. By that time, approximately 13,000–15,000 slaves a year were being imported through the efforts of Zanzibar-based slave trade organizations that had established posts deep in the African interior.

When Said died in 1856, Oman and Zanzibar were divided. Threatened with a British blockade of its ports in 1873, Zanzibar agreed to end the slave trade. However, smugglers continued to import between 10,000 and 12,000 slaves a year into the island until slavery itself was outlawed in 1889. Britain established a protectorate over Zanzibar and Pemba the following year. Three major political parties—two Arab and one African—emerged after World War II, and Zanzibar became internally self-governing in 1963. In 1964, the Afro-Shirazi Party (ASP) staged a bloody coup, and the sultan was forced into exile, the Arab-dominated political parties were banned, and many Arabs and Indians left the country. Zanzibar merged with Tanganyika in April 1964 to form the United Republic of Tanganyika and Zanzibar (changed to Tanzania six months later), although Zanzibar retained considerable control over its internal affairs.

Zimba (Wa-Zimba)

BANTU group that, in 1580, embarked on a bloody campaign of conquest across East Africa. The Zimba first attacked the towns of Tete and Sena on the Zambezi River, not only killing the people, but eating them as well. A force of 5,000 Zimba then marched toward Kilwa, reputedly "killing and eating every living thing, men, women, children, dogs, cats, rats, snakes, lizards."[1] Only those willing to join them were spared. The city of Kilwa had already been weakened by Portuguese assaults. When the Zimba attacked in 1587, 3,000 of its people were killed and eaten. The rest fled into the forests. Following the destruction of Kilwa, the Zimba forces continued northward toward MOMBASA, arriving there in 1589. Mombasa was then already under attack by the Portuguese, who left the weakened city to its fate. Many of Mombasa's residents ran into the sea, preferring possible attacks by sharks to capture by the Zimba. The Zimba then turned their attention to the city of Malindi but were themselves attacked by the Segeju people, who defeated them and put an end to the terror they had created. The origins of the Zimba are unknown, but it is thought they were runaway slaves who formed mercenary bands employed by the Lunda of Malawi. Their actions may have been in response to Portuguese efforts to control the ivory trade in East Africa.

Zimbabwe, Republic of

Country in south-central Africa. Capital: Harare. Zimbabwe was formerly known as Rhodesia. Tools dating from the second century have been found there, along with artifacts from BANTU-speaking peoples who moved into the area sometime after A.D. 400. Zimbabwe is also the site of the famous GREAT ZIMBABWE ruins, the remains of a Shona kingdom (ca. 1200–1450) that provided gold and ivory for KILWA's INDIAN OCEAN TRADE. Southwestern Zimbabwe was invaded in 1837 by the NDEBELE, who settled there, establishing a capital at Bulawayo. In 1888, the Ndebele chief, Lobengula, was tricked into turning most tribal land over to British businessman Cecil Rhodes, who arranged to exploit the region's mineral wealth

---

[1] Robert W. July, *A History of the African People.* New York: Scribner, 1970, p. 86.

through his British South Africa Company (BSAC). A year later, the BSAC received a charter from the British government to colonize the area, which was named Rhodesia in Rhodes' honor. The Ndebele rebelled in 1893 but were overcome by BSAC troops, who invaded Bulawayo and killed Lobengula. Another unsuccessful revolt by both the Ndebele and the Shona took place in 1896–97. Rhodesia became a self-governing colony in 1923; however, blacks continued to be denied political rights. In 1953, the British established the Federation of Rhodesia and Nyasaland, which linked Southern Rhodesia (now Zimbabwe) with Northern Rhodesia (now Zambia) and Nyasaland (now Malawi). Blacks received limited political rights under the government of Prime Minister Edgar Whitehead in 1960, but in 1962, the country came under the control of white conservatives who opposed black rights. The federation split apart the following year, and in 1964, Northern Rhodesia became independent. In 1965, Southern Rhodesia (or Rhodesia) declared its independence under Prime Minister Ian Smith. Britain refused to recognize the decree but would not use force to oust the white government. Two black groups, the Zimbabwe African National Union (ZANU) and the Zimbabwe African People's Union (ZAPU), began a guerrilla war, and in 1976 the white regime agreed to institute majority rule by 1978. Its failure to carry out its promise led to continued warfare. In 1980, Rhodesia became the Republic of Zimbabwe under Prime Minister Robert Mugabe's ZANU-PF (Patriotic Front) Party. The Mugabe government has been guilty of harassment and abuse of journalists and others. In 2000, a crisis situation arose when landless blacks occupied white-owned farmland and beat and sometimes murdered white farmers in an effort to take their land. Mugabe, who encouraged whites to remain in Zimbabwe after the civil war, has refused to condemn the action and has threatened to take the land of white farmers without compensation. Though whites number only 70,000 in a country of 12.5 million, they own more than half of the fertile land available.

Zong

British ship from which over 100 sick slaves were thrown overboard in 1781 so that its insurers would bear the cost of the loss rather than the ship's owners. The *Zong* had left West Africa on September 6 with 470 slaves aboard. After 12 weeks at sea and a loss of more than 60 slaves, water ran short because of navigational errors. The slaves, wearing manacles, were thrown overboard during a three-day period. Ten others jumped overboard, fearing otherwise they would be thrown over while chained. One slave managed to grab a rope and pull himself back on board. The decision to throw the sick slaves overboard was based on insurance laws that stated that ship owners must bear the cost of slaves who died "natural deaths" or by suicide. Insurance companies were required to pay only when deaths were caused during mutinies or to protect others. The ship company claimed that throwing the slaves overboard was necessary to save the lives of the rest, even though the murders had continued after two days of rain had allowed the *Zong* to collect six casks of water. Though there was a huge public outcry and the insurance company refused to pay, the ship's owners sued (*Gregson v. Gilbert*) and collected. In 1790, the British Parliament outlawed insurance payments for any slaves thrown overboard for any reason.

A variation of the *Zong* case occurred in 1796, when a slave ship company tried to collect on 128 slaves (77 percent of those aboard) who had starved to death during a voyage delayed by storms. The judge threw out the claim, pointing out that since the captain and crew had not starved, the slave deaths could not be attributed to natural risks of ocean passage.

Dysentery, smallpox, and ophthamalia, which often resulted in blindness, were major problems on slave ships, as was insanity brought about by cruel treatment. Slaves with contagious diseases and those who were not expected to survive or regain their sight or sanity were often thrown overboard. Schools of sharks regularly followed the slave ships, and a loss of only 10 percent of the slave "cargo" was considered extremely good.

Zulu

South African ethnic and linguistic group. Traditionally, Zulu clans live in large enclosed compounds called *kraals*. Cattle are extremely important as an indication of wealth and prestige. This is attested to by the fact that the Zulu have over 300 words to describe various cattle.

In the early 19th century, the Zulu were unified by SHAKA, who created a 50,000-man army and subjugated the surrounding tribes, extending his control over 200,000 square miles. Shaka was murdered by his half-brother Dingane, who later agreed to a peace treaty with the Boers (South African whites of Dutch and French Huguenot descent), then ambushed and killed about 70 of them in 1838. The Boers retaliated, killing approximately 3,000 Zulu at the Battle of Blood River. The British attacked the Zulus in 1878 after Chief Cetshwayo refused to submit to British rule. After several defeats the British finally overcame the Zulu forces and eventually annexed Zululand in 1887.

In 1959, under the white-ruled South African government, the Zulus were assigned to a homeland, or BANTUSTAN, called Kwazulu. Approximately half of South Africa's Zulu population still live there. The extended family, which is an important feature of Zulu life, suffered serious disruption when thousands of Zulu men were forced to leave their families to work in the mines and cities of South Africa. During the struggle against the white South African government, many Zulu migrant workers joined the Inkatha Freedom Party under Chief Gatsha Mangosuthu Buthelezi. Conflict between Inkatha and Nelson Mandela's AFRICAN NATIONAL CONGRESS, which also included many Zulus, frequently resulted in bloodshed.

A young Zulu woman, wearing samples of her beadwork, poses for a photograph while on her way to a wedding. (*Volkmar Wentzel/Archive Photos*)

BIBLIOGRAPHY

Adero, Malaika, ed. *Up South.* New York: New Press, City University of New York, 1993.

Adloff, Richard. *West Africa: the French-Speaking Nations, Yesterday and Today.* New York: Holt, Rinehart and Winston, 1964.

Africa Watch. *Mozambique: Conspicuous Destruction.* New York: Human Rights Watch, 1992.

———. *Children of Sudan: Slaves, Street Children and Child Soldiers.* New York: Human Rights Watch, 1995.

———. *Evil Days: 30 Years of War and Famine in Ethiopia.* New York: Human Rights Watch, 1991.

———. *Mauritania's Campaign of Terror.* New York: 1994.

Anderson, Jervis A. *Philip Randolph.* Berkeley, Calif.: University of California Press, 1986.

Aptheker, Herbert. *American Negro Slave Revolts.* New York: International, 1983.

———. *One Continual Cry.* New York: Humanities Press, 1971.

———. *To Be Free.* New York: International Publishers, 1969.

Appiah, Kwame Anthony, and Henry Louis Gates, eds. *Africana: The Encyclopedia of the African and African American Experience.* New York: Basic Ciritas Books, 1999.

Ashe, Arthur, and Arnold Rampersad. *Days of Grace.* New York: Knopf, 1993.

Atyeo, Don. *Blood and Guts: Violence in Sports.* New York: Paddington Press, 1979.

Ball, Howard. *A Defiant Life.* New York: Crown Publishers, Inc., 1998.

Baines, John, and Jaromir Malek. *Atlas of Ancient Egypt.* New York: Facts On File, 1980.

Banks, William M. *Black Intellectuals.* New York: W. R. Norton & Co., 1996.

Batchelor, Danzil. *Jack Johnson and His Times.* London: Weidenfeld and Nicolson, 1990.

Bates, Daisy. *The Long Shadow of Little Rock.* Fayetteville: University of Arkansas Press, 1987.

Beals, Melba Pattillo. *Warriors Don't Cry.* New York: Simon & Schuster, Pocket Books, 1994.

Bearden, Romare, and Harry Henderson. *A History of African American Artists: From 1792 to the Present.* New York: Pantheon Books, 1993.

Beckwith, Carol, and Angela Fisher. *African Ark.* New York: Abrams, 1990.

Bentsen, Cheryl. *Maasai Days.* New York: Doubleday, 1989.

Berry, Mary Frances. *Black Resistance/White Law.* New York: Penguin Books, 1994.

Bismauth, Dale. *History of Religions in the Caribbean.* Kingston, Jamaica: Kingston, 1989.

Blockson, Charles L. *The Underground Railroad.* New York: Berkely Books, 1994.

Botkin, B. A., ed. *Lay My Burden Down.* New York: Dell, 1994.

Branch, Taylor. *Parting the Waters America in the King Years, 1954–63.* New York: Simon & Schuster, 1988.

Brett, Michael Brett, and Elizabeth Fentress. *The Berbers.* Cambridge, Mass.: Blackwell Publishers Ltd., 1996.

Brodie, James Michael. *Created Equal: The Lives and Ideas of Black American Innovators.* New York: Morrow, 1993.

Brundage, W. Fitzhugh, ed. *Under Sentence of Death: Lynching in the South.* Chapel Hill: University of North Carolina Press, 1997.

Bullard, Sara. *Free at Last.* New York: Oxford University Press, 1993.

Burenhult, Goran, ed. *Traditional Peoples Today.* New York: HarperSanFrancisco, American Museum of Natural History, 1994.

Burner, Eric R. *And Gently He Shall Lead Them: Robert Parr Moses and Civil Rights in Mississippi.* New York: New York University Press, 1994.

Butler, Paul. *Racially Based Jury Nullification: Black Power in the Criminal Justice System.* The Yale Law Journal. Volume 105, December 1995.

Cagin, Seth, and Philip Dray. *We Are Not Afraid.* New York: Macmillan, 1988.

Campbell, James. *Talking at the Gates: A Life of James Baldwin.* New York: Viking, 1991.

Campbell, Horace. *Rasta and Resistance.* Trenton, N.J.: Africa World Press, 1987.

Canot, Theodore. *Adventures of an African Slaver.* New York: Dover, 1854/1969.

Carson, Ben. *Gifted Hands.* Grand Rapids, Mich.: Zondervan Publishing, 1990.

———. *The Big Picture.* Grand Rapids, Mich.: Zondervan Publishing, 1999.

Carter, Dan T. *Scottsboro: A Tragedy of the American South.* Baton Rouge: Louisiana State University Press, 1979.

Chalmers, David M. *Hooded Americanism: The History of the Ku Klux Klan.* Durham, N.C.: Duke University Press, 1987.

Chiasson, John. *African Journey.* New York: Macmillan, 1987.

Christian, Charles M. *Black Saga.* New York: Houghton Mifflin, 1995.

Cole, Bill. *John Coltrane.* New York: Da Capo Press, 1993.

Cole, David. *No Equal Justice.* New York: The New Press, 1999.

Collier, James Lincoln. *Duke Ellington.* New York: Oxford University Press, 1987.

Connah, Graham. *African Civilizations.* New York: Cambridge University Press, 1992.

Conniff, Michael L., and Thomas J. Davis. *Africans in the Americas.* New York: St. Martin's Press, 1994.

Cornish, Dudley Taylor. *The Sable Arm.* Lawrence: University Press of Kansas, 1990.

Costen, Melva Wilson. *African American Christian Worship.* Nashville, Tenn.: Abingdon Press, 1993.

Cottrell, Leonard. *Hannibal, Enemy of Rome.* New York: Plenum, Da Capo Press, 1992.

Cox, Clinton. *The Forgotten Heroes: The Story of the Buffalo Soldiers.* New York: Scholastic, 1993.

Crewe, Quentin. *In Search of the Sahara.* New York: Macmillan, 1983.

Crow, Bill. *Jazz Anecdotes.* New York: Oxford University Press, 1990.

Davidson, Art. *Endangered Peoples.* San Francisco, Calif.: Sierra Club, 1994.

Davidson, Basil. *Africa in History.* New York: Macmillan, Collier Books, 1991.

———. *African Civilization Revisited.* Trenton, N.J.: Africa World Press, 1991.

———. *The African Slave Trade.* Boston, Mass.: Little, Brown, 1988.

———. *The Lost Cities of Africa.* Boston, Mass.: Little, Brown, 1987.

Davis, David Brion. *Slavery and Human Progress.* Bridgewater, N.J.: Replica Books, Baker & Taylor, 2000.

Davis, Ian Carr. *Miles Davis: The Definitive Biography.* New York: Thunder's Mouth Press, 1998.

Davis, Miles, and Quincy Troupe. *Miles.* New York: Simon & Schuster, 1990.

Dittmer, John. *Local People.* Urbana and Chicago: University of Illinois Press, 1994.

Douglass, Frederick. *Life & Times of Frederick Douglass.* Secaucus, N.J.: Citadel Press, 1983.

———. *My Bondage and My Freedom.* Chicago: Johnson, 1970.

———. *Narrative of the Life of Frederick Douglass.* New York: Signet, 1968.

Dow, George Francis. *Slaving Ships and Slaving.* Salem, Mass.: Marine Research Society, Brattleboro, Vt.: Hildreth, 1927.

Driskell, David, David Levering Lewis, Deborah Willis Ryan, and Mary Schmidt Campbell. *Harlem Renaissance: Art of Black America.* New York: Aberdale Press, 1994.

DuBois, W. E. B. *Black Reconstruction in America 1860–1880.* New York: Macmillan, Atheneum, 1992.

———. *The Souls of Black Folk.* New York: Random House, 1996.

Dyson, Michael Eric. *I May Not Get There With You.* New York: The Free Press, 2000.

Edgerton, Robert B. *The Fall of the Asante Empire.* New York: Simon & Schuster, Free Press, 1995.

Englebert, Victor. *Wind, Sand & Silence: Travels with Africa's Last Nomads.* San Francisco, Calif.: Chronicle Books, 1992.

Estell, Kenneth. *African America, Portrait of a People.* Detroit, Mich.: Visible Ink Press, 1994.

———. *African-American Almanac.* 3 vols. Detroit, Mich.: Gale, 1992.

Evans, Ivor H. N. *The Negritoes of Malaya.* Cambridge, England: The University Press, 1937.

Evers, Charles. *Evers.* New York: World, 1971.

Evers, Myrlie B. *For Us, the Living.* Oxford: University of Mississippi Press, 1998.

Fage, J. D. "Slavery and the Slave Trade in the Context of West African History." No. 3 in Vol. 10 of *The Journal of African History.* New York: Cambridge University Press, 1969.

Fage, J. D., and Roland Oliver. *A Short History of Africa.* New York: Penguin Books, 1990.

Fairclough, Adam. *Race & Democracy: The Civil Rights Struggle in Louisiana 1915–1972.* Athens, Ga.: University of Georgia Press, 1995.

———. *To Redeem the Soul of America.* Athens, Ga.: University of Georgia Press, 1987.

Farmer, James. *Lay Bare the Heart.* Fort Worth: Texas Christian University Press, 1998.

Feather, Leonard. *From Satchmo to Miles.* New York: Da Capo Press, 1984.

Fogel, Robert William. *Without Consent or Contract.* New York: Norton, 1994.

Foner, Eric. *Reconstruction: America's Unfinished Revolution 1863–1877.* New York: Harper & Row, 1988.

Foner, Philip S., and Ronald L. Lewis. *Black Workers.* Philadelphia, Pa.: Temple University Press, 1989.

Forbath, Peter. *The River Congo.* New York: Harper & Row, 1977.

Fox, Matt J. F. S. S., ed. *New Guinea and the Philippines.* Sydney, Australia: Australia Story Trust, 1945.

Franklin, John Hope, and Loren Schweninger. *Runaway Slaves.* New York: Oxford University Press, 1999.

Franklin, John Hope. *From Slavery to Freedom: A History of African Americans.* New York: Knopf, 1994.

Friedman, Lawrence M. *Crime and Punishment in American History.* New York: BasicBooks/HarperCollins, 1993.

———. *George Washington Williams.* Durham, N.C.: Duke University Press, 1998.

Garrow, David J. *Bearing the Cross.* New York: Morrow, 1999.

Garvan, John M. *The Negritos of the Philippines.* Horn and Vienna, Austria: Verlag Ferdinand Berger, 1964.

Gates, Henry Louis, Jr. *Colored People.* New York: Random House, Vintage Books, 1995.

Gates, Henry Louis, Jr., ed. *Bearing Witness.* New York: Pantheon Books, 1991.

Genovese, Eugene D. *From Rebellion to Revolution.* Baton Rouge: Louisiana State University Press, 1992.

———. *Roll, Jordan, Roll.* New York: Random House, Vintage Books, 1976.

Giddings, Paula. *When and Where I Enter.* New York: Morrow, 1996.

Gillespie, Dizzy. *to BE or not to BOP.* Garden City, N.Y.: Doubleday, 1979.

Ginzburg, Ralph. *100 Years of Lynchings.* Baltimore, Md.: Black Classic Press, 1997.

Goggin, Jacqueline. *Carter G. Woodson: A Life in Black History.* Baton Rouge, La., and London: Louisiana State University Press, 1993.

Goldman, Roger, and David Gallen. *Thurgood Marshall: Justice for All.* New York: Carroll & Graf, 1992.

Grant, Donald L. *The Way It Was in the South: The Black Experience in Georgia.* New York: Carol, 1993.

Guralnick, Peter. *Searching for Robert Johnson.* New York: Dutton, Obelisk Books, 1998.

Gwaltney, John Langston. *Drylongso.* San Diego: Harcourt Brace Jovanovich, 1993.

Haber, Louis. *Black Pioneers of Science & Invention.* New York: Harcourt, Brace & World, 1992.

Halpern, Rick, and Roger Horowitz. *Meatpackers: An Oral History of Black Packinghouse Workers and the Struggle for Racial & Economic Equality.* New York: Monthly Review Press, 1999.

Hamdun, Said, and Noel King. *Ibn Battuta in Black Africa.* Princeton, N.J.: Markus Wiener, 1994.

Hampton, Henry, and Steve Fayer. *Voices of Freedom.* New York: Bantam Books, 1990.

Hansberry, Lorraine. *To Be Young, Gifted and Black.* New York: Signet, 1969.

Harding, Vincent. *There is a River.* New York: Harcourt Brace Jovanovich, 1993.

Harris, Joseph E. *Africans and Their History.* New York: Penguin Books, Mentor Book, 1998.

Haskins, James. *Pickney Benton Stewart Pinchback.* New York: Macmillan, 1973.

Hasse, John Edward, ed. *Jazz: The First Century.* New York: William Morrow, 2000.

Havecker, Cyril. *Understanding Aboriginal Culture.* Sydney, Australia: Cosmos, 1987.

Hayden, Robert C. *Eight Black American Inventors.* Reading, Mass.: Addison-Wesley, 1988.

Hentoff, Nat. *Listen to the Stories.* New York: HarperCollins, 1995.

Herzhaft, Gerard. *Encyclopedia of the Blues.* Fayetteville: University of Arkansas Press, 1992.

Higginson, Thomas Wentworth. *Army Life in a Black Regiment.* East Lansing: Michigan State University Press, 1997.

Hine, Darlene Clark, Elsa Barkley Brown, and Rosalyn Terborg-Penn, eds. *Black Women in America.* Vols. 1 and 2. Bloomington and Indianapolis: Indiana University Press, 1994.

Hochschild, Adam. *King Leopold's Ghost.* New York: Houghton Mifflin Company, 1998.

Holway, John B. *Black Diamonds.* New York: Stadium Books, 1991.

———. *Josh and Satch.* New York: Carroll & Graf/Richard Gallen, 1991.

———. *Voices from the Great Black Baseball Leagues.* New York: Da Capo Press, 1992.

Honey, Michael Keith. *Black Workers Remember: An Oral History of Segregation, Unionism, and the Freedom Struggle.* Berkeley: University of California Press, 2000.

Huggins, Nathan Irvin. *Harlem Renaissance.* New York: Oxford University Press, 1973.

———. *Slave and Citizen: The Life of Frederick Douglass.* Boston, Mass.: Little, Brown, 1980.

Hughes, Langston, Milton Meltzer, and C. Eric Lincoln. *A Pictorial History of Black Americans.* New York: Crown, 1990.

Hughes, Robert. *The Fatal Shore.* New York: Random House, Vintage Books, 1988.

Hurmence, Belinda, ed. *Before Freedom.* New York: Penguin Books, Mentor Book, 1990.

Iliffe, John. *The African Poor.* New York: Cambridge University Press, Redwood Burn Limited, Trowbridge, Wiltshire, 1992.

Inikori, Joseph E., and Stanley L. Engerman, eds. *The Atlantic Slave Trade.* Durham, N.C., and London: Duke University Press, 1992.

International Defence and Aid Fund for Southern Africa. *Children Under Apartheid.* Orpington, Kent, England: Bishop, 1956.

Jackson, John G. *Introduction to African Civilizations.* New York: Citadel Press/Carol, 1990.

Jacobs, Harriett. *Incidents in the Life of a Slave Girl.* New York: Oxford University Press, 2000.

James, C. L. R. *The Black Jacobins.* New York: Random House, Vintage Books, 1989.

Jones, Constance. *Africa 1500–1900.* New York: Facts On File, 1993.

Jones, Howard. *Mutiny on the Amistad.* New York: Oxford University Press, 1997.

Jones, James H. *Bad Blood: The Tuskegee Syphilis Experiment.* New York: Macmillan, Free Press, 1993.

July, Robert W. *A History of the African People.* Prospect Heights, Ill.: Waveland Press, 1998.

Junod, Henri Philippe. *Bantu Heritage.* Westport, Conn.: Negro Universities Press, 1970.

Katz, William Loren. *Black People Who Made the Old West.* Baltimore: Africa World, 1992.

———. *The Black West.* New York: Touchstone Books, 1996.

———. *Breaking the Chains.* New York: Simon & Schuster, 1998.

———. *Eyewitness.* New York: Simon & Schuster, Touchstone, 1995.

———. *The Invisible Empire.* Seattle, Wash.: Open Hand, 1986.

Keane, Fergal. *Season of Blood.* London, England: Penguin Books, 1996.

Kennedy, Randall. *Race, Crime, and the Law.* New York: Pantheon Books, 1997.

King, Martin Luther, Jr. *Stride Toward Freedom.* New York: HarperCollins, HarperSanFrancisco, 1958.

Klein, Herbert S. "The Trade in African Slaves to Rio de Janeiro 1795–1811: Estimates of Mortality and Patterns of Voyage." No. 4 in Vol. 10 of *The Journal of African History.* New York: Cambridge University Press, 1969.

Kluger, Richard. *Simple Justice.* New York: Random House, Vintage Books, 1977.

Kranz, Rachel. *Black Americans.* New York: Facts On File, 1992.

Kroeber, A. L. *Peoples of the Philippines.* Westport, Conn.: Greenwood Press, 1974.

Lamb, David. *The Africans.* New York: Random House, Vintage Books, 1987.

Landess, Thomas, and Richard Quinn. *Jesse Jackson and the Politics of Race.* Ottawa, Ill.: Jameson Books, 1985.

Lane-Poole, Stanley. *The Story of the Moors in Spain.* Baltimore, Md.: Black Classic Press, 1990.

Lanker, Brian. *I Dream a World.* New York: Stewart, Tabori & Chang, 1999.

Leeming, David. *James Baldwin.* New York: Knopf, 1994.

Lerner, Gerda, ed. *Black Women in White America.* New York: Random House, Vintage Books, 1992.

Levine, Ellen. *Freedom's Children.* New York: Putnam, 1993.

Levy, Eugene. *James Weldon Johnson.* Chicago, Ill.: University of Chicago Press, 1973.

Lewis, David Levering. *When Harlem Was in Vogue.* New York: Viking Penguin, 1997.

Lewis, John, with D'Orso Michael. *Walking With the Wind.* New York: Simon & Schuster, 1998.

Lieb, Sandra R. *Mother of the Blues: A Study of Ma Rainey.* Amherst, Mass.: University of Massachusetts Press, 1983.

Lincoln, C. Eric. *The Black Muslims in America.* Grand Rapids, Mich.: Trenton, N.J.: Africa World Press, 1994.

Litwack, Leon F. *Been in the Storm So Long.* New York: Random House, Vintage Books, 1980.

———. *Trouble In Mind.* New York: Vintage Books, Random House, 1999.

Lofton, John. *Denmark Vesey's Revolt.* Kent, Ohio: Kent State University Press, 1983.

Logan, Rayford W., and Michael R. Winston. *Dictionary of American Negro Biography.* New York: Norton, 1982.

Lyon, Danny. *Memories of the Southern Civil Rights Movement.* Chapel Hill, N.C.: University of North Carolina Press, 1992.

McAdam, Doug. *Freedom Summer.* New York: Oxford University Press, 1990.

McPherson, James M. *The Negro's Civil War.* New York: Ballantine Books, 1991.

Malcolm X and Alex Haley. *The Autobiography of Malcolm X.* New York: Ballantine Books, 1992.

Mandela, Nelson. *Long Walk to Freedom.* New York: Little, Brown, 1994.

Mann, Coramae Richey. *Unequal Justice: A Question of Color.* Bloomington & Indianapolis: Indiana University Press, 1993.

Mannix, Daniel P., and Malcolm Cowley. *Black Cargoes: A History of the Atlantic Slave Trade.* Viking Press, 1962.

Marable, Manning. *W. E. B. DuBois.* Boston, Mass.: Twayne, 1986.

Marable, Manning, and Leith Mullings, eds. *Let Nobody Turn Us Around.* Lanham, Md.: Rowman & Littlefield, 1998.

Mead, Chris. *Champion Joe Louis: A Biography*. New York: Viking Penguin, Penguin Books, 1995.

Megill, Donald D., and Richard S. Demory. *Introduction to Jazz History*. Englewood Cliffs, N.J.: Prentice-Hall, 1993.

Meillassoux, Claude. *The Anthropology of Slavery*. Chicago, Ill.: University of Chicago Press, 1991.

Mellon, James, ed. *Bullwhip Days*. New York: Avon Books, 1992.

Miers, Suzanne, and Igor Kopytoff, eds. *Slavery in Africa*. Madison: University of Wisconsin Press, 1977.

Miller, Joseph C. *Way of Death*. Madison: University of Wisconsin Press, 1988.

Mills, Kay. *This Little Light of Mine*. New York: Penguin Books, Plume, 1994.

Murphy, Dervla. *The Ukimwi Road*. London: HarperCollins, Flamingo, 1994.

Nelson, Samuel H. *Colonialism in the Congo Basin 1880–1940*. Athens, Ohio: Ohio University Center for International Studies, Ohio University Press, 1994.

Newman, James L. *The Peopling of Africa*. New Haven, Conn.: Yale University Press, 1995.

Nugent, Rory. *Drums along the Congo*. New York: Houghton Mifflin, 1993.

Oakley, Giles. *The Devil's Music*. New York: Da Capo, 1997.

Oliver, Roland, and Anthony Atmore. *The African Middle Ages 1400–1800*. New York: Cambridge University Press, 1989.

Oritz, Victoria. *Sojourner Truth, a Self-made Woman*. New York: Lippincott, 1974.

Osae, T. A., A. T. O. Odunsi, and S. N. Nwabara. *A Short History of West Africa*. New York: Hill & Wange, 1973.

Paige, Leroy (Satchel), and David Lipman. *Maybe I'll Pitch Forever*. Lincoln: University of Nebraska Press, 1993.

Pakenham, Thomas. *The Scramble for Africa*. New York: Avon Books, 1991.

Parkinson, Wenda. *This Gilded African: Toussaint L'Ouverture*. London and New York: Quartet Books, 1980.

Pearson, Hugh. *The Shadow of the Panther*. New York: Addison-Wesley, 1994.

Petterson, Donald. *Inside Sudan*. Boulder, Colorado: Westview Press, 1999.

Pryor, Richard, and Todd Gold. *Pryor Convictions*. New York: Pantheon Books, 1995.

Quarles, Benjamin. *Black Abolitionists*. New York: DaCapo Press, Plenum, 1991.

———. *The Negro in the Making of America*. New York: Touchstone Books, 1996.

Quirke, Stephen, and Jeffrey Spencer, eds. *Ancient Egypt*. New York: Thames & Hudson, 1993.

Raines, Howell. *My Soul Is Rested*. New York: Penguin Books, 1977.

Rampersad, Arnold. *The Life of Langston Hughes*. New York: Oxford University Press, 1986.

Ribowsky, Mark. *A Complete History of the Negro Leagues 1884–1955*. New York: Carol, Birch Lane Press, 1995.

———. *Don't Look Back*. New York: Simon & Schuster, 1994.

Ritter, E. A. *Shaka Zulu*. New York: Penguin Books, 1987.

Robeson, Paul. *Here I Stand*. Boston, Mass.: Beacon Press, 1988.

Robinson, Randall. *Defending the Spirit: A Black Life in America*. New York: Dutton, 1998.

Rowna, Carl T. *Dream Makers, Dream Breakers: The World of Justice Thurgood Marshall*. Boston, Mass.: Little, Brown, 1993.

Salzman, Jack, David L. Smith, and Cornel West, eds. *Encyclopedia of African-American Culture and History*. New York: Macmillan, 1995.

Shillington, Kevin. *History of Africa*. New York: St. Martin's Press, 1995.

Shostak, Marjorie. *Nisa: The Life and Words of a !Kung Woman*. New York: Random House, Vintage Books, 1983.

Smith, J. Clay, Jr. *Emancipation: The Making of the Black Lawyer 1844–1944*. Philadelphia: University of Pennsylvania Press, 1993.

Smith, Valerie, A. Walton Litz, and Lea Baechler, eds. *African American Writers*. New York: Macmillan, Collier Books, 1993.

Spring, Christopher. *African Arms and Armor*. Washington, D.C.: Smithsonian Institution Press, 1993.

Stampp, Kenneth M. *The Peculiar Institution*. New York: Random House, Vintage Books, 1989.

Stedman, John Gabriel. *Narrative of an Expedition Against the Revolted Negroes of Surinam*. Holland: University of Massachusetts Press, 1971. (Originally printed ca. 1795)

Stewart, Kilton. *Pygmies and Dream Giants*. New York: Norton, 1954.

Thiong'o, Ngugi Wa. *Detained: A Writer's Prison Diary*. Ibadan, Nigeria: Heinemann Educational Books, 1981.

Thomas, Elizabeth Marshall. *The Harmless People*. New York: Vintage Books, 1989.

Thomas, J. C. *Chasin' the Trane*. New York: Plenum, Da Capo Press, 1975.

Tibbles, Anthony, ed. *Transatlantic Slavery*. London: Merrell Holberton Publishers in Association with NMGM, 1994.

Tracy, Steven C., ed. *Write Me a Few of Your Lines: A Blues Reader*. Amherst: University of Massachusetts Press, 1999.

Turnbull, Colin M. *Tradition and Change in African Tribal Life*. New York: Avon, Camelot Books, 1966.

Tuttle, William M., Jr. *Race Riot*. Champaign: University of Illinois Press, 1997.

Tygiel, Jules. *Baseball's Great Experiment*. New York: Oxford University Press, 1997.

Ungar, Sanford J. *Africa*. New York: Simon & Schuster, Touchstone Books, 1989.

Van Sertima, Ivan. *The Golden Age of the Moor*. New Brunswick, N.J.: Transaction, 1993.

———. *They Came Before Columbus, the African Presence in Ancient America*. New York: Random House, 1976.

———, ed. *African Presence in Early Europe*. New Brunswick, N.J.: Transaction, 1993.

Voices of Triumph-Perseverance. Alexandria, Va.: Time-Life Books, 1993.

von Sodon, Wolfram. *The Ancient Orient*. Grand Rapids, Mich.: Eerdmans, 1994.

Voss, Frederick S. *Majestic in His Wrath: A Pictorial Life of Frederick Douglass*. Washington, D.C.: Smithsonian Institution Press, 1995.

Walvin, James. *Black Ivory*. Washington, D.C.: Howard University Press, 1994.

Warkow, Arther I. *From Race Riot to Sit-In, 1919 and the 1960s*. Glouster, Mass.: Doubleday, 1966.

Washington, Margaret, ed. *Narrative of Sojourner Truth*. New York: Random House, Vintage Books, 1993.

Weisbrot, Robert. *Freedom Bound*. New York: Penguin Books, Plume, 1991.

Welding, Pete, and Toby Byron, eds. *Bluesland*. New York: Penguin Books, Dutton, 1991.

Wells, Ida B. *Crusade for Justice: The Autobiography of Ida B. Wells*. Chicago: University of Chicago Press, 1972.

Wepman, Dennis. *Africa: The Struggle for Independence*. New York: Facts On File, 1993.

White, Deborah Gray. *Ar'n't I a Woman?* New York: Norton, 1999.

White, Rev. Gavin, R. A. Kea, Humphrey J. Fisher, and Myron J. Echenberg. "4 Papers on Firearms in Sub-Saharan Africa." No. 2 in Vol. 12 of *The Journal of African History*. New York: Cambridge University Press, 1971.

Whitfield, Stephen J. *A Death in the Delta*. Baltimore: Johns Hopkins Press, 1991.

Whitney, Malika Lee, and Dermott Hussey. *Bob Marley*. Rohnert Park, Calif.: Pomegranate Artbooks, 1994.

Wilkins, Roy, and Tom Mathews. *Standing Fast: The Autobiography of Roy Wilkins*. New York: Da Capo, 1994.

Williams, Eric. *Capitalism and Slavery*. Chapel Hill: University of North Carolina Press, 1994.

Williams, John A., and Dennis A. Williams. *If I Stop I'll Die*. New York: Thunder's Mouth Press, 1991.

Williams, Juan. *Eyes on the Prize*. New York: Viking Penguin, 1987.

Williams, Michael W., ed. *The African American Encyclopedia*. 6 vols. Tarrytown, N.Y.: Marshall Cavendish Books, 1993.

Willis-Braithwaite, Deborah. *Vanderzee, Photographer 1886–1983*. New York: Abrams, 1994.

Wilson, Francis. *South Africa: The Cordoned Heart*. Cape Town, South Africa: Gallery Press; New York: Norton, 1986.

Woods, Donald. *Biko: Cry Freedom*. New York: Holt, 1999.

Woodward, C. Vann, and Elisabeth Muhlenfield, eds. *The Private Mary Chesnut: The Unpublished Civil War Diaries*. New York: Oxford University Press, 1984.

Wright, Richard. *Black Boy*. New York: HarperCollins, HarperPerennial, 1993.

Yetman, Norman, ed. *Voices from Slavery*. Mineola, N.Y.: Dover Press, 2000.

INDEX

Page numbers in **boldface** indicate main essay headings; page numbers in *italic* indicate illustrations; page numbers followed by *m* indicate maps.

A

Aaron, Henry ("Hank") **1**, *1*
Abassids 99, 328
Abbas, Ferhat 14
Abbott, Robert Sengstacke **1–2**
Abd 198
Abdallah Ibn Yasin 16
Abele, Julian Francis 2
Abernathy, Ralph David **2**, 204, 278
Abidjan 148
Abolition Church 183
abolitionists **2–6**, 15, 16–17, 18, 28, 47, 58, 76, 183, 269, 303
    chronology of 4–5
    Dred Scott decision and 254
    education and 92
    political parties 5
    societies 3
    voting rights and 305
    writings of 3–5, 299, 312–313
    Abolition of Slavery in the United States, The
      (Pezzicar) *103*
Aborigines **6–7**, *6*
Abraham 7
Abubakari II 12, 194
Abu Bakr ibn Umar 16
Abu Simbal 236
Abyssinia 7, 105
Accompong 80, 210
Achebe, Chinua **7–8**, *8*
acquired immunodeficiency syndrome (AIDS) **8–9**, 45, 286, 298
ACTION 179
Adal 105
Adams, Abigail 2
Adams, Henry 107
Adams, John Quincy 17
Adarand Constructors v. Peña 10
Adjas 112–113
Admiralty Islands 199
Adowa 200
Aero-Foam 158

Aesop (Aethiop) **9**
Afar 86, 168
affirmative action **9–10**, 174
AFL (American Federation of Labor) 172, 173, 236
AFL-CIO 173, 237
Africa **10–12**, 49, 81, 84, 85, 90, 122, 132, 149, 177. *See also specific countries and kingdoms*
    education in 92, 273
    European influence in late 19th century
      64m
    military history of 39
    nations of *11m*
    Pan-Africanism 16, 53, 119, 136, **224–225**
    slavery and. *See* slavery, slave trade
African Agricultural Union 142
African contact with Americas before Columbus **12**
African Methodist Episcopal Church (A.M.E.) 15, 303
African National Congress (ANC) **12–13**, 193, 277, 278, 324, 331
African Union Society 182
Afrikaners 276
Agaja 82
age groups/age sets **13**, 188
Agriculture, U.S. Department of 173, 280
Ahidjo, Ahmadou 52
Ahmad, Muhammad 281
Ahmad ibn Ibrahim (Ahmad Gran) 105
Ahmadu 252
Ahmed, Mulay 284
AIDS. *See* acquired immunodeficiency syndrome **8–9**, 45, 286, 298
Ailey, Alvin **13**, 102
Air Force, U.S. 83. *See also* black soldiers
Aja 82
Akan **13–14**, 109, 125
Akwame 14
Alabama, University of 97, 185
Aldridge, Ira Frederick **14**
Alexander the Great 99, 134

Alexandria 92
Alfonso 165–166
Algeria **14**, 109, 157
Ali, Muhammad (Cassius Clay) **14–15**, *15*
Ali, Muhammad (ruler in Egypt) 99, 281
Allakoi Keita 282
Allen, Henry 101
Allen, Louis 206
Allen, Richard **15**, 40, 155
Almohads **16**, 180, 204, 205
Almoravids **16**, 34, 124, 180, 198, 204, 205, 258
Alodia (Alwa) 57
Alooma, Idris 56, 159
alphabet 227, 228
Alpha Suffrage Club 317
Amenhotep I 98–99
American and Foreign Anti-Slavery Society 3
American Anti-Slavery Society 3
American Colonization Society **16**, 179
American Federation of Labor (AFL) 172, 173, 236
American Moral Reform Society 113–114
American Revolution 21, 39–40, 113, 252, 270
America's Promise—The Alliance for Youth 230
Ames, Adelbert 306
Amin, Idi 286, 298
Amistad **16–17**, 58, 267
ANC. *See* African National Congress
Anderson, Marian **17–18**, *17*
Anderson, Osborne Perry **18**, 68
And the Migrants Kept Coming (Lawrence) 176
Andrianampoinimerina 189
Angelou, Maya (Marguerite Johnson) **18**, 201
Angola, People's Republic of **18**, 165, 210, 277
animism **18–19**, 124, 137, 281, 321
Anjouan 63
Annan, Kofi 125
Annie Allen (Brooks) 46
Anotchi 22
Anthony, Susan B. 301

antislavery movement. *See* abolitionist
    movement
Apache Indians 157
apartheid 13, **19**, 246, 258, 277, 278, 297
        Biko and **36**
        Mandela and 193
Apollo Theater **19**, 112, 135, 203, 302
Appiah, Kwame Anthony 123
apprenticeship system 6, **20**, 170
Aptidon, Hassan Gouled 86
Arabian Peninsula 147, 148
Arabs **20–21**, 34, 56, 99, 155, 160, 162, 180,
    197, 205, 286, 294–295, 328, 329
        slave trade and 264
Arap Moi, Daniel 160
Arawak Indians 130–131, 132
Arctic 140
Aristide, Jean-Bertrand 132
Arizona 201
armed forces, blacks in. *See* black soldiers
Armistead, James **21**
Armstrong, Daniel Louis **21–22**, *22,* 78, 150,
    151, 202, 235
Armstrong, Samuel 314
Army, U.S. 82. *See also* black soldiers
arson 271
Asclepius 147
Ashanti (Asante) 14, **22–23**, 39, 69, 109, 126,
    160, 284
Ashanti War 22
Ashe, Arthur Robert, Jr. **23**, *23*
Ashley, John 116
Ashmore, Harry 182
asiento **23–24**
Askia Muhammad Touré. *See* Muhammad Touré
Aspects of Negro Life (Douglas) 86
Assad, Hafez al- 149
Association for the Study of Negro Life and
    History (ASNLH) 322
Assoumani, Azaly 63
Assyrians 99, 285
Astaire, Fred 150
Aswan Dam 219
Atlanta Braves 1
Attucks, Crispus **24**, 138
Augustine, St. 14, **24**
Augustus 205
Auld, Thomas 87
Australia 200
Autobiography of an Ex-Colored Man, The
    (Johnson) 153
Autobiography of Miss Jane Pittman, The (Gaines)
    120
Axum (Aksum) **24–25**, 104, 105, 108, 124, 168,
    174

B

back-to-Africa movements 16
Baguirmi 56
Bailey, Alonzo 71
Bailey v. Alabama 71, 171
Baker, Ella Josephine **26**, 280
Baker, Josephine **26–27**, *26,* 43
Bakongo 165
Bakri, al- 124
Balanchine, George 27, 91
Baldwin, James Arthur **27**, 81
Balkans 149

Baltimore, Charles 143
Baltimore Colored Caulkers Trade Union Society
    171
Bambara **27**, *28,* 151, 198, 276
Banda, Hastings 190
Banneker, Benjamin **28**
Bantu **28–29**, 45, 51, 104, 120, 147, 160, 161,
    162, 165, 167, 189, 203, 204, 207, 212, 232,
    233, 282–283, 328, 329
        Zimba 162, 190, 203, 285, **329**
bantustans (homelands) 19, **29**, 277, 331
Baoule 148
Baptist War 6, **29**, 261
Baraka, Imamu Amiri (LeRoi Jones) **29**
Barca, Hamilcar 134
Barnett, Ferdinand 317
Barnett, Ross 200
barracoons 16, **30**, 58, 61, 165, 196, 267
Barre, Muhammad Siyad 275
Barry, Marion 280
Bar's Fight, The (Prince) 230
Barthe, Richmond **30**, 135, 182
Bartók, Béla 202
baseball leagues, Negro 1, **213–214**, *213,* 224,
    246
baseball players
        Aaron, Henry ("Hank") **1**, *1*
        Paige, Leroy Robert ("Satchel") 78, 214,
            223–224, *223*
        Robinson, Jack Roosevelt ("Jackie") 1, 184,
            214, **245–246**, *246*
Bashir, Omar Hassan 281
Basie, William ("Count") **30**, 142, 150, 156, 225,
    287
basket, Tutsi *50*
basketball 244
Basra 328
Basutoland 177
Bates, Daisy Lee Gatson **30–31**, *31,* 181–182
Bates, Ruby 75, 254–255
Batson v. Kentucky 76
Battle of Life, The (Tanner) 285
Bearden, Romare **31**
beauty 313
bebop 57, 125, 151, 204, 225, 247
Bechet, Sidney **31–32**
Bechuanaland 45, 177
Beckwith, Byron de la 76, 107
Beckwourth, James Pierson **32**, *32*
Bedie, Henri Konan 148
Belgian Congo **32–33**, 65, 68, 185
Belgium, Belgians 50, 67, 68, 185, 248
Belize 122
Bell, Alexander Graham 176
Bella, Ahmed Ben 14
Beloved (Morrison) 206, 321
Bengasi 180
Benin, Kingdom of 33, 82, 103, 107, 113,
    146–147, 191, 216, 217, 263, 290
Benin, Republic of **33–34**, 116
Benjamin-Constant, Jean-Jacques 285
Bennett, Ned and Rolla 303
Berbers 16, 21, **34**, 56, 124, 155, 180, 197, 204,
    205, 294, 295
        Almoravids **16**, 34, 124, 180, 198, 204, 205,
            258
Berbice 61
Beta Israel (Black Jews) **34–35**

Bethune, Mary Jane McLeod **35**, *35,* 322
Betsimisaraka 189
Beydanes 198
Biafra 7, 216, 278
Biko, Stephen **36**, 277
Bill of Rights 242
Bioko 104
Birmingham, Alabama 163
        King's Letter from Birmingham Jail 163,
            177–178
        Sixteenth Street Baptist Church bombing in
            177, **263**
Birney, James 5
Birth of a Nation 167, 292
Bismarck Archipelago 199
Bissel, F. W. 86
Biya, Paul 52
Black, Julian 183
Black Bourgeoisie, The (Frazier) 115
Black Boy (Wright) 186, 323
Black Codes **36**, 71, 169, 239, 240, 241, 305
Black Consciousness Movement 36
blackface 152
Black History Month 323
Black Jews (Beta Israel) **34–35**
Black Masons 132
Black Muslims 36, *208,* 211. *See also* Nation of
    Islam
Black Panther Party for Self-Defense **36–37**, *37,*
    53, 214
black power movement **37–38**, 47, 320
black Seminoles 38
Black Skin, White Masks (Fanon) 109
Blacksmith, Ben 70
black soldiers **39–43**, *39, 41,* 113, 186, 196,
    239
        Brownsville, Texas, Affair **47–48**, 77, 117,
            287
        Buffalo Soldiers 40, **48–49**, *48*
        Civil War 40, 42, 88, 103–104, *108,* 111,
            138, 179, 270, 271, 293
        Houston Mutiny 77, **143–144**, 243
        integration of armed forces 41, 150, 174,
            237, 248
        military justice 77–78
        Tuskegee Airmen **296**
Black Star Line 122, 123
Blair, Ezell 263
Blake, James Hubert ("Eubie") 26, **43**
Blakey, Art (Abdullah ibn Bulaina) **43**, 47, 246
Blanton, Jimmy 202
Blanton, Thomas E., Jr. 263
Blood River, Battle of 276, 331
blood storage and transport 89, 155–156
Bloody Sunday **43**, 74, 309
blues **43–45**, *44,* 127, 150, 235, 244
Bluest Eye, The (Morrison) 206
Bluford, Guion Stewart, Jr. **45**
Blyden, Edward W. 224
boat people 132
Boers 177, 212, 276, 324, 331
Boer War 276
Boganda, Barthélemy 55
Bogle, Paul **45**
Bokassa, Jean-Bedel 55
Bongo, Albert-Bernard 120
Bonny 216

Bontemps, Arna **45**, 136
Booth, Joseph 57
bop. *See* bebop
Bornu 159
Bostic, Earl 62
Boston Massacre 24
Boston Riot 292
Botswana, Republic of 8, **45**
Boukman Revolt **45–46**, 131, 290
Boulanger, Nadia 156
Boumédienne, Houari 14
Bourguiba, Habib 295
Bouteflika, Abdelaziz 14
boxing 14–15
Boxley, George 137
Bowler, Jack 231
Boyer, Jean-Pierre 132
Braddock, James 183
Bradford, Perry 235
Brando, Marlon 91
Bratton, O. S. 101
Brazil 224, 265, 266, 269, 273
Brazza, Pierre Savorgnan de 65–66
Bridges, Robert 113
Brillante 266–267
Bringing the Prisoners Out 137
Britain, British 33, 52, 104, 113, 128, 179, 210,
219, 222, 270, 275, 282, 283, 286, 327
    Ashanti and 22–23
    Cameroon and 52
    Cape Colony and 324
    Egypt and 99
    Ethiopia and 106, 130
    Gambia and 121
    Gold Coast and 22, 109, 124, **126**
    Haiti and 131
    Kenya and 160–161
    Lesotho and 177
    Maasai and 188
    Madagascar and 189
    Mau Mau and 160–161, **197**
    Mauritius and 198
    Mombasa and 203
    Ndebele and 212, 330
    Nigeria and 216
    Rhodesia and 329–330
    Samori and 252
    Senegal and 258
    Seychelles and 259
    slavery and 5–6, 20, 23–24, 29, 40, 81, 104,
        121, 198, 259, 261, 265, 266–267, 276,
        329
    Somaliland and 275
    South Africa and 276, 277
    Sudan and 281
    Togo and 290
    triangular trade and **291**, 292*m*
    Uganda and 298
    in War of 1812 15, 38, 40, 113
    Yoruba and 326
    Zanzibar and 329
    Zulus and 331
British South Africa Company (BSAC) 212, 327,
    330
Brodie, Steve 153
Brooklyn Dodgers 214, 246
Brooks, Gwendolyn **46**
Brotherhood of Sleeping Car Porters 173, 237

Brown, Charles A. 245
Brown, Claude **46–47**
Brown, Clifford 47
Brown, Henry ("Box") 299
Brown, James 47, 276
Brown, John 18, 68, 88, 128, 136–137, 144, 176,
    179, 270, 294
Brown, Minnijean 182
Brown, Oliver 95
Brown, William Wells 47
Brown, Willie 155
Brownsville, Texas, Affair **47–48**, 77, 117, 287
Brownsville Raid, The (Fuller) 117
Brown v. Board of Education of Topeka, Kansas **48**,
    59, 60, 79, 95–96, 98, 145, 196, 211–212, 241
Bruce, Blanche Kelso **48**, 115
Bryant, Carolyn 288
Bryant, Roy 288
Bubi 104
bubonic plague 264
Buffalo Soldiers 40, **48–49**, *48*
Buganda 298
Bullard, Eugene Jacques 41
bulldogging 228
Bunche, Ralph Johnson **49**
Bunyoro 298
Burke, Selma Hortense **49**, 135
Burkina Faso **49–50**, 116, 148, 191, 207
Burns, Tommy 153
Burris, Samuel 301
Burundi, Republic of **50**
Bush, George 230, 288
Bushmen **51**
    Khoi 51, **161**, 168, 210, 232
    !Kung San 45, 51, **167–168**, 210
Bush Negroes **51**
buses 204, 227
    freedom riders 68, 109–110, **115–116**, 162,
        163, 178, 280
    Montgomery Bus Boycott 2, 26, 59, 162,
        178, **204**, 226, 248
businesspeople, black 171, *171*
busing **51**, 97
Buyoya, Pierre 50
Byzantine Empire 294

C

Cable, George Washington 73
Cabral, Amilcar 53, 129
Cabral, Luis de Almeida 129
Cadamosto, Luigi da 53
Callahan, John 103
Callahan, William 255
Callender, James Thomson 139
Callender, Red 202
Calloway, Cab 125, 135, 311
calypso 52, 244, 276
Cambyses 99
Cameroon, Republic of **52**, 117
Camp Logan 143
Camus, Albert 206
Canary Islands 157
Cane (Toomer) 290
Cape Verde, Republic of **52–53**
capoeira 53
Caribbean 52, 254, 273
Carmichael, Stokely (Kwame Ture; Kwame
    Touré) 37, **53**, 179, 280

Carnera, Primo 183
Carney, William 111
Carr, Samuel 139
Carrido, Juan **53–54**
Carson, Benjamin S. **54**
Carter, Jimmy 207, 282, 326
Carthage 54, 134, 227, 294
Carver, George Washington **54–55**, *55*, 314
Casablanca 206
Casement, Roger 67–68
Cash, Herman 263
casting, bronze 252
Cast the First Stone (Himes) 141
Cayor 321
Central African Republic 55, 66, 120
Centralia 315
Central Intelligence Agency, U.S. (CIA) 65,
    185–186
Cesaire, Aimé 188, 213
Cetshwayo 331
Chad, Republic of **55–56**, 66, 120, 253
chain gangs 20, 72–73, *72*, 170, 248
Challenger 45
Chambliss, Robert 263
Champollion, Jean 140
Chaney, James 56, 59, 76, 110, 186, 227, 308
Changa 56, 204
Changamire 56, 204, 214
Charbonneau, Toussaint 325
Charles, Ray 156
Charles II 267
Cheng Ho 192
Cherry, Bobby Frank 263
Chesapeake Marine Railway and Dry Dock
    Company 209
Chesnutt, Charles Waddell 57
Chicago 91
Chicago blues 316
Chicago *Defender* 1–2, 134, 144, 217
Chicago World's Fair 317
children
    apprenticeship system and **20**, 170
    justice system and 78
Chilembwe, John 57
Chilembwe Uprising 57, 190
Chiluba, Frederick 327
China 147, 148, 192
Chisholm, Shirley 149
Chi wara kun headdress 28
Chocolate Dandies 26, 43
Christian, Charlie 57, 164, 204, 311
Christianity 24, 25, 92, 99, 105, 108, 113, 165,
    177, 189, 205, 220, 238, 294
    civil rights and 59
Christian Nubia **57–58**, 219, 281
Churchill, Winston 188, 206
CIA. *See* Central Intelligence Agency
Cinqué, Joseph 16–17, **58**
CIO (Congress of Industrial Organizations) 173
City of God (Augustine) 24
Civil Rights Act (1866) 71, 76, 169, 239, 241
Civil Rights Act (1964) 9, **58–59**, 60, 97, 164,
    173, 174, 263, 307, 319
Civil Rights Act (1968) 173
Civil Rights movement 27, 37, 38, 47, **59–60**, 72,
    79, 87, 98, 107, 127, 143, 150, 167, 174, 201,
    288, *312*. *See also specific issues, organizations
    and people*

Civil Rights movement (continued)
  Alabama rally *58*
  FBI and 72
  Harlem Renaissance and 135
  police and 74
  sit-ins 59, 68, 109, 149, **263**, *263,* 280
Civil War 5, 88, 89, 93, 103–104, 169, 270, 274, 305
    black soldiers in 40, 42, 88, 103–104, *108,* 111, 138, 179, 270, 271, 293
    medal of honor recipients in 42
Clark, Kenneth Bancroft **60**, 96
Clark, Mark 37
Clark, William 325
Clark Air Force Base 213
Clarke, Kenny 204
Clayton, Powell 167
Cleaver, Eldridge 37
Cleopatra 99
Cleveland, James 127
Cleveland Indians 224
Clinton, Bill 18, 83, 149, 249, 296
cloth 273
    kente 125, **160**
    mud **208**
Cobb, Jeremiah 295
Code Noir **60**, 269
Coffin, Levi 301
coffle **60–61**, *61*
Coffy's Rebellion **61**
COFO (Council of Federated Organizations) **69**, 280
COINTELPRO 72
Coleman, Elizabeth ("Bessie") **62**
Coleman, Ornette 151
Coleridge-Taylor, Avril 62
Coleridge-Taylor, Samuel 62
Colfax **62**, 240, 306
Collins, Addie Mae 263
Collins, Albert 311
Colored Caulkers' Trade Union Society 209
Colored Citizen 209
Colored National Labor Union 171–172
Color Purple, The (Walker) 156, 312, *312,* 321
Coltrane, John W. ("Trane") **62–63**, *63,* 83, 204
Columbus, Christopher 130
    African contact with Americas before **12**
Committee, the 107
Committee for Improving Industrial Conditions in New York 212
Committee for Industrial Organization (CIO) 173
Committee on Urban Conditions Among Negroes 212
Comoros, Federal Islamic Republic of the **63**
Compromise of 1850 117
confessions 74
Confessions (Augustine) 24
Congo, Democratic Republic of 32, **63–65**, 66, *93,* 185, 186, 249
Congo, Republic of the **65–66**, 120
Congo Free State 32, 63, **66–68**, 289, 320
Congo My Country (Lumumba) 185
Congo-Ocean Railroad 66
Congo River 63, 65, **68**, 165
Congressional Medal of Honor 40, 41, 48, 49, 111, 157
    list of recipients of 42

Congress of Industrial Organizations (CIO) 173
Congress of Racial Equality (CORE) 56, 59, **68**, 109, 110, 116, 227, 248, 280, 308
Conjure Woman, The (Chesnutt) 57
Conner, Eugene ("Bull") 116, 163, 178
Conrad, Earl 255
Conrad, Joseph 68
Constantine 108
Constitution, U.S. 60, 70, 242
    Sixth Amendment to 75–76
    Eighth Amendment to 79
    Thirteenth Amendment to 5, 71, 104, 122, 238, 241
    Fourteenth Amendment to 71, 76, 95, 169–170, 228, 229, 239, 240, 241–242
    Fifteenth Amendment to 71, 88, 136, 240, 241, 242, 304, 306, 318
Conte, Lansana 129
convict-lease programs 20, 73, 170, 240
Conyers, John 202, 227
Cooke, Sam 127, 276
Coolidge, Calvin 35, 123
Copeland, John Anthony, Jr. **68**
copper 327
Córdoba 204, 205
CORE. *See* Congress of Racial Equality
Corisco 104
Cornish, James 319
Cornish, Samuel 248
Cornwallis, Charles 21
Coromantees (Coramantines) **69**, 81, 267
Cortés, Hernán 53–54
Cosby, William Henry, Jr. ("Bill") **69**, *69,* 231
Cotton Club 102
Council of Federated Organizations (COFO) **69**, 280
cowboys 185
Craft, William and Ellen **69–70**, 138
Cray, Robert 44
Creole Mutiny **70**, 267
Creoles 261
Cresques, Abraham 194
Crête-à-Pierrot 84
crime 75, 240
criminal justice system, U.S. **70–80**
    chain gangs 20, 72–73, *72,* 170, 248
    convict leasing 20, 73, 170, 240
    death penalty 79, 143–144, 240
    jury system 75–76, 143, 240, 257
    juvenile justice 78
    malicious prosecution 75
    military justice 77–78
    police brutality 74–75
    police failure to protect blacks 73–74
    police harassment 75
    political and economic control maintained by 71–72
    sentencing and treatment of prisoners 78–79, 170
    Simpson case and 262
    Crisis 90, 136, 144, 153, 212, 319
Crite, Allan Rohan **80**
crop lien system 170
Crow Indians 32
Crucifixion, The (Fuller) 118
Crump, Edward ("Boss") 134
Cuba 254, 269, 273
Cuban Giants 213

Cudjoe 69, **80–81**, 196, 210
Cuffe, Paul 16, **81**, 224
Cullen, Countee Porter 27, 45, *80,* **81**, 136, 236
Cush. *See* Kush
Cyclone Eline 207
Cyrenaica 180

D

Dacko, David 55
Dagomba 207
Dahmer, Vernon 59
Dahomey 33–34, 39, **82**, 113, 116, 222, 264
Dako 82
Damas, Léon 213
Danakil 86, 168
Dance Theater of Harlem 203
Danforth, John 288
Daoud 284
Daughters of the American Revolution (D.A.R.) 17
David Walker's Appeal 3, 248, 312–313
Davies, Ronald 181
Davis, Benjamin Oliver, Sr. and Benjamin Oliver, Jr. **82–83**, 296
Davis, Edmund 167
Davis, Jefferson 83–84
Davis, Joseph 83–84
Davis, Miles Dewey III 43, 63, **83**, *83,* 133, 151, 156, 246
Davis Bend **83–84**, 305
Death and the King's Horseman (Soyinka) 278
death penalty 79, 143–144, 240
death rates, from slave trade 266–267
Debs, Eugene 172
debt peonage 20, 71, 170–171
Deby, Idriss 56
Decolonising the Mind (Ngũgĩ) 215
Defender (Chicago) 1–2, 134, 144, 217
Defiance Campaign 13
Delany, Martin Robinson 16, **84**, 224
Democratic Party 62, 202, 241, 308, 317
    Mississippi Freedom Democratic Party 26, 69, 133, 179, **202–203**, 206, 280, 308
Dempsey, Jack 154
Dengel, Leban 105
Denkyira 14
Depression, Great. *See* Great Depression
Deslondes, Charles 184
Dessalines, Jean-Jacques 30, **84–85**, 131, 291
Detained (Ngũgĩ) 215
Devany, Peter 303
Diallo, Amadou 74
Diggs, Charles 246
DiMaggio, Joe 224
Dingane 331
Dingiswayo 259, 260
Dinka 85, 282
Diop, Cheikh Anta 85
Dioulas (Dyulas) 85
discrimination. *See* Civil Rights movement; segregation
diversity 9, 10
Dixieland 150
Djenne. *See* Jenne
Djibouti, Republic of 86, 232
Djoser 147
Doe, Samuel K. 180
Dogon 86, *86, 192*

Dominican Republic 89, *304*, 326
Dorantes, Andres 105
Dorsey, Thomas A. 127, 149
Dos Santos, Jose Eduardo 18
Douglas, Aaron **86–87**, *87*, 135, 182
Douglas, Robert 244
Douglass, Frederick 3, 57, 84, **87–89**, *87, 88*, 92,
    103, 115, 128, 136, 138, 169, 183, 242, 287,
    293, 294, 301
draft riots **89**, 169
dragnets 75
Dreaming Emmett (Morrison) 206
Drew, Charles Richard **89**
DuBois, Nina Yolande 81
DuBois, William Edward Burghardt (W. E. B.) 72,
    81, **89–90**, *90*, 93, 209, 211, 212, 215, 224,
    225, 253, 292, 314, 322
    Talented Tenth concept of 90, 136, **285**
Dumas, Alexandre (Dumas Père [Sr.]) **90–91**
Dumas, Alexandre fils (Jr.) 91
Dumas, Marie Cessette 91
Dunbar, Paul Laurence **91**
Dunham, Katherine **91**
Dunn, Oscar 228
DuSable, Jean-Baptiste Pointe **91**
Dutch 51, 61, 127, 198, 224, 258, 276
Dutch Guyana 51
Duvalier, Francois ("Papa Doc") 132
Duvalier, Jean-Claude ("Baby Doc") 132
Dylan, Bob 176, 316

E

Ebony 154
Eckford, Elizabeth 182
Eckstine, Billy 83, 302
Edison, Thomas 176
education and schools **92–98**, *93, 94, 97*, 172,
    180, 240
    affirmative action **9–10**
    in Africa 92, 273
    Brown v. Board of Education of Topeka, Kansas
        48, 59, 60, 79, 95–96, 98, 145, 196,
        211–212, 241
    busing **51**, 97
    Freedmen's Bureau and 115
    Little Rock Nine 30–31, 59, 97, **181–182**,
        181
    movable schools 55
    school segregation and integration 30, 51,
        60, 92, 95–98, 128, 143, 181–182, 241
Edwards, Alonzo 143
Egypt, Arab Republic of 20, 39, 57, 85, **98–101**,
    98, 104, 194, 212, 219, 232, 278
    dynastic history 100–101
    Imhotep and **147**
    Kushites and 168
    pyramids in 98, 147, *233*, 233
    Ramses II and **236**, *236*
    Sudan and 281
    Taharqa and **284–285**
Eighth Amendment 79
Eisenhower, Dwight D. 35, 140, 182, 307
Elaine, Arkansas, incident 75, **101**, 172–173,
    211, 243
Elder, Lee 321
Eldridge, Roy 125
Elgar, Edward 62
Elizabeth I 267

Ellington, Edward Kennedy ("Duke") **101–102**,
    102, 135, 150, 202
Ellison, Ralph Waldo **102–103**, 176
Elmina Castle 22, **103**, 126
Elobey Chico 104
Elobey Grande 104
Emancipation Act 20, 29
Emancipation Proclamation 5, 40, 88, **103–104**,
    179, 241
Emerson, John 254
Emperor Jones, The (O'Neill) *245*
employment and labor rights 20, 116–117, 120,
    148, **169–174**, *174*, 179, 200, 217, 243, 257,
    290, 305, 317
    affirmative action **9–10**, 174
    blackbirders 200
    Black Codes **36**, 71, 169, 241
    black entrepreneurs and professionals 171,
        171
    child labor 20, 170
    debt peonage 20, 71, 170–171
    Exodusters and 107, 170
    prison labor 20, 72–73, *72*, 170
    sharecropping 26, 101, 170, 172–173,
        260–261, *260*
    unions 171–173, 209, 237, 261
    workplace segregation 174
England. *See* Britain, British
"Entertainer, The" (Joplin) 157
entrepreneurs and professionals, black 171, *171*
Equal Employment Opportunities Act (1972)
    9
Equal Employment Opportunity Commission
    (EEOC) 174, 288
Equatorial Guinea, Republic of **104**
Eritrea 24, **104–105**, 106, 232
Eschikagou 91
Estevanico (Esteban; Estevanillo) **105**
Ethiopia, Federal Democratic Republic of 24,
    34–35, 86, 104, 105, **105–106**, 275
    Lalibela and 105, **174–175**
    Menelik II and 106, **200**
    Ethiopia Awakening (Fuller) 118
Eucherius 251
Europe. *See also specific countries*
    influence in Africa in late 19th century
        64*m*
Evers, Charles 107
Evers, Medgar Wiley 59, 76, **106–107**, *106*, 133,
    307
Evers, Myrlie 107
"Everybody's Protest Novel" (Baldwin) 27
Ewe 290
Ewuare the Great 33, **107**
Exodusters (Exodus of 1879) **107**, 170, 262
extended family 9, 19, **108**
Eyadema, Ghansimgbe 290
Ezana 24, **108**

F

Fada-n-Gourma 207
Fairbank, Calvin 137–138, 301
Falashas 35
false pretense laws 71
family, extended 9, 19, **108**
Fang 120
Fanon, Frantz Omar **109**, 224
Fante 14, **109**

Fard, W. D. (Fard Muhammad) 208, 211
Farmer, James Leonard 68, **109–110**, *110*
farmers 172, *172*, 173, 305
    sharecroppers 26, 101, 170, 172–173,
        260–261, *260*
Farm Security Administration (FSA) 225
Farouk 99
Farrakhan, Louis Abdul (Louis Eugene Walcott)
    110–111, *110*, 201, 202, 211
Fatimid Dynasty 99
Faubus, Orval 31, 181, 182
Fauset, Jessie 135–136
FBI (Federal Bureau of Investigation) 72
Fernando Po 104
Ferres Galley 267
Fezzan 180
Fifteenth Amendment 71, 88, 136, 240, 241,
    242, 304, 306, 318
Fifty-fourth Massachusetts Regiment **111**, *111*
Fight Never Ends, The 184
Fiji 198
Fire! 145
First Seminole War 7
Fisk Jubilee Singers **111**, *112*
Fisk School 111
Fisk University 111, 158
Fitzgerald, Ella **112**
Flipper, Henry O. 40, 77, 326
Fon 34, **112–113**
Foraker, Joseph 47
for colored girls who have considered suicide/when
    the rainbow is enuf (Shange) 260
Ford, Gerald 221
Foreman, George 15
Forever Free (Lewis) 179
For Love of Imabelle (Himes) 141
Forman, James 280
Forrest, Nathan Bedford 113
Forrestal, James 78
Fort Dade, Treaty of 7, 142
Forten, James 15, **113–114**, 155
Fort Gibson, Treaty of 7
Fort James 121
Fort Jesus 203
Fort Negro 7, 38, **113**, 195
Fort Pillow 113
40 acres and a mule **114**, 170, 177
Fosse, Bob 150
Foster, Rube 214
4 Little Girls 177
Fourteenth Amendment 71, 76, 95, 169–170,
    228, 229, 239, 240, 241–242
    due process clause in 241–242
    equal protection clause in 241
Fouta Djalon 128
Fowler, John ("Bud") 213
France, French 99, 113, 179, 191, 222, 253, 270,
    295, 321
    Algeria and 14
    Benin and 33–34
    Berkina Faso and 49
    Cameroon and 52
    Central African Republic and 55
    Chad and 56
    Comoros and 63
    Congo and 65–66
    Dahomey and 82
    Djibouti and 86

France, French (*continued*)
  Gabon and 120
  Guinea and 128–129
  Haiti and 84–85, 131–132
  Ivory Coast and 116, 142, 148
  Jenne and 151–152
  Louisiana and 184
  Madagascar and 189
  Mauritania and 198
  Morocco and 205
  Niger and 215
  Saint-Domingue and 45–46, 85, 131, 290
  Samori and 252
  Senegal and 258, 259
  Seychelles and 259
  slavery and 23, 46, 60, 127, 269, 290
  Togo and 290
Frank, Leo 186
Franklin, Aretha **114**, *114*, 276
Franklin, Benjamin 3
Franklin, John Hope **114**, 320
Frazier, E. Franklin **114–115**
Frazier, Joe 15
Free African Society 15, 155
Freedman's Hospital 319
Freedman's Savings and Trust Company 48, 89, **115**
Freedmen's Bureau 20, 93, 94, 111, 115, **115**, 122, 238, 239
Freedom Ballot Campaign 69
Freedom Charter 13
freedom riders 59, 68, 74, 109–110, **115–116**, 162, 163, 178, 280
Freedom Schools 280, 308
Freedom's Journal 248
Freeland, William 87
Freeman, Elizabeth (Mum Bett or Mumbet) **116**
Free Soil Party 5
Free Speech and Headlight 316
Freetown 261
French and Indian Wars 39, 230
French Congo 120
French Equatorial Africa 120
French Somaliland 86
French Sudan 152, 191
French West African Federation **116–117**, 152, 191
Fresh Prince of Bel Air, The 156
Frey, John 214
Frick, Ford 246
Front de Libération Nationale (FLN) 14, 109
frontier wars 40
Fruit of Islam (FOI) 211
Fuentes, Carlos 123
Fugitive Slave Law **117**, *117*, 183
Fuhrman, Mark 74
Fulani (Foulas; Foulbe) **117**, 121, 128, 159, 215, 222, 275, 276
Fuller, Charles **117–118**
Fuller, Meta Vaux Warrick **118–119**, *118*, 135
Furman v. Georgia 79

G

Gabon, Republic of 66, **120**
Gaines, Ernest J. **120**
Gambia, Republic of the **121**, 321
Gamin (Savage) 253
Gandhi, Mohandas K. 13, 59, 162, 178, 179

Gao **121**, 151
Garcia, Jose Mauricio Nunes **121–122**
Garfield, James 89
Garifunas (Garinagus; Black Caribs) **122**
Garner, James 30
Garner, Margaret 206
Garnet, Henry Highland **122**
Garrett, Thomas 301
Garrison, William Lloyd 3, 113, 175
Garvey, Marcus 16, 72, **122–123**, *123*, 136, 188, 190, 224, 238, 253, 302
gas masks 205
Gates, Henry Louis, Jr. **123**
Gaye, Marvin **124**, 126, 276
Ge'ez **124**
General Electric Company *175*
Georgetown University 138
Georgia 271
Germany, Germans 50, 52, 210, 221, 248, 286, 290, 298
Get On the Bus 177
Ghaji, Ali 159
Ghana, Kingdom of 16, 23, 34, 69, **124**, 159, 160, 191, 198, 290
Ghana, Republic of 13, 14, 22, 23, **124–125**, 126, 216–217
ghettos 173
Giants of Jazz 204
Gibson, Josh 214
Giddings, Joshua 70
Gideon v. Wainwright 79
Gillespie, John Birks ("Dizzy") 62, 83, **125**, 151, 156, 202, 204, 225, 302
Gilliam, Sam **125–126**
Giovanni, Nikki **126**
Giovanni's Room (Baldwin) 27
Giza 233, 278
Glidden Paint Company 158
Glory 111
Gobir 117
God's Trombones: Seven Negro Sermons in Verse (Johnson) 86
gold 121, 124, 151, 160, 168, 207, 265, 276
Gold Coast 14, 22, 23, 69, 103, 109, 124, **126**, 217
Goldman, Ron 262
Gompers, Samuel 172
Goncharova, Natalia 232
Goodman, Andrew 56, 59, 76, 110, 186, 227, 308
Goodman, Benny 57, 141, 164
Goodman, Robert 149
Good Shepard, The (Fuller) 118–119
Gorbachev, Mikhail 230
Gordon, Charles 281
Gordone, Charles **126**
Gordy, Berry, Jr. **126**, 276
Gorée (Île de Gorée) **127**, 258
gospel music 127, 133, 235, 276
Gossec, François 250
Go Tell It on the Mountain (Baldwin) 27
Gowon, Yakubu 216
Graham, Henry 116
Grande Comore 63
grandfather clauses **127**
Grant, Charlie 214
Grant, Ulysses S. 84, 111, 209, 306
Granz, Norman 112

Great Britain. *See* Britain, British
Great Depression 44, 136, 173, 235, 237
Great Gabriel Conspiracy **231**
Great Migration (northern migration) 135, 212, **217**, 218*m*
Great Trek 276
Great White Hope, The 154
Great Zimbabwe (Great Enclosure) **127–128**, *128*, 329
Greece, Greeks 85, 228
Green, Ernest 182
Green, Shields 68, **128**
Green, Steve 317
Grey, Victoria 281
Griffin v. Prince Edward County, Virginia 128
Group Areas Act (1959) 277
Grunitzky, Nicolas 290
Guanches 157
Guardian 292
guardians 20, 170
Guei, Robert 148
Guelle, Ismail Omar 86
Guin 290
Guinea, Republic of 53, 116, 117, 121, **128–129**, 180, 191
Guinea-Bissau, Republic of 53, **129**
Gullah (Gulla) **129**
guns 265
Gurdjieff, Georgei 290
Guyana 51, 61, 270
Guyot, Lawrence 133, 280

H

Habashat 105
Habyarimana, Juvenal 50, 248–249
Hagar, Fred 235
Haile Selassie I (Ras Tafari Makonnen) 106, **130**, *130*, 238
Haiti, Republic of 45, 84–85, 89, **130–132**, 153, 196, 231, 270, 273, 290–291, 326
  Voodoo in **303–304**, *304*
Haitian Revolution 46, 84, 270, 290
Haley, Alex Palmer 121, **132**
Hall, George 322
Hall, Prince **132–133**
Halpulaar 198
Hamer, Fannie Lou Townsend **133**, 202, 280
Hammarskjöld, Dag 65
Hampton, Fred 37
Hampton, Lionel 47, 202
Hampton, Wade 184
Hancock, Herbie **133**, 287
Hancock, John 132
Handy, William Christopher **134**
Hannibal 39, 54, **134**
Hanno 54, 121, **134**
Hansberry, Lorraine Vivian **135**
Haratines 198
Harlan, John Marshall 95, 229
Harlem 102, **135**, 155, 225
  Apollo Theater **19**, 112, 135, 203, 302
  Dance Theater of Harlem 203
  Renaissance 43, 45, 81, 87, 135, **135–136**, 145, 153, 182, 188, 212, 253, 290, 313
  Harlem Shadows (McKay) 188
Harmon, Leonard Roy 41
Harp, The (Savage) 253
Harper, Frances Ellen Watkins **136**

Harpers Ferry Raid 18, 68, 88, 128, **136–137,** *137,* 144, 270, 294
Harrison, Benjamin 89, 287, 320
Hartgrove, W. B. 322
Harth, Mingo 303
Hassan 317
Hatshepsut 232
Hausa 39, **137,** 159, 215, 216, 275
Hawkins, Alfred 255
Hawkins, Coleman Randolph 83, **137,** 235, 246
Hayden, Lewis 76, **137–138**
Hayden, Palmer 135
Hayden, Robert Earl **138**
Hayes, Roland 135
Hayes, Rutherford B. 89, 139, 240, 306
headdress *28*
Healy, Eliza 138
Healy, James Augustine 138
Healy, Michael Augustine 138
Healy, Patrick Francis **138**
Heart of Darkness (Conrad) 68
Height, Dorothy 201
Hemings, Elizabeth 139
Hemings, Sally **139**
Henderson, Fletcher 135, 137, 150, 235
Hendrix, Jimi **139**
Henry, Aaron 69, 202
Henry I (Henry Christophe) 131–132
Henson, Josiah **139–140,** 299
Henson, Matthew Alexander **140,** *140*
Herero 210
Herodotus 168, 212
hieroglyphics **140,** *141,* 201
Hill, Anita 288
Hill, Robert L. 101
Hill, Teddy 125
Hillard, Ryder 78
Himes, Chester Bomar **141**
Hines, Earl ("Fatha") 302
Hispaniola 130, 269, 270
Hitler, Adolf 221
HIV (human immunodeficiency virus) 8
Hobson, Julius 72
Hodges, Johnny 62–63
Holiday, Billie **141–142,** *141,* 274
Homestead Act (1862) 107, 170, 262
Homestead Grays *171*
Hoover, Herbert 35
Hoover, J. Edgar 72
Hopwood v. State of Texas 10
Horse, John (Juan Caballo) **142**
Horton, James 255
Horus
    relief of *98*
    Temple of *141*
Hottentot Code 276
Houphouët-Boigny, Félix **142,** 148, 259
House, Eddie ("Son") 155, 315
housing 173, 196, 317
Houston, Charles Hamilton **142–143,** 211, 322
Houston Mutiny 77, **143–144,** 243
Howard, Oliver 115
Howard Law School 142, 143
Howard University 182, 183
Huddleston, Trevor 297
Hughes, Charles Evans 153
Hughes, James Mercer Langston 44, 45, 46, 135, 136, **144–145,** *144,* 145, 182, 188, 236

human immunodeficiency virus (HIV) 8
Humphrey, Hubert 195
Hunter, Alberta 44
Hunter, David 40
Hunter, Jesse 247
Hurst, E. H. 206
Hurston, Zora Neale 135, 144, **145,** *145,* 182, 322
Hutchinson, Jim 73
Hutton, Bobby 37
Hutu 50, 65, 248, 249
Hyksos 98

I

Ibadan 325, 326
Iberian Peninsula 264
Ibn Battuta **146,** 162, 284
Ibo 7, 216
Idris I 180
Ife **146–147,** *146,* 216, 217, 221, 325–326
"If We Must Die" (McKay) 188
Imhotep **147**
India 147, 148, 162
Indian campaigns, medal of honor recipients in 42
Indian Ocean 63, 259
    trade **147–148,** *147m,* 160, 162, 203, 207, 285, 328, 329
Indians. *See* Native Americans
Indonesia 147, 148, 189
Industrial Revolution 272–273
Industrial Workers of the World (IWW) 172
Ingram, Rosa Lee 288
Inkatha Freedom Party (IFP) 277
integration 98, 109, 200, 211. *See also* Civil Rights movement; segregation
    of armed forces 41, 150, 174, 237, 248
    freedom riders and 59, 68, 74, 109–110, **115–116,** 162, 163, 178
    of schools 51, 96–98, 128, 143, 181–182
International Association of the Congo 66
International Labor Defense (ILD) 255
Interpreters, The (Soyinka) 278
Invisible Man (Ellison) 102
Iraq 328
Iroquois Indians 270
Islam, Muslims 14, 16, 20, 21, 27, 57, 85, 99, 105, 117, 121, 124, 128, 137, 146, 147, 151, 159, 191, 193, 194, 198, 204, 207, 209, 252, 258, 259, 261, 264, 275, 281, 286, 289, 294, 295, 321, 328
    Nation of Islam. *See* Nation of Islam
Israel 295
Issa 86
Italian Somaliland 106
Italy 104, 264
    Ethiopia and 106, 130, 200
    Libya and 180
    Somaliland and 275
Ivory Coast, Republic of (Côte d'Ivoire) 13, 27, 116, 142, **148,** 191
I Will Marry When I Want (Ngũgĩ) 215

J

Jackson, Alexander 322
Jackson, Andrew 3, 7, 38, 40, 113
Jackson, James 209
Jackson, Jesse Louis 111, **149,** 202, 278

Jackson, Jimmie Lee 59, 309
Jackson, Mahalia 127, **149–150,** 274
Jackson, Michael **150,** 156, 276
Jackson, N. P. 320
Jackson, Rufus ("Sonnyman") *171*
Jackson Five 150
Jaga 166
Jamaica 196, 210, 244, 269, 273
    Baptist War in 6, **29,** 261
    Morant Bay Rebellion in 45
    slavery in 45, 261, 270
    Tacky's Rebellion in **284**
James, Daniel, Jr. ("Chappie") 150
Jamison, Judith 13
Jammeh, Yahya 121
Jawara, Dawda 121
Jay, John 3
jazz 30, 127, 135, 139, **150–151,** 164, 244. *See also specific musicians*
    avant-garde 151, 247
    bebop 57, 125, 151, 204, 225, 247
    cool 151
    electric 151
    fusion 151
    swing 30, 102, 150–151
Jazz at Home (Douglas) 87
Jazz Hounds 235
Jazz Messengers 43
Jefferson, Lemon ("Blind") 151, 164, 176, 311
Jefferson, Thomas 28, 139, 304, 313
Jeffries, Jim 154
Jemison, Mae Carol **152,** *152*
Jenkins Ferry 113
Jenne (Djenne) **151–152,** 191, 194, 275, 282
Jessup, Thomas 38
Jet 154
Jews, Judaism 59
    Black Jews **34–35**
Jim Crow **152**
Johannes IV 200
John VI 121
Johnson, American Jim 154
Johnson, Andrew 49, 115, 238–239, 305
Johnson, Charles 135
Johnson, Frank 143
Johnson, Henry 41, **152**
Johnson, Jack 154
Johnson, James Weldon 46, 86, 90, 136, 143, **153,** *153,* 188, 211, 243
Johnson, J. J. 246
Johnson, John Arthur (Jack) **153–154**
Johnson, John Harold 154
Johnson, John Rosamond 153
Johnson, June 133
Johnson, Lonnie 164
Johnson, Lyndon 9, 59, 60, 164, *196,* 197, 307, 309–310, *309,* 319
Johnson, Robert 139, **154–155,** 164, 315
Johnson, William Henry 135, 155
Johnson, Yormie 180
Johnson Publishing 154
Jolof 258, 321
Jones, Absalom 15, 40, **155**
Jones, Frederick McKinley **155–156**
Jones, James Earl 154
Jones, Jo 225
Jones, Lois Mailou 156
Jones, "Mother" Mary 172

Jones, Peter 36
Jones, Quincy Delight, Jr. 150, **156**, *156*
Joplin, Scott **156–157**
Jordan, George 40, **157**
Jordan, Michael Jeffrey **157**
Juba II **157**, 205
Judaism, Jews 59
    Black Jews **34–35**
Julian (monk) 57
Julian, Percy Lavon 49, **158**, *158*
Julian Laboratories 158
Juneteenth (Ellison) 103
jury nullification 76
jury system 75–76, 143, 240, 257
Just, Ernest Everett **158**
justice system. *See* criminal justice system, U.S.

K

Kabbah, Ahmad Tejan 261, 262
Kabila, Laurent 65
Kagame, Paul 249, 298
Kalahari Desert 51
Kalonga 190
Kanem-Bornu 56, **159**, 215, 216
Kanemi, Al- 159
Kanissa'ai **159**
Kano 117
Kansas, migration to 107, 170
Kansas City Call 319
Kanuri 159
Karenga, Maulana Ron 168
Karimojong 298
Karnak 236
Kasavubu, Joseph 65
Katakarmabi, Idris 159
Katanga 65, 185
Kati, Mahmud al- 121
Katsina 117
Kaunda, Kenneth 327
Kay, Ulysses **159–160**
Kayibanda, Grégoire 248
Kebbi 117
Keita, Modibo 191
Kennedy, John F. 59, 178–179, 190, 195, 197, 307
Kennedy, Robert F. 74, 116, 162, 179, 319
kente cloth 125, **160**
Kentucky Derby 209
Kenya, Republic of **160**, 187–188, 192, 197
Kenyatta, Jomo 160, **160–161**, 197, 224
Kerekou, Mathieu 34
Kerma **161**, 219, 281
Khama, Seretse 45
Khoi (Khoisan; Khoikhoi) 51, **161**, 168, 210, 232, 324
Kikuyu 160, **161**, *161*, 188, 197, 215
Kikuyu Central Association (KCA) 160
Kilwa (Kilwa Kisiwani) 128, 147, **161–162**, 190, 285, 329
King, Coretta Scott 162
King, Martin Luther, Jr. 2, 18, 59, 116, 119, 133, 149, 150, **162–164**, *162, 163*, 179, 195, 201, 203, 204, 248, 278, 307, 308–309, 326
    FBI and 72
    Letter from Birmingham Jail 163, **177–178**
King, Riley Ben ("B. B.") 44, 57, 139, **164**, *164*, 311
King, Rodney 74, 76

Kisama 61, **165**, 196
Kisangani 65
KKK. *See* Ku Klux Klan
Knights of Labor 171, 172
kola nuts **165**
Kolingba, André 55
Kololo 327
Konare, Alpha Oumar 192
Kongi's Harvest (Soyinka) 278
Kongo, Kingdom of 18, **165–166**
Korean War 41, 49, 60, 150
    medal of honor recipients in 42
Koroma, Johnny Paul 262
Kosovo 149
Kossoi 121
Krou 148
Ku Klux Klan (KKK) 36, 70, 74, 107, 113, 163, **166–167**, *166*, 170, 239, 240, 243, 263, 274, 280, 305, 306
    education and 93
Ku Klux Klan Act (1871) 167, 240
Kumasi 22, 23, 126
Kumbi-Saleh 124, 198
kung fu 189
!Kung San 45, 51, **167–168**, 210
Kush 25, 99, 108, 161, **168**, 201, 219, 236, 281, 284
Kwanzaa **168**, *168*
Kwazulu 331
kwosso **168**

L

labor rights. *See* employment and labor rights
Lafayette, marquis de (General Lafayette) 3, 21
Lafitte, Jean 40
Lagos 216
Lake Chad 56
Lake Nasser 219
Lake Nyos 52
Lake Okeechobee, Battle of 142
Lalibela 105, **174–175**
Lambarene 120
land acquisition 170
    40 acres and a mule **114**, 170, 177
landmines 207
Lane, Robert 127
Langston, Mary 144
Last Poets, The 237–238
Latimer, Lewis Howard **175–176**, *175*
Lawrence, Jacob Armstead, Jr. 176
League of Nations 104, 286, 290
Leakey, Louis 286
Learning Tree, The (Parks) 226
Leary, Lewis Sheridan 68
Le Cap François 84
Leclerc, Charles 84, 291
Ledbetter, Huddie ("Leadbelly") 43, 151, **176**
Lee, Bruce 189
Lee, George 59, 107
Lee, Herbert 59, 206
Lee, Robert E. 136
Lee, Shelton ("Spike") **176–177**
Leary, Lewis Sheridan 144
Leibowitz, Samuel 255
Lemba 35
Leo Africanus (Al-Hassan ibn Muhammad el-wazzan el Zayyati) 121, **177**, 289
Leopold II 32, 63, 66, 67, 68, 320

Leo X 177
Lesotho, Kingdom of **177**
Letter from Birmingham Jail (King) 163, **177–178**
Letters (Augustine) 24
Lewanika 327
Lewis, John Robert **178–179**, *178*, 195, 280
Lewis, Mary Edmonia **179**
Lewis and Clark expedition 325
Liberator 3, 113, 175, 188
Liberia, Republic of 16, 123, 129, **179–180**, 326
Liberty Party 5
Libya (The Socialist People's Libyan Arab Jamahiriya) 34, 56, **180**, 230
lien laws 170
"Lift Every Voice and Sing" (Johnson and Johnson) 153
Lift Every Voice and Sing (The Harp) (Savage) 253
light bulbs 175, 176
Lij Kassa Haylu 105–106
Lincoln, Abraham 88, 172, 238, *293*, 305
    Emancipation Proclamation of 5, 40, 88, **103–104**, 179, 241
Lincoln, C. Eric 36
Lindsay, Vachel 144
Lisbon 264
Lissouba, Pascal 66
Liston, Sonny 15
literacy requirements **180–181**
Little Rock Nine 30–31, 59, 97, **181–182**, *181*
Liuzzo, Viola 59
Livingstone, David 286, 289, 327
Livingstone Falls 68
Lobengula 212, 329, 330
Locke, Alain Leroy 86, *87*, 119, 136, **182–183**, 188, 254, 318, 322
Loguen, Jermain Wesley **183**
Lomax, John and Alan 176, 316
London, Jack 138
Longfellow, Henry Wadsworth 179
Lord's Resistance Army 298
Louima, Abner 74
Louis, Joe **183–184**, *184*, 245
Louisiana Purchase 325
Louisiana Slave Revolt **184**
Love, Nat (Deadwood Dick) **184–185**, *185*
Lovejoy, Elijah 3
Lowery, Joseph 278
Lozi 210
Lubi 148
Lucy, Autherine Juanita (Autherine Lucy Foster) 97, **185**
Lumumba, Patrice Emery 65, **185–186**
Lundu 190
Luo 160
Luthuli, Albert 13
Lyles, Aubrey 43
lynching 73, 76, 143, 153, 167, 171, **186**, *186*, 215, 217, 243, 287, 288
    Red Record report on **242–243**, 317

M

Maasai 117, 160, **187–188**, *187*, 285
McCartney, Paul 176
McClain, Franklin 263
McCoy, Elijah **188**
McDowell, Calvin 242

McEnery, Thomas 172
McGraw, John 214
McGuire, James 90
Machel, Grace 193
Machel, Samora Moises 207
Macias Nguema, Francisco 104
McKay, Festus Claudius (Claude) 45, 136,
    188–189, 236, 243–244
McNair, Denise 263
McNeil, Joseph 263
Madagascar, Republic of **189**
Magee House *299*
Mainassara, Ibrahim Bare 215
Maine 40
Makuria 57
Malagasy 189
Malawi, Republic of 57, **189–190**, 327, 329, 330
Malay Peninsula 199
Malaysia 189
Malcolm X (Malcom Little; El-Hajj Malik El-
    Shabazz) 110, 132, 138, **190–191**, *190*, 201,
    208, 211, 224
Mali, Empire of (Melle) 16, 27, 128, 146, **191**,
    194, 207, 258, 275, 282, 289, 293
Mali, Republic of 86, *86*, 116, 121, 124, 151,
    191–192, *192*, 205
Mali Federation 259
Malindi **192**, 329
Mamelukes 99
Mamprussi 207
Mancham, James 259
Manchild in the Promised Land (Brown) 46–47
Mandela, Nelson Rolihlahla 13, 19, 83, **192–193**,
    193, 277, 278, 324
Man Died, The (Soyinka) 278
Mandinka (Mandingo; Mandes) 27, 85, 117, 121,
    124, 148, **193–194**
Manhattan Music Shop and Sky Rocket Grill *171*
Manley, Michael 195
Mann, Woodrow 182
Mansa Kankan Musa 191, **194**, 289
Mansfield, Walter 15
Manuel 166
"Maple Leaf Rag" (Joplin) 157
Mapp v. Ohio 75
Ma Rainey's Black Bottom (Wilson) 320
Maravi 190
March on Washington 2, 150, 164, 179,
    194–195, *194*, 237, 248, 263, 319
Margold, Nathan Ross 95, 142–143
Margold Strategy 95
Mariam, Mengisu Haile 106
Marley, Robert (Nesta Bob Marley) 49, **195**, 238,
    244
Maroons (Outlayers) 61, 69, 80–81, **195–196**,
    210, 270, 284, 301
Marrakesh 16
Marrow of Tradition, The (Chesnutt) 57
Marshall, Thurgood 60, 77, 78, 96, 142,
    196–197, *196*, 211, 258
Martel, Charles 204
martial arts 53, 189
Mascarene islands 198, 207, 265
mask, Yaure *12*
Mason, John 301
Massounde, Tadjiddine Ben Said 63
Matabele (Ndebele) 177, **212**, 329, 330
Matamba 220

Matara III 248
Matope 204
Matzeliger, Jan Ernst **197**
Mau Mau 160–161, **197**, 215, 311
Mauretania 157, **197**, 205, 286
Mauritania, Islamic Republic of 16, 27, 34, 116,
    124, **198**, 205, 317
Mauritius (Saint Maurice) **251**
Mauritius, Republic of **198**, 207, 259, 265, 329
Mayotte 63
M'Ba, Leon 120
Mbeki, Thabo 193, 278
Medal of Honor. *See* Congressional Medal of
    Honor
Melanesia, Melanesians **198–200**, *199m*
Memphis sound 276
Menabe 189
Menelik II 106, **200**
Menes 98
"Men of Color to Arms" (Douglass) 103
mento 244
Mercury Records 156
Meredith, James 97, 107, **200–201**, *200*
Merinids 205
Merneptah 236
Meroe 25, 168, **201**
Messenger 236–237
Mexico 273
Mfume, Kweisi 202
Micanopy 7
Middle Congo 120
Middle Passage **201**
migration
    Exodus of 1879 107, 170, 263
    northern (Great) 135, 212, **217**, *218m*
    slavery and 272, 273
Milam, J. W. 288
military, blacks in. *See* black soldiers
Miller, Doris ("Dorie") 41, **201**
Miller, Flournoy 43
Million Man March 111, 177, **201–202**
Mina 290
Mingus, Charles ("Charlie") 151, **202**
minstrel shows 152
Mississippi, University of 97, 107, 200, *200*
Mississippi Freedom Democratic Party (MFDP)
    26, 69, 133, 179, **202–203**, 206, 280, 308
Mississippi Freedom Summer Project 56, 68, 74,
    110, **203**, 206, 227, 280, 307
Missouri Compromise 303
Mitchell, Arthur 91, **203**
Mitchell, Mitch 139
Mobutu Sese Seko (Joseph Mobutu) 65
Mogadishu 147, 275
Mohammed VI 206
Moheli 63
Mombasa **203**, 329
Momoh, Joseph Saidu 261
Monk, Thelonius Sphere 63, 151, 156, **203–204**,
    203, 225, 246
Monomotapa 56, **204**, 207
Monroe, James 231
Monroe v. Pape 75
Montes, Pedro 16
Montgomery, Alabama
    freedom riders 59, 68, 74, **115–116**, 162,
    163, 178, 280
    route from Selma to *308m*

Montgomery, Benjamin 84
Montgomery, Olen 255, 256
Montgomery Bus Boycott 2, 26, 59, 162, 178,
    204, 226, 248
Montgomery Improvement Association (MIA) 2,
    162, 204
Moors 16, 21, 34, **204–205**, 264, 286
    Almohads 16, 180, 204, 205
    Almoravids **16**, 34, 124, 180, 198, 204, 258
moraingy fighting 189
Morant Bay Rebellion 45
Morel, Edmund Dene 67–68
Morgan, Garrett A. **205**
Morgan v. Virginia 196
Morocco, Kingdom of 16, 121, 157, 191, 197,
    205–206, 276, 286, 317
Morris, Robert 95
Morrison, Toni **206**, 321
Moses 236
Moses, Robert Parris 69, 202, **206–207**, 280,
    308
Moshesh 177
Moss, Thomas 242
Mossi (Moro) 49, **207**, 276
Mothershed, Thelma 182
Motown Records 126, 150, 276
Mott, Lucretia 301
Movement for the Restoration of the Ten
    Commandments of God 298
Mozambique, Republic of 190, **207–208**, 214,
    266, 277
Msiri 66
Mswati III 283
Mubarak, Hosni 99
mud cloth **208**
Mugabe, Robert 8, 330
Muhammad, Elijah 110, 190, **208**, *208*, 211
Muhammad V 206
Muhammad bin Ali Sanusi 180
Muhammad Speaks 191
Muhammad Touré (Muhammad ibn Abu-Bakr)
    137, 207, **208–209**, 276, 282
Mule Bone (Hurston and Hughes) 144, 145
Muluzi, Bakili 190
Murphy, Isaac Burns **209**
Murray, Anna 87
Murray v. Pearson 95
Musa-ibn-Nusair 205, 286
Museveni, Yoweri 298
music. *See also specific musicians*
    blues **43–45**, *44*, 127, 150, 235, 244
    calypso **52**, 244, 276
    gospel **127**, 133, 235, 276
    jazz. *See* jazz
    race **235**
    ragtime 150, 157
    rap **237–238**
    reggae 52, **244**
    rhythm and blues 47, 244, *244*, 276, 316
    soul 276
    spirituals 43, 111, 127, **278–279**, 300–301
Muslim Brotherhood 99
Muslim Mosque 191
Muslims. *See* Islam, Muslims
Mutota 204
Mwene Mutapa kingdom 128
Mwinyi, Ali Hassan 286
Myers, Issac 171–172, **209**

Mystery 84
Mzilikazi Khumalo 212

N

NAACP. *See* National Association for the
  Advancement of Colored People
Nafata 275
Nairobi 188
Nalle, Charles 294
Namibia, Republic of 8, **210**
Nanas-Benz 290
Nanny ("Granny Nanny") **210**
Nanny Town 210
Napoleon I 39, 84, 131, 134, 140, 291
Narváez, Pánfilo de 105
Nascimento, Edson Arantes do (Pele) **211**
Nash, Diane 281
Nasser, Gamal Abdel 99
National Association for the Advancement of
  Colored People (NAACP) 26, 30, 31, 57, 59,
  77, 90, 107, 135–136, 142, 143, 153, 181, 185,
  186, 195, 202, **211–212**, 215, 226, 227, 287,
  292, 306, 317, 319, *319*
    Crisis magazine 90, 136, 144, 153, 212, 319
    Marshall and **196–197**
    school segregation and 95–96
    Scottsboro Boys and 255
National Association of Colored Women
  (NACW) 35, 287
National Ballet Company of Brazil 203
National Equal Rights League 292
National Guard 181, *181,* 182
National Labor Union (NLU) 171, 209
National League for the Protection of Colored
  Women 212
National Rainbow Coalition 149
National Urban League 35, 135, 136, 195, **212**
Nation of Islam (NOI; The Lost-Found Nation of
  Islam) 15, 36, 110, 111, 202, **211**
    Malcolm X and 190–191, 208, 211
Native Americans 12
    Apache 157
    Arawak 130–131, 132
    Crow 32
    Iroquois 270
    Plains 48
    Seminole. *See* Seminole Indians
    Native Son (Wright) 323, *323*
Navarro, Fats 202, 246
Ndadaye, Melchior 50
Ndebele (Matabele) 177, **212**, 329, 330
Ndongo kingdom 18, 219
Ndwandwe 259, 260
Neal v. Delaware 76
Neco (Neche) **212**, 227
Nectanebo II 99
Ned **212–213**
Negritos (Aeta) 199, **213**, 258
Negritude 85, **213**
Negro baseball leagues 1, **213–214**, *213,* 224,
  246
Negro Digest 154
Negro Family in the United States, The (Frazier)
  115
Negro Fellowship League 317
"Negro Speaks of Rivers, The" (Hughes) 144
Negro World 122
Netherlands. *See* Dutch

Newby, Dangerfield 68
New Caledonia 198, 200
New Deal 2, 35
New England Anti-Slavery Society 3
New Guinea 198, 199, 200
Newman, William 143
New Negro, The (Locke) 86, *87,* 182, 254
New Negro Movement 182
New Orleans Louisianian 28
Newton, Huey P. 36, 37, **214**
New York Age 317
New York City
    draft riots in **89**, 169
    Harlem. *See* Harlem
New York City Ballet 203
New York Slave Rebellion of 1712 **214**, 271
Ngoni 56, 190, **214–215**, 327
Ngũgĩ, Wa Thiong'o (James Ngũgĩ) **215**
Niagara Movement 90, 211, **215**, 292
Niama, Mulume 67
Nichols, Joseph V. 176
Niger, Republic of 16, 137, **215**
Nigeria, Federal Republic of 7, 33, 84, 117, 137,
  146, **215–216**, 217, 275, 278, 325
Niger River 293
Nile River 98, 140, 212, **216**, *216*
Nixon, Edgar Daniel 204, 227
Nixon, Richard 102, 316
Niza, Narcos de 105
Nkrumah, Kwame 53, 124–125, 126, 185,
  216–217, 224
Nobatia 57
Nobel Peace Prize 49
Nobody Knows My Name (Baldwin) 27
Nok 216, **217**
No Place To Be Somebody (Gordone) 126
Norris, Clarence 255, 256
Norris v. Alabama 75, 256
northern migration (Great Migration) 135, 212,
  217, 218*m*
North Pole 140
North Star 3, 84, 87, 183
Norton, Eleanor Holmes 281
Notes of a Native Son (Baldwin) 27
Ntaryamira, Cyprien 50, 249
Ntibantunganya, Sylvestre 50
Nuba (Nubians) 56, **217–219**, 282
    Christian **57–58**, 219, 281
Nubia 99, 168, **219**, 236, 281
Nuer **219**, 282
Nujoma, Sam 210
Numeiri, Jaafar al- 281
Numero, Joseph 155
Numidia 14, **197**
Nyasaland 57, 190, 327, 330
Nyerere, Julius Kambarage **219**, 224, 286
Nzinga Mbande 18, **219–220**

O

Obasanjo, Olusegun 216
Obiang Nguema Mbasogo, Theodoro 104
Obote, Milton 298
Oduduwa 146–147, 221, 325–326
Oglethorpe, James 271
Okeh Records 235
oil 281–282
Olduvai Gorge 286
Oliver, Joe ("King") 21, 150, 159

Olorun 146
Olympic Games 37, 221, 247
Olympio, Sylvanus 290
Oman 160, 329
Omani 203, 286
opera 17, 230
Operation Breadbasket 149, 278
Operation PUSH (People United to Save
  Humanity) 149
Opportunity 135, 136
Organisation de l'Armée Secrète (OAS) 14
Organization of African Unity 130
Oromo 105
Oromo Liberation Front (OLF) 106
Ory, Kid 202
Osai Tutu 22
Osceola 7, 38, 142
Ottoman Empire 99, 104, 105, 180, 295
Ouadai 56
Ouagadougou 207
Our Nig (Wilson) 123
Ovambo 210
Owen, Chandler 236, 237
Owens, James Cleveland (Jesse) **221**, *221*
Oyo 82, 146, 216, **221–222**, 325, 326

P

Pace, Harry 134
Pagalu 104
Paige, Leroy Robert ("Satchel") 78, 214,
  223–224, *223*
Pailleterie, Alexandre Davy de la 91
Paine, Thomas 3
Palmares, Republic of (Quilombo dos Palmares)
  195, **224**
Palmer, Henry 319
Pan-Africanism 16, 53, 119, 136, **224–225**
Pan Africanist Congress (PAC) 13
Panama 230
Papuans 199
Parker, Charles Christopher, Jr. ("Charlie";
  "Yardbird"; "Bird") 47, 83, 125, 151, 156, 202,
  204, **225**, 246, 302
Parker, Mack 186
Parks, Gordon **225–226**, *226*
Parks, Raymond 226
Parks, Rosa Louise McCauley 59, 162, 178, 201,
  204, **226–227**, *226*
pass laws 13, 36, 277
Patasse, Félix-Ange 55
"Pathology of Race Prejudice, The" (Frazier)
  114–115
Patterson, Haywood 255, *255,* 256
Patterson, John 116
Pattillo, Melba 182
Payne's Landing, Treaty of 7
Pearl Harbor 201
Peary, Robert E. 140
Peerboom Plantation 61
Pele (Edson Arantes do Nascimento) **211**
Pemba 329
Penn, Lemuel 186
Pennsylvania Railroad 217
peonage system 20, 71, 170–171
Perry, Oliver Hazard 40
Persian Empire 99
Persian Gulf 148, 230
Persian Gulf War 41, 99, 230

Pétion, Alexandre 131–132
Pettiford, Oscar 156
Pettigrew, Ben 171
Peul tribe 117
Pezzicar, F. 103
Philadelphia, Mississippi, Murders 110, 227, 308
Philippines 49, 199, 213
Phoenicians 54, 180, 227–228, 294, 328
Piankhi 284
Pickett, Bill 228
Pickett, Wilson 127
Pierre-Noel, Louis Vergniaud 156
Pinchback, Pinckney Benton Stewart 228, 290
Pitcairn, John 252
Plains Indians 48
plantations 268
Planter 40, 274
Plessy, Homer 95, 228
Plessy v. Ferguson 95, 96, 228–229
Poems on Miscellaneous Subjects (Harper) 136
poison 272
Poison Spring 113, 229
police 73
    brutality by 74–75
    failure to protect blacks 73–74
    harassment by 75
Polisario Front 317
political parties
    abolitionist 5
    Democratic Party 62, 202, 241, 317
    Mississippi Freedom Democratic Party 26,
        69, 133, 179, 202–203, 206, 280, 308
    Republican Party 5, 62, 172, 209, 228, 236,
        240, 273, 301, 314, 317
poll tax 229, 308
Porter, Kenneth 38
Portugal, Portuguese 53, 104, 148, 160, 162,
    190, 204, 224, 285–286, 321, 329
    Angola and 18
    Benin and 33, 103
    Gambia and 121
    Gold Coast and 126
    Guinea and 129
    Kongo Kingdom and 165
    Madagascar and 189
    Mombasa and 203
    Mozambique and 207
    Nzinga and 219–220
    São Tomé and 252–253
    Senegal and 258
    Sierra Leone and 261
    slavery and 18, 33, 103, 129, 165–166, 207,
        252, 261, 264
    Zanzibar and 328–329
Posey, Cum 171
Pottawatomie Creek 136
Powell, Adam Clayton, Jr. 229
Powell, Bud 246
Powell, Colin Luther 41, 49, 229–230, 230
Powell, Ozie 255, 256
Powell v. Alabama 75, 255
Poyas, Peter 303
Presley, Elvis 150, 244
Presley, Lisa Marie 150
Prester John 165
Préval, René 132
Price, Cecil 227
Price, Mary Violet Leontyne 230

Price, Victoria 75, 254–255
Prince, Abijah 231
Prince, Lucy Terry 230–231
prisons, prisoners 72–73, 78–79, 170
    chain gangs 20, 72–73, 72, 170, 248
    convict-lease programs 20, 170, 240
Pritchard, Gullah Jack 303
professionals and entrepreneurs, black 171, 171
profiling 75
Progressive Farmers and Household Union of
    America 101
property rights of African Americans in the
    United States 169, 170, 315
    40 acres and a mule 114, 170, 177
    housing 173, 196, 317
Proposition 209 10
Prosser, Gabriel 184, 231, 270
Provident Hospital 319
Pryor, Richard Franklin Lennox Thomas III
    231–232
Ptolemy 99, 216
Puerto Rico 254
Pulitzer Prize 46
Pullman porters 173, 237
Punic Wars 54, 134, 197, 294
Punt 232
Puryear, Martin 232
Pushkin, Alexander Sergeyevitch 232
Pygmies 29, 50, 120, 213, 232–233, 233, 248,
    249
pyramids 98, 147, 233, 233

Q
Qaddafi, Muammar al- 180
Qokli Hill 260
Quarles, Benjamin 234
Quelimane 207
Quest Broadcasting 156
Quest Records 156

R
Rabearivelo, J. J. 188
race records 44, 235
racism 273. See also Civil Rights movement;
    segregation
Rackley, Alex 37
Radama I 189
Radama II 189
ragtime 150, 157
Rainey, Gertrude Pridgett ("Ma") 44, 235, 236,
    274
Rainey, Lawrence 227
Raisin in the Sun, A (Hansberry) 135
Ramses II (Ramses the Great; Ramesses) 236,
    236
Randolph, Asa Philip 26, 136, 173, 174, 194,
    236–237, 237, 248
Rangel, Charles 229
rap 237–238
Rastafarianism 130, 195, 238, 244
Ratsimilaho 189
Ratsiraka, Didier 189
Rawlings, Jerry John 125
Ray, Gloria 182
Ray, James Earl 164
Reagan, Ronald 288
Reconstruction 20, 62, 71, 72, 93, 94, 107, 167,
    170, 217, 238–241, 238

end of 306
    lynchings and 243
    presidential 238–239, 305
    radical 239–240, 305–306
Reconstruction Act (1867) 36, 71, 93, 115, 239,
    242, 305–306
Reconstruction Amendments 71, 241–242
    Thirteenth 5, 71, 104, 122, 238
    Fourteenth 71, 76, 95, 169–170, 228, 229,
        239, 240, 241–242
    Fifteenth 71, 88, 136, 240, 241, 242, 304,
        306, 318
Redding, Noel 139
Red Record 242–243, 317
Red Sox 214
Red Summer of 1919 144, 237, 243–244
Reeb, James 59, 309
Regents of the University of California v. Bakke 10
reggae 52, 244
Reinhardt, Django 164
Reiss, Winold 86
religion 298
    animism 18–19, 124, 137, 281, 321
    Christianity. See Christianity
    Islam. See Islam, Muslims
    Rastafarianism 130, 195, 238, 244
    Voodoo 34, 303–304, 304
Renaissance Big Five 244
René, France-Albert 259
Reorganization Act (1866) 40, 48
Republican Party 5, 62, 172, 209, 228, 236, 240,
    273, 301, 314, 317
restrictive covenants 173, 196
Réunion 207, 265, 329
Revels, Hiram Rhoades 48, 244, 306
Revolutionary Petunias and Other Poems (Walker)
    312
Revolutionary War 21, 39–40, 113, 252, 270
Rhodes, Cecil 45, 190, 212, 327, 329–330
Rhodesia 246, 277, 327, 329. See also Zimbabwe
rhythm and blues 47, 244, 244, 276, 316
Richie, Lionel 150
Richmond, David 263
Rickey, Branch 246
Rillieux, Norbert 244–245
Rio Muni 104
riots 169, 244
    draft 89, 169
    race 70, 73, 243, 247
Roach, Max 47, 202
Roatan 122
Roberson, Willie 255, 256
Roberts, Needham 152
Roberts, Sarah 95
Roberts, Terrance 182
Robertson, Carole 263
Robeson, Paul 125, 135, 245, 245
Robinson, Bill ("Bojangles") 135
Robinson, Jack Roosevelt ("Jackie") 1, 184, 214,
    245–246, 246
Robinson, Randall 246
Robinson, Smokey 124, 126, 276
Rochambeau, Donatien 84–85
Rodin, Auguste 118
Rogers, Will 228
Rollins, Theodore Walter ("Sonny") 47,
    246–247
"Rollin' Stone" (Waters) 316

Rome, Roman Empire 14, 24, 54, 85, 99, 134, 197, 205, 294
Roosevelt, Eleanor 17, 35, 154
Roosevelt, Franklin D. 2, 35, 49, *130*, 174, 206, 237
Roosevelt, Theodore ("Teddy") 47, 48, 77, 153, 314
Roots (Haley) 121, 132, **247**
Rosewood **247**
Ross, Diana 142
Roxborough, John 183
Rozwi 204
Rudolph, Wilma Goldean **247**
Ruggles, David 293
Ruiz, José 16
Russwurm, John Brown **247–248**
Rustin, Bayard 26, 194, 237, **248**, 278
Ruth, Babe 1
Rwanda (Rwandese Republic) 50, *50*, 65, **248–249**, *249*, 298
Ryswick, Treaty of 131

S

Sacagawea 325
Sadat, Anwar El- 99
Sadiq el Mahdi 281
Sahara 14, 34, 56, **250**, 286, 293
    trans-Saharan trade routes 251*m*
Sahel 50, **250**, 293
Sahili, as- 194
Said, Sayyid 329
Saint-Domingue 85, 131
    Boukman Revolt in **45–46**, 131, 290
Saint-Georges, Joseph Boulogne, chevalier de **250–251**
Saint Maurice (Mauritius) **251**
St. Vincent 122
Saladin 99
Salem, Peter 40, **252**
Samori Touré 128, 148, 191, 194, **252**
Sanankoro **252**
Sanha, Malan Bacai 129
Sankara, Thomas 49–50
Sankoh, Foday 262
Sankor University 289
Santo Domingo 131, **290–291**
Sao 56, **252**
São Tomé e Príncipe **252–253**
Sara 56, **253**
Saro-Wiwa, Ken 216
Sartre, Jean-Paul 109
Sassou-Nguesso, Denis 66
Savage, Augusta Christine Fells 135, **253**
Savimbi, Jonas 18
scarification 219, **253**, *253*
Schmeling, Max 183–184
Schomburg, Arthur Alfonso 135, **254**
School Daze 177
schools. *See* education and schools
Schweitzer, Albert 120
Schwerner, Michael 56, 59, 76, 110, 186, 227, 308
Scipio Africanus 134
SCLC. *See* Southern Christian Leadership Conference
Scott, Dred 241, **254**, *254*
Scottsboro Boy (Patterson and Conrad) 255
Scottsboro Boys 75, 78, 226, **254–256**, *255*

Sea Islands 305
Seale, Bobby 36, 37, 214
searches 75
Sea Wolf, The (London) 138
Second Seminole War 32
Sedgwick, Theodore 116
Seeger, Pete 176
Segovia, Andres 202
segregation 95, 98, 172, 196, 240, 241, **256–258**, *256, 257*, 314. *See also* Civil Rights movement; integration
    apartheid. *See* apartheid
    on buses. *See* buses
    Clark's study on effects of 60, 96
    de facto 257
    de jure 257
    Jim Crow **152**
    Mingus and 202
    in schools 30, 60, 92, 95–98, 128, 143, 241
    sit-in movement and 59, 68, 109, 149, **263**, *263*
    in workplaces 174
Sekou Touré 53, 128–129, 191, 252
Selma, Alabama 43, 164, 179, **258**, *307, 308–309*
    route to Montgomery from 308*m*
Seminole Indians 7, 113, 142, 195, 240
    black **38**
Seminole Wars 7, 32, 38, 40, 113
Senegal, Republic of 85, 116, 121, 127, 191, 198, 205, 258, **258**, 321
Senegambia 121
Senghor, Léopold Sédar 85, 188, 213, 258, **258–259**
Senoufo 148
Senzangakona 259
"separate but equal" ruling 95, 228–229
Serko 121
Seychelles, Republic of **259**
Shabazz, Betty 201
Shaft 226
Shaka (Nodumehlezi; Sigidi) 39, 212, 214, **259–260**, 331
Shange, Ntozake **260**
sharecroppers 26, 170, **260–261**, *260*
    Elaine, Arkansas, incident **101**, 172–173, 243
Sharecroppers Union 261
Sharpe, Samuel 29, **261**
Sharpeville Massacre 13, 177, 193, 277
Shaw, Artie 142
Shaw, Robert Gould 111, 179
Shelley v. Kraemer 173, 196
Shepard, William 67
Sheppard, Mosby 231
Sherman, William T. 114
She's Gotta Have It 177
Shirazis 160
Shona 127–128, 329, 330
Shuffle Along 26, 43
Shuttlesworth, Fred 278
sickle-cell anemia 261
Sierra Leone, Republic of 40, 129, 180, **261–262**
Silent March 153
Silver, Horace 43
Simpson, Bryan 164
Simpson, Nicole Brown 262
Simpson, Orenthal James ("O. J.") 74, **262**
Singleton, Benjamin ("Pap") 107, 170, **262–263**

Singleton, Zutty 311
Sirius 86
Sissle, Noble 26, 43
Sisulu, Walter 193
sit-in movement 59, 68, 109, 149, **263**, *263*, 280
Sixteenth Street Baptist Church bombing 177, **263**
Sixth Amendment 75–76
ska 244
slave caravans 264, 265
Slave Coast 33, 82, **263–264**
slave codes 70, 269
slave revolts 127, 137, 252, 269–271, 284
    Boukman Revolt **45–46**, 131, 290
    Coffy's Rebellion **61**
    Gabriel Prosser conspiracy 184, **231**, 270
    Harpers Ferry Raid 18, 68, 88, 128, **136–137**, *137*, 144, 270, 294
    Louisiana Slave Revolt **184**
    Maroons and 195–196
    Nat Turner, uprising led by 92, 270, **295–296**
    New York Slave Rebellion of 1712 **214**, 271
    Stono, South Carolina, Rebellion 270, 271, **280**
    Tacky's Rebellion **284**
    Vesey uprising 184, 270, **302–303**
    Zanj Rebellion **328**
slavery, slave trade 12, 21, 22, 52, 55, 56, 62, 63, 65, 67, 82, 84, 89, 105, 106, 113, 121, 127, 128, 132, 137, 148, 159, 169, 189, 192, 200, 216, 219, 222, 242, 252, 254, 258, 259, **264–274**, *265, 268, 272*, 276, 282, 285–286, 290, 295, 329
    American Colonization Society and **16**
    asiento and **23–24**
    barracoons and 16, **30**, 58, 61, 165, 196, 267
    Black Codes and 36, 169, 239, 241
    in Brazil 224
    British and 5–6, 20, 23–24, 29, 40, 81, 104, 121, 198, 259, 261, 265, 266–267, 276, 329
    coffles and **60–61**, *61*
    criminal justice and 70–71
    Davis Bend and 84
    death rates and numbers of victims 266–267
    East Coast African trade 264–265
    education and 92–93
    Emancipation Proclamation and 5, 40, 88, **103–104**, 241
    end of 5–6, 104, 241
    free and slave areas in U.S. in 1860 271*m*
    Freeman and 116
    French and 23, 46, 60, 127, 269, 290
    in Haiti 84, 131, 270
    impact of 272–273
    in Jamaica 45, 261, 270
    in Mauritania 198
    merchant companies and 267
    Middle Passage and **201**
    migration forced by 272, 273
    Portuguese and 18, 33, 103, 129, 165–166, 207, 252, 261, 264
    resistance to 271–272. *See also* slave revolts
    slave life 267–268
    soldiers and 39–40, 49

spirituals and 43, 111, 127, **278–279**,
    300–301
  in Sudan 85
  Thirteenth Amendment and 5, 71, 104, 122,
    238, 241
  Tippu Tip and 66, 264, **289–290**, *289*
  transatlantic trade 265
  triangular trade **291**, *292m*
  Underground Railroad and. *See*
    Underground Railroad. *See also*
    abolitionist movement
slaves, former and runaway 24, 38, 113, 169, 293
  apprenticeship system and 6, **20**
  Bush Negroes **51**
  Davis Bend and 84
  Exodusters **107**, 170, 262
  40 acres and a mule for **114**, 170, 177
  Freedman's Savings and Trust Company 48,
    89, **115**
  Freedmen's Bureau 20, 93, 94, 111, 115,
    115, 122, 238, 239
  Fugitive Slave Law and **117**, *117*, 183
  Kisama settlement of 61, **165**
  Maroons 61, 69, 80–81, **195–196**, 210, 270,
    284, 301
  Palmares settlement of 195, **224**
  sharecropping and 170
  Underground Railroad and. *See*
    Underground Railroad
slave ships 267, 330
  Amistad **16–17**, 58, 267
  Creole **70**, 267
  Zong **330**
Sledge, Percy 276
Smalls, Robert 40, **274**
Smith, Bessie 44, 235, **274**, *274*
Smith, Ian 330
Smith, Lamar 59
Smith, Mamie 44, 137, 235
Smith v. Allwright 196, 318
SNCC. *See* Student Non-Violent Coordinating
    Committee
Snelgrave, William 267
Snow, Kneeland 143
Sobhuza II 283
soca 52, 276
Sofala 162, 207
Sokoto Caliphate 117, 159, 216, **275**
soldiers, black. *See* black soldiers
Soldier's Play, A (Fuller) 117–118
Soldier Vote Act (1942) 229
Solomon, King 227
Solomonid dynasty 105
Solomon Islands 198–199, 200
Somali Democratic Republic (Somalia) 232, **275**
Songhai, Empire of 92, 121, 151, 191, 207, 215,
    275–276, 282, 284, 293
Song of Solomon (Morrison) 206
Soninke 198
Sonning Music Award 83
Sonthonax, Léger Félicité 46, 84, 131
Soudan 116, 152, 191
soul **276**
Soul On Ice (Cleaver) 37
Souls of Black Folk, The (DuBois) 90
South Africa, Republic of 177, 210, 248,
    276–278, *277*
  African National Congress in **12–13**

apartheid in. *See* apartheid
Biko and **36**, 277
HIV in 8
South Carolina 269–270, 305
  Stono Rebellion in 270, 271, **280**
Southern Christian Leadership Conference
    (SCLC) 2, 18, 26, 149, 162, 163, 178, 248,
    278, 307, 326
  Operation Breadbasket 149, 278
Southern Homestead Act (1866) 170
Southern Regional Council (SRC) 179
Southern Tenant Farmers' Union (STFU) 173
Soviet Union 185, 275
  U.S. cold war with 18, 60, 65, 173
Soweto 13, 277
Soyinka, Wole (Akinwande Oluwold Soyinka)
    123, 215, **278**
Spain, Spanish 16, 23, 34, 104, 131, 184, 205,
    254, 264, 286, 290–291, 317
  Moors and 204–205
Spanish-American War 40–41, 49, 82
  medal of honor recipients in 42
Spear of the Nation 13
Sphinx **278**, *279*
Spielberg, Steven 156
Spinks, Leon 15
Spiral 31
spirituals 43, 111, 127, **278–279**, 300–301
Spivey, Victoria 44
"Spunk" (Hurston) 145
Sri Lanka 148
Stamps, J. E. 322
Stance, Emanuel 49
Staneyville 65
Stanley, Henry 63, 216, 289, 298
Stanley Falls 68
Stanton, Edward 239
Stark, John 157
State Press 30, 31
Stax Records 276
Steele v. Louisville & Nashville R.R. 173
stelae 25
Stevens, Siaka 261
Stevens, Thaddeus 301
Stewart, Eliza 228
Stewart, Henry 242
Still, William 136, **279–280**, 294
Stinney, George 78
Stokes, Moses 235
Stono, South Carolina, Rebellion 270, 271, **280**
Stowe, Harriet Beecher 3, 139, 299, 301
Strauder v. West Virginia 76
Strayhorn, Billy 102
strikebreakers 172
Struggle: From the History of the American People
    (Lawrence) 176
Stuart, Oscar 212–213
Student Non-Violent Coordinating Committee
    (SNCC) 26, 37, 53, 59, 107, 116, 133, 164,
    178, 179, 195, 263, **280–281**, 307
  Moses, Robert Parris and 206
Stuyvesant, Peter 135
Sudan, Republic of the 56, 85, 161, 168, 217,
    219, **281–282**, 298, 328
Sudd 216, 219, **282**
Suez Canal 106, 198
sugar 244–245, 265
Sumanguru 117, 191

Summer of Sam 177
Sumner, Charles 76, 95
Sundiata Keita 117, 191, **282**
Sunni Ali the Great (Ali Ber) 151, 208, 275–276,
    282, 289
Supreme Court, U.S. 9, 10, 51, 74, 75, 76, 78, 79,
    97, 115, 117, 127, 171, 173, 182, 196, 197,
    204, 227, 229, 240, 241, 245, 318
  Brown v. Board of Education of Topeka, Kansas
    48, 59, 60, 79, 95–96, 98, 145, 196,
    211–212, 241
  Dred Scott decision 241, **254**
  Griffin v. Prince Edward County, Virginia 128
  Plessy v. Ferguson 95, 96, **228–229**
  Scottsboro Boys case 255–256
Supremes 126
Suriname 51
Swahili 20, 29, 147, **282**
Swaziland, Kingdom of 8, 177, **282–283**
Sweatt v. Painter 10
swing 30, 102, 150–151
syphilis experiment, Tuskegee 296
Syria 99

T

Tacky 69
Tacky's Rebellion **284**
Taft, William Howard 48, 314
Taghaza **284**
Taharqa **284–285**
Talented Tenth 90, 136, **285**
Talking Skull (Fuller) 118
Tambo, Oliver 193
Tamerlane 264
Tan 154
Tanganyika 219, 285, 329
Tanner, Henry Ossawa **285**
Tanner, John 172
Tanzania, United Republic of 187–188, 219,
    285–286, 298, 328, 329
Tariq ibn Ziyad 204, 205, **286**
Tassili-n-Ajjer rock paintings 14, 250, **286**
Tatum, Art, Jr. **286–287**
Taylor, Charles 180, 262
Taylor, Fannie 247
Tecora 58
Temple, Lewis **287**
Temptations 126, 276
Tenkodogo 207
tennis 23
Terrell, Mary Eliza Church **287–288**
Terrell, Tammi 124
Terrell, Robert 287
Tewodros II 105–106
Thaba Bosiu 177
Theban Legion 251
Their Eyes Were Watching God (Hurston) 145
Thembu 192
Things Fall Apart (Achebe) 7
Thirteenth Amendment 5, 71, 104, 122, 238
Thomas, Clarence 258, **288**
Thomas, Jefferson 182
Thompson, William 41
Thoreau, Henry David 59, 178, 301
Thurman, Wallace 145
Tigre 106
Till, Emmett 76, 107, 154, 178, 186, 206,
    288–289

Timbuktu (Timbuctoo) 92, 151, 191, 194, 207, 275, 282, **289**, 293
Tindley, Charles 127
Tippu Tip (Hamidi bin Muhammed; Tippu Tib) 66, 264, **289–290**, *289*
Tlokwa 177
Togo, Republic of **290**
Tolbert, William 180
Toledo 205
Toomer, Nathan Eugene ("Jean") 136, **290**
Toscanini, Arturo 17
Touré, Sékou 53
Tours, Battle of 204
Toussaint Louverture, François Dominique (Toussaint Breda; L'ouverture) 30, 85, 131, 176, **290–291**, *291*, 326
traffic light, inventor of 205
TransAfrica 246
Transitions 123
Traoré, Moussa 191, 192
Travis, Brenda 281
Travis, Joseph 295
Treaty of Fort Dade 7, 142
Treaty of Fort Gibson 7
Treaty of Payne's Landing 7
Treaty of Ryswick 131
Treemonisha 157
triangular trade **291**, *292m*
Trinidad 52
Tripoli 180
Tripolitania 180
Trotter, William Monroe **291–292**
Truman, Harry S. 35, 41, 55, 74, 78, 140, 150, 174, 237, 248
Trumbauer, Horace 2
Truth, Sojourner **292–293**, *293*, 301
Tshombe, Moise 65, 185, 186
Tswana 45
Tuareg 39, 56, 159, 215, 250, 276, 282, 289, **293–294**
Tubman, Harriet Ross 138, 176, 183, **294**, *294*, 299
Tubman, William V. S. 179–180
Tukulors 191
Tunisia, Republic of 54, **294–295**
Turkey 99, 105, 180
Turko-Italian War 180
Turner, Henry McNeal 16, 224
Turner, Nat 92, 138, 270, **295–296**, *295*
Tuskegee Airmen **296**
Tuskegee Institute 55, 292, 296, *313*, 314
Tuskegee Negro Conference 314
Tuskegee syphilis experiment 296
Tutsi 50, 65, 248, 249, 298
    basket *50*
Tutu, Desmond Mpilo 83, **297**, *297*
Tuvalu 198
Twelve Million Black Voices (Wright) 323

U

Ubangi-Shari 66, 120
Uganda, Republic of 282, 286, **298**
Umayyad dynasty 20, 99, 204
Umkhonto we Sizwe 13
Uncle Tom's Cabin (Stowe) 3, 139, **299**, *299*
Uncle Tom's Children (Wright) 323
Underground Railroad 47, 84, 88, 136, 139, 287, 299, **299–301**, *299*
    routes of *300m*

    Still and 279–280
    Tubman and **294**
Undi 190
Union Conscription Act 89
Union League **301**
unions 171–173, 209, 237, 261
United Mine Workers 172
United Nations (UN) 6, 37, 65, 104, 106, 125, 130, 132, 180, 185, 210, 229, 248, 249, 262, 275, 323, 326
United Steelworkers v. Weber 9–10
Universal Negro Improvement and Conservation Association and African Communities League (UNIA) 122, 123, 302
University of Alabama 97, 185
University of Mississippi 97, 107, 200, *200*
Up From Slavery (Washington) 314
Upper Volta 49, 116
Usuman dan Fodio 117, 275
U.S. v. Reynolds 171
Utica 227

V

vagrancy 71, 169, 260
Van Buren, Martin 5
Vandals 294
VanDerZee, James 135, **302**
Vanuatu 198, 200
Vaughan, Sarah **302**
Vesey, Denmark 184, 270, **302–303**
Vibe 156
Victoria 111
Victorio Indian War 157
Vieira, Joao Bernardo 129
Vietnam War 41, 150, 164, 179, 229
    medal of honor recipients in 42
Voodoo (Vodun) 34, **303–304**, *304*
voting rights 43, 62, 69, 133, 169, 229, 238, 241, 242, 257, **304–310**, *304, 307*, 317, 318
    Civil Rights movement and 306–307
    Fifteenth Amendment and 71, 88, 136, 240, 242, 304, 306, 318
    grandfather clauses and **127**
    literacy requirements and **180–181**
    Mississippi Freedom Summer Project 56, 68, 74, 110, **203**, 206, 227, 280, 307
    poll tax and **229**, 308
    Reconstruction and 36, 239, 305–306
    registration 56, 59, 68, 107, 110, 149, 162, 164, 201, 202, 203, 206, 227, 278, 280
    white primary and **317–318**
    for women 88, 136, 242, 287
Voting Rights Act (1965) 60, 164, 181, 309–310, *309*, 319

W

Wadai 159
Walcott, Derek **311**
Walker, Aaron Thibeaux ("T-Bone") 164, **311–312**
Walker, A'Lelia 313
Walker, Alice Malsenior 44, 156, **312**, *312*, 321
Walker, David 3, 248, **312–313**
Walker, Madam C. J. (Sarah Breedlove) 171, **313**
Walker, Wyatt T. 278
Walls, Carlotta 182
Wanke, Daouda Mallam 215
War Department, U.S. 77, 82, 143

Warmoth, Henry 228
War of 1812 15, 38, 40, 113, 155
Warren, Earl 79, 96
Washington, Booker Taliaferro 48, 57, 90, 172, 285, 292, **313–314**, *313*
Washington, D.C.
    March on 2, 150, 164, 179, **194–195**, *194*, 237, 248, 263, 319
    Million Man March in 111, 177, **201–202**
Washington, George **314–315**, *315*
Washington, Madison 70
Waters, Ethel 135
Waters, Muddy (McKinley Morganfield) 139, **315–316**
Watts, Andre **316**
Watutsi 50
Wayles, John 139
"We Are the World" 156
Webb, William ("Chick") 112
Webster, Delia 137–138
Webster, Noah 3
Weems, Charley 255, 256
Weep Not, Child (Ngũgĩ) 215
Wegbaja 82
Weinberger, Caspar 230
Wells, Mary 124
Wells-Barnett, Ida Bell 171, 186, 242, 243, **316–317**, *316*
"We Shall Overcome" 127
Wesley, Cynthia 263
West, African-Americans in *108*
West, Cornel 123
Western Sahara **317**
West Indies 130
West Point 77, 82, 326
whaling 287
Wheatley, Phillis 231, **317**, *318*
White, George 111, 186
White, Thomas 189
White, Walter 90, 136, 186, 211, 319
Whitehead, Edgar 330
white primary 211, **317–318**
white supremacists 167, 240. *See also* Ku Klux Klan
Whitman, Walt 144
Whittaker, Johnson 48, 77, 326
Whittier, John Greenleaf 301
Wideman, John Edgar **318**
Wife of His Youth, The (Chesnutt) 57
Wild Cat 142
Wilkins, Roy 195, 211, 309, **319**, *319*
Willard, Jess 154
Williams, Daniel Hale **319**
Williams, Eugene 255, 256
Williams, George Washington 67, **319–320**
Williams, G. Mennen 256
Williams, Hosea 278
Williams, H. Sylvester 225
Wilson, August **320**
Wilson, Harriet 123
Wilson, Teddy 142
Wilson, Woodrow 132, 143, 153, 243
Winfrey, Oprah **321**
Witiza 286
Wobblies 172
Wolof 121, 198, 258, 259, **321**
women's rights 240
    suffrage 88, 136, 242, 287

Wonder, Stevie 126, 202, 276
Woodard, Isaac 74
Woods, Earl 321, 322
Woods, Granville T. **321**
Woods, Tiger (Eldrick Woods) **321–322**, *322*
Woodson, Carter Godwin **322–323**
Work. *See* employment and labor rights
Works Progress Administration (WPA) 176, 253
World View of Race, A (Bunche) 49
World War I 49, 205, 217, 237, 243, 292
    black soldiers in 41, 42
    medal of honor recipients in 42
World War II 49, 60, 82–83, 180, 201, 205, 213,
    217, 295
    black soldiers in 41, *41*, 42, 296
    medal of honor recipients in 42
    Tuskegee Airmen in **296**
wrestlers 217–218
Wretched of the Earth, The (Fanon) 109
Wright, Andrew 255, 256
Wright, Moses 288
Wright, Richard 27, 186, 225, **323**, *323*
Wright, Roy 78, 255, 256

Wright Surreying Party *108*

W

Xhosa 192, 276, **324**

Y

Yao 190
Yasu, Lij 200
Yatenga 207
Yaure mask *12*
York **325**
Yorktown 21
Yoruba 33, 82, 113, 146, 215, 216, 221,
    325–326, *325*
Young, Andrew Jackson, Jr. 278, **326**
Young, Charles **326**
Young, Lester 142, 225
Young, Whitney 195, 212
Yunfa 275
Yusuf ibn Tashufin (Yusuf I) 16

Z

Zafy, Albert 189

Zaghawa 159
Zagwe dynasty 105
Zaire 32, 65, 185, *249*
Zambia, Republic of 190, **327**, 330
    AIDS in 9
Zande (Azande) **328**
Zanj **328**
Zanj Rebellion **328**
Zanzibar (Unguja) 147, 189, 219, 265, 285, 286,
    289–290, **328–329**
Zaria 117
Zenagas 34, 124, 205
Zimba (Wa-Zimba) 162, 190, 203, 285, **329**
Zimbabwe, Republic of 8, 190, 195, 207, 212,
    214, 246, 327, **329–330**
    Great Zimbabwe in **127–128**, *128*, 329
    Zong 330
    Zooman and the Sign (Fuller) 117
Zoser 147
Zulu 177, 212, 214, 259–260, 276, 283,
    330–331, *331*
Zumbi 224
Zwide 259